Korea

North Korea
p306

Seoul
p38

Around Seoul
p94

Gangwon-do
p119

Chungcheongbuk-do
p293

Chungcheongnam-do
p276

Gyeongsangbuk-do
p147

Jeollabuk-do
p263

Busan &
Gyeongsangnam-do
p182

Jeollanam-do
p208

Jeju-do
p231

THIS EDITION WRITTEN AND RESEARCHED BY

Simon Richmond,
Megan Eaves, Trent Holden,
Rebecca Milner, Phillip Tang, Rob Whyte

Feb 2016

Contents

GANGNAM (P52), SEOUL

TRADITIONAL HANOK

Contents

Welcome to Korea

Split by a fearsome border, the Korean Peninsula offers the traveller a dazzling range of experiences, beautiful landscapes and 5000 years of culture and history.

Ancient & Modern

The blue and red circle at the heart of the South Korean flag neatly symbolises the divided Korean Peninsula, but also the fluid mix of the ancient and the modern in the country officially called the Republic of Korea (ROK), where the vast majority of visitors will spend their time. South Korea is a dream destination – an engaging, welcoming place where the benefits of a high-tech nation are balanced by a reverence for tradition and the ways of old Asia.

Urban Marvel

Korea might be known as the Land of the Morning Calm, but dive into its capital, Seoul, the powerhouse of Asia's third-largest economy, and serenity is the last thing you'll feel. This round-the-clock city is constantly on the move, with its work-hard, play-hard population the epitome of the nation's indefatigable, can-do spirit. You can hardly turn a corner without stumbling across a tourist information booth, a subway station or a taxi in this multifaceted metropolis where meticulously reconstructed palaces rub shoulders with teeming night markets and the latest technological marvel.

Gorgeous Countryside

South Korea's compact size and superb transport infrastructure mean that tranquillity can be found in easy reach of the urban sprawl. Hike to the summits of craggy mountains enclosed by densely forested national parks. Some of those same mountains transform into ski slopes come winter. Get further off the beaten path than you thought possible by sailing to remote islands, where farming and fishing folk welcome you into their homes and simple seafood cafes. Chill out in serene villages surrounded by rice fields, sleeping in rustic *hanok* (traditional wooden house) guesthouses.

Festivals & Food

Rest assured the ROK also knows how to rock. A packed calendar of festivals and events means there's almost always a celebration of some sort to attend wherever you are – it might be Boryeong for its mud fest, or Gwangju for its Biennale or its annual salute to that most Korean of foods: kimchi. Friendly Koreans are always delighted to share their culture with visitors – often that means over a shared meal with a tantalising array of dishes and plenty of toasts with local alcoholic beverages.

Why I Love Korea

By Simon Richmond, Author

For all of its headlong rush into the 21st century on a *hallyu* (Korean popular culture wave), what charms me most about the ROK is its proud promotion of age-old traditions and culture. I fondly recall meditating at a Buddhist temple retreat where the honk of traffic was replaced by the rhythmic predawn chants of shaven-headed monks; hiking along Seoul's 600-year-old city walls; and walking parts of the Jeju Olle Trail, connecting with history and island traditions on the way. My taste buds also tingle with the memory of one of Asia's least known, but most delicious, cuisines.

For more about our authors, see page 424

Korea

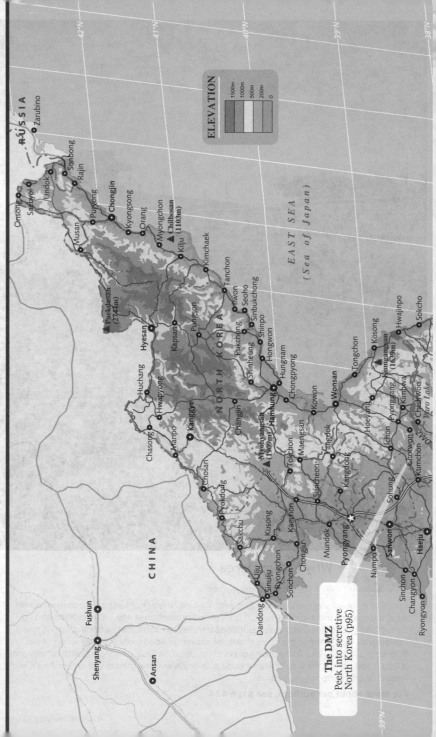

The DMZ
Peek into secretive
North Korea (p95)

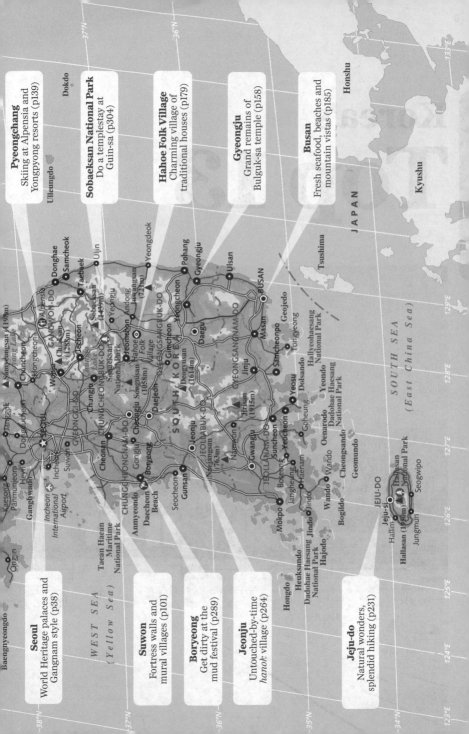

Pyeongchang
Skiing at Alpensia and
Yongpyong resorts (p139)

Sobaeksan National Park
Do a templestay at Guin-sa (p304)

Hahoe Folk Village
Charming village of
traditional houses (p179)

Gyeongju
Grand remains of
Bulguk-sa temple (p158)

Busan
Fresh seafood, beaches and
mountain vistas (p185)

Seoul
World Heritage palaces and
Gangnam style (p38)

Suwon
Fortress walls and
mural villages (p101)

Boryeong
Get dirty at the
mud festival (p289)

Jeonju
Untouched-by-time
hanok village (p264)

Jeju-do
Natural wonders,
splendid hiking (p231)

Korea's
Top 13

1

Changdeokgung

1 The 'Palace of Illustrious Virtue' (p43) was built in the early 15th century as a secondary palace to Gyeongbukgung, though these days this Unesco World Heritage–listed property exceeds Gyeong-bukgung in beauty and grace – partly because so many of its buildings were actually lived in by members of the royal family well into the 20th century. The most charming section is the Huwon, a 'secret garden' that is a royal horticultural idyll. Book well ahead to snag one of the limited tickets to view this special palace on a moonlight tour held on full-moon nights from April to June.

Hiking Around Jeju-do

2 The frequently dramatic volcanic land-scape of Jeju-do, the largest of South Korea's many islands, is best seen on foot. The Jeju Olle Trail (p259) is a network of 26 half- to full-day hiking routes that meander around the island's coast, part of the hin-terland and three other islands. Spending a day following all or part of a trail is a won-derful way to soak up Jeju's unique charms and beautiful surroundings. The summit of Hallasan (pictured below), the country's highest peak, is also very achievable and, in good weather, provides spectacular views.

HENDRIK H / SHUTTERSTOCK ©

FILIP NYMAN / 500PX ©

CHUNG SUNG-JUN / GETTY IMAGES ©

Boryeong Mud Festival

3 Every July, thousands of people converge on the welcoming seaside town of Boryeong and proceed to jump into gigantic vats of mud. Welcome to the Boryeong Mud Festival (p289). The official line is that the local mud has restorative properties, but one look around and it's clear that no one cares for much except having a slippery, sloshin', messy good time. Mud aside, this foreigner-friendly and high-profile festival also features concerts, raves and fireworks. A tip: don't wear anything you want to keep!

Suwon's Hwaseong Fortress

4 Built as an act of filial devotion and heavily damaged during the colonisation period of the early 20th century and again in the Korean War, the restoration of this Unesco World Heritage Site began in the 1970s and is now almost finished. A detailed 1801 record of its construction has allowed the 5.52km-long wall and the Hwaseong Haenggung (p101; a palace for the king to stay in during his visits to Suwon) to be rebuilt with great historical accuracy. A walk around the wall takes you through four grand gates.

Cheong-gye-cheon

5 A raised highway was demolished to allow reconstruction of this long-buried stream (p43). The effort has transformed central Seoul, creating a riverside park and walking course that provides a calm respite from the surrounding commercial hubbub. Public art is dotted along the banks of the stream and many events are held here, including a spectacular lantern festival in November, when thousands of giant glowing paper sculptures are floated in the water. There's also a good museum where you can learn about the history of the Cheon-gye-cheon.

4

5

RICHARD NEBESKY / GETTY IMAGES ©

MICHELE BURGESS / GETTY IMAGES ©

Skiing in Pyeongchang County

6 They say third time's a charm, and so Pyeongchang (p139) won the chance to host the Winter Olympics with its third bid. In 2018 the Games will be held at the Alpensia and Yongpyong ski resorts, as well as the Gangneung coastal area. Located near each other, Alpensia and Yongpyong have dozens of runs, including slopes for families and beginners, views of the East Sea (Sea of Japan) on clear days and some spanking-new accommodation and leisure facilities.

Jeonju Hanok Maeul

7 Jeonju's version of a traditional village (p265) is impressive. The slate-roof houses are home to traditional arts: artisans craft fans, hand-make paper and brew *soju* (local vodka). Foodies will be pleased that the birthplace of bibimbap (rice, egg, meat and vegies with chilli sauce) offers the definitive version of this dish. If you decide to stay (and you will), you'll find plenty of traditional guesthouses, where visitors sleep on a *yo* (padded quilt) in an *ondol* (underfloor heating) room. There's even one run by the grandson of King Gojong.

Gwangjang Market

8 During the day it's known for its secondhand clothes and fabrics, but it's at night that Gwangjang (p73) really comes into its own, when some of the market's alleys fill with vendors selling all manner of street eats. Stewed pigs' trotters and snouts, *gimbap* (rice, vegies and Spam wrapped in rice and rolled in sheets of seaweed) and *bindaettok* (plate-sized crispy pancakes of crushed mung beans and vegies fried on a skillet) are all washed down with copious amounts of *magkeolli* and *soju* (local liquors).

Busan

9 Mountains, beaches, street food and a cosmopolitan vibe make Korea's second-largest metropolis (p185) one of the country's most enjoyable cities. Its top attraction is the atmospheric waterside Jagalchi Fish Market, where you can try the freshest of seafood. Don't miss sunrise on Haeundae beach; the Busan Cinema Center (pictured above), an architecturally dazzling structure with the biggest screen in the country; strolling the lanes of Gamcheon Culture Village; sampling the local dessert *sulbing*; and knocking back shots of *soju* in a tent bar.

Bulguk-sa

10 It's hard to choose just one standout treasure in and around magnificent Gyeongju, but this Unesco World Heritage cultural site is most likely to take the honour, not least because it contains seven Korean 'national treasures' within its walls. The high point of the golden age of Shilla architecture, this incredibly sophisticated yet wonderfully subtle temple complex (p161), with its internal pagodas, external bridges and gorgeous, undulating scenery, is a monument to the skill of its carpenters, painters, craftspeople and architects.

Templestay at Guin-sa

11 A bell rings at 3.30am for a morning meditation session. Breakfast is an austere meal, taken in silence so you can contemplate the ache in your bones from bowing 108 times in front of Buddha. Later, you'll have more meditation time to contemplate the surrender of your body and mind in the search for inner peace. A templestay is the perfect antidote to fast-paced modern Korea, and while the country is awash with temples, the impressive fortress-like compound of Guin-sa (p304) is among the finest.

TRAVELASIA / GETTY IMAGES ©

10

Hahoe Folk Village

12 The closest thing Korea has to a time machine, the charming Hahoe Folk Village (p179), some way from Andong, is a truly wonderful experience for anyone wanting to get a sense of how Korea looked, felt, sounded and smelled before the 20th century changed the country forever. More than 200 people continue to live here, maintaining traditional ways and customs and even inviting people to spend the night in their *minbak* (private homes with rooms for rent). For a slice of old Korea, Hahoe should be at the top of your list.

The DMZ

13 It's known as the Demilitarized Zone (p95), but this 4km-wide, 250km-long heavily mined and guarded buffer, splitting North from South Korea, is anything but. An enduring Cold War symbol, the DMZ has become a surreal tourist draw, on both sides of the border. The tension is most palpable in the Joint Security Area, the neutral area built after the 1953 Armistice for the holding of peace talks, which can only be visited on an organised tour. Seven observations points along the South Korean side of the DMZ allow visitors to peer into the secretive North.

Need to Know

For more information, see Survival Guide (p387)

Currency
Korean won (₩)

Language
Korean

Visas
Australian, British, US
and most Western European citizens receive
a 90-day entry permit
on arrival. Five-day-only
stays on Jeju-do are visa
free.

Money
ATMs with a 'Global' sign
work with internationally issued cards; very
few are open 24 hours.
Credit cards are widely
accepted, except in the
countryside.

Mobile Phones
South Korea uses the
CDMA digital standard;
check compatibility with
your provider. Mobile
phones can be hired at
international airports
and elsewhere.

Time
Nine hours ahead of
GMT/UCT

When to Go

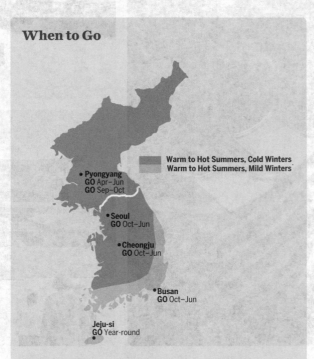

Warm to Hot Summers, Cold Winters
Warm to Hot Summers, Mild Winters

Pyongyang
GO Apr–Jun
GO Sep–Oct

Seoul
GO Oct–Jun

Cheongju
GO Oct–Jun

Busan
GO Oct–Jun

Jeju-si
GO Year-round

High Season
(Jun–Sep)

➡ Be prepared for
sweltering heat and
a very heavy rainy
season through July
across the peninsula.

Shoulder
(May, Oct)

➡ Late spring sees
the country bathed
first in blossoms
then fresh greenery.
In autumn you can
experience nature in
all its russet shades.

Low Season
(Nov–Apr)

➡ Temperatures
plummet and snow
falls. Best time for
skiing and visiting
museums and
galleries.

Useful Websites

Lonely Planet (www.lonely planet.com/south-korea) Best for pre-planning.

Korea Tourism Organization (KTO; www.visitkorea.or.kr) Official government-run site.

Korea4Expats (www.korea4 expats.com) Covers many aspects of Korean life.

Korea.net (www.korea.net) A treasure trove of background detail on the ROK.

Everyday Korea (http://wiki .everydaykorea.com) Info on a whole range of Korean topics.

Important Numbers

South Korea country code	☏82
International access code	☏00
Ambulance and fire	☏119
Police	☏112
Tourist information (English-speaking)	☏1330

Exchange Rates

Australia	A$1	₩830
Canada	C$1	₩885
Europe	€1	₩1311
Japan	¥100	₩978
UK	UK£1	₩1780
US	US$1	₩1176

For current exchange rates see www.xe.com.

Daily Costs

Budget:
Less than ₩100,000

➡ Dorm bed: ₩20,000

➡ Street food: ₩1000–₩5000

➡ Hiking: free

➡ Entry to National Museum of Korea: free

➡ Subway ticket: ₩1300

Midrange:
₩100,000–₩300,000

➡ *Hanok* guesthouse: ₩70,000

➡ Entry to Gyeongbokgung (Palace of Shining Happiness): ₩3000

➡ Barbecued pork meal: ₩40,000

➡ Theatre ticket: ₩40,000

Top End:
More than ₩300,000

➡ High-end hotel: ₩200,000

➡ Royal Korean banquet: ₩80,000

➡ Scrub and massage at a *jjimjil-bang* (luxury sauna): ₩60,000

➡ DMZ tour: ₩100,000

Opening Hours

Banks 9am to 4pm Monday to Friday, ATMs 7am to 11pm

Restaurants 11am to 10pm

Cafes 7am to 10pm

Bars 6pm to 1am, longer hours Friday and Saturday

Shops 10am to 8pm

Arriving in Korea

Incheon Airport (Seoul; p397)
Express trains (₩8000, 43 minutes) run every 30 minutes to Seoul; there are also commuter trains (₩3850, 53 minutes). Buses (₩10,000) and taxis (around ₩65,000) take an hour or more, depending on traffic.

Gimpo Airport (Seoul; p397)
Express trains (₩1400, 15 minutes) run regularly to Seoul station. You can also catch the subway (₩1400, 35 minutes). Buses (₩7500) and taxis (around ₩35,000) take 40 minutes to one hour to the city centre.

Gimhae Airport (Busan; p195)
Limo buses (₩6000 to ₩7000, one hour) and regular buses (₩1600, one hour) connect to Busan every 20 minutes. Or you can take the light rail line to Sasang subway station (₩2800, one hour). Taxis (around ₩40,000) take 30 minutes to one hour to the city.

Getting Around

Transport in South Korea is reasonably priced and efficient.

Plane There are dozens of local airports and reasonable fares to several destinations.

Train Excellent but not comprehensive network with clean, comfortable and punctual trains. It's worth looking into a KR Pass even for something as straightforward as a return Seoul–Busan train.

Bus Cheaper and slower than trains but serving every corner of the country.

Ferry Connecting the mainland to hundreds of islands.

Car Not recommended for first-time visitors. You must be over 21 and have an international driving permit.

For much more on **getting around**, see p397

First Time Korea

For more information, see Survival Guide (p387)

Checklist

➜ Check the validity of your passport

➜ If you plan to hire a car, bring a current international driving permit

➜ Check airline baggage restrictions

➜ Check government travel websites

➜ Call banks and credit card providers and tell them your travel dates

➜ Organise travel insurance

➜ Check whether your mobile phone is compatible with Korea's CDMA digital standard

What to Pack

➜ Passport

➜ Credit card

➜ Phrasebook or mini dictionary

➜ Slip-on shoes

➜ Travel plug

➜ Insect repellent

➜ Painkillers (or other hangover cure)

➜ Padlock

➜ Medical kit

➜ Sunscreen

➜ Torch (flashlight)

Top Tips for Your Trip

➜ It's worth investing in a KR Pass even if you make only one longish trip on a fast train, such as Seoul to Busan return.

➜ Save money on public transport fares (and also pay for taxis) using a touch-and-go T-Money Card.

➜ Check with local tourist offices about free guided tours with students and others citizens who speak English and other languages.

➜ Spend over ₩30,000 at shops participating in the Global Refund scheme and you can claim VAT back on leaving the country.

➜ Hops from Seoul to Jeju-do on budget airlines may seem cheap, but check on baggage restrictions and extra costs before deciding – flying with Korean Air or Asiana may work out a better deal.

What to Wear

The vast majority of Koreans wear Western-style dress these days, although you'll sometimes see people in *hanbok* (Korean clothing). The best version of this type of clothing – in fine silks and organza – are usually worn by women, and sometimes men, for formal occasions. More casual pyjama-style *hanbok* are made from cotton and are very comfortable for everyday wear.

For business, Koreans are quite formal and men wear suits and ties.

Sleeping

In general you don't need to worry about where to stay – hotels and motels are so numerous there's usually little need to book ahead.

➜ **Motels** The most common form of accommodation. Most offer well-equipped, if plain, rooms. Some can be fancy, particularly rent-by-the-hour love hotels.

➜ **Hanok Guesthouses** Often only have a few rooms, so advance booking is advised.

➜ **Hostels** Common in cities and the best place to meet fellow travellers and English-speaking Koreans.

Advance Planning

If you are travelling over any of Korea's major holidays, you should book all internal transport well ahead of time.

Think about booking ahead if you wish to stay at a *hanok* (traditional house), as these have only three or four guest rooms in total. Top-end international chain hotels can also fill up when conferences are in town.

Hiking on the weekend can be a madhouse – schedule your hikes for a weekday instead. The same goes for skiing trips in winter.

Book the USO tour to the DMZ as soon as you can, as it fills up.

Bargaining

Try bargaining if you're prepared to pay in cash and buy in bulk at markets, from street and subway vendors and even, occasionally, for big-ticket items in department stores.

Tipping

➡ **When to Tip** Generally not expected.

➡ **Restaurants** No need to tip; only top-end hotel restaurants will add a service charge.

➡ **Guides** Not expected; a small gift will be appreciated, though.

➡ **Taxis** No need to tip; fares are metered or agreed before you get in.

➡ **Hotels** Only in the most luxurious do you need to tip bellboys etc, and only if service is good.

Language

Korean is the common language. It's relatively easy to find English speakers in the big cities, but not so easy in smaller towns and the countryside. Learning the writing system, *hangeul,* and a few key phrases will help you enormously in being able to decode street signs, menus and timetables. In big cities, you'll find nearly all the street signs are in both Korean and English.

Etiquette

There are several social rules that Koreans stick to, although they will generally be relaxed about foreigners doing likewise. Follow these tips to avoid faux pas:

➡ **Meetings & Greetings** A quick, short bow is most respectful for meetings and departures. Give or receive any object using both hands – especially name cards (an essential feature of doing business in Korea), money and gifts.

➡ **Shoes** Remove your shoes on entering a Korean home, guesthouse, temple or Korean-style restaurant.

➡ **Eating & Drinking** Pour drinks for others and use both hands when pouring or receiving. Use chopsticks or a spoon to touch food and don't leave either sticking up in a bowl of rice.

➡ **Loss of Face** A mishandled remark or potentially awkward scene should be smoothed over as soon as possible, and if you sense someone actively trying to change the subject, go with the flow. An argument or any situation that could lead to embarrassment should be avoided at all costs.

ULLSTEIN BILD / GETTY IMAGES ©

If You Like...

Traditional Architecture

Changdeokgung The most attractive of Seoul's palaces, this World Heritage–listed site also has a 'secret garden'. (p43)

Bukchon Hanok Village Around 900 *hanok* (traditional wooden houses) make this Seoul's largest neighbourhood of traditional homes. (p43)

Seokbul-sa Hidden in the mountains of Busan, this temple perches daintily among enormous cliff-like boulders. (p187)

Jeonju Hanok Maeul Jeonju's sprawling *hanok* village is a charming nod to Korea's low-slung architectural style. (p265)

Seongeup Folk Village Step back in time in this walled village of thatched stone homes on Jeju-do. (p247)

Hahoe Folk Village People still live in the rustic homes in this beautiful riverside village complex. (p179)

Haein-sa This religious complex houses the Tripitaka Koreana: 81,258 wooden printing blocks containing Buddhist scriptures. (p156)

Crafts & Shopping

Namdaemun Market Open round the clock, with more than 10,000 stores dealing in everything from seaweed to spectacles. (p86)

Shinsegae Centum City Shop till you drop in Busan at the world's largest department store. (p194)

Icheon Ceramic Village See traditional kilns and buy beautiful pots directly from their makers. (p105)

Gangjin Celadon Museum Before you buy, watch celadon (green-glazed pottery) being crafted and kiln-fired here. (p222)

Daegu's Herbal Medicine Market Stock up on anything from cheap ginseng to reindeer horns at this fascinating market. (p149)

Damyang Long famed for its bamboo products, this town holds a bamboo crafts festival in May. (p215)

Daein Market Fifty-plus artists have studios beside regular stalls at this traditional market in Gwangju. (p214)

Outdoor Activities

Jeju Olle Trail Discover Jeju-do's byways on this excellent series of hiking routes around the volcanic island. (p259)

Cycle along the Han River Pedal the cycle lanes linking the parks strung along Seoul's major waterway. (p57)

Wolchulsan National Park Hike through Korea's smallest national park over a vertigo-inducing 52m-high bridge spanning two ridges. (p228)

Seogwipo Korea's best scuba-diving destination, with colourful corals, kelp forests and dolphins. (p249)

High1 Check out the ski season at this resort in the mountains west of Taebaek. (p141)

Seoul City Wall Hike beside these ancient walls as they snake over the capital's four guardian mountains. (p52)

Saryangdo Tackle jagged ridges, 400m peaks, ropes and ladders on the hike around this beautiful island off the coast of Tongyeong. (p199)

World Heritage Sites

Jongmyo The royal ancestral shrine set in peaceful wooded grounds is just one of several World Heritage Sites in Seoul. (p43)

Namhan Sanseong Hike beside 17th-century fortress walls surrounded by beautiful pine and oak forests and wild flowers. (p104)

Hwaseong Suwon's impressive fortress walls have been meticulously reconstructed with great historical accuracy. (p101)

Gochang Thousands of bronze-age tombs known as dolmen dot the hills around this small village. (p273)

Gyeongju Prime examples of Buddhist art in the form of sculptures, reliefs, temples and palace architecture. (p158)

Jeju-do The dormant volcanoes, Hallasan and Seongsan Ilchulbong, and a network of lava-tube caves are all World Heritage worthy. (p231)

Contemporary Buildings

Dongdaemun Design Plaza & Park Zaha Hadid's sleek building is straight out of a sci-fi fantasy. (p51)

Seoul City Hall This giant glass wave is a modern reinterpretation of traditional Korean design. (p45)

Busan Cinema Center Architecturally dazzling structure with the biggest screen in the country. (p189)

Paju Book City The hub of Korea's book industry is based in a complex of futuristic award-winning buildings that are a must for architectural buffs. (p99)

Songdo International City Marvel at this model urban development in the bay off Incheon. (p114)

Museums & Galleries

National Museum of Korea Packed with national treasures spanning the centuries. (p50)

Leeum Samsung Museum of Art Three top architect-designed buildings and a dazzling collection of art from ancient to contemporary. (p51)

Top: Wolchulsan National Park (p228), Jeollanam-do
Bottom: Namiseom Island (p121)

National Museum of Modern and Contemporary Art Make the trek out to Seoul Grand Park to see this classy art museum. (p378)

Asian Culture Complex New collection of galleries and performance spaces on the main site of Gwangju's May 18 uprising. (p212)

Arario Museum A quartet of renovated buildings in Jeju-si house showcase an outstanding collection of contemporary art. (p233)

Gyeongju National Museum Houses a superb collection of artefacts from the Shilla dynasty and beyond. (p159)

Top Tastes

Namdo Food Festival Tuck into hundreds of different dishes, including the love-it-or-loathe-it *hongeo samhap* (fermented skate). (p213)

Busan Sink your teeth into a twitching squid tentacle at Jagalchi Fish Market, or snack on the nether parts of chickens in tent bars. (p185)

Jeonju Eat bibimbap, Korea's most famous culinary export (after kimchi, of course), at its birthplace. (p264)

Boseong Try the green-tea ice cream, green-tea noodles and green-tea biscuits close by tea plantations. (p221)

Jeju Mawon Sample raw horsemeat at this restaurant in a mock-up of a Joseon Palace in Jungmun Resort. (p256)

Chuncheon Along Dakgalbi Geori there are 20-plus restaurants serving the town's famous spicy chicken dish, *dakgalbi*. (p121)

Gwangjang Market Sample super-tasty and cheap street food in one of Seoul's massive covered markets. (p73)

Sokcho Platters of raw fish and other seafood delights at this east-coast port. (p125)

Offbeat Experiences

Dragon Hill Spa & Resort Strip down for a communal steam and full-body scrub at this fancy *jjimjil-bang* (upmarket sauna) in Seoul. (p56)

Chamsori Gramophone & Edison Museum If you love music and the spirit of invention, don't miss this astounding collection of vintage machines. (p135)

Cheorwon March along a North Korean infiltration tunnel under the DMZ and peer into North Korea. (p129)

Haesindang Park Admire phallic sculptures in this park in the fishing village of Sinnam. (p144)

Sex Museums Gain a very adult education at Jeju-do's trio of nookie-obsessed exhibitions. (p238)

Kumsusan Sun Memorial Palace of the Sun Pay your respects to the embalmed body of Great Leader Kim Il-sung in his former palace. (p312)

Mr Toilet House Hilarious poo-related exhibits and more serious sanitation issues at this toilet-shaped museum in Suwon. (p102)

Scenic Spots

Suncheon-man Rich mud beneath the rustling reeds attracts migratory birds and, in turn, scores of tourists. (p217)

Paekdusan One of the best reasons to visit the DPRK is this stunning and fabled mountain. (p324)

Bukhansan National Park Sweeping mountaintop vistas, maple leaves and rushing streams all within easy reach of Seoul. (p110)

Heyri Wandering around this 'book village' with its contemporary buildings and quirky sculptures is a pleasure. (p98)

Ji-dong Mural Village Outside Suwon's city walls, this labyrinth of grungy alleyways bursts with vibrant wall murals. (p102)

Samjinae Village Enjoy the slow life in this village of centuries-old stone walls, homesteads and heritage houses. (p216)

Jikji-sa Popular templestay in a postcard-pretty temple in a quiet forest. (p158)

Island Life

Namhaedo You'll blink several times and think you've been transported to southern France on this gorgeous island. (p204)

Ulleungdo This East Sea island offers mist-shrouded volcanic cliffs, traditional harbour towns and a breathtaking jagged coastline. (p172)

Udo Admire the Seongsan Ilchulbong tuff cone volcano from the white coral-sand beach on this lovely island. (p250)

So-Muuido Stroll around this car-free island at the southeastern tip of lovely Muuido. (p114)

Jindo Spring tidal drops reveal a 2.8km-long causeway leading to the tiny island of Modo-ri. (p229)

Sapsido Offers undeveloped beaches, bucolic villages surrounded by rice paddies, and the salty smell of fish. (p290)

Namiseom Island Spot deer, ostriches and waterfowl on this wooded, lake-bound island southwest of Chuncheon. (p121)

Month by Month

January

Come prepared for freezing temperatures and snow across much of the country.

🏃 Taebaeksan Snow Festival

Marvel at giant ice sculptures and enjoy sledding fun at this winter celebration in Taebaeksan Provincial Park. (p144)

February

Local religious holidays and festivals follow the lunar calendar, while the rest follow the Gregorian (Western) calendar. Therefore, Seollal will sometimes occur in January.

🎆 Seollal (Lunar New Year)

Koreans visit relatives, honour ancestors and eat traditional foods over this three-day national holiday. There are a number of events in Seoul during this time. For more information visit www.visitseoul.net or www.visitkorea.or.kr. In 2017 Seollal begins on 28 January and in 2018 on 16 February.

April

Bring your raincoat and war clothes as the weather can still be wintry and wet. Early April is also when areas of Korea turn pink in a transient flurry of delicate cherry blossoms.

🎆 Yeongdeungpo Yeouido Spring Flower Festival

Masses of cherry blossoms around the Seoul island draw the biggest crowds, but you can also see the flowers on Namsan and at Ewha Woman's University. (p60)

🎆 GIC Biennale

Running into May, the world's largest biennale specialising in ceramics (www.kocef.org) is for people potty about pottery. It's held in odd-numbered years in Incheon.

🏃 Pyongyang Marathon

Held on the nearest Sunday to 15 April, Kim Il-sung's birthday, this event (www.pyongyangmarathon.com) is a unique chance to run through the mysterious North Korean capital.

May

One of the most pleasant months in which to visit Korea, with good weather and fewer problems finding accommodation than in the busy summer months.

🎆 Jongmyo Daeje

Held on the first Sunday of the month, this ceremony honours Korea's royal ancestors and involves a solemn, costumed parade through downtown Seoul to the royal shrine at Jongmyo, where spectators can enjoy traditional music and an elaborate, all-day ritual. (p61)

🎆 Lotus Lantern Festival

The weekend preceding Buddha's birthday, Seoul celebrates with a huge daytime street festival and evening lantern parade – the largest in South Korea. (p61)

✿ Buddha's Birthday

Brings a kaleidoscope of light and colour, as rows of paper lanterns are strung down main thoroughfares and in temple courtyards across Korea (celebrated on 14 May in 2016, 3 May in 2017 and 22 May in 2018).

☆ Chuncheon International Mime Festival

The lakeside city hosts street performers, magicians, acrobats and quirky shows such as a soap-bubble opera at this festival. (p121)

June

Warmer weather before the rains of July make this a great time to enjoy Korea's great outdoors on hiking trips and at the beach.

✿ Gangneung Danoje Festival

Recognised by Unesco as a Masterpiece of the Oral and Intangible Heritage of Humanity, Gangneung's version of the Dano Festival is held according to the lunar calendar and features shamanist rituals, mask dances and market stalls. (p135)

July

It can rain – a lot – during this month, so make sure you have appropriate gear and arrange your travel plans accordingly.

☆ Ansan Valley Rock Festival

One of Korea's premier summer music festivals (www.valleyrockfestival.com), with a stellar line-up of international headliners as well quality K-Indie bands.

🏃 Boryeong Mud Festival

Head to Daecheon Beach to wallow in mud pools and take part in stacks of muddy fun and games. (p289)

August

Head for breezy coastal areas and the loftier mountains to find some relief from the sweltering heat of high summer.

🏃 Chungju World Martial Arts Festival

This festival is held in the World Martial Arts Park, where you'll see all sorts of unusual martial arts with teams participating from across the world. (p299)

September

Book ahead for transport around Chuseok, when many Koreans are visiting family and friends.

✿ Gwangju Biennale

Korea's leading international art show is a two-month carnival of the avant-garde, held from September to November in even-numbered years. (p212)

☆ Mask Dance Festival

This 10-day festival in Andong, held at the end of the month and running into October, brings together more than 20 traditional dance troupes. (p178)

✿ Korea International Art Fair

Held at Seoul's COEX, KIAF is one of the region's top art fairs and a good opportunity to get a jump on the country's hot new artists. (p61)

October

Autumn is a great time to visit, particularly if you like hiking as this is when the mountains run through a palate of rustic colours.

☆ Busan International Film Festival

Korea's top international film festival, held in the architecturally stunning Busan Cinema Center, attracts stars from across Asia and beyond. (p189)

✿ Seoul International Fireworks Festival

Best viewed from Yeouido Hangang Park, this festival sees dazzling fireworks displays staged by both Korean and international teams. (p60)

✿ Baekje Cultural Festival

This major festival, packed with events, is held in Buyeo in even-numbered years and in Gongju in odd-numbered years. (p284)

🍴 Gwangju World Kimchi Culture Festival

Join the celebrations for Korea's most famous contribution to the culinary arts. For details see http://kimchi.gwangju.go.kr.

Itineraries

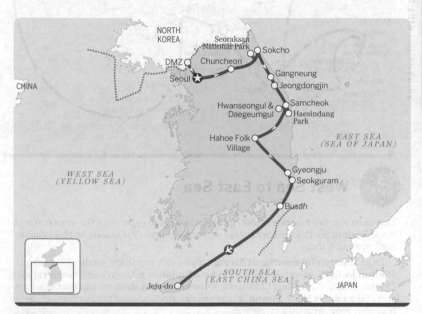

2 WEEKS **South Korea's Highlights**

Access the best of Korea on this trip taking in the dynamic capital Seoul, the southern port of Busan, lost-in-time country towns, quirky sights and beautiful Jeju-do.

Spend four or five days in **Seoul**, including a day trip north to the **DMZ**. Next head east to **Chuncheon**, where you can cycle around Uiam Lake and sample the town's famous chicken dish, *dakgalbi*.

Dine on fresh seafood in **Sokcho** then hike around the stunning peaks and waterfalls of **Seoraksan National Park**. Follow the coast south to **Gangneung** to view well-preserved Joseon-era buildings, quirky museums and a tiny North Korean spy submarine at Unification Park in **Jeongdongjin**. From **Samcheok** explore the huge **Hwanseongul** and **Daegeumgul** caves, as well as **Haesindang Park**, packed with phallic sculptures.

Delve into Korea's past at serene **Hahoe Folk Village** and **Gyeongju**, ancient capital of the Shilla kingdom, where you can spend a couple of days exploring royal tombs, the excellent museum and the World Heritage–listed grotto at **Seokguram**.

Busan, with its fish market, beaches and urban buzz, is worth a few days. From here fly to **Jeju-do**, where you can enjoy amazing volcanic scenery on leisurely hikes.

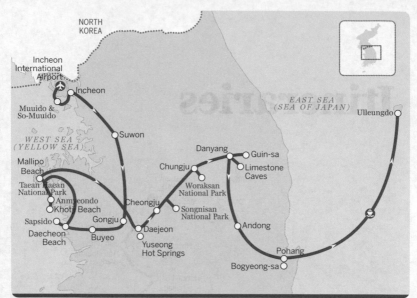

West Sea to East Sea

3 WEEKS

This cross-country itinerary is ideal for those looking to experience the more rustic and natural side of South Korea, with stops on ruggedly beautiful islands and hikes along leafy mountain trails.

From **Incheon International Airport** it's a quick hop to the small, idyllic island of **Muuido**, from where you can walk to **So-Muuido** or relax on lovely beaches. Enjoy Chinese food in the historic Chinatown of **Incheon**, then stroll around the Open Port area. Take a direct bus to **Suwon**, where you can stride around the ramparts of the meticulously reconstructed fortress wall.

Gongju and **Buyeo**, the ancient capitals of the Baekje kingdom, are your next stops – hillside tombs, a fortress and museum will give you an insight into Korea's oldest dynasty. After enjoying the sand, seafood and mud skincare spa of **Daecheon Beach**, sail to the serene island of **Sapsido**, where you can spend the night. Return to Daecheon and continue north by bus to **Anmyeondo**, the largest island in the Taean Haean National Marine Park. Continue working on your tan at either **Khotji Beach** or **Mallipo Beach**, or hike some the new Haebyeongil trails through the park.

Travel inland to **Daejeon** to soak at **Yuseong Hot Springs**. Continue to **Cheongju**, learn about the world's oldest printed book then move on to **Songnisan National Park**, covering central Korea's finest scenic area and home to a 33m-tall gold-plated Buddha statue.

Chungju is the gateway to lovely **Woraksan National Park** and for a two-hour scenic ferry trip across Chungju Lake to sleepy **Danyang**, which is small-town Korea at its most charming. Explore nearby **limestone caves** and the stately temple complex of **Guin-sa** within Sobaeksan National Park.

Use **Andong** as a base for exploring the surrounding area packed with attractive river and lakeside villages. It's only a couple of hours by bus from here to **Pohang**. From Pohang visit **Bogyeong-sa** temple in a gorgeous valley with 12 waterfalls, then board the ferry to **Ulleungdo**, a sparsely inhabited, volcanic island.

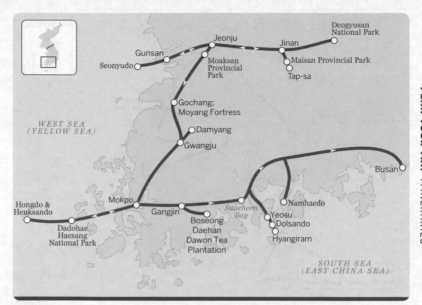

2 WEEKS The Deep South Trail

This 850km route around Korea's greenest and least-industrialised region offers the opportunity to visit scores of rural islands, dine in countless seafood restaurants and dig deep into artistic traditions.

Jeonju has a fascinating *hanok* village crammed with traditional houses and buildings. Use it as a base for visiting the 6th-century Geumsan-sa temple in **Moaksan Provincial Park**. Don't miss **Maisan Provincial Park**, where you can hike between a pair of 'horse ear' mountains and see a sculptural garden of stone pinnacles piled up by a Buddhist mystic at the **Tap-sa** temple. Alternatively, go hiking or skiing in beautiful **Deogyusan National Park**.

The industrial port city of **Gunsan** boasts Korea's largest collection of Japanese-colonial-period buildings. From here hop on a ferry to the relaxing island of **Seonyudo**, situated amid 60 mostly uninhabited small islands. When the tide is in and the sun is out, the views from here are unbelievably beautiful.

Bronze and Iron Age tombs dot the lush green hills around the small village of **Gochang**, where you can also explore the 15th-century, ivy-covered **Moyang Fortress**.

Further south, **Gwangju** is home to several interesting historical sites, museums and a major arts complex. Make a day trip to **Damyang** to stroll the sandy trails through its Juknokwon bamboo grove. Move on to the port of **Mokpo** to board boats to the remote havens of **Heuksando** and **Hongdo** in the **Dadohae Haesang National Park**.

Admire Korea's centuries-old tradition of pottery at **Gangjin** and taste products made from healthy green tea at the beautiful **Boseong Daehan Dawon Tea Plantation**.

Go bird spotting in the Ramsar-listed wetlands of **Suncheon Bay** then continue to **Yeosu**, site of Expo 2012 and access point for **Dolsando**, where you can hike up to **Hyangiram**, a Buddhist temple perched on a cliff.

For a final island experience, take in terraced rice paddies and misty temples on picturesque **Namhaedo**. The trail finishes at Korea's second-largest city, **Busan**.

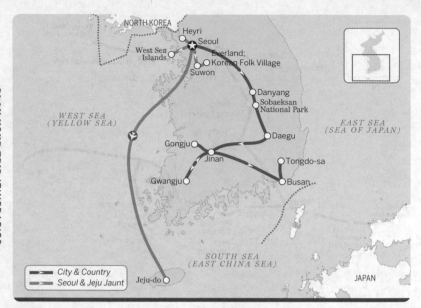

 ## City & Country

Some of South Korea's top temples feature on this route linking its two main cities.

In **Seoul** attend a Templelife program at Jogye-sa or Bongeun-sa. **Danyang** is the transit point for **Sobaeksan National Park**, where you'll find modern Guin-sa, headquarters of the Cheontae sect.

Daegu is the base for trips to stunning Haein-sa, housing a World Heritage–listed library of more than 80,000 14th-century woodblocks, and Jikji-sa, a magnificent temple dating to the 5th century.

Jinan is the access town for Tap-sa, a tiny temple surrounded by two 'horse ear' mountains and an extraordinary sculptural garden of 80 stone pinnacles (or towers). From **Gwangju**, visit Unju-sa, with its fine collection of stone pagodas and unusual twin and reclining Buddhas.

From **Gongju**, one-time capital of Korea's Baekje dynasty, visit remote Magok-sa, with a hall of 1000 pint-sized disciples who are all slightly different.

Finish just outside of **Busan** at **Tongdo-sa**, which has an excellent Buddhist art museum containing 30,000 artefacts.

Seoul & Jeju Jaunt

This two-centre itinerary is well suited to parents travelling with kids.

Seoul's many parks, interactive museums and, in summer, outdoor swimming pools are ideal for family fun. Older kids will most likely be happy cruising the capital's vast shopping malls and department stores looking for souvenirs of Korea's pervasive pop culture.

Day trips include the beaches of the **West Sea islands**; Korea's biggest amusement park, **Everland**; and the **Korean Folk Village**. The latter two can just as easily be visited from **Suwon**, where it's fun to walk around the walls of an 18th-century fortress. North of Seoul, the modern village of **Heyri** offers inventive sculptures and art exhibits.

Hop on a flight to **Jeju-do**, blessed with a fascinating volcanic landscape and dozens of sandy beaches. Amusement and water parks, cycle and skate hire and a whole raft of adventure activities, from quad biking to scuba diving, are possible on this fun-packed island with plenty of world-class resorts.

Gwanghwamun & Jongno-gu 광화문, 종로구

★Gyeongbokgung PALACE

(경복궁; Palace of Shining Happiness; Map p58; www.royalpalace.go.kr; adult/child ₩3000/1500; ⌚9am-5pm Wed-Mon Nov-Feb, to 6pm Mar-May, Sep & Oct, to 6.30pm Jun-Aug; [S] Line 3 to Gyeongbokgung, Exit 5) Like a phoenix, Seoul's premier palace has risen several times from the ashes of destruction. Hoards of tourists have replaced the thousands of government officials, scholars, eunuchs, concubines, soldiers and servants who once lived here. Watch the changing of the guard ceremonies at the main entrance **Gwanghwamun** (광화문; 161 Sajik-ro, Jongno-gu), then set aside at least half a day to do justice to the compound, which includes a couple of museums, ornamental gardens and some of Seoul's grandest architectural sights.

★Changdeokgung PALACE

(창덕궁; Map p58; http://eng.cdg.go.kr/main/main.htm; 99 Yulgok-ro, Jongno-gu; adult/child ₩3000/1500, plus Huwon ₩8000/4000; [S] Line 3 to Anguk, Exit 3) You must join a guided tour to look around World Heritage–listed Changdeokgung, the most beautiful of Seoul's four main palaces. English tours run at 10.30am and 2.30pm; if you don't care about the commentary then there are Korean tours on the hour. To see the palace's lovely Huwon section, join tours that run at 11.30am and 1.30pm, with an extra 3.30pm tour March to October. Book online or come early as the Huwon tours are restricted to 50 people at a time.

★Bukchon Hanok Village NEIGHBOURHOOD

(북촌한옥마을; Map p58; bukchon.seoul.go.kr; [S] Line 3 to Anguk, Exit 3) Meaning 'North Village', Bukchon, between Gyeongbokgung and Changdeokgung, is home to around 900 *hanok*, Seoul's largest concentration of these traditional Korean homes. It's a busy tourist area, but it's still a pleasure to get lost in the streets here admiring the patterned walls and tiled roofs contrasting with the modern city in the distance.

To find out more about the area before you set off to explore, drop by the **Bukchon Traditional Culture Center** (북촌문화센터; Map p58; ☎02-2171 2459; http://bukchon.seoul.go.kr/eng/exp/center1_1.jsp; 37 Gyedong-gil, Jongno-gu; ⌚9am-6pm Mon-Sat) [FREE].

★Jongmyo SHRINE

(종묘; Map p58; ☎02-765 0195; jm.cha.go.kr; 157 Jong-ro, Jongno-gu; adult/child ₩1000/500; ⌚9am-5pm Wed-Mon Mar-Oct, to 4.30pm Wed-Mon Nov-Feb; [S] Line 1, 3 or 5 to Jongno 3-ga, Exit 11) Surrounded by dense woodland, the impressive buildings of the Confucian shrine Jongmyo house the 'spirit tablets' of the Joseon kings and queens and some of their most loyal government officials. Their spirits are believed to reside in a special hole bored into the wooden tablets.

For its architecture and the special ceremonies that take place here, the shrine has been awarded World Heritage status: the most famous ceremony is the **Jongmyo Daeje** in early May.

★Jogye-sa TEMPLE

(조계사; ☎02-768 8600; www.jogyesa.kr/user/english; 55-Ujeongguk-ro, Jongno-gu; ⌚24hr; [S] Line 3 to Anguk, Exit 6) The focus of Jogye-sa is the giant wooden hall **Daeungjeon**, Seoul's largest Buddhist worship hall. Completed in 1938, its design followed the Joseon-dynasty style. The exterior is decorated with scenes from Buddha's life and carved floral latticework, while inside are three giant Buddha statues: on the left Amitabha, Buddha of the Western Paradise; in the centre is the historical Buddha, who lived in India and achieved enlightenment; on the right, the Bhaisaiya or Medicine Buddha, holds a medicine bowl.

★Cheong-gye-cheon RIVER

(청계천; Map p58; www.cheonggyecheon.or.kr; 110 Sejong-daero, Jung-gu; [S] Line 5 to Gwanghwamun, Exit 5) A raised highway was torn down and cement roads removed in this US$384-million urban renewal project to 'daylight' this stream. With its landscaped walkways, footbridges, waterfalls and a variety of public artworks, such as the enormous pink-and-blue shell entitled **Spring** in Cheong-gye Plaza (Map p56), the revitalised stream is a hit with Seoulites who come to escape the urban hubbub and, in summer, dangle their feet in the water.

★Arario Museum in SPACE MUSEUM

(Map p58; ☎02-736 5700; www.arariomuseum.org; 83 Yulgok-ro, Jongno-gu; adult/child/youth ₩10,000/4000/6000; ⌚10am-7pm; [S] Line 3 to Anguk, Exit 3) Korean business magnate and contemporary-art collector Kam Chang-il has found the perfect home for jewels from his collection at this ivy-clad brick building that's considered a seminal piece of early

TICKET TO THE PALACES

If you plan to visit Seoul's four main palaces – Gyeonbukgung, Changdeokgung, Changgyeonggung and Deoksugung – you can save some money by buying a combined ticket (₩10,000) valid for up to a month. The ticket is sold at each of the palaces and also covers entry to Huwon at Changdeokgung.

1970s architecture. The building's compact, low-ceilinged rooms and labyrinthine layout fit the conceptual pieces, by the likes of Nam Jun Paik, Koo Kang, Lee Ufan, Tracey Emin, Damien Hirst and Sam Taylor Johnson, like a glove – you never know what artistic wonder lies around the next corner.

MMCA Seoul   MUSEUM
(Map p58; ☑02-3701 9500; www.mmca.go.kr; 30 Samcheong-ro, Jongno-gu; admission ₩4000; ☉10am-6pm Tue, Thu, Fri & Sun, to 9pm Wed & Sat; Ⓢ Line 3 to Anguk, Exit 1) Combining architectural elements from several centuries of Seoul's history, this new branch of the city's premier contemporary-art museum is a work in progress. The melding of spacious new gallery buildings with the art-deco buildings of the former Defense Security Command compound is impressive, but at the time of research the facility had yet to get a director (because this a politically sensitive appointment) and its shows have met with muted critical reaction. Nonetheless, it's well worth a visit.

Seoul Museum of History   MUSEUM
(서울역사박물관; Map p58; ☑02-724 0114; www.museum.seoul.kr; 55 Saemunan-ro, Jongno-gu; ☉9am-8pm Tue-Fri, to 7pm Sat & Sun; Ⓢ Line 5 to Gwanghwamun, Exit 7) ꜰʀᴇᴇ To gain an appreciation of the total transformation of Seoul down the centuries, visit this fascinating museum that charts the city's history since the dawn of the Joseon dynasty. Outside is one of the old tram cars that used to run in the city in the 1930s as well as a section of the old Gwanghwamun gate. Inside there's a massive scale model of the city you can walk around as well as donated exhibitions of crafts and photographs.

National Museum of Korean Contemporary History   MUSEUM
(Map p58; ☑02-3703 9200; www.much.go.kr; 198 Sejong-daero, Jongno-gu; ☉9am-6pm Tue, Thu, Fri & Sun, to 9pm Wed & Sat; Ⓢ Line 5 to Gwanghwamun, Exit 2) ꜰʀᴇᴇ The last century has been a tumultuous time for Korea, the key moments of which are memorialised and celebrated in this museum charting the highs and lows of that journey. The displays are modern, multilingual and engaging, as well as proof of how far the country has come in the decades since its almost total destruction during the Korean War. Head to the roof garden for a great view of Gyeongbokgung and Gwanghwamun Square.

Gwanghwamun Square   SQUARE
(광화문광장; Map p58; Sejong-daero, Jongno-gu; Ⓢ Line 5 to Gwanghwamun, Exit 4) Upgraded in recent years this broad, elongated square provides a grand approach to Gyeongbukgong and is used for various events (as well as protests). Giant statues celebrate two national heroes: **Admiral Yi Sun-sin**, 1545–98, who stands atop a plinth at the square's southern end; and a **statue of King Sejong**, 1397–1450, who sits regally on a throne in the middle of the square. An entrance at the base of the statue leads down to an **underground exhibition** (Map p58; Gwanghwamun Sq, Jongno-gu; ☉10.30am-10pm Tue-Sun; Ⓢ Line 5 to Gwanghwamun, Exit 4) ꜰʀᴇᴇ with sections on both of the men.

National Folk Museum of Korea   MUSEUM
(국립민속박물관; Map p58; ☑02-3704 3114; www.nfm.go.kr; 37 Samcheong-ro, Jongno-gu; ☉9am-6pm Wed-Mon Mar-Oct, to 5pm Wed-Mon Nov-Feb; Ⓢ Line 3 to Anguk, Exit 1) ꜰʀᴇᴇ Give yourself at least an hour to do justice to this excellent museum, which has three main exhibition halls covering the history of the Korean people, the agricultural way of life and the life of *yangban* (aristocrats) during the Joseon era. Among the many interesting exhibits is an amazingly colourful funeral bier (it looks like a fantasy Noah's Ark) – these were used to give the deceased a great send-off.

Ⓞ Myeong-dong & Jung-gu
명동, 중구

★ **N Seoul Tower & Namsan**   TOWER
(Map p46; www.nseoultower.com; Namsan; adult/child ₩9000/7000; ☉10am-11pm; ꔧ shuttle buses 2, 3, 5) The iconic N Seoul tower (236m), atop the city's guardian mountain Namsan, offers panoramic views of this immense metropolis from its observation deck. Come at sunset and you can watch the city morph into a galaxy of twinkling stars. Up top is the

Plan Your Trip

Outdoor Activities

Korea's countryside, coastline and islands are a year-round outdoor playground with a range of activities, including hiking, cycling, diving, surfing, rafting and kayaking. With soaring mountains and a reliable snow record, it's ideal for winter sports and in 2018 it will host the Winter Olympics.

Hiking & Rock Climbing

Hiking is Korea's number-one leisure activity. There are 21 national parks and scores more provincial parks, threaded with thousands of trails – everything from leisurely half-day walks, such as those along the Jeju Olle Trail, to strenuous mountain-ridge treks. Basic shelters are available, but expect a full house during holidays, summer months and autumn weekends. If you're planning a major overnight mountain trek, shelter reservations two weeks in advance are recommended. About a quarter of the trails may be closed at any one time to allow areas to regenerate.

➡ **Korea National Park Service** (www. knps.or.kr) For trail information and online reservations for park accommodation.

➡ **Hike Korea** (www.hikekorea.com) Learn about Korean mountain culture as well as many of the country's best trails. The site's author, Roger Shepherd, is one of the authors of *Baekdu-Daegu Trail,* a book that details the 1400km-long 'White Head Great Ridge' down the southern Korean Peninsula.

➡ **Hiking Hub Korea** (www.hikinghubkorea. com/about-hiking-hub.html) Downloadable PDFs of English-language hiking guides for many of Korea's mountains.

➡ **Adventure Korea** (www.adventurekorea. com) In addition to running hiking trips,

Activity Tips

Top 5 Outdoor Adventures

Climb Halla-san, Jeju-do

Dive Seogwipo, Jeju-do

Ski at Alpensia, Pyeongchang

Cycle around Seonyudo

Hike through Jirisan National Park

Responsible Outdoors

Pay any entrance fees required by park authorities.

Obtain reliable information about route conditions and tackle only trails within your realm of experience and fitness level. Do not hike closed trails.

Be aware of local laws, regulations and etiquette about wildlife and the environment.

Be aware that the weather can change quickly and seasonal changes will influence how you dress and the equipment you need to carry.

Leave only footprints, take only photographs – don't litter and don't bring back souvenirs such as seashells or flowers.

this expat-focused operator offers other adventurous activities, including cycling and rafting trips.

➡ **Korea on the Rocks** (www.koreaontherocks.com) Details on rock and ice climbing across Korea.

Cycling

To hire a bike, some form of ID is usually required. A helmet or lock is almost never included unless you ask.

In major cities it's possible to rent bikes – Seoul has great bicycle trails along the Han River.

Resorts with waterfront and hordes of tourists are sure to have a stand where bikes can be hired. Most bike paths are geared towards leisure riders, with couples and families in mind, so expect well-marked, paved, flat trails designed for pleasure rather than intense cross-country exhilaration.

The 200km pedal around Jeju-do, Korea's largest island, takes from three to five days, depending on your level of fitness and how quickly you wish to take it. Hwy 1132 runs around the entire island and has bicycle lanes on either side.

Another lovely island to cycle around is Seonyudo at the centre of the Gogunsan Archipelago, off the coast of Jeollabuk-do.

Filthy (www.mtbk-adventure.com) Written by Korea-based expats, this site details a selection of mountain-biking trails.

Skiing & Snowboarding

In 2018 Pyeongchang (p139) county in Gangwon-do will host the Winter Olympic Games, with Alpensia (p139) serving as the main resort and the larger Yongpyong (p140) nearby hosting the slalom events.

Korea's snow season runs from December to March. Lift tickets cost about ₩65,000 and equipment rentals about ₩30,000 per day. Package deals from travel agents include transport, tickets, rentals and, if required, lessons and accommodation. Overnight packages vary

KOREA'S TOP PARKS

National Parks

PARK	AREA	FEATURES & ACTIVITIES
Bukhansan	78 sq km	Great hiking, subway access from Seoul
Dadohae Haesang	2344 sq km (2004 sq km marine)	A marine park of scattered, unspoilt islands
Deogyusan	219 sq km	Ski resort, a fortress and a magical valley walk
Gyeongju	138 sq km	A historic park strewn with ancient Shilla and Buddhist relics
Hallasan	149 sq km	An extinct volcano; Korea's highest peak
Jirisan	440 sq km	Straddling two provinces; high peaks popular with serious hikers
Seoraksan	373 sq km	Korea's most beautiful park
Sobaeksan	320 sq km	Limestone caves and Guin-sa, an impressive temple complex, to explore

Provincial Parks

PARK	AREA	FEATURES & ACTIVITIES
Daedunsan	38 sq km	Granite cliffs, great views, hot-spring bath
Gajisan	104 sq km	Scenic views; famous Tongdo-sa temple
Mudeungsan	30 sq km	Near Gwangju, with an art gallery and a green-tea plantation
Taebaeksan	17 sq km	Visit the Coal Museum, hike to Dangun's altar

THE WASHINGTON POST / GETTY IMAGES ©

Hikers at Odaesan National Park (p142)

from ₩60,000 for a night in a *minbak* (private room in a home) or basic hotel, to upwards of ₩250,000 for condos and upmarket suites. Weekends are often very crowded, especially at resorts near Seoul. Skiers and snowboarders alike are catered for; boarding has become especially popular with Koreans in recent years.

Many resorts run dedicated shuttle buses to/from pick-up points in Seoul, making for a long but easy day on the slopes.

Gangwon-do

High1 (p141) Modern ski resort with among the best facilities and snow in Korea. Set in the Taebaek Mountains and boasting 18 slopes, five lifts and four gondolas.

Yongpyong (p140) Korea's oldest and biggest resort, with slopes ranging from bunny options to advanced runs.

Alpensia (p139) The 2018 Winter Games host resort. Its compact size also makes it a good place for families and anyone learning to ski.

Elysian Gangchon (p106) Small, slick ski resort reachable by the Seoul subway.

Jeollabuk-do

Deogyusan Muju (p272) The only ski area inside a national park, its 26 slopes are set in an Austrian-themed village.

Chungcheongbuk-do

Eagle Valley Ski Resort (p301) Modest resort near the relaxing hot springs of Suanbo.

North Korea

Masik-Ryong Ski Resort (p322) A pet project of Kim Jong-un, offering several runs (one over 5km long), bunny slopes, Skidoos, skating and the luxurious Masik Ryong Hotel.

Ice Skating

Indoor ice skating is available year-round at Seoul's **Lotte World** (롯데월드 아이스 링크; Map p67; ☎for English 02-1330; www.lotteworld.com/icerink; B3 fl, Lotte World Adventure, 240, Olympic-ro, Songpa-gu; per session incl rental adult/child ₩15,000/14,000; 🕒hours vary; 👪; [S]Line 2 or 8 to Jamsil, Exit 1).

Top: Skiing in Pyeongchang (p139)

Bottom: Golf in Incheon (107)

In winter there's an **outdoor rink** (서울광장 스케이트장; Map p46; ☎for English 02-1330; www.seoulskate.or.kr; 110 Sejong-daero; per hr incl skate rental ₩1000; ⏰10am-10pm Sun-Thu, to 11pm Fri-Sat Dec-Feb; 👪; [S]Line 1 or 2 to City Hall, Exit 5) outside City Hall, and the Grand Hyatt (p67) and Sheraton Walkerhill hotels have temporary outdoor rinks.

Surfing

Haeundae (p187) and Songjeong beaches in Busan are among the best places to experience South Korea's surf. However, you'll need to suit up as the best time for surf conditions is winter, when waves are whipped up by strong winds from the north. Water temperatures at these times dip to 3°C, but could be as high as 10°C. If that's too chilly for you, head to balmy Jungmun Beach (p255) off Jeju-do's south coast.

Diving

Korea has an active scuba diving scene. The top dive site is just off Seogwipo on Jeju-do's south coast, with walls of colourful soft coral, 18m-high kelp forests (March to May), schools of fish and the occasional inquisitive dolphin. Diving here is a mixture of tropical and temperate – rather like diving in Norway and the Red Sea at the same time. Visibility is best from September to November, when it can be up to 30m (it's around 10m at other times) and water temperature varies from 15°C to 28°C.

Other good underwater sites on the east coast are Hongdo, off the south coast; Pohang, Ulleungdo and Dragon Head, off Sokcho; and a wreck dive off Gangneung. The west coast has some dive operators – at Daecheon beach, for instance – but visibility can be poor.

Golf

In 1998 Se Ri Pak put South Korea onto the golf map by winning the US Women's Open. Today, Korean women dominate the American LPGA Tour and golf is a national pastime with hundreds of courses dotting the country.

One of the most popular golfing destination is Jeju-do, where courses include Jungmun Beach Golf Club (p255) and Pinx Golf Club (p260).

Playing on a course in Korea isn't cheap. An average 18-hole round of golf may set you back ₩300,000. But for virtual golf, there are thousands of golf cafes around the country, so you'll find one in just about any city. A round of virtual golf at chains such as **Golfzon** (http://company.golfzon.com) costs about ₩30,000. Also common are golf practice ranges.

Birdwatching

With some of the widest and most extensive tidal flats in the world, the Korean Peninsula is a natural magnet for birds. More than 500 species have been spotted in Korea, including 34 threatened species. Most are on their migratory route between Siberia and Manchuria in the north and Southeast Asia and Australia in the south.

Popular birdwatching spots include the following.

➡ **Suncheon Bay** This wetland park on Jeollanam-do's south coast is where the hooded crane winters.

➡ **Demilitarized Zone (DMZ)** A preferred stop for migrating birds because it's been uninhabited for 50 years.

➡ **Bamseom Island Bird Sanctuary** This pair of islets in Seoul's Han River is off-limits to humans but birds – including mandarins, mallards, spotbills and great egrets – can be spotted from an observation platform in Yeouido's Han River Park.

Birds Korea (www.birdskorea.org) has photos of Korean birds and lots of info for bird lovers.

Kayaking, Canoeing & Rafting

Gangwon-do's northwest is the hotspot for kayaking, canoeing and rafting trips from mid-April to October. Adventure Korea (p29) and Koridoor (p60) also offer whitewater rafting trips.

Regions at a Glance

Seoul

History
Food
Shopping

Historic Landmarks

Given how thoroughly it was trashed during the Korean War, it's no small miracle that so many of Seoul's historic landmarks remain. A number of them are meticulous reconstructions, but that doesn't diminish their significance or impact.

Food & Drink

Seoul is the best place to sample the full range of Korean culinary delights – from hot kimchi stews and sizzling street snacks to the delicate morsels that make up a royal banquet.

Shoppers' Delight

At all times of day or night there's always somewhere to shop in Seoul. The teeming markets of Dongdaemun and Namdaemun are must-do experiences, as is cruising the boutiques and department stores of Myeong-dong or ritzy Apgujeong and Cheongdam.

p38

Around Seoul

Islands
History
Art

Island Escapes

Scores of islands flaking off like crumbs into the West Sea make for perfect escapes from the urban grip of Seoul and Incheon. Try historic Ganghwado or laid-back Muuido, which has gorgeous beaches.

Historic Sites

The DMZ splitting North and South Korea is a must-see, as are the Unesco World Heritage–listed fortress walls surrounding the inner core of Suwon.

Artistic Places

The pottery town of Incheon draws in ceramics lovers, and Heyri near the DMZ border is a serene village packed with small galleries. See something different in the exhibitions at Incheon Art Platform or the sculptures of Anyang Art Park.

p94

Gangwon-do

Hiking
Skiing
Quirky

Misty Mountains

Seoraksan National Park abounds with gorgeous vistas of mist-shrouded crags that rarely fail to stun. The valleys are full of quiet temples, hot springs and hiking trails.

Hit the Slopes

Host of the 2018 Winter Olympics, Pyeongchang's Yongpyong and Alpensia ski resorts aren't the biggest in the world but they pack in heaps of family-friendly options such as sledding and inner tubing.

The Unknown DMZ

Peek into North Korea at the northernmost point along the DMZ at the Goseong Unification Observatory, or go deep under the zone itself in the Second Infiltration Tunnel in Cheorwon.

p119

Gyeongsang-buk-do

Temples
History
Food

Idyllic Retreats

Topping mist-shrouded mountains are mysterious ancient temples, idyllically isolated from the neon-drenched cities of Gyeongsangbuk-do.

Historic Sites

Head to Gyeongju, the 'museum without walls', for a slice of Shilla history, be it the fabulous finds on display at the excellent National Museum, or the tombs and temples that surround the town.

Delicious Dishes

The island of Ul-leungdo offers the best seafood in Korea, or try Andong's famous mackerel. Don't miss Daegu or Gyeongju's innovative and superb eating options, surely some of the best in the country.

p147

Busan & Gyeongsang-nam-do

Food
Beaches
Islands

Fresh Fish

You'd have to be swimming in the ocean to get your hands on seafood fresher than the produce at Busan's Jagalchi Fish Market. Pick your creature from a tank and it'll be your next meal within minutes.

Sand Castling

Sure, Haeundae beach can be overcrowded and over-hyped, but it's the nation's most loved for good reason. Kick back in the sand, frolic in the waves and snack on barbecued shellfish in Cheongsapo.

Island-Hopping

The coastline has myriad islands to explore, but Nam-haedo, one of the largest, is stunningly beautiful, with mountaintop temples and terraced rice paddies sloping down to the sea.

p182

Jeollanam-do

Art & Culture
Islands
Quirky

Ceramics & Art

From Gangjin's ancient celadon (green-tinged pottery) kilns to Gwangju's brand-new Asian Culture Complex, Jeollanam-do has a long history of supporting the arts.

Islands Galore

The rolling hills lead down to the coastline, where you can hop on a boat to explore hundreds of islands. Don't forget to sample the local catch of the day: sashimi, abalone or even live octopus.

Eclectic Excursions

Hunting for murals in a traditional market (in Gwangju), getting steamy in a seawater sauna (in Hampyeong), gawking at sunken treasures (in Mokpo)... these are just some of the quirky sights and activities possible here.

p208

Jeju-do

Hiking
Art & Culture
Food

Hiking Trails

Discover the island the slow way, following one or more of the 26 routes on the Jeju Olle Trail. Alternatively, take one of four routes to the top of Hallasan (1950m), South Korea's tallest mountain.

Arty Stones & Sexy Art

Jeju-do is packed with all manner of galleries and museums, from the impressive Jeju Stone Park and stunning photos at Kim Young Gap Gallery Dumoak, to a trio of sex museums.

Local Delicacies

Jeju's separately developed island culture reveals itself in a distinct cuisine, heavy on seafood but also with cuts of black pig and horse on the menu.

p231

Jeollabuk-do

Hiking
Food
History

Head for the Hills

For a small province, Jeollabuk-do has an impressive amount of parkland. Choose from a number of national and provincial parks and join the droves of outdoor enthusiasts in exploring Korea's natural beauty.

Glorious Food

In the middle of an agricultural heartland, Jeonju is Korea's favourite foodie destination, home of the rice dish bibimbap and a lively street-food culture. After hours it's all about the *makgeolli* (milky rice wine).

Go Back in Time

History is celebrated in Jeonju's *hanok* village and its clusters of artisans. Other engaging reminders of the past include the Gochang fortress and the former colonial port of Gunsan.

p263

Chungcheongnam-do

Beaches
Festivals
History

Sunbathing Fun

There are opportunities galore to work on that tan at Korea's most popular beaches. Whether you like packed summer scenes or intimate small strips of sand, you'll find it here.

Mud Rollicking

Possibly Korea's most famous (some say infamous) festival, the Boryeong Mud Festival is a messy extravaganza that's hugely popular with foreigners.

Baekje History

The twin sleepy towns of Gongju and Buyeo were once the seat of power of Korea's earliest dynasty, the long-running Baekje kingdom. Festivals, fortresses, tombs and museums pay tribute to its legacy.

p276

Chungcheongbuk-do

Temples
Gentle Activities
History

Find Inner Peace

While Korea may be awash with temples, some of the most grand and glorious can be found here. The modern hillside complex of Guin-sa impresses, as does the 33m-high gold Buddha at Beopju-sa.

Slow it Down

This landlocked region, with its quiet towns, offers a chance for leisurely exploration of Korea's heartland. Take a meandering cruise along Chungju Lake or soak in an *oncheon* (hot-spring spa) at Suanbo.

Footnotes in History

The world's first book printed by movable type was created in Cheongju. Other historical footnotes, such as the Cheongnamdae presidential villa, will also vie for your attention.

p293

North Korea

Politics
Quirky
Scenery

Monuments and Propaganda

Any trip to North Korea is full of politics, from the ubiquitous propaganda to the museums, monuments and art. Coming here is a fascinating chance to see things from a different perspective.

Mind-Bogglers

Whether visiting an exhibition of Kim Jong-il's gifts housed in a mountainside warehouse, or taking a trip on the world's most secretive metro system, there's no trip weirder than a tour of the DPRK.

Spectacular Scenery

Beyond its unique political situation, North Korea is rich in natural beauty, with soaring mountains, sandy beaches and crystal-clear lakes, making it a great place for nature lovers.

p306

On the Road

Seoul

📖 02 / POP 10.01 MILLION

Includes ➜

Best Places to Eat

➜ Jungsik (p74)

➜ Noryangjin Fish Market (p73)

➜ Congdu (p70)

➜ Gwangjang Market (p73)

➜ Coreanos Kitchen (p74)

Best Places to Stay

➜ Hide & Seek Guesthouse (p63)

➜ Minari House (p65)

➜ Small House Big Door (p63)

➜ Itaewon G Guest House (p65)

➜ Park Hyatt Seoul (p68)

Why Go?

An old Korean proverb goes 'even if you have to crawl on your knees, get yourself to Seoul!' Never has this been more sound advice. Asia's second-richest city, Seoul (서울) is a dynamic mash-up of markets and K-Pop, teahouses and temples, palaces and mountains, skyscrapers and pulsing neon. This Unesco City of Design also offers several contemporary architectural marvels, including the Dongdaemun Design Plaza & Park and the giant glass wave of the new City Hall.

Gaze down on this sprawling metropolis of 10 million people from atop any of Seoul's four guardian mountains and you will innately sense the powerful *pungsu-jiri* (feng shui) that has long nurtured and protected the city. Public transport is brilliant and whatever you want, at any time of the day or night, Seoul can provide. The joys of eating, drinking, shopping and general merrymaking are in abundant evidence, from Apgujeong's chic boutiques to Hongdae's bars and restaurants.

When to Go

Seoul

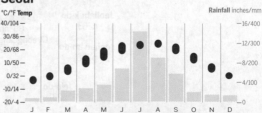

May Enjoy good weather and top events such as the Jongmyo Daeje and Lotus Lantern Festival.

Aug Cool off at the outdoor swimming pools along the Han River.

Oct Hike across mountains coated in brilliant autumn colours, and enjoy Seoul's fireworks festival.

History

When Seoul became the capital of Korea following the establishment of the Joseon dynasty in 1392, its population was around 100,000. Just over 600 years later this has ballooned to just over 10 million (or 25.6 million if you consider the wider metro area), making Seoul one of the world's largest cities, and the second richest in Asia in terms of GDP, after Tokyo.

During the 20th century the city suffered first under Japanese colonial rule and then during the Korean War when it was almost entirely destroyed. Rebuilt from the 1960s, Seoul is the country's centre of cultural, economic and political power. Past mayors have gone on to become South Korea's president, including Lee Myung-bak, who finished his term of office as president in December 2012.

When Park Won-soon, a former human rights lawyer and independent candidate, was elected Seoul's mayor in October 2011, it was a watershed moment not only for Korean politics but also for the city itself. Under previous mayors, top of the agenda had been construction-led growth that resulted in flashy, expensive projects such as the reclamation of the Cheong-gye-cheon and the commissioning of Dongdaemun Design Plaza.

Park has since aligned with the left-of-centre Democratic Party and won a second term as Seoul's mayor with policies such as building more footpaths and pedestrian-only zones, a bicycle-sharing scheme and expansion of the subway appealing to voters.

Sights

You'll spend the bulk of your time north of the meandering Han River that splits Seoul into two distinct regions, which are themselves split into 25 *gu* (administrative districts). This is home to historic Seoul, a relatively compact, walkable area.

Seoul's fascinating feudal past can be glimpsed in the palaces around Gwanghwamun (the main gate to Gyeongbokgung). Nearby Insa-dong (인사동), Samcheong-dong (삼청동) and Bukchon are all packed with souvenir shops, teahouses, restaurants and small museums, often in converted *hanok* (traditional wooden houses). Note that the narrow streets in these areas can get jammed on weekends and holidays. There are a few other sights of note further north around Seoul City Wall, which once encircled the city.

Namsan, crowned by N Seoul Tower, the green hill at the heart of the old city, is sandwiched between Myeong-dong shopping district to the north and the foreigner-friendly zone of Itaewon to the south. Not far to the west are the youthful party districts of Hongdae (the area around Hongik University), Sinchon and Edae.

South of the river, Gangnam and surrounding suburbs are best for shopping and entertainment.

SEOUL SIGHTS

SEOUL IN...

Two Days

Stroll around **Bukchon Hanok Village** (p43). Grab lunch and go shopping in **Insa-dong** (p86) then attend the changing of the palace guard at **Gyeongbokgung** (p43) or join the day's last tour of **Changdeokgung** (p43). Enjoy dinner in **Gwangjang Market** (p73). On day two visit the splendid **Leeum Samsung Museum of Art** (p51). Move on to either the **National Museum of Korea** (p50) or the **War Memorial of Korea** (p51). Freshen up at **Dragon Hill Spa & Resort** (p56), ride the cable car to **N Seoul Tower** (p44) atop Namsan then return to **Itaewon** for dining and late-night carousing.

Five Days

Follow Seoul City Wall up **Bukak-san** (p52) and down to the **Gilsang-sa** (p48) temple. Explore **Dongdaemun Design Plaza & Park** (p51), pick up a new outfit from the market here then follow the **Cheong-gye-cheon** (p43) back to the heart of the city. On day four visit **Seodaemun Prison History Hall** (p50) and hike up **Inwangsan Guksadang** (p50), where you might come across shamans performing ancient ceremonies. End the day with a traditional performing-arts show and royal-cuisine meal at **Korea House** (p85). Cap your visit off with a meal at **Noryangjin Fish Market** (p73), hire a bike in Yeouido and **cycle along the Han River** (p57) and soak up the buzzing nocturnal vibe of **Hongdae**.

Seoul Highlights

1 Soak up the serenity of the Secret Garden at World Heritage–listed **Changdeokgung** (p43).

2 Lose yourself in the picturesque streets of **Bukchon Hanok Village** (p43).

3 Take a break from the city with a stroll beside the **Cheong-gye-cheon** (p43).

4 Hike the old city walls to the summit of **Bukak-san** (p52) for panoramic views.

5 Shop until you drop in Myeong-dong and the all-night **Namdaemun Market** (p86).

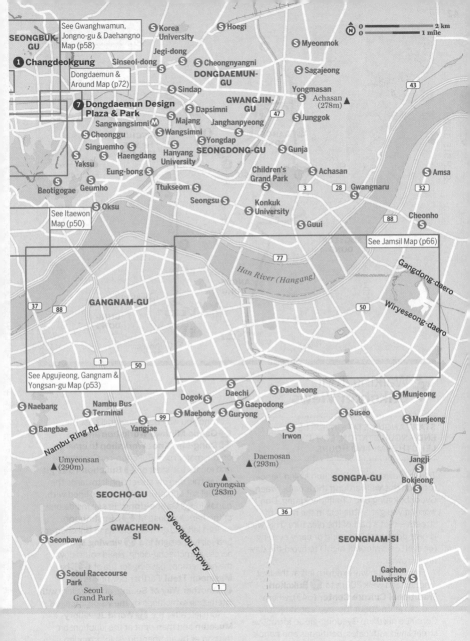

SEONGBUK-GU

See Gwanghwamun, Jongno-gu & Daehangno Map (p58)

❶ Changdeokgung

Sinseol-dong

Jegi-dong

Ⓢ Korea University

Ⓢ Hoegi

Ⓢ Myeonmok

Ⓢ Cheongnyangni

DONGDAEMUN-GU

Ⓢ Sagajeong

Dongdaemun & Around Map (p72)

Ⓢ Sindap

GWANGJIN-GU

Yongmasan

Ⓢ Junggok

Achasan (278m) ▲

43

❼ Dongdaemun Design Plaza & Park

Ⓢ Dapsimni

47

Sangwangsimni Ⓜ

Ⓢ Majang

Janghanpyeong

Ⓢ Cheonggu

Ⓢ Wangsimni

Ⓢ Yongdap

SEONGDONG-GU

Ⓢ Gunja

Singuemho Ⓢ

Haengdang

Hanyang University

Ⓢ Achasan

Ⓢ Amsa

Yaksu

Eung-bong Ⓢ

Children's Grand Park Ⓢ

3   28   Gwangnaru

32

Beotigogae

Ⓢ   Geumho

Ⓢ Ttukseom

Seongsu Ⓢ

Konkuk Ⓢ University

Ⓢ Oksu

Ⓢ Guui

88

Cheonho

See Itaewon Map (p50)

Ⓢ Seongsu

See Jamsil Map (p66)

Han River (Hangang)

77

Gangdong-daero

GANGNAM-GU

37   88

50

Wiryeseong-daero

1   50

See Apgujieong, Gangnam & Yongsan-gu Map (p53)

Ⓢ Daechi

Ⓢ Daecheong

Ⓢ Munjeong

Dogok Ⓢ

Ⓢ Gaepodong

Ⓢ Naebang

Nambu Bus Ⓢ Terminal

Ⓢ Maebong Guryong

Ⓢ Suseo

Ⓢ Munjeong

Ⓢ Bangbae

99

Yangjae

Ⓢ Irwon

Nambu Ring Rd

Ⓢ Jangji

Umyeonsan ▲(290m)

Daemosan ▲(293m)

SONGPA-GU

Bokjeong Ⓢ

Guryongsan (283m) ▲

36

SEOCHO-GU

GWACHEON-SI

Gyeongbu Expwy

SEONGNAM-SI

Ⓢ Seonbawi

Ⓢ Seoul Racecourse Park

Seoul Grand Park

1

Gachon University Ⓢ

❻ Party the night away at the bars and clubs of **Hongdae** (p74).

❼ Marvel at the space-age architecture of **Dongdaemun Design Plaza & Park** (p51).

❽ Listen to shamans' chants on the hills of **Inwangsan** (p50).

❾ Soak and sweat away your stresses at the **Dragon Hill Spa** (p56).

❿ Hire a bicycle and pedal around Yeouido and beside the **Han River** (p57).

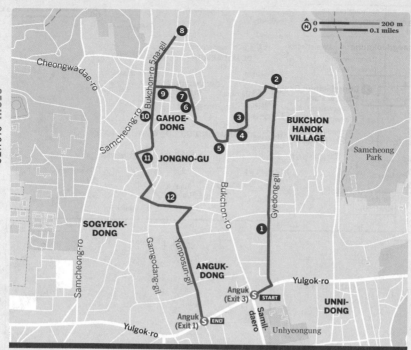

🏃 Walking Tour
Bukchon Views

START ANGUK STATION, EXIT 3
END ANGUK STATION, EXIT 1
LENGTH 3KM; TWO HOURS

Take in views across Bukchon's tiled *hanok* roofs on this walk around the area between Gyeonbokgung and Changdeokgung. Don't worry if you get a little lost in the maze of streets – that's part of the pleasure. This walk is best done early morning or early evening (or even on a moonlit night) to avoid the daytime crowds.

From the subway exit turn left at the first junction and walk 200m to **❶ Bukchon Traditional Culture Center** (p43), where you can learn about the area's architecture. Continue north up Gyedong-gil, an attractive street lined with cafes, boutiques and *hanok* guesthouses. At the T-junction at the top of the hill is the entrance to **❷ Choong Ang High School**, an attractive early 20th-century education complex that featured as a location in the hit Korean TV drama *Winter Sonata*.

Wind you way back downhill past the **❸ Gahoe Minhwa Workshop** and the **❹ Dong-Lim Knot Workshop** to emerge on the major road Bukchon-ro. Cross over and locate the start of **❺ Bukchon-ro 11-gil**. Follow this narrow street uphill towards the parallel set of picturesque streets lined with *hanok* in **❻ Gahoe-dong**. To see inside one of the *hanok*, pause at **❼ Simsimheon**.

Turn left and go a few blocks to Bukchon-ro 5na-gil; to the right is a **❽ viewing spot** across Samcheong-dong. Head south down the hill, perhaps pausing for tea at **❾ Cha Masineun Tteul**. Further downhill is **❿ Another Way of Seeing**, an art gallery with interesting exhibitions by the vision impaired.

Turn left after the **⓫ World Jewellery Museum** and then right at the junction; on the corner by another tourist information booth, walk up to the park at **⓬ Jeongdok Public Library**, a prime spot for viewing cherry blossoms in spring and the yellowing leaves of ginkgo trees in autumn. Return to the subway station via Yunposun-gil.

Myeong-dong

Skygarden PARK
(Map p46; Seoul Station; S Line 1 or 4 to Seoul Station, Exit 2) Earmarked for completion by the end of 2017, Seoul's Skygarden is proposed to be what the High Line is to New York, an elevated urban tree-filled park in the heart of the city. It will run along an abandoned stretch of highway overpass near Seoul Station.

◉ Western Seoul

Ewha Womans
University ARCHITECTURE, MUSEUM
(www.ewha.ac.kr; Ewhayeodae-gil, Seodaemun-gu; S Line 2 to Ewha Womans University, Exit 2) Come to this venerable university, founded in 1886 by American Methodist missionary Mary Scranton, to view Dominque Perrault's stunning main entrance, a building that dives six storeys underground and is split by a broad cascade of steps leading up to the Gothic-style 1935 Pfeiffer Hall. Walking through here feels like experiencing the parting of the Red Sea.

Jeoldusan Martyrs' Shrine MUSEUM
(절두산 순교성지; ☎02 3142 4434; www .jeoldusan.or.kr; 6 Tojeong-ro, Mapo-gu; museum by donation; ⊙ shrine 24hr, museum 9.30am-5pm Tue-Sun; S Line 2 or 6 to Hapjeong, Exit 7) Jeoldusan means 'Beheading Hill' – this is where up to 2000 Korean Catholics were executed in 1866 following a royal decree, most thrown off the high cliff here into the Han River. Next to

the chapel (where Mass is held daily at 10am and 3pm), the museum includes some of the grizzly wooden torture equipment used on the Catholic martyrs, 27 of whom have been made saints. There are also books, diaries and relics of the Catholic converts.

War & Women's Human Rights Museum MUSEUM

(전쟁과여성인권박물관; Map p49; ☎02-365 4016; www.womenandwar.net; 20 World Cup Buk-ro 11-gil, Mapo-gu; adult/child under 14yr/youth 14-19yr ₩3000/1000/2000; 🕐1-6pm Tue, Thu-Sat, 3-6pm Wed; 🚌6, 15, 7711, 7011, 7016 or 7737, [S] Line 2 to Hongik University, Exit 1, then) In Korea the survivors of sexual slavery by the Japanese military during WWII (know euphemistically as 'comfort women') are respectfully called *halmoni* (grandmother). When you enter this well-designed and powerfully moving museum you'll be given a card printed with the story of a *halmoni* helping you to connect with the tragic history of these women.

KT&G SangsangMadang ARCHITECTURE

(KT&G 상상마당; Map p49; ☎02-330 6200; www.sangsangmadang.com; 65 Eoulmadang-ro, Mapo-gu; 🕐shop noon-11pm, gallery 1-10pm; [S] Line 2 to Hongik University, Exit 5) Funded by Korea's top tobacco company, this visually striking building is home to an art-house cinema, a concert space (hosting top indie bands) and galleries that focus on experimental, fringe exhibitions. There's also a great design shop for gifts on the ground floor. The architect Bae Dae-yong called his design the 'Why Butter Building' as the pattern of concrete across its glazed facade is said to resemble both butterfly wings and butter spread on toast.

Northern Seoul

★Korea Furniture Museum MUSEUM

(한국가구박물관; ☎02 745 0181; www.kofum.com; 121 Daesagwan-ro, Seongbuk-gu; tour without/with tea ₩20,000/40,000; 🕐11am-5pm Mon-Sat; [S] Line 4 to Hangsung University, Exit 6) Advance reservations are required for the hour-long guided tours of this gem of a museum in which 10 beautiful buildings serve as the appetiser to the main course: a collection of furniture, including chests, bookcases, chairs and dining tables made from varieties of wood, such as persimmon, maple and paulownia, some decorated with lacquer, mother of pearl or tortoise shell. Take a taxi here from the subway exit.

★Gilsang-sa TEMPLE

(길상사; ☎02-3672 5945; www.gilsang sa.or.kr; 68 Seonjam-ro 50-gil, Seongbuk-gu; 🕐10am-6pm Mon-Sat; [S] Line 4 to Hangsung University, Exit 6) This delightful hillside temple is beautiful to visit at any time of year, but particularly so in May when the grounds are festooned with lanterns for Buddha's birthday. There's a small teahouse and the temple offers an overnight templestay program on the third weekend of the month.

A shuttle bus runs roughly once an hour between 8.30am and 4.30pm to the temple from near the subway exit.

Changgyeonggung PALACE

(창경궁; Palace of Flourishing Gladness; Map p58; ☎02-762 4868; http://english.cha.go.kr; 185 Changgyeonggung-ro, Jongno-gu; adult/child ₩1000/500; 🕐9am-6.30pm Tue-Sun; [S] Line 4 to Hyehwa, Exit 4) Originally built in the early 15th century by King Sejong for his parents, the oldest surviving structure of this palace is the **Okcheongyo** stone bridge (1483) over the stream by the main gate. The main hall, **Myeongjeongjeon** (Map p58), 1616, has lovely latticework and an ornately carved and decorated ceiling. Look out for dates (usually in early May) when the palace is open for night viewing and illuminated, making it a romantic spot – if you can ignore the crowds.

Ihwa Maeul NEIGHBOURHOOD

(이화 벽화 마을; Ihwa-dong, Jongno-gu; [S] Line 4 to Hyehwa, Exit 2) High on the slopes of Naksan is one of the city's old *daldongnae* (literally 'moon village') where refugees lived in shacks after the Korean War. Sixty years later it has morphed into a tourism hot spot thanks to a growing collection of quirky sculptures and imaginative murals on walls along the village's steep stairways and alleys. It's a great area for casual wandering, but if you drop by the **Lock Museum** (쇳대박물관; Map p58; ☎02-766 6494; 100 Ihwajang-gil, Jongno-gu; adult/child ₩4000/3000; 🕐10am-6pm Tue-Sun; [S] Line 4 to Hyehwa, Exit 2) you can pick up an English map to the village.

The euphemistic name *daldongnae* alludes to the fact that residents had a great view of the moon from their hovels high on the hillside. There are still wonderful views of the city but try to come early – and certainly avoid weekends – unless you like being surrounded by mobs of selfie-stick-toting tourists.

upmarket **N.Grill** (☎02-3455 9297; lunch/dinner from ₩55,000/95,000; ⏲11am-3pm & 5-11pm; [S] Line 4 to Myeongdong, Exit 3 then cable car) and a cafe. The tower has become a hot date spot with the railings around it festooned with locks inscribed with lovers' names.

Walking up Namsan isn't difficult, but riding the **cable car** (Map p46; one-way/return adult ₩6000/8500, child ₩3000/5500; ⏲10am-11pm; [S] Line 4 to Myeongdong, Exit 3) is popular for more good views.

★Deoksugung PALACE

(덕수궁; Map p46; www.deoksugung.go.kr; 99 Sejong-daero, Jung-gu; adult/under 7yr/child ₩1000/free/500; ⏲9am-9pm Tue-Sun; [S] Line 1 or 2 to City Hall, Exit 2) One of Seoul's five grand palaces built during the Joseon dynasty, Deoksugung (meaning Palace of Virtuous Longevity) is the only one you can visit in the evening and see the buildings illuminated. It first served as a palace in 1593 and is a fascinating mix of traditional Korean and Western-style neo-classical structures. The palace's main gate is the scene of the entertaining **changing of the guard** ceremony at 11am, 2pm and 3.30pm.

★Seoul City Hall ARCHITECTURE

(서울시청사; Map p46; http://english.seoul.go.kr; 110 Sejong-daero, Jung-gu; ⏲7.30am-6pm Mon-Fri, from 9am Sat & Sun; [S] Line 1 or 2 to City Hall, Exit 5) [FREE] Looking like a tsunami made of glass and steel, the Seoul City Hall was completely redeveloped in 2013. It is a modern reinterpretation of traditional Korean design; the cresting wave provides shade (like eaves found on palaces and temple roofs) over the handsome old City Hall, which was built from stone in 1926.

★Citizens Hall CULTURAL CENTRE

(Map p46; ☎02-739 7733; www.seoulcitizenshall.kr; basement, City Hall, 110 Sejong-daero, Jung-gu; ⏲9am-9pm Tue-Sun; [S] Line 1 or 2 to City Hall, Exit 5) [FREE] Head down to city hall's basement to reach Citizens Hall, a multipurpose space with an interesting mix of multimedia art exhibitions, design shops and a fair-trade cafe. There's also a 21st-century version of Speakers Corner and Media Wall where locals can express their views. Pick up a map and guide from its information desk.

Namsangol Hanok Village CULTURAL CENTRE

(남산골한옥마을; Map p46; ☎02-2264 4412; http://hanokmaeul.seoul.go.kr; 28 Toegye-ro 34-gil, Jung-gu; ⏲9am-9pm Wed-Mon Apr-Oct, to 8pm Nov-Mar, office 10am-5pm; [S] Line 3 or 4 to Chungmu-ro, Exit 4) [FREE] Located in a park at the foot of Namsan, this peaceful village is a wonderful spot to encounter traditional Korean culture. It features five differing *yangban* (upper class) houses from the Joseon era, all relocated here from different parts of Seoul. Also here is **Seoul Namsan Gugakdang** (☎02-2261 0512; tickets from ₩20,000; ⏲closed Tue; [S] Line 3 or 4 to Chungmuro, Exit 4) where traditional music and concerts are staged most evenings.

On the right of the entrance is an office that provides free one-hour tours around the village at 10.30am, noon, 2pm and 3.30pm.

Sungnyemun GATE

(남대문, Namdaemun; Map p46; ⏲9am-6pm Tue-Sun; [S] Line 4 to Hoehyeon, Exit 5) [FREE] Standing alone on an island – in direct contrast to the mayhem around it – Seoul's picturesque Great South Gate, Sungnyemun (also known as Namdaemun) is one of the capital's original four main gates built in the 14th century. Its arched brick entrance, topped by a double-storey pavilion, is accessed by pedestrian crossing from Gate 1 of Namdaemun Market. It's been reconstructed a number times over the years following damage under Japanese occupation and during the Korean War, and most recently after an arson attack in 2008.

Seoul Museum of Art GALLERY

(서울시립미술관, SEMA; Map p46; ☎02-2124 8800; www.sema.seoul.go.kr/; 61 Deoksugung-gil, Jung-gu; ⏲10am-8pm Tue-Fri, to 7pm Sat & Sun; [S] Line 1 or 2 to City Hall, Exit 2) [FREE] Hosting world-class exhibitions that are always worth a visit, SEMA has ultra-modern, bright galleries inside the handsome brick-and-stone facade of the 1928 Supreme Court building. For some special exhibitions an entrance fee is charged.

Myeong-dong Catholic Cathedral CHURCH

(명동성당; Map p46; ☎02-774 1784; www.mdsd.or.kr; 74 Myeong-dong-gil, Jung-gu; [S] Line 4 to Myeongdong, Exit 6) [FREE] Go inside this elegant, red- and grey-brick Gothic-style cathedral, consecrated in 1898, to admire the vaulted ceiling and stained-glass windows. The cathedral provided a sanctuary for student and trade-union protestors during military rule, becoming a national symbol of democracy and human rights. Its sleek modern plaza entrance adds an intriguing 21st-century touch with designer shops and cafes.

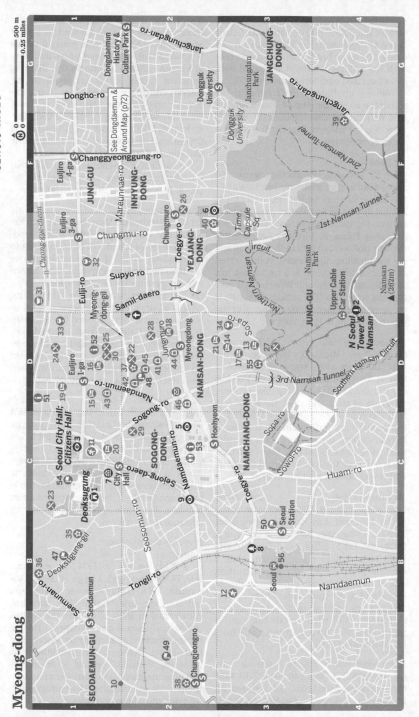

Myeong-dong

500 m
0.25 miles

Dongdaemun History & Culture Park

See Dongdaemun & Around Map (p72)

Dongho-ro

Jangchungno-ro

JANGCHUNG-DONG

Dongguk University

Janchungdan Park

Jangchungdan-ro

Changgyeonggung-ro

Euljiro 4-ga

JUNG-GU

Mareunnae-ro

INHYUNG-DONG

Dongguk University

2nd Namsan Tunnel

39

Euljiro 3-ga

Chungmu-ro

Chungmuro

26

Toegye-ro

YEAJANG-DONG

40 6

Time Capsule Sq

1st Namsan Tunnel

Cheong-gye-cheon

31

Eulji-ro

Myeong-dong-gil

Samil-daero

Supyo-ro

32

4

Northern Namsan Circuit

Namsan Park

Namsan (262m)

33

28

Jungmuro

Sopa-ro

34

Upper Cable Car Station

Namsan

JUNG-GU

24

52 25

30

22

45

Myeongdong

Myeongdong

21 14

18

13

N Seoul Tower & Namsan

2

Euljiro 1-ga

16

42 37

41 48

44

NAMSAN-DONG

17 55

27

3rd Namsan Tunnel

51

19

15

43

29

46

Hoehyeon

Southern Namsan Circuit

Namdaemun-ro

Sogong-ro

Seoul City Hall; Citizens Hall

3 11

20

SOGONG-DONG

5

53

Hoehyeon

NAMCHANG-DONG

Sopa-ro

Sowol-ro

Huam-ro

54

Deoksugung

7

City Hall

9

Sejong-daero

Namdaemun-ro

Toegye-ro

23

Seosomun-ro

50

Seoul Station

Deoksugung-gil

35

47

8

56

36

Deoksugung-gil

SEODAEMUN-GU

Seodaemun

Seoul

Namdaemun

Tongil-ro

12

Saemunan-ro

49

Chungjeongno

38

Hongdae

Hongdae

Seodaemun Prison History Hall MUSEUM

(서대문형무소역사관; www.sscmc.or.kr/culture2/foreign/eng/eng01.html; 251 Tongil-ro, Seodaemun-gu; adult/child/youth ₩3000/100/1500; ⏲9.30am-6pm Tue-Sun Mar-Oct, to 5pm Tue-Sun Nov-Feb; [S]Line 3 to Dongnimmun, Exit 5) Built in 1908, this one-time prison is a symbol of Japanese cruelty and oppression during their colonial rule of Korea from 1910 until 1945. However, it was also used by Korea's various postwar dictators up until its closure in 1987. View the original cell blocks where independence fighters and democracy campaigners were held. Of the hundreds of prisoners who died here the most famous is Ryu Gwan-sun, an 18-year-old Ewha high school student, who was tortured to death in 1920.

Inwangsan Guksadang SHRINE

(인왕산 국사당; Inwangsan, Seodaemun-gu; [S]Line 3 to Dongnimmun, Exit 2) This is Seoul's most famous shamanist shrine and a place where you may witness *gut*, sacrifices to the spirits made by *mudang* (shamans) who are usually female. The Japanese demolished the original shrine on Namsan in 1925, so Korean shamanists rebuilt it here. The simple shrine with turquoise painted doors is above the temple **Seonamjeong** (선암정사), marked by a bell pavilion and gates painted with a pair of traditional door guardians.

◎ Itaewon & Yongsan-gu 이태원, 용산구

★**National Museum of Korea** MUSEUM

(국립중앙박물관; www.museum.go.kr; 137 Seobinggo-ro; ⏲9am-6pm Tue, Thu & Fri, to 9pm Wed & Sat, to 7pm Sun; [S]Line 1 or 4 to Ichon, Exit 2) [FREE] The grand, marble-lined, modernist building cleverly channels plenty of natural light to show off Korea's ancient treasures. Among the must-see exhibits in the ground-floor galleries are the **Baekje Incense Burner**, an extraordinary example of the artistry of the 6th- to

Itaewon

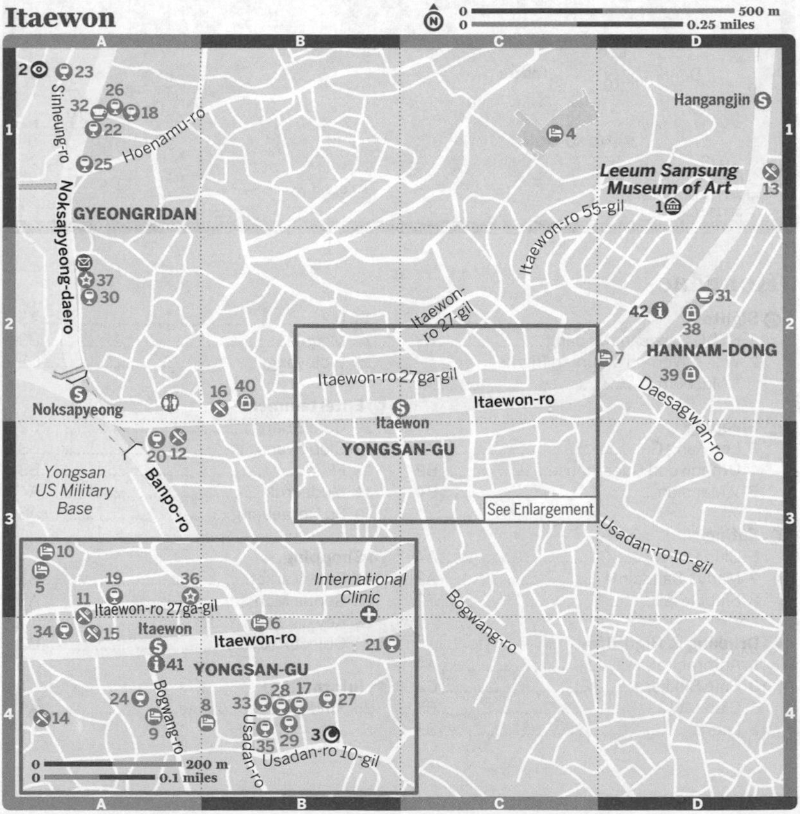

7th-century Baekje Kingdom, and the **Golden Treasures for the Great Tomb of Hwangham**. In the 3rd-floor sculpture and craft galleries, search out the **Pensive Bodhisattva** from the 7th century. Also look down on the top of the Goryeo-dynasty **Ten Story Pagoda** carved from marble.

★Leeum Samsung Museum of Art GALLERY

(Map p50; www.leeum.org; 60-16 Itaewon-ro 55-gil; adult/child ₩10,000/4000, temporary exhibition ₩7000/4000, day pass ₩13,000/6000; ⏲10.30am-6pm Tue-Sun; [S] Line 6 to Hangangjin, Exit 1) Korea's premier art gallery is divided into three main buildings, covering modern and traditional art. Contemporary-art lovers will want to focus on **Museum 2** featuring a mix of early- and mid-century paintings, sculptures and installations by esteemed Korean and international artists including Nam Jun Paik, Damien Hirst, Andy Warhol and Jeff Koons. For traditional Korean art, **Museum 1** is a must, with four floors of paintings, calligraphy, ceramics, celadon, metalwork and Buddhist art. The museum's third area is devoted to special exhibitions.

★War Memorial of Korea MUSEUM

(전쟁 기념관; www.warmemo.co.kr; 29 Itaewon-ro; ⏲9am-6pm Tue-Sun; [S] Line 4 or 6 to Samgakji, Exit 12) [FREE] This huge museum documents the history of the Korean War (1950–53) with heaps of black-and-white documentary footage (with English commentary) of the main battles and events. Along with photos, maps and artefacts, the films give a fascinating insight into what the war was like. There's plenty of military hardware outside – tanks, helicopters, missiles and planes, plus stirring war memorials. Time your visit to see the **Honour Guard Ceremony** (⏲2pm Fri early Apr-end Jun, mid-Oct–end Nov), an awesome display of military precision and weapon twirling by the armed forces.

Dongdaemun & Eastern Seoul

★Dongdaemun Design Plaza & Park CULTURAL CENTRE

(DDP; 동대문디자인플라자; ☎02-2153 0408; www.ddp.or.kr; 28 Eulji-ro, Jung-gu; ⏲10am-7pm Tue, Thu, Sat & Sun, to 9pm Wed & Fri; [S] Line 2, 4 or 5 to Dongdaemun History & Culture Park, Exit 1)

Itaewon

Top Sights
1 Leeum Samsung Museum of Art D1

Sights
2 HBC Art Village A1
3 Seoul Central Mosque B4

Sleeping
4 Grand Hyatt Seoul C1
5 Guesthouse Yacht A3
6 Hotel D'Oro B4
7 IP Boutique Hotel D2
8 Itaewon G Guest House B4
9 Itaewon Hostel & Inn A4
10 SP@Itaewon Guesthouse A3

Eating
11 Atelier du Saint-Ex A3
12 Linus' BBQ A3
13 Passion 5 .... D1
14 PLANT A4
15 Tartine A4
16 Vatos B2

Drinking & Nightlife
17 Always Homme B4
18 Booth A1
19 Booth Mansion A3
20 Cakeshop A3
21 Craftworks B4
22 Craftworks Taphouse A1
23 Damotori A1
24 Four Seasons A4
25 Made in Pong Dang A1
26 Magpie Brewing Co. A1
27 Miracle B4
28 Queen B4
29 Soho B4
30 Southside Parlor A2
31 Takeout Drawing D2
32 Takeout Drawing A1
33 Trance B4
34 Venue/ A4
35 Why Not B4

Entertainment
36 All that Jazz A3
37 Thunderhorse Tavern A2

Shopping
38 Millimetre Milligram D2
Post Poetics .... (see 38)
39 Steve J & Yoni P D2
40 What the Book B2

Information
41 Itaewon Subway Tourist Information Center A4
42 Itaewon Tourist Information Centre D2

Dongdaemun Design Plaza is architect Zaha Hadid's sleek concept dubbed the 'Metonymic Landscape'. The building, a curvaceous concrete structure with a silvery facade partly coated with lawns that rise up on to its roof, is a showcase for Korean and international design. It comprises multiple undulating levels of galleries, exhibition spaces, design shops and event halls. The attached Dongdaemun History & Culture Park includes museums that highlight past uses of this area, such as a 16th-century military camp.

Heunginjimun GATE

(Dongdaemun; [S]Line 1 or 4 to Dongdaemun, Exit 6) The Great East Gate to Seoul's City Wall has been rebuilt several times in its 700-year history, and, after recent renovations, it's looking majestic. It's not possible to enter the gate, stranded by a traffic island, but there are plenty of good photo ops from Naksan Park.

Seoul Forest PARK

(서울숲; http://parks.seoul.go.kr; 685 Seongsul-ga 1-dong, Seongdong-gu; ⏲24hr, rental stall 9am-10pm; [S]Bundang Line 2 to Seoul Forest, Exit 2) A hunting ground in Joseon times, this park makes for a very pleasant area to enjoy some time in natural surroundings. It's big, so to see it all it's best to hire a bicycle (₩3000 per 1½ hours) or a pair of rollerblades (₩4000 per hour) from the rental stall by Gate 2 across from Seoul Forest subway. Among the trees and lakes are deer enclosures, eco areas, an insect exhibition, a plant nursery and fountains. It's a lovely spot for a picnic.

Children's Grand Park PARK

(서울 어린이대공원; ☎02-450 9311; www.childrenpark.or.kr; 216 Neungdong-ro, Gwangjin-gu; amusement park rides ₩4000; ⏲5am-10pm, amusement park 9am-5pm, zoo 10am-6pm; 👪; [S]Line 5 or 7 to Children's Grand Park, Exit 1) [FREE] Let your little ones run wild in this enormous playground, which includes amusement rides, a zoo, botanical garden, wetland eco area and a giant musical fountain.

Gangnam & South of the Han River

★Olympic Park PARK

(올림픽 공원; www.olympicpark.co.kr; 424 Olympic-ro Songpa-gu; [S]Line 8 to Mongchontoseong, Exit 1 or Line 5 to Olympic Park, Exit 3) [FREE] This large and pleasant park was the focus of the 1988 Olympics. Strolling its paths takes you past its stadiums surrounded by plenty of greenery, ponds and open-air sculptures. There's a gallery of modern art and two museums on the history of the Baekje dynasty. The park contains the remains of the **Mongchon-toseong** (Mongchon Fortress), an earth rampart

SEOUL CITY WALL

Initially built in 1396, Seoul City Wall (http://seoulcitywall.seoul.go.kr) runs for 18.6km, connecting the peaks of Bukak-san (342m), Nak-san (125m), Namsan (262m) and Inwangsan (338m), all north of the Han River. It was punctuated by four major gates and four sub-gates, of which six remain.

Over time parts of the wall were demolished, but in an effort to have the entire structure designated by Unesco as a World Heritage Site, the city has been restoring some of the missing sections. At the time of writing, some 70% (12.8km) is in place and it's relatively easy to follow a hiking route beside and, in several cases, atop the walls.

The circuit can be accomplished in a day, but is better split over two if you prefer to take your time and do some sightseeing. Start at **Heunginjimun (Dongdaemun)**, near to which is the informative **Seoul City Wall Museum** (한양도성박물관; ☎02 724 0243; http://seoulcitywall.seoul.go.kr; 283 Yulgok-ro, Jongno-gu; ⏲9am-7pm Tue-Sun; [S]Line 1 or 4 to Dongdaemun, Exit 1) [FREE], and walk in an anticlockwise direction. This way you'll get the steepest section up and down Bukak-san done in the morning and could linger on Namsan later in the afternoon.

If you don't have time for this, opt to hike alongside the most spectacular section of the wall over **Bukak-san** (북악산; www.bukak.or.kr; ⏲9am-3pm Apr-Oct, from 10am Nov-Mar; 🚌1020, 7022, 7212 to Changuimun) [FREE]. You'll need to bring your passport to gain access. It's also open only during daylight hours and photography is allowed only at designated spots, such as Baekakmaru, the summit viewpoint. As it overlooks the presidential compound, there are plenty of soldiers and CCTV cameras, lending a vivid sense of the wall's original purpose as the city's last line of defence.

Apujeong, Gangnam & Yongsan-gu

Apujeong, Gangnam & Yongsan-gu

⦿ Sights
1 GT Tower East........................C4
2 Some Sevit.............................A2
3 Urban Hive.............................C3

✪ Activities, Courses & Tours
4 Kukkiwon...............................C3
5 Spa Lei..................................B2

⏢ Sleeping
6 24 Guesthouse Gangnam Center.........C3
7 24 Guesthouse Garosu-gil.................C2
8 H Avenue Hotel.....................D3
9 Kimchee Gangnam Guesthouse..........D2
10 La Casa................................C1
11 Mercure Seoul Ambassador
     Gangnam Sodowe...............D3

⊗ Eating
12 Coreanos Kitchen.................D1
13 Ha Jun Min..........................D1
14 Jungsik.................................D1
15 Nonhyeon Samgyetang..........D2
16 Samwon Garden...................D1

⦿ Drinking & Nightlife
17 Club Octagon.......................C3
18 Greenmile Coffee.................D2
19 Neurin Maeul.......................C4
20 SJ Kunsthalle.......................D2
     Take Urban.......................(see 3)

⦿ Entertainment
21 LG Arts Center.....................D3

🔒 Shopping
22 10 Corso Como Seoul...........D1
23 Galleria................................D1
24 Garosu-Gil...........................C2

ℹ Information
25 Gangnam Tourist Information
     Center.............................C1

ℹ Transport
26 Seoul Express Bus Station..........A3

LOCAL KNOWLEDGE

ARTY ITAEWON

If the top of the hill near **Seoul Central Mosque** (서울 중앙성원; Map p50; 732-21 Hannam2-dong; S Line 6 to Itaewon, Exit 3) in Itaewon wasn't intriguing enough with its extraordinary diversity that mixes Seoul's Islamic community with its GLBT community and red-light district, the enclave of artists who've recently moved into spaces along Usadan-ro, setting up studios, galleries, pop-up shops and cool hole-in-the-wall bars and eateries, adds another layer of interest. Aim to visit on the last Saturday of each month for its **Stairway Flea Market** (Usadan-ro), which has a street-party-like atmosphere as local artists sell their works on the stairs and stalls set up along the strip.

Also check out the adjoing suburb of Haebangchon (HBC), an historically impoverished neighbourhood that's undergone a dramatic gentrification. The **HBC Art Village** (Map p50; arthill 100.com; S Line 6 to Noksapyeong, Exit 2) has recently been developed with murals and art installments throughout its backstreets.

surrounded by a moat, built in the 3rd century AD during the Baekje dynasty.

★ **Bongeun-sa**　　　　　BUDDHIST TEMPLE
(봉은사; ☏ 02-3218 4895; www.bongeunsa.org; 531 Bongeunsa-ro, Gangnam-gu; S Line 2 to Samseong, Exit 6) Located in the heart of ritzy Gangnam, the shrines and halls of the Buddhist temple Bongeun-sa, with its tree-filled hillside location, stand in direct juxtaposition to its corporate high-rise surrounds. Founded in AD 794, the buildings have been rebuilt many times over the centuries. Entry to the temple is through **Jinyeomun** (Gate of Truth), protected by four king guardians. The main shrine, **Daewungjeon** has lattice doors and is decorated inside and out with Buddhist symbols and art that express Buddhist philosophy and ideals.

Lotte World Tower　　　　　BUILDING
(www.lwt.co.kr/en/main.do; 300 Olympic-ro, Songpa-gu; S Line 2 or 8 to Jamsil, Exit 1) Due for completion in late 2016, Seoul's latest landmark is the 555m-high Lotte World Tower – the tallest skyscraper in Korea (and sixth highest in the world). Its sleek contemporary design is loosely inspired by traditonal Korean ceramics, and will feature the world's highest observation deck with a glass-floored skywalk, art gallery, cafe, six-star hotel and the mega **Lotte World Mall** (☉ 10.30am-10pm) complex.

COEX Aquarium　　　　　AQUARIUM
(☏ 02-6002 6200; www.coexaqua.com; COEX Mall, 513, Yeongdong-daero, Gangnam-gu; adult/child under 13yr/child 13-18yr ₩22,000/16,000/19,000; ☉ 10am-8pm; S Line 2 to Samseong, Exit 6) Seoul's largest aquarium exhibits thousands of fish and other sea creatures from around the world. You can see live coral, sharks, turtles, rays, electric eels, octopus, evil-looking piranhas and pulsating jellyfish. Its only downside is the smallish enclosures for the seals and manatees.

Lotte World　　　　　AMUSEMENT PARK
(롯데월드; ☏ 02-1661 2000; www.lotteworld. com; 240 Olympic-ro, Songpa-gu; adult/child/youth ₩31,000/25,000/28,000, passport incl most rides ₩46,000/36,000/40,000; ☉ 9.30am-10pm; S Line 2 or 8 to Jamsil, Exit 3) This huge complex includes an amusement park, an ice-skating rink, a cinema multiplex, department store, folk museum, shopping mall, hotel, restaurants and more. Kids and adults alike will love the place, which is basically an indoor Korean version of Disneyland, complete with 'flying' balloons, 3D films, laser and music shows, screen rides, fantasy parades and thrill rides. The outdoor **Magic Island** is in the middle of Seokchon Lake, and that part may close in bad weather.

Seonjeongneung　　　　　ROYAL TOMBS
(선정릉; http://jikimi.cha.go.kr/english; Seonjeongneung Park, 1 Seolleung-ro 100-gil, Gangnam-gu; adult/child under 13yr/youth 13-18yr ₩1000/free/500; ☉ 6am-8pm Tue-Sun; S Line 2 or Bundang Line to Seolleung, Exit 8) Seonjeongneung Park contains two main burial areas for kings and queens from the Joseon dynasty. The first tomb is for King Seongjong, who reigned from 1469 to 1494, and who was prolific both as an author and as a father – he had 28 children by 12 wives and concubines. Go around the side and you can walk up to the tomb for a closer look. Nearby is the tomb of King Seongjong's second wife, Queen Jeonghyeon Wanghu.

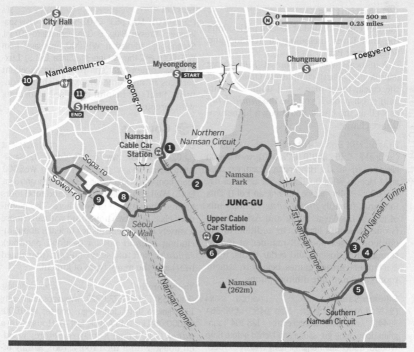

Walking Tour
Namsan Circuit

START LINE 4 TO MYEONGDONG, EXIT 4
END HOEHYEON STATION
LENGTH 6KM; THREE HOURS

Following pedestrian pathways and parts of the Seoul City Wall, this hike takes you around and over Namsan, providing sweeping city views along the way and a chance to enjoy the mountain's greenery and fresh air. It's best done early in the morning, but leafy trees do provide some shade most of the way.

From the subway exit walk up to the ❶ **cable car station** – just before you reach here you'll see steps leading up the mountainside to the pedestrian-only Northern Namsan Circuit. Walk left for five minutes, and pause to look around the ❷ **Waryong-myo** shrine before following the road as it undulates gently around the mountain. Pass routes down to Namsangol Hanok Village and Dongguk University until you reach the ❸ **outdoor gym**, uphill from the ❹ **National Theatre of Korea** (p80).

You can cut out the next bit by hopping on one of the buses that go to the peak from the bus stop near here. Otherwise, turn right at the start of the Southern Namsan Circuit road and you'll soon see the ❺ **city wall** (p52). A steep set of steps shadows the wall for part of the way to the summit. At the fork continue on the steps over the wall and follow the path to ❻ **N Seoul Tower** (p44) and the ❼ **Bongoodae** (signal beacons).

Grab some refreshments to enjoy at the geological centre of Seoul, before picking up the city wall trail down to pretty ❽ **Joongang Park**. On the left is ❾ **Ahn Jung-geun Memorial Hall**.

The park continues over a road tunnel down towards the Hilton Hotel with reconstructed sections of the wall. Finish up taking a look at the reconstruction of ❿ **Sungnyemun (Namdaemun)** (p45) then browsing ⓫ **Namdaemun Market** (p86).

Activities

Bicycles can be rented at several parks along the Han River, including on Yeouido and Seoul Forest Park.

Join locals sweating it out at *jjimjil-bang* (sauna and bath) complexes. Open round the clock, these places can double as bargain crash pads. If you use the *jjimjil-bang* as well as the baths, you'll pay a higher entrance charge.

Dragon Hill Spa & Resort SAUNA
(드래곤힐스파; ☎010 4223 0001; www.dragonhillspa.co.kr; 40-713, Hangangno 3(sam)-ga; day/night Mon-Fri ₩10,000/12,000, Sat & Sun all-day ₩12,000; 🕐24hr; [S] Line 1 to Yongsan, Exit 1) This foreigner-friendly *jjimjil-bang* – a noisy mix of gaudy Las Vegas bling and Asian chic – is one of Seoul's largest. In addition to the outdoor unisex pool, all manner of indoor saunas and ginseng and cedar baths, there is a cinema, arcade games, beauty treatment rooms and multiple dining options.

Silloam Sauna TRADITIONAL SAUNA
(실로암사우나찜질방; Map p46; ☎02-364 3944; www.silloamsauna.com; 128-104 Jungnim-dong, Jung-gu; sauna adult/child before 8pm ₩8000/6000, sauna & jjimjil-bang ₩10,000/7000; 🕐24hr; [S] Line 1 or 4 to Seoul Station, Exit 1) Across the street from Seoul Station, this spick-and-span foreigner-friendly *jjimjil-bang* has a wide range of baths and sauna rooms. It's also a shoestringer sleeping option if you need a place to stay for a night.

Eland Cruises CRUISE
(www.elandcruise.com; Han River Park, Yeouido; cruises from ₩12,000; 🕐11am-8.40pm; [S] Line 5 to Yeouinaru, Exit 3) A variety of day and night short sightseeing cruises depart from this Yeouido pier, one of three that the company's boats pause at along the Han River.

Kukkiwon TAEKWONDO
(국기원(세계태권도본부)); Map p53; ☎02-567 1058; www.kukkiwon.or.kr; 32 Teheran-ro 7-gil, Gangnam-gu; 🕐office 9am-5pm Mon-Fri; [S] Line 2 to Gangnam, Exit 12) There's no better place to see Korea's very own home-grown martial arts than here at the world headquarters for taekwondo. It hosts a regular schedule of taekwondo displays, training courses and tournaments. Call ahead to see when you might be able to see a training session. Also check out its **museum** while you're here.

Spa Lei SPA
(스파레이; Map p53; ☎02-545 4121; www.spalei.co.kr; Cresyn Bldg, 5 Gangnam-daero 107-gil, Seocho-gu; admission ₩14,000, massage from ₩30,000; 🕐24hr; [S] Line 3 to Sinsa, Exit 5) Luxurious women-only spa providing excellent services in an immaculate, stylish environment. Staff are helpful and used to dealing with foreigners.

Courses

O'ngo COOKING COURSE
(☎02-3446 1607; www.ongofood.com; 12 Samil-daero 30-gil, Jongno-gu; courses from ₩65,000, tours from ₩57,000; [S] Line 1, 3 or 5 to Jongno 3-ga, Exit 5) Well-run cooking classes and food tours around the city are offered here. The beginners' class lasts two hours and you can choose a variety of different dishes to learn about including *haemul pajeon* (seafood pancake), *sundubu* (soft tofu stew), bulgogi (marinated beef) and the many types of kimchi.

Yoo's Family COOKING COURSE
(Map p58; ☎02-3673 0323; www.yoosfamily.com; 19 Yulgok-ro 10-gil, Jongno-gu; courses ₩20,000-65,000; [S] Line 3 to Anguk, Exit 4) Housed in a *hanok* (traditional Korean one-storey wooden house with a tiled roof), Yoo's Family offers a variety of courses including learning how to make kimchi. You can also practise the tea ceremony, make prints from carved wooden blocks and dress up in *hanbok*. A minimum of two people is required.

Makgeolli Makers COURSE
(Map p46; www.facebook.com/makgeollimakers; Susubori Academy, 47 Kyonggidae-ro, Seodaemun-gu; course ₩45,000; [S] Line 2 or 5 to Chungjeongno, Exit 7) Run by Becca Baldwin and Daniel Lenaghan, two well-qualified brewing instructors, these fun courses will provide all you need to know about *makgeolli* (a mildly alcoholic drink made from rice, water and *nuruk*, a wheat-based mix of yeasts, enzymes and moulds) and how to make it.

YBM Sisa LANGUAGE COURSE
(Map p58; ☎02-2278 0509; http://kli.ybmedu.com; 104 Jong-ro, Jongno-gu; courses from ₩130,000; 🕐6.30am-9pm Mon-Fri, 9am-4pm Sat & Sun; [S] Line 1, 3 or 5 to Jongno 3-ga, Exit 15) Korean classes (maximum size 10) for all ability levels cover grammar, writing and conversation. Private tuition (₩50,000 per hour for one person) can also be arranged here.

Cycling Tour
Han River Cycle Ride

START LINE 5 TO YEOUINARU STATION, EXIT 3
END YEOUIDO PARK
LENGTH 15KM; THREE HOURS

It's possible to walk this 15km route around Yeouido and across the river, via the island park of Seonyudo, but it's quicker and more fun to use a bicycle, which you can rent at several outlets in Yeouido Hangang Park, the starting point for the ride. Walk east from the subway exit towards the Hangang Cruise Terminal in Yeouido Hangang Park where you'll find a ➊ **bicycle rental stall** (first hour ₩3000, every extra 15 minutes ₩500, open 9am to 5pm); bring some form of photo ID for it to keep as a deposit.

Cycle west out of the park and across the ➋ **Mapo Bridge**, taking the blue ramp down to the north bank of the river. Head west for about 4km until you reach a steep cliff, at the top of which is ➌ **Jeoldusan Martyrs' Shrine** (p47). Continue west to the Yanghwa bridge and carry your bike up the stairs to the path on the west side. On an island about halfway along the bridge is the beautifully landscaped ➍ **Seonyudo Park**. There are wonderful river views from the park (which used to be a water-filtration plant) as well as a cafe where you can take a break.

Continue from the park back to the south bank of the Han River and pedal back towards Yeouido. At the western tip of the island you can pause to view the ritzy ➎ **Seoul Marina** and the ➏ **National Assembly**. Also have a look around central ➐ **Yeouido Park**, which includes a traditional Korean garden.

Continue along the bike paths on the southern side of the island – ➑ **Yeouido Saetgang Eco Park** here is wilder and more natural. As you round the eastern tip of Yeouido, look up to see clouds reflected in the gold-tinted glass of the ➒ **63 City** skyscraper. After returning your bike to the rental stall, look out for the quirky ➓ **monster sculpture** based on the hit horror movie *The Host*.

Gwanghwamun, Jongno-gu & Daehangno

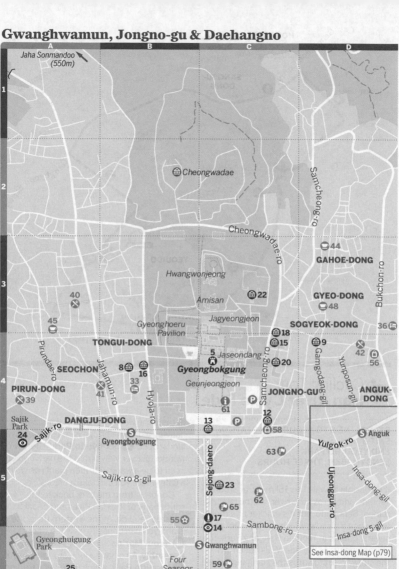

Jaha Sonmandoo
(550m)

Cheongwadae

Cheongwadae-ro

GAHOE-DONG

Samcheong-ro

Bukchon-ro

Hwangwonjeong

44

Amisan

22

GYEO-DONG

48

Jagyeongjeon

SOGYEOK-DONG

36

Gyeonghoeru
Pavilion

18
15

9

TONGUI-DONG

5 Jaseondang

Gyeongbokgung

20

42
56

40

45

8
16

33

Geunjeongjeon

Samcheong-ro

Gamgodang-gil

Yunposun-gil

ANGUK-
DONG

Pirundae-ro

SEOCHON

Jahamun-ro

41

Hyoja-ro

JONGNO-GU

PIRUN-DONG

39

61

DANGJU-DONG

Sajik
Park

24

Sajik-ro

Gyeongbokgung

13

12

58

Anguk

Yulgok-ro

Ujeongguk-ro

Insa-dong-gil

63

Sajik-ro 8-gil

Sejong-daero

23

62

Insa-dong 5-gil

See Insa-dong Map (p79)

Gyeonghuigung
Park

55

65

17
14

Sambong-ro

Gwanghwamun

Four
Seasons
Hotel

59

25

7

57

Saemunan-ro

27

Jonggak

Jong-ro

Seoul
Museum of
Art Annexe

26

Cheong-
gye Plaza

64 Bosingak

60 38

4 Cheong-gye-cheon

See Myeong-dong Map (p46)

Deoksugung-gil

Sejong-daero

Euljiro
1-ga

Deoksugung

Seoul
Plaza

Eulji-ro

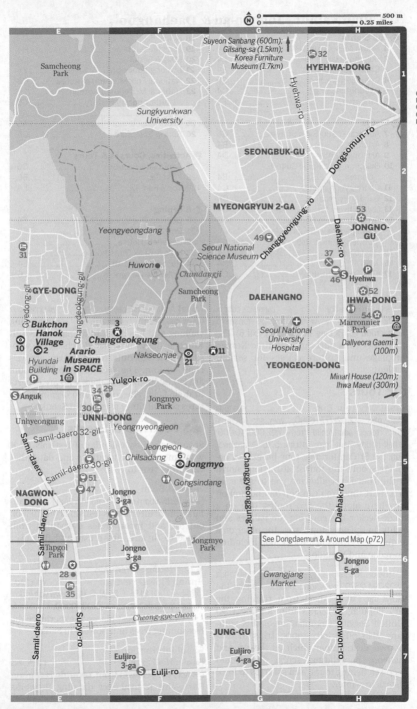

SEOUL

0 500 m
0 0.25 miles

Samcheong Park

Sungkyunkwan University

Hyehwa-ro

🚌 32
HYEHWA-DONG

SEONGBUK-GU

Dongsomun-ro

MYEONGRYUN 2-GA

Daehak-ro

53 ☆
JONGNO-GU

Yeongyeongdang

Changgyeonggung-ro

49 🍴

Seoul National Science Museum

37 ☆

🚇 31

Changdeokgung-gil

Gyedong-gil

Huwon ●

Chundangji

Samcheong Park

DAEHANGNO

46 🚇 S Hyehwa P

52 ☆
IHWA-DONG

GYE-DONG

Bukchon Hanok Village

3 🏛
Changdeokgung

54 ☆ 19

Seoul National University Hospital

Marronnier Park

Dallyeora Gaemi 1 (100m)

10 ◉
2 ◉

Nakseonjae

21 ◉

11 🍴

YEONGEON-DONG

Minari House (120m); Ihwa Maeul (300m)

Hyundai Building

Arario Museum in SPACE

1 🏛

Yulgok-ro

S Anguk

34 🏨
29 ●

30 🍴
UNNI-DONG

Jongmyo Park

Unhyeongung

Samil-daero 32-gil

Yeongnyeongjeon

Samil-daero

43

Changgyeonggung-ro

NAGWON-DONG

Samil-daero 30-gil

51 🍴
47 ◉

Jeongjeon
Chilsadang

6 ◉
Jongmyo

Jongno 3-ga

🍴 Gongsindang

50 🍴

Jongno 3-ga S

Jongmyo Park

See Dongdaemun & Around Map (p72)

Gwangjang Market

S Jongno 5-ga

Tapgol Park

28 ●
35 🍴

Daehak-ro

Hullyeonwon-ro

Cheong-gye-cheon

Samil-daero

Supyo-ro

JUNG-GU

Euljiro 3-ga S Eulji-ro

Euljiro 4-ga S

Gwanghwamun, Jongno-gu & Daehangno

Yonsei University   LANGUAGE COURSE
(☑ 02-2123 3465; www.yskli.com; 50 Yonsei-ro, Seodaemun-gu; Ⓢ Line 2 to Sinchon, Exit 6) The university runs part- and full-time Korean language and culture classes for serious students.

Tours

Seoul City Tour Bus   BUS TOUR
(Map p58; ☑ 02-777 6090; www.seoulcitybus. com; tours adult/child from ₩12,000/10,000; ⊙ half-hourly 9am-7pm; Ⓢ Line 5 to Gwanghwamun, Exit 6) Comfortable tour buses run between Seoul's top tourist attractions north of the Han River allowing you to see a lot in a short time. You can hop on and hop off anywhere along the two routes, one on a single-decker bus covering the palaces and sights on the downtown area, the other on a double-decker bus in a wider loop including Hongdae and Yeouido.

Koridoor Tours   BUS TOUR
(☑ 02-794 2570; www.koridoor.co.kr; Ⓢ Line 1 to Namyeong, Exit 2) Apart from running the very popular DMZ/JSA tour for the USO (United Service Organizations), this company also offers city tours; trips to out-of-town destinations, such as Suwon and Incheon; paragliding, scuba diving and deep-sea fishing tours; and ski trips to local resorts in winter.

Royal Asiatic Society   WALKING TOUR
(www.raskb.com) Organises enlightening walking and bus tours to all parts of South Korea, usually on weekends; check the website for the schedule. Nonmembers are welcome to join. The reasonably priced tours are led by English speakers who are experts in their field. The society also organises lectures several times a month in Seoul.

Festivals & Events

Seoul has a busy calendar of festivals. Visit www.knto.or.kr for locations and dates that vary from year to year.

Festival Bo:m   ART
(www.festivalbom.org; ⊙ late Mar–Apr) This annual multicultural arts festival is one to look out for, and incorporates everything from dance to theatre, art, music and film over two weeks.

Yeongdeungpo Yeouido Spring Flower Festival   CULTURAL
(영등포 여의도 봄꽃축제; www.ydp.go.kr/ english/page.do?mCode=D010000000; ⊙ early Apr) One of the best places to experience the blossoming trees and flowers in Seoul.

Seoul International Fireworks Festival   FIREWORKS
(⊙ Apr) Best viewed from **Yeouido Hangang Park**, this festival sees dazzling fireworks

displays staged by both Korean and international teams.

Jongmyo Daeje   CULTURAL
(www.jongmyo.net/english_index.asp; ⊘ May) On the first Sunday in May, this ceremony honours Korea's royal ancestors, and involves a costumed parade from Gyeongbokgung (p43) through central Seoul to the royal shrine at Jongmyo (p43), where spectators can enjoy traditional music and an elaborate ritual.

Lotus Lantern Festival   BUDDHIST
(Yeon Deung Ho; www.llf.or.kr/eng; ⊘ May) On the Sunday before Buddha's birthday, a huge parade is held from Dongdaemun to Jogye-sa starting at 7pm.

Seoul International Cartoon & Animation Festival   ART
(www.sicaf.org; ⊘ May) Half a million animation fans pack auditoriums in Seoul each year to see why the city is an epicentre of cartoon craftsmanship.

Seoul Fringe Festival   ART
(www.seoulfringefestival.net; ⊘ Aug) One of Seoul's best performing-arts festivals. Local and international artists converge on the Hongdae area.

Sajik Daeje   CULTURAL
(www.rfo.co.kr; ⊘ Sep) Normally held at Sajik-dan (사직단; Map p58; www.jongno.go.kr; Sajik Park, 89 Sajik-ro, Jongno-gu; Ⓢ Line 3 to Gyeong-bokgung, Exit 5) on the third Sunday of September, the 'Great Rite for the Gods of Earth and Agriculture' is one of Seoul's most important ancestral rituals and designated as an Important Intangible Cultural Property.

Seoul Drum Festival   MUSIC
(www.seouldrum.go.kr; Seoul Plaza; ⊘ Oct) Focusing on Korea's fantastic percussive legacy, this three-day celebrates all kinds of ways to make a lot of noise, bringing together different types of drumming from around the world.

Korea International Art Fair   ART
(www.kiaf.org; ⊘ Oct) The convention centre at COEX Mall (p89) is the location for this fair in which hundreds of local and international galleries participate.

Seoul Lantern Festival   CULTURAL
(http://blog.naver.com/seoullantern;   ⊘ Nov) Centred along the Cheong-gye-cheon (p43), this festival sees the stream park illuminated by gigantic fantastic lanterns made by master craftsmen.

🛏 Sleeping

Seoul has a good selection of budget accommodation, including many backpacker hostels. There's also no shortage of top-end places, but if you're looking for somewhere memorable rather than ubiquitously bland in the midrange, your options will be

GANGNAM ARCHI-TOUR

Given the generally blank historical canvas and wide-open spaces of Gangnam, architects have been able to push the envelope a bit more with their designs south of the river. Here are a few to look out for.

Some Sevit (세빛섬; Sebitseom; Map p53; www.somesevit.com; Hanggan Riverside Park; [S] Line 3, 7 or 9 to Express Bus Terminal, Exit 8-1) [FREE] On three islands on the Han River are these futuristic buildings with undulating glass facades covered in LEDs that glow colourfully each evening.

Tangent (Yeongdong-daero, Gangnam-gu; [S] Line 2 to Samseong, Exit 6) An enormous sculpture in glass, concrete and steel, reminiscent of a painting by Kandinsky.

Prugio Valley (337 Yeongdong-daero, Gangnam-gu; [S] Line 2 to Samseong, Exit 1) Looking like a giant music speaker crossed with a slab of Swiss cheese, this incredible steel-clad building was designed by Unsangdong Architects.

GT Tower East (Map p53; 411 Seocho-daero, Seocho-gu; [S] Line 2 to Gangnam, Exit 9) The slinky-like curvaceous styling rises like a giant sculpture.

Urban Hive (Map p53; 476 Gangnam-daero, Gangnam-gu; [S] Line 9 to Sinnonhyeon, Exit 3) Above Shinonyheon Station this building looks like an enormous concrete beehive and houses the stylish **Take Urban** (테이크어반; Map p53; ☎02-519 0001; www.takeurban.co.kr; 476 Gangnam-daero, Gangnam-gu; 🕒8am-midnight; [S] Line 9 to Sinnonhyeon, Exit 3) cafe on the ground floor.

narrowed to Bukchon's *hanok* guesthouses and a handful of design-conscious operations scattered around the city. Bear in mind that *hanok* rooms are small, bathrooms are cramped (but modern) and you sleep on a thin *yo* (padded-quilt) mattress on an *ondol*-heated floor.

For Seoul, budget places are those that offer double rooms with bathroom facilities for under ₩60,000, midrange places are ₩60,000 to ₩250,000 and top end is over ₩250,000. Prices don't normally change with the seasons, although some hotels and guesthouses may offer special deals online or at quiet times.

Gwanghwamun & Jongno-gu

★Hostel Korea 11th HOSTEL ₩
(Map p58; ☎070-4705 1900; www.cdg.hostelkorea.com; 85 Donhwamun-ro, Jongno-gu; dm/tr/q from ₩20,000/129,000/149,000, d & tw ₩99,000; ❄@📶; [S] Line 3 to Anguk, Exit 4) The best of the larger hostels popping up in this area occupying old office or apartment buildings. This one has a colourful, fun design, great location, roomy capsule-style dorm beds and a fabulous rooftop chill-out area with panoramic views.

Doo Guesthouse HANOK GUESTHOUSE ₩
(Map p58; ☎02-3672 1977; www.dooguesthouse.com; 103-7 Gyedong-gil; s/d/tr/q incl breakfast ₩50,000/60,000/100,000/120,000; ❄@📶; [S] Line 3 to Anguk, Exit 3) Mixing old and new is this enchanting *hanok* in a garden setting with a traditional-style room where breakfast is served. The shared bathrooms are high quality, with bidets and walk-in showers. The rooms have TVs and DVD players.

Beewon Guesthouse GUESTHOUSE ₩
(비원장; Map p58; ☎02-765 0677; www.beewonguesthouse.com; 77-4 Donhwamun-ro 11ga-gil; dm/d/tr ₩17,000/43,000/47,000; ❄@📶; [S] Line 3 to Anguk, Exit 4) Combining facility-filled motel-style rooms (some with *ondol* options) with free, guesthouse-style communal facilities, the clean-and-tidy Beewon is generally quiet and friendly, plastered with photos of happy past guests.

★Hotel the Designers BOUTIQUE HOTEL ₩₩
(Map p58; ☎02-2267 7474; www.hotelthedesigners.com; 89-8 Supyo-ro, Jongno-gu; r/ste from ₩90,000/150,000; ❄📶; [S] Line 1 or 3 Jongno 3-ga, Exit 15) Eighteen designers were given free reign to decorate the suites at this sophisticated love motel, tucked off the main road. Check the website for the different themes: our favourite is Camp Ruka-baik with a tent, deck chairs, tree bark–covered poles and guitar for a camping-in-the-city experience.

If you just want a taste of these fantasy rooms then short stays (fours hours Sunday to Thursday, three hours Friday and Saturday) are also available for ₩40,000.

Hide & Seek Guesthouse GUESTHOUSE **₩₩**
(Map p58; ☎02-6925 5916; www.hidenseek.co.kr; 14 Jahamun-ro 6-gil, Jongno-gu; s/tw/tr incl breakfast from ₩56,000/77,000/105,00; ❄📶; [S]Line 3 to Gyeongbokgung, Exit 5) Stylish design marks out this appealing five-room guesthouse, tucked away in Tongui-dong, beside the remains of an ancient pine tree, and occupying a modern, two-storey house with a broad outdoor terrace. Breakfast is served in the cute Stella's Kitchen cafe.

Hotel Sunbee HOTEL **₩₩**
(호텔썬비; ☎02-730 3451; www.hotelsunbee.com; 26 Insa-dong 7-gil, Jongno-gu; d/tw/ondol incl breakfast ₩100,000/120,000/140,000; ❄@📶; [S]Line 3 to Anguk, Exit 6) The friendly Sunbee offers huge double beds in tastefully decorated rooms with widescreen TVs and computers for a lower price than similar business hotels nearby. A simple breakfast is served in the ground-floor cafe.

Moon Guest House HANOK GUESTHOUSE **₩₩**
(☎02-745 8008; www.moonguesthouse.com; 31-16 Samil-daero 32-gil, Jongno-gu; s/d incl breakfast from ₩50,000/80,000; ❄📶; [S]Line 3 to Anguk, Exit 4) There are seven rooms at this 50-year-old *hanok,* which has been renovated to a high standard. Rooms are tiny and the cheapest have shared bathrooms. Various traditional cultural experiences are offered to guests.

★**Fraser Suites** APARTMENT **₩₩₩**
(☎02-6262 8888; www.frasershospitality.com; 18 Insa-dong 4-gil, Jongno-gu; 1-/2-/3-bedroom apt incl breakfast ₩330,000/440,000/550,000; ❄@📶🏊; [S]Line 1, 3 or 5 to Jongno 3-ga, Exit 5) These fully equipped serviced apartments are modern, light and spacious, great for a long-term stay for which discounts are available. Staff try hard to make this a home-away-from-home and its location, steps away from Insa-dong-gil, is ideal for sightseeing.

Rak-Ko-Jae HANOK GUESTHOUSE **₩₩₩**
(락고재; Map p58; ☎02-742 3410; www.rkj.co.kr; 98 Gyeo-dong; s/d ₩198,000/275,000; ❄@; [S]Line 3 to Anguk, Exit 2) This beautifully restored *hanok*, with an enchanting garden, is modelled after Japan's ryokan. The guesthouse's mud-walled sauna is included in the prices, as are breakfast and dinner. The en-suite bathrooms are tiny though.

Myeong-dong & Jung-gu

Zaza Backpackers HOSTEL **₩**
(자자 백팩커스; Map p46; ☎02-3672 1976; www.zazabackpackers.com; 32-3 Nansandong-2ga, Jung-gu; s/d ₩50,000/60,000; ❄@📶; [S]Line 4 to Myeondong, Exit 3) In the backpacker enclave that's sprung up along the hill to Namsan, Zaza is one of the best with its contemporary building full of design touches and a friendly young staff. It runs the nearby **Global Hostel** (서울 글로벌 호스텔; Map p46; ☎02-587 5776; www.seoulglobalhostel.com; 38 Sogong-ro 6-gil, Jung-gu; s/d/tr/q ₩50,000/60,000/80,000/100,000; ❄📶; [S]Line 4 to Myeongdong, Exit 3), which also resembles something out of an architectural magazine. It has modern, comfortable rooms and a spacious kitchen and dining area.

Namsan Guesthouse GUESTHOUSE **₩**
(남산게스트하우스; Map p46; ☎02-752 6363; www.namsanguesthouse.com; 79-3 Toegye-ro 18-gil, Jung-gu; dm/d/tr/q with breakfast ₩30,000/55,000/85,000/95,000; ❄@📶; [S]Line 4 to Myeongdong, Exit 2) Taking over the neighborhood on the slopes of Namsan, this long-running backpacker now has five locations in the immediate area. While each varies from the others – some with pod-style dorms fitted with TVs, others with rooftop terraces – all make for good budget choices. See the website for specifics of each branch.

★**Small House Big Door** BOUTIQUE HOTEL **₩₩**
(스몰 하우스 빅 도어; Map p46; ☎02-2038 8191; www.smallhousebigdoor.com; 6 Namdaemun-ro 9-gil, Jung-gu; r incl breakfast from ₩115,000-250,000; ❄📶; [S]Line 2 to Euljiro 1-ga, Exit 1, 2) Down a narrow street in downtown Seoul, this suave little art hotel is quite the find. Its white-toned rooms all feature locally designed, handmade furniture and beds, and maximise the use of space with ingenious slide-out desks and TVs. Pricier rooms have outdoor sitting areas and sky windows.

Metro Hotel HOTEL **₩₩**
(메트로호텔; Map p46; ☎02-2176 3199; www.metrohotel.co.kr; 14 Myeong-dong 9ga-gil, Jung-gu; s/d incl; breakfast from ₩110,000/143,000; ❄@📶; [S]Line 2 to Euljiro 1-ga, Exit 6) An excellent midrange choice, this small professionally run hotel has boutique aspirations.

Splashes of style abound, from the flashy, metallic lobby to its laptops. Room size and design vary – ask for one of the larger ones with big windows (room numbers that end in 07).

Crib49 GUESTHOUSE ₩₩
(크립 49 게스트하우스; Map p46; ☎070-8128 5981; www.crib49.com; 49 Toegye-ro 20na-gil, Jung-gu; d/tr incl breakfast from ₩80,000/100,000; ✳@ক; ⓢLine 4 to Myeongdong, Exit 3) Up the hill near Namsan's cable car, the *ondol* rooms at this smart guesthouse have mattresses on the floor, and a minimalist decor with Scandanavian-style shelving and plasma TVs. Its rooftop deck has Namsan views and there's a small kitchen.

Nine Tree Hotel Myeong-dong HOTEL ₩₩
(나인 트리 호텔 명동; Map p46; ☎02-7500 999; www.ninetreehotel.com; 51 Myeong-dong 10-gil, Jung-gu; s/d incl breakfast ₩170,000/190,000; ✳ক; ⓢLine 4 to Myeong-dong, Exit 8) There's plenty to like about this snazzy hotel well placed in the heart of Myeong-dong's shopping district. The smart boutique-y rooms have city views, a pillow menu of nine different types, Japanese-style electronic toilets, clothes press, foot massage machines, minibar and coffee maker. Plus there's substantial discounts if you book online.

Plaza HOTEL ₩₩₩
(더 플라자; Map p46; ☎02-771 2200; www. hoteltheplaza.com; 23 Taepyeong-ro 2-ga; r from ₩300,000; ✳@ক✳; ⓢLine 1 or 2 to City Hall, Exit 6) Opposite the striking rising glass edifice of City Hall, you couldn't get more central than the Plaza. Rooms sport a smart design with giant anglepoise lamps, circular mirrors and crisp white linens contrasting against dark carpets. It also has some chic restaurants and a good fitness club with a swimming pool.

Lotte Hotel Seoul HOTEL ₩₩₩
(롯데호텔서울; Map p46; ☎02-771 1000; www. lottehotelseoul.com; 30 Eulji-ro; r from ₩380,000; ✳@ক✳; ⓢLine 2 to Euljiro 1-ga, Exit 8) The natural extension to its Myeong-dong shopping empire, this twin-towered hotel with more than a thousand rooms has a marble-lined lobby long enough for Usain Bolt training runs. The new wing's standard rooms are bigger than those in the old, but don't have as modern a design; some come with City Hall views. There's also a ladies-only floor with a book-lined lounge.

🛏 Western Seoul

★V Mansion HOSTEL ₩
(Map p49; ☎070-8877 0608; http://mansion .com; 133 Tojeong-ro, Mapo-gu; d ₩80,000, dm/s/tw with shared bathroom & breakfast ₩28,000/50,000/70,000; ✳@ক; ⓢLine 6 to Sangsu, Exit 3) Offers something quite unexpected from a Seoul backpackers – space and a big garden! Exhibitions by local artists and various arty events are held here to help visitors connect with Seoul's creative spirits.

Urbanwood Guesthouse HOSTEL ₩
(Map p49; ☎070-8613 0062; www.urbanwood.co.kr; 3rd fl, 48-20 Wausan-ro 29-gil, Mapo-gu; s/d incl breakfast from ₩60,000/80,000; ✳ক; ⓢLine 2 to Hongik University, Exit 8) Creatively decorated in bright colours and modern furnishings, this cosy guesthouse feels more like a cool arty apartment. Martin, the convivial English-speaking host, knows the area well and whisks up a mean coffee on the professional barista machine in the well-appointed kitchen. It also has apartments to rent in the area.

Roi House GUESTHOUSE ₩
(☎070-811 2626; http://roihouse.wix.com/english; 14 Donggyo-ro 41-gil, Mapo-gu; dm/tw/q incl breakfast from ₩22,000/70,000/130,000; ✳@ক; ⓢLien 2 to Hongik University, Exit 3) Modern, with larger rooms than most guesthouses and a quiet location on a tree-lined street in Yeon-nam-dong, this is a very pleasant place to stay that's within walking distance of Hongdae. Owner Park Simon speaks good English.

★Lee Kang Ga GUESTHOUSE ₩₩
(Map p49; ☎02 323 5484; www.leekanghouse. com; 4th fl, 12 World Cup-buk-ro 11-gil, Mapo-gu; d incl breakfast from ₩80,000; ✳@ক; 🚌15, 7711, 7737 or 7016, ⓢLine 2 to Hongik University, Exit 1) Near the War and Women's Human Rights Museum, this appealing guesthouse is worth the schlep from Hongdae. Rooms are attractively decorated with *hanji* (traditional paper) wallpaper, silky pillows and pine-wood furniture and a few have balonies and washing machines. There are great views from the rooftop kitchen and garden.

Conrad Seoul HOTEL ₩₩₩
(☎02-6137 7000; http://conradseoul.co.kr; 23-1 Yeouido-dong, Yeongdeungpo-gu; s/d from ₩330,000/374,000; ✳@ক✳; ⓢLine 5 or 9 to Yeouido, Exit 3) Superior service, luxe rooms decorated in natural tones, and sweeping views of the Han River and city are what you'd expect

here – and it absolutely delivers. The natural choice for business travel on the island.

Northern Seoul

★**Minari House** GUESTHOUSE ₩₩
(미나리 하우스; ☎070-8656 3303; www.minarihouse.com; 3 Ihwajang 1na-gil, Jongno-gu; dm/s/d/tw incl breakfast ₩35,000/70,000/100,000/130,000; ❄📶; [S] Line 4 to Hyehwa, Exit 2) Designed as a base for artists and creatives, the four appealing rooms here sport minimalist design and arty touches. Breakfast is served in a lovely gallery cafe on the ground floor, which opens out onto a spacious tiered garden. Located near Ihwadong, and overlooking the grand *hanok* of Korea's first president Syngman Rhee, it also runs an artist residency.

Eugene's House HANOK GUESTHOUSE ₩₩
(Map p58; ☎02-741 3338; www.eugenehouse.co.kr; 36 Hyehwa-ro 12-gil, Jongno-gu; s/d incl breakfast from ₩70,000/110,000, s/tw with shared bathroom ₩50,000/100,000; ❄📶; [S] Line 4 to Hyehwa, Exit 1) The friendly family who runs this *hanok* homestay (named after their daughter) speak English and have another *hanok* around the corner where they also conduct various cultural experiences. These homes have larger courtyards than similar places in Bukchon, and a pleasing, lived-in quality. The rooms are all different and uniquely furnished.

Itaewon & Yongsan-gu

★**Itaewon G Guest House** HOSTEL ₩
(이태원 G 게스트하우스; Map p50; ☎010 8774 7767; www.gguest.com; 14-38 Bogwang-ro 60-gil; dm/s/d incl breakfast ₩15,000/40,000/70,000; ❄📶; [S] Line 6 to Itaewon, Exit 3) Owned by the ultra-friendly couple – Shrek and Fiona – this hostel stands above others for its attention to thought and detail. Set in a renovated industrial-chic apartment building, its private rooms and dorms are clean, spacious and have quality, thick mattresses. There's also **G Guest Home** in a nearby residential street that'll suit those looking for a more a low-key stay.

It's a good place to meet others, whether hanging out in its basement or on the awesome rooftop with weekly barbecues. Other perks include free laundry, filter coffee and bikes for the nearby Han River cycling path. Room rates go up around ₩5000 on weekends.

TEMPLE PROGRAMS

At the **Templestay Information Centre** (☎02-2013 2000; www.templestay.com; 56 Ujeonggguk-ro, Jongno-gu; [S] Line 3 to Anguk, Exit 6) you can find out all about – and book overnight stay programs at – many beautiful temples in Seoul and around Korea.

Visit **Bongeun-sa** (p54) on Thursday if you want to take part in its **Templelife program** (tour ₩20,000; 🕑2-4pm Thu), which includes lotus-lantern making, *dado* (tea ceremony), a temple tour and Seon (Zen) meditation. Book three weeks in advance to take part in its overnight templestay program (₩70,000).

A similar Temple Life program (₩30,000, 1pm to 4pm) is offered at **Jogye-sa** (p43) every Saturday, while shorter programs (for a donation) are available daily. **Gilsang-sa** (p48) also runs an overnight templestay program (₩50,000) on the third and fourth weekends of the month.

SP@Itaewon Guesthouse HOSTEL ₩
(SP@이태원게스트하우스; Map p50; ☎02-796 6990; www.spguest.com; Itaewon-dong 112-11; dm/s/f from ₩15,000/32,000/70,000; ❄📶; [S] Line 6 to Itaewon, Exit 1) Run by a friendly team of international staff, this Serbian-owned hostel has a prime location just up the hill from Itaewon's main drag. It attracts an eclectic crowd of backpackers, long-term residents and local students who congregate in the old-school party-house garage downstairs. The same owners also run the more laid-back **Itaewon Hostel & Inn** (이태원 인; Map p50; ☎02-6221 0880; www.itaewoninn.com; 103-2 Bogwang-ro; dm ₩16,000, s/d ₩50,000/70,000, s with shared bathroom ₩35,000; [S] Line 6 to Itaewon, Exit 4) with a cool rooftop.

Guesthouse Yacht GUESTHOUSE ₩
(요트게스트하우스; Map p50; ☎010 6556 1125; www.guesthouseyacht.com; 23 Itaewon-ro 23-gil; dm/s/d incl breakfast ₩20,000/40,000/60,000; ❄@📶; [S] Line 6 to Itaewon, Exit 1) Steered ably by 'the Captain' (the owner was the first Korean to sail by yacht across the Pacific) and his trusty crew, this friendly guesthouse has a good selection of rooms with shared bathrooms, including it's 'penthouse' with its own piano. The highlight is the small rooftop

Jamsil

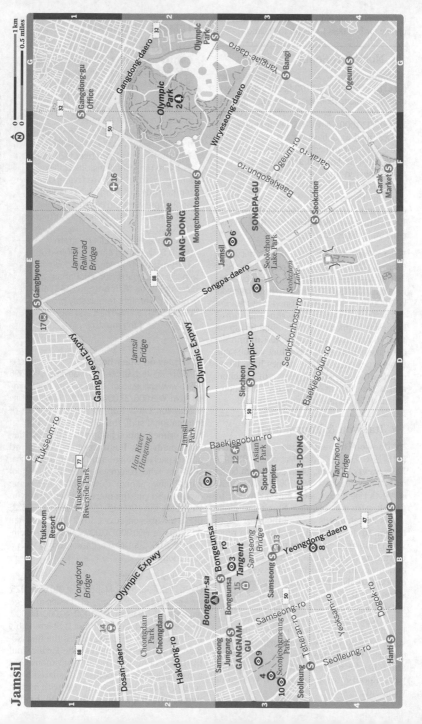

Jamsil

decked out in astroturf. Once a month guests are invited on sailing trips to the West Sea.

IP Boutique Hotel
HOTEL ₩₩

(IP 부티크 호텔; Map p50; ☏02-3702 8000; www.ipboutiquehotel.com; 737-32 Hannam-dong; r from ₩170,000; ✳@🛜🌊; ⒮Line 6 to Itaewon, Exit 2) Trying a bit too hard to be hip with bold contemporary artworks and quirky interior-design choices, this boutique wannabe slightly misses the mark. Still, it's in a great location and in a city of fairly generic-style hotels it certainly stands out.

Hotel D'Oro
LOVE MOTEL ₩₩

(디오로호텔; Map p50; ☏02-749 6525; 34-34 Itaewon-ro 27-gil, Yongsan-gu; d from ₩88,000; ✳@🛜; ⒮Line 6 to Itaewon, Exit 2) This above-average love motel offers some style, modern equipment and furnishings, plus free soft drinks rather than an expensive minibar. The entrance is up the hill off the main road.

Grand Hyatt Seoul
HOTEL ₩₩₩

(그랜드 하얏트 서울; Map p50; ☏02-797 1234; www.seoul.grand.hyatt.com; 322 Sowol-ro; r from ₩360,000; ✳@🛜🌊; ⒮Line 6 to Hangangjin, Exit 1) Making the most of its hilltop views, the Grand Hyatt oozes class. Rooms are a bit smaller than at rivals, but all have been freshly renovated and sport a contemporary look. Pamper yourself in the spa, dance the night away at popular club JJ Mahoney's or swim in the excellent outdoor pool which, come winter, is turned into an ice rink.

▦ Dongdaemun & Eastern Seoul

★ K Hostel
HOSTEL ₩

(케이 호스텔; ☏02-2233 9155; www.khostel.net; 384 Jong-ro, Jongno-gu; dm/s/tw incl breakfast & with shared bathroom ₩20,000/30,000/50,000, d with private bathroom ₩55,000; ✳🛜; ⒮Line 2 to Dongmyo, Exit 2) Your quintessential Western-style backpacker, this lively hostel (one of many branches in Seoul) is within a high-rise building featuring vibrant decor, homely kitchen, comfy lounge and sensational rooftop with barbecue, couches and temple views. Rooms are clean and more spacious than most. It's a 15-minute walk to Dongdaemun market.

Dongdaemun Hostel & Inn
HOSTEL ₩

(동대문 호스텔; ☏070-7785 8055; www.dongdaemunhostel.com; 43-1 Gwanghui-dong 2-ga, Jung-gu; s/d/tr from ₩20,000/40,000/50,000; 🛜; ⒮Line 2, 4 or 5 to Dongdaemun History & Culture Park, Exit 4) A lot is crammed into the tiny single rooms at this backpackers guesthouse including computer, desk and a shower/toilet cubicle. In the laneway behind is Dongdaemun Inn with doubles and triples.

Toyoko Inn Seoul Dongdaemun
HOTEL ₩₩

(토요코인 서울 동대문; ☏02-2267 1045; www.toyoko-inn.com; 337 Toegye-ro, Jung-gu; s/d incl breakfast from ₩60,500/77,000; ✳@🛜; ⒮Line 2, 4 or 5 to Dongdaemun History & Culture Park, Exit 4) The small, clean and well-equipped rooms at this Japanese business hotel are great value, and well located for Dongdaemun's main sights.

JW Marriott Dongdaemun Square HOTEL ₩₩₩
(JW 메리어트 동대문 스퀘어 서울; ☎02-2276 3000; www.jwmarriottdongdaemun.com; 279 Cheonggyecheon-ro, Jongno-gu; r from ₩300,000; [S]Line 1 or 4 to Dongdaemun, Exit 9) A prime location next door to Dongdaemun Market and opposite from Heunginjium Gate, the five-star Marriot is a smaller, more intimate branch compared to usual. All rooms have desks, bathrooms/tubs and are equipped with TVs, top-notch sound systems and coffee capsules, however it's worth upgrading to a room with views of Heunginjium and retractable blinds that open to the stars.

🛏 Gangnam & South of the Han River

Kimchee Gangnam Guesthouse HOSTEL ₩
(김치 강남 게스트하우스; Map p53; ☎02-518 6696; www.kimcheeguesthouse.com; 23 Seolleung-ro 133-gil, Gangnam-gu; dm/s/d incl breakfast ₩25,000/35,000/60,000; ❄@📶; [S]Line 7 to Gangnam-gu Office, Exit 3) A rare budget choice for ritzy Gangnam, this friendly guesthouse is set in a posh-looking old apartment building in a residential street. The mixed dorms are modern and spacious, while private rooms are more on the boxy side. Unwind in the basement with stylish cafe, vintage furniture and full kitchen.

24 Guesthouse Gangnam Center GUESTHOUSE ₩
(24게스트하우스 강남 센터점; Map p53; ☎02-538 1177; gangnamcenter.24guesthouse.co.kr; 52 Bongeunsa-ro 20-gil, Gangnam-gu; dm/s/d/tr incl breakfast ₩30,000/50,000/60,000/80,000; ❄📶; [S]Line 2 to Yeoksam, Exit 4) Hidden away in a residential backstreet of Gangnam, this double-storey guesthouse has an appealing location that's close enough to the action, yet far enough away to enjoy a peaceful stay. Rooms all share bathrooms and lack character, but make up for it with a laid-back homely atmosphere and full kitchen. There's also a pricier branch along **Garosu-gil** (Map p53; ☎02-540 7742; 31-5 Dosan-daero 13-gil, Gangnam-gu; s/d incl breakfast with shared bathroom ₩60,000/70,000, r with private bathroom ₩80,000; ❄📶; [S]Line 3 to Sinsa, Exit 6).

★**La Casa** HOTEL ₩₩
(라까사 호텔 서울; Map p53; ☎02-546 0088; www.hotellacasa.kr; 83 Dosan-daero 1-gil, Gangnam-gu; s/d incl breakfast from ₩178,000/215,000; ❄@📶; [S]Line 3 to Sinsa, Exit 6) The first venture into the hospitality business by classy Korean furniture and interior design store Casamia packs plenty of chic style. The rooms are attractive and spacious with quirky details such as the travel-themed pillow cases, while the lobby also has plenty of design features and art books. It's handy for Garosu-gil.

Mercure Seoul Ambassador Gangnam Sodowe HOTEL ₩₩
(머큐어 서울 앰배서더 강남 쏘도베; Map p53; ☎02-2050 6000; www.mercureseoul.com; 642 Teheran-ro 25-gil, Gangnam-gu; r from ₩147,400; ❄@📶; [S]Line 2 to Yeoksam, Exit 4) Well located, this business-smart hotel is decorated in candy colours and arty flourishes. Rooms with city views cost extra, as does the sauna (₩5000), but laundry is included and good discounts are available by booking online. There's also the upstairs Rooftop Kloud bar with a great view and single-malt selection.

H Avenue Hotel LOVE MOTEL ₩₩
(에이치 에비뉴 호텔; Map p53; ☎02-508 6247; 12 Teheran-ro 29-gil, Gangnam-gu; r from ₩60,000; ❄@📶🏊; [S]Line 2 to Yeoksam, Exit 8) Fantastic value, this hotel is most notable for its roof-terrace rooms, which come with their own roof-deck swimming pools and views over Namsan and the nearby cathedral; stay midweek for the best deals. While essentially a love motel, it comes without all the usual, weird trappings.

★**Park Hyatt Seoul** HOTEL ₩₩₩
(파크 하얏트 서울; ☎02-2016 1234; www.seoul.park.hyatt.com; 606 Teheran-ro, Gangnam-gu; r from ₩450,000; ❄@📶🏊; [S]Line 2 to Samseong, Exit 1) A discrete entrance – look for the rock sticking out of the wall – sets the Zen-minimalist tone for this gorgeous property. Each floor only has 10 rooms, with spotlit antiquities lining the hallways. Spacious open-plan rooms are glassed in with floor-to-ceiling windows that boast city views and come with luxurious bathrooms classed among the best in Asia.

🍴 Eating

Dining out is one of the great pleasures of Seoul, with literally tens of thousands of options, from cheap street stalls proffering deep-fried snacks and *tteokbokki* (rice cakes in a sweet sauce), to fancy restaurants serving royal Korean cuisine and seafood so fresh it's still wriggling on the plate.

✕ Gwanghwamun & Jongno-gu

★ Rogpa Tea Stall
VEGETARIAN ₩

(록바; Map p58; blog.naver.com/rogpashop; 16 Sajik-ro 9-gil, Jongno-gu, noon-8pm Tue-Sun; mains ₩6000-8000; ⌕; ⓢ Line 3 to Gyeongbokgung, Exit 1) You'll feel whisked to the Himalayas at this charming fair-trade cafe that raises awareness about the Tibetans' situation (Rogpa is Tibetan for friend and helper). Everything is vegetarian and freshly made, beautifully presented and rather delicious. Dig into a mild curry followed by a sweet *dosa* (crispy lentil pancake) and chai made with soy milk.

★ Tongin Market Box
Lunch Cafe
KOREAN ₩

(통인시장; Map p58; tonginmarket.co.kr; 18 Jahamun-ro 15-gl, Jongno-gu; meals ₩5000; ⌚ 11am-4pm Tue-Sun; ⓢ Line 3 to Gyeongbokgung, Exit 2) For a fun lunch, buy 10 brass coins (₩5000) at the cafe about halfway along this old-school covered market. You'll be given a plastic tray with which you can then go shopping in the market. Exchange your coins for dishes such as savoury pancakes, *gimbap* (seaweed covered rice rolls) and *tteokbokki*.

You can buy more coins, if needed, and use them (or cash) to pay for rice and soup (₩1000 each, kimchi is free) back at the cafe.

Tobang
KOREAN ₩

(토방; ☎ 02-735 8156; 50-1 Insa-dong-gil, Jong-no-gu; meals ₩6000; ⌚ 11.30am-9pm; ⓢ Line 3 to Anguk, Exit 6) A white sign with two Chinese characters above a doorway leads the way to this excellent value eatery, where you sit on floor cushions under paper lanterns. Order spicy stews *sundubu jjigae* or *doenjang jji-gae* for some Korean home-cooking flavour and excellent side dishes that include bean sprouts, cuttlefish, raw crab in red-pepper sauce, soup and rice.

Koong
DUMPLINGS ₩

(궁; ☎ 02-733 9240; www.koong.co.kr; 11-3 Insa-dong 10-gil, Jongno-gu; dumplings ₩10,000; ⌚ 11.30am-9.30pm; ⓢ Line 3 to Anguk, Exit 6) Koong's traditional Kaeseong-style dump-lings are legendary and more than a mouthful. Only order one portion, unless you're super hungry, or enjoy them in a flavourful soup along with chewy balls of rice cake.

Osegyehyang
VEGAN ₩

(오세계향; ☎ 02-735 7171; www.go5.co.kr; 14-5 Insa-dong 12-gil, Jongno-gu; meals from ₩7000; ⌚ noon-3pm & 4.30-9pm; ⌕; ⓢ Line 3 to Anguk, Exit 6) Run by members of a Taiwanese reli-gious sect, the vegetarian food combines all sorts of mixtures and flavours. The barbecue-meat-substitute dish is flavoursome.

Wood and Brick
BAKERY ₩

(Map p58; ☎ 02-747 1592; www.woodnbrick.com; 3 Bukchon-ro 5-gil, Jongno-gu; baked goods ₩5000-10,000; ⌚ cafe 8am-10pm, restaurant noon-10pm; ⓢ Line 3 to Anguk, Exit 2) The terrace seating at this combined bakery cafe and restaurant is a great spot from which to watch the com-ings and goings of Bukchon. Their baked goods, sandwiches and European deli-style eats are top notch.

Tosokchon
KOREAN ₩₩

(토속촌; Map p58; ☎ 02-737 7444; 5 Jahamun-ro 5-gil, Jongno-gu; mains ₩15,000-22,000; ⌚ 10am-10pm; ⓢ Line 3 to Gyeongbokgung, Exit 2) Spread over a series of *hanok*, Tosokchon is so fa-mous for its *samgyetang* (ginseng chicken soup) that there is always a long queue wait-ing to get in, particularly on weekends. Try the black chicken version, which uses the silkie breed with naturally black flesh and bones.

Gogung
KOREAN ₩₩

(고궁; ☎ 02-736 3211; www.gogung.co.kr; 44 Insa-dong-gil, Jongno-gu; meals ₩8000-12,000; ⌚ 11am-10pm; ⓢ Line 3 to Anguk, Exit 6) In the basement of Ssamziegil is this smart and stylish restaurant, specialising in Jeonju (capital of Jeollabuk Province) bibimbap, which is fresh and garnished with nuts, but contains raw minced beef. The *dolsot bibim-bap* is served in a stone hotpot. Both come with side dishes. Also try the *moju*, a sweet, cinnamon homebrew drink.

Bibigo Gyejeolbabsang
KOREAN ₩₩

(비비고 계절밥상; ☎ 02-2223 2551; B1 Insa-dong Maru, 35-4 6 Insa-dong-gil, Jongno-gu; buffet lunch Mon-Fri/Sat & Sun ₩13,900/22,900, dinner ₩22,900; ⌚ 10.30am-10.30pm; ⓢ Line 3 to An-guk, Exit 6) There's usually a line for 'Season's Table', a good-value *hansik* (Korean food) buffet in the basement of Insa-dong Maru. A wide range of dishes are temptingly laid out and include items such as hot-stone bibim-bap, which you need to order with one of the chits on your table. Desserts and some drinks are included.

[i] SEOUL DINING WEBSITES & BLOGS

ZenKimchi (www.zenkimchi.com)

Seoul Eats (www.seouleats.com)

Korea Taste (www.koreataste.org)

Alien's Day Out (www.aliensdayout.com)

★ **Congdu** KOREAN ₩₩₩
(Map p46; www.congdu.com; 116-1 Deoksugung-gil, Jung-gu; set course lunch/dinner from ₩36,800/58,800, mains from ₩29,800; 🕑11.30am-1.50pm & 5.30-8.30pm; [S] Line 5 to Gwanghwamun, Exit 6) Feast on elegantly presented, contemporary twists on Korean classics, such as pinenut soup with soy milk espuma (foam) or raw blue crab, at this serene restaurant tucked away behind the British Embassy. The main dining room becomes an open roof terrace in good weather.

Balwoo Gongyang VEGETARIAN ₩₩₩
(발우공양; ☎02-2031 2081; www.balwoogongyang.or.kr; 5th fl, Templestay Information Center, 56 Ujeongguk-ro, Jongno-gu; lunch/dinner from ₩27,500/39,600; 🕑11.40am-3pm & 6-8.50pm; ✍; [S] Line 3 to Anguk, Exit 6) Reserve three days in advance for the delicate temple-style cuisine served here. Take your time to fully savour the subtle flavours and different textures of the vegetarian dishes, which range from rice porridge and delicate salads to dumplings and fried shitake mushrooms and mugwort in a sweet and sour sauce.

Min's Club FUSION ₩₩₩
(민가다헌; ☎02-733 2966; www.minsclub.co.kr; 23-9 Insa-dong 10-gil, Jongno-gu; set course lunch/dinner from ₩32,000/70,000; 🕑noon-2.30pm & 6-9.30pm; [S] Line 3 to Anguk, Exit 6) Old-world architecture meets new-world cuisine in this classy restaurant housed in a beautifully restored turn-of-the-20th-century *hanok*, said to be the first in Seoul to incorporate Western features such as en-suite bathrooms. The European-Korean meals (more European than Korean) are beautifully presented and there's an extensive wine selection.

Hanmiri KOREAN ₩₩₩
(한미리; Map p58; ☎02-757 5707; www.hanmiri.co.kr; 2nd fl, Premier Pl, 8 Cheonggyecheon-ro, Jongno-gu; lunch/dinner from ₩30,000/50,000; 🕑noon-3pm & 6-10pm; [S] Line 5 to Gwanghwamun, Exit 5) Sit on chairs at tables for this modern take on royal cuisine; book a table with windows overlooking the Cheong-gyecheon. It's gourmet and foreigner-friendly. There's another branch in Gangnam.

🍴 Myeong-dong & Jung-gu

Myeong-dong Gyoja NOODLES ₩
(명동교자; Map p46; www.mdkj.co.kr; 29 Myeongdong 10-gil, Jung-gu; noodles ₩8000; 🕑10.30am-9.30pm; [S] Line 4 to Myeongdong, Exit 8) The special *kalguksu* (noodles in a meat, dumpling and vegetable broth) is famous, so it's busy, busy, busy. Fortunately it has multiple levels and a nearby branch to meet the demand.

Mokmyeoksanbang KOREAN ₩
(목멱산방; Map p46; Northern Namsan Circuit, Jung-gu; mains ₩8000-10,000; 🕑11.30am-8pm; [S] Line 4 to Myeongdong, Exit 3) Order and pay at the till, then pick up delicious and beautifully presented bibimbap from the kitchen when your electronic buzzer rings. The traditional wooden house in which the restaurant is based is named after the ancient name for Namsan (Mokmyeok); it also serves Korean teas and *makgeolli* (rice wine) in brass kettles.

Wangbijip KOREAN ₩₩
(왕비집; Map p46; www.wangbijib.com; 2nd fl, 34-1 Myeongdong 1-ga, Jung-gu; mains from ₩12,000; 🕑11.30am-11pm; [S] Line 4 to Myeongdong, Exit 8) Head upstairs to this tasteful Korean restaurant popular for grilled meats and other traditional dishes such as *samgyetang* (chicken stuffed with ginseng) and bibimbap.

Baekje Samgyetang KOREAN ₩₩
(백제삼계탕; Map p46; 50-11 Myeongdong 2-ga; mains from ₩15,000; 🕑9am-10pm; [S] Line 4 to Myeongdong, Exit 6) This 2nd-floor restaurant, marked by a sign with red Chinese characters, offers reliable *samgyetang*. Put salt and pepper into the saucer and dip the pieces of chicken into it. Drink the herbal soup at the end.

Soo:P Coffee Flower CAFE ₩₩
(Map p46; www.soopcoffeeflower.com; 97 Sogong-ro, Jung-gu; coffee ₩2500, sandwiches ₩8000; 🕑11am-10pm Mon-Sat; 📶; [S] Line 1 or 2 to City Hall, Exit 7) A slice of arty Hongdae in downtown Seoul, this earthy light-filled cafe is filled with pot plants and makes a great spot for a light meal such as gourmet sandwiches, organic vegie bibimbap and homemade cakes. They also do good coffee.

Hadongkwan KOREAN ₩₩
(하동관; Map p46; www.hadongkwan.com; Myeongdong 1-ga, Jung-gu; soup ₩12,000-15,000; ⏲7am-4pm; [S] Line 4 to Myeongdong, Exit 8) In business since 1935, the big bowls of wholesome beef broth and rice at this popular pit stop come either in the regular version with slices of meat or the more expensive one with added tripe. Add salt and masses of sliced spring onions to taste.

Gosang KOREAN ₩₩₩
(고상; Map p46; ☎02-6030 8955; www.barugosang.com; 67 Suha-dong, Jung-gu; lunch/dinner set course ₩39,900/50,000; ⏲11.30am-3.30pm & 5.30-10pm; 🥕; [S] Line 2 to Euljiro 1-ga, Exit 4) One worth dressing up for, this classy restaurant specialises in vegetarian temple dishes that date from the Goryeo dynsasty. It's all set-course, traditional-style banquets here, and there's also a meat option. It's in a posh food court in the basement of the Center 1 Building.

Western Seoul

★Menya Sandaime JAPANESE ₩
(Map p49; ☎02-332 4129; www.menyasandaime.com; 24 Hongik-ro 3-gil, Mapo-gu; mains ₩7000-9000; ⏲noon-10pm; [S] Line 2 to Hongik University, Exit 9) On a street with several other Japanese restaurants, this atmospheric ramen shop is the real deal and proof that being part of a chain need not compromise food quality. It's a great place for single diners who can sit at the counter by the open kitchen watching the hip, tattooed chefs carefully craft bowls of delicious noodles.

★Tuk Tuk Noodle Thai THAI ₩
(☎070-4407 5130; blog.naver.com/tuktuknoodle; 37 Yeonhui-ro, Mapo-gu; mains ₩7500-12,000; ⏲noon-3pm & 5-10.30pm; [S] Line 2 to Hongik University, Exit 3) Credited with kicking off a trend for more authentic Thai restaurants in Seoul, Tuk Tuk is a jauntily decorated basement space close by Dongjin Market. Thai chefs whack out a broad menu of spicy dishes that don't compromise on flavour.

Slobbie KOREAN ₩₩₩
(Map p49; ☎02-3143 5525; www.facebook.com/slobbie8; 5th fl, 10 Hongik-ro 6-gil, Mapo-gu; meals ₩8000; ⏲11.30am-11.30pm Mon-Sat; 📶; [S] Line 2 to Hongik University, Exit 9) 🍃 Simple, tasty dishes such as bibimbap and *jjigae* (stews) are served in pleasant, modern surroundings at this admirable social enterprise training young chefs from challenged backgrounds and providing jobs for single mothers. The restaurant name is pronounced Slow-bee, indicating its aim to promote a slower, healthier and more organic lifestyle for Seoulites.

Ciuri Ciuri ITALIAN ₩₩
(Map p49; ☎02-749 9996; www.ciuriciuri.co.kr; 2nd fl, 314-3 Sangsu-dong, Mapo-gu; mains ₩7000-18,000; ⏲noon-3pm & 6-11pm Mon-Fri, noon-11pm Sat & Sun; [S] Line 6 to Sangsu, Exit 1) At this eatery run by Italian couple Enrico and Fiore, the tasty and unusual – for Seoul – specialities hail from Sicily, such as *arancine* (saffron-flavoured risotto balls), *anelletti* (small ring pasta) and a special type of sausage. The place is decorated as if you're on holiday in Sicily itself, with straw hat lampshades and colourfully painted tiled tables and water bottles.

Northern Seoul

★Jaha Sonmandoo KOREAN ₩
(자하손만두; ☎02-379 2648; www.sonmandoo.com; 12 Baekseondong-gil, Jongno-gu; mains ₩7000-10,000; ⏲11am-9.30pm; 🚌1020, 7022, 7212, [S] Line 3 to Gyeongbokgung, Exit 3) Around lunchtime and on weekends, Seoulites flock to this mountainside dumpling house for the steamed and boiled vegetable and beef and pork parcels. A couple of plates is enough of these whoppers; the sweet cinnamon tea to finish is free.

Deongjang Yesool KOREAN ₩₩
(된장예술; Map p58; ☎02-745 4516; 9-2 Daehak-ro 11-gil, Jongno-gu; set meal ₩9500; ⏲9am-11pm; 🥕; [S] Line 4 to Hyehwa, Exit 3) Serves a tasty fermented-bean-paste-and-tofu stew with a variety of nearly all vegetarian side dishes at a bargain price – no wonder it's well patronised by the area's student population.

Look for the stone carved lions flanking the door.

Itaewon & Yongsan-gu

Vatos MEXICAN ₩
(Map p50; ☎02-797 8226; www.vatoskorea.com; 2nd fl, 1 Itaewon-ro 15-gil; 2 tacos from ₩6900; ⏲11.30am-11pm Sun-Thu, from noon Fri & Sat; 📶; [S] Line 6 to Itaewon, Exit 4) Tacos have long been popular as a snack of choice for GIs and expats in Itaewon, but these guys make the shift from Tex Mex to hipster LA food

Dongdaemun & Around

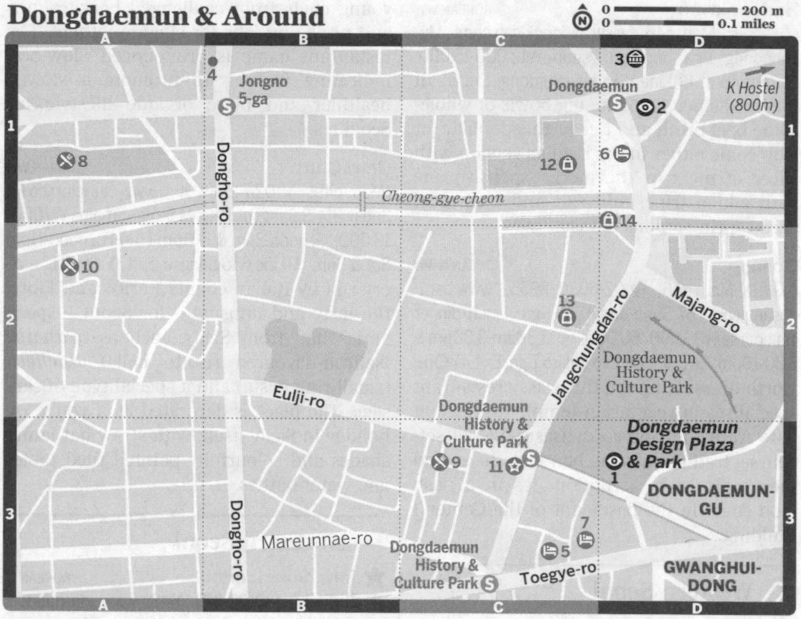

Dongdaemun & Around

⊙ Top Sights
1 Dongdaemun Design Plaza & Park D3

⊙ Sights
2 Heunginjimun D1
3 Seoul City Wall Museum D1

Activities, Courses & Tours
4 Royal Asiatic Society B1

Sleeping
5 Dongdaemun Hostel & Inn C3
6 JW Marriott Dongdaemun Square D1
7 Toyoko Inn Seoul Dongdaemun C3

🍴 Eating
Dongdaemun Market .... (see 12)
8 Gwangjang Market A1
9 Samarkand C3
10 Woo Rae Oak A2

Entertainment
11 Klive C3

Shopping
12 Dongdaemun Market C1
Dongdaemun Shopping Complex .... (see 12)
13 Doota C2
Gwangjang Market .... (see 8)
14 Pyoung Hwa Clothing Market D1

truck-style tacos with a Korean twist. Expect soft corn tortillas filled with *galbi* short rib, a side of kimchi carnitas fries and cocktails like its 'makgeolita'.

PLANT VEGAN ₩

(Map p50; www.facebook.com/studioplant; 20 Itaewon-ro 16-gil; mains from ₩10,000; ⏰11am-8pm Tue-Sat; 🌱; [S] Line 6 to Itaewon, Exit 4) Set up by the creator of the popular vegetarian blog **Alien's Day Out** (www.aliensdayout.com), this cosy vegan cafe specialises in dairy- and meat-free baked goods. The menu changes daily, but you can expect the likes of tempeh meatball subs, mock-chorizo pasta and awesome cakes such as salted-caramel pumpkin pie.

Passion 5 BAKERY, DESSERTS ₩

(Map p50; 272 Itaewon-ro; sandwiches from ₩5000; ⏰7.30am-10pm; [S] Line 6 to Hangangjin, Exit 2) Offering a Fortnum & Mason–like experience, this homage to fine food is a good place to do a few laps of the gleaming arcade to check out a gourmet choice of goods from house-baked breads and sandwiches, soups (including a sourdough clam chowder), to handmade chocolates, lavish cakes, as well as a champagne bar and European-style deli items.

Linus' BBQ AMERICAN, BARBECUE ₩₩
(Map p50; www.facebook.com/linusbbq; 136-13 Itaewon-ro; mains from ₩15,000; ⏲11.30am-3.30pm & 5.30-10pm; [S] Line 6 to Itaewon, Exit 4) Specialising in authentic southern-style American barbecue, Linus' does a range of Alabama- and Texan-style dishes which involves heaped plates of pulled pork or beef brisket, and excellent sandwiches. There's a *M*A*S*H* theme going (less tacky than it sounds) with its khaki-canvas-covered terrace, combined with a 1950s Americana soundtrack.

Tartine CAFE ₩₩
(Map p50; ☎02-3785 3400; www.tartine.co.kr; 4, Itaewon-ro 23-gil; mains ₩9000-38,500; ⏲10am-10.30pm; [S] Line 6 to Itaewon, Exit 1) Looking for dessert? You won't go wrong with the sweet pies at this charming bakery-cafe run by an American baker. It also has a diner opposite with plenty of brunch options.

Atelier du Saint-Ex FRENCH ₩₩₩
(Map p50; ☎02-795 2465; Itaewon 2-gil; mains ₩21,000-49,000; ⏲noon-11pm, to 2am Fri & Sat; 📶; [S] Line 6 to Itaewon, Exit 1) A revamped version of this acclaimed French bistro has seen it converted to a more casual affair while maintaining the quality service and delicious dishes such as grilled herb chicken and caramelised pork belly.

🍴 Dongdaemun & Eastern Seoul

★Gwangjang Market KOREAN ₩
(광장시장; Kwangjang; www.kwangjangmarket.co.kr; 88 Changgyeonggung-ro, Jongno-gu; dishes ₩4000-10,000; ⏲8.30am-10pm; [S] Line 1 to Jongno-5ga, Exit 8, or Line 2 or 5 to Euljiro 4-ga, Exit 4) Best known as Seoul's largest food alley (or *meokjagolmok*), the market is home to some 200 stalls set up among kimchi and fresh seafood vendors. Its speciality is the golden fried *nokdu bindaetteok* (mung-bean pancake; ₩5000) – paired beautifully with *makgeolli* (rice wine). Otherwise go for the healthier option of bibimbap or *boribap* (mixed rice and barley topped with a selection of vegies).

DON'T MISS

NORYANGJIN FISH MARKET

Providing terrific photo opportunities, **Noryangjin Fish Market** (노량진 수산시장; www.susansijang.co.kr; 688 Nodeul-ro, Dongjak-gu; ⏲24hr; [S] Line 1 to Noryangjin, Exit 1) supplies every kind of aquatic life form to restaurants, fish shops and the general public. At the time of research, a state-of-the-art multistorey complex was nearing completion and should now be open, housing the 700 stalls and numerous restaurants that make up the market.

If you want to view the market at its liveliest, get here for the auctions, which kick off around 1am. Otherwise, visit around meal times when the apron-clad vendors will happily sell you produce directly – be it live crabs, prawns, the dark-orange-and-red *meongge* (Korean sea squirt, very much an acquired taste), or prepared platters of *hoe* (raw fish slices). You can then take your seafood to several restaurants within the market who will either serve it up with a variety of side dishes (usually around ₩3000 per person), or prepare and cook it (starting from an extra ₩5000, depending on the creature). A good one is **Busan Ilbeonji** (부산일번지; ☎02-813 7799; 2nd fl, Noryangjn Market; mains ₩15,000-30,000; ⏲10.30am-10.30pm).

★Woo Rae Oak NOODLES, BARBECUE ₩₩
(우래옥; ☎02-2265 0151; 62-29 Changgyeonggung-ro, Jung-gu; mains ₩11,000-43,000; ⏲11.30am-10pm; [S] Line 2 or 4 to Euljiro 4ga, Exit 4) Tucked away in the sewing-machine parts section of Dongdaemun's sprawling market streets is this elegant old-timer specialising in *bulgogi* and *galbi* (barbecued beef; from ₩29,000, could feed two). But its delicious *naengmyeon* (buckwheat cold noodles) make the best lunch paired with delicious kimchi.

Samarkand CENTRAL ASIAN ₩₩
(사마르칸트; 159-10 Mareunnae-ro, Jung-gu; mains from ₩8000; ⏲10am-11pm; [S] Line 2, 4 or 5 to Dongdaemun, Exit 12) This family-run Uzbekistan restaurant is a part of Dongdaemun's 'Little Silk Road', an intriguing district that's home to a community of Russian-speaking traders from the 'stans,

Mongolia and Russia. It has delicious halal home-cooking, including lamb shashlyk that goes beautifully with fresh *lepeshka* bread and Russian beer. The area is worth a look around, signage is in Cyrillic.

🍴 Gangnam & South of the Han River

Coreanos Kitchen MEXICAN ₩

(Map p53; www.coreanoskitchen.com; Basement, 25 Seolleung-ro 157-gil, Gangnam-gu; tacos from ₩3300, burritos from ₩9000; 🕒noon-11pm; [S] Bundang Line to Apgujeong Rodeo, Exit 5) What was originally a hipster food truck in Austin, USA, Coreanos (which is Spanish for Korean) brings its winning formula of kimchi tacos to Seoul. Tastes here are a fusion of authentic Mexican street food with Korean flavours, with its hand-pressed, soft-corn tortilla tacos filled with anything from *galbi* (beef ribs) to kimchi pork belly.

Nonhyeon Samgyetang KOREAN ₩

(Map p53; 720 Eonju-ro, Gangnam-gu; mains ₩8000-18,000; 🕒24hr; [S] Line 7 to Hak-dong, Exit 10) The original branch of this popular restaurant is a good place to sample Korean specialities such as *samgyetang* (ginseng chicken soup) or steaming bowls of hearty *juk* (rice porridge) done with seafood or vegetarian servings.

Ha Jun Min KOREAN ₩

(Map p53; 332 Apgujeong-ro, Gangnam-gu; buffet ₩8000; 🕒24hr; 🥬; [S] Bundang Line to Apgujeong Rodeo, Exit 6) Keeping it real in the heart of ritzy Apgujeong Rodeo St, this long-established no-frills Korean restaurant offers amazing-value, all-you-can-eat dishes, including great vegetarian options. For barbecue it's ₩18,000, but you'll need two people. There's no English sign but it's 200m west across the road from Galleria.

★ **Jungsik** NEO-KOREAN ₩₩₩

(정식당; Map p53; ☎02-517 4654; jungsik.kr; 11 Seolleung-ro, 158-gil, Gangnam-gu; 4-course lunch/dinner from ₩50,000/90,000; 🕒noon-3pm & 5.30-10.30pm; [S] Bundang Line to Apgujeong Rodeo, Exit 4) Voted number 10 in *Asia's 50 Best Restaurants* in 2015, neo-Korean cuisine hardly gets better than this. At the Apgujeong outpost of the New York restaurant named after creative chef-owner Yim Jungsik, you can expect inspired and superbly presented contemporary mixes of traditional and seasonal ingredients over multiple courses. Book at least one month in advance.

Samwon Garden KOREAN ₩₩₩

(삼원가든; Map p53; ☎02-548 3030; www.samwongarden.com; 835 Eonju-ro, Gangnam-gu; mains from ₩43,000; 🕒11.30am-10pm; [S] Line 3 to Apgujeong, Exit 2) Serving top-class *galbi* for more than 30 years, Samwon is a Korean idyll, surrounded by beautiful traditional gardens including several waterfalls. It's one of the best places in the city for this kind of barbecued-beef meal. There are also more inexpensive dishes such as *galbitang* (beef short-rib soup) for ₩13,000.

🍷 Drinking & Nightlife

From rustic teahouses and gourmet coffee shops to craft-beer pubs and cocktail bars, Seoul offers an unbelievable number of places to relax over a drink. No-frills *hof* (pubs) are common, and don't miss that quintessential Seoul nightlife experience: *soju* (local vodka) shots and snacks at a *pojangmacha* (street tent bar).

For clubbing, hit Hongdae, Itaewon and Gangnam. Most clubs don't start becoming busy until 10pm and only start buzzing after midnight. Friday and Saturday nights have a real party atmosphere. Except in the classiest of Gangnam clubs, dress codes are generally not too strict.

🍷 Gwanghwamun & Jongno-gu

★ **Sik Mool** BAR

(식물; Map p58; ☎02-747 4858; 46-1 Donhwamun-ro 11da-gil, Jongno-gu; 🕒11am-midnight; [S] Line 1, 3 or 5 to Jongno 3-ga, Exit 6) Four *hanok* were creatively combined to create this chic designer cafe-bar that blends old and new Seoul. Clay-tile walls, Soviet-era propaganda posters, mismatched modern furniture and contemporary art surround a young crowd sipping cocktails, coffee and wine and nibbling on house-made pizza.

★ **Daeo Sochom** CAFE

(대오서점; Map p58; ☎010 570 1349; 55 Jahamun-ro 7-gil, Jongno-gu; 🕒noon-8pm Tue-Sun; [S] Line 3 to Gyeongbokgung, Exit 2) Opened as a bookstore in 1951 by Mrs Kwong and her husband Mr Cho, this charming cafe is still run by the same family and oozes bygone-days atmosphere with lots of memorabilia and quirky decor. Entry is ₩5000 which gets you a choice of drink.

GLBT SEOUL

Squished between 'Hooker Hill' and the Little Arabia strip by the Seoul Mosque, 'Homo Hill' is a 50m-long alley so called because of its cluster of GLBT-friendly bars and clubs. Most hardly have room to swing a handbag, so on warm weekends the crowds often spill onto the street. All genders and sexual persuasions will feel welcome here.

At the bottom of the hill on the left is **Trance** (Map p50; cafe.daum.net/trance; Usadan-ro; admission incl 1 drink ₩10,000; ⏰10.30pm-5am; ⚐; ⓢLine 6 to Itaewon, Exit 3), a basement club with pouting drag queens and late-night shows. Next door is the eternally popular **Queen** (Map p50; www.facebook.com/queenbar; 7, Usadan-ro 12-gil; ⏰8pm-5am Tue-Sun; ⓢLine 6 to Itaewon, Exit 3), which offers sit-and-chat zones, though it usually gets very crowded with almost everyone dancing.

Flirty, friendly staff and a cosy style mark out **Always Homme** (올웨이즈옴므; Map p50; facebook.com/AlwaysHommeBar; Usadan-ro 12-gil; ⏰8pm-4am Sun-Thu, to 6am Fri & Sat; ⓢLine 6 to Itaewon, Exit 3). The same management runs **Why Not** (Map p50; Usadan-ro; ⏰7.30pm-3am Sun-Thu, to 5am Fri & Sat; ⓢLine 6 to Itaewon, Exit 3), a dance club across the alley with lights and lasers – expect plenty of K-Pop. On the same side of the street, higher up the hill, is the slightly roomier and relaxed **Soho** (Map p50; Usadan-ro; ⏰10pm-5am; ⓢLine 6 to Itaewon, Exit 3), while at the top of the hill is the lesbian bar **Miracle** (Map p50; Usadan-ro; ⏰8pm-5am; ⓢLine 6 to Itaewon, Exit 3).

Between Tapgol Park and Jongno 3-ga subway station is an area that supports scores of gay bars and small clubs. Not all are welcoming of foreigners, or might expect patrons to pay a hefty admission for *anju* (snacks). 'One-shot bars', where you can drink without an admission fee, include **Barcode** (Map p58; 41-1 Donhwamun-ro, Jongno-gu; ⏰7pm-4am; ⓢLine 1, 3 or 5 to Jongno 3-ga, Exit 3), run by friendly English-speaking Kim Hyoung-Jin; and **Shortbus** (Map p58; korea-shortbus.wix.com/shortbus; 45 Donhwamun-ro, Jongno-gu; ⏰7pm-5am; ⓢLine 1, 3 or 5 to Jongno 3-ga, Exit 3), an appealing wine and cocktail bar. Both have English signs. Alternatively, drop by the outdoor *pojangmacha* food stalls around Jongno 3-ga to sink cheap beer, *soju* (local vodka) and snacks with the gay community.

In Hongdae is the long-running **Labris** (라브리스; Map p49; ☎02-333 5276; 81-Wausan-ro, Mapo-gu; ⏰7pm-2am Mon-Thu, to 5am Fri-Sun; ⓢLine 6 to Sangsu, Exit 1), a women-only social/dance club that attracts locals and foreigners; and **Club MWG** (Map p49; www.facebook.com/clubmwg1; 6-5, Wausan-ro 19-gil, Mapo-gu; ⏰10pm-5am Fri & Sat; ⓢLine 2 to Hongik University, Exit 2), which hosts the GLBT-friendly **Meet Market** (www.facebook.com/meetmarketseoul) queer party events.

In June, Seoul pins up its rainbow colours for the **Korean Queer Festival** (www.kqcf.org), which includes a parade through central Seoul.

⭐**Brew 3.14**   BAR
(Map p58; ☎070-4178 3014; www.facebook.com/brew314; 39 Donhwamun-ro 11-gil, Jongno-gu; ⏰4pm-midnight; ⓢLine 1, 3 or 5 to Jongno 3-ga, Exit 6) Along with sibling operation Brew 3.15 across the road, Brew 3.14 has carved a name for itself with its great selection of local craft beers, delicious pizza (which they call by the American name 'pie') and moreish fried chicken. Both bars are quiet, convivial places to hang out over pints and eats.

⭐**Dawon**   TEAHOUSE
(다원; ☎02-730 6305; 11-4 Insa-dong 10-gil, Jongno-gu; teas ₩7000; ⏰10.30am-10.30pm; ⓢLine 3 to Anguk, Exit 6) The perfect place to unwind under the shady fruit trees in a courtyard with flickering candles. In colder weather sit indoors in *hanok* rooms decorated with scribbles or in the garden pavilion. The teas are superb, especially *omijacha hwachae* (fruit and five-flavour berry punch), a summer drink.

Kopi Bangatgan   CAFE
(커피 방앗간; Map p58; 118-11 Bukchon-ro 5ga-gil, Jongno-gu; ⏰8.30am-10.30pm; ⓢLine 3 to Anguk, Exit 1) Based in a *hanok*, 'Coffee Mill' is a charming spot decorated with retro pieces and the quirky, colourful artworks of owner Lee Gyeong-hwan whom you're likely to spot painting at the counter. Apart from various coffees they also serve waffles.

Story of the Blue Star BAR

(푸른별 주막; ☎02-734 3095; 17-1 Insa-dong 16-gil, Jongno-gu; ⏰3pm-midnight; [S]Line 3 to Anguk, Exit 6) Owned by a stage actor this rustic hang-out, plastered with posters, is an atmospheric place to sample *makgeolli* (rice wine) served out of brass kettles into brass bowls. Flavours include mulberry leaf, green tea and taro. Order slices of their homemade organic tofu and kimchi to eat as you drink.

Cha Masineun Tteul TEAHOUSE

(차마시는뜰; Map p58; 26 Bukchon-ro 11na-gil, Jongno-gu; ⏰10.30am-10pm; [S]Line 3 to Anguk, Exit 1) Overlooking Samcheong-dong and Gwanghwamun is this lovely *hanok* with low tables arranged around a courtyard. They serve traditional teas and a delicious bright-yellow pumpkin rice cake that is served fresh from the steamer.

Dalsaeneun Dalman Saenggak Handa TEAHOUSE

(달새는 달만 생각한다; ☎02-720 6229; 14-3 Insa-dong 12-gil, Jongno-gu; teas ₩7000-9000; ⏰10am-11pm; [S]Line 3 to Anguk, Exit 6) 'Moon Bird Thinks Only of the Moon' is packed with plants and rustic artefacts. Bird song, soothing music and trickling water add to the atmosphere. Huddle in a cubicle and savour one of their teas, which include *gamnipcha* (persimmon-leaf tea). *Saenggangcha* (ginger tea) is peppery but sweet.

Ikdong Dabang BAR

(익동다방; Map p58; ☎070-8690 2759; www.facebook.com/ikdongdabang; 17-19 Supyo-ro 28-gil, Jongno-gu; ⏰11am-11pm; [S]Line 1, 3 or 5 to Jongno 3-ga, Exit 6) More evidence of the evolution of Ikseon-dong's cluster of *hanok* into cool cafe-bars and guesthouses is this arty *dabang* (an old Korean name for a cafe). Look for the bright yellow-and-blue, painted-steel-frame sculpture that leads into a courtyard sometimes used for musical performances.

🍷 Myeong-dong & Jung-gu

Walkabout BAR

(Map p46; blog.naver.com/walkaboutnu; 49 Toegye-ro 20-gil, Jung-gu; ⏰10am-midnight Mon-Sat, 2-10pm Sun; 📶; [S]Line 4 to Myeongdong, Exit 3) Among Myeong-dong's backpacker enclave leading up to Namsan, this travel-themed bar is run by a couple of young travel nuts who serve Korean craft beers on tap.

Caffe Themselves CAFE

(Map p46; www.caffethemselves.com; 388 Samil-daero, Jongno-gu; coffee ₩5500; ⏰10am-10pm; 📶; [S]Line 1 to Jonggak, Exit 12) A worthy stop for those who take their coffee seriously, here baristas know how to do a decent single-origin espresso, slow drip or cold brew. They roast their own beans, which they sell by the bag, as well as having ready-made samples to try.

🍷 Western Seoul

★**Wolhyang** BAR

(Map p49; ☎02-332 9202; www.tasteofthemoon.com; 27 Wausan-ro 29-gil, Mapo-gu; ⏰11.30pm-2am Mon-Sat, to 1am Sun; 📶; [S]Line 2 to Hongik University, Exit 8) Specialising in *makgeolli* (milky rice wine) from around Korea, and other local liquors, this brightly decorated, spacious 2nd-floor bar is a great place to sample traditional alcoholic drinks. They also have various fruity and nutty flavours of *makgeolli* as well as decent food such as savoury pancakes.

★**Anthracite** CAFE

(Map p49; www.anthracitecoffee.com; 10 Tojeong-ro 5-gil; ⏰11am-midnight; 📶; [S]Line 6 to Sangsu, Exit 4) An old shoe factory is the location for one of Seoul's top independent coffee-roaster and cafe operations. Drinks are made using the hand-drip method at a counter made out of an old conveyor belt. Upstairs is a spacious lounge and there's outdoor seating on the roof.

Café Sukkara CAFE, BAR

(Map p49; ☎02-334 5919; www.sukkara.co.kr; Sanullim Bldg, 327-9 Seogyo-dong, Mapo-gu; ⏰11am-midnight Tue-Sun; 📶; [S]Line 2 to Hongik University, Exit 9) There's a fantastic range of drinks and some very tasty things to eat (try their butter-chicken curry) at this shabby-chic, farmhouse-style cafe with a contemporary Japanese flair. They make their own juices and liquors – try the black shandy gaff, a mix of homemade ginger ale and Magpie Brewery dark beer.

M2 CLUB

(Map p49; ☎02-3143 7573; www.ohoo.net/m2; 20-5 Jandari-ro, Mapo-gu; Sun-Thu ₩10,000, Fri & Sat ₩20,000; ⏰9.30pm-4.30am Sun-Thu, 8.30pm-6.30am Fri & Sat; [S]Line 6 to Sangsu, Exit 1) Deep underground is M2, one of the largest and best Hongdae clubs. It has a high ceiling and plenty of lights and visuals. Top local and international DJs spin mainly progressive house music.

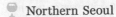

Northern Seoul

Mix & Malt BAR

(Map p58; ☎02-765 5945; www.facebook.com/MixMalt; 3 Changgyeonggung-ro 29-gil, Jongno-gu; 🕒7.30am-2am Sun-Thu, to 3am Fri & Sat; 📶; [S] Line 4 to Hyehwa, Exit 4) Even without the advantage of the owner's delightful golden retriever Louis padding around, this would be a superb cocktail and malt-whiskey bar (some 50 plus single malts) to hunker down in. It also serves tasty US comfort food and has plenty of room on two levels, with sofas and a fireplace for winter and an outdoor deck for warmer days.

★ **Suyeon Sanbang** TEAHOUSE

(수연산방; 8 Seongbuk-ru 26-gil, Seongbuk-gu; 🕒11.30am-10pm; 🚌1111, 2112, [M] Line 4 to Hangsung University, Exit 6 then) Seoul's most charming teahouse is based in a 1930s *hanok* that was once the home of novelist Lee Tae-jun and is surrounded by a peaceful garden. Apart from medicinal teas and premium-quality, wild green tea, they also serve traditional sweets; the salty-sweet pumpkin soup with red-bean paste is a taste sensation.

Dallyeora Gaemi 1 BAR

(달려라 개미 1; ☎02-3676 5955; 22-14 Naksan-gil, Jongno-gu; 🕒4-11pm; [S] Line 4 to Hyehwa, Exit 2) Purists may snub their fruit-flavoured slushies made from *makgeolli* (a mild milky rice alcohol) but the fact is that they are not a bad choice at this fun update on a *pojangmacha* (tent bar). There's a second branch

DON'T MISS

CRAFT BEER VALLEY

At the epicentre of the craft-beer revolution in Seoul, Noksapyeong (in Gyeongridan, up from Itaewon) is home to a string of brewers who have set up shop in what's now known locally as Craft Beer Valley.

Craftworks Taphouse (Map p50; craftworkstaphouse.com; 651 Itaewon 2-dong, Gyeongridan; 🕒11am-midnight Mon-Fri, to 2am Sat & Sun; [S] Line 6 to Noksapyeong, Exit 2) The original brewer to kick off Noksapyeong's craft-beer scene, Craftworks has secured a treasured place in the hearts of Seoul's ale lovers. Order the paddle to sample its seven beers (₩10,500) and then decide which one to savour in a pint. They also feature guest breweries, house wine and a quality menu of pub grub. Happy hour is 4pm to 6pm.

Also has branches in Itaewon (Map p50; www.craftworkstaphouse.com/itaewon; 214-1 Itaewon-ro; [S] Line 6 to Itaewon, Exit 3) – which has a greater beer selection – and downtown at Euljiro (Map p46; www.craftworkstaphouse.com/downtown; Pine Avenue Mall, 100 Eulji-ro, Jung-gu; [S] Line 2 or 3 to Euljiro 3-ga, Exit 12).

Magpie Brewing Co. (Map p50; www.magpiebrewing.com; Noksapyoungro 54gil 7, Gyeongridan; 🕒3pm-1am; [S] Line 6 to Noksapyeong, Exit 2) A big player in Seoul's craft-beer movement, this brew pub is split into two parts. Downstairs is **Magpie Basement**, a beer bunker with low-lying lamps, serving its eight beers on tap and pizza (from ₩9000). Otherwise there's the more intimate **Brew Shop**, which does occasional home-brew classes and tastings for ₩60,000. They've also opened bars in Hongdae (Map p49; www.magpiebrewing.com; 6-15 Wausan-ro 19-gil, Mapo-gu; 🕒5pm-2am Tue-Thu, 5pm-3am Fri, 2pm-3am Sat, 2pm-2am Sun; [S] Line 2 to Hongik University, Exit 9) and Jeju Island.

Booth (Map p50; www.theboothpub.com; Itaewon-dong 705, Gyeongridan; 🕒noon-1am; [S] Line 6 to Noksapyeong, Exit 2) The original Booth brew pub has pop-art murals on its walls, and is known for its flagship Bill's pale ale and pepperoni pizza by the slice. There's also a divey industrial Booth Mansion (Map p50; www.theboothpub.com; 36 Itaewon-ro 27ga-gil; beer ₩5000; 🕒5pm-1am Sun-Thu, 2pm-3am Fri & Sat; [S] Line 6 to Itaewon, Exit 1) branch near Itaewon station, and in Gangnam.

Made in Pong Dang (Map p50; www.pongdangsplash.com; 222-1 Noksapyeong, Gyeongridan; 🕒4pm-midnight Sun-Thu, 2pm-2am Fri & Sat; [S] Line 6 to Noksapyeong, Exit 2) In a scene dominated by North Americans, Pong Dang is an all-Korean affair, producing six of its own beers on taps pulled from the wood-panelled bar, including pale ale, Belgian Blonde ale and seasonals such as oatmeal stout.

ⓘ TICKETS

Interpark (http://ticket.interpark. com) Tickets for theatre, concerts and sporting events.

KTO Tourist Information Centre (p91) Sells discount tickets for shows.

XIndie Ticket Lounge (Map p49; ☑02-322 2218; www.ticketlounge.co.kr; Eoulmadang-ro, Mapo-gu; ⊗1-9pm Tue-Sun; ⓢLine 6 to Sangsu, Exit 1) Hongdae hub for gig tickets.

higher up the hill in the heart of Ihwa Maeul also serving breads and other bakes made with *makgeolli*. The name means 'Ants Run'.

Hakrim CAFE
(Map p58; www.hakrim.pe.kr; 119 Daehak-ro, Jongno-gu; ⊗10am-midnight; �🐱; ⓢLine 4 to Hyehwa, Exit 3) Little has changed in this retro Seoul classic since the place opened in 1956, save for the price of drinks. Apart from coffee they also serve tea and alcohol. The cosy wooden booths and dark corners make it popular with couples.

🍷 Itaewon & Yongsan-gu

Southside Parlor COCKTAIL BAR
(Map p50; www.facebook.com/Southside-Parlor; 218 Noksapyeong-daero, Gyeongridan; ⊗6pm-midnight; ⓢLine 6 to Noksapyeong, Exit 2) Having outgrown their roots in a hipster food truck in Texas, these artisan cocktail makers have set up shop in Itaewon. Here mixologists know their stuff, concocting labour-intensive original and classic cocktails, served at an old-school copper bar counter. If the weather is nice, check out the Astroturf rooftop. If you're hungry they've got a quality menu of pulled-pork sandwiches, burgers etc.

Damotori BAR
(다모토리; Map p50; 31 Sinheung-ro, Haebangchon; ⊗6pm-1am Sun-Thu, to 2am Fri & Sat; 🐱; ⓢLine 6 to Noksapyeong, Exit 2) A locals' favourite along HBC's main strip, the dimly lit Damotori specialises in quality *makgeolli* (milky rice wine), hand-picked from provinces around the country. The food is also excellent, especially the seafood pancakes.

Four Seasons BAR
(사계; Map p50; www.facebook.com/craftpub4seasons; Basement, 7 Bogwang-ro 59-gil; ⊗6pm-1am

Mon-Thu, to 2am Fri, 2pm-2am Sat, to midniight Sun; ⓢLine 6 to Itaewon, Exit 4) Set up by a bunch of local beer geeks who brew their own ales, this basement bar has 10 craft beers on tap and a good stock of bottled varieties in the fridge.

Takeout Drawing CAFE
(Map p50; www.takeoutdrawing.com; Noksapyeong-daero, Gyeongridan; ⊗2pm-10am; ⓢLine 6 to Noksapyeong, Exit 2) This arty cafe is a cool place to hang out and enjoy graphic art, books and magazines with coffee, organic teas and other beverages. There's another branch in **Hannam** (Map p50; Itaewon-ro; 🐱; ⓢLine 6 to Hanganjjin, Exit 3).

🍷 Gangnam & South of the Han River

Greenmile Coffee CAFE
(Map p53; www.facebook.com/greenmilecoffee; 11 Seolleung-ro 127-gil, Gangnam-gu; coffee from ₩3500; ⊗8am-9pm Mon-Fri; 🐱; ⓢLine 7 to Gangnam-gu Office, Exit 2) Fitted out in designer furniture and caffeine-related paraphernalia, this cool little cafe is one of Seoul's best spots for coffee. They roast all their single-origin beans on-site, sourced from Africa to Latin America. As well as offering the usual espresso, pour-overs and cold drip, they're also the proud owners of laboratory-like, halogen-powered equipment that does sensational siphon brews.

Neurin Maeul BAR
(느린마을; Map p53; ☑02-587 7720; 7 Seocho-daero 73-gil, Seocho-gu; ⊗11am-11pm; ⓢLine 2 to Gangnam, Exit 9) The Gangnam branch of this Baesangmyeon Brewery bar is a bit snazzier than others, but remains a good place to sample quality traditional Korean alcohol. Its signature Neurin Maeul *makgeolli* (milky rice wine) is the standout – divided into the four 'seasons', which refers to the differing production stages; you can sample each before ordering. You're likely to have to order food here.

Jugs cost ₩8000 per litre (₩3000 takeaway). Sign up for free membership to get two-hours of unlimited *makgeolli* for ₩10,000. There's another **branch** (Map p46; ☑02-587 7720; Center 1, 26 Eulji-ro 5-gil, Jung-gu; ⓢLine 2 to Euljiro 1-ga, Exit 3 or 4) in Myeongdong.

★ SJ Kunsthalle CLUB, BAR
(Map p53; ☑010 2014 9722; sjkunsthalle.com; 5 Eonju-ro 148-gil; ⊗11am-1am Mon-Sat; 🐱; Ⓜ Line

Insa-dong

Insa-dong

3 to Apgujeong, Exit 3) What's not to love about this bar/gallery/events space created like a giant's Lego set from old shipping containers. There's live music and a wide variety of other events. Opening hours vary, so check the website for upcoming events.

★ **Club Octagon** CLUB
(Map p53; www.cluboctagon.co.kr; 645 Nonhyeon-ro, Gangnam-gu; admission before 11pm & after 4am ₩10,000, 11pm-4am ₩30,000; ⏲Thu-Sat 10pm-6am; [S] Line 7 to Hak-dong, Exit 4) Voted number 6 in the world's top clubs by *DJ Mag* in 2015, Octagon is one of Gangnam's best for serious clubbers. High-profile resident and guest DJs spin house and techno over its powerful Funktion 1 sound system to an appreciative crowd here to party till dawn.

Ellui CLUB
(www.facebook.com/ellui.club; 551 Dosan-daero, Gangnam-gu; admission ₩30,000; ⏲10pm-8am Fri & Sat ; [S] Line 7 to Cheongdam, Exit 13) If you're going to visit just one mega club in Gangnam, Ellui is the one. It's a massive space with a dazzling light and sound system and multiple dance floors.

☆ Entertainment

☆ Gwanghwamun & Jongno-gu

Sejong Center for the Performing Arts THEATRE
(세종문화회관; Map p58; ☎02-399 1114; www.sejongpac.or.kr; 175 Sejong-daero, Jongno-gu; [S] Line 5 to Gwanghwamun, Exit 1 or 8) One of Seoul's leading arts complexes, with several performance and exhibition spaces, puts on major drama, music and art shows – everything from large-scale musicals to fusion *gugak* (traditional Korean music) and chamber orchestras.

☆ Myeong-dong & Jung-gu

Jeongdong Theater THEATRE
(Map p46; ☎02-751 1500; www.jeongdong.or.kr; 43 Jeongdong-gil, Jung-gu; tickets ₩30,000-40,000; ⏲4pm & 8pm Tue-Sun; [S] Line 1 or 2 to City Hall, Exit 2) Most famous for its critically acclaimed musical *Miso*, this theatre company also produces a number of traditional non-verbal musicals.

National Theater of Korea THEATRE
(Map p46; ☎02-2280 4122; www.ntok.go.kr; 59 Jangchungdan-ro, Jung-gu; [S] Line 3 to Dongguk University, Exit 6) The several venues here are home to the national drama, *changgeuk* (Korean opera), orchestra and dance companies. Free concerts and movies are put on in summer at the outdoor stage. Walk 10 minutes here or hop on bus 2 at the stop behind Exit 6 of the subway.

☆ Western Seoul

★ **Mudaeruk** LIVE MUSIC
(무대륙; Map p49; ☎02-332 8333; www.mudaeruk.com; 12 Tojeong-ro 5-gil, Mapo-gu; admission from ₩10,000; 📶; [S] Line 6 to Sangsu, Exit 4) The 'Lost Continent of Mu' has been hiding out in Sangsu-dong all these years? Join in-the-

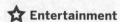

SEOUL SHOWTIME

Running for over 15 years, with no end in sight, is Korea's most successful non-verbal performance, **Nanta**. Set in a kitchen, this highly entertaining 1½-hour show mixes up magic tricks, *samulnori* ('traditional' Korean farmers' dance) folk music, drumming with kitchen utensils, comedy, dance, martial arts and audience participation. A hit wherever it plays, Nanta is staged at two venues:

Myeongdong (눈스퀘어; Map p46; ☎02-739 8288; www.nanta.co.kr; 3rd fl, Unesco Bldg, 26 Myeongdong-gil, Jung-gu; tickets ₩40,000-60,000; ⏲2pm, 5pm & 8pm; [S] Line 4 to Myeong-dong, Exit 6)

Chungjeongo (Map p46; ☎02-739 8288; www.nanta.co.kr; 476 Chungjeongno 3-ga, Seodaemungu; tickets ₩40,000-60,000; ⏲shows 5pm & 8pm; [S] Line 5 to Chungjeongo, Exit 7)

Other recommended shows include **Jump** (Map p46; ☎02-722 3995; www.hijump.co.kr; 22 Jeong-dong, Jung-gu; tickets from ₩40,000; ⏲4pm Mon, 4pm & 8pm Tue-Sat, 3pm & 6pm Sun; [S] Line 5 to Gwanghwamun, Exit 6), featuring a wacky Korean family all crazy about martial arts; and **Bibap** (Map p46; ☎02-766 0815; www.bibap.co.kr; 386, Samil-daero, Jongno-gu; tickets from ₩40,000; ⏲8pm Mon, 5pm & 8pm Tue-Sat, 3pm & 6pm Sun; [S] Line 1 to Jonggak, Exit 12), a comedic Iron Chef–style contest that adds beatbox and a cappella into the mix.

know hipsters for shows by bands and DJs specialising in electronic music in the basement on weekends. Upstairs is a stylish cafe-bar with craft beer, sharing boards of food and great fish and chips.

Club Evans
JAZZ

(Map p49; ☎02-337 8361; www.clubevans.com; 63-Wausan-ro, Mapo-gu; admission ₩10,000; ⓘ7.30pm-midnight Sun-Thu, to 2am Fri & Sat; Ⓢ Line 6 to Sangsu, Exit 1) Appealing across the generations, Evans offers top-grade jazz and a great atmosphere. Get here early if you want a seat or book ahead. They release their own label CDs, too. Monday is jam night.

Café BBang
LIVE MUSIC

(카페 빵; Map p49; cafe.daum.net/cafebbang; 12 Wausan-ro 29-gil, Mapo-gu; ⓘ7pm-6am; Ⓢ Line 2 to Hongik University, Exit 8) You're sure to catch something interesting here – apart from gigs by indie artists and bands, it also hosts film screenings, art exhibitions and parties.

CLUB FF
LIVE MUSIC

(Map p49; ☎011 9025 3407; Hongdae; admission ₩10,000; ⓘ7pm-6am; Ⓢ Line 6 to Sangsu, Exit 1) A top live venue with up to eight local indie bands playing at the weekend until midnight. Afterwards it becomes a dance club with DJs.

Su Noraebang
KARAOKE

(수노래방; Map p49; ☎02-322 3111; www.skysu.com; 67 Eoulmadang-ro, Mapo-gu; per hr ₩2000-20,000; ⓘ24hr; Ⓢ Line 6 to Sangsu, Exit 1) Sing your heart out and be noticed: some rooms have floor-to-ceiling windows fronting onto the street so you can show off your K-Pop moves. Rates rise from noon to 6am with the most expensive period from 8pm to the early hours.

World Cup Stadium
STADIUM

(월드컵주경기장; www.seoulworldcupst.or.kr; 240, World Cup-ro, Mapo-gu; Ⓢ Line 6 to World Cup Stadium, Exit 1) Built for the 2002 Football World Cup, this 66,000-seat venue is still used as a sports and events stadium. Die-hard soccer fans may want to visit the small **museum** (adult/child ₩1000/500; ⓘ9am-5.30pm) here that focuses on the World Cup event.

Cinemateque KOFA
CINEMA

(한국영상자료원; ☎02-3153 2001; www.kore-afilm.org; 400 World Cup buk-ro, Mapo-gu; Ⓢ Line 6 to Susaek, Exit 2) **FREE** Free classic and con-

---

GYEONGBOKGUNG'S TURBULENT HISTORY

Originally built by King Taejo in 1395, Gyeongbokgung served as the principal royal residence until 1592, when it was burnt down during the Japanese invasion. It lay in ruins for nearly 300 years until Heungseon Daewongun, regent and father of King Gojong, started to re-build it in 1865. Gojong moved in during 1868, but the expensive reconstruction project bankrupted the government.

In the early hours of 8 October 1895, Japanese assassins broke into the palace and murdered Empress Myeong-seong (Queen Min), one of the most powerful figures at that time in Korea. She was targeted because of her attempts to modernise Korea and protect its independence.

During Japanese colonial rule, the front section of the palace was again destroyed in order to build the enormous Japanese Government General Building. This was itself demolished in the 1990s to enable Gwanghwamun to be rebuilt to how you see it today.

---

temporary Korean films are on the bill at one of the three cinemas in this home of the Korean Film Archive. See the website for directions from the subway exit.

☆ Northern Seoul

Jazz Story
JAZZ

(Map p58; ☎02-725 6537; www.jazzstory.co.kr; 86 Daehak-ro 12-gil, Jongno-gu; admission ₩5000; ⓘ5pm-3am; Ⓢ Line 4 to Hyehwa, Exit 2) Lined with shelves of old LPs and some rather extraordinary metalwork decor, this shack-like building is certainly one of Seoul's more striking bars, where you can catch live sets by the house jazz band at 8.30pm (8pm on Sunday).

ArkoPAC
THEATRE

(Map p58; ☎02-3668 0007; www.koreapac.kr; 17 Daehak-ro 10-gil, Jongno-gu; Ⓢ Line 4 to Hyehwa, Exit 2) In this large, red-brick complex, designed by Kim Swoo-geun, are the main and small halls of both the Arko Art Theater and Daehangno Arts Theater. Come here for a varied dance-oriented program of events and shows.

1. Gyeongbokgung (p43)
The beautiful grounds of the 'palace of shining happiness' contain islands on an artifical lake

2. Dongdaemun Design Plaza & Park (p51)
At Seoul's stylish plaza you'll find sculptures on display including the haechi, the symbol of the city

3. Cheong-gye-cheon (p43)
This revitalised stream runs through the centre of the capital

SEOUL FOR CHILDREN

Seoul is a safe and family-friendly city with plenty of interesting museums (including several devoted to kids themselves) as well as parks, amusement parks and fun events that will appeal to all age groups.

The best way to cut down on child grumbles is to mix your sampling of traditional Korean culture with things the kids are more likely to enjoy. Fortunately, thanks to the global appeal of local pop culture, the young ones are likely to be more au fait with contemporary Korean pop culture than you! Be prepared to search out shops stocking Girls Generation posters, DVDs of the latest Korean TV soap opera, or *manhwa* (Korean print comics and graphic novels): **Kyobo Bookshop** (p85) is a good place to start.

Not that museums and other traditional culture centres here need be boring. The **National Museum of Korea** (p50) and the **National Folk Museum of Korea** (p44) have fun, hands-on children's sections, and the **War Memorial of Korea** (p51) has outdoor war planes and tanks that make for a popular playground. Various events, some involving dressing up in traditional costumes or having a go at taekwondo, happen at **Namsangol Hanok Village** (p45).

Amusements parks include the theme-park extravaganzas of **Lotte World** (p54) and **Everland Resort** (p107), easy day trips from the city. There are also scores of free city-managed parks – places such as **Seoul Forest** (p52), **Olympic Park** (p52) and the string of bicycle-lane-connected parks that hug the banks of the Han River. Each summer, six big outdoor pool complexes open in the Han River parks, too.

Korea 4 Expats (www.korea4expats.com) has more child-related information on Seoul.

Dongsoong Arts Center THEATRE
(Map p58; ☎02-766 3390; www.dsartcenter.co.kr; 122 Dongsung-gil, Jongno-gu; [S] Line 4 to Hyehwa, Exit 1) Major theatre complex where you can see Korean and international performance arts in a variety of genres. The centre includes a puppet theatre, smaller performances spaces and a museum devoted to *kokdu* (wooden dolls and effigies with spiritual properties).

☆ Itaewon & Yongsan-gu

★Cakeshop CLUB
(Map p50; www.cakeshopseoul.com; 134 Itaewon-ro; entry incl 1 drink ₩20,000; ⏲Tue-Sat 10pm-5am; [S] Line 6 to Noksapyeong, Exit 2) Head underground to Itaewon's hippest club for electronic beats spun by international and top local DJs. Its attracts a lively, mixed crowd and is very popular so expect long queues.

Venue/ CLUB
(Map p50; facebook.com/venuerok; 165-6 Itaewon-ro; ⏲10pm-6am; [S] Line 6 to Itaewon, Exit 1) This dive-y basement club attracts a fun-loving, unpretentious crowd for quality DJs spinning hip hop and electronica. There's no cover charge, but there's a queue after midnight.

Thunderhorse Tavern LIVE MUSIC
(Map p50; www.thunderhorsetavern.com; Noksapyeong 220, Gyeongridan; ⏲8.30pm-midnight; [S] Line 6 to Noksapyeong, Exit 2) Take the stairs down to this dingy basement venue for a regular roster of local and expat bands playing anything from indie and punk to metal.

All that Jazz JAZZ
(Map p50; ☎02-795 5701; www.allthatjazz.kr; 3rd fl, 12 Itaewon-ro 27ga-gil; admission ₩5000; ⏲6pm-1am Sun-Thu, to 2.30am Fri & Sat; [S] Line 6 to Itaewon, Exit 2) A fixture on the Seoul jazz scene since 1976, top local musicians regularly perform here; table reservations are recommended for the weekend. During the week live music starts at 8.30pm, with additional earlier 6.30pm shows on Fridays and weekends. There's also a late 11.30pm show on Friday and Saturday.

☆ Dongdaemun & Eastern Seoul

Klive LIVE PERFORMANCE
(☎02-2265 0810; www.klive.co.kr; 9th fl, Lotte Fitin Bldg, 264 Eulji-ro, Jung-gu; adult/child ₩33,000/16,000; ⏲shows 2pm, 4pm, 6pm & 8pm Tue-Sun; [S] Line 2, 4 or 5 to Dongdaemun History & Culture Park, Exit 11) One for the K-Pop fans out there, with nightly concerts using state-

of-the-art hologram technology with scarily real effects. It's all in Korean, but there are English subtitles.

☆ Gangnam & South of the Han River

Seoul Arts Center
PERFORMING ARTS

(서울 예술의전당; SAC; ☑02-580 1300; www.sac.or.kr; 2406 Nambusunhwan-ro, Seocho-gu; tickets from ₩10,000; ⓢLine 3 to Nambu Bus Terminal, Exit 5) The national ballet and opera companies are based at this sprawling arts complex, which includes a circular opera house with a roof shaped like a Korean nobleman's hat. It also houses a concert hall and a smaller recital hall in which the national choir, the Korea and Seoul symphony orchestras and drama companies stage shows.

National Gugak Center
TRADITIONAL MUSIC

(☑02-580 3300; www.gugak.go.kr; 2364, Nambusunhwan-ro, Seocho-gu; tickets from ₩10,000; ⓢLine 3 to Nambu Bus Terminal, Exit 5) Traditional Korean classical and folk music and dance are performed, preserved and taught at this centre, which is home to the Court Music Orchestra, the Folk Music Group, Dance Theater and the Contemporary Gugak Orchestra. The main theatre, Yeak-dang, puts on an ever-changing program by leading performers every Saturday, usually at 3pm.

LG Arts Center
PERFORMING ARTS

(Map p53; ☑02-2005 0114; www.lgart.com; 508 Nonhyeon-ro, Gangnam-gu; ⓢLine 2 to Yeoksam, Exit 7) Major local and international artists and companies perform at this multi-hall, state-of-the-art venue.

Seoul Sports Complex
SPORTS

(서울종합운동장; Jamsil Sports Complex; ☑02-2240 8800; http://stadium.seoul.go.kr; 10 Jamsil-dong, Songpa-gu; tickets from ₩7000; ⓢLines 2 or 8 to Sports Complex, Exit 6) A part of the Seoul Sports Complex, even if you're not a baseball fan it's worth coming along to Jamsil Baseball Stadium (admission ₩15,000-25,000) for a game for its raucous atmosphere and off-field entertainment such as K-Pop cheerleaders. Also here is Olympic Stadium, which is used for major concerts.

🛍 Shopping

Whether it's traditional items such as *hanbok* (clothing) or *hanji* (handmade paper),

WORTH A TRIP

KOREA HOUSE

Scoring a hat-trick for high-quality food, entertainment and shopping is **Korea House** (한국의집; Map p46; ☑02-2266 9101; www.koreahouse.or.kr; 10 Toegye-ro 36-gil, Jung-gu; set menu lunch/dinner ₩45,000/68,200, performances ₩50,000; ⓒlunch noon-2pm Mon-Fri, dinner 5-6.30pm & 7-8.30pm, performances 6.30pm & 8.30pm, shop 10am-8pm; ⓢLine 3 or 4 to Chungmuro, Exit 3). A dozen dainty, artistic courses make up the royal banquet. The *hanok*, the *hanbok*-clad waitresses, the *gayageum* (zither) music and the platters and boxes the food is served in are all part of the experience.

The intimate theatre stages two traditional, hour-long **dance and music performances**, which you can see independently of eating here. Put on by a troupe of top musicians and dancers, the shows have some English commentary on a screen.

Rounding out the experience is Korea House's **shop**, which stocks an expertly edited selection of quality-design goods, traditional crafts, books and cards.

or digital gizmos and K-Pop CDs, chances are slim that you'll leave Seoul empty-handed. Seoul's teeming markets, electronics emporiums, underground arcades, upmarket department stores and glitzy malls are all bursting at the seams with more goodies than Santa's sack.

🔒 Gwanghwamun & Jongno-gu

★Kyobo Bookshop
BOOKS, MUSIC

(Map p58; ☑02-3973 5100; www.kyobobook.co.kr; B1, Kyobo Bldg, 1 Jong-ro, Jongno-gu; ⓒ9.30am-10pm; ⓢLine 5 to Gwanghwamun, Exit 4) Kyobo's flagship branch sells a wide range of English-language books and magazines (you'll find them on the left from the main entrance), as well as stationery, gifts, electronics and CDs and DVDs in their excellent **Hottracks** (www.hottracks.co.kr) section.

Seoul Selection
BOOKS, DVDS

(Map p58; ☑02-734 9565; www.seoulselection.co.kr; 6 Samcheong-ro, Jongno-gu; ⓒ9.30am-6.30pm Mon-Fri, 1-6pm Sat; ⓢLine 3 to Anguk, Exit 1)

Staff speak English here and can recommend titles published by Seoul Selection as well as a wide range of other publishers' books in English on Korean culture, along with Korean CDs and Korean movies and drama series on DVD (with English subtitles). The website has an excellent monthly newsletter about what's on in Seoul.

★KCDF Gallery CRAFTS

(☎02-793 9041; www.kcdf.kr; 8 Insa-dong 11-gil, Jongno-gu; 🕐10am-7pm; [S]Line 3 to Anguk, Exit 6) The Korean Craft and Design Foundation's gallery has a shop on the ground floor showcasing some of the finest locally made products including woodwork, pottery and jewellery. It's the ideal place to find a unique, sophisticated gift or souvenir.

★Insa-dong Maru CRAFTS

(☎02 2223 2500; www.insadongmaru.co.kr; 35-4 6 Insa-dong-gil, Jongno-gu; 🕐10.30am-8.30pm Sun-Fri, to 9pm Sat; [S]Line 3 to Anguk, Exit 6) Around 60 different Korean designer shops selling crafts, fashion and homewares are gathered at this slick, new complex spread over several levels around a central rest area where there's a piano available for impromtu concerts by passers-by.

Ssamziegil HANDICRAFTS

(www.ssamzigil.com; 42 Insa-dong-gil, Jongno-gu; 🕐10.30am-8.30pm; [S]Line 3 to Anguk, Exit 6) An arty four-storey complex built around a courtyard that's a popular stop for one-off clothing, accessories or household goods.

Jonginamoo HOMEWARES

(종이나무; Map p58; jonginamoo.com; 3 Bukchon-ro 5-gil, Jongno-gu; 🕐10am-10pm Mon-Sat, from noon Sun; [S]Line 3 to Anguk, Exit 2) Selling beautiful traditional-styled furniture and decorative pieces for your home including a variety of lamps with shades made of *hanji* (handmade paper).

Dolsilnai FASHION

(돌실나이; ☎02-737 2232; www.dolsilnai.co.kr; 35 Insa-dong-gil, Jongno-gu; 🕐10.30am-8pm; [S]Line 3 to Anguk, Exit 6) Come here for beautifully designed, casual *hanbok* (traditional Korean clothing) made from natural fabrics in a variety of soft natural and pastel colours. There's always a selection of garments for men and women that are discounted.

Myeong-dong & Jung-gu

Myeong-dong is home to all the major global fast-fashion labels, including Asian faves Uniqlo, Basic House and Bean Pole. The streets fill up every evening with shoppers, hawkers and people shouting out the latest sale through megaphones. It all borders on sensory overload, but shouldn't be missed.

Namdaemun Market MARKET

(Map p46; www.namdaemunmarket.co.kr; 21 Namdaemun-sijang 4-gil, Jung-gu; 🕐24hr; [S]Line 4 to Hoehyeon, Exit 5) You could spend all day in this swarming night-and-day market and not see it at all. The largest market in Korea, each section has hundreds of stalls, from clothing to handicrafts and accessories. Its market food, though, is the highlight, with dozens of stalls selling *sujebi* (dough and shellfish soup), homemade *kalguksu* noodles and bibimbap (mixed rice, meat and vegetables). **Restaurant Alley** has a huge range of Korean food – all with plastic replicas outside to make choosing easy.

Shinsegae DEPARTMENT STORE

(신세계백화점; Map p46; ☎02-2026 9000; www.shinsegae.com; 63 Sogong-ro, Jung-gu; 🕐10.30am-8pm; [S]Line 4 to Hoehyeon, Exit 7) Wrap yourself in luxury inside the Seoul equivalent of Harrods. It's split over two buildings, the older part based in a gorgeous 1930 colonial building that was Seoul's first department store, Mitsukoshi. Check out local designer fashion labels and the opulent supermarket in the basement with a food court; another food court is up on the 11th floor of the building with an attached roof garden to relax in.

Lab 5 FASHION

(Map p46; 5th fl, Noon Sq, Myeongdong 2-ga, Jung-gu; [S]Line 2 to Euljiro 1-ga, Exit 6) No need to root around Dongdaemun Market for the latest hot K-designers, with this store showcasing the designs of 100 rising stars including participants of *Project Runway Korea.*

Åland FASHION

(Map p46; www.a-land.co.kr; 30 Myeongdong 6-gil, Jung-gu; 🕐10.30am-10.30pm; [S]Line 4 to Myeongdong, Exit 6) Spread over three levels, this multi-label boutique mixes up vintage and garage-sale items with new designer pieces to wear and decorate your home. For menswear head to the building across the street.

Primera ACCESSORIES

(Map p46; www.primera.co.kr; 22 Myeongdong 4-gil, Jung-gu; ⏲10am-10pm; [S] Line 4 to Myeongdong, Exit 5) The flagship store of this Korean cosmetics store specialises in organic skin products and essential oils using germinated sprouts.

Lotte Department Store DEPARTMENT STORE

(롯데백화점; Map p46; ☎02-771 2500; http://store.lotteshopping.com; 81 Namdaemun-ro, Jung-gu; ⏲10.30am-8pm; [S] Line 2 to Euljiro 1-ga, Exit 8) Retail behemoth Lotte spreads its tentacles across four buildings: the main department store, Lotte Young Plaza, Lotte Avenue and a duty-free shop. Also here is a multiplex cinema, restaurants and hotel.

Migliore Mall FASHION

(밀리오레 명동점; Map p46; ☎02-2124 0005; www.migliore.co.kr; 115 Toegye-ro, Jung-gu; ⏲11am-11.30pm Tue-Sun; [S] Line 4 to Myeongdong, Exit 6) Always teeming with young trendsetters, this high-rise mall is packed with small fashion shops.

Western Seoul

★Key ARTS, CRAFTS

(Map p49; www.welcomekey.net; 48-5 Wausan-ro 29-gil; ⏲noon-10pm Tue-Sun; [S] Line 2 to Hongik University, Exit 8) Representing scores of artists and craftspeople, several of whom also sell their goods at the Free Market on Saturday, this small gallery and showroom offers affordable, exclusive items, from jewellery to pottery to fabric art and paintings.

Free Market SOUVENIRS

(Map p49; www.freemarket.or.kr; Hongik University Playground, 19-3 Wausan-ro 21-gil, Mapo-gu; ⏲1-6pm Sat Mar-Nov; [S] Line 2 to Hongik University, Exit 9) Going strong since 2002, this lively weekly market helps to propel talented young creatives on to big-time retail. It's a great opportunity to meet the crafters and buy a unique souvenir, be it a hand-painted baseball cap, a colourful piece of jewellery or a leather bag. A good line-up of singers and bands play all afternoon, too.

★Gentle Monster ACCESSORIES

(Map p49; www.gentlemonster.com; 48 Dongmak-ro 7-gil, Mapo-gu; [S] Line 2 or 6 to Hapjeong, Exit 3) Sunglasses at night is *the* Hongdae look and this hip place is where to pick up the edgiest of shades and frames as worn by K-Popsters and TV stars. Imaginative and fun art installations change roughly every 25 days on the ground floor.

Object Recycle ACCESSORIES

(Map p49; www.insideobject.com; 110 Wausan-ro, Mapo-gu; ⏲11am-10pm; [S] Line 2 to Hongik University, Exit 9) 🍃 Although there's a bigger branch of Object in Hongdae, this one is notable for specialising in products that involve some element of re- or up-cycling, such as jeans and shirts made into bags, clocks from LP records and sidetables from cardboard boxes.

Itaewon & Yongsan-gu

Millimetre Milligram STATIONERY, BAGS

(Map p50; www.mmmg.net; Itaewon-ro; ⏲11am-9pm; [S] Line 6 to Itaewon, Exit 3) Usually shortened to MMG, this is the spot to pick up quirky stationery and bags, including the Swiss brand Freitag. There's a cafe as well as a basement gallery/furniture store and, on the 3rd floor, the boutique art-book and magazine shop **Post Poetics** (⏲1-8pm Mon-Sat).

Yongsan Electronics Market ELECTRONICS

(용산전자랜드; 125 Cheongpa-ro; ⏲10am-7.30pm; [S] Line 1 Yongsan, Exit 3) If it plugs in, you can find it at this geeky universe of high-tech marvels. Computer prices are usually marked but prices on other goods are lacking, so do what the locals do – check out the prices online before arriving. It's also a good spot for well-priced (and barely used) secondhand phones. The area is being redeveloped, and is now spread across several buildings.

What the Book BOOKS

(Map p50; ☎02-797 2342; www.whatthebook.com; 151 Itaewon-ro; ⏲10am-9pm; [S] Line 6 to Itaewon, Exit 3) Itaewon's best bookshop sells new releases and secondhand English-language fiction and nonfiction, plus an interesting range on Korean culture and international magazines.

Steve J & Yoni P FASHION

(Map p50; ☎02-796 4766; www.stevejandyonip.com; Hannam-dong; ⏲11.30am-7.30pm; [S] Line 6 to Hanganjin, Exit 3) Collaborating on the super-fashionable streetwear in this boutique are local designers Steve J and Yoni P. Their T-shirts, sweatshirts and colourful printed clobber is stocked by high-class boutiques around the world, but their flagship store is down this happening little street in Hannam-dong.

GALLERIES GALORE

Seoul's eclectic contemporary-art scene is mainly clustered on either side of Gyeongbuk-gong, in Samcheon-dong, Tongui-dong and Insa-dong. The many commercial galleries here put on regularly changing shows of both local and international artists, which, unless otherwise mentioned, are free to browse. Useful resources include the free monthly art magazine **ArtnMap** (www.artnmap.com) and **Seoul Art Guide** (in Korean).

Samcheong-dong

Artsonje Center (Map p58; ☑ 02-733 8945; www.artsonje.org/asc; 87 Yulgok-ro 3-gil, Jongno-gu; adult/child ₩3000/1000; ⊙ 11am-7pm Tue-Sun; Ⓢ Line 3 to Anguk, Exit 1) Founded in 1998, Artsonje supports experimental art, runs workshops and has lectures as well as an annual Open Call for new works. Also here is a cafe and arthouse cinema. They are also the Seoul outpost for the fascinating **Real DMZ Project** (http://realdmz.org), an annual show with artworks based on research carried out in the DMZ.

Gallery Hyundai (Map p58; ☑ 02-287 3500; www.galleryhyundai.com; 8 Samcheong-ro, Jongno-gu; ⊙ 10am-6pm; Ⓢ Line 3 to Anguk, Exit 1) The trailblazer for Korea's contemporary commercial-gallery scene, Hyundai has been going strong since 1970 and represents some of the giants of the scene including Lee Joong-seop and Paik Nam June. As well as this exhibition space it has another branch nearby at 14 Samcheong-ro.

Hakgojae (Map p58; ☑ 02-720 1524; www.hakgojae.com; 50 Samcheong-ro, Jongno-gu; ⊙ 10am-7pm Tue-Sat, to 6pm Sun; Ⓢ Line 3 to Anguk, Exit 1) This elegant gallery is easily spotted by the robot sculpture on the roof of its modern section. Entry is via the converted *hanok* building, which neatly symbolises the gallery's aim: 'to review the old to learn the new'.

Kukje (Map p58; ☑ 02-735 8441; www.kukjegallery.com; 54 Samcheong-ro, Jongno-gu; ⊙ 10am-6pm Mon-Sat, to 5pm Sun; Ⓢ Line 3 to Anguk, Exit 1) Kukje's two main gallery spaces are found

🍴 Dongdaemun & Eastern Seoul

★ **Dongdaemun Market**   MARKET
(동대문시장; Dongdaemun; ⊙ 7-10pm Mon-Sat; Ⓢ Line 1 or 4 to Dongdaemun, Exit 8) Take Seoul's commercial pulse at this colossal retail and wholesale market. It sprawls across a wide area on both sides of the Cheong-gye-cheon. On one side is the multilevel **Pyoung Hwa Clothing Market** (평화시장; ⊙ 7-10pm) crammed with stalls selling wholesale clothing and accessories. The other side of the stream is **Dongdaemun Shopping Complex** (⊙ 9am-6pm Mon-Sat), with a more eclectic range of goods, plus atmospheric **food alleys** (동대문시장; dishes from ₩6000; ⊙ 10am-10pm).

Doota   DEPARTMENT STORE
(☑ 02-3398 3114; www.doota.com; 275 Jangchungdan-ro, Jung-gu; ⊙ 10.30am-midnight Sun-Thu, to 5am Fri & Sat; Ⓢ Line 2, 4 or 5 to Dongdaemun History & Culture Park) Cut through Dongdaemun's commercial frenzy by heading to its leading fashion mall full to the brim with domestic brands. Ten floors above and below ground are dedicated to clothing, accessories, beauty items and souvenirs. When you start flagging, there are plenty of cafes and a good food court on the 7th floor.

Seoul Yangnyeongsi
Herb Medicine Market   TRADITIONAL MEDICINE
(www.seoulya.com; Jegi-dong; ⊙ 9am-7pm; Ⓢ Line 1 to Jegi-dong, Exit 2) Also known as Gyeongdong Market, Korea's biggest Asian medicine market runs back for several blocks from the traditional gate on the main road and includes thousands of clinics, retailers, wholesalers and medicine makers. If you're looking for a leaf, herb, bark, root, flower or mushroom to ease your ailment, it's bound to be here.

Seoul Folk Flea Market   FLEA MARKET
(서울풍물시장; 19-3 Cheonho-daero 4-gil, Dongdaemun-gu; ⊙ 10am-7pm, closed 2nd & 4th Tue of month; Ⓢ Line 1 or 2 to Sinseol-dong, Exit 6 or 10) Spilling out of a two-storey building into the surrounding area, here you'll find a fascinating collection of artworks, collectables and general bric-a-brac from wooden masks and ink drawings to Beatles LPs and valve radios.

off the main road, behind their restaurant building, which has the running woman sculpture on its roof by Jonathan Borofsky. It's a leading venue for international artists to exhibit, with the likes of Damien Hirst, Anish Kapoor and Bill Viola all having shows here.

Tongui-dong

Jean Art Gallery (Map p58; ☎ 02-738 7570; www.jeanart.net; 25 Hyoja-ro, Jongno-gu; ⏲ 10am-6pm Tue-Fri, to 5pm Sat & Sun; [S] Line 3 to Gyeongbokgung, Exit 3 or 4) Pioneer of the Tongui-dong gallery scene and specialising in representing contemporary Korean and Japanese artists, such as Naru Yoshitomo and Yayoi Kusama. One of Yayoi's 2m-tall dotted pumpkin sculptures stands in a courtyard outside one of the gallery's buildings.

Artside (Map p58; ☎ 02-725 1020; www.artside.org; 15 Jahamun-ro 6-gil, Jongno-gu; ⏲ 10am-6.30pm Tue-Sun; [S] Line 3 to Gyeongbokgung, Exit 3 or 4) Since 1999, Artside has taken a leading role in artistic exchange between Korea and China by regularly staging exhibits by contemporary Chinese artists such as Zhang Xiaogang.

Insa-dong

Hwabong Gallery (☎ 02-737 0057; www.hwabong.com; 10 Insa-dong 7-gil, Jongno-gu; ⏲ 10am-7pm; [S] Line 3 to Anguk, Exit 6) Cutting-edge Korean art is usually on show in this basement space alongside permanent displays of the smallest book in the world (no more than a dot), and the largest book.

Sun Art Center (☎ 02-734 0458; www.sungallery.co.kr; 8 Insa-dong 5-gil, Jongno-gu; ⏲ 10am-6pm Tue-Sun; [S] Line 3 to Anguk, Exit 6) One of Seoul's longest running commercial-art galleries, in business since 1977, Sun Art specialises in early-20th-century Korean art and awards an annual prize to the most promising local artist.

Dapsimni Antiques Market ANTIQUES
(⏲ 10am-6pm Mon-Sat; [S] Line 5 to Dapsimni, Exit 2) One for serious collectors, this sprawling collection of antique shops is spread over three separate precincts. Here you can browse through old dusty treasures – from *yangban* (aristocrat) pipes and horsehair hats to wooden shoes, fish-shaped locks and embroidered status insignia – dating anywhere from 100 to 600 years ago.

Gangnam & South of the Han River

COEX Mall MALL
(☎ 02-6002 5300; www.coexmall.com; 513 Yeongdong-daero, Gangnam-gu; ⏲ 10am-10pm; [S] Line 2 to Samseong, COEX Exit) One of Seoul's premier malls, the shiny COEX is a vast maze of department stores loaded with shops selling fashion, lifestyle, accessories and electronics, as well as a multiplex cinema and aquarium (p54). It's also a launching point to the airport (p91), and has several hotels.

10 Corso Como Seoul FASHION
(Map p53; www.10corsocomo.co.kr; 416 Apgujeong-ro, Gangnam-gu; ⏲ 11am-8pm; [S] Bundang Line to Apgujeong Rodeo, Exit 3) Inspired by its shopping complex in Milan, this outpost of the fashion and lifestyle boutique is about as interesting as Gangnam retail can get. The blend of fashion, art and design includes several local designers. There's also a brilliant selection of international books and CDs to browse, and a chic cafe for an espresso or glass of wine.

Galleria DEPARTMENT STORE
(Map p53; ☎ 02-344 9414; http://dept.galleria.co.kr; Apgujeong-ro, Gangnam-gu; ⏲ 10.30am-8pm; [S] Line Bundang to Apgujeong Rodeo, Exit 7) Department stores in Seoul don't get more luxurious than this. If you want to play Audrey Hepburn staring wistfully into Tiffany's, don a Helen Kaminski hat, try on a Stella McCartney dress or slip into a pair of Jimmy Choos; the east wing of fashion icon Galleria is the place to be.

Garosu-Gil STREET
(Map p53; [S] Line 3 to Apgujeong, Exit 5) One of Gangnam's most famous strips, this tree-lined street is worth a stroll for brand-name stores and cute fashion boutiques, plus art galleries, restaurants and cafes.

> ### ⓘ TRANSLATION & COUNSELLING SERVICES
>
> **Tourist Phone Number** (☏ 1330) Call any time of the day or night if you need interpretation help or information on practically any topic.
>
> **Seoul Global Center** (p396) At this support centre for Seoul's foreign residents there are volunteers who speak a range of languages, as well as full-time staff who can assist on a range of issues.

ⓘ Information

DANGERS & ANNOYANCES

A common sight on central Seoul's streets – particularly around Gwanghwamun and Seoul Plaza – are squadrons of fully armed riot police. Student, trade-union and other protests occasionally turn violent. Keep well out of the way of any confrontations that may occur.

Drivers tend to be impatient, with kimchi-hot tempers, and most of them, including bus drivers, routinely go through red lights. Don't be the first or last person to cross at any pedestrian crossing. Keep two eyes out for cars parking on footpaths, and for motorcyclists who speed along footpaths and across pedestrian crossings.

EMERGENCY

If there are no English-speaking staff available, ring the 24-hour tourist information and help line: ☏ 1330.

Ambulance (☏ 119)
Fire Brigade (☏ 119)
Police (Map p58; ☏ 112)

INTERNET ACCESS

Wi-fi is universal and usually free. Most hotels offer it; if they don't, they'll have LAN cables for wired access in rooms. If you need a computer, look for the 'PC방' signs. These places charge around ₩2000 per hour and are invariably packed with teenage online gamers.

LEFT LUGGAGE

Most subway stations and bus terminals have lockers. Small lockers cost ₩1000 a day and the ones large enough to fit a backpack are ₩2000.

MEDIA

Print and online magazines in English include **Seoul Magazine** (http://magazine.seoul-selection.com), **10 Magazine** (www.10mag.com) and **Groove Korea** (http://groovekorea.com).

MEDICAL SERVICES

Most facilities don't accept international insurance, so bring cash or credit cards.

Asan Medical Center (☏ 02-3010 5100; http://eng.amc.seoul.kr; 88 Olympic-ro 43-gil, Songpa-gu; ☺ international clinic 8.30am-5.30pm Mon-Fri; Ⓢ Line 2 to Seongnae, Exit 1) A 10-minute walk from the subway exit.

International Clinic (Map p50; ☏ 02-790 0857; www.internationalclinic.co.kr; 211 Itaewon-ro, Yongsan-gu; ☺ 9am-6.30pm Mon-Wed & Fri, to 4pm Sat; Ⓢ Line 6 to Itaewon, Exit 2) Appointments are a must.

Severance Hospital (☏ 02-2228 5800; www.yuhs.or.kr; 50-1 Yonsei-ro, Seodaemun-gu; ☺ international clinic 9.30-11.30am & 2-4.30pm Mon-Fri, 9.30am-noon Sat; Ⓢ Line 2 to Sinchon, Exit 3) A 15-minute walk from the subway exit.

MONEY

Credit cards are readily accepted and many ATMs accept foreign credit cards – look for one that has a 'Global' sign or the logo of your credit-card company. Many banks offer a foreign-exchange service. There are also licensed moneychangers, particularly in Itaewon, that keep longer hours than the banks and provide a faster service, but may only exchange US cash.

POST

Central Post Office (Map p46; ☏ 02-6450 1114; 70 Sogong-ro, Myeong-dong; ☺ 9am-8pm Mon-Fri, to 1pm Sat & Sun; Ⓢ Line 4 to Myeong-dong, Exit 5) This basement post office sells train tickets and offers free internet.

TOILETS

There are plenty of clean, modern and well-signed public toilets, virtually all free of charge. It's wise to carry a stash of toilet tissue around with you, just in case there's none available.

TOURIST INFORMATION

There are scores of tourist information booths around the city. In major tourist areas, such as Insa-dong and Namdaemun, look for red-jacketed city tourist guides who can also help with information in various languages.

Cheong-gye-cheon Tourist Information Center (Map p58; Sejong-daero, Gwanghwamun; ☺ 9am-6pm; Ⓢ Line 5 to Gwanghwamun, Exit 5)

Gangnam Tourist Information Center (Map p53; http://tour.gangnam.go.kr; 161 Apgujeong-ro, Gangnam-gu; ☺ 10am-7pm; Ⓢ Line 3 to Apgujeong, Exit 6) A shiny new information centre with helpful staff and a stack of brochures on Gangnam. It also has the K-Pop Experience and the Gangnam Medical Tour Center.

Gyeongbokgung Tourist Information Center (Map p58; 161 Sajik-ro, Jongno-gu; ☺ 9am-6pm; Ⓢ Line 3 to Gyeongbokgung, Exit 5)

Insa-dong Tourist Information Center (☎ 02-734 0222; Insa-dong 11-gil; 🕒 10am-10pm; [S] Line 3 to Anguk, Exit 6) Two more centres are at the south and north entrances to Insa-dong-gil.

Itaewon Subway Tourist Information Center (Map p50; ☎ 02-3707 9416; Itaewon Station; 🕒 9am-10pm; [S] Line 6 to Itaewon) Located beside the gate to subway lines in the station.

KTO Tourist Information Center (Map p46; ☎ 02-1330; www.visitkorea.or.kr; Cheonggye-cheon-ro, Jung-gu; 🕒 9am-8pm; [S] Line 1 to Jonggak, Exit 5) The best information centre; knowledgeable staff, free internet and many brochures and maps.

Myeong-dong Tourist Information Center (Map p46; ☎ 02-778 0333; http://blog.naver.com/mdtic1129; 66, Eulji-ro, Jung-gu; 🕒 9am-8pm; [S] Line 2 to Eulji-ro 1-ga, Exit 6)

Namdaemun Market Tourist Information Center (Map p46; ☎ 02-752 1913; Gate 5 or 7; 🕒 10am-7pm; [S] Line 4 to Hoehyeon, Exit 5) You'll find two info kiosks within the market.

WEBSITES

➜ **Lonely Planet** (www.lonelyplanet.com/south-korea/seoul) For planning advice, author recommendations, traveller reviews and insider tips.

➜ **Seoul Sub-Urban** (http://seoulsuburban.com) Explore the city by subway.

➜ **Visit Seoul** (www.visitseoul.net) Official website of Seoul City Tourism.

Getting There & Away

AIR

Seoul has two airports. The main international gateway, Incheon International Airport (p397), is 52km west of central Seoul on Yeongjongdo island. This top-class operation also has a few domestic connections.

> **CITY AIR TERMINALS**
>
> If you're flying Korean Air, Asiana or Jeju Air, you can check in your luggage and go through immigration at **City Airport Terminal** (Map p46; http://english.arex.or.kr/jsp/eng/terminal/introduction.jsp; Seoul Station; 🕒 5.20am-7pm; [S] Line 1 or 4 to Seoul Station), then hop on the A'rex train to Gimpo or Incheon. South of the river, a similar service operates from **CALT** (☎ 02-551 0077; www.calt.co.kr; COEX Mall, 22 Teheran-ro 87-gil, Gangnam-gu; 🕒 5.30am-6.30pm; [S] Line 2 to Samseong, Exit 5) at the COEX Mall and includes most major airlines. From here limo buses run to either airport.

The bulk of domestic flights (and a handful of international ones) arrive at Gimpo International Airport (p398), 18km west of the city centre.

BUS

Seoul is well served by very frequent intercity buses – outside of busy holidays you can turn up, get your ticket and go. The prices quoted here are for regular services – you'll pay more for deluxe and night buses.

Dong-Seoul Bus Terminal (☎ 02-1688 5979; www.ti21.co.kr; 50 Gangbyeonnyeok-ro; [S] Line 2 to Gangbyeon, Exit 4) Serves the eastern part of Korea (1st floor) and major cities (2nd floor). Sample fares include Icheon (₩3800), Gongju (₩7700), Chuncheon (₩7800), Buyeo (₩12,700), Jeonju (express/deluxe ₩12,200/17,900) and Busan (express/deluxe ₩19,900/29,500).

Nambu Bus Terminal (☎ 02-521 8550; www.kobus.co.kr/web/eng/index.jsp; 292 Hyoryeong-ro; [S] Line 3 to Nambu Bus Terminal, Exit 5) Serves destinations south of Seoul such as Daecheon Beach.

BUS SERVICES FROM SEOUL

DESTINATION	PRICE EXPRESS/DELUXE (₩)	DURATION
Busan	23,00/34,200	4hr 15min
Buyeo	11,600	2hr 30min
Chuncheon	6800	1hr 10min
Gongju	8000/9000	1hr 30min
Gwangju	17,000/26,100	3hr 20min
Gyeongju	20,400/30,300	3hr 45min
Jeonju	12,800/18,700	2hr 35min
Mokpo	20,000/30,000	3hr 40min
Sokcho	18,100	2hr 30min

Seoul Express Bus Station (Map p53; ☎ 02-536 6460-2; Ⓢ Lines 3, 7 or 9 to Seoul Express Terminal) Long-distance buses arrive at the major station Seoul Express Bus Terminal, split across two separate buildings: **Gyeongbu Line Terminal** (www.kobus.co.kr) serves mainly the eastern region, and **Central City Terminal** (www.hticket.co.kr) serves the southwestern region.

TRAIN

Most trains leave **Seoul Station** (Map p46; Ⓢ Line 1 or 4 to Seoul Station), which has high-speed Korea Train Express (KTX), *saemaul* (express) and *mugunghwa* (semi-express) services to many parts of the country. **Yongsan Station** (Ⓢ Line 1 & Jungang Line) handles KTX and train connections with South Chungcheong and the Jeolla provinces. For current fares and detailed schedules, visit the website of the **Korea National Railroad** (www.letskorail.com).

East of central Seoul, long-distance services to destinations in eastern Gyeonggi-do and Gangwon-do leave from **Cheongnyangni Station** (청량리역; Ⓢ Line 1 to Cheongnyangni). South of the Han River, **Yeongdeungpo Station** (영등포역; Ⓜ Line 1 to Yeongdeungpo) is a major *saemaul/mugunghwa* station for services heading south.

ⓘ Getting Around

TO/FROM INCHEON INTERNATIONAL AIRPORT

Bus

City limousine buses (₩9000, every 10 to 30 minutes, 5.30am to 10pm) take around an hour to reach central Seoul, depending on traffic. There are also **KAL deluxe limousine buses** (www.kallimousine.com; ₩14,000), which drop passengers off at hotels around Seoul.

Taxi

Expect to pay anything between ₩65,000 and ₩100,000 for the 70-minute journey to central Seoul, depending on traffic – meters run on a time basis when the taxis aren't moving. From midnight to 4am, regular taxis charge 20% extra.

Train

A'rex express trains to Seoul Station (43 minutes) are ₩8000; the commuter trains (53 minutes) cost ₩4050.

TO/FROM GIMPO INTERNATIONAL AIRPORT

Bus

Limousine buses (₩6500, around 40 minutes depending on traffic) run between Gimpo and Incheon airports. Both City (₩5000) and KAL (₩7000) deluxe limousine buses also run every 10 minutes to central Seoul.

Subway

Subway Lines 5 and 9 connect the airport with the city (₩1450, 35 minutes).

Taxi

A taxi costs around ₩35,000 to the city centre.

Train

A'rex trains run to Seoul Station (₩1300, 15 minutes).

PUBLIC TRANSPORT

All fares can be paid using the rechargeable, touch-and-go **T-Money card** (http://eng.t-money.co.kr), which provides a ₩100 discount per trip. The basic card can be bought for a non-refundable ₩2500 at any subway station booth, bus kiosk and convenience store displaying the T-Money logo. Reload it with credit at any of the aforementioned places and get money refunded that hasn't been used (up to ₩20,000, minus a processing fee of ₩500) at subway machines and participating convenience stores before you leave Seoul.

Bus

Seoul has a comprehensive and reasonably priced **bus system** (www.bus.go.kr; ◷ 5.30am–midnight). Some bus stops have some route maps in English and most buses have major destinations written in English on the outside and a taped announcement of the names of each stop in English, but few bus drivers understand English.

Long-distance-express red buses run to the outer suburbs, green buses link subways within a district, blue buses run to outer suburbs and yellow short-haul buses circle small districts. Using a T-Money card saves ₩100 on each bus fare and transfers between bus and subway are either free or discounted. Place your T-Money card on the screen as you exit as well as when you get on a bus, just as you do on the subway.

Subway

Seoul has an excellent, user-friendly **subway system** (www.smrt.co.kr; ◷ 5.30am–midnight), which connects with destinations well beyond the city borders, including Suwon and Incheon. The minimum fare of ₩1350 (₩1250 with a T-Money card) takes you up to 12km. In central Seoul the average time between stations is just over two minutes, so it takes around 25 minutes to go 10 stops.

Most subway stations have lifts or stair lifts for wheelchairs. Escalators are common, but you'll do a fair amount of walking up and down stairs and along corridors. Neighbourhood maps inside the stations, including ones with digital touch screens, help you figure out which of the subway exits to take.

Taxi

Ideal for short trips, regular taxis have a basic charge of ₩3000 for 2km, rising ₩100 for every 144m or 35 seconds after that if the taxi is travelling below 15km/h. A 20% surcharge is levied between midnight and 4am. Deluxe taxis are black with a yellow stripe and cost ₩4500 for the first 3km and ₩200 for every 164m or 39 seconds, but they don't have a late-night surcharge. Few taxi drivers speak English, but most taxis have a free interpretation service whereby an interpreter talks to the taxi driver and to you by phone. Orange **International Taxi** (☏ 02-1644 2255; www.internationaltaxi. co.kr) has English-speaking drivers – these can be reserved in advance for an extra 20% on the regular fare and can be chartered on an hourly or daily basis for longer journeys. All taxis are metered; tipping is not required.

Around Seoul

Why Go?

Though Seoul is one of the world's busiest, most populated and modern cities, remarkably only within a 45-minute journey by road, you can be transported to rural, mountainous surrounds that feel an entire world away.

In the provinces surrounding the capital – Gyeonggi-do and Incheon-gwangyeok-si – you'll find illustrious World Heritage–listed historical sites, snaking fortress walls, enchanting palaces, timeless temples, cultural villages, lively cities, national parks, sandy beaches, remote islands and picturesque mountains perfect for hiking and skiing.

From the thrilling trip to the North Korean border along the Demilitarized Zone (DMZ), to staying overnight in Buddhist temples, the diversity of experiences is impressive. And beyond the traditional sites are ski resorts and world-class theme parks, plus cutting-edge contemporary art, meaning there's pretty much something for everyone.

Best Traditional Sights

➜ Hwaseong (p101)

➜ Namhansanseong (p104)

➜ Jeondeung-sa (p117)

➜ Bomun-sa (p117)

➜ Bukhansan National Park (p110)

Best Art & Culture

➜ Anyang Art Park (p104)

➜ Heyri (p98), Paju (p99)

➜ Suwon's Mural Villages (p102)

➜ Nam June Paik Art Center (p102)

➜ Cerapia (p105)

➜ Incheon Art Platform (p107)

When to Go

Incheon

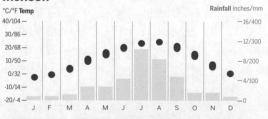

Dec–Feb Hit the slopes at Gyeonggi-do's ski resorts for skiing and snowboarding.

Apr & Oct Head to the hills to hike among cherry blossoms in spring or colourful foliage in autumn.

Jul Enjoy summer by the beach at Muuido, or further afield at Deokjeokdo.

GYEONGGI-DO 경기도

Gyeonggi-do was designated as a province after the Korean War. The seat of regional government has been Suwon since 1967. You can find out more about what this province offers the visitor at http://english.gg.go.kr.

The Demilitarized Zone (DMZ) & Joint Security Area (JSA)

The 4km-wide, 240km-long buffer known as the Demilitarized Zone (DMZ) slashes across the peninsula, separating North and South Korea. Lined on both sides by tank traps, electrical fences, landmines and armies in full battle readiness, it is one of the scariest places on earth. It is also one of the most surreal, since it has become a major tourist attraction with several observatories allowing you to peek into North Korea (aka the DPRK; Democratic People's Republic of Korea). For history buffs and collectors of weird and unsettling experiences, a visit here is not to be missed.

The place most people want to go is the Joint Security Area (JSA), 55km north of Seoul, inside of which is the truce village of Panmunjeom – there's nowhere else in South Korea where you can get so close to North Korea and DPRK soldiers without being arrested or shot, and the tension is palpable.

The only way into this heavily restricted area is on an organised tour. To visit the JSA you'll need to bring your passport. Note citizens of certain countries are not allowed on these tours. There are also strict dress and behavioural codes; usually collared shirts for men, and no ripped jeans, revealing clothing or open-toed shoes. Alcohol consumption is also prohibited. Only children over 10 years are permitted.

⊙ Sights

JSA (Panmunjeom)　　MILITARY SITE
Unquestionably the highlight of any trip to the DMZ is the JSA at Panmunjeom. An improbable tourist destination, it's here where the infamous Military Demarcation Line separates South and North Korea. Soldiers from both sides often stand metres apart eyeballing one another from their respective sides of the blue-painted UN buildings. You'll be taken inside the meeting room – where the truce between North and South Korea was signed –

the only place where you can safely walk into North Korea from South Korea.

Tours kick off with a briefing by US or ROK (Republic of Korea) soldier guides at Camp Bonifas, the joint US-ROK army camp just outside the DMZ, before being transferred to another bus to the JSA.

Within the blue conference room at the JSA, where official meetings are still sometimes held, microphones on the tables constantly record everything said, while ROK soldiers stand guard inside and out in a modified taekwondo stance – an essential photo op. Their North Korean counterparts keep a steady watch, usually, but not always, from a distance.

Though your tour will be a quiet one, the soldier guide will remind you that this frontier is no stranger to violent incidents. One of the most notorious was in 1976 when two US soldiers were hacked to death with axes by North Korean soldiers after the former tried to chop down a tree obstructing the view from a watchtower. Camp Bonifas, the joint US-ROK army camp just outside the DMZ, is named after one of the slain soldiers.

Back on the bus you'll be taken to one of Panmunjeom's lookout posts from where you can see the two villages within the DMZ: Daeseong-dong in the South and Gijeong-dong in the North. You'll also see the site of the axe-murder incident and the Bridge of No Return where the POW exchange took place following the signing of Armistice Agreement in 1953.

The forested surrounds are Korea's most ecologically pristine and allegedly home to the Siberian tiger.

Dora Observatory　　OBSERVATORY
(binoculars ₩500; ☉10am-5pm Tue-Sun) Peer through binoculars for a closer look at Kaesong city and Kaesong Industrial Complex in the DPRK, where cheap North Korean labourers are employed by South Korean conglomerates.

Third Infiltration Tunnel　　TUNNEL
(제3땅굴; ☉9am-5pm Tue-Sun) Since 1974, four tunnels have been found running under the DMZ, dug by the North Koreans so that their army could launch a surprise attack. Walking along 265m of this 73m-deep tunnel is not for the claustrophobic or the tall: creeping hunched over, you'll realise why they issue hard hats. The guide will point out how the North Koreans painted

Around Seoul Highlights

1 Fathoming the bizarre terror-meets-tourism experience of a trip to the **DMZ** (p95).

2 Discovering a colonial past, Chinatown and contemporary art on a walk through **Incheon** (p107).

3 Striding along the World Heritage–listed fortress wall before browsing street art in **Suwon** (p101).

4 Meandering around **Heyri** (p98), a community village set up by artists and designers devoted to art and contemporary architecture.

5 Sampling traditional Korean liquors at **Sansawon Brewery** (p105).

6 Hiking to the granite peaks and mountainside temples in **Bukhansan National Park** (p110).

7 Climbing the steps to view the grotto and 10m-tall Buddha rock carving at **Bomun-sa** (p117) on the island of Seongmodo.

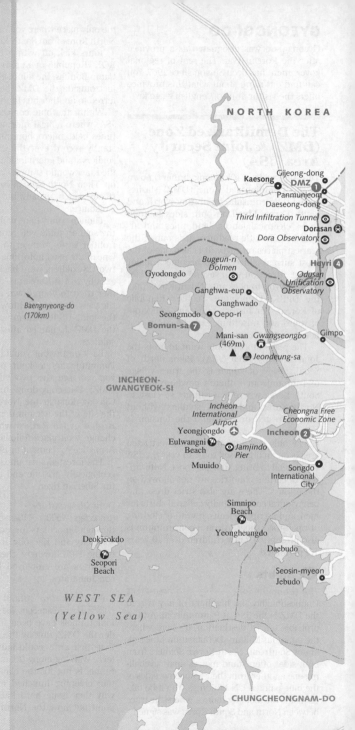

LIVING INSIDE THE DMZ

The 1953 *Korean Armistice Agreement* created two villages in the Demilitarized Zone (DMZ). On the south side is **Daeseong-dong** (대성동 or 'Freedom Village') less than 1km from Panmunjeom, where around 200 people live in modern houses with high-speed internet connection and earn a tax-free annual income of more than US$80,000 from their 7-hectare farms. There's an 11pm curfew, and soldiers stand guard while the villagers work in the rice fields or tend their ginseng plants.

On the North Korean side of the line is **Gijeong-dong** (기정동). The North translates this as 'Peace Village' but the South calls it Propaganda Village because virtually all the buildings are believed to be empty or just facades – the lights all come on and go off here at the same time at night. The village's primary feature is a 160m-high tower flying a flag that weighs nearly 300kg, markedly larger than the one on the South Korean side. It's believed that some workers from the nearby Kaesong Industrial Complex may now be living in Gijeong-dong.

the rocks black so they might claim it was a coal mine.

Dorasan Train Station
LANDMARK
(admission ₩500) Awaiting the next departure to Pyongyang (and onward Trans Eurasian intercontinental travel), Dorasan train station stands as a symbol of hope for the eventual reunification of the two Koreas. The shiny international customs built in 2002 remains unused. Trains to Seoul still run here four times daily.

Imjingak
MEMORIAL
FREE This park is dedicated to the 10 million South Koreans separated from their familes when the peninsula was divided postwar. Also here is Freedom Bridge, connecting North and South, where 13,000 POWs were exchanged in 1953. There is also a steam train derailed during the war.

Odusan Unification Observatory
OBSERVATORY
(오두산통일전망대; www.jmd.co.kr; adult/child/teen ₩3000/1000/1600; ⊙9am-5.30pm Apr-Sep, to 5pm Oct-Mar, to 4.30pm Nov-Feb) In between Heyri and Paju, this observation deck provides another chance to gaze across the DMZ into North Korea. There's also an exhibition hall with interesting displays on the conflict.

☞ Tours

The only way to visit the DMZ is on a tour. Prices vary from ₩70,000 to ₩135,000, depending on the length of the tour and whether lunch is included. Be sure to check tours include a visit to the JSA, as not all companies go there.

Before booking check refund and rescheduling options if a tour is cancelled – this can occasionally happen.

Koridoor Tours
ADVENTURE TOUR
(☏02 795 3028; www.koridoor.co.kr; ₩96,000; ⊙office 8am-5pm Mon-Sat; Ⓢ Line 1 to Namyeong, Exit 2) Run by the USO, the US army's social and entertainment organisation, these tours have long been regarded as one of the best. Book at least one week in advance. Lunch isn't included.

Panmunjom Travel Center
ADVENTURE TOUR
(☏02 771 5593; http://panmunjomtour.com; Lotte Hotel Main Bldg, 6th fl; tour from ₩77,000-120,000) A reputable company with knowledgeable guides, and notable for having a North Korean defector who comes along (but not always) to answer your questions. Prices include lunch.

Heyri
헤이리
☑031
Less than 10km south of the DMZ, Heyri is a charming village of small-scale contemporary buildings that couldn't be more of a contrast to the heavily fortified, doom-laden border. Conceived as a 'book village' connected to the nearby publishing centre of Paju Book City (p99), it has blossomed into a community of artists, writers, architects and other creative souls.

Get your bearings at the **Tourist Information Office** (☏031 946 8551; www.heyri. net; Gate 1; ⊙10am-6pm Tue-Sun), where you can pick up a map showing the scores of small art galleries, cafes, boutique shops and quirky private collections turned into minimuseums.

Just wandering around the village is a pleasure. Be sure to check out the residential area with its interesting examples of modern architecture. Most are created with materials that reflect and fit in with the natural environment. Roads twist naturally, the village is beautifully landscaped and sculptures abound.

On Mondays most places shut down in Heyri.

◉ Sights

There are around 30 galleries in Heyri. Some are world-class art spaces, while others trade in kitsch, particularly around Gate 4 where you'll find toy and Elvis museums.

Blume Museum of Contemporary Art   GALLERY
(BMOCA; www.bmoca.or.kr; Gate 3; admission ₩3000; ⊙11am-6pm Mon-Sat, 1-6pm Sun) Within in a post-modern building that incorporates a giant tree into its facade, this contemporary gallery exhibits a mix of emerging and established artists across all mediums.

Gallery SoSo   GALLERY
(☑031 949 8154; www.gallerysoso.com; Gate 7; ⊙11am-6pm Tue-Sun) There's nothing so-so about this classy gallery inside a modernist building backing on to the forest. It offers artist residency programs and has a guesthouse too.

White Block Art Center   GALLERY
(www.whiteblock.org; Gate 1; ⊙11am-6.30pm) In the centre of the village, this is one of Heyri's larger-scale galleries with three floors showcasing contemporary art. Outside stands the blue *Greeting Man* sculpture.

Gallery MOA   GALLERY
(www.heyrimoa.com; Gate 1; entry ₩1000) In an award-winning modernist building listed in the book *1001 Buildings to see Before You Die,* this boutique gallery exhibits conceptual art in rotating monthly shows.

🛏 Sleeping

★ Motif #1   GUESTHOUSE ₩₩
(☑031 949 0901; www.motif1.co.kr; Gate 1; d weekday/weekend ₩120,000/140,000; ❈ ⊛) The bohemian-chic home of Ansoo Lee – traveller, writer and president of the art council – is typical of Heyri. It's packed with art and has beautifully designed rooms worthy of a boutique hotel, plus a library of 10,000 books to browse. All four doubles and one family room have bathrooms, and guests can use the kitchen.

★ Forest Garden   GUESTHOUSE ₩₩₩
(☑010 4363 2660, 031 8071 0127; www.forestgarden.kr; Gate 1; d weekday/weekend incl breakfast ₩170,000/200,000; ❈ ⊛) English-speaking Mr Kim, retired from the Korea Tourism Organisation, and his artist wife Son Yeong-won, own this award-winning home that was built climbing up the hillside. Large rooms are comfortable and stylish, and there is a lovely lounge and rooftop sitting area.

WORTH A TRIP

PAJU BOOK CITY   파주출판도시

If you enjoyed Heyri's arty vibe and contemporary architecture, you should definitely add a stop to nearby Paju. The hub of Korea's book industry, there are some 300 publishing houses and bookstores set within a complex of futuristic award-winning buildings, a must for architectural buffs.

Your first port of call should be the **Asia Publication Culture & Information Centre** (아시아출판문화정보센터; www.pajubookcity.org/english; ⊙10am-5pm) to pick up a walking-tour map and guide to the area. Check out the 'Forest of Wisdom' a corridor lined with towering 8m-high shelves containing 200,000 books; titles on its top shelf are accessed by crane.

If you want to stay the night, the boutique **Guesthouse Jijihang** (☑031 955 0090; http://pajubookcity.org/jijihyang; Asian Publication Culture Centre; d/tr ₩132,000/154,000; ❈ ⊛) is attached to the centre, which also has an Italian restaurant and book cafe. Across the street, **Café Hesse** (sandwiches ₩4500; ⊙9am-8pm Sun-Thu, 10am-9pm Fri & Sat) is just the place to soak up Paju's literary vibes.

Paju Book City is 10km south of Heyri. Bus 2200 and 200 both stop en route to Seoul; disembark at Eunseokgyo bus station.

Suwon

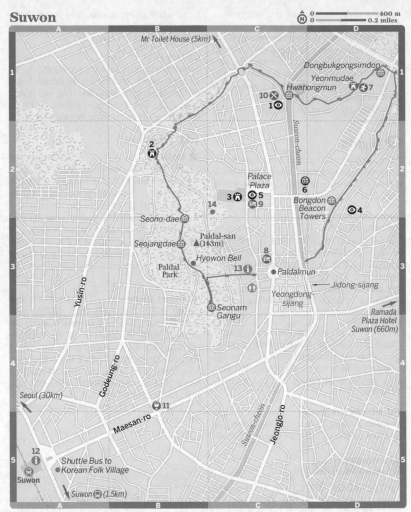

✗ Eating & Drinking

In Heyri practically every gallery (and there are a lot of them) has an attached cafe or restaurant.

Foresta Book Cafe CAFE ₩₩
(www.heyribookhouse.co.kr; Gate 3; drinks from ₩5000, pizza ₩15,000; ⊙10.30am-9pm; 🐾)
Foresta's backdrop comprises a colossal floor-to-ceiling wall of books, with plenty of tables to enjoy house-roasted Ethiopian coffee, sandwiches and pizzas. The attached bookstore sells art books on Heyri.

Homeo CAFE
(www.homeo.kr; Gate 3; ⊙10am-9pm) This vintage-themed cafe-cum-furniture-store, decked out in industrial decor and Chesterfield couches, has a menu of cakes, sandwiches and coffee.

Kokopelli BAR
(http://blog.daum.net/lookipc; Gate 4; beer ₩5500; ⊙noon-midnight) A good spot for a drink, Kokopelli stays true to its motto of 'Not war, make beer' by brewing its own ales. Its sign is the cover of Sonic Youth's *Goo* album.

Suwon

◎ Sights
Alternative Art Space Noon .... (see 1)
1 Haenggung-dong Mural Village C1
2 Hwaseong B2
3 Hwaseong Haenggung C2
4 Ji-dong Mural Village D2
Space Bom .... (see 1)
5 Suwon Cultural Foundation C2
6 Suwon Hwaseong Museum C2

⊕ Activities, Courses & Tours
7 Yeonmudae Archery Centre D1

⊜ Sleeping
8 Hwaseong Guest House C3
9 Suwon Hostel C2

⊗ Eating
Seongil .... (see 1)
10 Yeonpo Galbi C1

⊜ Drinking & Nightlife
Bom Cafe .... (see 1)
11 Bulgeun Sutalk B4

ⓘ Information
12 Suwon Tourist Information Centre A5
13 Tourist Information Booth C3

ⓘ Transport
14 Hwaseong Trolley C2

ⓘ Getting There & Away

Express Bus 2200 (₩2000, 45 minutes) and local bus 200 (₩1800, 1 hour 20 minutes) both leave from stop 16 near Hapjeong station on subway lines 2 and 6 in Seoul. Both pass through Paju on the way to Heyri; the local bus also stops near Odusan. The last bus back is around 10.30pm.

Suwon & Around   수원

♩ 031 / POP 1.07 MILLION

Around 30km south of Seoul, sprawling Suwon is the largest city in Gyeonggi-do province. It's most known for its World Heritage–listed fortifications built by Joseon dynasty ruler King Jeongjo, who had the idea of moving the capital from Seoul to Suwon in 1794. The fortress wall that surrounded the city was constructed but the king died and power stayed in Seoul.

While it can easily be visited as a day trip, there's a lot to see. So it's worth staying for a night or two.

◎ Sights & Activities

Hwaseong FORTRESS
(화성; http://ehs.suwon.ne.kr; adult/child ₩1000/500; ⊙24hr) The World Heritage–listed fortress wall that encloses the original town of Suwon is what brings most travellers to the city. Snaking up and down Paldal-san (143m), the fortification wall stretches a scenic 5.7km past four majestic gates, command posts, pavilions, observation towers and fire-beacon platforms. Built by King Jeongjo and completed in 1796, it was constructed of earth and faced with large stone blocks and grey bricks, nearly all of which have been restored.

It takes around two hours to complete the circuit. Try to go outside the wall for at least part of the way, as the fortress looks much more impressive the way an enemy would see it.

Start at **Paldalmun**, also known as Nammun (South Gate), and follow the steep steps off to the left up to the **Seonam Gangu**, an observation point near the peak of Paldal-san. Near the command post, **Seojang-dae**, is the large **Hyowon Bell** you can toll (₩1000) and **Seono-dae**, a tower on the summit that was used by crossbow archers, and has spectacular panoramic views of the city.

On the wall's north side is **Hwahongmun**, a watergate over a stream. Nearby **Dongbukgongsimdon**, another watchtower, has a unique design – a high, tapering structure with rounded corners, stone base and brick tower. Further on, the **Bongdon Beacon Towers** were used to send messages around the country.

If you don't fancy the walk, head up the hill at the rear of the palace to the find the 54-seat **Hwaseong Trolley** (adult/child/teen ₩1500/700/1100; ⊙10am-5.20pm) that winds in and out of the fortress wall to the archery field at Yeonmu-dae.

Hwaseong Haenggung PALACE
(화성행궁; adult/child ₩1500/700; ⊙9am-6pm, changing of the guard 2pm Sun, martial-arts display 11am & 3pm Tue-Sun) Sitting at the base of Mt Paldal, King Jeongjo's palace was built in the late 18th century as a place for him to stay on his visits. It's been meticulously reconstructed after being destroyed during the Japanese Occupation. From March to November, various traditional performances are held at the plaza in front of the palace, including a changing of the guard ceremony and martial-arts display.

DON'T MISS

SUWON'S MURAL VILLAGES

A must for lovers of urban art, the villages of Haenggung-dong and Ji-dong are both in gritty neighbourhoods that have recently been decorated by local artists with colourful murals – equal to Seoul's Ihwa-dong, but without the hordes of tourists.

Haenggung-dong Mural Village is the more established of the two, featuring work by a mix of international muralists. You can pick up a map from the **Alternative Art Space Noon** (☑ 031 244 4519; www.spacenoon.co.kr; ⊗ noon-7pm) FREE, a renovated house that's now a cool little gallery. It stands alongside **Space Bom** (⊗ noon-10pm), which also exhibits local artists.

Ji-dong, just outside the city walls, is arguably more interesting with its expansive labyrinth of grungy alleyways bursting with vibrant murals. To get here, head through Jidgan Market arcade and take the first left at Changnyongmon-ro, from where it's a further 500m.

Find out how detailed court records aided the reconstruction process and see how the area used to look at the **Suwon Cultural Foundation** (⊗ 9.30am-6pm Mar-Oct, to 5pm Nov-Feb) FREE on the south side of the plaza in front of the palace.

Every October a grand royal procession is reenacted as part of Suwon's annual festival.

Suwon Hwaseong Museum MUSEUM
(http://hsmuseum.suwon.ne.kr; adult/child ₩2000/free; ⊗ 9am-6pm) This modern, well-presented museum details the palace and fort's construction, including dioramas of the building process.

Mr Toilet House MUSEUM
(Haewoojae; ☑ 031 271 9777; www.haewoojae.com; 458-9 Jangan-ro, Jangan-gu; ⊗ 10am-6pm Tue-Sun, to 5pm winter) FREE A contender as Korea's wackiest museum, Mr Toilet House is the former residence of Suwon's mayor, the late Sim Jae-duck – appropriately designed like a toilet. As well as hilarious poo-related exhibits and a sculpture garden, it also covers more serious sanitation issues. Kids especially will love it, and there's a children's museum across the road with an observatory deck for viewing the toilet house.

Jae-duck was famous for his efforts in beautifying Suwon's public toilets during the lead-up to the 2002 Soccer World Cup, decorating them with art, flowers and classical music – most of which remain around the city today.

It's important to note it's not just a quirky museum, but an NGO that was established to improve public health worldwide. Visit its website for more details.

To get here take bus 64, 65 or 98 from Hwasseong Haenggung (25 minutes) and

get off at Dongwon High School, from where it's a 10-minute walk.

Korean Folk Village CULTURAL CENTRE
(한국민속촌; ☑ 031 288 0000; www.koreanfolk. co.kr; 90 Minsokchon-ro, Yongin-si; adult/child/teen ₩15,000/10,000/12,000; ⊗ 9.30am-6.30pm May-Sep, to 6pm Oct-Apr) Showcasing traditional Korean culture, this 99-hectare folk village comprises thatched and tiled traditional houses and buildings from around Korea. It takes at least half a day to wander the picturesque grounds where you'll encounter artisans wearing *hanbok* (traditional clothing) making pots and handmade paper, while others tend to vegetable plots and livestock. The **Folk Museum** offers a fascinating snapshot of 19th-century Korean life.

Throughout the day traditional musicians, dancers, acrobats and tightrope walkers perform, and you can watch a staged wedding ceremony. There are also kid-specific attractions including an amusement park, which costs extra, plus several traditional restaurants.

A free shuttle bus leaves Suwon's main tourist information centre (30 minutes, at 10.30am, 12.30 and 2.30pm). The last shuttle bus leaves the folk village at 4.30pm (5pm on weekends). After that time, walk to the far end of the car park and catch city bus 37 (₩1300, one hour, every 20 minutes) back to Suwon station.

Nam June Paik Art Center GALLERY
(☑ 031 201 8500; http://njpac-en.ggcf.kr; 10 Paiknamjune-ro, Giheung-gu, Yongin-si; admission ₩4000; ⊗ 10am-6pm) Not far from the Korean Folk Village, this gallery features the work of internationally acclaimed avante-garde artist Nam June Paik (1932–2006). It shows a changing collection of his

pioneering new-media work, namely his signature TV sets.

From Suwon station take bus 10, 66, 66-4, 10-5 or 37; from Seoul take the Budang line subway to Sanggal station, from where it's a 10-minute walk. En route you'll pass **Gyeong-gi Provincial Museum** (http://old.musenet.or.kr/ english; 6 Sanggal-ro, Giheung-gu, Yongin-si; ☉ 10am-8pm Mon-Fri, to 10pm Sat & Sun) 𝗙𝗥𝗘𝗘, worth a stop for its fine collection of cultural artefacts.

Yeonmudae Archery Centre   OUTDOORS

(10 arrows ₩2000; ☉ 9.30am-5.30pm, every 30min) In the northeast corner of the fortress, this archery centre allows you to fire arrows at targets; a sport Koreans dominate at the Olympics.

🛏 Sleeping

Hwaseong Guest House   GUESTHOUSE ₩

(☑ 010   5316   3419;   www.hsguesthouse. com;   11-801 Beong-gil, Jeongju-ro;   dm/s/d ₩18,000/30,000/35,000;   ✳@🛜) An old backpacker favourite, Hwaseong's spacious rooms all share bathrooms and a communal kitchen with full cooking facilities. To find it turn left at the road with the bakery opposite the 7-11 on Jeongjo-ro, north of Paldalmun.

Suwon Hostel   HOTEL ₩

(수원호스텔; ☑ 031 245 5555; www.sarangchae. org; 4 Paldallo 2-ga, Paldal-gu; d from ₩30,000; ✳🛜) More of a hotel than hostel, Suwon Hostel offers exceptional value for money with large Western-style rooms or *on-dol* (traditional, sleep-on-a-floor-mattress rooms) with retro antique furnishings. Note the 'no alcohol' policy.

Ramada Plaza Hotel Suwon   HOTEL ₩₩₩

(☑ 031 230 0031; www.ramadaplazasuwon.com; 150 Jungbu-daero; r from ₩165,000; ✳@🛜) About five minutes by taxi east of Suwon's fortress, the Ramada is a stylish affair with contemporary rooms and top-grade facilities, including a gym, deli and restaurants.

🍴 Eating & Drinking

Suwon is renowned for its *galbi* (beef rib) dishes.

Seongil   NOODLES ₩

(Haenggung-dong Mural Village; mains from ₩5000) This humble restaurant, run by a friendly owner, is popular with local artists for cheap and tasty traditional Korean noodles and dumplings. It's opposite the *hanok* (traditional wooden home) decorated with the fish mural.

Yeonpo Galbi   KOREAN ₩₩

(연포갈비; 56-1 Jeongjo-ro 906beon-gil; meals ₩10,000-40,000; ☉ 11.30am-10pm) Down the steps from Hwahongmun, this famous restaurant serves up its special Suwon version of *galbitang* (₩10,000) – big ribs in a seasoned broth with noodles and leeks – only served at lunch.

Bom Cafe   CAFE

(Haenggung-dong Mural Village; ☉ noon-10pm) A cool, arty cafe attached to its eponymous gallery (p102), Bom specialises in traditional Korean teas and also sells quality homemade crafts.

Bulgeun Sutalk   BAR

(붉은수닭; ☉ 5pm-3am) Look for the iron rooster marking the entrance to this dimly lit bohemian bar with plenty of scatter cushions, where you can enjoy a chilled evening drinking cheap draft beer. It's five minutes' walk northeast of Suwon station.

ℹ Information

The **main tourist information centre** (☑ 031 228 4673; english.swcf.or.kr; ☉ 9am-6pm; ⓢ Suwon, exit 4) is on the left outside the railway station. There are several **tourist information booths** (☑ 031 228 4672; ☉ 9am-6pm) located at several other points around the walls, but English is limited.

The **Suwon City Tour** (☑ 031 256 8300; www.suwoncitytour.kr; adult/child/youth ₩11,000/4000/8000; ☉ 10am & 2pm Tue-Sun) is a good option for those short on time.

ℹ Getting There & Away

BUS

Long-distance buses depart from **Suwon bus terminal** (www.suwonterminal.co.kr), heading to major cities incuding Incheon (₩4500, 1½ hours, every 15 minutes), Busan (₩24,800, five hours, 10 daily), Daegu (₩19,900, 3½ hours, six daily) and Gwangju (from ₩16,000, three hours, every 30 minutes).

There's also an airport bus (₩12,000, 70 minutes) leaving every 30 miunutes opposite the Suwon tourist information centre.

TRAIN

From Seoul, the Budang line and Line 1 run to Suwon (₩1850, one hour). KTX trains from Seoul are speedier (from ₩4600, 30 minutes) but not as frequent.

From **Suwon train station**, high- and regular-speed trains depart frequently to cities all over Korea, including Busan (from ₩25,900, 5½ hours), Daegu (from ₩18,200, three hours),

Daejeon (from ₩8100, 70 minutes) and Jeonju (from ₩15,100, three hours). High-speed trains take about half the time, but are double the cost.

ℹ️ Getting Around

Outside Suwon train station on the left, buses 11, 13, 36 and 39 go to Paldalmun (₩1100, 10 minutes). A taxi is ₩5000.

To get to the city's bus terminal catch bus 5, 5-1 or 7-1 (₩1100, five minutes) outside Suwon train station.

Anyang Art Park
안양예술공원

A short bus ride north of Anyang, 20km south of Seoul, is Anyang Art Park FREE, an open-air sculpture park. Set among the trees of a wooded valley and along the rocky river bank, it comprises 52 quirky pieces by Korean and international artists. Highlights include the spinning *Dancing Buddha*, the *Dimensional Mirror Labyrinth*, the *Anyang Crate House Dedicated to the Lost (Pagoda)*, made of multicoloured plastic German beer crates, and the freaky *Boy + Girl* that messes with perspective. Climb up the spiralling *Anyang Peak*, a 141m-high observatory, for fantastic views across the valley.

Back by the river, drop in to see what's happening at Anyang Pavilion (📞031 687 0548; https://apap.or.kr/en; 1½hr guided tour ₩1000; ⊘9am-6pm Tue-Sun; tours 11am & 3pm Wed-Fri, 10am, 2pm, 4pm Sat & Sun Mar-Nov), a sleek minimalist building designed by Portuguese architect Álvaro Siza. Here you can pick up a map to the art park, as well as join a guided tour.

Grab an outdoor table overlooking the river at Coo Coffee Roasting House (http://blog.naver.com/coocoffee; brunch ₩11,000; ⊘10am-11pm; 🛜) for all-day brunch and single-origin coffees. There's also jazz on Saturday evenings. Alternatively, enjoy *mechuri* (메추리; quail roasted over charcoal), available at several stalls near Anyang Pavilion.

Anyang station is on Line 1 of the subway. Take Exit 1 and then bus 2 on the left outside Lotte Department Store, disembarking at the last stop (₩800, 10 minutes).

Donggureung 동구릉

The largest and most attractive of the World Heritage–listed royal tombs scattered around Seoul and Gyeonggi-do, Donggureung (동구릉; www.jikimi.cha.go.kr/english; adult/child ₩1000/500; ⊘6am-5pm Tue-Sun) is the burial place of seven kings and 10 queens from the Joseon dynasty.

Located 20km northeast of central Seoul in Guri, the tombs are set over 196 hectares of forested paths; it takes around 1½ hours to explore its entirety. All tombs are similarly arranged on large grassy mounds according to the rules of Confucianism and Feng Shui. The entrances are marked by a simple red-painted wooden gate, stone pathway and hall for conducting rites in front of the humped burial mounds decorated with stone statuary – typically a pair of civil officers and generals, plus horses and protective animals such as tigers and rams.

A walking-tour map is available from the History Centre Museum (⊘9am-4.40pm) inside the gate's entrance, which also has a good overview of the area.

The most notable tomb is that of King Taejo (1335–1408), the founder of the Joseon dynasty. In contrast to the other neatly clipped plots in this leafy park, his mound is covered in bushy pampas grass from his hometown of Hamhung (now in North Korea) that – in accordance with the king's predeath instructions – has never been cut. Also don't miss the tombs at Mongneung, the only ones you can scramble up and explore close-up.

To reach the complex take subway line 2 to Gangbyeon to connect with bus 1, 1-1 or 1115-6, around 40 minutes from central Seoul.

Namhansanseong
남한산성 도립공원원

The World Heritage–listed fortress of Namhansanseong, 20km southeast of central Seoul, once guarded the city's southern entrance. Today it's famous for hiking trails which hug the 17th-century fortress walls, of which 12.3km still remain, taking you through beautiful pine and oak forests, and wild flowers.

Your first stop should be Namhansanseong Emergency Palace (adult/child ₩2000/1000; ⊘10am-5pm Tue-Sun), the beautifully reconstructed complex of the king's quarters, which also has a hiking map of the complex.

The most popular hiking route is the two-hour loop that leads you past the main gates of Bukum (North Fortress), Seomun (West), Nammun (South) and South Command Post,

WORTH A TRIP

SANSAWON BREWERY

If you're the kind who's impartial to a day out at a winery, brewery or distillery, mixed in with a bit of culture amid nature, then a day trip to **Sansawon Brewery & Museum** (☑ 031 531 9300; www.sansawon.co.kr; 25 Hwadong-ro 432beon-gil, Hwahyeonmyeon, Pocheon-si; ⏱ 8.30am-5.30pm) is a must. Set up by Baesangmyun Brewery, a producer of traditional Korean liquors, Sansawon is all about quality, chemical-free craft *makgeolli* (milky rice wine), *soju* (local vodka) and rice wines; far removed from nasty hangovers from convenience-store items. For only ₩2000 you get a sampler and shot glass for unlimited tasting. Also here is a museum of traditional brewery equipment (no English signage, unfortunately).

Outside stand rows of ceramic vats containing *soju* left to age. It's a lovely outdoor area and we highly recommend packing a picnic lunch and buying a bottle to enjoy on the lawn.

It's worth getting in touch with **Makgeolli Mamas & Papas** (MMPKorea; https://mmp-korea.wordpress.com), experts in the field, to see if they're running tours.

Otherwise, take the bus from Dong Seoul terminal (across from Gangbyeon subway on line 2) to Pocheon (₩6000, one hour and 10 minutes). From here it's a 10-minute taxi ride for around ₩8000.

---

with sweeping panoramas. Or you can trek the entire wall's perimeter in around seven hours. Be sure to mix up trails that lead in and out of the wall to change your views.

To get here, take subway line 8 to Sanseong, then get a taxi or take bus 9 from Exit 2 of the station to the park's south gate, a total journey of around one hour from central Seoul.

Icheon 이천

☑ 031 / POP 195,175

Surrounded by mountains, the famed pottery centre of Icheon (not to be confused with Incheon) has origins in the craft that date back to the Joseon dynasty. It's a tradition that continues today with quality ceramics to admire and purchase. Only 60km southeast from Seoul, it makes for an easy day trip.

◉ Sights & Activities

Seolbong Park   SCULPTURE, PARK
(설봉공원; http://tour.icheon.go.kr; ⏱ 9am-5pm) Head here first to pick up a good local area map at the visitors' centre, then stroll around the parklands admiring the variety of ceramic sculptures that surround the scenic lake. Plus there are galleries, museums and an impressive **rock-climbing** wall. The park is also the venue for the annual **Icheon Ceramic Festival** (www.ceramic.or.kr; ⏱ late Apr–mid-May).

Cerapia   ARTS CENTRE
(www.kocef.org; gallleries ₩2000; ⏱ 9am-6pm Tue-Sun) An art complex within Seolbong Park, Cerapia focuses on contemporary rather than traditional ceramics. It comprises several quality galleries with rotating shows, a sculpture garden and show room. There's also an opportunity to partake in resident artist workshops (₩30,000), from pottery to glassblowing, and kids programs too. Head around the back to check out the traditional kiln with its multiple chambers.

Icheon Ceramic Village   NEIGHBOURHOOD
(이천 도예촌; www.ceramic.or.kr) Located north of downtown, the Icheon Ceramic Village dates back to the Joseon dynasty and continues today with hundreds of producers offering a quality selection of traditional wares for sale. Spread over a wide urban area, it's centred at **Sagimakgol Ceramics Village** where most shops open daily from mid-morning.

To make your own pottery, head to **Hankook Dojakwon** (Korean Ceramic Gallery; Icheon Pottery Village; from ₩20,000; ⏱ 10am-6pm), at the village's entry.

Catch a taxi (₩5000) or local bus 24-4, 24-5, 24-11 or 114-1 (₩1500, 15 minutes) from outside the bus terminal and get off at the village denoted by arched gates with giant pots out front.

Haegang Ceramics Museum   MUSEUM
(해강 도자 미술관; www.haegang.org; admission ₩2000; ⏱ 9.30am-5.30pm) A beautiful collection of celadon pottery is on display at this museum, 1km north of the ceramics village.

WINTER SPORTS NEAR SEOUL

A number of ski/snowboard resorts are located about an hour from Seoul. Resort shuttles (often free) depart from pickup points around the city. Most resorts offer equipment rental (including clothing) and English-speaking instructors, and night skiing is increasingly popular.

Elysian (엘리시안 강촌 스키장; www.elysian.co.kr; 688, Bukhangangbyeon-gil, Namsan-myeon, Chuncheon-si; lift tickets per day adult/child ₩62,000/43,000, gear rental per day adult/child ₩50,000/30,000) Small-but-slick resort located on the Seoul subway (line 7) with 10 runs that see decent snowfall.

Bears Town Ski Resort (베어스타운리조트 스키장; ☑ 031 540 5000; www.bearstown.com; 27, Geumgang-ro 2536beon-gil, Naechon-myeon, Pocheon-si; 匣) Eleven wide, easy slopes that cater well for beginners. There's also a sledding hill, a youth hostel and condominium.

Konjiam Ski Resort (곤지암리조트 스키장; ☑ 02 3777 2100; www.konjiamresort.co.kr; San 23-1, Doung-ri, Docheok-myeon, Gwangju-si; lift tickets per day adult/child ₩77,000/52,000, equipment rental per day adult/child ₩30,000/25,000; 匣) A choose-your-own-time ticketing system and electronic lift-ticket readers make this an easy one-hour day trip from Seoul.

Jisan Resort (지산 포레스트 리조트; ☑ 031 644 1200, free shuttle reservation 031 644 1552 3; www.jisanresort.co.kr; lift tickets per day adult/child ₩73,000/49,000, equipment rental per day adult/child ₩24,000/19,000) Small resort 56km south of Seoul with five lifts and a variety of slopes to keep all skill levels happy.

Yangji Pine Resort (양지파인리조트스키장; ☑ condos 02 516 7161 ext 3, hostel 02 511 3033; www.pineresort.com; 34-1, Namgok-Ri, Yangji-Myun, Cheoin-Gu; lift tickets per day adult/child ₩63,500/41,000, equipment rental per day adult/child ₩45,000/33,000; 匣) One of the closest resorts to Seoul with six slopes and lifts, a sledding hill, and a youth hostel plus condos.

Miranda Spa Plus SPA
(미란다호텔 스파플러스; www.mirandahotel.com/new/SPA/eng/index.asp; adult/child spa only ₩12,000/8000, all facilities ₩27,000; ⊙6am-10pm) Attached to the Miranda Hotel Icheon (p106), this large complex has ultramodern facilities with indoor and outdoor baths.

Icheon Termeden SPA
(www.termeden.com/english; adult/child Mon-Fri ₩32,000/22,000, Sat & Sun ₩36,000/26,000; ⊙8am-8pm) A German-style spa resort, 10km south of the town centre and surrounded by a forest. It has Jacuzzi-style pools, and lots of indoor and outdoor pools. A free shuttle bus runs here from SC Bank across from Icheon bus terminal.

🛏 Sleeping & Eating

Miranda Hotel HOTEL ₩₩₩
(미란다호텔; ☑ 031 639 5000; www.mirandahotel.com; r ₩236,000; 🅿@🛜) Icheon's snazziest hotel overlooks a lake with a pavilion on an island. There's also a bowling alley.

★Deokjegung KOREAN ₩₩
(덕제궁; ☑ 031 634 4811; set lunch ₩12,000; ⊙10.30am-9.30pm) On a hillside outside town, this traditional restaurant serves a wonderful assortment of courses among the paper screens, floor seating and floral-wallpapered walls. It's a treat worth the taxi ride out here – about ₩7000 from Seolbong Park.

❶ Getting There & Away

Buses run from Dong-Seoul Bus Terminal to Icheon (₩4500, one hour, every 15 to 40 minutes). Once in Icheon most places are accessible by bus, or are around a ₩5000 taxi ride away.

INCHEON-GWANGYEOK-SI

The provice Incheon-gwangyeok-si was separated from Gyeonggi-do in 1981. It continues to grow with giant areas of landfill in the West Sea having been converted recently into the new urban centres such as Songdo International City.

EVERLAND RESORT

Set in lush hillsides 40km south of Seoul, this mammoth amusement park is regarded as one of Korea's best.

The main theme park **Everland** (📞 031 320 5000; www.everland.com; adult/child/teen ₩48,000/31,000/34,000; ⏱ 9.30am-10pm Sep-Jun, to 11pm Jul & Aug) has fantasy buildings, fairground attractions, impressive seasonal gardens, live music and parades. Lit up at night, the park takes on a magical atmosphere and there are always fireworks. The highlight for many is the wooden rollercoaster, supposedly the steepest in the world. Expect long queues for all rides.

Next door is **Caribbean Bay** (adult/child from ₩35,000/27,000; ⏱ 10am-5pm Sep-Jun, 9.30am-11pm Jul & Aug), a superb indoor and outdoor water park. The outdoor section is usually open from June to September (there's a higher entrance charge in July and August) and features a huge wave pool that produces a mini-tsunami every few minutes, plus water-based thrill rides.

A free shuttle bus runs from Everland's main entrance to the **Hoam Art Museum** (http://hoam.samsungfoundation.org; adult/child ₩4000/3000, free with Everland ticket; ⏱ 10am-6pm Tue-Sun) and you are well advised to take it. The serenely beautiful Hee Won traditional Korean gardens induce a calm frame of mind so that visitors can fully appreciate the gorgeous art treasures inside the museum, including paintings, screens and celadon.

To get here from Seoul take bus 5002 (₩2000, 50 minutes, every 15 minutes) from Gangnam. From outside Suwon's train station, hop on bus 66 or 66-4 (₩1700, one hour, every 30 minutes).

Incheon 인천

📞 032 / POP 2.9 MILLION

South Korea's third largest city, this expanding metropolis and industrial port – 36km west of Seoul – is the place where Korea opened up to the world in 1883, ending centuries of self-imposed isolation. In 1950, during the Korean War, the American General Douglas MacArthur led UN forces in a daring landing behind enemy lines here.

Fragments of this history can be seen in Incheon today, particularly in the colourful **Chinatown** and **Open Port** areas, the most interesting areas to explore and easily accessible via subway. Come here to eat Chinese food, stroll along the Wolmido waterfront and visit the fish market at Yeonan, where you can catch ferries to China or the West Sea islands.

Note the Incheon international airport isn't located in Incheon itself, but rather on Yeongjongdo, over one hour away by bus.

◉ Sights

Incheon Art Platform ARTS CENTRE
(www.inartplatform.kr; Open Port; ⏱ 9am-6pm Tue-Sun) FREE This attractive complex of 1930s and '40s brick warehouses was turned over to the Incheon Foundation for Arts and Culture, and they've created gallery spaces and artist residency studios. Performances and events are also held here, and there is a light-filled cafe with plenty of art books.

They offer three-month residency programs for artists; visit the website for more info.

Jayu Park PARK
(Open Port) This beautiful hillside park, designed by a Russian civil engineer in 1888, makes a good spot for a stroll. It contains the monument for the centenary of Korea–USA relations and a statue of General MacArthur.

Incheon Grand Fishery Market MARKET
(www.asijang.co.kr; Yeonan; ⏱ 5am-9pm; 🍽) Even if you've already visited Noryangjin (p73) in Seoul, this fish and seafood market is still worth seeing. It's a more intimate, brightly lit place displaying hundreds of types of marine products, all of which you can eat on the spot at several small restaurants and cafes. Bus 12 and 24 will get you here from Dongincheon subway station.

Incheon Open Port Museum MUSEUM
(인천개항박물관; www.icjgss.or.kr/open_port; Open Port; adult/child/teen ₩500/200/300; ⏱ 9am-6pm) One of three former Japanese bank buildings along the same street, this is an interesting museum of the history of Incheon since the port's opening in 1883.

Modern Architecture Museum MUSEUM
(Open Port; adult/child/youth ₩500/200/300; ⊙9am-6pm) Housed within a former colonial Japanese bank, this museum sheds insight into Incheon's multiculturalism through its varied architecture. It includes displays of Incheon's buildings, ranging from modernism, gothic, French rennaissance, Japanese imperial and Chinese styles.

Songwol-dong Fairy Tale Village PUBLIC ART
(인천 송월동 동화마을) Like a princess who's waved a magic wand over its streets, this once gritty neighbourhood has been transformed into a children's wonderland of brightly coloured fairy-tale-themed murals. While it's aimed at kids, it's quirky enough to warrant a visit for all.

Jjajangmyeon Museum MUSEUM
(Chinatown; admission ₩1000; ⊙9am-6pm) A noodle museum with engaging visual displays about the famous Chinese dish of *jjajangmyeon*, invented as a cheap eat for local workers at Incheon's port town.

Wolmido NEIGHBOURHOOD
(월미도; http://wolmi.incheon.go.kr) Once an island, Wolmido was later a military base

Incheon

and site of the Incheon Landing Operation during the Korean War. Today it's a leisure area with atmospheric Coney Island–style waterfront boardwalk and amusement park. It also has the forested **Wolmi Park** (월미공원; http://wolmi.incheon.go.kr/index.do; Wolmi-do; ⊙6am-10pm, garden 9am-8pm) FREE with tranquil walking trails leading to traditional gardens and the hilltop **Wolmi Observatory** (Wolmi Park; ⊙6am-10pm) FREE with wonderful 360° views of Incheon and beyond.

At the base of the park, the **Korean Emigration History Museum** (http://mkeh. incheon.go.kr; ⊙9am-6pm Tue-Sun) FREE offers an interesting insight to the journey of Korean migrants, with a focus on settlers' experiences in the US and the Americas.

Incheon Landing Operation Memorial Hall
MUSEUM

(인천상륙작전기념관; www.landing915.com; Song-do; ⊙9am-6pm Tue-Sun) FREE Some 70,000 UN and South Korean troops took part in the surprise landing in Incheon in 1950, supported by 260 warships. Find out about this daring attack at this sombre, strikingly designed museum. The displays include newsreel films of the Korean War, plus guided missiles and LVT landing crafts. Bus 6-1, 8 and 16 come here from Dongincheon subway.

Incheon Metropolitan City Museum
MUSEUM

(인천광역시립박물관; Song-do; ⊙9am-6pm Tue-Sun) FREE Next to the Incheon Landing Operation Memorial Hall is the city's main museum, offering an excellent collection of celadon pottery and some interesting historical displays dating from the Three Kingdoms.

☞ Tours

You can pick up two city-run tours outside Incheon station.

Incheon City Tour
BUS TOUR

(http://english.visitincheon.org; 4hr tour ₩7000-10,000; ⊙11am, noon, 1.30pm & 2.30pm Tue-Sun) These four-hour bus tours have interchangeable itineraries that stop at places such as Incheon's port, Songdo, Incheon Bridge and Eurwangi Beach.

Ganghwa Tour
TOUR

(8hr tours ₩10,000; ⊙Sat & Sun Apr-Oct) Weekend tours of Ganghwa islands leave only if there are enough people booked.

🛏 Sleeping

Eden Motel
MOTEL ₩

(☏032 763 9598; Beon-gil; d ₩25,000) Slightly rundown, but excellent value nevertheless, the Eden Motel has large rooms with bathrooms and is run by a friendly couple.

Hotel Atti
MOTEL ₩₩

(호텔 아띠; ☏032 772 5233; ymj5599@naver. com; 88, Sinpo-ro 35beon-gil, Open Port; r from ₩60,000; ❅@☎) A comfortable and stylish midrange option located at the base of Jeju Park, with varying styles of room featuring anything from claw-foot baths to arty decor and computer terminals.

Harbor Park Hotel
HOTEL ₩₩

(하버 파크 호텔; ☏032 770 9500; www. harborparkhotel.com; 217 Jemullyang-ro; r from ₩110,000; ❅@☎) Sporting a sleek contemporary design inside and out, the rooms at the Harbor Park provide great views of the working harbour and hillsides. There's

WORTH A TRIP

BUKHANSAN NATIONAL PARK

Bukhansan National Park (북한산 국립공원; ☎031 873 2791; bukhan.knps.or.kr; Ⓢ Line 1 to Dobong-san) Granite-peak-studded Bukhansan National Park is so close to Seoul that it's possible to visit by subway – which partly accounts for why it sees more than 10 million hikers a year. It offers sweeping mountaintop vistas, maple leaves, rushing streams and remote temples. Even though it covers nearly 80 sq km, the park's proximity to the city (45 minutes by subway) means it gets crowded, especially on weekends.

Popular for **hiking** and **rock climbing**, the park is divided into two sections, the Bukhan-san and Dobong-san areas. Both are separate destinations that feature multiple scenic trails leading to mountain peaks. Neither are a stroll in the park, and are quite strenuous. Bring plenty of water.

In the northern area a popular hike is the climb up **Dobong-san** (740m), which climaxes with the spectacular ridge-top peak climb. Along the way be sure to take signed detours to visit atmospheric forested temples **Cheonchuk-sa** (천축사) on the way up and **Mangwol-sa** (망월사) upon descent – around a four-hour trek in total.

The southern part has South Korea's highest peak, **Baegundae** (836m), a 3½-hour return trip via the Bukhansanseong trail. For rock climbers, nearby **Insu-bong** (810m) has some of the best multipitch climbing in Asia and routes of all grades.

Getting There & Away

For Dobong-san, take subway line 1 to Dobongsan station, a 15-minute walk from **Dobong Park Information Centre** (☎031 954 2566; ⊙sunrise-sunset), which has a basic hiking map in English. If you take the route down via Wondol-bong (recommended) you'll finish at Mangwolsa station.

Baegundae is accessed from Bukhansanseong or Jeongneung; both have information centres with maps. For Bukhansanseong take subway line 3 to Gupabal station and then take bus 70. For Jeongneung take line 4 to Gireum station and bus 110B or 143.

---

a good gym and tempting top-floor buffet restaurant (adult/child ₩35,000/23,000), also with stellar views.

✕ Eating

In Chinatown you can sample local variations on Chinese cuisine including *jjajangmyeon* (noodles in a savoury-sweet, black-bean sauce), *jjampong* (noodles in a spicy seafood soup) and *onggibyeong* (crispy meat- or veg-filled dumplings baked inside large clay jars).

Tochon KOREAN ₩
(토촌; Open Port; mains ₩8000-15,000; ⊙10am-10pm) At the bottom of Jayu Park, Tochon is one of Incheon's most atmospheric Korean restaurants with decor comprising traditional ceramics, lush greenery, a small waterfall and aquarium-lined walls. It's a sit-down affair serving bulgogi (grilled marinated beef) and bibimbap (rice, egg, meat and vegies with chilli sauce) with an impressive array of sides.

Samchi St SEAFOOD ₩
(동인천 삼치거리; Dongincheon; from ₩6000; Ⓢ Exit 8, Dongincheon) This strip of lively restaurants all specialise in cheap, delicious grilled *samchi* (Spanish mackerel), which when accompanied by a few bottles of *makgeolli* (milky rice wine), makes for a fun boozy evening out. It's a short walk from Dongincheon station.

Dada Bok CHINESE ₩
(dumplings ₩4500; ⊙11am-8pm) Just back from the bedlam of Chinatown, this unassuming restaurant is the local pick for Incheon's tastiest dumplings. There's a choice of pork or shrimp, either steamed or pan-fried.

Shinpo-sijang KOREAN ₩
(신포시장; Shinpo-dong; street eats ₩1000-10,000; ⊙10am-8pm) Locals line up at stalls here for takeaway boxes of *dakgangjeong* (spicy sweet and sour deep-fried chicken). It's well worth sampling, as are other street eats available along the twin covered arcades, including giant candy-coloured *mandu* (dumplings).

Pungmi CHINESE ₩
(풍미; ☎032 772 2680; Chinatown; meals ₩5000-10,000; ⊙9am-9.30pm) In business since 1957, this is a good place to sample *jjajangmyeon*, a local speciality.

Wonbo CHINESE ₩
(원보; Chinatown; dumplings ₩2000; ⏲11am-9pm) Charcoal-fired pork-filled dumplings are the speciality of this no-frills corner takeway.

Mandabok CHINESE ₩₩
(만다복; ☎032 773 3838; www.mandabok.com; Chinatown; mains ₩7000-30,000; ⏲11am-10pm) Guarded by a pair of terracotta warriors, this is one of Chinatown's fanciest restaurants, with a refined interior and top-notch cuisine. Try the sweet-and-sour pork (₩20,000). There's often a long queue.

🍷 Drinking

★**Min** BAR
(민; ⏲6pm-midnight) Translated as 'the People', this cosy bar, part of a row of colonial-era shophouses, is a hang-out for students from the local art college who sip beers and traditional Korean alcohol while tucking into savoury pancakes. There's no sign so look for the mural of a tiger smoking a pipe.

Bboya BAR
(뽀야; Open Port; ⏲6pm-1am) This unique cafe-bar is covered inside and out by colourful mosaics, created from plastic and metal caps from bottles of beer and soft drinks.

Kudo Siktak CAFE
(구두; 232 Beon-gil, Open Port; ⏲1-11pm Mon-Sat) An arty cafe with retro-style furniture and clothing displays, which feels more like a vintage clothes store, with good coffee, cheap draft beer and tasty meals you'll need to order in advance.

Café Castle CAFE
(Cafe 성; ☎032 773 2116; www.cafecastle.com; Chinatown; ⏲noon-10am) Enjoy coffee, tea, cocktails and snacks at this intimate cafe with a fantastic harbour view from its rooftop garden.

[i] Information

Tourist Information Centre (http://english.incheon.go.kr) The tourist information centres at Incheon station (☎032 777 1330; eng.icjg.go.kr/index.asp; Incheon Station; ⏲9am-6pm); Wolmido Promenade (☎032 765 4169; Wolmido Promenade; ⏲6am-9pm); and the bus terminal (☎032 430 7257; Bus terminal; ⏲10am-6pm) have very helpful staff, particularly outside the subway station, with lots of excellent maps, tourist info and suggestions for Incheon and beyond.

[i] Getting There & Away

BOAT

Yeonan Pier (☎032 885 0180; www.icferry.or.kr) and **International Ferry Terminal 2** (☎1599 5985; www.icferry.or.kr) are the departure points for regular international ferries to a number of Chinese cities, as well as the islands of the West Sea.

To/From China

Ferries link 10 Chinese ports with Incheon, including Tianjin (for Beijing), Dalian, Qingdao, Yingkou, Qinhuangdao, Yantai, Shidao, Lianyungang, Weihai and Dadong. They're suitable for those with a penchant for slow travel, as they can get crowded. Also, they're not much cheaper than flying if your journey takes from 15 to 24 hours. The cheapest fares offer a thin mattress on a dormitory floor, while the more expensive fares give you a small cabin with a bunk bed and TV.

Child fares are usually half the adult fare, and some companies offer students a 20% discount. Most ferries leave from Yeonan Pier, but the larger boats depart from International Ferry Terminal 2. You'll need to arrange visas in advance.

To/From West Sea Islands

Yeonan Pier has a domestic ferry terminal where boats leave for 14 of the larger inhabited islands in the West Sea, including Deokjeokdo and Baengnyeongdo. Cancellations aren't uncommon due to bad weather (particularly windy conditions), so allow for enough time if you have a flight to catch.

To find out more about these and other West Sea islands see www.ongjin.go.kr.

BUS

From **Incheon Bus Terminal** (☎032 430 7114; www.ictr.or.kr/eng/index.asp; [S] Incheon Line 1 to Incheon Bus Terminal) you can take direct long-distance buses all over South Korea, from Suwon (₩4500, one hour) to Busan (from ₩24,100, 4½ hours). For Seoul it's faster, cheaper and easier to connect via the subway.

SUBWAY

Subway Line 1 from Seoul (₩1650) takes around 70 minutes; the line branches at Guro so make sure you're on an Incheon-bound train.

[i] FREE AIRPORT TOURS

For those with time on their hands waiting for a flight at Incheon Airport, the **transit tours** (☎1577 2600; www.airport.kr; Incheon Airport) [FREE] are a good option. Tours vary from to one to five hours, covering sights in Incheon and Seoul.

ⓘ Getting Around

BUS & TAXI

Buses (₩1200) and taxis leave from outside Dongoincheon and Incheon stations. To the airport and Yeongjongdo, take bus 306 from Incheon station (₩2800, every 15 minutes, 70 minutes). To get to Yeonan Pier take bus 12 or 24 from Dong-Incheon, or hail a taxi (₩8000). For International Ferry Terminal 2, take bus 23 from Incheon station or a taxi (₩3000). It's a 20-minute walk from Incheon station to Wolmido, or hop on bus 2, 23 or 45. A taxi costs ₩3000.

SUBWAY

Incheon's Line 1 runs in a north–south direction and intersects with Seoul's Line 1 subway at Bupyeong (부평). At its northern terminus the line connects with the A'rex express to Incheon International Airport at Gyeyang (계양), while in the south it terminates at the International Business District of Songdo International City. The basic fare is ₩1300.

Yeongjongdo 영종도

ⓙ 032

Home to Korea's busiest international airport, Yeongjongdo's best western beaches aren't disturbed by air traffic. **Eulwangni Beach** (을왕리 해수욕장) is the most popular. Despite its commercial setup it's an attractive place framed by hillside pine forests, which can get busy on weekends.

Next to Eulwangni's Youngjong Sky Resort is a **spa** (spa adult/child ₩10,000/6000; ⏰7am-8pm) and **water park** (low-/high-season adult ₩25,000/40,000 child ₩20,000/30,000; ⏰10am-7pm).

Just up from Eulwangni is **Wangsan Beach** (왕산 해수욕장), which has a less developed beachfront.

🛏 Sleeping & Eating

It's only worth staying here if you have an early-morning departure or late-arrival flight. Just outside Incheon International Airport is the Airport Business District, not to be confused with Airport Town Square, two stops away on the A'rex train at Unseo.

Hotel Ray LOVE MOTEL ₩₩

(ⓙ 032 752 8333; iamhangang@gmail.com; Eulwangni Beach; r from ₩55,000; ✳🛜) Shaped like a ship and just steps away from Eulwangni Beach, this love motel offers wonderful ocean views from the 'porthole' windows. Cheaper rooms on the ground floor have no views.

Global Guesthouse APARTMENT ₩₩

(ⓙ 032 743 0253; www.globalgh.com; Airport Business District; apt ₩50,000; ✳🛜) These spacious studio apartments all come with a washing machine and cable TV. Rates include free pickup from the airport.

Incheon Airport Hotel HOTEL ₩₩

(인천에어포트호텔; ⓙ 032 752 2066; www.incheonairporthotel.co.kr; Airport Town Sq; r weekday/weekend ₩89,000/99,000; ✳@) Well-priced hotel with triangular whirlpool baths, desktop PCs and airport pickup.

Youngjong Sky Resort HOTEL ₩₩₩

(ⓙ 032 745 9000; www.yjskyresort.com; 379 Yongyuseo-ro; r from ₩180,000; ✳🛜🐟) Eulwangni's fanciest resort makes a good spot to finish your trip. Its rooms have sweeping views across the beach and it offers discount rates for its attached spa and water park. There is a free shuttle bus to the airport too.

Caffe Ora INTERNATIONAL ₩₩

(Eulwangni Beach; meals ₩15,000-20,000; ⏰10am-11pm) Overlooking the Eulwangni and Wangsan beaches, this modernist piece of architecture could be mistaken for the villain's headquarters in a James Bond movie. It's actually nothing more sinister than a high-class multicuisine restaurant.

ⓘ Getting There & Away

From Incheon subway, bus 306 (1½ hours) runs every 15 minutes.

Ferries (adult/child ₩3500/1500, 15 minutes, every 30 minutes from 7am to 6pm) shuttle between Wolmido promenade and Yeongjongdo. From there catch bus 5 to the airport.

A'rex trains run to Incheon International Airport, from where you can connect to bus 301, 306 or 316 to reach Eulwangni Beach. There's a ₩6000 toll to drive to the island via the 12.4km-long Incheon Bridge.

Muuido 무의도

ⓙ 032

If you're looking for a beachside escape within easy reach of Seoul, Muuido fits the bill perfectly. Much less developed than Yeongjongdo, the island has several lovely beaches. However swimming is only possible during high tide; during low tide the water recedes substantially, turning it into mudflats.

Yeongjongdo & Muuido

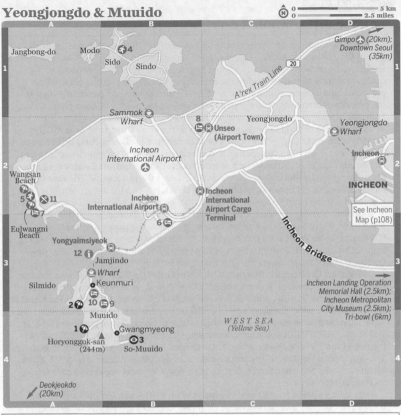

Yeongjongdo & Muuido

◉ Sights
1 Hanagae Beach	A4
Hanagae Beach Huts	(see 1)
2 Silmi Beach	A3
3 So-Muuido	B4

◆ Activities, Courses & Tours
4 Bicycle Hire	B1
5 Eulwangni Beach Spa & Jjimjil-bang	A2
Eulwangni Beach Water Park	(see 5)

⌂ Sleeping
6 Global Guesthouse	B3
7 Hotel Ray	A2
8 Incheon Airport Hotel	B2
9 Island Garden	B3
10 Seaside Hotel	A3
Youngjong Sky Resort	(see 5)

✖ Eating
11 Caffe Ora	A2

ℹ Information
12 Muuido Tourist Information Centre	A3

The **Muuido Tourist Information Centre** (◷ 9am-6pm Tue-Sun) is on the Jamjindo side, and has an English brochure.

◉ Sights

Hanagae Beach   BEACH
(하나개 해수욕장; www.hanagae.co.kr; adult/child ₩2000/1000) Hanagae Beach is Muui-

do's best, with plenty of golden sand, a handful of seafood restaurants and basic beach huts under the pine trees or on the beach.

Silmi Beach   BEACH
(실미 해수욕장; ☎ 032 752 4466; adult/child ₩2000/1000) The laid-back Silmi Beach has a nice patch of sand, plus a freshwater

WORTH A TRIP

SONGDO INTERNATIONAL CITY

An intriguing futuristic smart city created out of landfill in the bay, **Songdo International City** (www.songdo.com) is connected to Yeongjeong-do by the 21.38km Incheon Bridge. In the works since 1994, Songdo is billed as a model urban development. It's designed around high-tech buildings and networks, using best-practice ecofriendly principles, and includes a business district, convention centre and parkland. However, the economic turndowns of recent years have dented the most ambitious plans, leaving Songdo a work in progress, and it sometimes feels like a ghost town.

To get an idea of Songdo's master plan drop by the sleek **Compact Smart City** (Songdo International City; ⊙9am-6pm; Ⓢexit 4 Incheon line 1 to Central Park) FREE a multi-level display centre with scale models and exhibitions covering Incheon's past, present and future. Next door is the helpful **Songdo Tourist Information Centre** (⊙9am-6pm) which has a useful walking-tour map. Also here is the photogenic **Tri-bowl** (www.tribowl.kr; Songdo; ⊙1-6pm Wed, Fri-Sun; Ⓢ Central Park, exit 4), a futuristic piece of architecture that's part giant sculpture, part performance hall and hosts regular free concerts.

From here it's a short walk to **Central Park**, built on reclaimed land and a pleasant place to stroll with a pretty lake with salt-laced breeze. At the park's northwest corner is **NC Canal Cube Walk**, a shopping and eating district that runs along a canal. Heading back southwards is **G-Tower** (Songdo; ⊙9am-6pm) FREE with sensational 360° views from its I-Vision Centre observatory deck on the 33rd floor.

Overlooking Central Park, **Sheraton Incheon Hotel** (☑032 835 1000; www.sheraton.com/incheon; 153 Convensia Rd; r from ₩380,000; ❋@☎☀; Ⓜ Incheon Line 1 to University of Incheon) is Songdo's most upmarket accommodation choice, while **Central Park Hotel** (☑032 310 5000; www.centralparkhotel.co.kr; 193 Technopark-ro; r from ₩120,000; ❋☎) is a more affordable business hotel. A more memorable option is **Gyeongwonjae** (경원재앰배서더; ☑032 729 1101; gyeongwonjae.ambatelen.com; Songdo; r from ₩170,000), within the new **Hanok Village** cultural precinct in Central Park. It offers traditional style rooms and restaurants, including **Hanyang** (Songdo; from ₩8000; ⊙11.30am-4pm & 5-9.30pm), which does affordable and tasty bibimbap (rice, egg, meat and vegies with chilli sauce) and bulgogi dishes.

The city is very bike friendly, and free **bicycle hire** (GT Tower; ⊙9am-5pm Mon-Fri) is available from GT Tower on weekdays for three hours; bring photo ID. Otherwise, on weekends you can rent a pricey bike from East Boat House in Central Park for around ₩10,000 per half hour.

To get to Songdo take the Incheon 1 subway line to Central Park station, around one hour from Incheon station.

swimming pool during summer. At low tide you can walk to Silmido (실미도), an uninhabited island. At time of research the beach was in the process of being redeveloped by new Filipino owners.

So-Muuido ISLAND
(admission ₩2000) Don't miss the tiny car-free island of So-Muuido connected by foot bridge to Muuido's southeastern tip. It's a charming fishing village with a clifftop walk that offers good seaside panoramas.

🛏 Sleeping & Eating

Both Hanagae and Silmi beaches offer camping (BYO tent) and basic accommodation in **beach huts**. Rates at hotels and pensions rise on weekends and during July and

August. At **Keunmuri wharf** there's a row of seafood restaurants.

Hanagae Beach Huts HUT ₩
(Hanagae Beach; huts without bathroom ₩30,000) The best budget choice on the island is this row of stilted beach boxes plonked directly on Hanagae Beach. Rooms are basic heated *ondol*, with *very* thin bedding. There's a ₩10,000 key deposit, and showers costs ₩1000. There are also private pension rooms for ₩100,000 which offer value for groups.

Island Garden PENSION ₩₩
(☑010 3056 2709; www.islandgardenkr.com; camping ₩50,000 r weekday/weekend ₩100,000/150,000; ❋☎) Still under construction at the time of research, but definitely one to look out for with its own

private beach, all rooms looking out to the water and a grassy plot for camping. The friendly owners speak good English.

Seaside Hotel
HOTEL ₩₩

(☏032 752 7737; www.seasidehotel.co.kr; r from ₩77,000; ❉⌗) All the pleasantly decorated rooms at this hotel (both large Western-style and *ondol*) have sea views – it's a little lacking in atmosphere but the price is right. Wi-fi is in the lobby only, but there's free pickup from the jetty.

❶ Getting There & Around

To get here, head to Incheon Aiport from where you catch bus 222 and 2-1 (₩1000, 20 minutes, hourly) to the islet of Jamjindo (장진도), connected by causeway to Yeongjongdo. From here you catch the ferry for the short five-minute crossing to Muuido (₩3000 return, half-hourly until 7pm, 6pm in winter). Bus 306 is also an option from Incheon, but involves a 15-minute walk to the jetty.

Transport on Muuido comprises a bus service that loops around the island in 30-minutes intervals scheduled to connect with ferry arrivals before heading to Hanagae, Silmi and So-Muuido.

West Sea Islands

For those seeking something a bit different, well away from the mainland, the West Sea Islands are worthy of exploration. Comprising seven main islands scattered in the Yellow Sea, it offers a unique brand of tourism attracting anyone from adventure travellers wanting a glimpse of the frontline with North Korea, to hikers and beach lovers in search of somewhere to camp on the sand with a bonfire.

Deokjeokdo
덕적도

Deokjeokdo, 70km southwest of Incheon, is one of the most scenic of the West Sea islands. The main reason to come here is for the beach, so it's more a summertime destination. It's particularly popular with the local expat community given its proximity to Seoul.

Along Deokjeokdo's southern shore, the most popular beach is spectacular 2km-long **Seopori Beach** backed by a thick grove of 200-year-old pine trees. Here you can also climb the highest peak, **Bijo-bong** (292m), for the grand view. Nearby **Batjireum Beach**, 4km north of Seopori, is also a nice spot to hang out.

🛏 Sleeping & Eating

There are plenty of *yeogwan* (small, family-run hotels) and *minbak* (private homes with rooms for rent) as well as free camping at the foreshore of Seopori Beach (shower use ₩1000). There's also a convenience store, which is handy for alcohol. During warmer months it can get busy on weekends, so book ahead.

Beach Love
PENSION ₩₩

(비치사랑펜션; ☏010 5248 0007; www.beachlove.co.kr; Seopori Beach; r from ₩40,000; ❉⌗) In the heart of Seopori, these units lend a beachy vibe. The spacious rooms have their own balconies and picnic tables. The friendly owner speaks good English.

Sum Love
PENSION ₩₩

(섬사랑; ☏032 832 9660; www.mydeokjeokdo.com/~sumlove; Seopori Beach; r ₩40,000) Overlooking the football stadium, this pension has a mix of Western-style and *ondol* rooms, plus enticing outdoor areas, BBQs and free bicycles.

Ole
NOODLES ₩

(Seopori Beach; noodles ₩7000; ⏱10.30am-9pm) Next door to the convenience store, this laid-back floor-seated restaurant specialises in steaming bowls of clam noodles.

❶ Getting There & Away

Several daily ferries depart Incheon's Yeonan Pier for the one-hour journey that costs around ₩46,000 return.

Baengnyeongdo
백령도

If you got a thrill out of visiting the DMZ, Baengnyeongdo beckons as an equally surreal destination. On the frontline with North Korea, it forms the Northern Limit maritime demarcation line, and here things feel noticeably more real and twitchy. Among the razor wire, land-mine warning signs and trenches, you'll encounter pill boxes manned by soliders in full combat gear with fingers on triggers, and tanks and artillery guns all squarely pointed towards North Korea.

Lying 222km northwest of Incheon, Baengnyeongdo is South Korea's westernmost point. Though the island has an isolated outpost feel, there's a surprising number of things to see. The main township is Baengnyeong, 3km north of Yonggipo Port.

While Baengnyeongdo has never been targeted, it's a destination not without its risks; locals get paid $50 a month in 'danger money'. Several clashes in the region have occurred over the years, most significantly in 2010 when a South Korean vessel was sunk 2km offshore, allegedly by a North Korean torpedo. The same year nearby Yeonpyeong island was fired at by North Korea, killing four people.

◉ Sights

While there's no tourist information office, there's a good English map available from the jetty. The island has several hiking routes, but keep to the signed paths as there are landmines in the area.

★ Dumujin   BAY

On the northwest tip of the island, this series of stunning rock formations – named after their resemblance to generals gathered at a meeting – jut out spectacularly to sea. A decked walkway snakes up and down to different vantage points.

Kkeutseom Observatory   LOOKOUT

(⊘ 9am-6pm Tue-Sun) Atop a hill shared by the military, Kkeutseom Observatory has binoculars looking towards North Korea, plus an auditorium with interactive map and a room dedicated to wishes of unification. There are also displays of artillery shells fired by the North that hit Yeonpyeong in 2010. It's on the eastern tip of the island near the port.

Simcheonggak Pavilion   VIEWPOINT

(entry ₩1000) This attractive hilltop pavilion stands peacefully gazing out to sea; across the sea lies Jangsan Peninsula in North Korea. There are binoculars for a closer peek, plus a display of a tank and artillery gun.

Cheonan Warship Memorial   MEMORIAL

This sombre memorial is dedicated to the 46 crewmen from the *Cheonan* warship who lost their lives in 2010 after being hit by a torpedo allegedly fired by a North Korean vessel. The incident occurred 2.5km out to sea from this site.

Sagot Beach   BEACH

Sagot Beach is 3km long; its tanned diatomite of sands is packed so hard that people can (and do) drive cars on it. It was used as a landing strip during the Korean War.

⬛ Sleeping & Eating

There's a number of small restaurants and pensions in town, plus a 24-hour convenience store.

Island Castle   PENSION ₩₩

(아일랜드캐슬; ☑ 032 836 6700; www.island-castle.kr; Banengnyeong; r weekday/weekend ₩60,000/70,000; ❋ ⊚) On the edge of town, 3km from the port, this is Banengnyeong's most comfortable option with spacious, modern rooms with cable TV, wi-fi and private balconies. There's also a restaurant and tennis court.

Moonhwa Motel   PENSION ₩₩

(☑ 032 836 7001; www.0328367001.co.kr; Banengnyeong; r ₩40,000; ⊚) In town, Moonhwa is a decent budget choice with large, clean Western-style rooms.

❶ Getting There & Away

The island is served by two daily high-speed ferries from Incheon's Yeonan Pier, including **Korea Express Ferry** (KEF; ☑ 1577 2891; http://kefship.com/english; Yeonan Pier) departing at 8.30am (around ₩65,000 return, 4½ hours). A local bus runs infrequently around the island, otherwise you can hire a taxi for half a day for around ₩50,000.

Ganghwado   강화도

☑ 032 / POP 57,700

For a brief period in the mid-13th century, when the Mongols were rampaging through the mainland, the island of Ganghwado (now linked by bridge to the mainland) became the location of Korea's capital. Situated at the mouth of the Han River, South Korea's fifth-largest island continued to have strategic importance – it was the scene of bloody skirmishes with French and US forces in the 19th century as colonial powers tried to muscle in on the 'hermit kingdom'.

It's not just Ganghwado's fascinating history that makes it worth visiting. Given over to small-scale agriculture (it's famous for its 'stamina-producing' ginseng), the island provides a welcome rural respite from the sometimes craziness of Seoul.

Ganghwado's main town, **Ganghwa-eup** (강화읍), located 56km from Seoul, is not particularly scenic, but is just 2km beyond the northern bridge. It acts as a base on the surprisingly large island for visiting all attractions by bus. The **tourist information centre** (☑ 032 930 3515; www.ganghwa.incheon. kr; Ganghwa-eup Bus Terminal; ⊘9am-6pm) in the bus terminal should be your first port of call, and can provide you with English maps and bus schedules.

⦿ Sights & Activities

The island is big, and buses infrequent, so you'll need a day or two to do it properly. If time is tight, consider taking a tour: several leave from Seoul (check with the KTO Tourist Information Center, p91) and there's also one from Incheon on Sundays.

A 15km **cycle path** runs alongside the seaside highway passing fortifications that line the east coast including **Gwangseong-bo** (광성보) and **Chojijin** (초지진). Bikes (per day ₩9000) can be rented from 9am to 4pm at the souvenir stall beside the fortification Gapgot Dondae (갑곶돈대), close to the northern bridge.

Bomun-sa   TEMPLE
(보문사;   Seongmodo;   adult/child/youth ₩2500/1000/1700; ⊙9am-6pm) Situated high in the pine-forested hills of the west-coast island of Seongmodo (steep walk and many stairs - catch your breath at the top), this temple has some superbly ornate painting on the eaves of its buildings. The grotto and 10m-tall Buddha rock carving are standouts.

To get here, take bus 31 from Ganghwa-eup terminal to Oepo-ri (₩1200, 20 minutes), 13km away on the west coast, and take a ferry across to Seongmodo (adult/child ₩2000/1000, cars ₩16,000; 10 minutes, every 35 minutes; 7am to 9pm March to November, 7am to 5.30pm December to February). From here there's a bus (₩1200; hourly on weekdays, every 30 minutes on weekends) to the temple.

Jeondeung-sa   BUDDHIST TEMPLE
(전등사; ☑032 937 0125; www.jeondeungsa. org;   adult/child/youth   ₩3000/1000/2000; ⊙7am-sunset) In Ganghwado's southeast, Jeondeung-sa has a tranquil forested hilltop setting within the walls of Samrangseong Fortress. Founded in 1259, it's one of Korea's oldest Buddhist temples. It comprises various halls, gates, temples and pavilions. Here the *Tripitaka Koreana*, 80,000 wooden blocks of Buddhist scriptures were carved between 1235 and 1251.

A free vegetarian lunch is served from around noon; wash your own dishes afterwards. You can also stay overnight and sip traditional teas at the charming teahouse.

Mt Mani-san   HIKING
(마니산; adult/child ₩2000/700; ⊙9am-6pm) It's a steep one-hour climb, with more than 900 steps, to reach the top of scenic Mt Mani-san (469m). At its summit is

Chamseongdan (참성단; 10am to 4pm), a large stone altar said to have been originally built and used by Dangun, the mythical first Korean. There's also a helipad and rocky outcrops, which both offer splendid views. It's 14km from Ganghwa-eup; bus 41 leaves here hourly (30 minutes).

Ganghwa Peace
Observation Deck   OBSERVATORY
(adult/child ₩2500/1700, binoculars per 2min ₩500; ⊙9am-6pm; ▣1, 2) Only 2km from North Korea, this multiplex observatory offers prime views into the hermit kingdom. Through binoculars you can spy villages, workers in rice fields, military towers and distant mountain ranges. There's a short, introductory video in English, but you'll need to request it to be played. Bus 1 will get you here, with bus 2 returning to Ganghwa-eup terminal.

Ganghwa History Museum   MUSEUM
(museum.ganghwa.go.kr;   adult/child/youth ₩1500/1000/1000; ⊙9am-6pm Tue-Sun; ▣1, 2, 30) Covering 5000 years of the island's history, this museum's range of exhibits is engaging and modern. There's good info on Ganghwa's Unesco Heritage-listed dolmen sites, while the replica of the US Navy attack on Ganghwado in 1871 takes you into the thick of the battle. It's a 30-minute bus ride from Ganghwa-eup bus terminal.

Ganghwa Dolmen Park   PARK
(⊙24hr) FREE Across from Ganghwa History Museum this grassy site features **Bugeun-ni Dolmen** (부근리 고인돌), the biggest such Bronze Age stone relic, with a top stone weighing more than 50 tonnes. It's one of 150 dolmen scattered around Ganghwa, 70 of which are World Heritage-listed.

Goryeogungji Palace   PALACE
(고려궁지; Ganghwa-eup; adult/child ₩900/600; ⊙9am-6pm) In Ganghwa-eup are the remains of the small palace built in 1231, once surrounded by an 18km fortress wall. The fortress was destroyed in 1866 by French troops, who invaded Korea in response to the execution of nine French Catholic missionaries. Some 2km of walls and three major gates have since been renovated. It's a 10-minute walk from the bus terminal.

Directly down the hill from the palace is **Ganghwa Anglican Church** (c 1900), built in traditional Korean-style with arched-tiled roof. Follow the alleyway down to the

Yongheunggung Royal Residence, where King Cheoljong used to live.

🛏 Sleeping

Ivy Tourist Hotel
LOVE HOTEL ₩

(아이비호텔; ☎032 932 9811; Ganghwa-eup; r from ₩35,000; ❋⓪) A well-priced love hotel, the Ivy has clean, but dark, rooms with unique touches such as Jacuzzi-style jet showers. It's opposite the bus stop after crossing the northern bridge. It's a further 10 minutes by bus to the main terminal.

Jeondeung-sa Temple
TEMPLESTAY ₩₩

(☎032 937 0152; http://eng.templestay.com; dm incl food & activities from ₩60,000) Part of the templestay program, Jeondeung-sa is a good choice for experiencing life in a Buddhist temple. Prices include vegetarian meals, a two-day cultural program and 4am wake-ups.

★ Namchidang
HANOK GUESTHOUSE ₩₩₩

(남취당; ☎010 9591 0226; http://kyl3850.com/pension/index.php?uid=3; Tosuk Tofu Maeul; r from ₩100,000; ❋🐾) In the south of the island, a couple of kilometres from Jeondeung-sa, this beautiful purpose-built *hanok* has traditional wood-fired *ondol* rooms.

There are free bikes to get around, and lessons in traditional painting on cotton. Buses 2, 3 and 41 run here from Ganghwa-eup.

🍴 Eating & Drinking

Gourmands flock to Ganghwado to sample seafood at the different fishing villages on the island. At Bomun-sa there are heaping plates of inexpensive *twigim* (tempura) seafood and mugwort, accompanied by local ginseng *makgeolli*. On the east coast head to Deurih-mi for seaside restaurants specialising in local eel dishes. At Jeondeung-sa there are many traditional restaurants, or drop by for a free vegetarian lunch in the temple.

Wangjajeong
KOREAN ₩₩

(왕자정; Ganghwa-eup; meals ₩7000-25,000; ⊙10am-9.30pm; ✍) Dine on the terrace, enjoying healthy, delicious vegetarian dishes such as *mukbap* (acorn jelly rice) and *kong-piji* (bean soup), while overlooking the walls of Goryeogungji Palace (p117).

Jungnim Dawon
TEAHOUSE

(죽림다원; Jeongeungsa Temple; tea ₩5000; ⊙8.30am-7.30pm May-Oct, 9.30am-4.30pm Nov-Apr) Within Jeondeung-sa, this atmospheric tea garden is frequented by resident monks and pilgrims sipping on Korean teas.

ℹ Getting There & Around

There are frequent buses running to Ganghwa-eup (₩2100, 1½ hours, every 10 minutes from 4am to 10pm), near Seoul's Sinchon station. From Incheon, you can jump on bus 90 from Bupyeong subway. While buses from Ganghwa-eup connect all points of the island, they run infrequently, usually on the hour, so it pays to get info on bus schedules.

Gangwon-do

Why Go?

Mountainous Gangwon-do (강원도) gives you some of South Korea's most spectacular landscapes, up-close Demilitarized Zone (DMZ) experiences, and laid-back coastal towns and beaches on the East Sea. This is where many Seoulites escape – to get lost in the mountains, to chow down on Chuncheon's fiery chicken dish *dakgalbi* or the raw fish of the coastal towns, or to leap into a frenzy of sports such as skiing in Pyeongchang county, host of the 2018 Winter Olympics.

While the province may not have that much by way of cultural antiquities, what it does have – Gangneung's 400-year-old Dano Festival, for instance – it celebrates with zest. And Gangwon-do can be quirky too. Near Samcheok you'll find a park full of unabashed phallic sculptures standing cheek by jowl with a humble fishing village, while Gangneung has a museum dedicated to its founder's lifelong obsession with all things Edison.

Best Places to Eat

➡ 88 (p126)

➡ Byoldang Makguksu (p122)

➡ Todam Sundubu (p137)

Best Places to Stay

➡ House Hostel (p125)

➡ Kensington Stars Hotel (p133)

➡ Chuncheon Tourist Hotel (p122)

➡ Haslla Museum Hotel (p139)

When to Go

Chuncheon

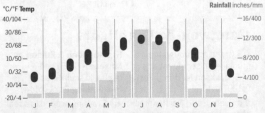

Jan–Mar This is the best time to hit the ski slopes at Yongpyong and Alpensia.

Jun–mid-Aug Head to Gyeongpo from mid-July to enjoy beach season.

Oct–Nov Feast your eyes on the autumn colours at Seoraksan National Park.

History

Gangwon-do is the southern half of a province that once straddled the border (the North Korean half is romanised as Kangwon-do). Some areas north of the 38th parallel belonged to North Korea from 1945 till the end of the Korean War, and it's not uncommon to come across families with relatives in North Korea.

During the war this province saw many fierce battles for strategic mountaintops. Subsequently its rich natural resources, such as coal and timber, were industrialised, spurring the development of road and rail links. When many coal mines closed in

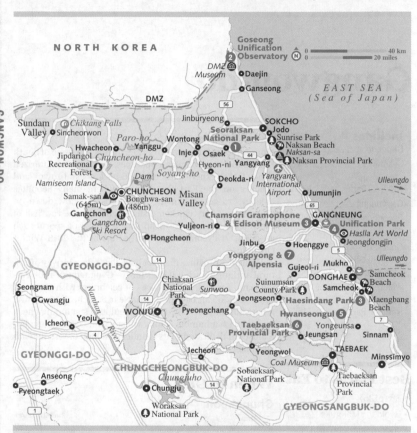

Gangwon-do Highlights

❶ Climbing through the stunning, misty mountains of **Seoraksan National Park** (p129).

❷ Peering into North Korea at **Goseong Unification Observatory** (p127), the northernmost point of the DMZ.

❸ Getting your fill of quirky at the **Chamsori**

Gramophone & Edison Museum (p135) and of phallic sculptures at **Haesindang Park** (p144).

❹ Crawling around in a real North Korean submarine at the **Unification Park** (p138).

❺ Marvelling at the limestone wonders of cathedral-like cave **Hwanseongul** (p144).

❻ Making a pilgrimage to the mountaintop altar to Dangun in **Taebaeksan Provincial Park** (p144).

❼ Taking the kids skiing at the 2018 Winter Olympic venues in Pyeongchang's **Yongpyong** (p140) and **Alpensia** (p139) ski resorts.

the 1990s, the province had to create alternative employment opportunities, such as tourism.

ⓘ Getting There & Away

AIR

In some years, not a single flight took off from the derided **Yangyang International Airport** (www.airport.co.kr/yangyangeng/index.do) along the coast south of Sokcho. However, a surge in visitors from across China began in 2013, and **Jin Air** (www.jinair.com) plans flights to and from 23 Chinese cities in 2016. In mid-2015, Yangyang was also designated a nonvisa transfer airport, seeing another spike in Chinese visitors who can stay without a visa for 120 hours.

BUS

Because of their frequency and wide coverage, buses are your best way in and out of Gangwon-do in all areas except the Chuncheon region, which has good rail links to Seoul. From the southeast coast, it's best to bus to cities such as Busan rather than go by train, which may require several transfers.

TRAIN

Korail (www.letskorail.com) only covers the western and southern areas of Gangwon-do, with links to Chuncheon, Gangneung, Wonju, Taebaek and several other towns. Services may be infrequent and require transfers depending on your destination.

ⓘ Getting Around

Bus routes are excellent, while train lines cover only the southeast of the province and, in the west, Chuncheon and Gangchon. You can rent a car in cities such as Chuncheon, Sokcho and Gangneung; highways are excellent, though tolls and speed cameras are frequent. **Kumho Rent A Car** (www.ktkumhorent.com) is a relatively pricey rental agency but will serve foreign travellers with international licences.

Chuncheon 춘천

 033 / POP 275,000

While it's surrounded by gorgeous mountains, the charms of Gangwon-do's capital are mostly artificial: shimmering lakes created by dams, the fiery chicken dish *dakgalbi,* and well-loved (if schmaltzy) settings for the enormously popular TV drama *Winter Sonata*. Still, it's a good base for outdoor activities and its proximity to Seoul makes it a popular weekend getaway. With several universities here, Chuncheon is also shaking off some of that small-town feel with a burgeoning shopping and nightlife scene, and a Legoland theme park drawing visitors from 2017. In late May it hosts the very popular **Chuncheon International Mime Festival** (www.mimefestival.com; ⊙ late May), which is a raucous collection of street performances and even water fights.

◉ Sights

Uiam-ho LAKE
(의암호; bicycle rental per hr/day ₩3000/15,000, ID required; ⊙ bicycle rental 9am-7pm) A flat bicycle path skirts the peddle-boat filled lake from Ethiopia Café (next to a **Sculpture Park** of bizarre statues) round to the **Korean War Memorial**, the **Soyang-gang Maiden** statue and beyond. The memorial is dedicated to a Korean War battle, when outnumbered South Korean defenders at Chuncheon held back the invading North Koreans.

GANGWON-DO CHUNCHEON

WORTH A TRIP

ISLAND OF TREES

Chuncheon is known for the filming of popular TV drama *Winter Sonata,* and part of the series was set on **Namiseom Island** (남이섬; www.namisum.com), in an artificial lake southwest of Chuncheon. It's home to rows of majestic redwoods, ginkgos and pines, making it ideal for strolling. The island is also home to roaming deer, ostriches and various waterfowl, and hosts rotating art and photography exhibits. It's a touristy park with a zip wire (₩38,000 with island entry), electric triway (₩18,000 per hour) and plenty of *Sonata* kitsch – it calls itself the Naminara Republic and visitors need 'visa' tickets (foreigners ₩8000, kids under three are free), which include a return ferry trip (7.30am to 9.40pm) – but it's a fine spot for a breath of fresh air. To get there, hop on a train from Chuncheon to Gapyeong (₩3000, 17 minutes, hourly) and then walk 1.6km (25 minutes) or bus it (₩1300, three minutes) to Gapyeong Wharf.

The easy route makes a particularly attractive ride just before sunset.

There's **bicycle rental** (per hr/day ₩3000/10,000, ID required; ⊙9am-7pm) from a stall opposite the Ethiopia Café, or from a **bike store** (per 1hr/2hr/day ₩3000/5000/10,000; ⊙9am-7pm) behind the restaurants at Chuncheon station, where you can also buy clear cycling-route maps.

🛏 Sleeping

★ Chuncheon
Tourist Hotel   BUSINESS HOTEL ₩₩
(춘천관광호텔; ☎033 257 1900; www.hotelchuncheon.com; 30-1 Nagwon-dong; d/tw/ste from ₩77,000/88,000/110,000; ❋@🤶) This friendly hotel stands out for its central location steps away from the Myeong-dong shopping district (yes, the same name as the one in Seoul), its 43in flat-screen TVs and comfy beds, large spiffy rooms, and especially Mr Tony, its gregarious English-speaking manager.

There's a Chinese restaurant on the premises and breakfast is available for ₩10,000. It's about a two-minute taxi ride to Chuncheon station or 10 minutes from the Express Bus Terminal.

Sejong Hotel Chuncheon   HOTEL ₩₩
(춘천 세종 호텔; ☎033 252 1191; www.chunchonsejong.co.kr; d/tw from ₩133,100, ondol ste ₩175,450; ❋❋@❋) Nestled on the slope of Bongui-san, this hotel offers unrivalled views of Chuncheon and the surrounding countryside. Rooms have a warm glow, with all the mod cons, and some ground-floor rooms have a patio.

Grand Motel   MOTEL ₩₩
(그랜드모텔; ☎033 243 5022; Okcheon-dong 39-6; r ₩40,000; P❋@🤶) This motel run by a kind and helpful family stands out from the surrounding love motels for comfortable, good-sized rooms without any tackiness. There's a free pick-up service

from the train station, and the family can also provide information for sightseeing in Chuncheon and nearby. Rates rise by 25% on Friday and Saturday.

🍴 Eating

Chuncheon's gastronomical pride and joy is spicy *dakgalbi* (닭갈비) chicken pieces, *tteok* (rice cakes) and vegetables cooked with spicy chilli paste on a sizzling hot iron plate in the middle of the table. Off the downtown Myeong-dong shopping area, Dakgalbi Geori (닭갈비 거리; Dakgalbi St) is a lively street with more than 20 restaurants (meals around ₩10,000) offering such fare. Most places will only serve *dakgalbi* to at least two diners, and a serving for two is often enough to feed three.

Jangwon Myeongga   KOREAN ₩
(장원명가; ☎033 254 6388; Dakgalbi Geori; dakgalbi ₩10,000; ⊙10am-midnight) A tiny place where you sit on the floor to eat platters of *dakgalbi* with big, chicken flavour. Half way down Dakgalbi Geori on the east side.

Byoldang Makguksu   NOODLES ₩₩
(별당막국수; ☎033 254 9603; meals ₩5000-35,000) Housed in a 40-year-old building, this atmospheric restaurant serves up delicious *makguksu*, a Gangwon-do speciality. The buckwheat noodles are served cold, garnished with vegies, pork slices and half a hard-boiled egg. Set back from the main road on a side street, the restaurant has a vertical red sign with white lettering and a parking lot out front.

You can have *makguksu* dry or add broth from a kettle, as well as mustard, sugar, vinegar and spicy *gochujang* (red-pepper paste) to taste.

Bistro Tasty   ITALIAN ₩₩
(☎010 9371 8616; meals ₩7000-14,000; ❋🤶) Oodles of space and mismatched-furniture chic make this low-lit restaurant a stylish

BUS DEPARTURES FROM CHUNCHEON

DESTINATION	PRICE (₩)	DURATION	FREQUENCY
Cheongju	14,400	3hr	every 10min
Cheorwon	15,100	3½hr	every 30min
Dong-Seoul	6800	70min	every 10min
Gangneung	11,700	2hr	every 30min
Sokcho	13,400	2hr	every 1-1½hr

date spot for locals, yet it's equally comfortable for solo diners. Set dishes, such as seafood linguine (₩12,000) with bread and a glass of wine, are excellent value.

Drinking

Party-goers can head to the back gate of **Kangwon National University** (Gangwon-dae humun; 강원대 후문) where there are plenty of bars and cafes. Another magnet for

Chuncheon

Chuncheon

◎ Sights
1 Korean War Memorial C1
2 Sculpture Park B3
3 Soyang-gang Maiden C1
4 Uiam-ho B1

🛏 Sleeping
5 Chuncheon Tourist
   Hotel C2
6 Grand Motel D2
7 Sejong Hotel Chuncheon D2

🍽 Eating
8 Bistro Tasty C2
9 Byoldang Makguksu D3
10 Jangwon Myeongga C3

🍸 Drinking & Nightlife
11 Ethiopia Café B3
12 J Cat Cafe D3
13 Jackson Bill C2
14 R Mutt 1917 ....A3

ℹ Information
15 Chuncheon City Hall Department of
   Tourism D2
16 Tourist Information Booth C2
   Tourist Information Office ....(see 19)

ℹ Transport
17 Bicycle Rental C2
18 Bicycle Rental B3
19 Express & Intercity Bus Terminals C4

young people is the cafes of Myeong-dong shopping street.

★ Jackson Bill
BAR

(☑010 2993 7754; 50-6 Joyang-dong) This loveable watering hole between Myeong-dong and the bend of Dakgalbi Geori feels like the sort of place where everyone knows your name. Drawing a mix of expat teachers and Koreans, veteran bartender and owner Mr Oh has 8000 vinyl records and takes requests; he'll dig out oldies from the '70s and '80s if you like.

Look for the orange sign at street level and head up to the bar on the 2nd floor.

Hard Rock
BAR

(☑033 243 0516; 628-12 Hyoja-Samdong) There are cocktails and an impressive imported beer list including Guinness on tap and North Korea's Taedonggang. Hard Rock is on the main strip of bars running parallel to the main road near the back gate of Kangwon National University.

J Cat Cafe
CAFE

(http://cafe.naver.com/gwcat; smoothies ₩4500; ☉12.30-9.30pm) A dozen cats mostly to yourself to admire, take selfies with and tease with toys. You can't pet the kitties, but you can get good smoothies and tea, which are your ticket in. Look for the cat banner on the street with Tommy Hilfiger on the corner and head to the 2nd floor.

Ethiopia Café

(이디오피아; ☉10am-9pm) Ethiopia Café is the main establishment at the lakefront, near the Memorial Hall for Ethiopian Veterans of the Korean War with its triple-pointed roof.

R Mutt 1917
CAFE

(☑033 254 1917; www.artncompany.kr; ☉10am-11pm) Part of the Art n Company gallery, this stylish hillside cafe dedicated to Marcel Duchamp commands lovely views of Uiam-ho from its patio. Rotating painting and sculpture exhibitions are held here. It's in the MBC broadcasting building; from downtown, take a taxi (about ₩4000) since the closest bus stop is down the hill.

🛍 Shopping

Chuncheon's main shopping area is the Myeongdong-gil pedestrian lane, while a

ℹ LEGOLAND ON JUNGDO

Directly across from Chuncheon on Uiam-ho (Uiam Lake), the little island of Jungdo was once an outdoor-activity playground but closed in 2014. The big-name thrill as of 2017 will be a Legoland theme park, the largest Legoland in the world, with a hotel, condos and a water park.

dozen outdoor-supplies stores line the south side of Geumgang-no. There's an extensive underground arcade with mostly clothing boutiques running under Myeongdong-gil and Geumgang-no.

ℹ Information

The best place for tourist information for the region is the **Chuncheon City Hall Department of Tourism**. There is also a basic **tourist information office** (☑033 250 3896) at the bus terminal, and a **tourist information booth** (☑033 250 4312) outside Chuncheon station, both have maps in English, but staff only speak Korean.

ℹ Getting There & Away

BUS

The **Express & Intercity Bus Terminals** are beside each other. Departures from the latter include Gwangju (₩24,500, five hours, hourly); while buses leave either terminal for Daegu (₩18,300, four hours, hourly). A short taxi ride takes you downtown; the highway is unpleasant to walk along.

TRAIN

ITX trains run on the Gyeongchun line from Seoul's Cheongnyangni train station (₩6000, one hour, hourly) and Yongsan station (₩6900, 80 minutes, hourly) to Chuncheon station, also stopping at Namchuncheon in Chuncheon, which is a little further to downtown Myeongdong-gil. From either station it's a quick taxi ride to downtown Chuncheon, though it is an easy walk from Chuncheon station.

Seoul's Gyeongchun metro line also runs trains from Sangbong to Namchuncheon and Chuncheon stations (₩2850, one hour, 15 minutes), taking in scenic mountain views.

ℹ Getting Around

Most short taxi rides around Chuncheon cost about ₩5000. The local train between Chuncheon and Namchuncheon stations is ₩1150.

Sokcho

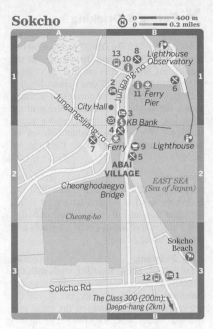

GANGWON-DO SAMAK-SAN

Samak-san   삼악산

The highest mountain near Chuncheon, **Samak-san** (📞 ticket office 033 262 2215; adult/youth/child ₩1600/1000/600; ⏲ sunrise-sunset) offers incredible views of the town and surrounding lakes. The hike up to the peak (645m) can be strenuous and takes at least two hours, passing pretty waterfalls near the base and several temples.

To get to the ticket office, take bus 3, 5, 50 or 50-1 (₩1300, 15 minutes) heading south along Jungang-no in Chuncheon. Get off after about 10km, when you see the green road sign saying 'Seoul 79km'.

Sokcho   속초

📞 033 / POP 100,000

Despite its proximity to Seoraksan National Park, **Sokcho** (http://sokcho.gangwon.kr) is more of a fishing town than a tourist town. The main commercial activity – and its attendant aromas – are clustered along the waterfront. For most domestic tourists the main draw is the chance to sup on fresh raw fish with the tang of salt in the air. Abai Shikdang has been particularly attractive to visitors since its vintage restaurants appeared

in the K-Drama *Autumn in My Heart*. The beaches also get crowded on New Year's Eve when people gather to watch the first sunrise of the year.

Sokcho is only about 60km from the border and was part of North Korea from 1945 to the end of the Korean War. Most of the coastline is lined with barbed wire. At night, remember that lights in the water are to attract squid; lights on the beaches are to detect infiltrators.

There are small **tourist information booths** (in English 📞 1330; 9am-6pm, closed Jan) outside the express and intercity bus terminals and the ferry pier (9am to 4pm). English-speaking staff alternate between them on different days.

🛏 Sleeping

In July and August room rates can double or triple. You can camp on the beach in these months too (₩4000 to ₩8000 per night, shower ₩2000, lockers ₩2000 to ₩4000). A cluster of motels are around the lighthouse area.

★ **House Hostel**   HOSTEL ₩
(더하우스 호스텔; 📞 033 633 3477; www.thehouse-hostel.com; dm/s/d ₩18,000/23,000/35,000, Jul & Aug dm/s/d ₩30,000/40,000/60,000; ❄@🛜) Within a five-minute walk of the intercity bus terminal, this is

everything good budget accommodation should be. It combines the niceties of Korean motel rooms – water dispenser, minifridge and basic toiletries – with free amenities such as bikes, laundry and breakfast (cereal, bread and coffee). The quirky common lounge and charming, light-filled breakfast room are great for meeting travellers.

The English-speaking young owner sits down with all guests for a thorough and excellent overview of the area with a map.

James BLuE Hostel
HOSTEL ₩

(☑ 033 637 2789; www.hostel-jamesblue.com; 466-36 Dongmyeong-dong, off Jungang-no; dm/r ₩20,000/40,000; ❄✳@🖤) This is a hostel all grown up. Rooms are clean and common areas close at night for proper rest for all. Bonuses include heated flooring, strong showers, reliable wi-fi and a helpful English-speaking owner. Buses to Seorak-san are nearby, though early risers note: breakfast starts at 8am. Rates increase 25% Friday and Saturday, and 50% July to August and October.

Class 300
BUSINESS HOTEL ₩₩

(더클래스300; ☑ 033 630 9000; www.theclass300.com; 1288-22 Joyang-dong; d Sun-Thu ₩95,000, d Fri & Sat ₩140,000; ✳@🖤) Although far from central Sokcho, the Class 300 is one of the classier joints in town, with stylish decor (though a tad worn), relatively soft beds and English-speaking staff. There's a breakfast buffet on the 15th floor with good views of the city and beach.

Good Morning Family Hotel
HOTEL ₩₩

(굿모닝가족호텔; ☑ 033 637 9900; Sokcho Rd; r ₩60,000; ✳@) This spiffy nine-storey hotel is one of the nicest near the beach. Rooms have contemporary dark-wood floors, tasteful decor and floor-to-ceiling windows to take advantage of the view. Rates rise by ₩20,000 on Saturday.

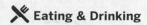 Eating & Drinking

88
SEAFOOD ₩₩

(88생선구이; ☑ 033 633 8892; barbecue per person ₩10,000; ⏱4-8.30pm) On a corner on the waterfront, 88 just does delicious fish barbecue at your table. Staff don't speak English (Mandarin, yes) but you needn't say a thing. Plonk down and they handle the grilling, checking and dishing up of tender squid, mackerel, flounder and other fish served with rice and kimchi. Look for the large '88' signs.

Wangsibri
BARBECUE ₩₩

(왕십리; ☑ 033 636 7849; meals ₩10,000; ⏱3pm-midnight) If seafood isn't your thing, fill up at this no-frills all-you-can-eat barbecue joint, where locals perch on stools and feast till closing time.

Abai Shikdang
SEAFOOD ₩₩

(아바이식당; ☑ 033 635 5310; meals ₩10,000-30,000) A fine place to try squid *sundae* (sausage) in Abai, a collection of vintage seafood restaurants between the canal and the sea, made famous by the K-Drama *Autumn in My Heart*. To get there, take the (also famous) old-fashioned ferry (a floating platform attached to a hand-pulled cable; ₩200) across the harbour and walk under the elevated-bridge road on the other side.

Cafe Nadoo
CAFE

(☑ 033 635 9773; Abaimeul-gil 24; drinks ₩4000; ⏱10am-9pm; 🖤) In the old-timey Abai district, this chic spot hewn from raw concrete serves coffee, tea and lemonade.

ℹ Getting There & Away

AIR

Yangyang International Airport (p121) is a 120-hour, visa-free airport for the Chinese and has flights with Jin Air (p121) that connect to 23 cities in China, such as Harbin and Dalian.

BUS DEPARTURES FROM SOKCHO

DESTINATION	PRICE (₩)	DURATION (HR)	FREQUENCY
Busan	41,800	7½	11 daily
Chuncheon	13,400	2	every 1-1½hr
Daegu	25,300	3½	5 daily
Dong-Seoul	17,300	3½	hourly
Gangneung	6300	1	every 20min

SOKCHO'S SEAFOOD DELIGHTS

Seafood is what Sokcho does best and it is at its freshest and most fragrant at the waterfront market stalls where you can pick your tasty victim from the tanks.

The mainstay of the local cuisine is *modeumhoe* (모듬회; assorted raw fish), served with *banchan* (side dishes), *ssam* (vegetable leaves) and *ganjang* (soy sauce) with wasabi, and spicy soup.

A large platter of *modeumhoe* costs ₩30,000 to ₩100,000. Order from the tanks, or tell your hosts your budget and let them assemble a meal for you. Don't forget the *soju* (local vodka).

Another local speciality is squid *sundae* (sausage). *Sundae* is usually made with a pork casing, but here with *ojingo sundae*, squid is stuffed with minced noodles, tofu, onion, carrot, seaweed and seasoning, then sliced and fried in egg.

Daepo-hang (대포항; Daepo-dong) At the southern harbour of Daepo-hang you can poke around seafood market stalls or bump elbows with the locals at casual eateries where the proprietor will kill, slice and serve your meal within minutes of scooping it live out of the tank. Alternatively partake of a more civilised (though not necessarily quiet) meal at a seafood restaurant.

Daepo-hang is the largest (and marginally priciest) seafood market in Sokcho. It is to the south, on the way to Nak-san and Seorak-san, making it popular for pre- or post-climbing. Take bus 1, 1-1, 7, 7-1, 9 or 9-1 (₩1200, 10 minutes) heading south and get off at the giant parking lot for the harbour.

Jungang-sijang (중앙시장; Jungangsijang-ro; ☉10am-10pm) The basement of this fish market has plentiful indoor casual restaurants with tanks of (soon to be) seafood. Most places are perched away from the constantly wet floor.

Dongmyeong-hang Sokcho's northern harbour provides the seafood market experience in a proper building, with a communal eating hall upstairs. You can also take away your meal to eat on the breakwater.

BUS

Buses leave Sokcho **Express Bus Terminal** for Seoul Gangnam (₩18,100, 2½ hours, every 30 minutes). Bus departures for Busan, Chuncheon, Daegu, Dong-Seoul and Gangneung leave from Sokcho **Intercity Bus Terminal**.

Getting Around

Many local buses (1, 1-1, 7, 7-1, 9 and 9-1) connect the intercity bus terminal, via the town's main street Jungang-no, to the express bus terminal and Daepo-hang. Buses 7 and 7-1 go to the Seoraksan area and national-park entrance, while buses 9 and 9-1 link Sokcho with Nak-san and Yangyang.

Around Sokcho

👁 Sights

Goseong Unification
Observatory Building   HISTORIC BUILDING
(📞033 682 0088; adult/child ₩3000/1500, parking ₩3000; ☉9am-4pm, to 5.30pm 15 Jul–20 Aug) While this area was part of North Korea

from 1945–53, today this building is the closest most South Koreans can get to glimpsing that world. There are binoculars (₩500 for two minutes) installed on the viewing deck, and inside the observatory is a large map labelled (in Korean only) with mountain names and the locations of military installations (red text for North Korea, white text for South Korea). Kiosks here sell liquor, cash, postage stamps and other souvenirs from North Korea.

On a clear day, you can get a good view of Kumgang-san, about 20km to the west. The North-bound highway and railroad fell quiet after South Korea suspended Kumgang-san tours in July 2008, when a South Korean tourist was shot by North Korea.

Despite the solemnity of the place, the parking lot is cluttered with souvenir shops and restaurants. On the other side of the lot is the Korean War Exhibition Hall, which provides something of a primer on the war.

DMZ Museum   MUSEUM
(DMZ박물관; 📞033 680 8463; www.dmzmuseum.com; adult/child ₩2000/1000; ☉9am-5.30pm

GET YOUR ADRENALINE GOING

With rushing rivers, rugged mountains and fairly unspoiled scenery, Gangwon-do's northwest has become a hotbed for kayaking, canoeing and rafting trips from mid-April to October. Trips from **Cheorwon** (철원; www.cwg.go.kr/site/english) make forays onto the Hantan-gang (*gang* means river) in the Sundam Valley, while those from **Inje** (인제; www.inje.go.kr) head to the Naerincheon river. Neither course is extremely difficult unless monsoon rains whip them up; occasional drought can leave water levels very low.

Kayaking and rafting trips cost ₩35,000 (three hours) to ₩60,000 (seven hours) – add ₩5000 in the peak season – including instruction, and most companies offer pickup from Seoul. Companies based in Cheorwon include **Hanleisure** (☑ 033 455 0557; www.hanleisure.com) and **Sundam Leisure** (☑ 033 452 3034; www.leports114.com). In Inje, try **X-Game** (☑ 033 462 5217; www.injejump.co.kr), which also offers bungee jumping (₩40,000 to 60,000).

Intercity buses from Dong-Seoul serve Sincheorwon (₩8700, two hours, every 25 minutes) and Inje (₩12,200, two hours, every 30 minutes).

Mar-Oct, to 5pm Nov-Feb) This large museum is inside the Tongil Security Park, on the left side of the road as you approach the Goseong Unification Observatory (p127). It has a surprising amount of English in its narration of the history of the DMZ, as well as exhibits such as US POW letters and extensive photos.

From downtown Sokcho or the bus stop right outside the intercity bus terminal, catch bus 1 or 1-1 (₩5020, 1½ hours, 44km, every 15 minutes) headed north, but ask if they go to the DMZ as not all do. Get off at Machajin (마차진; a round-trip taxi from Sokcho might cost ₩70,000) and walk about 10 minutes up to the Tongil Security Park (통일안보공원). Here you present identification and purchase your admission ticket. If you don't have your own vehicle, the staff might be able to help you hitch a ride, but don't count on it. It's 10km to the observatory; pedestrians, bicycles and motorbikes are not allowed.

Naksan Provincial Park   PARK
(☑ 033 670 2518; http://eng.yangyang.go.kr) **FREE** This small coastal park south of Sokcho is home to the temple **Naksan-sa** (낙산사; ☑ 033 672 2448; adult/youth/child ₩3000/1500/1000; ⏰ 5am-7pm), established in AD 671 and enjoying glorious sea views all around. A majestic 15m-tall statue of the Goddess of Mercy, Gwaneum, presides over the East Sea from a promontory. Notably it has never fallen victim to the forest fires that have periodically razed the temple buildings (most recently in 2005).

Most of the temple complex has been stoutly rebuilt since the last fire and the surrounding pine forest is recovering as well. Immediately below the statue is a small shrine, with a window strategically constructed so that a kneeling devotee can look up and gaze upon the statue's face. Further down a side path is a pavilion with a glass-covered hole through which you can see the sea cave below. From 11.30am to 1.30pm, complimentary vegetarian noodle soup is served at the temple cafeteria.

Below the temple is **Naksan Beach** (낙산해수욕장), considered one of the best on the east coast and phenomenally busy in summer, when accommodation prices can triple. At other times it's a pleasant place to stay if you want to avoid Sokcho's fishing-town feel.

🛏 Sleeping

The Suites Hotel Naksan   HOTEL ₩₩
(☑ 033 670 1100; http://naksan.suites.co.kr/eng; 440-5 Bunji, Josan-ri; r from ₩95,000; ✲✳ @ 🛈) That beach is glistening right outside your balcony, or ascend to the roof terrace for even more spectacular views from a sun lounger. Rooms are spacious, plush and bright in modern, muted colours. The karaoke lounge, free laundry and table tennis are family-friendly additions.

Euisangdae Condotel   MOTEL ₩₩
(의상대콘도텔; ☑ 033 672 3201; r ₩40,000-75,000; ✳ @ 🛈) It doesn't look like much from the outside, but rooms are clean and sharp and enjoy great views right on the beachfront. They also come with kitchenettes and desktop computers.

❶ Getting There & Away

Bus 9 and 9-1 (₩1500, 15 minutes, every 15 minutes) can be picked up outside either of Sokcho's bus terminals, heading in the direction of Yangyang. Get off at Naksan Beach. You can approach Naksan-sa via the beach, or walk backwards along the highway and follow the signs to approach it from the landward side.

Seoraksan National Park
설악산 국립공원
☑ 033

This **park** (☑ 033 636 7700; http://english.knps. or.kr; adult/child ₩3500/500; ☉ sunrise-sunset) is one of the most beautiful and iconic on the entire Korean Peninsula. Designated by Unesco as a Biosphere Protection site, it boasts oddly shaped rock formations, dense forests, abundant wildlife, hot springs and ancient Shilla-era temples. Seorak-san (Snowy Crags Mountain) is the third-highest mountain in South Korea, with its highest peak, Daecheong-bong, standing at 1708m. Set against this landscape are two stately temples, **Sinheung-sa** and **Baekdam-sa**.

Peak season is July and August, while in mid-October visitors flock to see the changing colours of the autumn leaves – best appreciated over a bottle of *meoruju* (wild fruit wine). Given the park's size (nearly 400,000 sq km), sections are sometimes closed for restoration or preservation, or to prevent wildfires. Check with the **Visitor Centre** (☑ 033 636 7700; ☉ 10am-5pm Tue-Sun, closed Mon) before you head out.

The park is divided into three sections, unconnected by road: Outer Seorak is the most accessible and popular area, nearest to Sokcho and the sea. Seorak-dong has hotels, motels, *minbak* (private homes with rooms for rent), restaurants, bars, *noraebang* (karaoke rooms) and general stores; Inner Seorak covers the western end of the park and is the least commercialised; Southern Seorak is the name given to the Osaek

---

A DIFFERENT SIDE TO THE DMZ

Say 'DMZ' (Demilitarized Zone) and most people think of Panmunjeom. But the little-touristed town of **Cheorwon** (철원; www.cwg.go.kr) presents a more haunting version. Under North Korea's control from 1945, it saw fierce fighting during the Korean War and was built anew after the war, as part of South Korea. But even today it abounds with army trucks and military checkpoints. It's one way to see the DMZ without paying an exorbitant fee and being hustled onto coaches.

Most of the war sites lie within the Civilian Control Zone that spans 20km from the border, so visitors must present identification and register with the **Hantan-gang Tourism Office** (한탄강관광지 관리사무소; ☑ 033 450 5558) at the Iron Triangle Memorial Hall (철의 삼각 전적관) for an official 2½-hour **tour** (adult/youth/child without transport ₩4000/3000/2000; ☉ 9.30am, 10.30am, 1pm & 2.30pm or 2pm in winter, closed Tue). You must have your own vehicle or hitch a ride. There's usually a tour shuttle bus (₩8000) available on weekends. If not, a three-hour taxi ride to cover the sights would be about ₩100,000. Bring your passport.

The first stop is the **Second Tunnel**, dug by North Korea in 1975. About 1km of it lies in South Korea and it's large enough for purportedly 16,000 soldiers to stream through per hour. A 150m staircase leads down to the tunnel, then it's a well-lit, albeit damp, 500m stretch to where the tunnel was discovered, just 300m from the border.

The next stop is the **Cheorwon Peace Observatory**, 1km from the DMZ. There are coin-operated binoculars for gazing at North Korea and its 'propaganda village' Seonjeon. A short drive down the road is the petite **Woljeong-ri Station**, left as a memorial to the railway line between Seoul and Wonsan, and housing the battered, twisted remains of a bombed train.

After passing a few battle-scarred buildings, the tour ends at the former Labor Party (that is, Communist Party) HQ. The surviving facade is evocative, but its associations are less than pleasant: when Cheorwon was part of North Korea, many civilians were imprisoned and tortured here.

Buses from Dong-Seoul run to Sincheorwon (₩8700, two hours, every 25 minutes), where a taxi will get you to the Iron Triangle Memorial Hall in about 15 minutes.

Seoraksan National Park

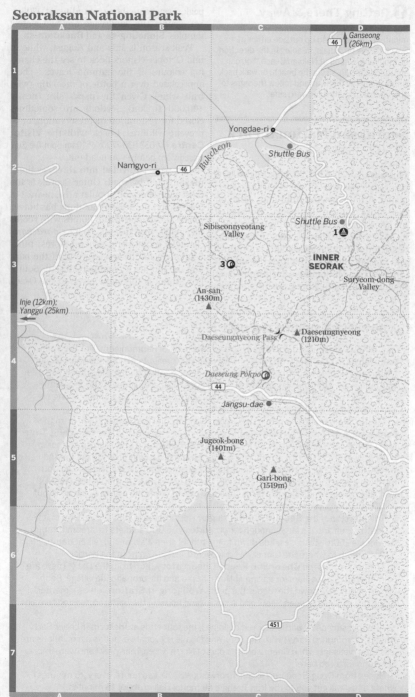

Ganseong
(26km)

Yongdae-ri

Shuttle Bus

Namgyo-ri

Bukcheon

Sibiseonnyeotang
Valley

Shuttle Bus

1

INNER
SEORAK

3

Suryeom-dong
Valley

An-san
(1430m)

Inje (12km);
Yanggu (25km)

Daeseungnyeong Pass

Daeseungnyeong
(1210m)

Daeseung Pokpo

Jangsu-dae

Jugeok-bong
(1401m)

Gari-bong
(1519m)

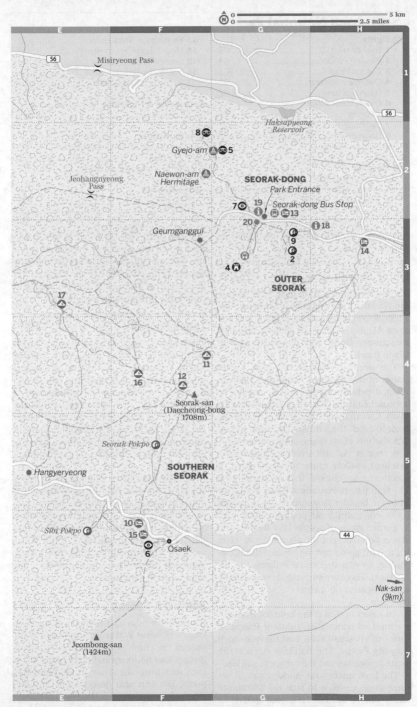

N
0 ———— 5 km
0 ———— 2.5 miles

56 Misiryeong Pass

Haksapyeong Reservoir

56

8

Gyejo-am 5

Naewon-am Hermitage

Jeohangnyeong Pass

SEORAK-DONG
Park Entrance

7 19 Seorak-dong Bus Stop
20 13
18

Geumganggul

9
2

14

4

OUTER SEORAK

17

11

16 12

Seorak-san
(Daecheong-bong
1708m)

Seorak Pokpo

SOUTHERN SEORAK

Hangyeryeong

Sibi Pokpo 10
15
6 Osaek

44

Nak-san
(9km)

Jeombong-san
(1424m)

Seoraksan National Park

(Five Colours) area, which is famous for its mineral springs.

Outer Seorak   외설악

Within 20 minutes' walk inside the Seoraksan National Park entrance is **Sinheung-sa**, a temple complex that has stood on this site since AD 652. From here, paths diverge for **Daecheong-bong** and the rocky face of **Ulsan Bawi**.

The ascent to Daecheong-bong is a solid tramp of five to seven hours and 10km to 14km, depending on the route. It can also be approached from Osaek in Southern Seorak. Many Korean hikers time their arrival at the peak to catch the sunrise. There are mountain shelters of varying quality en route.

A shorter but still strenuous hike is the two-hour, 4.3km route to Ulsan Bawi, a spectacular granite cliff that stands at 873m. The trail passes **Heundeul Bawi**, a massive 16-tonne boulder balanced on the edge of a rocky ledge, which can be rocked to and fro by a small group of people. It's a lookout and also a popular spot for photos. From here, it's a hard-going but rewarding climb (including an 808-step metal staircase) to Ulsan Bawi. There are stupendous views all the way to Sokcho on a clear day – well worth the effort.

An easier option is the hour-long hike to a couple of waterfalls: **Yukdam Pokpo**, a series of six small falls, and the 40m-high **Biryong Pokpo**. The 2km hike starts at the stone bridge beyond the cable-car station.

The least taxing and quickest way to get some good views is to ride the 30-minute **cable car** (☑ 033 636 7362; adult/child return ₩10,000/7000; ⊙ 8.30am-5pm, to 6pm in summer), which drops you a 20-minute walk from the remains of the fortress **Gwongeum-seong**, believed to date to the 13th century. The cable car runs every 20 minutes, more frequently during peak season.

Inner Seorak   내설악

The relatively uncrowded river valleys in the northwestern section of the park are well worth exploring. From the park entrance near Yongdae-ri, take a shuttle bus or walk 6.5km to the serene temple of **Baekdam-sa** (☑ 033 462 2554; ⊙ sunrise-sunset), which faces east and is best appreciated in the morning. From there, you can ramble along the Suryeom-dong Valley for an hour or two, or even connect to Outer Seorak (seven hours, 14km).

Alternatively, from Namgyo-ri there's a splendid 2½-hour hike in the Sibiseonnyeotang Valley to **Dumun Pokpo**. After another two hours uphill you can turn right for a 30-minute hike up **An-san** (1430m) or turn left for **Daeseungnyeong** (1210m), which takes the same amount of time. You can also approach An-san from the south, via a hiking trail from Jangsu-dae.

Southern Seorak   남설악

It's easier to hike up Daecheong-bong from **Osaek Mineral Water Spring** in the south, though the climb is still steep and difficult. Budget four hours up and three hours down, then soak away the strain in the hot-spring pools. You can also descend on the other side to Seorak-dong (six hours).

🛏 Sleeping

The widest range of accommodation is at Seorak-dong. Accommodation rates can double in July and August, and also tend to inflate in October. At other times, the upmarket hotels offer significant discounts. Basic camping facilities (₩3500 to ₩7000) are available in Seorak-dong, Jangsu-dae and Osaek.

There are four mountain **shelters** (₩7000 to ₩8000) along the Outer Seorak routes to Daecheong-bong – at Jungcheong, Yangpok, Huiungak and **Socheong**. Reservations are accepted only for **Jungcheong** (☑ 033 672 1708; http://english.knps.or.kr; Dec-Apr ₩7000, May-Nov ₩8000) and **Huiungak** (☑ 033 672 1708; http://english.knps.or.kr; Dec-Apr ₩7000, May-Nov ₩8000), which is just 100m below the peak. **Suryeom-dong Shelter** (☑ 033 462 2576) is located on the trail from Baekdam-sa.

Check for shelter closures at http://english.knps.or.kr/experience/shelters/default.aspx.

🛏 Seorak-dong 설악동

Mount Sorak Youth Hostel HOSTEL ₩
(설악산 유스호스텔; ☑ 033 636 7116; www.sorakyhostel.com; dm/f ₩25,000/50,000, Fri & Sat ₩30,000/75,000; ❋ @) The cheapest option for solo travellers, but you'll have to bus it to the park entrance (₩1200, five minutes, every 10 minutes).

★ Kensington Stars Hotel LUXURY HOTEL ₩₩₩
(켄싱턴호텔; ☑ 033 635 4001; www.kensington.co.kr; d & ondol ₩209,000, tw ₩300,000; ❋ @ 🛜) Just 300m from the park entrance, in the crook of a mountain, is this English oasis – with Edwardian armchairs in the lobby, and red double-decker buses outside. The floors have themes such as movies and sports, and autographed memorabilia abound; check out the Beatles records in the Abbey Road lounge.

🛏 Inner Seorak

The road from Yongdae-ri to the park entrance (1km) is flanked by farmhouses, **minbak** (per room from ₩20,000) and restaurants. It's a good place to spend the night if you'd like to wake up to your own slice of rural Korean idyll.

🛏 Southern Seorak

Seorak Oncheonjang MOTEL ₩
(설악온천장; ☑ 033 672 2645; r ₩30,000; ❋ @ 🛜) This motel has pleasant rooms spread over two neat white buildings, with the lobby in the rear one. The *oncheon* (hot-spring spa; summer and autumn only) is free for guests, as is internet use. Owner Mr Lim can speak some English. Rates rise to ₩40,000 on Friday and Saturday, and go up to ₩70,000 during peak periods.

Green Yard Hotel HOTEL ₩₩
(그린야드호텔; ☑ 033 670 1000; www.greenyardhotel.com; r & ondol from ₩102,000; ❋ @) The only high-end hotel, this mountain chalet–inspired complex has smart rooms with all the creature comforts (oddly wi-fi is only in the lobby). The *oncheon* (guests/nonguests ₩7000/11,000) looks a little industrial from the entrance, but has lovely outdoor bath areas. Rates rise 20% on weekends.

✗ Eating & Drinking

As in many national parks, various restaurants around Seoraksan serve popular fare such as *sanchae* bibimbap (₩9000) and *sanchaejeongsik* (mountain-vegetable banquet dishes; ₩11,000), both of which feature local vegetables.

Seolhyang CAFE
(drinks ₩8000; ⊙ 8am-6.30pm) Inside the park and on the outskirts of Seorak-dong, this charming traditional Korean cafe built with thick logs sits by a bridge leading to the main pavilion of Sinheung-sa temple. It's the perfect spot to refuel with a coffee and a cookie or two.

ⓘ Information

The Seoraksan National Park Visitor Centre (p129) at the entrance to Outer Seorak has some information in English as well as maps. A **tourist information office** (⊙ 9.30am-5.30pm) inside the park entrance has a smaller selection as well as lockers (per hour ₩2000 to ₩3500).

ⓘ Getting There & Away

The access road to Outer Seorak branches off the main coast road at Sunrise Park, halfway between Sokcho and Nak-san. From outside Sokcho's intercity bus terminal, along Jungang-no, or opposite its express bus terminal, catch bus 7 or 7-1

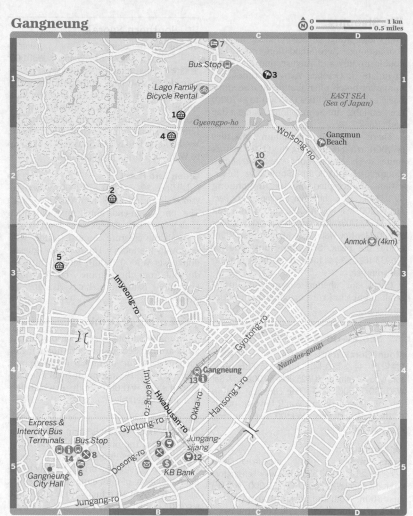

(₩1200, 30 minutes, every 10 minutes), which terminates at the park entrance at Seorak-dong.

Buses from Sokcho's intercity bus terminal run every hour to Osaek (₩4000) and Jangsu-dae (₩5600). From Dong-Seoul, there are also eight buses daily to Osaek (₩19,400). At Osaek, buy your bus ticket (cash only) at the general store about 10m from the bus stop on the highway.

Also from Sokcho's intercity bus terminal, buses bound for Jinburyeong (six daily from 6.30am to 5.50pm) make stops at Yondae-ri (₩6800) and Namgyo-ri (₩7100). From Yongdae-ri, it's a 1km walk to the park entrance. There, you can hike or take a shuttle bus (adult/child one way ₩1800/1000, 15 minutes, every 20

minutes) to Baekdam-sa; it runs from 7am to 5.30pm.

Gangneung   강릉

☑ 033 / POP 200,000

Gangneung is the largest city on the Gangwon-do coast. Its pockets of attractiveness lie towards the sea, particularly near Gyeongpo, while its cultural hotspots – well-preserved Joseon-era buildings and the 400-year-old shamanist Dano Festival (p135) – are matched by quirky modern

Gangneung

attractions, such as a museum lovingly dedicated to Thomas Edison and a North Korean submarine on display in nearby Jeongdongjin. With natty motels and a decent bar scene as well, the town is a good place to linger for a few days if you're looking for an experience that's off the beaten track without being too small-town.

The **tourist information centre** (☑ 033 640 4537; www.gntour.go.kr; ☺ 9am-8pm) is beside the bus terminal, with English-, Mandarin- and Japanese-speaking staff who can book accommodation for you.

There is also a small booth in front of the train station, and another at Gyeongpo Beach. The main shopping area is downtown, in the warren of lanes near Jungang-sijang.

◉ Sights

Chamsori Gramophone
& Edison Museum   MUSEUM
(참소리 축음기 에디슨 과학 박물관; ☑ 033 655 1130; www.edison.kr; adult/youth/child ₩7000/6000/5000; ☺ 9am-5pm; ⊞) This whimsical museum is a sheer delight. It combines the two loves of private collector Son Sung-Mok: gramophones and Thomas Edison. There are hundreds of antique gramophones (or phonographs, as Edison termed them) and music boxes, as well as a colourful collection of Edison's other inventions and related devices, from cameras and kinetoscopes to toys, TVs and typewriters. Some of these items are the only one of their kind.

Though the tour is in Korean only, the guide demonstrates the use of some antique music boxes and other contraptions – good fun for children and anyone interested in 'retro' technology. Take bus 202 for Gyeongpo and get off at the Gyeongpo Beach stop (five minutes after Seongyojang) from where it's a five- to 10-minute walk back.

Ojukheon   HISTORIC BUILDING
(오죽헌; ☑ 033 648 4271; adult/youth/child ₩3000/2000/1000; ☺ 8am-6pm) Revered as the birthplace of the paragon of Korean womanhood, Sin Saimdang (1504–51), and her son, the philosopher and government

GETTING INTO THE SPIRIT

The highlight of Gangneung's calendar is the shamanist **Dano Festival** (Danoje; 단오제), celebrated for one week on the fifth day of the fifth lunar month (usually in June). It's one of the biggest holidays in Korea and has been recognised by Unesco as a 'Masterpiece of the Oral and Intangible Heritage of Humanity'. For foreigners, it's a great opportunity to revel it up Korean-style, while learning about some of the country's oldest spiritual beliefs.

Danoje is the climax of a month-long series of shamanist and Confucian ceremonies for peace, prosperity and bountiful harvests. On the first day there's a lantern parade to welcome a mountain spirit, who unites with his 'wife', another spirit dwelling in Gangneung. During the festival people present their wishes to both, while female shamans perform the *dano gut*, a rite of singing, dancing and sacrifice offering to the spirits to implore their blessings. On the final day the people send the male spirit back to the mountain.

LOCAL KNOWLEDGE

GRAMOPHONES & GIZMOS GALORE

Ask Mr Son Sung-Mok about any item in his **Chamsori Gramophone & Edison Museum** (p135), and he'll tell you a story about it. He has amassed more than 10,000 gramophones, Edison inventions and their technological descendants from around the world, only a fraction of which are on public display.

Mr Son's best story just might be the one about his very first gramophone, a Columbia G241 made in the 1920s and given to him by his parents when he was a boy in Wonsan (in what is today North Korea). When the family fled south during the Korean War, the 12kg phonograph was the only possession he lugged along. It now takes pride of place beside the entrance to the museum shop.

As for Mr Son's favourite story, he'll point at the American coin-slot phonograph on the museum's 2nd floor in the middle of the main gallery; it's tall like a grandfather clock. Dating from the 1900s, it's the only one of its kind left, so when it came up for auction in Argentina, Mr Son was determined to get it. Even falling victim to an armed robbery en route didn't stop him from making it to the auction and putting in a successful bid.

Mr Son's fascination with gramophones extends to the man who invented and patented the phonograph, Thomas Edison. Mr Son notes that Edison didn't do well in school yet was curious enough to learn on his own. Through this museum, Mr Son hopes to inspire Korean children to be likewise curious and interested in many things. He also has plans for a children's museum, a movie museum and perhaps a school to train curators.

Gramophones are still his first love, though, whether he's tinkering with one, savouring its music or looking for new acquisitions. A consummate collector for over 40 years, he declares, 'I will keep collecting till I die'.

official Yi Yulgok (1536–84), this complex contains one of the oldest surviving Joseon-dynasty homes. The sprawling space has the feel of an elegant park, with buildings nestled amid punctiliously maintained gardens, lotus pools and the black-stemmed bamboo groves for which the property is named.

Many of Sin's paintings are on display at Ojukheon, including a delicate folding screen with eight studies of flowers and insects. The building, Eojegak, preserves a children's textbook which Yi authored and hand-wrote, *Gyeokmongyogyeol*.

Sin Saimdang was an accomplished poet and artist, and is traditionally regarded in Korea as a model daughter, wife and mother. Her visage graces the ₩50,000 note – a move that irked some women's groups, who say it reinforces the idea that women should devote themselves to their children at home as Sin did, teaching her son the Confucian classics.

Yi Yulgok, also known by his pen name Yiyi, appears on the ₩5000 note, with Ojukheon on its front and back. Yi won first prize in the state examination for prospective government officials and went on to serve the king. Unfortunately his advice to prepare

against a possible invasion by Japan was ignored – to the kingdom's peril after Yi's death, when the Japanese invaded in 1592.

Ojukheon is 4km from downtown Gangneung. From right outside the bus terminal, take bus 202 (₩1200, 10 minutes, every 30 minutes) and make sure it's the one heading to Gyeongpo (경포). The bus stop outside Ojukheon is well signposted.

Gangneung Seongyojang HISTORIC BUILDING (강릉선교장; ☎033 640 4799; adult/youth/child ₩3000/2000/1000; ◐9am-6.30pm) Dating to the late Joseon dynasty, this national cultural property was for 300 years the home of a *yangban* (aristocratic) family. It was built for a descendant of the brother of King Sejong (the monarch who invented *hangeul*, the Korean phonetic alphabet), and has been restored in keeping with the original floor plan and architectural style. The complex includes residential quarters, a library and a pavilion overlooking a lotus pond.

It's very pretty but somewhat lifeless, like a movie set; in fact, a number of Korean films and TV shows have been shot here. The servants quarters have unfortunately been turned into a gift shop, but you can try your hand at some traditional games outside.

To get here, take bus 202 and get off about five minutes after Ojukheon.

Gyeongpo Beach
BEACH

(경포해수욕장; ☑ tourist info booth 033 640 4537; ⏱ tourist info booth 9am-5pm) The largest beach on the east coast, and the third-busiest in South Korea, has 1.8km of flat, white sand running down to moody, steel-grey waters. It's besieged by visitors during the official season (13 July to 20 August). At other times, the noisy strip of beachside restaurants and motels doesn't detract too much from the charm of the famous wind-twisted pine trees. There is a small **tourist information booth**.

Gyeongpo-ho & Gyeongpodae Pavilion
HISTORIC BUILDING

(경포호 | 경포대) Immediately behind Gyeongpo Beach is Gyeongpo-ho, which attracts local residents looking for a little peace and quiet. There's a 4km bicycle path along the lakeshore, passing traditional pavilions. The most prominent is Gyeongpodae, from which it is poetically said that you can see five moons: the moon itself and its four reflections – in the sea (now obscured by pine trees), in the lake, in your obligatory glass of alcohol and in your own mind.

It hosts a Cherry Blossom Festival in early April. Rent a bike from **Lago Family** (☑ 010 2068 8808; per hr ₩5000; ⏱ 10am-6pm) at the north of the lake next to the bus stop. Gyeongpodae is a short walk from the Chamsori Gramophone & Edison Museum (p135).

🛌 Sleeping

MGM Hotel
HOTEL ₩₩

(MGM 호텔; ☑ 033 644 2559; www.mgmhotel.co.kr; d from ₩77,000, deluxe tw from ₩88,000; ❈ @) North of Gyeongpo-ho but close to the shore, the MGM sure isn't Vegas but it's comfortable enough, with relatively soft beds and all the mod cons (go for the deluxe rooms). There's an on-site spa with large baths, too. Staff can speak a little English. Prices can double in summer and rates rise by ₩11,000 on weekends.

Equus Motel
MOTEL ₩₩

(에쿠스모텔; ☑ 033 643 0114; r ₩40,000; ❈ @) This love motel has sleek rooms that are the best value for money around the bus terminal. Rooms have neat black decor and enormous TVs, and better rooms come with

treadmills and whirlpool baths. No English is spoken here. Rates rise by ₩10,000 on Saturday.

🍴 Eating & Drinking

There are heaps of raw-fish and seafood restaurants along the beach, but Gangneung's prized speciality is *sundubu* (순두부), soft or uncurdled tofu made with sea water in **Chodang**, the 'tofu village'. At its plainest, *sundubu* is served warm in a bowl, with *ganjang* (soy sauce) on the side. It can also be prepared in *jjigae* (순두부찌개; stew) or *jeongol* (순두부전골; casserole).

★ Todam Sundubu
VEGETARIAN ₩

(토담 순두부; ☑ 033 652 0336; meals ₩7000-10,000; ☑) In Chodang, this rustic eatery serves up simmering *sundubu* inside a quaint wooden house with floor seating. Look for the white vertical sign with red lettering beside Heogyun-Heonanseolheon Park (허균·허난설헌 기념공원). To get to Chodang, take bus 206, 207 or 230 (₩1200, 30 minutes) from outside the bus terminal.

Terarosa
ITALIAN ₩

(테라로사; ☑ 033 648 2760; www.terarosa.com; meals ₩6000-10,000; ⏱ 9am-10pm; ❈ 🐾 🍴) If it's good coffee or bread-packed breakfasts you're craving, check out this polished cafe that roasts and brews about 20 varieties of coffee, bakes its own bread and serves sandwiches, pasta, and wraps with chilli con carne. Facing McDonald's on Jungang-ro, take the lane on the left.

Haengun Sikdang
KOREAN ₩

(행운 식당; ☑ 033 643 3334; meals ₩6000-9000) Offers good, simple fare such as *kimchi jjigae* (kimchi stew) or *doenjang jjigae* (soybean-paste stew); if you like squid or octopus, try the stir-fried *ojing-eo bokkeum* (오징어볶음) or *nakji bokkeum* (낙지볶음). Look for the light-brown sign and blue umbrella outside.

Bumpin' Bar
BAR

(☑ 033 644 3574; ⏱ 7pm-1am) This gem, down an alley opposite Terarosa, lives in a ramshackle wooden house with a low ceiling. Park yourself at the beautiful, dark bar, constructed of old pine planks from a Buddhist temple, and make a request from the English-speaking owner's vinyl collection of classic rock.

Rush BAR

(☑ 070 8202 3233; 31-2 Gunghak-dong) This laid-back basement club has a stage with live music every weekend. Its burgers (₩7000) are worth a try if you're craving a break from Korean food. Facing Starbucks on Jungang-ro, take the first lane on the left to near the end.

❶ Getting There & Away

BOAT

Gangneung has a ferry to the island of Ulleungdo. Services depart from the **Anmok Ferry Terminal** (☑ 033 653 8670; one-way/return ₩54,000/108,000) at 8.40am or 9am daily (2½ hours). To get to the terminal, take buses 202 or 303 (₩1300) from the bus terminal or a taxi (₩6000, 15 minutes).

BUS

Gangneung's **Express & Intercity Bus Terminals** share the same building, near the entrance to Hwy 7. Express buses from Gangneung head to Dong-Seoul (₩15,000, 2½ hours, every 40 minutes) and Gangnam (₩21,000, every 20 minutes).

TRAIN

Seven *Mugunghwa* (semiexpress) trains connect Gangneung (₩21,900, six hours) daily with Seoul's Cheongnyangni station via Wonju. There is also a special 'seaside train' to Samcheok.

❶ Getting Around

Buses 202 and 303 (every 25 minutes) connect the bus terminal with the train station. Bus 202 goes directly to Gyeongpo (경포). Bus 202-1 travels between Gyeongpo and downtown (시내) and terminates at Gangneung station.

A useful bus timetable in English is available at tourist information centres.

Around Gangneung

The coast south of Gangneung has a couple of unique sights that merit a day trip if you

have the time. Where else can you get inside a North Korean submarine?

Sights

Unification Park HISTORIC SITE

(통일 공원; ☑ 033 640 4469; adult/youth/child ₩3000/2000/1500; ⊙ 9am-5.30pm Mar-Oct, to 4.30pm Nov-Feb) The park consists of two areas, the main attraction being a seafront display of a warship and North Korean submarine. You can enter both for a fascinating insight into the confined spaces that both North and South Koreans lived in. The distant second area displays military planes and a retired presidential plane set up for photo ops. There is also an underwhelming 'security exhibition hall' and you won't miss much if you skip this area and head to the seafront.

The 35m-long **submarine** was spying on military facilities near Gangneung in 1996 when it ran aground off Jeongdongjin. The commander burnt important documents (the fire-blackened compartment is still visible) and the 26 soldiers made a break for shore, hoping to return to North Korea. It took South Korea 49 days to capture or kill them (except one, who went missing); during the manhunt 17 South Korean civilians and soldiers were killed and 22 injured.

The **warship**, while considerably larger than the submarine, has a less dramatic story: built in America in 1945, it saw action in WWII and the Vietnam War, and was donated to South Korea in 1972. Its interior has been refurbished as an exhibition on Korean naval history with interesting glimpses at sleeping quarters and mess halls.

Unification Park is 4km north of the Jeongdongjin train station along the coastal road. As you exit the train station, turn left and look for the bus stop along the row of restaurants. Take bus 111, 112 or 113 (₩1300, 20 minutes, hourly) from downtown Gangneung and get out right after the warship, at the third stop once you hit the coastal

BUS DEPARTURES FROM GANGNEUNG

DESTINATION	PRICE (₩)	DURATION (HR)	FREQUENCY
Chuncheon	11,700	2	every 40min
Daejeon	17,400	3½	10 daily
Samcheok	5300	1	every 10min
Sokcho	8200	1½	every 20-30min
Wonju	7900	1½	hourly

road. The military planes are at the second stop, an exposed 20-minute walk along the highway.

Haslla Art World ARTS CENTRE
(하슬라아트월드; ☑ 033 644 9419; www.haslla.kr; 33-1 Gangdong-myeon, Jeongdongjin-ri San; adult/child ₩10,000/9000; ⊙ 8.30am-6pm; ⊕) Sitting atop a hill, this park has contemporary Korean sculptures set amid a pleasant 11-hectare garden with winding paths and boardwalks. On a clear day, there are incredible sea views. It's a nice ramble for an hour or so, but the artworks are generally underwhelming, albeit quirky. They include enormous midair stones suspended by cables, as well as cow-dung art by Choi Ok-yeong.

Round up your visit with some traditional Korean tea at the **Sea Café** (a drink is included in the admission price).

The adjacent Haslla Museum Hotel (p139) has five art galleries, with exhibitions on subjects such as *Pinocchio*; they're also open to ticket holders.

The park is 1.5km north of the Jeongdongjin train station. Take bus 11, 112, 113, or 114 (₩1300, five minutes, hourly), and walk up a steep slope to the park entrance.

🛌 Sleeping

⭐**Haslla Museum Hotel** HOTEL **WWW**
(하슬라호텔; ☑ 033 644 9411; www.haslla.kr; d from ₩198,000; ❄ 🛜) This architectural oddity by the Haslla Art World is an oasis of design: beds are shaped like large wooden bowls, rooms are furnished with quirky pieces of art and all have great ocean views. Rates rise 20% on Friday and Saturday and nearly double during peak times in summer.

ℹ Getting There & Away

BUS
Bus 109 (₩1700, 45 minutes, every one to two hours) leaves from the bus stop outside Gangneung's bus terminal for Jeongdongjin, which is located 20km south. Buses 111, 112 and 113 (₩1300, 35 minutes, hourly) leave from downtown Gangneung.

TRAIN
Eleven trains daily connect Jeongdongjin to Gangneung (₩2600, 15 minutes). Jeongdongjin is also a stop on the 'seaside train' that runs between Gangneung and Samcheok.

ℹ Getting Around

Local buses are infrequent; taxis are a better option. A trip between any of the sights costs ₩5000 to ₩8000.

Pyeongchang 평창
☑ 033

Pyeongchang county is the host of the 2018 Winter Olympics. Two main ski resorts in the area, Alpensia (p139) and Yongpyong (p140), will host most of the events. Alpensia has the main Olympic Village, hosting the ski jumping, luge, bobsleigh and cross-country skiing, while Yongpyong, which is one of northeast Asia's better ski resorts, will host the downhill slalom events. The ceremonies will be held in a purpose-built temporary stadium about two kilometres from Alpensia Olympic Village.

The town of **Hoenggye** (횡계) serves as a transit hub for both ski resorts and provides cheaper eating options, a bit of nightlife, and basic accommodation such as **Boutique Olive** (부티크 올리브; ☑ reservations 033 336 3444; 314-1 Hoenggye-ri, Daegwanryeong-myeon; condos from ₩100,000; P ❄ @ 🛜), which has clean, reasonably priced condo rooms.

Alpensia 알펜시아

🏃 Activities

Alpensia Ski Resort SKIING, SNOW SPORTS
(알펜시아리조트 스키장; ☑ 033 339 0000; www.alpensia.co.kr; 325, Solbong-ro; lift tickets per day adult/child ₩68,000/50,000, equipment rental per day adult/child ₩32,000/24,000; ⊕) With just six runs, Alpensia is a small but well-serviced resort and host of the 2018 Winter Olympics. Far less crowded than its neighbour, Yongpyong (p140), Alpensia is a fine place for family skiing and beginners, with one long easy slope, several intermediate runs and an advanced run, as well as an alpine coaster. There's also very scenic night skiing.

The resort village at the bottom of the slope has three hotels (guests get a 30% discount on lift tickets), restaurants and a water park, and nearby is a ski-jump stadium, cross-country and biathlon courses, and a golf course. There are also several summertime-only hiking trails surrounding the resort.

Odaesan National Park

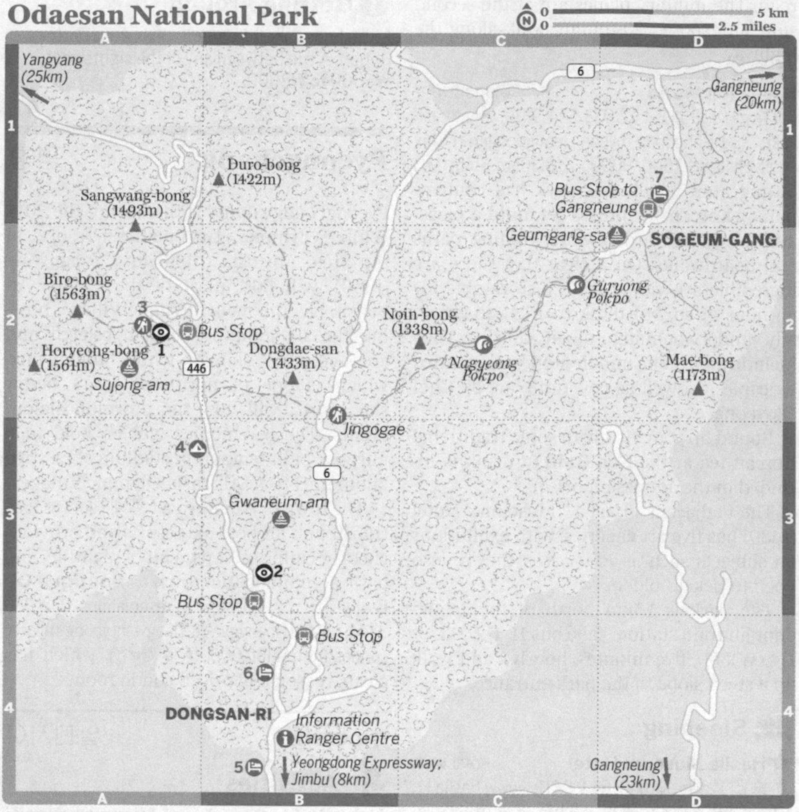

Odaesan National Park

Sights

1 Sangwon-sa A2
2 Woljeong-sa B3

Activities, Courses & Tours

3 Hiking Trails A2

Sleeping

4 Dongpigol Camping Ground A3
5 Kensington Flora Hotel B4
6 Minbak Village B4
7 Sogeum-gang Minbak Village D1

Sleeping

Alpensia has several dedicated hotels steps from the slopes, including the luxurious **InterContinental Alpensia Pyeongchang Resort** (인터컨티넨탈 알펜시아 평창 리조트; ☎front desk 033 339 0000; www.ihg.com; 225-3 Yongsan-ri; r ₩180,000, ste ₩385,000; P⊜❄@📶🏊) and two Holiday Inns, one a **resort** (홀리데이인 알펜시아 평창 리조트; ☎033 339 0000; www.holidayinn.com; 225-3 Yongsan-ri; r ₩162,000; P⊜❄@📶) and the other an **all-suite hotel** (홀리데이인 알펜시아 평창 스위트; ☎033 339 0000; www.holidayinn.com; 225-3 Yongsan-ri; ondol ₩224,500, ste ₩302,000; P⊜❄@📶).

Yongpyong 용평

Activities

Yongpyong Ski Resort SKIING, SNOW SPORTS
(용평리조트 스키장; ☎033 335 5757; www.yongpyong.co.kr; 715, Olympic-ro, Daegwanryeong-myeon; lift tickets per day adult/child ₩72,000/55,000, equipment rental per day adult/child ₩35,000/27,000; 👪) Korea's most beloved ski resort, and one of its largest with 31 slopes and 15 lifts, Yongpyong is a perennial favourite with snow-seekers each winter.

The resort gets an average of 250cm of snow (season runs November to March), and on a clear day it's possible to glimpse the East Sea from the slopes.

The surrounding buildings, including the giant Dragon Plaza ski house, manage to be charming but not kitschy. The resort also has cross-country trails and two half-pipes, and lessons are available in English.

🛏 Sleeping

Yongpyong has a number of condos and hotels near the slopes. The nicest is **Dragon Valley Hotel** (드래곤밸리호텔; ☎02 3270 1231; www.yongpyong.co.kr; r ₩300,000; ❈🛜🏊), which sells out quickly, and there's a **youth hostel** (용평호스텔; ☎02 3270 1231; www. yongpyong.co.kr; dm ₩13,000, r up to 14 people ₩80,000; ❈) open during ski season and high summer.

ℹ Getting There & Away

Most travellers arrive to Yongpyong or Alpensia via private shuttle buses (₩19,000 one way, three hours) departing from various pick-up points around Seoul. Tickets can be booked in advance (see resort websites for details) or bought from the driver, though spots tend to fill up, especially on weekends.

Buses run to Hoenggye from Dong-Seoul (₩14,500, hourly). From here, free shuttle buses (10 minutes, 15 daily, 5.30am to 11.30pm) depart for Yongpyong from the post office next to the bus terminal, but you'll have to take a taxi (₩11,000, 10 minutes) to Alpensia. A taxi from Hoenggye to Yongpyong costs ₩10,000.

Intercity buses also go from Gangneung's bus terminal to Hoenggye (₩2600, 30 minutes, every 10 to 15 minutes).

A high-speed KTX service connecting Seoul to Pyeongchang is under construction and set to open in time for the 2018 Games.

There is no regular transport between the two resorts; a taxi can cost upwards of ₩20,000 for the 15-minute one-way journey and can be arranged by a hotel concierge on either side.

Gohan 고한

☎ 033 / POP 5384

This tiny mountain village is the epicentre for skiing at the slick High1 Ski Resort. The one street through town is lined with snow-gear rental shops, small hotels and chicken-and-beer restaurants. There's not much to draw a traveller here beyond the ski resort, but the town has all the basic amenities for a snow-filled weekend.

🏃 Activities

★ **High1 Ski Resort** SKIING, SNOW SPORTS (하이원리조트 스키장; www.high1.co.kr; 500, High1-gil; lift tickets per day adult/child ₩57,000/43,000, gear rental per day adult/child ₩32,000/26,000; ➹; 🚇 Gohan, 🚌 O to Gohan) In the mountains west of Taebaek, High1 is a modern ski resort that ranks among the better snow facilities in South Korea. At 1340m, the resort sees plenty of powder on its 18 slopes, which are served by five lifts and four gondolas. Rental gear, including clothing, is available and in decent condition, and you can hire demo skis and boards for a little more.

The slopes present a good spread of difficulties, with long, relaxed baby runs that commence from the top of the mountain (meaning even beginners can take in the panoramic views), alongside several advanced runs, where depending on the time of year, you may find moguls.

🛏 Sleeping

High1 Hotel HOTEL ₩₩ (하이원호텔; ☎bookings 033 1588 7789; www. high1.com; 399, Gohan 7-gil; d ₩175,000; P❈❄ @🛜) One of the cheaper High1 Ski Resort accommodation options, High1 Hotel does the job well, with a sparkling lobby and spacious rooms with views over the valley or mountains. It suffers a little from being located a 30-minute shuttle bus ride from the main resort area, but makes up for it with frequent discounts and a gondola to the peak.

Staff speak English and there's an on-site sauna. On-site eating options are scarce and expensive – pack in food and drink, or catch the free shuttle to town or the main resort area for dinner.

Kangwonland Hotel RESORT ₩₩₩ (강원랜드호텔; ☎033 1588 7789; www.high1. com; 265, High1-gil, Sabuk-eup; d ₩300,000, ondol ₩320,000; P❈❄@🛜❄) The main hotel at High1 Ski Resort is this high-rise hotel complete with casino (South Korea's largest) and convention centre. Rooms are of a high standard with prices to match, and there are several on-site dining options, as well as a pool, sauna, wine shop and theatre.

GANGWON-DO GOHAN

In exchange for the prices, you get easy access to the slopes via a free five-minute shuttle ride.

ⓘ Getting There & Around

Intercity buses run from Dong Seoul Bus Terminal to (Sin) Gohan Bus Stop (₩14,500, three hours, eight daily). Trains depart for Gohan from Seoul's Cheongnyangni station (₩14,400, four hours, seven daily). On weekends, the tourist O-train, which goes to Gohan from Seoul station (₩26,400, 7:45am, 3½ hours) is a lot of fun, kitted out in kitschy 1970s decor.

A free shuttle bus connects Gohan with all areas of High1 Ski Resort. Turn right out of the train station, walk down the drive and look for the bus shelter on the right.

Odaesan National Park
오대산 국립공원

This park has great hiking, superb views and two prominent Buddhist temples, Woljeong-sa and Sangwon-sa.

⊙ Sights & Activities

Odaesan National Park　　NATIONAL PARK
(☑ 033 332 6417; http://english.knps.or.kr; ⊙ 9am-7pm) **FREE** Like Seorak-san, Odae-san (Five Peaks Mountain) is a high-altitude massif; the best times to visit are late spring and early to mid-autumn, when the foliage colours are richest.

There are two main entrances to the park: from the south at Dongsan-ri and from the northwest at Sogeum-gang. The former leads to the temples and the main hiking trail.

Woljeong-sa　　TEMPLE
(월정사; ☑ 033 339 6800; www.woljeongsa. org; admission incl Sangwon-sa adult/youth/child ₩3000/1500/500; ⊙ 5am-9pm, museum 9.30am-5.30pm Apr-Oct, to 4.30pm Nov-Mar, closed Tue) This Shilla-era temple was founded in AD 645 by the Zen Master Jajang to enshrine relics of the historical Buddha. Although it fell victim to fires and was even flattened during the Korean War, one treasured structure that has survived from the Goryeo dynasty is the octagonal nine-storey pagoda in the main courtyard, with the figure of a kneeling bodhisattva before it. The younger buildings around it are decorated with intricate religious art.

There is a museum of Joseon-era Buddhist art and you can arrange a templestay here.

Sangwon-sa　　TEMPLE
(상원사; ☑ 033 332 6666; www.woljeongsa. org; admission incl Woljeong-sa adult/youth/child ₩3000/1500/500) Sangwon-sa, 10km beyond Woljeong-sa (p142), is where a hiking trail (p142) begins. The temple's intricately decorated bronze bell was cast in AD 725 and is the oldest bell in Korea (and one of the largest as well). Another prized object is the wooden statue of the bodhisattva of wisdom Munsu (in Sanskrit, Manjusri) – made in the 15th century, it is said, on the order of King Sejo after the bodhisattva cured his skin disease.

Hiking Trails　　HIKING
The main hiking trail begins at Sangwon-sa (p142) and is a fairly steep 6.5km climb to the highest peak **Biro-bong** (1563m), about three hours round-trip. Gung-ho hikers can continue from Biro-bong along a ridge to **Sangwang-bong** (1493m), then back down to the road and to the temple (12.5km, five hours).

A separate trail runs 13.3km from Sogeum-gang to **Jingogae**, passing several waterfalls, including **Guryong Pokpo** and **Nagyeong Pokpo**, and **Noin-bong** (1338m). The route takes about seven hours one way. The trail linking Jingogae to the western half of Odaesan is currently closed for restoration.

🛏 Sleeping & Eating

A small **minbak village** with restaurants is on the left side of the access road, about 1km from the turnoff from Hwy 6. It's a 40-minute walk south of Woljeong-sa, or you can take the bus. Halfway between the temples is **Dongpigol Camping Ground** (per tent ₩3000-6000). Sogeum-gang also has a **minbak village** and **camping ground**.

Kensington Flora Hotel　　LUXURY HOTEL **www**
(켄싱턴플로라호텔; ☑ 033 330 5000; www. kensingtonflorahotel.co.kr; r ₩180,000, ste ₩280,000; ❋🐾🛜🅿) Formerly known as the Odaesan Hotel, this tall deluxe hotel is about 2.5km from the southern park entrance, with sweeping views all around. Rooms are suitably plush and during low season discounts of up to 50% are possible.

ℹ Getting There & Away

To get to the southern park entrance near Dongsan-ri, take an intercity bus from Gangneung (₩3900, 50 minutes, every 10 minutes) to Jinbu. At Jinbu, local buses (₩1300, 12 per day) run from the bus terminal to Woljeong-sa (20 minutes) and Sangwon-sa (another 20 minutes). Look out for the white buses towards the rear of the terminal lot. Bus schedules are helpfully posted at all these stops, or you can get them from Gangneung's tourist information centres.

To get to Sogeum-gang, take local bus 303 (₩1300, 50 minutes, hourly) from right outside the Gangneung bus terminal. It drops you at the *minbak* village; it's 500m to the park-ranger station and the hiking trail begins another 500m beyond.

Samcheok 삼척

✍ 033 / POP 80,000

Sedate little Samcheok is the gateway to an unusual mix of sightseeing spots. Within an hour's bus ride are spectacular limestone caves, an inimitable 'penis park' (phallic sculptures, not body parts) and pretty beaches tucked away in quiet coves. The town has a rousing **Full Moon Festival** in February, with tug-of-war competitions.

The only sightseeing spot in town is the **Mystery of Caves Exhibition** (동굴 신비관; ✍ 033 574 6828; adult/youth/child ₩3000/2000/1500; ⊙ 9am-6pm Mar-Oct, to 5pm Nov-Feb; 👪), housed in a building that resembles a wedding cake dripping with brown icing. The exhibits (some in English) contain elaborate detail on cave formation and there's a 20-minute IMAX film at 10.30am, 2pm and 3pm.

The **tourist information centre** (✍ 033 575 1330; http://eng.samcheok.go.kr; ⊙ 9am-6pm) is beside the express bus terminal. Staff speak English and Japanese and detailed bus schedules are available in English for buses to Hwanseongul and Haesindang Park.

🛏 Sleeping & Eating

Moon Motel   MOTEL ₩₩

(✍ 033 572 4436; 432-63, Jeongsang-dong; d ₩50,000, deluxe tw/tr ₩60,000) Standing tall conveniently just a block back from the bus terminals is this love motel. Deluxe rooms are neat and massive – with huge flat screen TVs and sofas, beds that are sprawl-worthy after lengthy travels, and bathrooms with a spa and cavernous echo.

Eunmi Gamjatang   KOREAN ₩

(은미 감자탕; ✍ 033 573 5911; meals ₩5000-8000) This friendly eatery specialises in hearty *gamjatang* (meaty bones and potato soup) served in a *jeongol* (hotpot) or *ttukbaegi* (뚝배기; earthenware dish); you'll need at least two people to order it. Solo diners can try the *galbitang* or *yukgaejang* (spicy beef soup with vegetables).

Buona Pizza   ITALIAN ₩₩

(✍ 033 574 8030; meals ₩7500-18,000) If you need a break from Korean cuisine, this pizzeria across from Samcheok Post Office does a decent enough job.

ℹ Getting There & Away

BUS

The express and intercity bus terminals sit beside each other. Express buses to Seoul (₩17,500, 3½ hours) run to Gangnam (every 35 minutes) and Dong-Seoul (hourly).

TRAIN

A special 'seaside train' runs between Samcheok and Gangneung. Train carriages have been remodelled so that passengers face the extra-large windows looking out to sea (instead of the conventional front-back arrangement). From Samcheok, the train makes stops at Donghae, Jeongdongjin and several beach

GANGWON-DO SAMCHEOK

BUS DEPARTURES FROM SAMCHEOK

DESTINATION	PRICE (₩)	DURATION (HR)	FREQUENCY
Busan	30,200	4½	3 daily
Daegu	29,000	5	6 daily
Gangneung	5300	1	every 15min
Sokcho	11,600	3½	3 daily
Taebaek	6300	1	hourly
Wonju	12,700	3½	1 daily

WORTH A TRIP

BIG WHITE MOUNTAIN

In the heart of 'Korea's alps', Taebaeksan (태백산) is one of the most sacred mountains in the country. The small town of Taebaek (태백) is a jumping-off point for exploring **Taebaeksan Provincial Park** (태백산도립공원; ☑ 033 552 1360; http://taebaek.go.kr; San 80, Sodo-dong; adult/youth/child ₩2000/1500/700; ☉ sunrise-sunset), which offers year-round hiking on trails that snake up to **Janggun-bong** (1568m) and **Cheonjedan** (천제단), an altar connected with Korea's mythical founder, Dangun. Included in the park ticket is admission to the **Taebaek Coal Museum** (태백 석탄 박물관; ☑ 033 552 7730; www.coalmuseum.or.kr; Taebaek-san Provincial Park; adult/student/child ₩2000/1500/700; ☉ 9am-6pm; 🅿️), which documents the history of coal mining in the region.

Each winter in the park, the **Taebaeksan Snow Festival** (태백산 눈축제; ☑ info 033 550 2828; http://festival.taebaek.go.kr; 4834-31, Taebaeksan-ro; adult/youth/child ₩2000/1500/700; 🅿️ ; 🚍 6, 7) features giant snow sculptures and other wintery activities, including an igloo restaurant and K-pop performances. It is among the largest and most well-attended ice festivals in the country and a highlight on the festival calendar.

Buses connect Taebaek to Dong-Seoul (₩22,900, three hours, hourly), Samcheok (₩7100, 2½ hours, hourly), and Busan (₩29,400, four hours, six daily). Seven trains run to Seoul's Cheongnyangni station (₩17,600, four hours) daily. The flashy, retro tourist O-train (₩27,800, four hours, 7.45am) from Seoul station is a fun way to get here. It runs a loop and returns to Seoul from Taebaek at 6pm.

Buses 6 and 7 leave from Taebaek's bus terminal (₩1500, 20 minutes, every 30 minutes) for the provincial park. To find the right bus, go inside the bus station and find the glass doors in the right-hand waiting area.

stations before terminating at Gangneung (₩12,000 or ₩15,000, one hour 20 minutes). The sea views are lovely, but the route also passes some unattractive stretches of industrial landscape.

Trains depart Samcheok at 12.10pm and 3.42pm, and return from Gangneung at 10.24am and 2.10pm. There are extra services in May and August.

Trains take a scenic route to Andong (₩11,500, 3½ hours, daily) from Donghae, which you can get to by local bus 11 from outside the intercity bus terminal (₩1550, 25 minutes, every 10 minutes).

Around Samcheok

⊙ Sights

Hwanseongul
CAVE

(환선굴; ☑ 033 570 3255; adult/youth/child ₩4000/2800/2000; ☉ 8.30am-6.30pm Mar-Oct, 9.30am-5.30pm Nov-Feb) Hwanseongul is one of the largest caves in Asia; almost 2km of steel stairways take visitors through its cathedral-sized caverns – up, down and around its varied formations. Some curious formations to look out for are the heart-shaped hole over the correspondingly

named Bridge of Love, the rimstone that resembles a fried egg, and a difficult-to-spot calcite growth that resembles a tiny statue of the Virgin Mary.

As with many caves in Korea, Hwanseongul's natural beauty is breathtaking but, unfortunately, garish lighting and kitschy names have been added to 'enhance' the experience.

Bus 60 (₩2900, 45 minutes, departures 8.20am, 10.20am, 2.20pm) heads from Samcheok's intercity bus terminal for the cave. The last bus leaves the cave at 7.30pm.

Haesindang Park
PARK

(해신당 공원; ☑ 033 570 3568; adult/youth/child ₩3000/2000/1500; ☉ 9am-6pm Mar-Oct, to 5pm Nov-Feb, closed 18th each month) Of all the things you'd expect to find in a fishing village like Sinnam (신남), a 'penis park' is probably not one of them. There are more than 50 phallic sculptures, some taking the form of park benches or drums. These carvings were entered for a contest in Samcheok's now-defunct Penis Sculpture Festival; today they attract joshing *ajumma* and *ajeossi* (married or older women and men). It's a cheeky, eye-opening 20 to 30 minute walk if you don't stop, but you *will* stop.

Chiaksan National Park

The phallic obsession originates with a local legend about a drowned virgin whose restless spirit was affecting the village's catch. A fisherman discovered that she could be appeased if he answered the call of nature while facing the ocean, so the village put up phalluses to placate her. A small shrine to this spirit stands at the seaward tip of the park and binoculars look out to the statue commemorating where she drowned.

There's an elaborate series of penis sculptures representing the 12 animals of the Chinese zodiac and outside the park stands a red lighthouse with the same, uh, peculiarities. The park has impressive sea views and also contains the **Fishing Village Folk Museum** (어촌 민속 전시관; closed Monday), focusing on the history of fishing and shamanist rituals in the region, and sexual iconography in other cultures.

From Samcheok's intercity bus terminal, take bus 24 (₩1800, 40 minutes, 20km, hourly) from the platform on the right. You can enter Haesindang Park from the top of the headland (where there's a huge parking lot) or from the entrance in Sinnam. The easier walk is to start at the top, work your way down and exit at the village.

Beaches

The closest beaches are **Samcheok Beach** (삼척 해수욕장), found immediately to the north of town, and **Maengbang Beach** (맹방 해수욕장), about 12km south. The former has shallow waters, making it popular with families, and the usual assortment of motels and restaurants. Maengbang Beach has no buildings, although tented stalls spring up during beach season (10 July to 20 August). It's less frantic than Samcheok Beach, but the downside is that it's about a 2km walk (20 minutes) from the bus stop.

Bus 11 (₩1800, 20 minutes, five daily) runs from Samcheok's intercity bus terminal to Samcheok Beach. Maengbang Beach is on the route for bus 21, 23 and 24 (₩1800, 25 minutes).

Wonju   원주

📞033 / POP 306,000

The closest major town to Chiak-san National Park, **Wonju** (http://english.wonju.go.kr) is home to several universities and military bases. If you must spend the night, there are decent restaurants and love motels around the express bus terminal. There is no tourist information centre here.

ℹ️ Getting There & Away

From the express bus terminal buses run to Seoul Gangnam (₩10,000, 1½ hours, every 10 to 15 minutes) and Gangneung (₩7600, 1½ hours, hourly). Buses from the intercity bus terminal head to Cheongju (₩8400, 1½ hours, hourly) and Gwangju (₩7,900, two to four hours, every 1½ hours).

Trains (₩6300, 1¼ hours, hourly) run between Wonju and Seoul's Cheongnyangni station.

Chiaksan National Park
치악산 국립공원

This **park** (📞033 732 5231; http://english.knps. or.kr; parking ₩2000; ☉sunrise-sunset) **FREE** may be the smallest of the national parks in Gangwon-do, but it offers challenging **hikes** and is a very doable weekend trip from Seoul. A popular but strenuous route starts from **Guryong-sa** (구룡사; Nine Dragon Temple) up to 1288m-high Biro-bong (three hours, 5.6km); it's possible to continue another 5.4km (two hours) down to **Hwanggol** (황골).

Hiking trails also go from **Geumdae-ri** and **Seongnam-ri**, running about 6km to the peak Namdae-bong (1181m).

The main *minbak* and restaurant village is outside the Guryong-sa entrance. There are **camping grounds** (☑ 033 731 1289; ₩7000-9000) in summer available at **Daegok** near Guryong-sa and Geumdae-ri – pass the temple and walk 10 minutes. There are no mountain shelters.

ℹ Getting There & Away

To get to Guryong-sa, exit Wonju's intercity bus terminal and take a taxi (₩2200) to Wonju train station. Take bus 41 (₩2000, 40 minutes, every 25 minutes), which terminates at the car park near the park entrance. Guryong-sa is 800m further.

Bus 82 runs a loop service to Hwanggol (₩1200, 30 minutes, hourly), while bus 21 runs to Geumdae-ri and Seongnam-ri (₩1200). At Hwanggol, the bus can be picked up at the stop opposite the Italian restaurant Pino.

Gyeongsangbuk-do

Includes ➡

Best Places to Eat

➡ Dosolmaeul (p165)

➡ Gaejeong (p152)

➡ Kisoya (p165)

➡ Little Italia (p152)

➡ 99 Sikdang (p175)

Best Places to Stay

➡ Grand Daegu Hotel (p151)

➡ Sarangchae (p164)

➡ Baramgot Guesthouse (p164)

➡ Rak Ko Jae Hahoe (p179)

➡ Design Motel A2 (p171)

Why Go?

Korea's cultural warehouse, Gyeongsangbuk-do (경상북도) is a region resplendent both in natural beauty and heritage sites, including many fascinating temples, ancient pagodas, rock-carved Buddhas and tombs. Gyeongju is often called 'the museum without walls' for its historical treasures, many of which are outdoors. The oddly symmetrical *tumuli* (burial mounds) in the centre of town are serene pyramids – stately reminders of the dead they still honour.

The region's major city, Daegu, is a sprawling place with an excellent medicinal-herb market, a downtown drenched in neon and superb restaurants. Elsewhere, don't miss Haein-sa; this must-see temple-library amid gorgeous mountain scenery contains the Tripitaka Koreana, 1000-year-old wooden tablets inscribed with sacred Buddhist texts and ingeniously preserved in a building so ahead of its time that modern science hasn't improved it. Off the coast is the rugged island of Ulleungdo, with seemingly endless opportunities to enjoy spectacular coastal landscapes.

When to Go
Daegu

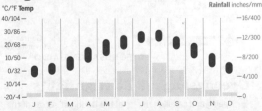

| Apr–Jun Lovely temperatures and low humidity; a great time to travel here. | Mid-Aug Catch Ulleungdo's squid festival and enjoy delicious seafood in a unique island setting. | Late Sep–early Oct Andong's Mask Dance Festival, a highlight of the Korean arts calendar. |

History

This area was once the capital of the Shilla empire (57 BC–AD 935), and as such was a central part of Korean government and trade. During this almost 1000-year-long empire, alliances were created with China to defeat Japanese threats, as well as to repel other Korean invaders. During this time Confucian laws were widely adopted and informed all aspects of Korean life, including who, where and when a person could marry.

Daegu 대구

☑ 053 / POP 2.45 MILLION

South Korea's fourth largest city is a pleasant and progressive place with a fascinating traditional-medicine market, some excellent eating options and a humming downtown that's good fun to explore. The city is a popular place for exchange students and English teachers, and the large student population gives Daegu a young and carefree feel.

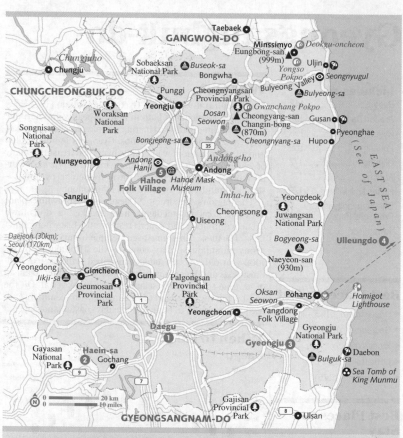

Gyeongsangbuk-do Highlights

❶ Seeing and smelling the fascinating **medicinal herbs** (p149) in Daegu before partaking of great eating in the city's downtown.

❷ Marvelling at the 80,000-plus wooden tablets of the Buddhist sutras at the temple **Haein-sa** (p156).

❸ Slipping back into the Shilla era in **Gyeongju** (p159), the 'museum without walls'.

❹ Walking along the rocky coastline and enjoying the stunning scenery and great seafood of **Ulleungdo** (p172).

❺ Admiring centuries-old architecture and an unchanged way of life in **Hahoe Folk Village** (p179).

A simple, two-line subway system makes getting around easy, and Daegu (sometimes spelled Taegu) is also a great hub for day trips; be sure to check out Haein-sa and Jikji-sa, both of which offer templestays for those wishing to immerse themselves in traditional local culture.

Sights & Activities

Daegu National Museum   MUSEUM
(국립대구박물관; Map p150; ☎053 768 6051; http://daegu.museum.go.kr; ⏰9am-7pm Tue-Sun, closed Mon) FREE This excellent museum has English labelling throughout most of its collection – and what a collection. Armour, jewellery, Buddhist relics from various different eras, Confucian manuscripts, clothing and textiles are all beautifully displayed in well-lit glass cases, and there's normally at least a couple of temporary exhibits here also. From Banwoldang subway, take bus 414 or 349; or from Dongdaegu station take bus 414 from across the road on the bridge. The electric boards inside the bus announce 'Nat'l Museum'.

Bullo-dong Tumuli-gongwon   TOMB
(불로동 고분 공원; ☎053 940 1224; ⏰9am-6pm) FREE If you're already in the north end of the city, stop by Bullo-dong Tumuli-gongwon, an enormous open space covering some 330,000 sq metres. The grassy hillocks that rise like bumps across the valley are *tumuli* (burial mounds, similar to those in Gyeongju (p159)). Dating from the 2nd to the 6th century AD, the *tumuli* are for both nobles and commoners – the higher the location on the hill, the higher the status of the person.

Greenvill   BATHHOUSE
(그린빌 찜질방 사우나; Map p153; sauna ₩5000, sauna & bed ₩7000; ⏰24hr; Ⓜ Line 1 or 2 to Banwoldang, Exit 1) This centrally located bathhouse and *jjimjilbang* (upmarket sauna) is not huge, but is clean and has a soothing mixture of hot, warm and cold tubs, plus scorching-hot (81°C) and ice-cold rooms. It's a 24-hour facility, so guests can sleep overnight on wooden pillows, making it a budget sleeping option if you're just staying one night. Take the lift to the basement.

Life Spa   BATHHOUSE
(수목원 생활 온천; ☎053 641 0100; www.lifespa.co.kr; admission ₩10,000; ⏰24hr; Ⓜ Line 1 to Jincheon) Located in western Daegu, this spa is a beautiful facility with 1100 sq metres of tubs and sweat rooms, a fitness centre and rooftop pools. Take the subway to Jincheon station, Exit 3. Walk to the intersection and turn right. From here, it's a quick taxi ride; ask for '*sumokwon saengwol oncheon*' (수목원 생활 온천).

Tours

Daegu City Tour   BUS TOUR
(Map p150; ☎053 603 1800; http://daegucitytour.com; adult/child ₩5000/3000; ⏰from 9.30am, every 40min, 12 daily) Travellers with limited time might consider Daegu's official double-decker tour. Jump on and off the bus at some of the area's best sites. Buy a ticket and get a full list of hop-on points from tourist information centres, such as at Dongdaegu station, where tours start.

GYEONGSANGBUK-DO DAEGU

DON'T MISS

DAEGU'S HERBAL MEDICINE MARKET

Daegu's Herbal Medicine Market (대구약령시; Map p153; Ⓜ Line 1 or 2 to Banwoldang, Exit 4), west of the central shopping district, has a history as vast as its scope. It dates from 1658, making it Korea's oldest medicine market and still one of its largest. The stores spill onto the street with fragrant curiosities from lizards' tails to magic mushrooms (the latter only with a prescription); you might also catch a glimpse of someone receiving acupuncture.

Start nearby at the **Daegu Yangnyeongsi Museum of Oriental Medicine** (Map p153; ☎053 257 4729; ⏰10am-5pm Tue-Sun, closed Mon; 🚻; Ⓜ Line 1 or 2 to Banwoldang, Exit 14) FREE to learn the uses of every spiky herb. An interactive museum on the upper two levels has re-creations of traditional clinics, video quizzes and many a stuffed animal – enough to even keep kids entertained. It's a visually exciting introduction to oriental medicine such as *insam* (ginseng) and reindeer horns, and the people who popularised it, with audio guides in English, Japanese and Chinese. On the days ending with 1 or 6 (except the 31st), *yangnyeong-sijang* (wholesale market) takes place downstairs.

Daegu

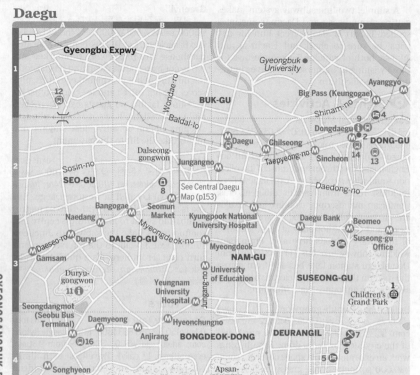

🛏 Sleeping

Danim Backpackers HOSTEL ₩
(다님; ☎ 010 6713 0053; www.danimbackpackers.
com; dm incl breakfast ₩22,000; ⊖❉@🛜;
Ⓜ Line 1 or 2 to Banwoldang, Exit 9) This tiny place
has an apartment feel, with just 12 beds in
two dorms (one female only). However, it has
all the necessities, including a great location
a short stroll from the neon-drenched streets
of downtown, communal kitchen, free use
of laundry facilities, rooftop and nearby bar.
Staff speak English and are very keen to help.

Rojan Motel MOTEL ₩
(로잔 모텔; Map p150; ☎ 053 766 0336; r
₩30,000; ❉; Ⓜ Line 2 to Beomeo, Exit 4) One of
the best deals in Daegu – if not the whole region – is this spotless, no-frills motel, which
offers clean, crisp sheets and a private bathroom. Credit cards are accepted, but there's no
internet. The location is good, with access to
downtown and plenty of nearby restaurants.

Empathy Guesthouse GUESTHOUSE ₩₩
(공감 게스트 하우스; Map p153; ☎ 070 8915
8991; http://empathyguesthouse.blogspot.kr; 32
Jungangdaero 79-gil, Jung-gu; dm/tw incl breakfast
₩23,000/55,000; ⊖❉@🛜; Ⓜ Line 1 to Jungangno, Exit 1) This guesthouse is part of the
Center for North Korean Defectors (www.
nkpeople.or.kr), and 20% of proceeds go to
resettlement elsewhere. It's a great place to
stay with heated flooring, rooftop terrace,
curfew-free independent entry, free laundry
and ample quiet despite rubbing shoulders
with downtown's drinkers. The sociable
lounge is good for hearing insights from
English-speaking volunteers about life for
defectors.

Hera Motel LOVE HOTEL ₩₩
(헤라모텔; Map p150; ☎ 053 958 2200; www.헤
라모텔.com; d/tw from ₩50,000/70,000; ❉@;
Ⓜ Line 1 to Dongdaegu, Exit 1) Very conveniently
located next to Dongdaegu station, this fab-
ulously kooky love hotel is a reliable choice

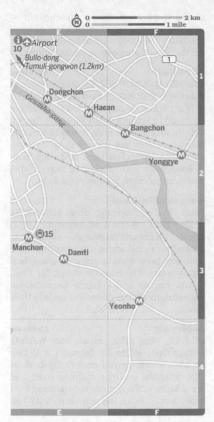

GYEONGSANGBUK-DO DAEGU

in an area dominated by downtrodden inns with ₩30,000 rooms. Enormous rooms with queen-sized beds and modern bathrooms (including cushions in the tubs) make a stay here comfortable, even if the decor can be garish. Prices rise ₩10,000 Friday and Saturday.

Turn right out of Dongdaegu station, walk down to the pedestrian bridge, but do not cross. Walk right down the steps to the street. It's straight ahead on the right.

Hotel Ariana HOTEL ₩₩
(호텔 아리아나; Map p150; ☑ 053 765 7776; www.ariana.co.kr; r from ₩120,000; ❋☎; Ⓜ Line 2 to Beomeo, Exit 4) This smart, well-run property has anodyne rooms, but they're comfortable and spacious, and each room has a double and single bed. It's in a good location near the Deurangil restaurant district, and is an easy bus ride to downtown. The friendly staff speak limited English. No breakfast, but the good Cafe Boccaccio on the ground floor serves pastries and pizzas.

**Novotel Daegu
City Center** LUXURY HOTEL ₩₩₩
(대구 노보텔; Map p153; ☑ 053 664 1101; http://novoteldaegu.co.kr; 611 Gukchaebosang-ro, Jung-gu; r from ₩185,900; ❋@☎; Ⓜ Line 1, Jungangno, Exit 3) There's a real lack of sleeping options in Daegu's busy downtown and, if you want to sleep in comfort, this sleek and modern high-rise Novotel is your best bet. Reception is on the 8th floor and all the rooms have great views, even if they can be a little on the small side.

Other attractions include a sauna, a superb breakfast buffet (₩24,000) and a smart terrace bar for evening drinks.

Grand Daegu Hotel LUXURY HOTEL ₩₩₩
(대구 그랜드 호텔; Map p150; ☑ 053 742 0001; www.daegugrand.co.kr; 563-1 Beomeo 1-dong, Susung-gu; r from ₩249,000; ❋@☎; Ⓜ Line 2, Beomeo, Exit 3) This immaculate property blends minimalism with style and touches such as king-sized beds and widescreen TVs. The location is great and the rooms are extremely comfortable, and there are more

liveried bellboys and pruned bonsai trees than you'll know what to do with.

Eating

Areas worth checking out for good restaurant selection include Deurangil in the south, which specialises in Korean *hanu* beef as well as a variety of other Asian cuisines, and the busy area around Gyeongbuk University in the north, which is full of student bars and restaurants serving cheap and delicious chicken dishes. Seomun-sijang has good street eats.

★ Gaejeong   KOREAN ₩

(개정; Map p153; dishes ₩6000-11,000; ⊙11am-10pm; Ⓜ Line 1 to Jungangno, Exit 2) This excellent-value place serves up divine but healthy traditional Korean food over three floors, so even if it's packed they'll usually be able to find you a seat. Don't hesitate to order the special rice with vegetables in a stone pot – surely one of the best dishes in Daegu. Calvin Klein is on the corner.

Happy Noodle Making   KOREAN ₩

(행복제면소; Map p153; ☑ 053 428 5900; dishes ₩4000-6000; ⊙11am-9.30pm; Ⓙ) This is a model cheap-eats restaurant. Take the tofu triple-threat *dubugugsu* (두부국수) – fresh, fried and with their signature noodles, all in a pretty stack to make a master chef proud. The picture and English menus have plenty more satisfying Korean dishes. Look for the green awning.

Geumgok Samgyetang   KOREAN ₩₩

(금곡 삼계탕; Map p153; mains ₩12,000; ⊙11am-10pm; Ⓜ Line 1 to Jungangno, Exit 2) A local, stylish favourite in easy walking distance of the downtown markets. Order one of the three menu items: ginseng-infused chicken, barbecue chicken, or a half-order of the latter (₩6000) – all are sublime. Look for the arched windows opposite Adidas.

Little Italia   ITALIAN ₩₩

(Map p153; ☑ 053 426 3992; 45-1 Gongpyeong-dong; dishes ₩9800-29,900; ⊙10am-2.30pm & 5-10pm; ❇ 🛜 ☑ ; Ⓜ Line 1 to Jungangno, Exit 2) A tranquil diamond in Daegu's rough shopping district. Bring a date like many do to this bistro's cottage cuteness, or love yourself up with risotto, steak, hand-stretched pizza and surprisingly good pasta and salads. The berry sorbet makes an excellent not-too-sweet finish.

Bongsan Jjim-Galbi   KOREAN ₩₩

(봉산 찜갈비; Map p153; dishes from ₩8000; ⊙10am-10pm; Ⓜ Line 1 to Jungangno, Exit 2) Located on Daegu's famous *jjim-galbi* (slow-cooked beef ribs) street, this quaint restaurant has been serving spicy steamed beef for 40 years. The friendly owner, Mr Choi, speaks English and is happy to accommodate customers who prefer less spice in their food.

Seokryujip   KOREAN ₩₩

(석류집; Map p150; meals from ₩10,000; ⊙10am-10pm; Ⓜ Line 2 to Beomeo, Exit 3) Dog or goat, which do you prefer? Try both at this delightful traditional dining room and see if Korea's fabled stamina-producing food really works. From the main street, it's just next to the SK petrol station – look for the traditional tiled roof.

🍷 Drinking & Nightlife

Around the Yasigolmok downtown district you'll find literally hundreds of cafes, bars and nightclubs – endless choice for

---

WAITING FOR DOKDO

In 1905, during the Japanese occupation, Japan annexed Dokdo – fishing grounds marked by two small, rocky islands – and renamed it Takeshima. Korea protested, but as a colony did not have much say. Following WWII, US general Douglas MacArthur designated the island part of Korea, and US forces erected a monument there to Korean fishermen accidentally killed nearby by American ordnance. However, Japan destroyed the monument in 1952, prompting Korea to send a defence unit and Japan to put the island under surveillance.

In August 2012, Lee Myung Bak became the first sitting South Korean President to visit Dokdo, causing tension between South Korea and Japan and bringing the disputed claims back to international prominence. They flare again twice a year when South Korea performs military drills on the island. While the two countries remain economically close and otherwise enjoy good relations, the disputed issue of Dokdo's ownership doesn't seem to be going anywhere quickly.

Central Daegu

Central Daegu

all forms of entertainment. The central shopping district is teeming with *hof* (local pubs), singing rooms, bars and cafes. There's a small gay district (map at www. utopia-asia.com) with a few bars near the Express Bus Terminal.

Buda   BAR
(부다; Map p153; ⊘5pm-5am; Ⓜ Line 1 or 2 to Banwoldang, Exit 3) One of the city's coolest bar-restaurants: wine bottles and candles

line the entrance, there's a hint of incense in the air and private rooms are created by sheer drapes. Remove your shoes as you enter. It's between the Bus pub and Club Egg.

Bus   PUB
(버스; Map p153; ⊘5pm-10am; Ⓜ Line 1 or 2 to Banwoldang, Exit 3) This unmistakable bus-turned-pub is on a side street right near Club Egg. It's a popular hang-out with students, and serves food and drink all night.

Club Egg
CLUB

(Map p153; ☉8pm-9am; Ⓜ Line 1 or 2 to Banwol-dang, Exit 3) Bump around in trance-inducing, black-lit darkness. The hip-hop, R&B and reggae are ear-splitting – just the way most of the crowd wants it. Look for the pink and black exterior.

Frog
CLUB

(Map p153; admission ₩15,000, US soldiers ₩8000; ☉9pm-6am; Ⓜ Line 1 or 2 to Banwoldang, Exit 3) Five floors of hip-hop and electronic music for you and a few thousand of your closest friends.

☆ Entertainment

There is a huge XN Milano complex that houses the **Hanil Gukjang cinema** (Map p153; Ⓜ Line 1 to Jungangno, Exit 2), where there are often English-language movies.

🛍 Shopping

Daegu is a shopper's dream. In addition to good prices on brand-name goods (clothes, shoes, bags etc) at the various department stores and amid the neon of downtown, Daegu has numerous speciality markets that make for a fascinating stroll even if you're not going to part with any won.

Seomun-sijang
MARKET

(서문시장; Map p150; ☉9am-6pm Mar-Oct, to 5pm Nov-Feb, closed 2nd & 4th Sun; Ⓜ Line 2 to Seomun Market, Exit 1) This hulking, multi-storey complex has more than 4000 stalls in six sections including clothing, silk and street food. Bustling yet orderly, it's been one of Korea's big three markets since 1669, even if the current buildings have little of that historic character. Outside the subway exit, turn 180° and walk around the corner.

Yasigolmok
MARKET

(야시골목; Ⓜ Line 1 to Jungangno, Exit 2) This is the heart of Daegu's shopping district, with clothing and fashion outlets and boutiques, bustling day and night.

ℹ Information

Daegu has a **tourist information centre** (Map p153; ☎1330, 053 627 8900; ☉9am-6pm) at all major transit points and destinations including the airport, outside Dongdaegu station, at Duryu-gongwon, in the central shopping district and by the herbal medicine market. All have helpful English-speaking staff, comprehensive local maps in English and reams of pamphlets.

ℹ Getting There & Away

AIR

Asiana, Korean Air and T'way Air connect Daegu with Seoul and Jeju. International destinations include Shanghai, Bangkok and Beijing on Air China and Jeju Air.

BUS

There are five bus terminals in Daegu: an **Express (Gosok) Bus Terminal** (Map p150; ☎053 743 3701; Ⓜ Line 1 to Dongdaegu, Exit 4) by Dongdaegu train station, plus **Dongbu** (East; Map p150; ☎053 756 0017; Ⓜ Line 1 to Dongdaegu, Exit 4), **Seobu** (West; Map p150; ☎053 656 1583; Ⓜ Line 1, Seongdangmot, Exit 3), **Nambu** (South; Map p150) and **Bukbu** (North; Map p150; ☎053 357 1851; Ⓜ Line 2, Duryu, Exit 1) intercity terminals. Note that buses to some destinations leave from multiple terminals, so it may be worth checking departure times of several terminals if you're looking for a bus at a specific time.

The express bus terminal is four separate buildings, each housing different companies with destinations including Andong, Busan, Daejeon, Gyeongju, Jinju and Seoul.

TRAIN

Dongdaegu station on the east side of the city is the main station for long-distance trains. It's near the express bus terminal. Daegu station, closer to downtown, is mostly for *tonggeun* (commuter-class) and *mugunghwa* (semi-express) trains.

You'll find good connections to Seoul including KTX (high-speed) trains (every 10 to 30 minutes to Seoul, ₩42,500, two hours) and budget *mugugahwa* (₩21,100, four hours). A frequent KTX service to Busan is available (₩17,100, one hour), though consider *saemaul* (express, ₩11,000, 1¼ hours) or *mugunghwa* (₩7500, 1½ hours) services to increase your departure options without adding a significant amount of travel time. A new KTX train between Daejeon and Daegu was due to open at the time of writing. Check www.korail.go.kr for schedules and fares.

ℹ Getting Around

TO/FROM THE AIRPORT

Daegu's airport is northeast of the city, about 2km from the express bus terminal. From downtown, take Line 1 to Ayanggyo station, Exit 3, and catch bus 401, 101 or Express 1. A taxi from the airport to the centre will cost around ₩10,000 and take about 20 minutes.

BUS & SUBWAY

Local bus fares are ₩1200, but can vary with longer routes. To get to Deurangil from central Daegu or Dongdaegu station, take bus 401. From

Dongdaegu train station, exit the building and walk right to the pedestrian bridge. Do not cross the bridge, instead walk right down the stairs. The bus stop is down the road. Two subway lines crisscross the city centre; train tokens also cost ₩1200.

Around Daegu

Palgongsan Provincial Park
팔공산 도립공원

Just 20km north of Daegu, this park is sprawling, mountainous and well visited. Its highest peak, Palgong-san ('Mountain of the Eight Meritorious Officers', 1192m) received its name around the end of the Shilla period after eight generals saved Wang-Geon, the founding king of the Goryeo kingdom.

◉ Sights

Donghwa-sa   TEMPLE
(동화사; admission ₩2500; ⊙9am-6pm) The park's most popular destination is the province's leading temple, with a history stretching back to AD 493.

Gatbawi   SHRINE
(갓바위; www.seonbonsa.org) **FREE** Gatbawi is a medicinal Buddha shrine and national treasure, some 850m above sea level and said to date back to AD 638. This Buddha is famed for the flat stone 'hat' hovering over its head, 15cm thick. Incense wafts and mountain mist make it quite a spiritual experience. Plan on a challenging, though enjoyable, two-hour (return) hike. About 20 minutes into the hike, the trail leads to a small temple.

For a longer and not-as-steep hike, pick up the dirt trail behind the temple. For a shorter but steeper walk up stone steps, turn left at the small pagoda in the temple compound. Note: the trails are often packed on weekends.

Bus 401 (₩1200) runs here from outside Dongdaegu station to Gatbawi bus stop, where the hikes begin.

Palgong-san Skyline Cable Car   CABLE CAR
(adult/child return ₩9000/5000; ⊙9.45am-sunset Tue-Sun, closed Mon) The quickest way to ascend Palgong-san. The 1.2km-long ride drops you at the observatory (820m), which affords a panoramic view of Daegu.

DAEGU BUS DEPARTURES
Departures from the Express Bus Terminal

DESTINATION	PRICE (₩)	DURATION	FREQUENCY
Andong	9300	1¾hr	every 20min
Busan	9700	1¾hr	hourly
Daejeon	13,600	2hr	hourly
Dongseoul	25,400	4hr	hourly
Gyeongju	4900	50min	every 40min
Jinju	13,100	2¼hr	hourly
Seoul Gangnam	25,200	4hr	every 10min

Departures from the Intercity Bus Terminals

DESTINATION	TERMINAL	PRICE (₩)	DURATION (HR)	FREQUENCY
Andong	Bukbu	6900	1½	every 30min
Busan	Seobu	9900	2	every 1½hr
Chuncheon	Bukbu	18,300	5½	5 daily
Gyeongju	Dongbu	4900	1	every 15min
Haein-sa	Seobu	7100	1½	every 40min
Jinju	Seobu	9300	2	hourly
Pohang	Dongbu	7400	1½	every 10min
Tongyeong	Seobu	12,800	2½	every 50min

Palgongsan Provincial Park

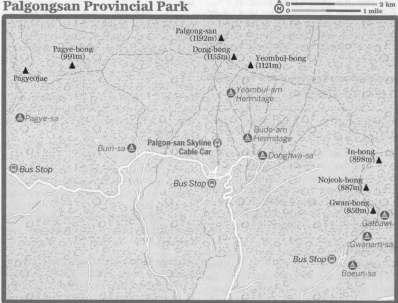

Bus 401 (₩1200) runs between Dong-daegu station and the tourist village below Gatbawi. Bus 급행 (Geuphaeng; ₩1300) connects Donghwa-sa and the bus stop near Dongdaegu station, running at least once every 12 minutes and taking 50 minutes to complete the journey.

Haein-sa   해인사

A small village surrounds the incredible Haein-sa complex, which is the main draw for visitors here.

◉ Sights

Haein-sa   TEMPLE
(☑ 055 934 3105; www.haeinsa.or.kr; admission ₩5000; ◷ 8-11am & noon-5pm Wed-Mon) This Unesco World Heritage–listed temple should be on every visitor's not-to-be-missed list. As well as being one of Korea's most significant temples, Haein-sa is also one of the most beautiful. Part of its beauty lies in the natural setting of mixed deciduous and coniferous forest surrounded by high mountain peaks and rushing streams. At **prayer times** (3.30am, 10am and 6.30pm) the place can feel otherworldly.

Haein-sa holds 81,258 woodblock scriptures, making it one of the largest Buddhist libraries of its kind.

Known as the Tripitaka Koreana, the blocks are housed in four buildings at the temple's upper reaches, complete with simple but effective ventilation to prevent deterioration. Although the buildings are normally locked, the blocks are easily visible through slatted windows.

The main hall, Daegwangjeon, was burnt down in the Japanese invasion of 1592 and again (accidentally) in 1817, though miraculously the Tripitaka survived. It escaped a third time, during the Korean War, when a South Korean pilot working for the Allied forces refused to allow them to bomb it.

The recently refurbished **Haein-sa Museum** showcases temple treasures including replicas of the scriptures, Buddhist art and other artefacts. It is a short walk from the main road, while the temple itself is a further kilometre up the hillside.

Hikers will want to challenge **Gaya-san** (1430m), the main peak in the national park, and a pretty one, though the 1100m stretch up from Haein-sa is known to be tough.

🛏 Sleeping & Eating

Haein-sa is a popular day trip from Daegu, but there are options to spend the night.

Haein-sa
TEMPLESTAY ₩

(http://80000.or.kr; weekday/weekend ₩40,000/60,000) Probably the most interesting sleeping option is to stay at the temple itself. Don't expect luxury – men and women sleep in separate *ondol* (underfloor-heated) dorms, but it's a worthwhile option to experience the otherworldly 3.30am prayer service.

Gobau
GUESTHOUSE ₩

(고바우; ✆ 055 932 5599; r ₩40,000; meals ₩8000-15,000; ⊙ restaurant 7am-midnight) A beautiful place to stay with kind owners. Rooms are simple, comfy, clean and floor-heated, with yellow linoleum. Try the **restaurant** where *sanchae jeongsik* (산채정식; rice with vegetables) is the main dish. It's in the centre of Haein-sa, up the hill beyond the bus terminal.

Haeinsa Tourist Hotel
HOTEL ₩₩

(해인사 관광 호텔; ✆ 055 933 2000; d/tw ₩79,000, ste ₩150,000; ❄) The most comfortable option in Haein-sa is at the top of the hill opposite the bus terminal, with fountains, a polished lobby, coffee shop, restaurant and sauna – even if it is often eerily deserted. Rates rise roughly 40% on Friday and Saturday.

Jeonju
KOREAN ₩₩

(전주; www.jjbab.com; dishes ₩8000-15,000; ⊙ 7am-9pm) Who would have imagined bus-terminal food could be this good? On the 2nd floor above the tiny terminal, this place serves tasty bibimbap (비빔밥; rice, egg, meat and vegies with chilli sauce), a good-value set menu with bulgogi and stir-fried shiitake mushrooms.

ℹ Getting There & Away

Although it's in Gyeongsangnam-do, Haein-sa is most easily accessed by bus (₩6600, 1½ hours, every 40 minutes) from Daegu's Seobu (South) intercity bus terminal. While the bus terminates at Haein-sa's small bus terminal at the top of the hill, tell the driver you're going to Haein-sa and they will drop you one stop earlier – look out for the traditional-style building on your right with 'shopping centre' written on it in English, and follow the crowds 1.2km up the hillside to the temple complex. All the hotels and the restaurants are around the bus terminal, a further 500m uphill along the main road.

TRIPITAKA KOREANA

The Tripitaka Koreana, also known as the Goryeo Buddhist canon, is one of the world's most significant Buddhist sacred texts. Tripitaka literally means 'three baskets', representing the three divisions of Buddhism: the Sutra (scriptures), Vinaya (laws) and the Abhidharma (treatises).

The Tripitaka Koreana has been preserved on more than 80,000 beautifully carved woodblocks, which took 16 years to complete. The first set of blocks, completed in 1087, was destroyed by Mongolian invaders in 1232. A reconstructed set, the one on display today, was completed in 1251. From carefully selecting appropriate birch wood, then soaking it in brine and boiling it in salt before drying it, to locating and constructing a sophisticated repository, the techniques involved were so complex and the artwork so intricate that they remain an inspiration today. The woodblocks are housed and preserved in the 15th-century hall, **Janggyong Pango**, a masterpiece of ingenuity in its own right; its techniques include charcoal beneath the clay floor and different-sized windows to minimise variations in humidity. Despite the ravages of Japanese invasion and fires that destroyed the rest of the temple complex, the repository remained standing with the woodblocks preserved intact.

During the 1970s, President Park Chung-hee ordered the construction of a modern storage facility for the woodblocks. The facility was equipped with advanced ventilation, temperature and humidity control. However, after some test woodblocks began to grow mildew the whole scheme was scrapped. Today the four storage halls and woodblocks are inscribed on the Unesco World Heritage list to ensure their continued preservation. In a bold attempt to ensure accessibility to more people, Haein-sa's monks have completely transcribed the works onto digital formats and translated the classical Chinese text into modern-day Korean.

Jikji-sa 직지사

📑 054

The lovely slowness of Jikji-sa convinces many visitors to linger a whole weekend, making it particularly popular for templestays.

⊙ Sights

Jikji-sa TEMPLE
(📑 054 436 6174; www.jikjisa.or.kr; adult/child/youth ₩3000/1500/2000; ⊙7am-6.30pm Mar-Oct, to 5.30pm Nov-Feb) Jikji-sa is a postcard-pretty temple in a quiet forest. The delicate paintings on the temple buildings have a refinement and an appealing grace, as do the giant timbers that support the structures, and the faded, cracked wood.

Of the 40 original buildings, about 20 still exist, the oldest dating from the 1602 reconstruction. Highlights include the **Daeungjong**, with stunning Buddhist triad paintings on silk (1774) that are national treasures, and the rotating collection in the temple's **Jikji Museum of Buddhist Arts** (📑054 436 6009; admission ₩2000; ⊙9am-5.30pm Mar-Oct, to 4.30pm Nov-Feb, closed Mon).

⊨ Sleeping & Eating

Many visitors day trip to Jikji-sa, while some join the Templestay program (p65). There's a well-established tourist village by the bus stop with *minbak* (private homes with rooms for rent), *yeogwan* (small, family-run hotels) and restaurants.

ℹ Getting There & Away

Jikji-sa is reached via Gimcheon (population 152,000), about 20 minutes by bus. Local buses 11, 111, and 112 (₩1400) depart every 10 minutes from Gimcheon's **intercity bus terminal** (📑 054 432 7600). The temple complex is a pleasant 15-minute walk from the bus stop.

Gimcheon can be reached by train on the line connecting Daegu (50 minutes) and Seoul. If you're using KTX from Seoul, transfer at Daejeon and take a local line to Gimcheon.

Gyeongju 경주

📑 054 / POP 280,000

Known as 'the museum without walls', Gyeongju holds more tombs, temples, rock carvings, pagodas, Buddhist statuary and palace ruins than any other place in South Korea.

Most visitors touring the city centre are taken aback by the distinctive urban landscape created by round grassy tombs – called *tumuli* – and traditional architecture with colourful hip roofs set against a canvas of green rolling mountains.

Two of Gyeongju's most not-to-be-missed sites – Bulguk-sa and Seokguram – are in the outlying districts and within reach via public transport. Gyeongju covers a vast area – some 1323 sq km – so you should plan on several days of travel if you want to visit some of the lesser-known places. Bus transport out to these areas is satisfactory, though personal transport is a better option if you value speed and flexibility.

In 57 BC, around the same time that Julius Caesar was subduing Gaul, Gyeongju became the capital of the Shilla dynasty, and it remained so for nearly a thousand years. In the 7th century AD, under King Munmu, Shilla conquered the neighbouring kingdoms of Goguryeo and Baekje, and Gyeongju became the capital of the whole peninsula. The population of the city eventually peaked at around one million people, but the Shilla fell victim to division from within and invasion from without.

The city began a cultural revival in the late 20th century – with much preservation and restoration work thanks to President Park Chung-hee in the 1970s.

⊙ Sights

Central Gyeongju is compact, encompassing the bus and train terminals (20 minutes' walk apart) and, between them, sights, lodgings and dining.

BUS DEPARTURES FROM GIMCHEON

DESTINATION	PRICE (₩)	DURATION (HR)	FREQUENCY
Andong	13,400	2	every 1-2hr
Daegu	6000	1¼	every 30min
Daejeon	6600	1¼	hourly
Gochang*	8000	1¼	hourly

*for Haein-sa & Gayasan National Park

About 5km east of the centre is Lake Bomun Resort, with a golf course, luxury hotels and posh restaurants. A 16km drive southeast brings you to Bulguk-sa, one of Korea's most famous temples. From here it's a quick ride to Seokgur-am, a mountain grotto with a historic Buddha.

⊙ Central Gyeongju

Gyeongju National Museum MUSEUM
(국립경주박물관; Map p164; ☑ 054 740 7537; http://gyeongju.museum.go.kr; ☉ 9am-6pm Tue-Fri & Sun, to 9pm Sat & holidays Mar-Dec, closed Mon) **FREE** Arguably the best history museum in Korea, the Gyeongju National Museum is where you can appreciate the significance of this ancient city in one fell swoop. The main archaeological hall has dazzling displays of jewellery, weaponry and other ceremonial items from the Shilla dynasty, including a 5th-century gold crown that looks like something out of *Game of Thrones*. The museum is an easy 150m walk from the east side of Wolseong-gongwon and is well signed.

You'll find an entire building devoted to the findings at Anapji Pond, an art hall focusing on Buddhist works and a temporary exhibition hall.

Outside the main hall, the **Emille Bell** (King Seongdeok's Bell) is one of the largest and most beautifully resonant bells ever made in Asia. It's said that its ringing can be heard over a 3km radius when struck only lightly with the fist. Unfortunately, you aren't allowed to test this claim.

There is English labelling throughout and an interesting multilingual audioguide is available too (₩3000). English-speaking tours run Saturdays starting at 1.30pm (March to November).

Tumuli-gongwon TOMB
(대릉원; Map p162; admission ₩1500; ☉ 9am-10pm) The huge, walled park has 23 tombs of Shilla monarchs and family members. From the outside, they look like grassy hillocks – much more subtle than the Egyptian pyramids, but they served the same purpose; many of the *tumuli* have yielded fabulous treasures, on display at the Gyeongju National Museum. On colder days, the park closes at sunset.

One tomb, **Cheonmachong** (Heavenly Horse Tomb), is open to visitors. A cross-section display shows its construction.

The tomb is 13m high and 47m in diameter and was built around the end of the 5th century. Facsimiles of the golden crown, bracelets, jade ornaments, weapons and pottery found here are displayed in glass cases around the inside of the tomb.

Noseo-dong Tombs TOMB
(노서동 고분; Map p162) **FREE** Near the main shopping area is the Noseo-dong district, where you'll find Shilla tombs. **Seobongchong** and **Geumgwanchong** are adjacent tombs built between the 4th and 5th centuries. They were excavated between 1921 and 1946; the finds included two gold crowns. Across the road is **Bonghwadae**, the largest extant Shilla tomb at 22m high and with a 250m circumference; adjoining it is **Geumnyeongchong**. Houses covered much of this area until 1984, when they were removed.

Bunhwang-sa PAGODA
(분황사; www.bunhwangsa.org; admission ₩1500; ☉ sunrise-sunset) This large pagoda was built in the mid-7th century during Queen Seondeok's reign, making it the oldest datable pagoda in Korea. It's a rare example of one made from brick. The magnificently carved Buddhist guardians and stone lions are a main feature; it is unique in that each entrance is protected by two guardians.

To get here, follow the willow-lined road across from the Gyeongju National Museum until you reach the first intersection. Turn right at the intersection and then take the first lane on the right. The walk will take about 20 to 25 minutes and is well sign-posted.

Cheomseongdae OBSERVATORY
(첨성대; Map p162; ☑ 054 772 5134; ☉ 8am-6pm Apr-Oct, 9am-6pm Nov-Mar) **FREE** Southeast of Tumuli-gongwon in the attractive sprawl of Wolseong-gongwon is the Far East's oldest astrological observatory, constructed between AD 632 and 646. Its apparently simple design conceals amazing sophistication: the 12 stones of its base symbolise the months of the year. From top to bottom there are 30 layers – one for each day of the month – and a total of 366 stones were used in its construction, corresponding (approximately) to the days of the year.

Numerous other technical details relate, for example, to the tower's position in relation to certain stars.

The visitor centre just outside the entrance has a digital display in English about the building's construction.

GYEONGSANGBUK-DO GYEONGJU

Gyeongju

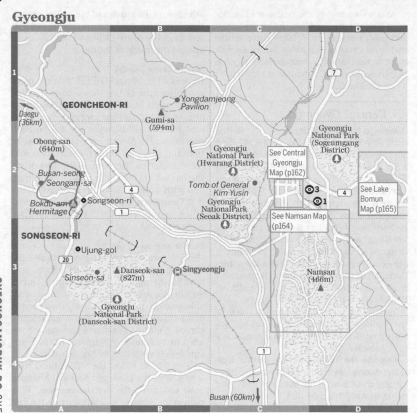

Gyeongju

◎ Sights

1 Anapji Pond D2
2 Bulguk-sa E3
3 Bunhwang-sa D2
4 Girim-sa F2
5 Golgul-sa F3
6 Seokguram F3

⊗ Eating

7 Gampo Hogung Raw Fish Center H3

ⓘ Information

8 Tourist Information Booth E3

Banwol-seong
RUINS

(반월성; Map p164; Castle of the Crescent Moon) **FREE** A few minutes' walk south from Cheomseongdae (p159), Banwol-seong is the site of a once-fabled fortress. Now it's attractive parkland, where you can see some walls

and ruins. The only intact building is **Seokbinggo** (Stone Ice House; early 18th century, restored 1973), which was once used as a food store.

Anapji Pond
POND

(안압지; Map p160; admission ₩2000; ⊙8am-sunset Sep-May, 7.30am-7pm Jun-Aug) This is a popular spot for couples to take prewedding photos. From June to early August, magnificent lotus blossoms seem to fill the horizon.

In the past, it was a pleasure garden to commemorate the unification of the Korean Peninsula under Shilla. The buildings here burned in 935 and many relics ended up in the pond itself, to be rediscovered only when it was drained for repair in 1975.

Thousands of well-preserved relics were found including wooden objects, a die used in drinking games, scissors and a royal barge – you can see them in the Gyeongju National Museum (p159).

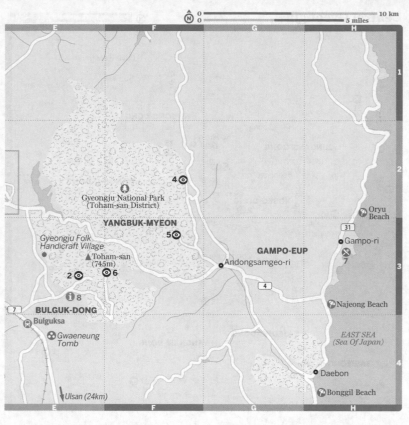

Eastern Gyeongju

Bulguk-sa
TEMPLE

(불국사; Map p160; www.bulguksa.or.kr; adult/child/youth ₩5000/2000/3000; ⏰7am-6pm Mar-Oct, to 5pm Nov-Feb) On a series of stone terraces about 16km southeast of Gyeongju, set among gnarled pines and iris gardens that would make Van Gogh swoon, this temple is the crowning glory of Shilla architecture and is on the Unesco World Cultural Heritage list. The excellence of its carpentry, the skill of its painters (particularly the interior woodwork and the eaves of the roofs) and the subtlety of its landscapes all contribute to its magnificence.

The approach to the temple leads you to two national-treasure **bridges**. One of these bridges has 33 steps, representing the 33 stages to enlightenment. Two more national treasures are the pagodas standing in the courtyard of the first set of buildings that somehow survived Japanese vandalism. The first, **Dabotap**, is of plain design and typical of Shilla artistry, while the other, **Seokgat-ap**, is much more ornate and typical of the neighbouring Baekje kingdom. The pagodas are so revered that replicas appear in the grounds of the Gyeongju National Museum (p159).

You can reach Bulguk-sa by loop buses 10 or 11 (₩1500, 30 minutes), though from central Gyeongju 11 is much quicker. There's a **tourist information booth** (☎046 746 4747) in the car park, near the bus stop.

Golgul-sa
BUDDHIST TEMPLE

(골굴사; Map p160; ☎054 744 1689; www.sunmudo.com; templestay per night incl meals ₩50,000; ⏰8am-6pm) **FREE** Finally, a temple where you can do more than just look around. The Buddha carved out of solid rock by Indian monks in the 6th century is fairly interesting but the real draw here

Central Gyeongju

is *sunmudo,* a Korean martial art that blends fighting skills with meditation. Short 20-minute demonstrations take place at 3pm Sundays at Sunmudo University on the temple grounds and *sunmudo* training is available through the **Templestay Program**. Reservations recommended. Most of the program is taught in English.

From Gyeongju intercity bus terminal, take a bus towards Gampo-ri or Yangbuk-myeon (bus 100 or 150) and ask the driver to drop you at Andongsamgeo-ri, where the turnoff to the temple is off to the left. Golgul-sa is a 20-minute walk down the road.

Lake Bomun Resort RESORT

(보문 단지; Map p165) Bomun is a tourist district around an artificial lake 5km east of central Gyeongju. Tradition-seekers will find the tandem bikes, paddle boats, conference centres and such less appealing, but it is home to Gyeongju's top-end lodgings. The lake and extensive parklands are great for strolling or bike riding, though the area doesn't have the character of the town centre.

Traditional dancing and musical performances are held on a regular basis from April to October at **Bomun Outdoor Performance Theatre**, located below the information centre by the lake.

Wooyong Museum of Contemporary Art MUSEUM

(우양미술관; Map p165; ☑ 054 745 7075; http://wooyangmuseum.org; admission ₩700; ☺ 10am-6pm Tue-Sun, closed Mon; P) This modern art museum behind the Hilton Hotel (p165) is the sister to Artsonje Center Seoul (Wooyong was previously called Sonje) and holds three exhibition spaces with seasonal exhibitions plus a permanent collection containing paintings, sculpture and mixed media. It's a worthwhile stop if you're in the area.

Central Gyeongju

Seokguram
GROTTO

(석굴암; Map p160; adult/child/youth ₩3500/
2500/2000; ⊙6.30am-6pm Apr-Oct, 7am-5.30pm
Nov-Mar) In the mountains above Bulguk-sa is
this famous Unesco World Cultural Heritage–
listed grotto. It can be a magical place,
especially when rain and mists cloak the
mountaintops. Chipmunks dance in the thick
woods leading up to the rotunda, where sits
an image of the Sakyamuni Buddha surrounded by more than three dozen guardians and
lesser deities. His position gazing over the East
Sea (visible in clear weather) has long made
him regarded as a protector of his country.

Seokguram was quite a feat of engineer-
ing when it was constructed in the mid-8th
century. Huge blocks of granite were quar-
ried far to the north at a time when the only
access to the Seokguram site (740m above
sea level) was a narrow mountain path.

Bus 12 runs hourly between the car parks
for Bulguk-sa and Seokguram (₩1500, 20
minutes). From the Seokguram car park, it
is a 400m walk along a shaded gravel track
and up the stairs to the grotto. Alternatively,
there is a hiking trail between the Seokguram
ticket office and Bulguk-sa (about 3.2km).

Girim-sa
TEMPLE

(기림사; Map p160; admission ₩4000; ⊙8am-
8pm) About 3.5km down the road from Golgul-
sa (p161), Girim-sa is one of the largest
complexes in the vicinity of the Shilla capital.
Its size (14 buildings and growing) compares
with that of Bulguk-sa, but the compound
lacks a 'wow' factor, which might explain
why it receives comparably fewer visitors.

From Golgul-sa, there is no public transport to Girim-sa. If you're without personal

transport, the choices are walking 3.5km
down the road alongside rice paddies, or
asking for a lift.

◎ Southern Gyeongju (Namsan) 남산

The mountain Nam-san (466m), south of
the city centre, is one of the region's most
rewarding areas to explore, a place where
you can easily combine the athletic with
the spiritual. It's beautiful, and strewn with
relics, active temples, monasteries and sites
for impromptu religious observance. Among
the relics that have been found here are 122
temple sites, 64 stone pagodas, 57 stone
Buddhas, and many royal tombs, rock-cut
figures, pavilions and the remains of fortresses, temples and palaces.

You can choose from hundreds of paths,
many of which run alongside streams that
tumble down the mountain. The paths and
tracks are well trodden, though at times you
will need to head off the main trails to scout
for relics that are not immediately visible,
since only a few of them are signposted.

You can also check with tourist offices
at Gyeongju or Lake Bomun for additional
maps and information about trail conditions.

Buses 11, 500, 501, 503, 505, 506, 507 and
591 all pass by Nam-san and take 20 minutes
from the city centre.

Samneung
ROYAL TOMBS

(삼릉; Map p164; ⊙24hr) **FREE** The reason
to come to this pine grove is to start a hike
up Nam-san. On your way up, you may pass
the *tumuli* of three Shilla kings. Another
tomb, located away from the others, is said

Namsan

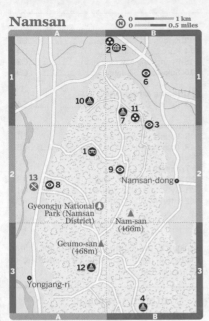

Namsan

⊙ Sights

1 Badukbawi	A2
2 Banwol-seong	B1
3 Bori-sa	B1
4 Chilbul-am	B3
5 Gyeongju National Museum	B1
6 Mangdeok-sa	B1
7 Ongnyong-am	B1
8 Samneung	A2
9 Sangsabawi	B2
10 Sangseon-am Hermitage	A1
11 Tapgol	B1
12 Yongjangsaji	A3

⊗ Eating

13 Sigol Yeohaeng	A2

to contain King Gyeongae, who was killed when robbers raided Poseokjeongji during an elaborate banquet, setting the stage for the dynasty's collapse.

☞ Tours

Numerous Korean-language **tour buses** (six- to nine-hour tours excluding lunch and admissions, ₩20,000) access all the sights and depart from the intercity bus terminal at various times each morning. Ask at the nearby tourist information kiosk for exact timings and costs.

🛏 Sleeping

Lodgings are everywhere, so finding a room in and around the bus and train stations to match your budget won't be a problem. Higher-end lodgings and restaurants are at Lake Bomun, with some less expensive options just east from the lake.

★ Sarangchae   HANOK GUESTHOUSE ₩

(사랑채; Map p162; ☎054 773 4868; www.kjstay.com; s/d incl breakfast ₩35,000/45,000, s/tw without private bathroom ₩30,000/40,000; @⊚) This charmingly traditional yet simple guesthouse to one side of Tumuli-gongwon has existed for 120 years and offers cosy rooms with *ondol* or beds scattered around a courtyard. The friendly owner speaks English and offers plenty of travel advice, including maps. There's free laundry, a left-luggage room and even log fires in the courtyard on some nights. Reservations essential.

Hanjin Hostel   HOSTEL ₩

(한진장여관; Map p162; ☎054 771 4097; http://hanjinkorea.wo.to; dm/s/tw ₩15,000/25,000/40,000; ⊚) Open since 1977 (and showing its age), this centrally located hostel is run by the friendly English-speaking Clint Kwon, who shares excellent local advice and history (his father accommodated probably the first Korea travel writer). The rooms are dingy, but bathrooms are modern. The kitchen, courtyard and roof deck are great for chatting with other travellers. Laundry is ₩6000 per load.

Taeyang-Jang Motel   LOVE HOTEL ₩

(태양장 여관; Map p162; ☎054 773 6889; r/ste ₩30,000/40,000; ✳@) This spotless motel has a rock garden in the lobby and a friendly owner. Rooms are spacious, with good bathrooms and all modern conveniences including huge widescreen TVs and in-room PCs.

Arirang-jang Yeoinsuk   GUESTHOUSE ₩

(아리랑장 여인숙; Map p162; ☎054 772 2460; r ₩20,000) Shabby but inexpensive, this place has tiny, odd-shaped *ondol* rooms. It's near the train station, to the left and behind the largest bakery.

Baramgot Guesthouse   GUESTHOUSE ₩₩

(바람곳게스트하우스; Map p162; ☎054 771 2589; www.baramgot.kr; 137 Wonhyo-ro; dm/d incl breakfast ₩18,000/50,000; ⊜✳@⊚) You'll love returning to Baramgot at the end of a day of walking. Drop a cushion onto the wooden floor of the charming sitting area and meet other travellers or watch a projected movie.

Bathrooms are reassuringly spotless and modern, and shared ones sport ample showers. Finally, get true rest on the plumpest mattresses in town. Basic English spoken.

Gyeongju Guest House
HOSTEL **₩₩**

(경주 게스트 하우스; Map p162; ☑054 745 7101; www.gjguesthouse.com; dm/tw/tr incl breakfast ₩18,000/45,000/65,000; ☺❋@☎) Just a short distance from the train station, this gleamingly presented guesthouse has a spacious and modern communal area, a sparkling kitchen and very clean dorm and room accommodation. Guests also get a free laundry and discounted bicycle rental (daily ₩5000). Staff speak basic English and this is a solid budget option.

Gyeongju Hilton
LUXURY HOTEL **₩₩**

(경주 힐튼호텔; Map p165; ☑054 745 7788; www.hilton.com; 484-7, Bomun-ro; r from ₩121,500; ❋☎≋) A real Miró hangs in the lobby of this Art Deco Hilton by the lake. It has a sauna, squash courts, pool and gym, not to mention spacious rooms with marble bathrooms. A good choice if you're looking for smart comfort.

Show Motel
LOVE HOTEL **₩₩**

(쇼모텔; Map p162; ☑054 771 7878; r from ₩60,000; ❋@) One of the snazziest of the multiple flashing love hotels behind the bus terminal. There's lots of attention to detail in the rooms from desktop computers and spacious interiors to saunas in the bathroom and complimentary drinks. Large bathrooms and general cleanliness make up for the gaudy decor.

Commodore Hotel
Gyeongju Chosun
HOTEL **₩₩₩**

(코모도호텔 경주; Map p165; ☑054 745 7701; www.commodorehotel.co.kr/eng; r from ₩144,000, sauna ₩5400; ❋@) Perhaps the best located of the lakeside hotels, with some of the most attractive grounds, the Commodore is less impressive on the inside, where rooms need a bit of updating. That said there is nice woodwork in the rooms, Gyeongju green and terracotta-coloured motifs downstairs, and one of the city's favourite saunas. Rates increase 25% Friday and Saturday.

✕ Eating & Drinking

Gyeongju provides plenty of good eating opportunities with the greatest concentration of choice in the city centre. Southeast of Tumuligongwun is a street full of *ssambap* **restaurants** (쌈밥집), where you order lots of side dishes and wrap them up in lettuce and other leaves.

Lake Bomun

Daebak Jip
KOREAN **₩**

(대박집; Map p162; mains ₩2500-10,000; ⊙11am-2pm) A good place to eat late, this local hangout does excellent barbecue pork and beef dishes at low prices. The service is friendly, even if there's no English menu or English spoken – the pictorial menu saves the day.

Sigol Yeohaeng
KOREAN **₩**

(시골 여행; Map p164; meals ₩5000-12,000; ⊙9am-9pm) Opposite the entrance to Samneung (p163), this 20-year-old restaurant specialises in *mukun kimchi* (묵은 김치), a spicy noodle-and-broth dish made with kimchi aged at least three years.

★ Dosolmaeul
KOREAN **₩₩**

(도솔마을; Map p162; mains ₩15,000; ⊙11.30am-9pm Tue-Sun) Definitely the most atmospheric place to eat in Gyeongju, this traditional courtyard restaurant beside Tumuligongwun has a delicious and broad menu featuring lip-smacking dishes such as steamed octopus with hot sauce, or seafood, meatball and vegetable stew. The best deal however is the ₩18,000 traditional Korean set dinner for two, a feast of around 20 small dishes.

Kisoya
JAPANESE **₩₩**

(기소야; Map p162; ☑054 746 6020; meals ₩10,000-30,000; ⊙10am-3pm & 5-10pm) Spotless and friendly Kisoya serves up mouthwatering Japanese dishes with a Korean slant. Mains are generous set meals of the classics from bento boxes to sashimi and noodle soups. Don't miss the chicken-fillet bento box.

Pyongyang Naengmyeon
NOODLES **₩₩**

(평양냉면; Map p162; meals ₩7000-12,000; ⊙11am-9pm) This bustling place always attracts crowds of locals who come here for the excellent Pyongyang Cold Noodles as well as the spicy bulgogi. It has a pleasant outdoor-seating area complete with a garden and a little fountain. Ask for the English menu.

Kuro Ssambap
KOREAN ₩₩

(구로쌈밥; Map p162; per person ₩12,000; ⊙11am-9pm) Eclectic collections of birds, rocks, figurines, pottery and other folk arts make this a unique place to dine on this strip of otherwise rather similar *ssambap* restaurants just to the north of Wolseong-gongwon. Orders include 28 refillable side dishes.

Sukyeong Sikdang
KOREAN ₩₩

(숙영 식당; Map p162; mains from ₩9000; ⊙11am-8.30pm) Since 1979, this cosy restaurant with a delightfully cluttered and rustic interior has been serving tasty *pajeon* (파전; green-onion pancake) made from organic ingredients and homemade *dongdongju* (동동주; rice wine). It's near the east wall of Tumuli-gongwon.

Gampo Hogung Raw Fish Center
SEAFOOD ₩₩₩

(감포 호궁 회센타; Map p162; crab meals from ₩30,000 person; ⊙7am-midnight) King crab and raw fish are the specialities of this bustling restaurant near Gampo harbour. Crab dinners

---

NAMSAN DAY HIKES

Central Namsan

There are numerous trails through Namsan, the most convenient starting at Samneung. Whichever route you take, be sure to include detours – necessary to hunt for relics off-track. There's virtually no English signage, but with some *hangeul* (Korean phonetic alphabet) skill you should do fine.

Three-hour course Head up from Samneung, breaking to take in several relief carvings and statues along the way, to the hermitage **Sangseon-am** (상선암; Map p164), where you'll find lovely views across the valley and maybe a monk chanting. Continue up past the rock formation **Badukbawi** (바둑바위; Map p164) and along the ridge to **Sangsabawi** (상사바위; Map p164), then walk back the way you came.

Five-hour course Instead of doubling back from Sangsabawi, continue on to the summit of **Geumo-san** (금오산, 468m) to **Yongjangsaji** (용장사지, Yongjang Temple Site; Map p164), where you can view the seated Buddha image carved in stone and the three-storey stone pagoda. Descend to **Yongjang-ri** (용장리, Yongjang village), from where you can catch a bus back to central Gyeongju.

Eight-hour course Follow the route as far as Yongjangsaji, but instead of heading down towards Yongjang-ri, head across the ridge to **Chilbul-am** (칠불암, Hermitage of Seven Buddhas; Map p164), Namsan's largest relic with images carved in natural rocks and stone pillars. From here it's mostly downhill towards the road and about another kilometre to **Namsan-ni** (남산리) (남산리, Namsan village) on the eastern side of the park, from where it's an easy bus ride back to town.

Northeastern Namsan

Take local bus 11 from Gyeongju and get off as soon as the bus crosses the river, about 2.5km past the **Gyeongju National Museum** (p159). Off the main road is a fork – take the left branch and you can wind your way to **Bori-sa** (보리사; Map p164), a beautifully reconstructed nunnery set amid old-growth trees and ancient images. It is possible to head over the hill behind Bori-sa to **Tapgol** (탑골, Pagoda Valley; Map p164), but it's a rough climb. It's easier to backtrack down to the fork and take the other branch. Follow the river for several hundred metres until you come to a small village. Turn left here and head up the road through Tapgol and you'll reach the secluded hermitage **Ongnyong-am** (옥룡암; Map p164). In the upper corner are ponderous boulders covered with Korea's greatest collection of relief carvings.

Returning to the bridge and looking towards the main road, you will see two stone pillars standing in a thicket of trees amid rice paddies. These pillars are all that remain standing of **Mangdeok-sa** (Map p164), a huge Shilla-era temple complex. From there it's an easy trip back towards the National Museum, about 20 minutes. Depending on your route, this itinerary might take you half a day.

start with a small selection of sides and finish with a pot of spicy fish soup. It's customary to negotiate the price of a crab meal before entering, although English isn't spoken, so bring a Korean friend or prepare for some interesting bargaining.

Gallery Cafe   CAFE
(Map p162; coffee ₩4000; ⊙9am-11pm) Finally, somewhere for a coffee with a view of a *tumuli* before you and bronze sculptures all around. This calm cafe bucks the trend of the surrounding chain coffee joints with some vinyl from the '60s, vintage furniture and tempting homemade green-tea smoothies.

☆ Entertainment

There are outdoor traditional dance and music performances every Saturday during April, May, September and October (3pm to 5pm) on the performance stage in Wolseong-gongwon. More regular modern and traditional performances are held at Lake Bomun between April and October. Weekend performances of Korean dance and music at Lake Bomun start at 7.30pm or 8.30pm with additional Thursday and Friday shows in May, July and August. Check with the tourist office for information about what's going on while you're in town.

❶ Information

There is central tourist information kiosks at the **train station** (☎ 054 772 3843; ⊙9am-6pm) and the **express bus terminal** (☎ 054 772 9289), as well as one in the car park near Bulguk-sa, all with English-speaking staff and comprehensive English-language maps.

For planning advice, author recommendations, traveller reviews and insider tips, see **Lonely Planet** (www.lonelyplanet.com/south-korea/gyeongsangbuk-do/gyeongju).

❶ Getting There & Away

AIR
There is no airport at Gyeongju, but the airports at Busan (Gimhae) and Ulsan are readily accessible. Ulsan's airport is closer, but Gimhae has more flights.

BUS
Gyeongju's **express bus terminal** (☎ 054 741 4000) and **intercity bus terminal** (☎ 054 743 5599) are adjacent to one other.

TRAIN
Gyeongju has a direct KTX service with regular services from here to Seoul (₩45,900, two hours) and Busan (₩11,000, 30 minutes), but it serves the out-of-town Singyeongju station, rather than the conveniently central Gyeongju station. Arriving at Singyeongju station, take bus 50, 60, 61, 70, 201 or 700 to the city centre (15 minutes).

From **Gyeongju train station** (☎ 054 743 4114) there are services to Pohang (₩2600, 30 minutes, every one to two hours) and Daegu (₩5200, one hour 20 minutes, hourly), but you need to go to Daegu or Pohang and change trains to reach Seoul. Change at Daegu to reach Busan.

❶ Getting Around

TO/FROM THE AIRPORT
Several buses link Gyeongju's main intercity bus terminal with both the Ulsan airport (₩4900, one hour, four daily) and Busan's Gimhae airport (₩14,100, 3½ hours, 10 daily).

GYEONGSANGBUK-DO GYEONGJU

GYEONJU BUS DEPARTURES
Departures from the Express Bus Terminal

DESTINATION	PRICE (₩)	DURATION (HR)	FREQUENCY
Busan	4800	1	hourly
Daegu	4900	1	every 40min
Daejeon	17,200	3¼	5 daily
Seoul	20,200	4½	hourly

Departures from the Intercity Bus Terminal

DESTINATION	PRICE (₩)	DURATION (HR)	FREQUENCY
Busan	4500	1	every 15min
Daegu	4200	1	every 40min
Pohang	4900	1	every 40min
Ulsan	3100	1	4 daily

BICYCLE

Hiring a bicycle is a great way to reach the sights. There are some bike trails around Namsan (but it's rather hilly) and Lake Bomun. There are bicycle-rental shops everywhere, including several scattered around the town centre and one opposite the Gyeongju National Museum (p159). The rates are approximately ₩3000 to ₩4000 hourly or ₩12,000 to ₩15,000 daily. Check your hostel for bike deals.

BUS

Many local buses (₩1500) terminate just outside the intercity bus terminal, alongside the river. For shorter routes (eg to Bulguk-sa), buses can be picked up along Sosong-no and Daejeong-no.

Buses 10 (which runs clockwise) and 11 (counterclockwise) run a circuit of most of the major sights including Bulguk-sa, Namsan and Lake Bomun, as well as the bus terminals and Gyeongju train station (every 15 minutes). Bus 150 departs from the train station to the eastern sights, via the Lake Bomun Expo arena (every 30 minutes). Bus 100 makes a similar initial route.

Buses make announcements in English for major attractions but can be standing-room only on busy weekends.

TAXI

If your time is limited and you want to cover a lot of ground in a short time, taxis are often available for day hire outside train and bus stations. Rates are negotiable but hover around ₩150,000/200,000 for five/seven hours. One way between Lake Bomun and the city centre is ₩10,000.

Around Gyeongju

Yangdong Folk Village
경주 양동마을

Yangdong Folk Village   VILLAGE
(경주 양동마을) Getting here is not easy, but your journey to this Joseon-dynasty village will be rewarded with an up-close, intimate look at superb traditional architecture in a decidedly noncommercial setting. Designated as a cultural-preservation area, the entire village (replete with stone walls, straw-thatched roofs and green gardens) is a photographer's dream. Set aside a half-day to admire the 180 or so houses typical of the *yangban* class – a largely hereditary class based on scholarship and official position.

Most of the homes here are still lived in, so you need to observe the usual courtesies when looking around; some of the larger mansions stand empty and are open to the public. There are descriptive plaques with English explana-tions outside some of the more important structures. If buildings are locked, you may be able to ask for a key nearby. There are no entry fees to any of the buildings.

When it's time for a break, try one of the area teashops, like **Uhyangdaok** (우향다옥; dishes ₩5000-15,000; ⊙noon-10pm), which is in a rustic building with simple treats such as green tea, wine and light meals. No English is spoken here but the owner goes to much effort to ease communication. If you want to stay the night, there are two small *ondol* rooms (₩35,000) for rent. Early breakfast is possible but you need to ask ahead of time.

From Gyeongju, buses 200, 201, 202, 203 and 206 will get you to within 1.5km of Yangdong. From the bus stop, follow the train line and then go under it. There's only one road into the village, about a 30-minute walk.

Oksan Seowon & Around
옥산 서원
☑ 054

Established in 1572 in honour of Yi Eon-jeok (1491–1553), Oksan Seowon was one of the most important *seowon*, or Confucian academies. It was enlarged in 1772 and was one of the few to escape destruction in the 1860s. However, an early-20th-century fire destroyed some of the buildings; today only 14 structures remain.

⊙ Sights

Dongnakdang   HISTORIC SITE
(독락당; ⊙by appointment) FREE A 10-minute walk beyond Oksan Seowon up the valley road will bring you to Dongnakdang, a beautiful collection of well-preserved buildings, constructed in 1515 and expanded in 1532 as the residence of Yi Eon-jeok after he left government service. The walled compound is partly occupied by descendants of Master Yi himself.

Due to past vandalism, the family requests visitors to book appointments in advance (ask at tourist offices). They will open up the inner rooms and answer any questions (in Korean).

🛏 Sleeping & Eating

Oksan Motel   MOTEL ₩
(옥산 모텔; ☎ 054 762 9500; www.oksanmotel. com; r from ₩35,000; ❄) About 500m from Dongnakdang, the Oksan has modern *ondol* or bedrooms with a shower, and a patio in front of the property.

Sanjang Sikdang
KOREAN ₩₩

(산장식당; ☎ 054 762 3716; chicken/duck stew for 2-4 people ₩30,000/35,000) This place specialises in free-range duck and chicken. *Tojongdak baeksuk* (토종닭 백숙) and *orihanbang baeksuk* (오리한방 백숙) are chicken and duck stews served with rice porridge. Note: stews take up to 50 minutes to prepare, so you can relax in the outdoor seating area or have a Korean speaker call before you arrive. It's between Dongnak-dang (p168) and the Oksan Motel (p168).

ⓘ Getting There & Away

Bus 203 (₩1800, six daily) to Angang-ri connects Gyeongju train station and Oksan Seowon.

Songseon-ri
송선리

Close to the summit of the thickly forested Obong-san (640m), **Bokdu-am** hermitage features a huge rock face out of which 19 niches have been carved. The three central niches hold a figure of the historical Buddha flanked by two bodhisattva (Munsu and Bohyeon); the remainder house the 16 arhat monks who have attained nirvana. The carving is recent and although there's an unoccupied house up here, the actual hermitage was burned down in 1988 after an electrical fault started a blaze. There is also a statue of Gwanseeum, the Goddess of Mercy, just beyond the rock face. Just below the hermitage is a stunning viewpoint from the top of a couple of massive boulders. It's a great place for a picnic lunch.

The trail is easy to follow, but bring water as there are no springs along the way. The walk up will take around an hour. From the bus stop in Songseon-ri, follow the creek up along the narrow road about 500m to a small temple, **Seongam-sa**. The trail starts just to the left of this temple and is well marked in Korean.

A further 3.8km up the road from the bus stop for Bokduam and Jusaam, remote **Sinseon-sa** near the top of Danseok-san (827m), is believed to be one of the oldest cave temples in Korea. About 50m to the right as you face the temple are some ancient rock carvings in a small grotto. The temple was used as a base by General Kim Yu-shin in the 7th century and has seen some renovation work since then. It's about a two-hour circuit walk from the bus stop. There's a little village along the way, about 2.5km from the bus stop.

Bus 300 (₩1800, every 25 minutes) travels to Obong-san and stops near Jusaam. If you're looking for a more direct route to Sinseon-sa, take bus 350 (₩1800, every one to two hours) and get off at Ujung-gol (우중골). From the intercity bus terminal, catch either bus at the stop near Paris Baguette.

Pohang
포항

☎ 054 / POP 508,000

If you've ever wanted to swim on a beach in full view of the world's second-largest steel plant, Pohang is the place for you. A large and rather bland city best known as home to Posco (Pohang Iron and Steel Company), Pohang does actually boast a pretty decent beach, though a fairly unpleasant smell pervades much of the place. Most people pass through here on the way to the island of Ulleungdo, but it's a convenient place to spend the night, with plenty of accommodation choices and beachside restaurants open until sunrise.

◉ Sights

Bogyeong-sa
TEMPLE

(보경사; admission ₩2500; ⏰ 7am-7pm) You'll need a full day to explore the offerings in and around this temple. About 30km north of Pohang, Bogyeong-sa is a gateway to a beautiful valley boasting 12 waterfalls, gorges spanned by bridges, hermitages, stupas and the temple itself. There are good **hikes** including Naeyeon-san (930m). The 20km return trip to the summit – Hyangno-bong – from Bogyeong-sa takes about six hours.

The well-maintained trail to the gorge and waterfalls branches off from the tourist village. It's about 1.5km to the first waterfall, 5m-high Ssangsaeng Pokpo. The sixth waterfall, Gwaneum Pokpo, is an impressive 72m and has two columns of water with a cave behind it. The seventh waterfall, about 30m high, is called Yeonsan Pokpo. Further up the trail, the going gets difficult; the ascent of Hyangno-bong should only be attempted if the day is young.

The temple is 15 minutes' walk from where the buses from Pohang terminate, and there's a tourist village with souvenir shops, restaurants, *minbak* and *yeogwan*.

Bus 500 (₩1600, 45 minutes, every 30 to 90 minutes) runs between Pohang's intercity bus terminal and the temple, though some require a transfer at Cheongha. The easiest route is to catch one the buses that travel directly to the temple; check with the tourist

Pohang

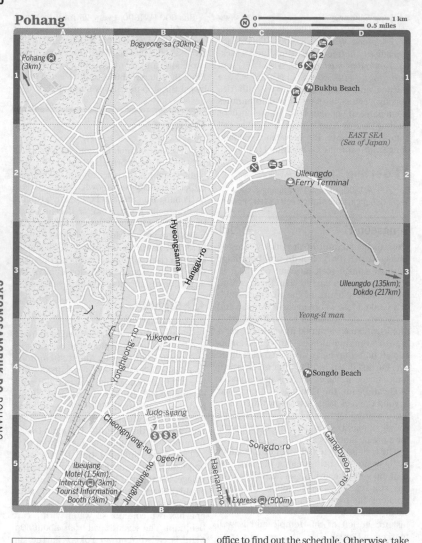

Bogyeong-sa (30km)

Pohang (3km)

4

2

6

Bukbu Beach

1

EAST SEA (Sea of Japan)

5

3

Ulleungdo **Ferry Terminal**

Ulleungdo (135km); Dokdo (217km)

Yeong-il man

Songdo Beach

Hyeongsanna

Hanggu-ro

Yongheong-no

Yukgeo-ri

Judo-sijang

7

8

Cheongnyong-no

Ogeo-ri

Songdo-ro

Gangbyeon-no

Haenam-no

Junghung-no

Ibeujang Motel (1.5km); Intercity (3km); Tourist Information Booth (3km)

Express (500m)

office to find out the schedule. Otherwise, take bus 500 to Cheongha, get off at the tiny terminal and wait for a connecting bus (₩1300, 15 minutes, every 10 to 90 minutes). A taxi from Cheongha to the temple costs ₩15,000.

🛏 Sleeping

Ibeujang Motel   LOVE HOTEL ₩
(이브장 모텔; ☎054 283 2253; d from ₩35,000; ❇) Small but clean rooms with bright furnishings and huge old-school TVs, the red lamps being the only hint that this is a love hotel. It's very conveniently located for the intercity bus terminal.

Design Motel A2　　　　　MOTEL **₩₩**
(디자인 모텔 A2; ☑054 249 5533; r/ste from ₩50,000/60,000; ❋☏) Right on the beachfront, this hotel with a design sensibility and boutique pretensions offers slightly more imaginative accommodation than its neighbours, with free coffee and popcorn, bathtubs in the middle of the rooms and 3D TVs. Each room is decorated differently (choose carefully from the room menu) and those with sea frontage really make the most of their views.

Blue Ocean Motel　　　　MOTEL **₩₩**
(블루오션 모텔; ☑054 232 2100; s/tw/ste ₩50,000/60,000/80,000; ❋@) With a prime location right on the beachfront, the Blue Ocean has comfortable and tasteful – if forgettable – rooms with PCs and all creature comforts, many with great views of the sea. Add ₩20,000 on weekends and during summer.

Motel Pacific　　　　　MOTEL **₩₩**
(모텔 퍼시픽; ☑054 252 8855; r from ₩45,000; ❋@☏) On the beachfront strip, this clean and efficiently run place has well-equipped rooms with fridge, TV and some ocean views. There are in-room PCs in the pricier rooms.

Manstar Motel　　　　　MOTEL **₩₩**
(맨스타 모텔; ☑054 244 0225; r ₩40,000-45,000; ❋@) Down a street off the main drag, the Manstar has decent rooms for budget travellers, seashell-design baths and the owner speaks English. Some rooms have a computer.

Eating

For fresh seafood head to Bukbu Beach, where there's a string of restaurants with your meal waiting in tanks along with some good barbecue options. Pohang's unique dish is *mulhoe* (물회), a spicy soup with raw fish.

Jju Jju Mi　　　　　　KOREAN **₩₩**
(쭈쭈미; servings from ₩8000; ☻5-10pm) Come here for unique *samgyupsal* (삼겹살): tangy pork on a skewer, cooked at your table on a rotisserie. It's behind the Manstar Motel (p171).

Yuk Hae Gong　　　　SEAFOOD **₩₩₩**
(육해공; dishes from ₩25,000; ☻noon-5am) Take a seat in the outdoor patio overlooking the beach and enjoy *jogae gu-e* (조개 구이), barbecued shellfish. Shells filled with seafood, cheese and onion look, smell and taste wonderful. It's often brimming with a boisterous late-night crowd – look for the restaurant with a gravel patio floor. If full, many nearby shops have a similar menu.

ⓘ Information

Bukbu Beach, adjacent to the ferry terminal, is 1.7km long, making it one of the longest sandy beaches on Korea's east coast. There's no English spoken at the **tourist information booth** (☑054 245 6761; ☻9am-6pm Mon-Sat Jul & Aug, to 5pm Sep-Jun) outside the **intercity bus terminal**, nor at **Pohang station**, but there are plenty of English-language brochures and maps. A booth outside the ferry terminal is not regularly staffed.

ⓘ Getting There & Away

AIR
Asiana and **Korean Air** both have daily Seoul–Pohang services.

POHANG BUS DEPARTURES
Departures From the Intercity Bus Terminal

DESTINATION	PRICE (₩)	DURATION (HR)	FREQUENCY
Andong	12,700	2	every 1-2hr
Busan	7700	1½	every 10min
Daegu	6700	2	every 10min
Seoul	23,300	4½	every 30min

Departures From the Express Bus Terminal

DESTINATION	PRICE (₩)	DURATION (HR)	FREQUENCY
Daejeon	19,800	3¼	hourly
Gwangju	25,800	4	5 daily
Masan	11,400	2¼	5 daily
Seoul	27,000	4½	every 40min

BOAT

There are ferry services to Ulleungdo.

BUS

Buses depart from Pohang's **intercity bus terminal** (☑ 054 272 3194) and the express bus terminal (a five-minute taxi ride from the intercity bus terminal).

TRAIN

In 2015 a new Pohang station was unveiled in a location north of the old one. There are now speedier KTX trains from **Pohang station** (☑ 054 275 2394; 137-1 Lin-ri, Heunghae-eup) to Seoul (₩53,600, 2½ hours, eight daily).

❶ Getting Around

Local buses cost ₩1000/1500 (regular/deluxe). Bus 200 runs between the airport and the intercity bus terminal. Bus 105 and 200 run between the intercity bus terminal and the **Ulleungdo ferry terminal** south of Bukbu Beach. A taxi between Pohang station and Bukbu Beach takes 20 minutes and costs ₩6000.

Ulleungdo   울릉도

☑ 054 / POP 10,235

This island (www.ulleung.go.kr), the top of an extinct volcano that rises majestically from the sea floor and has incredibly steep cliffs as a result, offers some of the most spectacular scenery in Korea; think mist-shrouded volcanic cliffs, traditional harbour towns and a breathtaking jagged coastline.

In the rainy season the green hues are even more vivid, saturating the hills like an overtoned colour photograph. In autumn, the hills are a patchwork of reds, greens and yellows from the turning leaves.

Located 135km east of the Korean Peninsula, Ulleungdo today is mainly a fishing community that sees enough tourism to warrant a sprinkle of (sadly) fairly mediocre hotels and far better restaurants.

◉ Sights

Dodong-ri   PORT

(도동리) Dodong-ri is the island's main tourist hub, meaning the greatest selection of lodging and dining options. Behind the ferry terminal, a spiral staircase leads to a seaside **walking trail** offering spectacular views of the sea crashing into jagged rocks. About 1.5km down the path is a **lighthouse** and a trail leading to Jeodong-ri (it's a two-hour return trip). The one-hour return walk to the lighthouse is an incredible highlight, but you'll need a flexible schedule as the path closes with strong ocean tides.

Dodong-ri is the island's administrative centre and largest town. Like a pirate outpost, its harbour is almost hidden away in a narrow valley between two forested mountains, making it visible only when approached directly.

Mineral Spring Park   PARK

(약수 공원) The highlight of this park, a 350m climb above Dodong-ri, is the **cable car** (return ₩8500; ⊙ 6am to 8pm) across a steep valley to Manghyang-bong (316m). The ride up affords stunning views of the sea and a bird's-eye view of Dodong-ri. Visit early or late in the day to avoid crowds, and avoid the weekends entirely, if possible.

The park's namesake *yaksu gwangjang* (mineral-water spring) is near the top. The water has a distinctive flavour (think diet-citrus-soda-meets-quartz) and some claim drinking it has all sorts of medicinal benefits.

Taeha-ri   VIEWPOINT

(태하리; admission ₩5000; ⊙ 8am-5pm) There is a terrific view of the northern coastline from Hyangmok Lighthouse (향목 등대) in the northwest corner of the island, about 20km from Dodong-ri. To get there you take a **monorail** on a six-minute, 304m ride up a sharp cliff (39° angle). You will be dropped off at the base of a 500m trail leading up to the lighthouse.

Buses to Taeha-ri leave the Dodong-ri terminal (₩1700, 40 minutes, every 40 minutes).

Namyang-Dong   VILLAGE

(남양동) The coastal road from Dodong-ri to Taeha-ri leads through Namyang, a tiny seaside community with spectacular cliffs covered with Chinese juniper and odd rock formations.

Sunset Point Pavilion   VIEWPOINT

Sunset Point Pavilion (Ilmoljeon Mang-dae) is a steep 15-minute walk above Dodong-ri town, commanding great views of the ocean and the sunset. To get there, follow the western creek out of town and cross the bridge after the school. An overgrown small trail continues up to the pavilion.

Jeodong-ri   PORT

(저동리) Jeodong-ri is a fishing village with picturesque sea walls, fishing nets, and seagulls. The boats with the lamps strung around like oversize holiday lights are for catching squid.

Ulleungdo

EAST SEA
(SEA OF JAPAN)

Samseonam Rock

Gwaneum-do

Gongam
(Elephant Rock)

Cheonbu-ri

JUGAM

SEOMMOK

Juk-do

Jukdo

HYEONPO

926

Nari-bunji
(Nari Basin)

Chinese
Juniper
Forest

Hyangmok
Lighthouse

Hyeongje-bong

Nari-dong

Monorail

Taeha-ri

Hyeongje-bong
(712m)

Sillyeong
Su

Road closed
to vehicles

(under construction)

Mireuk-san
(900m)

Bongnae
Pokpo

Naessujeon

Seongin-bong
(984m)

Cheonyeon
Natural Air
Conditioner

Jeodong-ri

Nokdu Bindaeddeok

Dodong-ri

Lighthouse

Sucheung-dong

Daea Ulleung Resort

926

Sadong-ri

Namyang-dong

Tonggumi

Turtle
Rock

Lighthouse

Pohang
(135km)

GYEONGSANGBUK-DO ULLEUNGDO

Bongnae Pokpo WATERFALL
(봉래폭포; admission ₩1400; ⏰6am-7pm Apr-Oct, 8am-5pm Nov-Mar) A steep 1.5km walk from Jeodong-ri is Bongnae Pokpo. Source of the island's drinking water, the waterfall is quite spectacular during summer.

On the return trip, cool down in **Cheonyeon Natural Air Conditioner** (천연에어콘 풍혈), a cave that maintains a year-round temperature of 4°C.

Buses serve the car park from Dodong-ri via Jeodong-ri (₩1700, 15 minutes, every 40 minutes).

🏃 Activities

Boat Trips
Boats ferry passengers on tours to various points around the island and to other islands.

With a reservation and sufficient demand, speedy boats (₩50,000, 3¼ hours) run out to politically disputed **Dokdo**, but you can't go onto the island.

During the annual **squid festival** (three days in mid-August), you may be able to board boats and even ride a vessel out to sea. The rest of the year it's interesting to watch the boats in the evening when they head out to sea with their lanterns glaring.

Round-Island Tour BOAT TOUR
(₩25,000; ⏰departs 9am & 3pm, six daily Jul & Aug) A round-island tour is a great way to admire Ulleungdo's dramatic landscape. Tours depart from Dodong-ri ferry terminal and last around two hours.

Jukdo Sightseeing Boats BOAT TOUR
(₩18,000; ⏰10am & 3pm) Sightseeing boats run to Jukdo, a nature preserve 4km from Ulleungdo. Visitors are welcome to take a picnic to eat on the island. It takes about 1½ hours including walk or picnic time. Most hotels and hostels can help you book these trips, which depart from the ferry terminal at Dodong-ri.

Dodong-ri

Dodong-ri

Hiking

Seongin-bong
HIKING

Various pathways lead to the summit of Seongin-bong (984m), but the two main routes run from Dodong-ri (about five hours return) or Nari-bunji (four to five hours return).

From Dodong-ri, take the main road towards **Daewon-sa**. Just before you reach the temple, there is a fork in the trail and a sign (in Korean) pointing the way to Seongin-bong (a steep 4.1km).

From Nari-bunji, enter the thick forest, adhering to the right-hand path, and you'll arrive at fields of chrysanthemum. Further on you'll pass a traditional home. Finally, at the entrance to the virgin forest area and picnic ground, the steep ascent of Seongin-bong takes you (one hour) through a forest of Korean beech, hemlock and lime.

Just below the peak, as you descend to Dodong-ri, is a trail off to the right, down to **Namyang-dong** (1½ hours).

Sillyeong Su
HIKING

(신령수) If you're not up for a major hike, try the 5km-return trip from the Nari basin bus stop to Sillyeong Su (신령수), a mountain spring. The walk cuts through a thick forest and is an easy one-hour stroll while waiting for the van to take you back to Cheonbu for a connection back to Dodong-ri.

🛏 Sleeping

Ulleungdo has lots of choices for those on a budget, but is very poorly set up for those wanting more comfort or luxury. Room rates rise steeply in peak season (from ₩50,000 to ₩100,000 in July, August and holidays) – coinciding with a flood of boisterous Korean travellers on package tours – so book ahead. Most hotels are in or around Dodong-ri.

Khan Motel
HOTEL ₩₩

(칸모텔; ☑ 054 791 8500; d from ₩80,000; ❋ @) One of the best options on the island is this classy if rather minimalist place with *ondol* and Western-style rooms. The rooms are on the small side, though the large TVs and computers are pluses. The owner is a great resource for guests looking for hard-to-find ferry tickets during the busy travel season.

Hotel Ulleungdo
HOTEL ₩₩

(울릉도 호텔; ☑ 054 791 6611; ondol/r ₩50,000/80,000; ❋) While it's the only hotel in Dodong-ri officially accredited for tourism, the Ulleungdo remains a large *yeogwan* with lots of simple but clean *ondol* rooms. It's a popular choice for groups who want to economise by sharing a room and don't mind the minimal furnishings.

Pension Skyhill
PENSION **WW**

(스카이힐 펜션; ☏054 791 1040; www.skyhill. or.kr; d/ondol from ₩70,000/60,000; ❋) Near the top of town, it's a popular destination for groups of university students, so the rooms and communal areas – such as a shared kitchen and rooftop barbecue facilities – look a little worn out. However, it's a convenient stroll from several restaurants and one of the cheapest deals in town.

Daea Ulleung Resort
HOTEL **WWW**

(대아 리조트; ☏054 791 8800; www.daearesort. com; r/ste from ₩160,000/230,000; ❋@⌘) Definitely the island's most expensive property, this impressive resort has amazing mountaintop views of the sea, but the rooms are rather overpriced for what they are: unexciting and smallish, albeit perfectly comfortable and clean. From mid-July to August there's an outdoor swimming pool, and room prices spike. The hotel is in Sadong-ri, a ₩5000 taxi ride from Dodong-ri.

✖ Eating & Drinking

Outdoor seafood stalls are ubiquitous in Ulleungdo. There are a few scattered traditional Korean food shops, where you can eat for as little as ₩3000, and some casual restaurants by the harbour with outdoor seating. Most restaurants are in Dodong-ri.

Nokdu Bindaeddeok
KOREAN **WW**

(녹두 빈대떡; Jeodong-ri; dishes from ₩10,000; ☺9am-8pm) Definitely the coolest and most unique of the island's eating options is this friendly place with outdoor floor seating under trees, overlooking a landscaped garden filled with statues, pagodas and a crane. The food is delicious; try the crispy *bindaetteok* (빈대떡; mung-bean pancake) and a platter of homemade *muk* (묵; acorn jelly) mixed with spicy onions and carrots.

Nokdu Bindaeddok is on the path leading to Bongnae Pokpo just outside Jeodong-ri. Look for two Korean totems in front of a black gate.

99 Sikdang
SEAFOOD **WW**

(99 식당; dishes ₩6000-23,000; ☺6.30am-10pm) One of the island's most famous restaurants – its owner will tell you proudly about its many appearances on Korea's famously food-obsessed TV channels – this is a place to delight in seafood barbecue and dishes such as *ojing-eo bulgogi* (오징어 불

고기; squid grilled at the table with vegetables and hot-pepper sauce) and *ttaggaebibap* (딱개비밥; shellfish with rice).

Yong Gung
SEAFOOD **WW**

(용궁; dishes from ₩16,000; ☺8am-10pm) Sit near the seafront with a bottle of *soju*, a platter of raw fish and watch the ocean crash onto the rocky shoreline at this ramshackle but quietly charming place. Mr Jeong (who speaks passable English) and his brother personally catch the seafood by diving for sea creatures each morning.

It's about 500m from the ferry terminal on the seaside walking trail.

Sanchang-Hoe Sikdang
SEAFOOD **WW**

(산창회식당; mains ₩7500-18,000; ☺6pm-midnight) Downstairs from Sanchang-jang Yeogwan, it specialises in *honghapbap* (mussel rice) served with a locally cultivated mountain plant called *myeong-e* (명이) and a generous bowl of *miyeokguk* (미역국; seaweed soup).

ℹ Information

The helpful **information booth** (☏054 790 6454; ☺9am-6pm) by the Dodong-ri ferry terminal occasionally has English speakers on duty, but this can't be relied upon. You can change money or withdraw cash from the 24-hour bank machine at Nonghyup Bank in Dodong-ri.

ℹ Getting There & Away

FERRY

You can get to Ulleungdo by **ferry** (☏054 242 5111; www.daea.com) from Pohang (standard/1st class ₩64,500/70,700, three hours). There is one departure daily year-round (weather permitting; strong winds or even morning rain means cancellations), and there are two daily departures during summer. If assigned seats are unavailable you can buy a floor-seating ticket in a common room for a slight discount. It's possible to take vehicles on the standard daily ferry, the *Sunflower* (₩5000 per vehicle), but not on the supplementary summer ferry, the *Ocean Flower*.

It is best to reserve (no deposit required) your tickets to and from the island, especially during summer – ask at a tourist office for someone to do this for you. Otherwise you can buy your ticket at the terminal first thing in the morning, but go early and expect to wait.

ℹ Getting Around

BUS

Buses run between Dodong-ri and Jeodong-ri every 30 minutes (₩1200, 10 minutes). There are 18 buses daily from Dodong-ri via

Namyang-dong (₩1700, 25 minutes) to Cheonbu-ri (₩1700, 65 minutes), where you can transfer to Nari-bunji via a van (₩1200, 10 minutes, eight daily). Timetables are posted at the Dodong-ri bus terminal.

TAXI

Taxis, usually 4WD, regularly ply between Dodong-ri and Jeodong-ri (₩5000). All-day trips can be arranged for about ₩150,000.

Andong 안동

📞 054 / POP 184,000

Famous for its mackerel, strong *soju* (local vodka) and wooden masks, Andong makes a good base for exploring the numerous historical and cultural sights outside the city. The city itself has a very laid-back vibe and is strikingly friendly, with a good selection of places to eat and stay.

⊙ Sights

Andong Folk Village VILLAGE

(안동민속촌) On a hillside above the town, Andong Folk Village is a repository for homes moved to prevent them from being submerged by the construction of Andong Dam in 1976. Relocated and partially reconstructed traditional-style buildings range from peasant farmhouses to elaborate mansions of government officials with multiple courtyards. The village looks so authentic that the TV network KBS has used it as a set for historical dramas on multiple occasions.

The village is about 4km east of Andong, close to the dam wall on the opposite side of the river from the main road. Take buses 3, 3-1 or 3-2 (₩1200) from next to the tourist office and hop off at *minsokchon* (folk village). A taxi costs about ₩6000.

Andong Folklore Museum MUSEUM

(안동 민속박물관; 📞 054 821 0649; admission ₩1200; ⊙9am-6pm Mar-Oct, to 5pm Nov-Feb) Next door to the folk village, it offers clear displays of Korea's folk traditions from birth through to death.

Soju Museum MUSEUM

(소주 박물관; www.andongsoju.net; ⊙9am-5pm Mon-Sat) FREE The heady 45% *soju* of Andong may not be to your taste, but its significance has been preserved with its designation as an intangible cultural property. On the grounds of the **Andong Soju Brewery**, the museum houses a couple of displays that detail the distilling process, the drinking ceremony and a history of *soju* labels. A

(thimble-sized) taste of the liquor is given at the end of your visit.

The museum is in the south of Andong, across the Nakdong-gang, and is best reached by taxi (₩5000). Catch bus 80 (₩1200, 10 minutes) from opposite the Kyobo building.

Jebiwon SHRINE

(제비원; ⊙24hr) FREE The body and robes of this Buddha are carved on a boulder over 12m high, on top of which are the head and hair – carved out of two separate pieces of rock. It's an impressive stark sight to behold emerging from the tall greenery.

Catch bus 54 (₩1200, every 30 minutes) from opposite the Kyobo building and ask the driver to drop you off at Jebiwon. Moving on to the next destination requires some imaginative travel techniques because there are no obvious bus stops on the street. You could stand on the street and wait for a bus or taxi, or ask anyone nearby for directions to Andong or Yeongju, which is 45km north. Don't be surprised if someone offers you a lift.

✲ Festivals & Events

Andong Mask Dance Festival (⊙late Sep–early Oct) is a great time to visit Andong. It brings together a colourful array of national and international mask-dance troupes. It is usually held in tandem with the **Andong Folk Festival** (⊙late Sep–early Oct), showcasing performances of traditional music and dance. Check with the tourist office for details.

🛏 Sleeping

★ Happy Guesthouse HOSTEL ₩

(해피 게스트하우스; 📞 010 8903 1638; s/d incl breakfast ₩25,000/40,000; ❄@) Things are happy a short walk from the action. Incense infuses the traditional downstairs dining room, while upstairs there are spotless new rooms with private bathrooms and mats for sleeping rolled directly onto the floor. There are PCs, Korean breakfast options (pumpkin rice porridge), and a helpful English-speaking owner.

Andong Hotel HOTEL ₩

(안동 호텔; 📞 054 858 1166; www.andonghotel.net; s/d/ste from ₩40,000/50,000/70,000; ❄@ 🛜) One of the best choices in town, the Andong Hotel is right in the centre of Andong and despite an incredibly kitschy decor capable of making any African

Andong

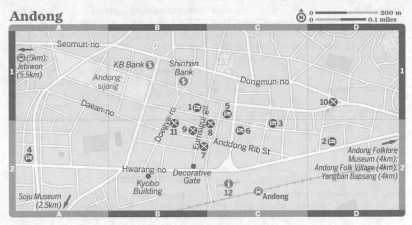

dictator feel right at home, it has spacious rooms (the suites are huge), good bathrooms, desktop PCs in each room and helpful staff. Rates rise ₩10,000 Friday and Saturday.

Gotaya Guesthouse GUESTHOUSE ₩
(☑ 010 4367 0226; 205-17 Dongbu-dong; dm incl breakfast ₩20,000; ❄❅@❆) If the drab apartment facade causes doubt in your heart, the warm kitchen and living-room atmosphere on the 5th floor will be a relief. The smiles continue with a free laundry on the ramshackle but sunny roof terrace, English-speaking staff, warm, clean dorms and small spaces that lend themselves to meeting travellers.

Andong Park Hotel HOTEL ₩₩
(안동 파크관광 호텔; ☑054 853 1501; www.andongparkhotel.com; d/tw/VIP ₩50,000/60,000/70,000; ❅@❆) Andong's establishment choice boasts friendly English-speaking staff and surprisingly reasonable prices given the quality of accommodation. The suites are spacious, with their own lounges, smart bathrooms with old-fashioned wooden bath tubs and flat-screen TVs. Standard rooms are smaller, but well-maintained and clean.

Munhwa Motel MOTEL ₩₩
(문화 모텔; ☑054 857 7001; r ₩35,000-45,000; ❅@) With its smart and surprisingly unhideous room decor, this unfussy motel in the centre of town is good value. The owners are very friendly, though they speak no English.

Andong

Sleeping
1	Andong Hotel	B1
2	Andong Park Hotel	D2
3	Gotaya Guesthouse	C2
4	Happy Guesthouse	A2
5	Munhwa Motel	C1
6	Sharp Motel	C2

Eating
7	Jaerim Galbi	B2
8	Jangsu Andong Jjimdak	C2
9	Lavender	B2
10	Loving Hut	D1
11	Mammoth Bakery	B2

Information
12	Tourist Office	C2

Some rooms have internet access with PCs, but there is no wi-fi.

Sharp Motel LOVE HOTEL ₩₩
(샵 모텔; ☑054 854 0081; http://sharphotel.com; s/d ₩40,000/50,000; ❅@) Centrally located and offering good-standard, relatively tasteful rooms, all with huge flat-screen TV, in-room PCs and fridges. The Sharp is a love hotel, but not obviously so.

🍴 Eating

You could eat each meal in Andong on Eumsigui-gil (aka Food St), the restaurant row in the town centre, marked by the decorative gate and lit-up archways, or the next door Andong Rib St, where there's a proliferation of tasty rib joints.

Loving Hut
VEGAN ₩

(러빙 헛; ₩5000-8000; ⊙noon-10pm) This simple place may look like nothing special but will thrill vegans and vegetarians with its bibimbap, kimchi stew, cold noodles and even a vegan burger.

Mammoth Bakery
BAKERY ₩

(맘모스 베이커리; coffee ₩3000, breads ₩1000-4000; ⊙8am-10pm) Friendly owner with good espresso and fresh tasty treats. If the weather is nice, enjoy your drink on the outdoor patio.

Jaerim Galbi
KOREAN ₩₩

(재림 갈비; servings ₩9000-22,000; ⊙10am-11pm) A good-value barbecue place serving pork ribs, bulgogi, prime beef rib and grilled beef steaks. The menu is very simple but the smell from the street is mouthwatering.

Lavender
INTERNATIONAL ₩₩

(라벤더; ☑054 855 8550; set meals ₩8000-20,000; ⊙11am-10pm Tue-Sun) White and airy, this is a civilised pasta and salad place – pastas come with garlic bread, salad and coffee.

Yangban Bapsang
KOREAN ₩₩

(양반 밥상; meals ₩8500-18,000; ⊙10am-9pm) Mackerel served golden – skin crispy, flesh tender – melts on the tongue the way mackerel was meant to. Not far from Andong Folk Village (p176), it's across the street from the entrance to the wooden bridge.

Jangsu Andong Jjimdak
KOREAN ₩₩₩

(☑054 852 4568; jjimdak from ₩25,000; ⊙11am-8pm) A *jjimdak* (simmered chicken, Andong's speciality) eatery where the owner speaks no English? Simple, just sit and choose either the large or even larger platter of the signature dish. Even easier is thinking the large is too much, but eating everything anyhow because the peppery-sweet, vegetable and glass-noodle stew is so addictive. Look for the pink awning.

ℹ Information

The **tourist office** (☑054 852 6800; www.andong.go.kr; ⊙9am-6pm) is outside the train station. The staff are very helpful and English is spoken.

ℹ Getting There & Away

Andong mainly uses the newer **bus terminal** (☑857 8296; www.andongterminal.co.kr) around 5km northwest from the town centre. To get into town take bus 0, 1, 2,11, 46, 51 or 76 (₩1200) and get out at Andong station, or it's a quick ₩5000 cab ride.

ℹ Getting Around

The tourist office hands out a helpful local bus timetable with English explanations. The town is small enough to get around on foot, and local buses serve all the sights.

ANDONG'S MASKED BALL

In late September/early October, masks and their admirers come from all over the world to join in a host of mask-related festivities. In Hahoe Folk Village (24km from Andong), masked dancers perform traditional dances in the pine forests to the delight of crowds. Andong City has numerous mask-related shows, and a mask-making contest pits artisan against artisan in a delightful 'mask off'. Firework displays are another popular attraction.

A must-see is a **Byeolsingut Talnori** (FREE; ⊙3pm Sat & Sun May-Oct; 3pm Sun Mar, Apr & Nov) performance, which takes place in a small stadium near Hahoe's car park. They're free, although donations are demanded by hard-working *halmeoni* (grandmas). If you can't make it to a performance, you can view many masks at the **Hahoe Mask Museum** (p179).

According to legend, the Hahoe mask tradition came about when the residents of Hahoe got frustrated with their hoity-toity noble clan. One clever craftsman carved a likeness of one of the most obsequious, much to the delight of his peers. Byeolsingut Talnori is a traditional dance style created by the common folk to satirise the establishment. Characters wear masks representing social classes including corrupt monks and the rich, some with bulging eyes and crooked mouths. The conflicts among them are portrayed in amusing combinations of popular entertainment and shamanism. Accompanying the dance are the sounds of *nong-ak*, a traditional farmers' musical-percussion quartet. For more information, visit www.maskdance.com or Andong's tourist office.

DEPARTURES FROM ANDONG
Bus

DESTINATION	PRICE (₩)	DURATION	FREQUENCY
Busan	16,200	2½hr	every 30-60min
Daegu	9700	1½hr	every 30min
Daejeon	15,000	3hr	every 30min
Dongseoul	16,500	3hr	every 30min
Gyeongju	12,000	1¾hr	7 daily
Juwangsan	8600	35min	6 daily
Pohang	15,000	2hr	every 2hr
Ulsan	15,900	2¾hr	8 daily

Train

DESTINATION	PRICE (₩)	DURATION (HR)	FREQUENCY
Daegu	8000	2	1 daily
Dongdaegu*	8200	2	3 daily
Gyeongju	8300	2	3 daily
Seoul	24,100	4	8 daily
Seoul	16,500	5½	2 daily

* transfer to Busan

Hahoe Folk Village
안동 하회마을

Now a Unesco World Heritage Site, **Hahoe Folk Village** (Andong Hahoe Maeul; admission ₩3000; ⊘9am-6pm Mar-Oct, 9am-sunset Nov-Feb) is the outstanding attraction of the region around Andong. Arrive early in the morning and the mystical beauty creates the illusion that you are in another time.

Walk down the dirt road and you'll pass small garden plots of squash vines, corn and green chilli peppers, all overshadowed by riverbank escarpments. Down the road, farm fields stretch out to the horizon. On your left is a magnificent village of centuries-old homes, so impeccable in design you'd swear you were living in the Joseon dynasty.

While other Korean folk villages can be tourist productions, this one has 230 residents maintaining old ways, and the government helps with preservation and restoration. There is a tourist information booth at the entrance to the village – where you can pick up a free multilingual **audio guide** (ID needed) – and a lotus pond that (in season) is filled with beautiful blooms.

Remember to respect people's privacy if you step beyond the entrance gates.

Two kilometres back in the direction of Andong, **Hahoe Mask Museum** (admission ₩3000; ⊘9.30am-6pm) houses a remarkable collection of traditional Korean masks, as well as masks from across Asia and countries as diverse as Nigeria, Italy and Mexico. The two daily buses to and from Hahoe follow a bumpy dirt road and make a 10-minute stop at **Byeongsan Seowon** (⊘9am-6pm Apr-Oct, to 5pm Nov-Mar) **FREE**, a former Confucian academy dating from 1572.

Many homes in Hahoe have *minbak* for rent from around ₩50,000. But for more luxury and privacy, try **Rak Ko Jae Hahoe** (⊘010 8555 1407, 054 857 3410; www.rkj.co.kr; d from ₩160,000, from ₩180,000 Apr-Oct; ❄☎), a four-room, upmarket guesthouse facing the river and blending seamlessly with the surrounding thatched-roof *hanok*. Each traditional room comes with modern comforts such as cable TV and a fridge plus an odd *hinoki* (pine) bathtub. There's a mud-walled *jjimjilbang* as well, for that true traditional bathing experience.

Bus 46 (₩1800, 50 minutes, eight daily) runs to Hahoe from Andong.

Juwangsan National Park

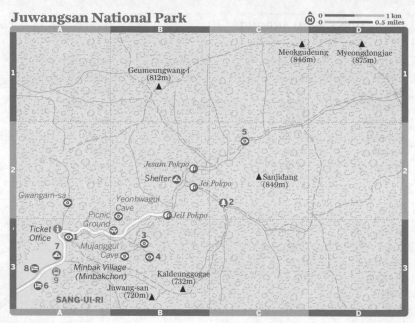

N
0 _____ 1 km
0 _____ 0.5 miles

Juwangsan National Park

◉ Sights
1 Daejeon-sa...A3
2 Hurimaegi..C2
3 Juwang-am Hermitage B3
4 Juwanggul Cave B3
5 Naewonmaeul C2

🛏 Sleeping
6 Bangalo Minbak A3
7 Campground A3
8 Hyangchon Sikdang-Minbak..............A3

ⓘ Information
Information Centre ....(see 9)

ⓘ Transport
9 Bus Terminal A3

Juwangsan National Park
주왕산 국립공원

of tracks radiates out from Cheongnyang-sa, most well marked. The largest temple in the park is **Cheongnyang-sa** and there are a number of small hermitages. Built in AD 663, the temple is quite scenic, sitting in a steep valley below the cliffs. **Ansimdang**, at the base of the temple, is a pleasant teahouse.

It takes about five hours to complete a round trip of the peaks, returning to the bus stop, or 90 minutes to the temple and back.

Across the street from the park entrance, there are a dozen *minbak,* shops, restaurants and the **Cheongnyangsan Museum** (⊙9am-6pm) FREE, a modest effort with artefacts related to the area's agricultural history, and clean public toilets.

From Andong, bus 67 (₩2200, one hour, six daily) continues past Dosan Seowon to the park.

Far to the east of Andong and reaching almost to the coast, the 106-sq-km **Juwangsan National Park** (admission ₩2000; ⊙sunrise-1hr before sunset) is dominated by impressive limestone pinnacles that seem to appear from nowhere. Beautiful gorges, waterfalls and cliff walks also feature, and

Cheongnyangsan Provincial Park
청량산 도립공원

Beyond Dosan Seowon, this **park** (⊙8.30am-6pm) boasts spectacular views and tracks wandering along cliff precipices. In addition to the mountain Cheongnyang-san, the summit of which is Changin-bong (870m), there are 11 scenic peaks, eight caves and a waterfall, **Gwanchang Pokpo**. A spiderweb

BUS DEPARTURES FROM JUWANGSAN

DESTINATION	PRICE (₩)	DURATION	FREQUENCY
Andong	7600	1½hr	4 daily
Busan	19,300	3¾hr	daily
Cheongsong	1600	20min	every 30min
Dongdaegu	16,400	3hr	3 daily
Dongseoul	24,100	5hr	6 daily
Yeongcheon*	13,000	2hr	3 daily

* transfer to Gyeongju

with any luck you'll see an otter or protected Eurasian flying squirrel, among the 900-plus wildlife species here.

☉ Sights & Activities

Most of the visitors to the park are content to see the **waterfalls** and **caves**, but for a more rigorous experience you can try **hiking** up from **Daejeon-sa**, a small, noble temple built just inside the entrance to the Juwangsan National Park, to **Juwang-san** (720m; 1¼ hours), once known as Seokbyeong-san or 'Stone Screen Mountain', along the ridge to **Kaldeunggogae** (732m, 15 minutes) and then down to **Hurimaegi** (50 minutes), a beauty spot, before following the valley back to Daejeon-sa (1¾ hours).

On the way back down take the side trip to **Juwanggul Cave**. The track first passes the hermitage **Juwang-am**; from here a steel walkway takes you through a narrow gorge to the modest cave.

Also within the park is **Naewonmaeul**, a tiny village where craftspeople do woodworking.

🛏 Sleeping & Eating

The *minbak* village *(minbakchon)* opposite the Juwangsan bus terminal has 50-plus properties of varying quality, so shop around before paying. The room rates can double on weekends and in July, August and October.

Hyangchon Sikdang-Minbak   B&B ₩
(향촌 식당 민박; ☑054 873 0202; r from ₩35,000) With the largest sign near the park entrance, this *minbak* and restaurant is hard to miss. It also has some of the area's nicest rooms. Downstairs in the **restaurant**, the *jeongsik* meal (₩10,000) comes with soup and a colourful array of leafy side dishes from the local mountains, some of which are picked by the owner.

Campground   CAMPGROUND ₩
(☑054 873 0014; sites adult/child/youth ₩2000/1000/1500) The campground, on the other side of the stream of the *minbak* village, has basic facilities and rents tents (₩5000 to ₩10,000).

Bangalo Minbak   CHALET ₩₩
(방갈로 민박; ☑054 874 5200; r weekdays/weekends ₩30,000/60,000) About 500m from the park entrance, this place has a log-cabin exterior with central courtyard. Rooms have *ondol* or beds and there's also a simple on-site **restaurant**.

❶ Information

The main gateway to the park is the town of Cheongsong, about 15km away. At the park entrance, the **information centre** (☑054 873 0014; 2nd fl, bus terminal; ☺9am-5.30pm) has English and Korean maps detailing hiking routes, distances and estimated calories burned. Be sure to check here for local trail conditions.

❶ Getting There & Away

Virtually all buses to Juwangsan stop in Cheongsong (₩1600, 20 minutes, every 30 minutes). Check the timetable inside the Juwangsan **bus terminal** for detailed schedules.

GYEONGSANGBUK-DO JUWANGSAN NATIONAL PARK

Busan & Gyeongsangnam-do

Why Go?

The best sites in Korea either awe with beauty or deepen your understanding of the culture. Busan (부산) and Gyeo-ngsangnam-do (경상남도) do both.

Busan's easily accessible mountains, beaches and hiking trails, as well as its colourful seafood and drinking scene, make it very easy to love. It's also home to the world's largest shopping and entertainment complex and a bedazzling world-class cinema centre.

Gyeongsangnam-do's natural beauty is closer than you think, thanks to an efficient transport system. Hop on a bus and you'll be rewarded with outstanding trails on Jirisan, glorious temples in hideaway locations and lush rice paddies in just about every rural community. For marine treasures, board a ferry and go island-hopping around Tongyeong. On land or by sea, Gyeongsangnam-do is accessible, affordable and waiting to be explored.

Best Places to Eat

➡ Jackie's Seafood (p190)

➡ Noran Mahura (p192)

➡ Sulbing (p190)

➡ Ddungbo Halmae Gimbap (p201)

➡ Dajeong Sikdang (p204)

Best Places to Stay

➡ Ibis Ambassador Busan City Centre Hotel (p189)

➡ Paradise Hotel (p190)

➡ Westin Chosun Beach Hotel (p189)

➡ Dong Bang Hotel (p202)

➡ Nexun (p201)

When to Go
Busan

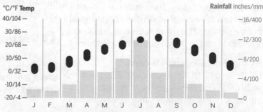

Apr–May Cherry blossoms make spring a great time for hiking.

Jul–Aug Haeundae and Gwangan beaches are in full swing.

Oct Busan International Film Festival runs through mid-October.

History

Gyeongsangnam-do has a long history of warfare, though it's difficult to beat the Imjin War for destruction, treachery and the birth of an icon. In 1592 the Japanese were eager to secure a land route to China, but the Joseon government refused assistance, so the Japanese attacked. Led by Toyotomi Hideyoshi, the Japanese landed 160,000 troops at several places, including Busan and Jinju, where the Koreans made an unsuccessful stand against a superior enemy.

The war's local star was Admiral Yi Sunsin, a brilliant tactician credited with the development of the turtle ship, an ironclad vessel instrumental in harassing Japanese supply lines. Despite his significant wartime contributions, Yi was arrested for disobeying orders thanks to a clever ruse concocted by the Japanese, who were eager to see the good admiral removed from the war. With Yi behind bars, the Japanese launched a massive assault that destroyed all but 13 of Joseon's 133 vessels. Shaken by the loss, the king released Yi and put him in charge of the

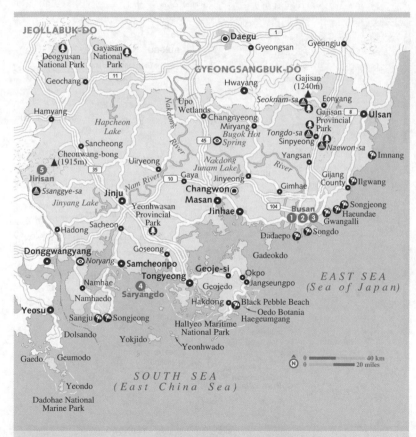

Busan & Gyeongsangnam-do Highlights

1 Shocking your taste buds with raw fish at **Jagalchi Fish Market** (p190).

2 Exploring the back alleys of **Gamcheon Culture Village** (p187).

3 Attending **BIFF** (p189), a world-class film festival.

4 Challenging yourself by hiking **Saryangdo** (p199), a beautiful island off the coast of Tongyeong.

5 Exploring **Jirisan** (p206), one of the best places to hike in Korea.

Busan

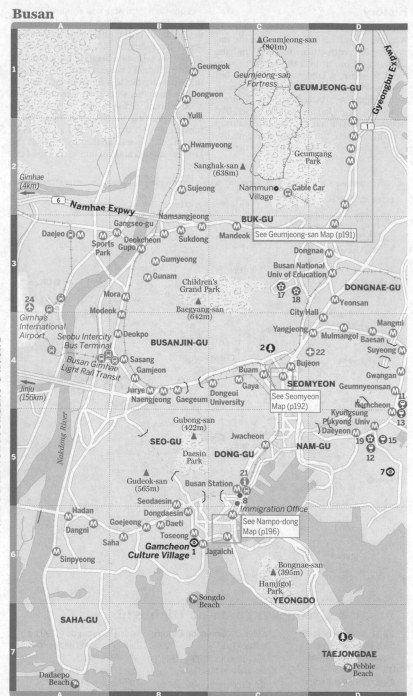

▲Geumjeong-san
(801m)

Geumjeong-san
Fortress

GEUMJEONG-GU

Geumgok

Dongwon

Yulli

Hwamyeong

Geumgang
Park

Sanghak-san ▲
(638m)

Sujeong

Nammun○ ○Cable Car
Village

Gimhae
(4km)

Namhae Expwy

Namsangjeong

BUK-GU

Daejeo

Gangseo-gu

Deokcheon

Mandeok

See Geumjeong-san Map (p191)

Gupo

Sukdong

Sports
Park

Gumyeong

Dongnae

Gunam

Busan National
Univ of Education

DONGNAE-GU

Mora

Children's
Grand Park

17 18

Yeonsan

Gimhae
International
Airport

Modeok

Baegyang-san
(642m)

City Hall

Deokpo

BUSANJIN-GU

Yangjeong

Mulmangol

Mangmi

Baesan

Seobu Intercity
Bus Terminal

Jinju
(156km)

Busan Gimhae
Light Rail Transit

Sasang

Gamjeon

2

Buam

Bujeon

22

Suyeong

Gaya

SEOMYEON

Geumnyeonsan

Jurye

Naengjeong

Gaegeum

Dongeui
University

Gwangan

See Seomyeon
Map (p192)

Namcheon

11

Gubong-san
(422m)

Kyungsung
Pukyong Univ

Daeyeon

13

SEO-GU

Jwacheon

NAM-GU

19 15

Daesin
Park

DONG-GU

12

Gudeok-san
(565m)

21

7

Seodaesin

Busan Station

8

Hadan

Dongdaesin

Daeti

Immigration Office

Dangni

Goejeong

See Nampo-dong
Map (p196)

Saha

Toseong

Gamcheon
Culture Village 1

Jagalchi

Sinpyeong

Bongnae-san
(395m)

Hamjigol
Park

YEONGDO

SAHA-GU

Songdo
Beach

6

TAEJONGDAE

Dadaepo
Beach

Pebble
Beach

Gyeongbu Expwy

tattered navy. In a classic case of size doesn't matter, the admiral destroyed or damaged 133 Japanese vessels. One year later, Yi defeated a Japanese armada near Namhaedo, costing the invaders 450 ships. It also cost Admiral Yi his life. In September of 1598, Hideyoshi died and the Japanese leadership lost its appetite for the war.

❶ Getting Around

For regional trips, bus is usually the best option, with departures from Seobu Terminal and **Busan Central Bus Terminal** (부산종합버스터미널; Map p191; www.bxt.co.kr; Ⓜ Line 1 to Nopo, Exit 3), both close to subway stations. Most train trips begin at Busan station, a glassy facility close to the city centre, or west-end Gupo station, which is closer to the airport. Busan's third train station – Bujeon, behind the Ibis Hotel in Seomyeon – has limited departures for destinations such as Gyeongju, Jinju, Hadong and Mokpo, on the slower *mugunghwa* service.

Busan   부산

☑ 051 / POP 3.6 MILLION

Bursting with mountains and beaches, hot springs and seafood, South Korea's second-largest city is a rollicking port town with tonnes to offer. From casual tent bars and chic designer cafes to fish markets teeming with every species imaginable, Busan has something for all tastes. Rugged mountain ranges criss-crossing the city define the urban landscape, while events such as the Busan International Film Festival underscore the city's desire to be a global meeting place. Note that Busan is within the boundaries of Gyeongsangnam-do but is a separate administrative unit with its own telephone area code.

◉ Sights & Activities

Beomeo-Sa   BUDDHIST TEMPLE
(범어사; Map p191; ☑ 051 508 3122; www.beomeo-osa.co.kr; ⊙ 8.30am-5.30pm; Ⓜ Line 1 to Beomeo-sa, Exit 5) This magnificent temple is Busan's best sight. Despite its city location, Beomeo-sa is a world away from the urban jungle, with beautiful architecture set against an extraordinary mountain backdrop. Beomeo-sa can be a busy place on weekends and holidays, as the path leading to the temple is the northern starting point for trails across Geumjeong-san. Before heading back to the city, visit the *pajeon* (파전; green onion pancake) restaurants near the bus stop.

Busan

At street level from Beomeosa station, spin 180 degrees, turn left at the corner and walk 200m to the terminus. Catch bus 90 (₩1200, 20 minutes, every 15 minutes) or take a ₩5000 taxi to the temple entrance.

To fully appreciate the beauty of this temple, sign up for the templestay program. The pre-dawn chanting is hauntingly extraordinary. Signing up for a templestay is usually completed online. Reservations, often two weeks in advance, are required by most temples. Payment in Korean won is typically completed by bank transfer.

Geumgang Park Cable Car CABLE CAR
(금강공원 케이블카; Map p191; http://geumgangpark.bisco.or.kr; one way/return adult ₩5000/8000, child ₩4000/6000; ⊗9am-5pm; Ⓜ Line 1 to Oncheonjang, Exit 1) Add this cable car to your list of must-do activities. The panoramic view of development coursing through valleys of verdant mountains is breathtaking. Most days the view extends from Asiad Stadium (p194) northward. On a clear day the Gwangan bridge is visible. Atop Geumjeong-san, you're well positioned for a short stroll to Geumjeong Fortress, a four-hour hike to Beomeo-sa, or a two-hour adventure to Seokbul-sa.

Near to the mountain-top cable-car platform there are plenty of tables serving food and drink, all run by women who pursue customers with zeal. Grilled goat meat is a speciality. Near a cliff, look for the boulder providing sweeping city views. It's a popular place for pictures and picnics.

The cable car is a 15-minute walk from Oncheonjang station. From Exit 1, walk left to the intersection. Cross the street and turn right at the first corner. Follow the road sign pointing to Geumgang Park. The cable car is 150m from the park entrance; look for the 'Ropeway' sign.

Geumjeong Fortress HISTORIC SITE
(금정산성; Map p191) FREE Travellers climbing Geumjeong-san (금정산; Geumjeong Mountain) expecting to see a fort will be disappointed because there isn't one. Geumjeong Fortress is four gates and 17km of stone walls encircling 8 sq km of mountaintop land. Not all is lost because this is where you'll find some of the city's best hiking, and the opportunity to see Korean hikers sporting the very latest in alpine fashion. Most hikers start at Beomeo-sa or the Geumgang Park Cable Car.

Hikers looking for a sturdy workout begin at the northern leg of the trail, which is on the left side of Beomeo-sa. The steep walk to the main ridge takes about an hour. Follow the trail left and head to Bukmun (북문; North Gate). The 8.8km hike from

Beomeo-sa to Nammun (남문; South Gate) is a comfortable walk with a couple of steep stretches.

The least arduous route is by cable car from Geumgang Park at the southern base of the mountain. From the mountaintop cable car platform, it's a 20-minute walk to the South Gate.

Seokbul-sa
BUDDHIST TEMPLE

(석불사; Map p191; ⊙7am-7pm) Hard to find, difficult to reach and a wonder to behold, this hermitage has Buddhist images meticulously etched into stone. Visually powerful in scale and impact, it's the kind of work that moves visitors to exclaim 'wow' as they step back and arch their necks to get the full picture. The quickest route here begins with a cable car ride (p186); up top, follow the trail signs.

The most interesting – and strenuous – route to Seokbul-sa is to add it to your Geumjeong Fortress (p186) hike (carry plenty of water). From Nammun, the path indicated by the Mandeokchon (만덕촌) sign leads to a collection of restaurants and a foot volleyball court. Keep going straight until you can't go any further, then turn right onto a narrow path. Eventually this leads to a larger path heading down the mountainside. Look for a sign that reads '석불사 입구' (Seokbul-sa entrance), which points you down a steep, rocky trail. Way down at the bottom, turn right at the cement road and walk uphill to the temple.

On the way back, you can either return to Nammun and then follow the signs to the cable car, or keep walking down the cement road from the temple – you'll end up near Mandeok station on Line 3.

★Gamcheon Culture Village
ARCHITECTURE

(감천문화마을; ⊙24hr; Ⓜ Line 1 to Toseong-dong station, Exit 8) FREE This historically rich, mountainside slum became a famous tourist destination after getting an arty makeover in 2009 when students decided to brighten up the neighbourhood with clever touches up the stairs, down the lanes and around the corners. Today it's a colourful, quirky community of Lego-shaped homes, cafes and galleries, ideal for an hour or two of strolling and selfies. Buy a map (₩2000) and join the scavenger hunt. Comfortable walking shoes recommended.

From the metro station, cross the street and walk to the bus stop in front of the hospital. Catch minibus 2 or 2-2 (₩900, 10 minutes) up the steep hill to the village. A taxi from the hospital (₩3000) is faster.

Haeundae
BEACH

(해운대해수욕장; Ⓜ Line 2 to Haeundae, Exit 3 or 5) Haeundae is the country's most famous beach. During the peak August travel season, umbrellas mushroom across the 2km-long beach while frolickers fill the water with inner tubes rented from booths behind the beach. It's a fun outing with 100,000 friends, though the marketing portraying Haeundae as a world-class resort is bunkum.

Gwangan
BEACH

(광안리해수욕장; Ⓜ Line 2 to Geumnyeonsan, Exit 3) Among the city's seven beaches, Gwangan is the best option for access and quality (the other beaches are Haeundae, Dadaepo, Songdo, Songjeong, Ilgwang and Imnang). Although the ugly wall of commercial development behind the beach diminishes the daytime experience, Gwangan shines at night. The multicoloured light show illuminating the Diamond Bridge is grand.

Outside the metro station, rotate 180 degrees and turn right at the corner. Or take Line 2 to Gwangan station, Exit 3 or 5.

Igidae
PARK

(이기대; Ⓜ Line 2 to Namcheon, Exit 3) If the trails of Geumjeong Fortress seem more like work than pleasure, there are opportunities to explore Busan's natural beauty at a more leisurely pace. Igidae is a nature park that's ideal for a two-hour stroll. Most visitors take the coastal route for the sweeping views of Haeundae across the bay.

From the metro station, walk to the first major intersection and turn left. The park is a 20-minute walk down the road.

Taejongdae Park
PARK

(태종대유원지; Ⓜ Line 1 to Nampo, Exit 6) On the southern tip of Yeongdo (영도; Yeong Island), experience the city's rugged coastline along a well-groomed walking path and the Korean penchant for shouting in parks.

Exit the metro station and walk along the Jagalchi side of the street towards Lotte department store; turn right at the main road. The bus stop (₩1200, bus number 8, 30, 88) is down the street, or take a taxi from the metro station (₩8000).

UN Cemetery
CEMETERY

(재한 유엔 기념공원; ☑051 625 0625; www.unmck.or.kr; 93, UN Pyeonghwa-ro, Nam-gu; ⊙9am-5pm; Ⓜ Line 2 to Daeyeon, Exit 3) This is the

Haeundae

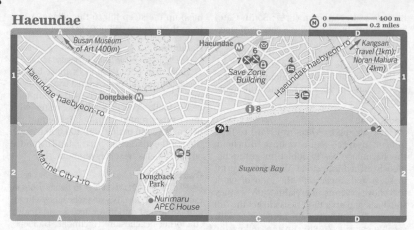

only United Nations cemetery in the world and is the final resting place of 2300 men from 11 nations, including the UK, Turkey, Canada and Australia, that supported the South in the 1950–53 Korean War. There's a moving photo exhibit, along with knowledgeable volunteers who share stories about the people in the images. The cemetery is a 15-minute walk from the station.

Yongdu-san Park   PARK
(용두산 공원; ☎ 051 860 7820; http://yongdusanpark.bisco.or.kr; Busan Tower adult/child ₩5000/3000; ⊙ tower 9am-10pm; Ⓜ Line 1 to Nampo, Exit 1) Close to the shopping in Nampo-dong, this humble park is home to the 118m-high **Busan Tower** (부산타워). If the haze is not too thick, daytime views of container-ship traffic in the harbour provide a sense of the port's scale of operations.

Busan Modern History Museum   MUSEUM
(부산 근대역사관; http://engmuseum.busan.go.kr; ⊙9am-6pm Tue-Sun; Ⓜ Line 1 to Jungang, Exit 5) **FREE** The hour it takes to walk through this small museum will be time well spent. There's a surprising amount of English material documenting the history of the Busan port, the Japanese influence and the Korean War.

It's in a building north of Yongdu-san Park, 300m west of the central post office.

Busan Museum of Art   MUSEUM
(부산 시립 미술관; ☎ 051 744 2602; ⊙10am-8pm Tue-Sun; Ⓜ Line 2 to Busan Museum of Art, Exit 5) **FREE** A modest gallery – hardly a must-see – but an interesting diversion on a rainy day.

Spa Land   SPA
(www.shinsegae.com; 1st fl, Shinsegae Centum City; adult/youth weekdays ₩13,000/10,000, weekends ₩15,000/12,000; ⊙6am-midnight, last entry 10.30pm; Ⓜ Line 2 to Centum City, Exit 3) You can't really experience Busan unless you've been naked in a room full of strangers inside Asia's largest bathhouse. The bathing area in Spa Land isn't particularly impressive, but the *jjimjilbang* (the area where people wear loose-fitting clothes) is immense – there's a panoply of relaxation rooms of various temperatures and scents.

Kids under 13 are not permitted.

Tours

From Taejongdae, a noisy 45-minute cruise (adult/child ₩10,000/7000, 9am to 5pm) runs along the coast with views of Igidae.

City Tour Busan
BUS TOUR

(부산 시티 투어버스; ☑ 051 464 9898; www. citytourbusan.com; adult/child ₩12,000/8000; ☺ tour times vary; Ⓜ Line 1 to Busan Station, Exit 1) City Tour runs six daytime routes with different themes. Buy a Loop Tour ticket and you can jump on and off that bus all day. Three different evening tours drive towards Haeundae, Gwangan bridge and the major hotels. All buses start at Busan station.

Mipo Wharf
BOAT TOUR

(미포 선착장; adult/child ₩22,000/13,000; ☺ hourly departures 10am-10pm; Ⓜ Line 2 to Haeundae, Exit 3 or 5) The small pier at the eastern end of Haeundae beach runs 50-minute return trips to the nearby Oryuk-do Islets and Gwangan bridge.

✸✸ Festivals & Events

Busan International Film Festival
FILM

(부산국제영화제; ☑ +82 1688 3010; www.biff. kr) It's all glitter, glamour and gossip in October when the Busan International Film Festival (BIFF) takes centre stage. Not just about movies – 319 films from 79 countries in 2014 – the real buzz centres on which Korean female starlet will wear the most revealing dress on the red carpet.

Screenings are at six theatres, including **Busan Cinema Center**, a magnificent complex with the world's longest cantilever structure. The 127,000 LED lights streaming across its concave surface create an urban architectural spectacle at night.

Busan International Fireworks Festival
FIREWORKS

(BIFF; 부산국제불꽃축제; ☑ 051 441 3121; www. bff.or.kr) In October the Busan International Fireworks Festival lights the sky. In 2014 there were two locations and times. A Friday evening show in **Busan Citizens Park** (부산 시민공원; http://citizenpark.busan.go.kr) and a bedazzling Saturday night choreography of light and colour, lasers and music near Gwangan beach set against the glimmering Diamond Bridge.

🛏 Sleeping

Seomyeon, at the intersection of two subway lines, is a practical choice for travellers who plan on seeing the sights. Between Haeundae station and the beach, there's a swathe of choices, from guesthouses to luxury rooms. Prices here are higher in July and August.

Pobi Guesthouse
HOSTEL ₩

(포비 게스트 하우스; ☑ 051 746 7990; www. pobihouse.com; 1394-328, 2nd fl, Jung-dong, Haeundae-gu; dm from ₩15,000, higher on weekends; ✳@🖘; Ⓜ Line 2 to Haeundae, Exit 3 or 5) Everything a guesthouse needs is here: Haeundae beach locale, knowledgeable staff and a friendly cat.

From the metro exit, walk straight and turn left at the Haeundae Market entrance. Walk to the end of the street and turn right. The guesthouse is down the road on the left.

Blue Backpackers
HOSTEL ₩

(☑ 051 634 3962; www.bluebackpackers. com; 454-1, Bujeon 2-dong, Busan Jin-gu; dm/r ₩20,000/₩40,000; ✳@🖘; Ⓜ Line 1 or 2 to Seomyeon, Exit 7) Rooms with individual baths, a central location and free toast on the roof make this a great budget choice. It's a 10-minute walk behind Lotte Hotel in Seomyeon.

★ Ibis Ambassador Busan City Centre Hotel
BUSINESS HOTEL ₩₩

(이비스 앰배서더 부산; ☑ 051 930 1110; https://ibis.ambatel.com/busan/main.amb; d from ₩100,000; ✳@🖘✱; Ⓜ Line 1 to Bujeon, Exit 1) Towering over Bujeon Market (p194), Ibis wins for location (a five-minute walk from Seomyeon), cheery staff and understated, chic rooms, which have LCD TVs. Starbucks and a convenience store are on street level.

Toyoko Inn Busan Seomyeon
BUSINESS HOTEL ₩₩

(토요코인 부산서면; ☑ 051 638 1045; www.toyoko-inn.com; d/tw ₩58,300/80,300; ✳@🖘✱; Ⓜ Line 1 or 2 to Seomyeon, Exit 8) One of several branches of the Toyoko Inn in Busan, this property caters to Japanese businessmen and offers rather cramped, no-frills rooms and a modest-but-free breakfast. It's a few minutes' walk from Seomyeon.

★ Westin Chosun Beach Hotel
LUXURY HOTEL ₩₩₩

(웨스틴 조선 비치 호텔; ☑ 051 749 7000; www.starwoodhotels.com; d from ₩230,000; ✳@🖘✱; Ⓜ Line 2 to Haeundae, Exit 3 or 5) Busan's oldest international hotel gets better with age. A hint of retro shaken, not stirred, with modern touches creates a James Bond – a la Sean Connery – sort of dashing cool. It's a little removed from the main action on Haeundae beach, which gives the place a secluded feel.

★ **Paradise Hotel** LUXURY HOTEL **www**
(파라다이스 호텔; ☎051 749 2111; http://paradisehotel.co.kr; tw from ₩240,000; ❄@🛜❄; Ⓜ Line 2 to Haeundae, Exit 3 or 5) Fantastic views of Haeundae beach, grovelling service and decent on-site dining make the Paradise stand out. The rooms are somewhat worn and the casino is modest, but amenities like the outdoor rooftop hot spring make up for that.

Lotte Hotel BUSINESS HOTEL **www**
(롯데 호텔; ☎051 810 1000; www.lottehotelbusan.com; d & tw from ₩430,000; ❄@🛜❄; Ⓜ Line 1 or 2 to Seomyeon, Exit 5 or 7) This business-class hotel in Seomyeon has many contemporary rooms, but the older ones are uninspiring and the quality of staff service at times seems gauche. There's a casino here but it's small, though the Japanese tourists don't seem to mind.

Eating

★ **Sulbing** DESSERTS **₩**
(설빙; http://sulbing.com; desserts from ₩6000; ⏰10.30am-10.30pm; Ⓜ Line 2 to Haeundae, Exit 5) No serious foodie should visit Busan without trying *sulbing,* a wonderfully subtle dessert invented in this city. It's a bowl of shaved frozen milk topped with soybean powder and sliced almonds. A splash of condensed milk adds a hint of sweetness. New variations experiment with yogurt, fruit and chocolate.

From the metro station, walk 100m; it's on the 2nd floor of a building near a small

---

BUSAN'S SPECIALITY FOOD

Busan is a coastal city, so it's not surprising that seafood flavours much of the local cuisine. Raw fish, called *hoe* (회; sounds like 'when' without the 'n'), is a popular dish enjoyed with a group of friends and is widely available and affordably priced (compared to most cities).

A typical *hoe* dinner starts with appetisers such as raw baby octopus still wiggling on the plate. A platter of sliced raw fish is the main course. Fish is dipped into a saucer of *chogochujang* (초고추장), a watery red-pepper sauce, or soy sauce (간장) mixed with wasabi (와사비). The meal is customarily finished with rice and a boiling pot of *maeuntang* (매운탕; spicy fish soup).

Most Koreans say *hoe* has a delicate taste and smooth texture. Western travellers may find the taste bland and chewy. A small platter starting at ₩40,000 is rarely sufficient for a pair of raw-fish fans. Raw fish is often accompanied with *soju* (local vodka).

Jagalchi Fish Market (자갈치 시장; http://jagalchimarket.bisco.or.kr; ⏰8am-10pm, closed 1st & 3rd Tue of month; Ⓜ Line 1 to Jagalchi, Exit 10) Anyone with a love of seafood and a tolerance for powerful odours could easily spend an hour exploring the country's largest fish market. Narrow lanes outside the main building teem with decades-old stalls and rickety food carts run by grannies who sell an incredible variety of seafood, including red snapper, flounder and creepy-crawly creatures with undulating tentacles.

Inside the main building, dozens of 1st-floor vendors sell just about every edible sea animal, including crabs and eels, two Busan favourites. After buying a fish, the fishmonger will point you to a 2nd-floor seating area where your meal will be served (₩4000 per person service charge). Halfway up the stairs, the din of flowing dinner chatter and the unmistakable thud-thud-thud of butcher knives whacking wooden chopping blocks becomes palpable. This is where raw-fish aficionados indulge themselves with meals from the fish tank, via the chopping block.

Jackie's Seafood (돼지초밥 횟집; ☎051 246 2594; ⏰10am-10pm, closed 1st & 3rd Tue of month; Ⓜ Line 1 to Jagalchi, Exit 10) Buying a raw-fish dinner couldn't be easier thanks to Jackie, the affable owner of this seafood restaurant. He speaks fluent English and uses signboards to help customers make smart seasonal food choices. It's on the 2nd floor of the main Jagalchi building.

Millak Town Raw Fish Centre (민락회센터; ⏰10am-1am; Ⓜ Line 2 to Gwangan, Exit 5) Buy a fish for ₩30,000 (or more) and walk upstairs to eat; the woman selling you the fish will indicate which floor. Inside the seating area, your fish will be prepared and served for ₩5000 per person. It's the tall building at the northeast end of Gwangan beach. Little English is spoken here, so you'll need to rely on body language.

parking lot. Sulbing shops can be found in most busy areas, such as Seomyeon, Kyungsung-Pukyung and Nampo-dong.

Dolgorae
KOREAN ₩

(돌고래; meals from ₩5000; ⊘7am-10pm; Ⓜ Line 1 to Nampo, Exit 1) The interior looks like a penitentiary, but this humble restaurant near the Gukje Market (p194) serves up tasty standards such as *doenjang jjigae* (된장찌개; soybean stew) and *soondubu jjigae* (순두부찌개; spicy tofu stew). Each dish comes with a kimchi that's sweeter than most. It's down a narrow lane; look for the yellow sign.

Yetnal Jjajang
KOREAN ₩

(옛날짜장; meals from ₩4000; ⊘9.30am-10.30pm; Ⓜ Line 1 or 2 to Seomyeon, Exit 7) A sterling example of a successful restaurant owner who won't update the interior. According to superstition, the good fortune a successful shop enjoys can be lost if the interior were changed. Consequently, some shoddy-looking restaurants, like this one, serve great food. The *jjajangmyeon* (짜장면; black bean-paste noodles) and *jjambbong* (짬뽕; spicy seafood soup) are excellent.

Gyeongju Gukbap
KOREAN ₩

(경주국밥; soup ₩6500; ⊘24hr, closed holidays; Ⓜ Line 1 or 2 to Seomyeon, Exit 3) It may look like all the other *dwaeji gukbap* (돼지국밥; pork and rice soup) restaurants on Seomyeon's Youth St but, judging by the number of celebrity autographs on the wall, this one is special. Hard to find outside the province, this must-try authentic Busan dish is simple, hearty and straightforward, just like the people of this fair city.

Podo Cheong
BARBECUE ₩

(포도청; ☑051 806 9797; per serving ₩7000; ⊘noon-midnight; Ⓜ Line 1 or 2 to Seomyeon, follow underground signs to Judies Taewha Exit) It's not the best *sutbul galbi* (숯불갈비; charcoal-fired barbecue) restaurant, but it is good. The main draw at this busy place is the backyard barbecue feel in the patio. Lean *moksal* (목살; pork chop) tastes great, though most Koreans will choose *samgyeopsal* (삼겹살; fatty pork).

Boribap & Cheonggukjang
KOREAN ₩

(보리밥 앤 청국장; meals from ₩6000; ⊘11am-9.30pm Wed-Mon; Ⓜ Line 2 to Haeundae, Exit 3 or 5) This small shop in Haeundae serves excellent traditional Korean meals featuring stews made from pungent *cheonggukjang*

Geumjeong-san

Geumjeong-san

⊙ Sights
1 Beomeo-Sa	A1
2 East Gate	A3
3 Geumgang Park Cable Car	A4
4 Geumjeong Fortress	A2
5 North Gate	A2
6 Seokbul-sa	A4
7 South Gate	A3
8 West Gate	A3

🛍 Shopping
9 Lotte Department Store Dongnae	B4

ℹ Transport
10 Busan Central Bus Terminal	B1
11 Busan Express Bus Terminal	B1
12 Busan Intercity Bus Terminal	B1

(청국장; fermented soybean paste). The mackerel set (고등어 정식) comes with a fish baked to perfection.

BUSAN & GYEONGSANGNAM-DO BUSAN

Seomyeon

It's on a lane on the north side of the Save Zone building.

True Octopus Restaurant KOREAN ₩₩
(소문난문어집; small/large set ₩20,000/ 40,000; ☺5pm-2am Mon-Sat; Ⓜ Line 1 or 2 to Seomyeon, Exit 7) There's no need to read a menu here because this shop serves only one thing: a humongous octopus tentacle with an amazing array of side dishes. Your only choice is between the small set (good for two people) or the large (three to four people). The taste and texture is similar to high-quality tuna or steak, though saltier.

✗ Cheongsapo 청사포

This out-of-the-way fishing port is a must-visit for the barbecued shellfish, arguably the best food in Busan. A ₩7000 taxi from Haeundae is the only practical way to get here.

★**Noran Mahura** SEAFOOD ₩₩
(청사포 노란 마후라; ☎051 703 3586; set meals from ₩30,000; ☺2pm-sunrise; Ⓟ) This cosy restaurant, not far from a lighthouse, is where people come for a drink to watch the sunset and unexpectedly stay for the sunrise. Meals include barbecued shellfish (조개 구이; *jogae gui*) with an amazing salsa-like sauce. It tastes even better with *soju* (local vodka) at sunrise.

🍺 Drinking

The busy commercial district around Pusan National University is a good bet for low-cost bars.

🍺 Gwangan

Beached SPORTS BAR
(☺4pm-late; Ⓜ Line 2 to Geumnyeonsan, Exit 1) Craig, the owner, calls it a dive bar with the best view of the Gwangan bridge. And he's

Seomyeon

right. A busy expat tavern, it's one of the few places in town to watch rugby, drink Kiwi beer and listen to Led Zeppelin.

From the metro station, turn right at the first corner, walk down to the beach road and look left.

Galmegi Pub   MICROBREWERY
(📱 010 4469 9658; www.galmegibrewing.com; 3-4 Namcheon 2-dong, Suyeong-gu; ⊘6pm-midnight Mon-Thu, until 1am Fri & Sat, closed Sun; Ⓜ Line 2 to Geumyeonsan, Exit 3) Craving craft beer? Busan's first craft brewery has an evolving menu, including black, blonde and pale ales. There are two other locations in Busan, but this one has the advantage of being close to Gwangan beach.

From the metro exit, spin 180 degrees, turn right at the first street and walk towards the beach road. It's near Starbucks.

HQ Gwangan   BAR
(⊘7pm-late Mon-Sat, 4pm-midnight Sun; Ⓜ Line 2 to Gwangan, Exit 3 or 5) This busy expat bar has cheap shots, pub grub, trivia nights, TV sports and a splendid view of Gwangan bridge.

From the metro station, walk to the beach road and turn left at the Lotteria fast-food restaurant.

Thursday Party   BAR
(⊘6pm-5am; Ⓜ Line 2 to Gwangan, Exit 3 or 5) This bar is a regular date spot for the university crowd because of the cheap draught, free curry-flavoured popcorn and pounding K-Pop. There are two locations on the Gwan-

gan beach road, plus branches in Seomyeon, Haeundae and Kyungsung-Pukyoung.

🍷 Kyungsung-Pukyong Universities

The neon burns brightly in this popular nightlife district frequented by hungry, thirsty, frugal students from two nearby universities.

★**The Comonplace**   WINE BAR
(문화골목 다반; 📱 051 625 0730; ⊘5pm-1am; Ⓜ Line 2 to Kyungsung-Pukyong, Exit 3) There's nothing common about this exceptional coffee and wine bar. Stylishly decorated, with an ubercool vibe, comfy sofas, friends dissecting existentialism over a glass of red wine, it's on the 1st floor of the architecturally intriguing **Golmok** (골목) complex. For something less Sartre and more Chomsky, try **Nogada**, the downstairs beer bar.

From the metro station, turn right at the first street then left at the second street. It's on a lane 40m down the road.

Eva's Ticket   BAR
(www.evasticket.com; Ⓜ Line 2 to Kyungsung-Pukyong, Exit 5) Weary English instructors flock to this spacious bar to unwind over cheap draught after a hard day of teaching phonics.

From the metro station, spin 180 degrees and turn right at the intersection then right again at the first street. It's down the road on the right.

🍵 Seomyeon

★**Maru**   TEAHOUSE
(마루; 📱 051 803 6797; Saesak-ro 17-1, Jin-gu; ⊘10am-10pm; Ⓜ Line 1 or 2 to Seomyeon, Exit 9) Splendid herbal teas and a warm interior make this an excellent alternative to the sterile sameness of chain coffee shops. The dark and earthy twin flower tea (쌍화차) is a speciality.

Exit the Yeonggwang Bookstore (p194), turn left and walk left around the corner. Look for a green signboard with 마루 150m down the street.

Emo   BAR
(이모; ⊘8pm-7am; Ⓜ Line 1 or 2 to Seomyeon, underground exit for Lotte department store) One of many orange *pojangmacha* (tented street stall) tents behind Lotte department store in Seomyeon serving drinks and unusual side dishes, such as grilled chicken anus.

BUSAN & GYEONGSANGNAM-DO BUSAN

☆ Entertainment

Sport

There's pro football here, but Busan is a baseball town at heart.

Lotte Giants BASEBALL
(롯데 자이언츠; ☑ 051 590 9000; www.giants-club.com/eng; ticket prices from ₩7000; Ⓜ Line 3 to Sports Complex, Exit 9) The Lotte Giants baseball experience inside Sajik stadium neatly captures the essence of Busan: boisterous, fun-loving and occasionally naughty (especially when the visiting pitcher holds the man on first base). Expect cheap tickets, no limit on how much food and drink fans can bring in and good fun with the orange bags.

From the metro station, walk towards HomePlus.

Busan IPark FOOTBALL
(부산 아이파크; ☑ 051 941 1100; www.busani-park.com; best seat ₩10,000; Ⓜ Line 3 to Sports Complex, Exit 9) Busan IPark, the city's pro football team, plays 19 home matches between March to November at **Asiad Stadium**, a giant 53,000-seat facility that sits empty most of the year. Games are thinly attended, so getting a good seat won't be a problem. Occasionally the stadium hosts K-Pop concerts. It's located behind Home-Plus.

Live Music

Monk JAZZ
(http://cafe.daum.net/clubmonk; cover ₩5000; ☉ 6.30pm-2am Mon-Sat; Ⓜ Line 2 to Kyungsung-Pukyong, Exit 3) The sweet sound of live jazz fills the room most nights from 9pm to 11pm with professional Korean performers – expats jam Wednesday nights.

From the station, turn right at the first street. Walk to the third intersection; it's on the right.

🛍 Shopping

Shinsegae Centum City DEPARTMENT STORE
(신세계 센텀시티; www.shinsegae.com; ☉ 10.30am-8pm; Ⓜ Line 2 to Centum City, Shinsegae Exit) The world's largest shopping complex – bigger than Macy's in New York – with everything you'd expect in a temple of commerce. There's a skating rink, indoor golf driving range, shops with seemingly every brand name in the universe and a place to recuperate – Spa Land (p188) – before you do it again.

Bujeon Market MARKET
(부전시장; ☉ 4am-8pm; Ⓜ Line 1 to Bujeon, Exit 5) You could easily spend an hour getting lost in this enormous traditional market specialising in produce, seafood and knick-knacks.

Gukje Market MARKET
(국제시장; ☉ 8.30am-8.30pm; Ⓜ Line 1 to Jagalchi, Exit 7) West of Nampo-dong, this traditional market has hundreds of small booths with a staggering selection of items, from leather goods to Korean drums.

**Lotte Department Store
Centum City** DEPARTMENT STORE
(롯데백화점 센텀시티점; www.lotte.co.kr; ☉ 10.30am-8.30pm; Ⓜ Line 2 to Centum City, Lotte Exit) Need to buy a $5000 handbag? You can probably find one at this Lotte outlet in Haeundae beside Shinsegae. Or you could try one of the other three outlets across the city in **Seomyeon** (☉ 10.30am-8pm; Ⓜ Line 2 to Seomyeon, Lotte Exit), **Dongnae** (Map p191; ☉ 10.30am-8pm; Ⓜ Line 1 to Myeongnyun, Exit 1) and **Gwangbok-dong** (☉ 10.30am-8pm; Ⓜ Line 1 to Nampo, Exit 10).

Yeonggwang Bookstore BOOKS
(영광도서; ☑ 051 816 9500; www.ykbook.com; Ⓜ Line 1 or 2 to Seomyeon, Exit 9) One of the city's oldest bookstores, with a decent selection of English books.

ℹ Information

EMERGENCY

Fire & Rescue (☑ 119)
Police (☑ 112)

INTERNET ACCESS

Busan is a wired city, but that doesn't mean internet access is free. Many public areas and cafes have password-protected wi-fi. Foreign devices might have trouble connecting to local networks.

MEDICAL SERVICES

Dong-Eui Medical Centre (동의의료원; ☑ 051 850 8941; http://eng.demc.kr; San 45-1, Yangjung 2 dong, Jin-gu; ☉ 8.30am-4.30pm Mon-Fri, to noon Sat; Ⓜ Line 1 to Yangjeong, Exit 4) English-speaking staff at this large medical complex can help travellers. Outside the metro station exit, take local bus 8.

MONEY

Most banks exchange currency, though the level of service varies. For international withdrawals, your best bet is a KB Kookmin Bank ATM. Look for the yellow asterisk and 'b' logo, and the 'global' ATM inside. If you need to get US dollars outside banking hours, go to Nampo-dong and look for the old women sitting on chairs whispering 'changee'.

Gimhae International Airport currency exchange Branches in the domestic terminal (⊘ 6am-4pm) and international terminal (⊘ 6am-9pm).

POST
Central Post Office (부산 중앙 우체국; www.koreapost.go.kr; ⊘ 9am-6pm Mon-Fri; Ⓜ Line 1 to Jungang, Exit 9) Busan's main post office is near the ferry terminal.

TOURIST INFORMATION
Busan Station Tourism Office (부산역 관광안내소; ☑ 051 441 6565; ⊘ 9am-8pm; Ⓜ Line 1 to Busan station, Exit 8 or 10) There's knowledgeable staff and a modest selection of maps on the 2nd floor.

Gimhae Airport – Domestic Terminal Info (☑ 051 974 3774; ⊘ 6am-11pm or last arrival) Useful information and helpful staff.

Gimhae Airport – International Terminal Info (☑ 051 974 3772; ⊘ 6am-11pm or last arrival) Loads of information and helpful staff, especially if you need to find a bus to a regional city.

Haeundae Tourism Office (해운대 관광안내소; ☑ 051 749 4335; http://eng.haeundae.go.kr; ⊘ 9am-6pm; Ⓜ Line 2 to Haeundae, Exit 3 or 5) A great selection of material.

Kangsan Travel (☑ 051 747 0031; www.kangsantravel.com; ⊘ 9am-noon & 1-6pm Mon-Fri; Ⓜ Line 2 to Jangsan, Exit 9) Provides English-language services geared towards expats.

WEBSITES
Lonely Planet (www.lonelyplanet.com/south-korea/gyeongsangnam-do/busan) For planning advice, author recommendations, traveller reviews and insider tips.

City Government (http://english.busan.go.kr) For basic socio-economic and travel data.

Gyeongsangnam-Do (http://english.gsnd.net) Learn about Gyeongsangnam-do's sites and geography.

Busan Haps (http://busanhaps.com) Free entertainment magazine filled with local ads and stories about which bar has a new hamburger on the menu.

ⓘ Getting There & Away

Domestic travellers usually come to Busan via KTX train service, though there are good bus connections from most major destinations. International travellers can fly directly to **Gimhae International Airport** (김해 국제 공항; ☑ 051 974 3114; www.airport.co.kr/gimhaeeng/index.do; Ⓜ Busan-Gimhae LRT, Exit Airport), 27km west of Busan's city centre.

AIR
There are frequent international flights to Japan and regional cities such as Beijing, Hong Kong, Bangkok, Chiang Mai and Cebu.

On domestic routes, the Busan–Seoul flight on Korean Air, Asiana or Air Busan (one hour, every 30 minutes from 7am to 9pm) usually requires reservations on weekends and holidays. Most flights from Busan to Seoul land at Gimpo airport, which has few international connections. If you're flying out of the country, catch the A'rex,

BUSAN BUS DEPARTURES

Departures from Busan Central Bus Terminal

DESTINATION	PRICE (₩)	DURATION	FREQUENCY
Gyeongju	5200	50min	every 30min
Pohang	8100	1½hr	every 15min
Seoul	37,600	4½hr	every 30min
Tongdo-sa	2000	25min	every 20min

Westbound Departures from Seobu Intercity Bus Terminal

DESTINATION	PRICE (₩)	DURATION	FREQUENCY
Gohyeon	13,400	2¾hr	every 30-40min
Hadong	11,000	2½hr	every hr
Jinju	7700	1½hr	every 15-25min
Namhae	11,900	2½hr	every 20-60min
Ssanggyae-sa	14,000	3½hr	10am & 4pm
Tongyeong	10,900	1¾hr	every 20-30min

Nampo-dong

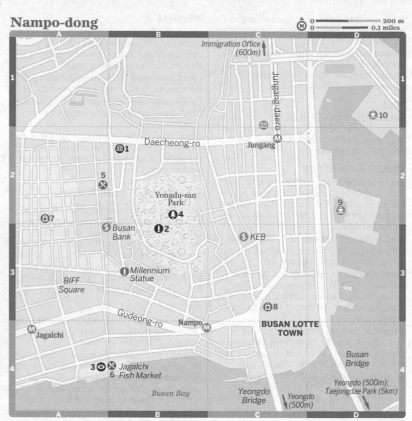

Immigration Office
(600m)

Daecheong-ro

Jungang-daero

Jungang

1

Yongdu-san
Park 4

5

7

$ Busan
Bank

2

KEB

9

Millennium
Statue

BIFF
Square

Gudeong-ro

Nampo

8

BUSAN LOTTE
TOWN

Jagalchi

3 Jagalchi
6 Fish Market

Busan Bay

Busan
Bridge

Yeongdo
Bridge

Yeongdo
(500m)

Yeongdo (500m);
Taejongdae Park (5km)

which runs between Seoul station and Incheon International with a stop at Gimpo airport. Flights also connect Busan and Jeju-do (one hour, every 30 to 90 minutes from 7am to 8pm).

BUS

Buses run every 30 to 60 minutes from the airport's domestic terminal to regional cities, including Gyeongju (₩9000), Changwon (₩8000) and Ulsan (₩7900).

Intercity (부산 시외 버스터미널; Map p191; ☑ 051 508 9966; http://dbterminal.co.kr/; Ⓜ line 1 to Nopo, Exit 3) and **express** (부산 고속 버스터미널 ; Map p191; ☑ 051 508 9201; www. kobus.co.kr; Ⓜ Line 1 to Nopo, Exit 3) buses depart from the Central Bus Terminal (p185) at Nopo-dong station.

Seobu intercity bus terminal (부산 서부 시 외 버스터미널; ☑ 051 559 1000; www.busantr. com; Ⓜ Line 2 to Sasang, Exit 3 or 5) is outside Sasang station, with street-level access through a department store.

BOAT

To find the **International Ferry Terminal** (국제 여객터미널; ☑ 051 465 3471; Ⓜ Line 1 to Jungang, Exit 12), exit the metro, walk towards the containers visible down the road and cross the major street. Continue straight and turn right just past the customs and immigration office. The terminal is about 150m down the path.

First-floor booths in the terminal sell tickets to three Japanese cities: Fukuoka (☑ 1688 7447, ₩90,000, departs 10.30pm, check in 7pm, eight hours); Shimonoseki (☑ 051 462 3161, ₩95,000, departs 9pm, 13 hours); Osaka (☑ 462 5482, ₩129,350, departs 3pm Sunday, Tuesday, Thursday, 18 hours).

On the 2nd floor there's a jet ferry to Tsushima (☑ 1599 0255, ₩75,000, two to three daily departures, 1½ to two hours) and a hydrofoil to Fukuoka (☑ 1599 0255, ₩115,000, two to four daily departures, three hours). Discounts are possible if you book ahead through a travel agent.

Nampo-dong

Ferries to Jeju-do (one way from ₩51,500) depart Busan's **Coastal Ferry Terminal** (부산항 연안여객터미널; Ⓜ Line 1 to Jungang, Exit 2) on Monday, Wednesday and Friday at 7pm and arrive 12 hours later.

TRAIN

Most trains depart from and arrive at Busan's downtown station. There are also departures from Gupo, a western station with easy access to metro Line 3 that saves the hassle of going downtown. Between Busan and Seoul (adult/child ₩58,800/29,400, every 30 to 60 minutes), KTX is the quickest service, with most trips taking three hours or less.

Saemaul services take five hours to reach Seoul (adult/child ₩42,600/21,300, eight daily departures). The *mugunghwa* service is only about 30 minutes slower and quite a bit cheaper (adult/child ₩28,600/14,300, 14 departures).

Busan's smallest station, Bujeon, services regional cities and towns such as Gyeongju (adult/child ₩6700/3300, 20 departures), Hadong (adult/child ₩11,000/5500, four departures) and Mokpo (adult/child ₩25,100/12,500, departs 6.25am). Check **Korea Rail** (www.letskorail.com) online for fares and schedules.

If you're heading to Japan, a **Korea-Japan Co-Ticket** (aka Korea-Japan Joint Ticket) provides discounted travel between the two countries. It covers Korea Rail services, the ferry crossing between Busan and Fukuoka or Shimonoseki and Japan Rail services. The application procedure is slightly complicated and tickets must be reserved seven days in advance; see www.korailtours.com for details.

❶ Getting Around

TO/FROM THE AIRPORT

A limousine bus from Gimhae airport (p195) runs to Seomyeon and the major hotels in Haeundae (₩7000, one hour, every 30 minutes). A second route goes to Seomyeon, Busan station and Nampo-dong (₩6000, one hour, every 40 minutes).

A taxi from the airport to Seomyeon takes 30 minutes and costs ₩40,000, depending on traffic. A 10-minute taxi from Deokcheon station costs ₩8000.

The most economical link between the airport and city (₩1600) is bus 307 from Gupo station, or 201 from Seomyeon (opposite Lotte department store).

The Busan–Gimhae Light Rail line connects Sasang and Daejeo stations with the airport (₩1300, 15 minutes). Buy a chip from the vending machine. Put the chip on the magnetic reader when entering the turnstile. When leaving the station, put the chip in the turnstile.

BUS

Adult cash fares are ₩1200/1600 for regular/express buses. Slight discounts are available when paying with a Hanaro card.

SUBWAY

Busan's four-line subway uses a two-zone fare system: ₩1300 for one zone and ₩1500 for longer trips. Purchasing a **Hanaro** (₩6000 plus travel credits, available at subway vending machines) is handy for long stays – you get a small discount on fares and avoid the hassle of buying a ticket for each trip. A one-day pass costs ₩4500. Subway trains generally run between 5.10am and 12.30am.

TAXI

Basic taxi fares start at ₩2800 (with a 20% night premium). Avoid black-and-red deluxe taxis if possible, because the fares can run high.

Gajisan Provincial Park 가지산 도립공원

This park has three sections. The northernmost section, not far from Gyeongju, is known for rocky terrain. This is where you'll find **Gajisan** (가지산; Mt Gaji; 1240m), the park's highest peak. Tongdo-sa, one of the country's most commercialised Buddhist temples, is in the smallest of the three sections.

◎ Sights

Seoknam-Sa
BUDDHIST TEMPLE

(석남사; www.seoknamsa.or.kr; park entrance adult/youth ₩1700/1300; ⊘3am-8pm; 🚌Eonyang terminal) This temple is a visual masterpiece filled with enchanting contours, colours and contrasts. And it all begins at the park entrance with an 800m walk through a heavily wooded forest where patches of sunlight struggle to break through the thick canopy of foliage. Home to female monks, the temple is just beyond a fork in the path that is the starting point for a 6.4km hike up Gajisan.

From Busan's Central Bus Terminal, catch a bus to the small but confusing Eonyang terminal (₩3300, 35 minutes, every 20 minutes) and buy a ticket for Seoknam-sa (bus 1713, ₩2000, 20 minutes, every 15 to 30 minutes). On the way back, bus 807 is another option to Eonyang (₩1200, every 15 to 30 minutes). It stops outside the bus terminal.

Tongdo-Sa
BUDDHIST TEMPLE

(통도사; 🕿055 384 7085; www.tongdosa. or.kr; adult/child/youth ₩3000/1000/1500; ⊘8.30am-5.30pm; 🚇Line 1 to Nopo, Exit 3) Tongdo-sa is noted for a *sari*, a crystalline substance thought to develop inside the body of a pure monk. The *sari* is enshrined in a fenced area and cannot be seen. It is a focal point of devotion, which is why Tongdo-sa does not have a Buddha statue in the main hall, a rarity in Korea. Tongdo-sa operates an English-language templestay program.

Inside the temple compound, stop by the **Tongdo-Sa Museum** (통도사 성보 박물관; www.tongdomuseum.or.kr; adult/youth ₩2000/1000; ⊘9.30am-5.30pm Wed-Mon; 🚇Line 1 to Nopo, Exit 3) to view a collection of Buddhist paintings along with 30,000 artefacts.

Buses to Tongdo-sa depart Busan's Central Bus Terminal (₩2200, 25 minutes, every 20 minutes) and stop at Sinpyeong bus terminal. Exit the terminal through the back lot, turn right and walk 10 minutes to the gate.

Geojedo
거제도

🕿055 / POP 243,000

Connected to the mainland by the 8km Busan-Geoje Fixed Link bridge and tunnel, Korea's second-largest island is famous for its massive shipbuilding industry and natural beauty. The coastal scenery varies between pastoral and industrial, with the best views in and around **Haegeumgang** (해금강). Geoje-do has one of the highest income levels in Korea, which accounts for the high cost of travelling in some parts of the island and the surprisingly intense traffic congestion in downtown Geoje-si. Geoje-si is sometimes called Gohyeon, a name that refers to the city's downtown area.

◎ Sights

Historic Park of Geoje POW Camp
MUSEUM

(거제도 포로수용소 유적공원; 🕿055 639 8125; www.pow.or.kr; adult/child/youth ₩7000/3000/5000; ⊘9am-6pm Apr-Oct, to 5pm Nov-Mar) In Geoje-si, this modest but worthwhile museum provides hard-to-find information about the POW camp experience during the Korean War. Just by the gate is a tourist info centre that has maps but no English-speaking staff.

From the Gohyeon intercity bus terminal, it's a 30-minute walk; a ₩5000 taxi ride will get you here in a few minutes.

Hakdong Mongdol Beach
BEACH

(학동 몽돌해변) About 30 minutes by car from Geoje-si, the black-pebble beach in **Hakdong** is a cosy destination for family outings and romantic getaways. Summer crowds flock to the 1.2km-long beach to laze on the bumpy rocks (bring a thick blanket), throw stones and fish off the pier. The rest of the year is rather quiet.

Haegeumgang
NATIONAL PARK

(해금강) Haegeumgang is a collection of breathtaking rocky islets and a jagged coastline, part of the **Hallyeo Maritime National Park**, which is famous for life-affirming sunrises, stirring sunsets and exhilarating drives. About an hour by car from Geoje-si, the road to Haegeumgang is filled with twists and turns requiring caution as drivers occasionally stop in unusual places to admire ocean views or buy snacks from roadside vendors.

Oedo Botania
ISLAND

(외도; 🕿070 7715 3330; www.oedobotania.com; adult/child/youth ₩11,000/5000/8000; 🚻; 🚢11) Geojedo's busiest tourist attraction is a tiny island-cum–botanical garden 4km off the coast. It's popular with Korean travellers, but unless you absolutely adore manicured gardens, long waits (if ferries are cancelled

FERRY EXCURSIONS

It's impossible to describe the full range of ferry trips to the magical islands around Tongyeong. Below is a sample of what's possible. The first three excursions depart the passenger **ferry terminal** (p200) near Gangguan harbour. The ferry to Saryangdo departs the Gaochi terminal in the northwest part of the city. Be sure to pack enough food; groceries on the islands are scant or expensive.

Yeonhwado (연환도; ☑ 055 641 6184) Peaceful and remote, Yeonhwado is a small island ideal for three-hour hikes. From the ferry (return ₩18,400, one hour, departs 6.30am, 9.30am, 11am, 1pm and 3pm), follow the path left past the brown cow up to the mountain ridge where you'll find **Yongmeori**, a spectacular arrangement of rocks that look like a dragon's head. There are a couple of *minbak* (private homes with rooms for rent) here, but Yeonhwado is usually a day trip.

Bijindo (비진도; ☑ 055 645 3717) Bijindo is actually two islands joined together by a sand bridge, which makes for some outstanding photography. It's a popular getaway destination for couples and families looking for a place to picnic amid sandy beaches and a quiet sense of bliss. Weekends and summer months can be busy and less blissful. Local accommodation is available but expensive.

The ferry crossing (return ₩17,250, departs 7am, 11am and 2.30pm) takes one hour.

Somaemuldo (소매물도; ☑ 055 645 3717) Sharp cliffs and crashing waves on dramatic rock formations make this a worthwhile journey. At low tide, walk across the land bridge and climb to the lighthouse. Some accomodation is available on the island.

The ferry (return ₩16,050, 1½ hours) departs Gangguan at 7am, 11am and 2.30pm.

Saryangdo (사량도; ☑ 055 647 0147) Jagged ridges, 400m-high peaks, ropes, ladders and awe-inspiring views await travellers looking for a challenging hike. Most travellers depart the ferry (return ₩10,000, 40 minutes, departs 7.30am, 9.30am, noon, 2pm and 4.10pm) on Saryandgo and catch a bus to the other side of the island to begin the five-hour trek.

From Tongyeong's bus terminal, catch bus 10-5 (₩1200, 40 minutes) or a taxi (₩14,000, 20 minutes) to the Gaochi ferry terminal (가오치 사량도행 여객터미널).

or delayed) and pushy lines, consider avoiding the place.

By car from Geoje-si, follow the road signs to Jangsangpo and look for the sign pointing to Oedo terminal.

🛏 Sleeping & Eating

There's a collection of motels a few blocks behind the Gohyeon bus terminal. You'll have no problem finding a place to eat in Hakdong, if you like raw fish.

Hotel B　　　　　　　　　　　　　HOTEL ₩₩
(☑ 055 635 9797; www.hotelb.net; r from ₩50,000; P❄@🛜) If you need to stay overnight in Geoje-si, try first this newer property with stylish rooms with different wallpaper themes. The larger, more expensive, rooms have spacious bathrooms. It's one of the taller buildings behind the bus terminal.

Geoje Tiffany Pension　　　　MOTEL ₩₩
(거제 티파니 리조텔; ☑ 055 636 8866; http://geojetiffany.co.kr; r from ₩50,000; ❄) Hakdong

has an impressive selection of motels of varying quality, some closer to the beach than others. Geoje Tiffany Pension is beside the beach. It's nothing fancy; just nice, clean rooms with bathroom and a friendly owner who speaks English. It's a short walk to nearby restaurants.

Palm Tree Pension　　　　PENSION ₩₩₩
(☑ 055 636 2241, 010 3566 6645; www.palmtree.kr; standard/deluxe r ₩100,000/300,000, higher on weekends; ❄🛜🏊) Beautiful and private, the Palm Tree is a gorgeous pension with balconies overlooking the sea. The snazzy boutique rooms have kitchenettes and spas. It's in a secluded area and a couple of kilometres from Hakdong's black pebble beach (p198). About 30 minutes by car along the coastal road from Geoje-si, look for the property with a windmill.

Samsung Hotel　　　　　　　HOTEL ₩₩₩
(☑ 055 631 2114; www.sghotel.co.kr; r from ₩310,000; P❄@🛜🏊) Here's the

business-class property that engineers, technicians and ship-industry professionals choose when visiting Geojedo. Not far from the Samsung shipyard, this upmarket property is one of the few hotels in Gyeongsangnam-do with an indoor swimming pool.

Green Restaurant
KOREAN ₩₩
(그린 식육 식당; ☑ 055 636 7535; servings from ₩9500) If the dozen-or-so raw-fish restaurants near the black pebble beach (p198) in Hakdong don't look appealing, try the barbecued pork at this small shop. Both *samgyupsal* (삼겹살; fatty pork belly) and *moksal* (목살; pork chop) are available.

❶ Getting There & Around

From the Gohyeon intercity bus terminal, there are frequent connections to Busan's Seobu terminal (₩7200, 1½ hours, every 10 to 30 minutes), Tongyeong (₩3400, 25 minutes, every 20 minutes) and Jinju (₩11,100, one hour, hourly).

Outside Geoje-si, the island's biggest town, public transport is not well developed. Although there are local buses, connections are inconvenient so personal transport on the island is recommended. It's relatively easy to drive to and from Busan thanks to the Busan-Geoje Fixed Link bridge but you'll have to pay the ₩10,000 toll for cars.

Tongyeong
통영

☑ 055 / POP 134,000

On the southern tip of Goseong Peninsula, Tongyeong is a coastal city wedged between Namhaedo and Geojedo. Most of the picturesque sights are in and around Gangguan (강구안), a pretty harbour made for sunset strolls. Visiting Tongyeong's truly spectacular sights – any one of the 151 islands dotting the coastline – usually requires an overnight stay and early morning ferry departure to some of the most pristine territory in the province.

There are three tourist information booths. Outside the intercity bus terminal and on Gangguan harbour (both open 9am to 6pm), there's a decent selection of material, though you'll need to rely on body language because no one speaks English. Ferry schedules are available from the desk inside the coastal passenger **ferry terminal** (☑ 055 642 8392; ⊙ 9am-4pm).

◉ Sights & Activities

Gangguan
HARBOUR
(강구안) It's not the only harbour in the city but Gangguan is the prettiest. It's also a busy pier anchored by a promenade that serves multiple civic functions, including dock, basketball court and picnic ground for package-tour travellers who aren't squeamish about a mid-morning *soju* pick-me-up.

Turtle Ship Replicas
HISTORIC SITE
(거북선; adult/youth ₩2000/1600; ⊙ 9am-6pm) Towards the north end of the Gangguan promenade, there are four turtle ships. Definitely worth a look. While ducking your head inside the ship, try to imagine how 50 sailors and 70 oarsmen might have functioned in these cramped quarters.

Hallyeosudo Cable Car
CABLE CAR
(한려수도 케이블카; ☑ 055 649 3804; http://cablecar.ttdc.kr; one way/return adult ₩6500/10,000, child ₩4000/6000; ⊙ 9.30am-5.30pm Sep-Mar, to 7pm Apr-Aug, closed 2nd & 4th Mon of month; ⊒ 141) Stretching out 1975m, this is Korea's longest cable-car ride. Near the top of Mireuk-san (461m), the view of Hallyeo Maritime National Park is dramatic. If you're up for a two-hour hike, buy a one-way ticket, walk down the back end of the mountain and head towards the Undersea Tunnel. Pick up a map from the booth near the ticket window. If you're coming here on the weekend, arrive early because wait times can be long.

The cable-car ticket office is a ₩7000 taxi ride from the passenger ferry terminal and ₩10,000 from the intercity bus terminal.

Jungang Live Fish Market
MARKET
(중앙활어시장; ⊙ 8am-8pm) Sure there's lots of fish, but this open-air market, filled with grannies selling food out of plastic tubs, is a good place to buy fruit and vegies before heading out on a ferry trip. The front entrance is near Gangguan harbour.

Nammang-san
MOUNTAIN
(남망산) Set aside an hour or more to enjoy the views atop this mountain beside Gangguan harbour. On the way up, you'll pass a modest sculpture park with 15 pieces of art. Up top there's a statue of Yi Sun-shin and a pavilion providing panoramic harbour views.

Undersea Tunnel
TUNNEL
(해저 터널; ⊙ 24hr) **FREE** The journey to the Undersea Tunnel is more interesting

than the sight itself. Constructed in the early 1930s, the 483m-long tunnel connects both sides of Seoho Bay (서호만). Not much more than a cement corridor, it does make for a pleasant evening stroll towards the Tongyeong Grand Bridge.

Tongyeong Sea Land   BATHHOUSE
(통영 해수랜드; ☎055 645 7700; public bath/jjimjilbang adult ₩6000/10,000, youth 5000/9000; ☺24hr) This is a 24-hour spa and *jjimjilbang*, so guests can sleep here overnight. Incredible value for budget travellers, but don't expect a good rest: you're on a hard floor surrounded by cranky babies, drunken snorers and people tiptoeing to the toilet all night. On the bright side, take a bath any time you want. It's on the Gangguan harbour road.

⏏ Sleeping

Around Gangguan there's a handful of motels near the ferry terminal and further down the road near the KB Bank, which is where Tongyeong's seedy side comes to life at night.

★ Nexun   MOTEL ₩₩
(넥슨모텔; ☎055 643 6568; r from ₩50,000; P ❄ @) The modern design and central location make this motel one of the nicer properties around Gangguan. Decent restaurants and waterfront strolls are minutes from your room. The passenger ferry terminal is across the street, which is ideal for travellers catching an early ferry to a nearby island.

Napoli Motel   MOTEL ₩₩
(나폴리모텔; ☎055 646 0202; http://tynapoli.co.kr; r from ₩50,000; ❄ @) This serviceable motel by the northern end of the Gangguan promenade has fairly modern rooms with harbour views. Expect to pay ₩70,000 and up in July and August.

✖ Eating & Drinking

★ Ddungbo Halmae Gimbap   KOREAN ₩
(뚱보 할매 김밥; ☎055 645 2619; per serving ₩4500; ☺7am-midnight) Hungry travellers with limited Korean skills come here because there's no need to speak or read a menu: this place only serves *chungmu gimbap* (충무 김밥), a spicy squid-and-radish dish. The waitress will ask how many servings you want and, if necessary, she'll use her fingers to count. It's opposite the turtle ships in Gangguan.

One serving of this spicy dish, which will test the red-pepper tolerance of the hardiest Korean food lover, should be enough for a single person.

Ae Gul Bang   BAKERY ₩
(통영애꿀빵; ☎055 648 8583; 6 balls for ₩6000; ☺8am-9pm) Stroll the Gangguan harbour road and it's impossible to miss the incredible number of shops selling a honey-covered sticky ball of bread with a paste filling called *gul bang*. Ae Gul Bang is a little different because its made with rice flour, which gives the bread a soft texture. Yummy but very sweet.

Dong Hae Sikdang   KOREAN ₩₩
(동해 식당; ☎055 646 1117; meals from ₩8000; ☺8am-8pm) A few scruffy tables with boisterous fishermen polishing off their third bottle of *soju* may not look inviting, but this small eatery serves excellent food. The *maeuntang* (매운탕; spicy seafood soup) is brimming with flavour and comes with a wonderful array of side dishes. It's behind the Palace Motel (팔레스 모텔) near the Gangguan harbour.

❶ Getting There & Around
The bus terminal is on the city's northern fringe. Local buses 10, 20, 30 and 40 run to Gangguan (₩1200, 25 minutes) from the terminal. A taxi to Gangguan costs ₩7000.

Express buses connect Tongyeong with Jinju (₩7600, 1½ hours, every 30 to 60 minutes), Busan (₩14,600, two hours, every 20 minutes), Gohyeon (₩3400, 25 minutes, every 15 minutes), Gimhae airport (₩10,400, 1½ hours, five daily departures) and Seoul (₩21,600, 4½ hours, every 30 to 50 minutes).

Jinju   진주
☎055 / POP 340,000
Famous for bibimbap (rice, egg, meat and vegies with chilli sauce) and its role in the Japanese invasions of the 16th century, Jinju is a laid-back city with a park-like fortress by the Nam-gang (Nam River). It's the largest city in the area and a convenient transport hub from which to explore the province's western region. With excellent bus connections, it's an easy day trip from Busan.

◉ Sights & Activities
Jinju's interesting sights are north of the Nam-gang. East of Jinju Fortress, Jinju-daero separates two worlds: a traditional

Jinju

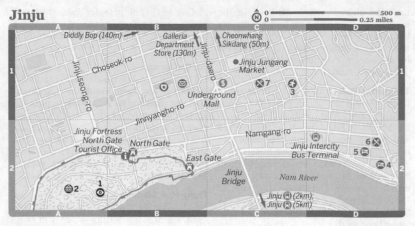

0 — 500 m
0 — 0.25 miles

Diddly Bop (140m)
Galleria Department Store (130m)
Cheonwhang Sikdang (50m)
Jinju Jungang Market
Choseok-ro
Jinju-daero
Jinjuseong-ro
Underground Mall
Jinnyangho-ro
Jinju Fortress North Gate Tourist Office
North Gate
Namgang-ro
Jinju Intercity Bus Terminal
East Gate
Jinju Bridge
Nam River
Jinju (2km);
Jinju (5km)

BUSAN & GYEONGSANGNAM-DO JINJU

market to the east and modern trappings such as cafes, bars, restaurants, cinemas and oodles of retail to the west.

Jinju Fortress   HISTORIC SITE
(진주성; Map p202; adult/child/youth ₩2000/600/1000; ◎9am-6pm Sun-Fri, to 7pm Sat) Local street signs call it a castle, but it's actually a well-preserved fortress that was partially destroyed during the Japanese invasion of 1592. One of the major battles of that campaign, in which 70,000 Koreans lost their lives, was fought here. Inside the fortress, traditional gates and shrines dot the grassy knolls of the heavily wooded park.

The small but interesting **Jinju National Museum** (국립진주박물관; Map p202; http://jinju.museum.go.kr; ◎9am-6pm Tue-Fri, to 7pm Sat, Sun & holidays) **FREE**, inside the fortress, has a worthwhile Imjin War exhibition.

Jageum Seong   BATHHOUSE
(자금성; Map p202; jjimjilbang ₩8000; ◎24hr) In Jinju's red-light district, take a bath and relax in the *jjimjilbang* before heading out for dinner and drinks. Then come back and sleep on the floor.

Exit the bus terminal, cross the street, walk left and then turn right at the first corner. Turn left at the small children's playground. It's in the tall building.

🎉 Festivals & Events

Around 50,000 glowing tigers, dragons and folk-tale characters light up the river during the **Nam-gang Lantern Festival** (www.yudeung.com) in early October.

🛌 Sleeping

There are half a dozen or more budget motels behind the intercity bus terminal.

★ Dong Bang Hotel   BUSINESS HOTEL **₩₩**
(동방호텔; Map p202; ☑055 743 0131; www.hoteldongbang.com; r from ₩145,000; **P❋🛜**) Jinju's only business-class hotel has perfectly cosy rooms with superb river views, although the decor feels somewhat 1980s. The cordial, English-speaking staff make this a very handy property to use as a base for touring the region. Prices jump in July and August. It's a 20-minute walk to Jinju Fortress and the city centre.

S+ Motel   MOTEL **₩₩**
(S+모텔; Map p202; ☑055 742 8580; regular/special/VIP r ₩40,000/50,000/70,000; **P❋@**) Wondering what the 'S' stands for? It might be 'snazzy' because the room

decor uses funky tiles and vibrant colours such as cherry red, tangerine orange and lime green. The rooms aren't especially spacious, though the VIP option comes with a king bed.

✖ Eating & Drinking

For something different, try one of the eel restaurants (₩15,000 to ₩20,000 per person) along the waterfront near the fortress. Pyeongan-dong, the area behind the Galleria department store, has a good number of bars and restaurants.

★ Zio Ricco
ITALIAN ₩₩

(Map p202; ☑ 055 741 7776; meals ₩10,000-20,000; ⊙ 10am-11pm; ✖) With low chairs and cool music, Zio Ricco is popular with locals and expats. Pasta and pizza are the specialities – they're decent enough and make for a nice break from Korean food, if you need one. On the 2nd floor, the restaurant owner sometimes (8pm to 10pm one Saturday night a month) plays sax with a surprisingly good band.

Cheonwhang Sikdang
KOREAN ₩₩

(천황식당; meals ₩9000-20,000; ⊙ 9.30am-9pm, closed 1st & 3rd Mon of month) Housed in a rustic post-war building, Cheonwhang is the place for bibimbap, a bowl of vegies, rice and a splotch of red-pepper paste served with *seonji guk* (선지국; beef-blood soup). Traditionalists might opt for the regional speciality, *yukhoe bibimbap* (육회비빔밥), which adds raw beef seasoned with soy sauce and sesame oil to the mix.

Walk up Jinju-daero towards Galleria and turn right at the first lane past Cho-seok-ro. Look for the old tile roof, wooden doors and grey-white exterior.

Poong Nyun
KOREAN ₩₩

(풍년; Map p202; ☑ 055 746 0606; pork per serving ₩8000, jeongol ₩10,000; ⊙ 11.40am-2.30pm & 5.30-10pm) A cosy meat restaurant

to enjoy barbecued *samgyeopsal* (삼겹살; fatty pork) and hard-to-find *beoseot jeongol* (소고기버섯전골), a beef-and-mushroom casserole.

Diddly Bop
BAR

(디들리밥; ⊙ 5pm-3am) It may not have all the trappings of a traditional Irish pub, such as patrons shouting 'How's the craic?', but it does have some good beer on tap, a respectable vinyl collection and decent chips. It's on a lane in Pyeongan-dong, behind the Galleria department store.

ℹ Getting There & Around

AIR
The closest airport is in Sacheon, 20km from Jinju. Two daily flights connect with Gimpo airport in Seoul via Korean Air, which also runs two flights a week to Jeju-do (as does Asiana). Local buses connect Jinju's north-end bus terminal to Sacheon airport (₩3000, 30 minutes).

BUS
There's an express bus terminal south of the river with services to Seoul (₩23,000, every 20 minutes), Daegu (₩13,100, hourly) and Gwangju (₩14,900, every 1½ hours). Most regional travellers use the terminal (시외버스터미널; Map p202) north of the river, which is close to the city centre.

TRAIN
The train station is south of the Nam-gang. There is KTX service connecting with Seoul (adult/child ₩56,600/28,300, 3½ hours, five daily), Dongdaegu (adult/child ₩16,300/8100, 1½ hours, twice daily) and Daejeon (adult/child ₩33,300/16,000, 2½ hours, twice daily).

Slower *mugunghwa* (adult/child ₩7400/3700, two hours, four daily) and *saemaeul* (adult/child ₩12,500/8000, 1½ hours, departs 7.26pm) services run to Gupo station in Busan.

BUSAN & GYEONGSANGNAM-DO JINJU

BUS DEPARTURES FROM JINJU (NORTH TERMINAL)

DESTINATION	PRICE (₩)	DURATION	FREQUENCY
Busan	7700	1½hr	every 10-20min
Hadong	5000	1hr	every 30min
Namhae	5700	1½hr	every 15-30min
Ssanggyae-sa	7300	2hr	departs 7.10pm
Tongyeong	4900	1½hr	every 50min

Namhaedo 남해도

☑ 055 / POP 49,000

Namhaedo, the country's third-largest island, is famous for garlic and a slower pace of life so clearly evident in the countryside, where some farmers continue to use oxen to plough fields. The drive around the island is arguably one of the most scenic routes in Korea. Rugged ocean views, dense forests and tiny fishing ports untouched by tourist development are best appreciated by travellers with their own transport and an unhurried sense of exploration.

◉ Sights & Activities

Bori-am   BUDDHIST TEMPLE

(보리암; depending on car size parking ₩4000-7000; ⊘8am-8pm) Between Namhae-si and Sangju beach, Bori-am is a busy Buddhist hermitage on Geum-san (금산; Geum Mountain, 681m) famous for brilliant sunrises and mesmerising vistas, the kind that move people to reconsider the meaning of life. The hermitage is a 30-minute drive from Namhae-si, or catch the Bori-am shuttle bus (hourly departures 8am to 8pm) near the front door of the Namhae-si bus terminal.

Getting to the mountaintop requires Buddha-like patience. The easiest way up is to take a shuttle bus from the entrance-level parking lot to the upper-level parking area (per person ₩1000, minimum 15 people before bus departs). From there it's a 30-minute walk to the hermitage. Some travellers with cars forgo the shuttle bus, preferring to drive to the upper parking area. Space up top is limited, so expect to wait an hour or more if you arrive in the afternoon.

Sangju   BEACH

(상주 해수욕장) For most of the year this pretty beach with 2km of soft white sand and shallow water is a quiet destination. During summer it's packed with fun-seeking frolickers, triggering 400% price spikes at the nearby motels. The beach is about a 30-minute drive south from Namhae-si.

Mijo   VILLAGE

(미조) This rustic fishing village is an ideal roadside diversion. Walk along the port, zigzag through narrow alleys and sample superb rural food. It's a short drive down the road from Sangju beach.

German Village   ARCHITECTURE

(독일 마을; ⊘24hr) FREE Here's a destination people visit because it's popular, not because it's interesting. Local marketing bumf calls it one of the island's best sites, but the German Village is yawningly underwhelming. There's nothing to do except walk on the street and remark how different the architecture looks compared to the Soviet-inspired apartment blocks spanning Seoul's Han River. If you do come, be prepared for crowds and traffic.

🛏 Sleeping & Eating

Byzantine Motel   LOVE HOTEL ₩₩

(비잔틴 모텔; ☑055 864 1515; standard/special r ₩40,000/50,000; ✳@) If you need to sleep in Namhae-si, the Byzantine Motel is down a side road outside the bus terminal. It's a standard love hotel, but rooms are slightly above average. The town centre is a 10-minute walk away.

Oasis Pension   PENSION ₩₩

(오아시스펜션; ☑055 862 6232; standard/ocean view r ₩50,000/70,000; ✳🖥) If you're spending the night in Sangju beach, try this pension where most rooms come with a double bed and a basic kitchen. Prices jump to ₩200,000 during summer, when the beach is packed. It's on the road running parallel to the beach.

★ Dajeong Sikdang   KOREAN ₩₩

(다정식당; ☑055 867 7334; meals from ₩8000; ⊘7am-7pm) In Mijo this modest restaurant serves outstanding twenjang jjigae (된장찌개; soybean stew). The soft tofu with vegetables and seafood is a welcome treat for travellers who need a break from spicy food. Facing the police station, walk left and turn right at the corner. Walk straight, turn left at the store and take the first right. It's down the road.

❶ Getting There & Around

There are frequent bus connections to Namhae-si from Seobu terminal in Busan and Jinju. Leaving the island, buses run to Hadong (₩4700, one hour, depart 6am, 7.10am, 10.05am and 4pm), Jinju (₩5700, 1½ hours, every 15 to 30 minutes) and Busan (₩11,900, 2¼ hours, every 30 to 45 minutes).

Local buses from Namhae-si to Sangju beach (₩2500, 40 minutes, every 20 to 40 minutes) and Mijo (₩3400, one hour, every 20 to 40 minutes) are available, but the return trip can involve long roadside waits.

Jirisan National Park

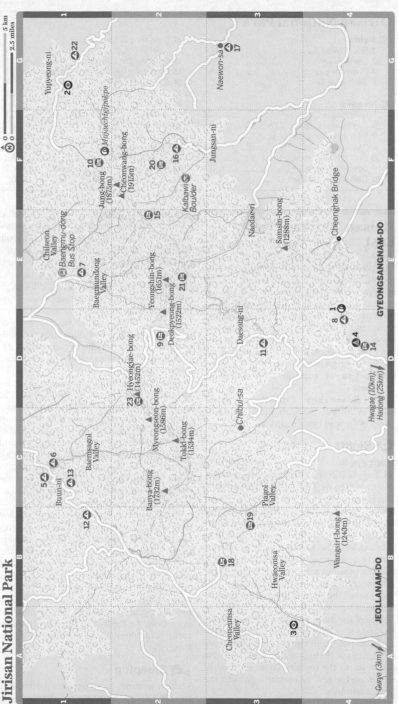

Jirisan National Park

Jirisan National Park – East   지리산 국립공원

♪ 055

This park offers some of Korea's best hiking opportunities, with 12 peaks over 1000m forming a 40km-long ridge. Many peaks are over 1500m, including **Cheonwang-bong** (1915m), the country's second-highest mountain. There are three principal entrances, each with a temple. Two of the three temples, Ssanggye-sa and **Daewon-sa**, are in Gyeongsangnam-do. From the west, **Hwaeom-sa** is accessible via Gurye in Jeollanam-do.

The **Jirisan Bear Project** was established in 2004 to build up a self-sustaining group of 50 wild bears in Jiri-san.

◉ Sights & Activities

Ssanggye-Sa   BUDDHIST TEMPLE
(쌍계사; ☎ 055 883 1901; www.ssanggyesa.net; adult/child/teen ₩2500/500/1000; ☸ 8am-6pm) The visual imagery of this temple is a feast for the eyes and, like any exquisite dinner, should be savoured with deliberation. Stone walls supporting multiple levels of buildings notched into the mountainside, combined with mature trees and a trickling creek, create a pleasant sensory experience. Three gates mark the path to the main hall – take time to read the signs to appreciate the symbolism of your visit.

One of the most attractive temples in the province, it's a long day trip from Busan. For a relaxed pace, consider an overnight stopover in Jinju or Hadong and an early morning departure to the temple. There are budget rooms and a few restaurants outside the temple entrance.

Jirisan Hiking Trails   HIKING
(지리산 하이킹 트레일; http://eng.jirisan-tour.com/; park entrance adult/child/youth ₩2500/500/1000) It's impossible to describe the myriad trails within this great park. The traditional course runs east to west (Daewon-sa to Hwaeom-sa), which experienced hikers say requires three days. Travellers from Busan and Gyeongsangnam-do often begin their journey via Ssanggye-sa, which is close to a bus stop, budget motels and restaurants. Infrequent direct buses depart Busan; otherwise travel to Hadong and catch a bus to the temple.

Some Lonely Planet readers have suggested a three-night route that puts hikers in position for a sunrise view on top of Cheonwang-bong. The route starts with a night at the Nogodan shelter. The next two nights are spent at the Baemsagol camping ground and Jangteomok shelter. On the final day, follow the trail to Jungsan-ri and then catch a bus to Jinju or Busan. Most shelters require reservations, which usually need to be made 15 days in advance.

Travellers with less ambitious plans, but who want to experience Jirisan's beauty, hike to **Buril Pokpo** (불일폭포). Starting from Ssanggye-sa, the mildly challenging trail (2.4km each way, three hours return) winds through a forest along a rippling creek. About two-thirds along the way, just when you've noticed the sound of the creek has disappeared, the trail bursts onto an open field. At the foot of the falls, there's a rocky pool where hikers meditate to regain their chi.

🛏 Sleeping

There are nine camping sites (from free to ₩2000): **Somakgol**; **Naewon-sa**;

Jungsan-ri; Baengmu-dong; Buril Pokpo; Daeseonggyo; Baemsagol 1; Baemsagol 2 and Deokdong. Facilities are basic. Travellers with a camper might try a car camping space at Naewon-sa, Dalgung and Deokdong (from ₩9000).

There are eight shelters (₩5000 to ₩8000). From west to east: Nogodan Piagol, Yeonhacheon, Byeoksoryeong, Seseok, Jangteomok, Rotari and Chibanmok. Jangteomok has enough space for 135 bodies, and sells torches, noodles and drinks. Seseok is the largest shelter, with space for 190 people. For overnight hikes, bring bedding, food, tea and coffee, as most shelters have limited supplies.

Multi-day treks require a hiking plan and bookings made 15 days in advance – available spots are often booked up within minutes after the reservation period opens during summer, autumn and weekends. Planning, perseverance and a flexible schedule are required if you want to stay at a shelter. Online reservations (page in Korean only) can be made at the website of Korea National Park Service (http://english.knps.or.kr).

Gilson Minbak INN ₩₩
(길손민박; ☑ 055 884 1336; ondol ₩40,000-70,000) Not far from the road leading to Ssanggye-sa, this place has clean rooms with private bathrooms. It's a brown-beige building on a small road off to the right as you walk up to the temple admission gate. No English is spoken here. If full, there are a dozen more *minbak* (private homes with rooms to rent) in the area.

ⓘ Getting There & Away

Buses to Ssanggye-sa often pass through Hadong, a small village and useful transfer point in the region. If you can't get a direct bus to Ssanggye-sa, travel to Hadong and catch one of the frequent buses to the temple (₩2800, 30 minutes, every 30 to 90 minutes). En route to Ssanggye-sa from Hadong, buses pass a large bridge and shortly thereafter make a quick stop in Hwagae; don't get off there. Further down the road (usually the next stop), the bus stops in front of a seafood restaurant beside a concrete bridge. Get out here, cross the bridge and follow the winding road to the park entrance. Buy your return bus ticket inside the seafood restaurant beside the bridge. The signboard lists times for several destinations, though most travellers are best served by heading to Hadong, where buses connect to Busan (₩11,000, 2½ hours, hourly) and Jinju (₩5000, 1½ hours, every 30 to 45 minutes).

Jeollanam-do

Why Go?

This beautiful southwest province is one of Korea's least developed and greenest. The heartland of Jeollanam-do (전라남도) has rolling hills, the towering Sobaek Mountains to the east and 6100km of coastline to the south and west, with more than 2000 islands offshore – less than 300 of which are inhabited. The province was largely isolated for centuries and it retains an off-the-beaten-track feel. It also has a rebel edge, and is proud of its ceramic and artistic traditions, its exiled poets and its prodemocracy martyrs.

With a comparatively balmy climate, Jeollanam-do is famous for its bountiful harvests, fresh seafood and green tea, celebrated in several festivals. For all its rural atmosphere, Jeollanam-do has urban elements too: Gwangju, the province's largest city, has a hip vibe and an active arts scene centred around a new, much-hyped cultural centre. It's also more accessible than ever, thanks to a faster KTX line that opened in 2015.

Best Places to Eat

➜ Dokcheon (p227)

➜ Wonjo Jangsu
Tongdak (p223)

➜ Jeonsama (p224)

➜ Yeongran Hoet-jip (p227)

Best Places to Stay

➜ Pedro's House (p212)

➜ Yuseongwan (p223)

➜ Sinsiwa (p212)

When to Go
Gwangju

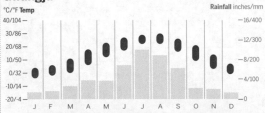

Jun–Aug Summer is the season for ferries to far-flung islands and lazing on sandy beaches.

Sep The Gwangju Biennale festival brings the glamour of the art world to town.

Oct The Gwangju Kimchi Festival *and* the Namdo Food Festival happen this month.

History

Far from Seoul during the Joseon era, Jeollanam-do was a place of exile, often used as a dumping ground for political and religious dissidents. The tradition of political dissent has continued; the province was a hotbed of opposition to the military governments that ruled South Korea in the 1960s and '70s. Students and trade unionists led countless prodemocracy protests and demonstrations, culminating in the 1980 uprising in Gwangju. As a result, development funds were withheld from the region for decades, something that is being rectified today with a flurry of new projects.

Gwangju 광주

☎062 / POP 1.48 MILLION

Gwangju (http://utour.gwangju.go.kr), Korea's sixth-largest city, may look like any other city but its history sets it apart: in 1980 a peaceful prodemocracy demonstration, known as the May 18 Democratic Uprising, was brutally put down by the then military government. Gwangju also has a long history of harbouring artists and this is reflected in civic support for the arts.

👁 Sights & Activities

The museum district is northwest of downtown. It's a 10-minute walk through a tunnel under the expressway from the Gwangju National Museum to the Gwangju Art Museum and the Gwangju Folk Museum, which are next to each other in a park along with the Biennale Exhibition Hall.

Gwangju National Museum MUSEUM
(국립광주박물관; ☎062 570 7000; http://gwangju.museum.go.kr; 110 Haseo-ro, Buk-gu; ⏲9am-6pm Tue-Sun; 🚌48) [FREE] The Gwangju National Museum's collection traces the

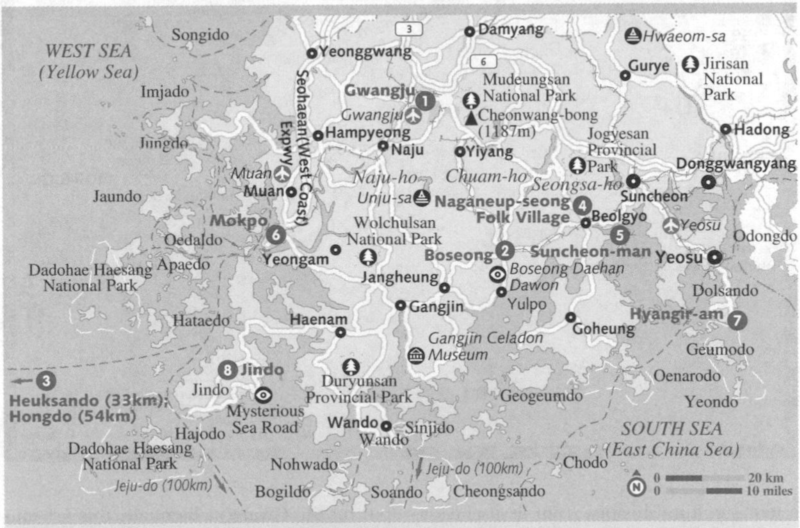

Jeollanam-do Highlights

1 Visiting **Gwangju** (p209) for its vibrant arts and nightlife scene, urban hiking opportunities, and solemn memorials.

2 Savouring the scenery and flavours of the **Daehan Dawon Tea Plantation** (p221) in Boseong.

3 Voyaging to the scattered, unspoilt islands of **Heuksando** (p230) and fabled **Hongdo** (p229).

4 Marvelling at the thatched-roofed houses of the immaculately preserved fortress town of **Naganeup-seong Folk Village** (p217).

5 Spotting migratory birds feasting in the rich wetlands at **Suncheon-man** (p217).

6 Eating still-wriggling octopus and seeing sunken ships in **Mokpo** (p225).

7 Watching the sunrise from the seaside hermitage **Hyangir-am** (p219).

8 Partaking in the mysterious 'parting of the sea' phenomenon known as the Ganjuyuk Gyedo in **Jindo** (p229).

Gwangju

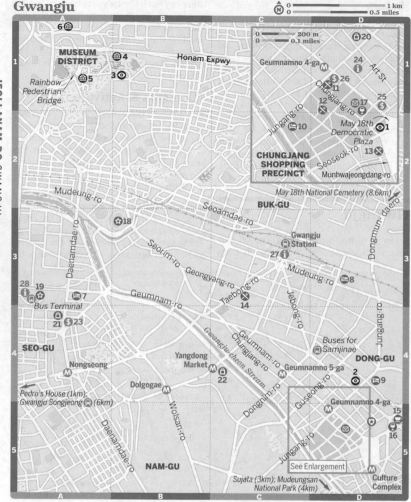

region's cultural history, from its prehistorical beginnings through the Joseon period (1392–1897), via artifacts, paintings and calligraphy. Look out for the Chinese ceramics salvaged from a 14th-century shipwreck.

Get the bus (20 minutes, every 30 minutes) from in front of the bus terminal or the train station.

Gwangju Museum of Art MUSEUM
(광주시립미술관; ☎062 613 7100; www. artmuse.gjcity.net; 52 Haseo-ro, Buk-gu; adult/child/youth ₩500/200/300; ⊘9am-6pm Tue-Sun; 🚌64) Managed by the same folks who

put on the Gwangju Biennale, this art museum shows up-and-coming Korean artists along with more established local names, such as Heo Baek-ryeon (pen name Uijae) and Oh Ji Ho.

Take the bus (every 20 minutes) from in front of the bus terminal to the Biennale Exhibition Hall stop. Bus 95 (every 15 minutes) also runs here from in front of the Asian Culture Complex.

Gwangju Folk Museum MUSEUM
(광주민속박물관; ☎062 613 5337; http://gjfm.gwangju.go.kr; 48-25 Seoha-ro, Buk-gu;

Gwangju

adult/child/youth ₩500/200/300; ⊘9am-6pm Tue-Sun; 📷64) Learn about traditional life in Jeollanam-do through the somewhat retro-looking dioramas and models here, which cover everything from kimchi and clothing to courtship rituals and shamanism.

See Gwangju Art Museum transport info.

Mudeungsan National Park NATIONAL PARK (무등산국립공원; ☎062 265 0761; 📷1187) **FREE** Overlooking Gwangju, Mudeungsan National Park is a gorgeous green mountain range with a spider's web of well-signed trails leading to the peak, **Cheonwang-bong** (1187m), and up to the towering rocky outcrops **Seoseok-dae** and **Ipseok-dae**. Just 30 minutes by bus from central Gwangju, it's naturally packed on weekends.

The most popular route starts at the temple **Wonhyo-sa**, which has an ornate pavilion overlooking the park and a bronze bell dating to 1710. The temple is just uphill from the bus stop. Double back and take the main path 4km up to Seoseok-dae and Ipseok-dae; it's steep going as you get towards the top. Then continue down through Jangbuljae pass to the temple **Jeungsim-sa** (another 6km), Gwangju's oldest temple. It has a Shilla-era iron Buddha backed by red-and-gold artwork, housed in an insignificant-looking shrine behind the main hall. The tiny shrine perched on a rock next to it is dedicated to the Shamanist Mountain God.

Around 250m past Jeungsim-sa, on the way to the bus stop, is **Uijae Museum of Korean Art** (의재미술관; ☎062 222 3040; www.ujam.org; 55 Jeungsimsa-gil, Dong-gu; adult/child ₩2000/1000; ⊘9.30am-5pm Tue-Sun; 📷9). This art gallery displays the gorgeous landscape, flower and bird paintings by the famed Heo Baek-ryeon (1891–1977), whose pen name was Uijae. The artist lived in a hermitage here in the shadow of the mountains.

The hike takes about five hours; if you're pressed for time, just visit Jeungsim-sa and the Uijae Museum.

The cleverly named bus 1187 (the height in metres of Cheonwang-bong) terminates near Wonhyo-sa; you can catch the bus (every 20 minutes) from the bus terminal or in front of the train station. Bus 9 (every 10 minutes) runs to the Jeungsim-sa area from Geumnam-no 4-ga and the bus terminal.

May 18th National Cemetery MEMORIAL (국립 5.18민주묘지; ☎062 266 5187; http://518. mpva.go.kr; 200 Minju-ro, Buk-gu; ⊘8am-6pm Mar-Oct, to 5pm Nov-Feb; 📷518) **FREE** Opened in 1997, this is the final burial place for victims of the May 18 Democratic Uprising of 1980, one of the most tragic incidents in modern Korean history. Officially, the casualties include 228 dead or missing and 4141 wounded, but the real numbers are believed to be much higher. A small but emotionally charged museum shows photographs, blood-stained flags, and a hard-hitting film that gives a dramatic account of the traumatic events that still scar the country's political landscape.

On the right, a memorial hall displays photographs of the ordinary folk – from students to grandmothers – who paid the ultimate price during the military government's crackdown. A five-minute walk through the memorial park leads to the reinstated original cemetery, where the victims were hurriedly buried without proper ceremony. The bodies were later reinterred in the new cemetery.

Get the bus (one hour, every 30 minutes) in front of the the bus terminal, train station or along Geumnam-ro.

Asian Culture Complex
ARTS CENTRE
(국립아시아문화전당; www.cct.go.kr; M Culture Complex) This ambitious arts complex, still under construction at the time of research, houses galleries, performance spaces, a library and plazas – all designed to boost Gwangju's capital in the art world. It's located on the main site of the May 18 Uprising; the old Provincial Hall building, the target of the protests, has been retained.

★☆ Festivals & Events

Gwangju Kimchi Festival
FOOD
(http://kimchi.gwangju.go.kr) Every October, Gwangju hosts a five-day kimchi (pickled vegetables) extravaganza with a fairground, market stalls, pottery making, folk music and a *hanbok* (traditional clothing) fashion show. Shuttle buses run to the often-changing venue.

Gwangju Biennale
ART
(www.gb.or.kr) This three-month contemporary art festival takes place every two years (due to be held in autumn 2016). Based at the **Biennale Exhibition Hall** (111 Biennale-ro, Buk-gu; 🖵 64), it features more than 500 artists and foreign curators from 60 countries. On odd-numbered years, the city holds the Design Biennale.

🛏 Sleeping

The downtown Chungjang nightlife district has a handful of love motels and there are more basic options around the bus terminal. New luxury hotels such as the Holiday Inn and Ramada are in the Sangmu district near City Hall.

★ Pedro's House
GUESTHOUSE ₩
(📵 mobile 010 9592 9993; www.pedroshouse.com; 18-3 Sangmu-daero 935beon-gil, Seo-gu; dm/d from ₩25,000/50,000; 🌬✳@🛜; M Ssangchon-dong) Gwangju local and veteran traveller Pedro Kim runs this homey guesthouse filled with books and travel souvenirs. The rooms (some with private baths) are spotless, and Kim, who speaks fluent English, knows pretty much everyone and everything in the city. Pedro's is west of the city center, on the metro.

Windmill Motel
LOVE MOTEL ₩
(윈드밀 모텔; 📵 062 223 5333; 150-8 Jun-gang-ro, Dong-gu; r ₩35,000-60,000; 🅿✳@🛜) The Windmill, on the west end of the Chungjang nightlife district, is a local landmark (there's a windmill on top). The staff are friendly and the rooms are clean, if not kitschy, and include flat-screen TVs, fridges and water coolers.

Ballade Motel
MOTEL ₩
(발라드 모텔; 📵 062 366 3307; 11 Jukbong-daero 78beon-gil, Seo-gu; r ₩35,000-45,000; 🅿✳@🛜) The pick of the bunch near the bus terminal, Ballade has rooms kitted out with a sofa, large TV and PCs. Prices jump by ₩10,000 on the weekend. It's 500m east of the Shinsegae Department Store.

Sinsiwa
HANOK GUESTHOUSE ₩₩
(신시와; 📵 062 233 2755; http://cafe.naver.com/sinsiwaguesthouse; 81-3 Chungjang-ro, Dong-gu; d/q from ₩50,000/100,000; 🌬🛜) Park Sung-hyun, one-time curator of the Gwangju Biennale, restored this 60-year-old *hanok* (traditional wooden home) himself, opening it as a guesthouse in 2015. The three rooms (two with private baths) are simple yet beautiful, decorated with an ever-changing display of works by local artists.

Geumsoojang Tourist Hotel
HOTEL ₩₩
(금수장 관광 호텔; 📵 062 525 2111; www.geumsoojang.co.kr; 2 Mudeung-ro, 321 beon-gil, Dong-gu; r ₩110,000-240,000; 🅿✳🛜) Classy in a retro sort of way, this hotel near the train station has English-speaking staff and comfortable rooms. Book online for a 50% discount. The in-house restaurant serves up a delicious rendition of the Korean *hanjeonsik* (banquet; ₩50,000).

🍴 Eating

Both the bus terminal and Shinsegae department store have food courts.

Cheongwon Momil   NOODLES **₩**
(청원모밀; ☑062 222 2210; 174-1 Jungang-ro, Dong-gu; noodles from ₩5000; ◷10.30am-8.30pm; 🅜Geumnamno 4-ga) This humble noodle shop, which specialises in *momil* (모밀; buckwheat noodles) is a Gwangju institution, in business since 1960 (as the sign out front proudly boasts). Dishes to try include *bibim-momil* (비빔모밀; buckwheat noodles in spicy sauce) and *momil-jjajang* (모밀짜장; buckwheat noodles in black soybean sauce).

Sujata   VEGETARIAN **₩₩**
(수자타; ☑062 222 1145; 3 Dongsan-gil 7beon-gil, Dong-gu; meals ₩8000; ◷11.30am-8.30pm; 🖉; 🖵15, 🅜Hakdong/Jeungsimsa) Run by Buddhist monks, Sujata puts on what is possibly the world's best salad bar. It includes soups, stews, noodles, a dozen different greens, countless pickled things, a make-your-own bibimbap (rice, egg and vegies with chilli sauce) section and even cake. It's all vegetarian, but even non-vegies will get their fill here: it's all you can eat.

Look for the red building halfway between the Uijae Museum of Korean Art and the Hakdong/Jeungsimsa subway station.

Minsokchon   KOREAN **₩₩**
(민속촌; ☑062 224 4577; 16-10 Jungang-ro 160beon-gil, Dong-gu; meals ₩8000-18,000; ◷11.30am-midnight; 🅜Culture Complex) Deservedly popular, Minsokchon serves up lean cuts of *so galbi* (소갈비; beef) and *dwaeji galbi* (돼지갈비; pork), set to sizzle over charcoal braziers set into the tables. It has a stylish, rustic interior; look for the traditional facade.

First Alleyway   INTERNATIONAL **₩₩**
(☑mobile 070 4127 8066; 5-4 Chungjang-ro an-gil, Dong-gu; meals ₩10,000-13,000; ◷noon-9.30pm Tue-Thu, to 11pm Fri, to midnight Sat, 11am-8pm Sun; 🅜Geumnamno 4-ga) Longtime expat Tim Whitman leads the kitchen here, turning out burgers, pizzas and – as befitting a Canadian – poutine. There's Sunday brunch, too. First Alleyway naturally draws an international crowd. It's a few doors down from H&M.

Yeongmi   KOREAN **₩₩₩**
(영미; ☑062 527 0249; 126 Gyeongyang-ro, Buk-gu; meals ₩28,000-48,000; ◷10.30am-2am, closed first Mon) There's a whole string of restaurants specialising in *oritang* (오리탕; duck stew) along the aptly named Duck St, but this 80-year-old joint, which seasons its stew with ginseng and jujube, is the most

famous. It's pricey, but dishes are meant for sharing.

🍷 Drinking

Chungjang-ro, the city's buzzing, semi-pedestrian shopping district, is also Gwangju's prime nightlife spot with hundreds of bars, nightclubs, restaurants and cafes.

Dadam   TEAHOUSE
(다담; 062 236 3606; 200-9 Dongmyeong-ro, Dong-gu; drinks from ₩5000; ◷11am-11pm; 🅜Culture Complex) Among all the cafes in town Dadam stands out for serving tea – all kinds of traditional Korean teas, from the medicinal *ssanghwatang* to the fruity *sujeonggwa*. There are traditional desserts too, such as rice cakes and sweet bean soup.

There's another outpost attached to the Gwangju Art Museum.

Kunst Lounge   LOUNGE
(☑062 223 0009; www.kunst-lounge.com; 4 Dongmyeong-ro, Dong-gu; drinks from ₩8000; ◷10am-midnight Mon-Sat; 🅢Culture Complex) Gwangju's most sophisticated spot does wine by the glass, German beers and a fantastic cheese platter. Located across from the new Asian Culture Complex, Kunst has a suitably artsy vibe.

Speakeasy   BAR
(☑mobile 010 4713 3825; 160 Jungang-ro, 31-31beon-gil, Dong-gu; drinks ₩6000-8000; ◷8pm-3am Thu-Sun; 🅜Geumnamno 4-ga) This

LOCAL KNOWLEDGE

DAEIN-SIJANG

By the early 2000s, **Daein-sijang** (대인시장; 10 Jebong-ro 184beon-gil, Dong-gu; ⊙6am-8pm; Ⓜ Geumnamno 4-ga), a traditional market in the city centre, was nearly shuttered. 'A new shopping mall had opened nearby. People didn't want to shop at traditional markets anymore. Now over 50 artists have their studios here,' explains Cho Seung-ki, director of the NPO Mite-Ugro (www.mite-ugro.org), which runs an artist residency program inside the market.

Daein Market's revival was part of the 2008 Gwangju Biennale, which saw artists add murals to the market walls; cheap rents encouraged them to stay. Of course there are still traditional stalls too, side-by-side with newer cafes and galleries. There's a night market here on the fourth Friday and Saturday of the month, June through October.

2nd-floor bar hidden down an alley is a favourite with foreigners and has a good selection of imported beers. Bands sometimes play on Fridays or Saturdays. From the front of Burger King go left for 40m and down the alleyway.

☆ Entertainment

The **U-Square Culture Centre** (유·스퀘어 문화관; www.usquareculture.co.kr; 904 Mujin-daero, Seo-gu), adjoining the bus terminal, houses cinemas and performance halls.

Gwangju Kia Champions Field BASEBALL
(광주기아챔피언스필드; ☑062 525 5350; www.tigers.co.kr; 10 Seorim-ro, Buk-gu; tickets from ₩7000; 🖵38) Catch the Kia Tigers professional baseball team in action from April through November at their new stadium. Stock up on snacks from the street vendors outside the stadium, where prices are cheaper. You're permitted to bring in food, beer, coolers and cameras. Games usually start at 5pm or 6.30pm.

Get the bus from in front of the bus terminal; or you can walk from there in 20 minutes (or in 30 minutes from Nongseong metro station).

🛍 Shopping

Chungjang is bursting with youth-oriented clothing, shoes and accessory stores.

Art Street STREET
(예술의 거리; Yesurui Geori; Ⓜ Geumnamno 4-ga) This cobblestone road is lined with art galleries, studios and stores selling *hanbok*, *hanji* (handmade paper), art books, calligraphy brushes and tea sets.

Yangdong-sijang MARKET
(양동시장; 238 Cheonbyeonjwa-ro, Seo-gu; ⊙9am-9pm; Ⓜ Yangdong Market) Voted Korea's best traditional market, sprawling Yangdong sells just about everything, from traditional medicines to clothing.

E-Mart HYPERMARKET
(20-11 Gwangju-daero 71beon-gil, Seo-gu; ⊙10am-midnight) Stock up on cheap food, drinks and supplies.

ℹ Information

Tourist Information Centres Bus terminal (☑062 365 8733; bus terminal; ⊙9am-6pm); Gwangju airport (☑062 942 6160; Gwangju airport; ⊙9am-6pm); train station (☑062 233 9370; train station; ⊙9am-6pm).
Gwangju International Centre (☑062 226 2733; www.eng.gic.or.kr; Samho Center 1-2F, 196 Jungang-ro, 5beon-gil, Dong-gu; ⊙9am-6pm Mon-Sat; Ⓜ Geunamno 4-ga) This expat organisation offers guidebooks, tourist information, Korean-language classes, tours and social events.

ℹ Getting There & Away

AIR

Eight Gwangju–Seoul and 10 Gwangju–Jeju flights run daily; for the latter, look for budget flights on the new T'Way Airlines (www.twayair.com).

BUS

Express and intercity buses to more than 100 destinations depart from the U-Square complex, 1km north of the Nongseong subway station.

TRAIN

KTX trains (₩46,800, two hours, eight daily) run between Yongsan station and the new Gwangju-Songjeong station on the west side of the city. *saemaeul* (₩34,300, four hours, four daily) and *mugunghwa* (₩23,000, 4½ hours, four daily) trains run to the older, more central Gwangju station. Trains also continue to Mokpo and Yeosu from both stations.

ℹ️ Getting Around

TO/FROM THE AIRPORT
Bus 1000 (30 minutes, every 15 minutes) runs from the airport to the bus terminal and Geumnam-ro. You can also take the metro. A taxi costs around ₩12,000.

BUS
Gwangju has more than 80 city bus routes, and most run past the bus terminal with bus stops on all sides. Bus 30 (20 minutes, every 15 minutes) runs between the bus terminal and Gwangju train station. City buses cost ₩1200.

METRO
Currently there is one line that stretches west to the airport and Gwangju-Songjeong station. A single ride is ₩1200; trains run from 5.30am until midnight.

TAXI
Flagfall is ₩2800. The YMCA is an easy drop-off spot for points downtown.

Damyang

Damyang (http://eng.damyang.go.kr/index.damyang) is famous for its bamboo and has a long tradition of bamboo craftwork. Sadly few artisans remain today, though the spirit of former times returns in May for the annual **bamboo festival** (www.bamboofestival.co.kr).

◉ Sights

Juknokwon GARDENS
(죽녹원; ☏061 380 2680; 119 Juknok-ro; adult/child/youth ₩2000/1000/1500; ⏰9am-6pm; 🚌311) Sandy walking trails wend through this bamboo grove, past pavilions and film locations for Korean dramas. It's one of the area's most popular attractions and can get crowded on weekends. But if you get a quiet moment – enough to hear the wind rustle the leaves – it can be enchanting.

Korea Bamboo Museum MUSEUM
(한국대나무박물관; ☏061 380 2909; www.damyang.go.kr/museum; 35 Jukhyangmunhwa-ro; adult/child/youth ₩2000/1000/1500;

BUS DEPARTURES FROM GWANGJU
Express Bus Destinations

DESTINATION	PRICE (₩)	DURATION (HR)	FREQUENCY
Busan	16,800	3½	hourly
Daegu	13,500	3½	every 40min
Daejeon	11,100	2½	every 30min
Incheon Airport	32,300	4½	every 30min
Jeonju	6600	1¼	every 30min
Seoul	17,600	4	every 10min

Intercity Bus Destinations

DESTINATION	PRICE (₩)	DURATION	FREQUENCY
Beolgyo	8900	1½hr	every 30min
Boseong	8400	1½hr	every 30min
Gangjin	9800	1½hr	hourly
Haenam	11,100	1½hr	every 40min
Jindo	12,200	3hr	hourly
Mokpo	5700	50min	every 20min
Songgwang-sa	7500	1½hr	5 daily
Suncheon	6900	1½hr	every 30min
Wando	16,500	2½hr	hourly
Yeongam	6900	1½hr	hourly
Yeosu	10,300	2hr	every 30min

SAMJINAE VILLAGE

South Korea may have developed at a breakneck speed, but it was also the first Asian country to sign on to the international *cittaslow*, or 'slow city' movement. One such city, or village rather, is **Samjinae** (삼지내마을; also called Changpyeong Slow City; http:// eng.slowcp.com), population 4105. There's little to do here but wander the dusty lanes, lined with centuries-old stone walls, past homesteads and heritage houses – but that's the point. There are a handful of *minbak* (rooms for rent in private houses; from ₩50,000) here. The tourist information centre in Gwangju can arrange your stay.

Samjinae is in the direction of Damyang. Take bus 303 (hourly; 40 minutes, ₩1750) from Daein Gwangjang and get off at Changpyeong Police Station, where you'll see a sign noting the entrance to the village. Alternatively you can take a taxi from Damyang bus terminal (approximately ₩20,000).

⏰9am-6pm; 📖311) Lightweight and durable, bamboo can be made into pretty much anything – as you'll see at this museum, which is basically a showroom for bamboo products, both traditional and modern.

✗ Eating

Bakmulgwan Ap-jip   KOREAN ₩₩
(박물관앞집; ☎061 381 199; 22 Jukhyangmunhwa-ro; meals ₩12,000-25,000; ⏰10am-9.30pm; 📖311) Damyang's signature dish is *daetongbap* (대통밥), rice and nuts cooked inside a bamboo stem. Try it here, across the street from the Korea Bamboo Museum. The spread of side dishes is huge.

ℹ Getting There & Away

The bus (₩2800, 40 minutes, every 15 minutes) departs from Gwangju bus terminal. Stay on until the end (past Damyang bus terminal) for Juknokwon; the Korea Bamboo Museum is one stop before Damyang bus terminal. It's about a 30-minute walk between the two sights.

Unju-sa

The temple compound Unju-sa occupies a river valley and its hillsides in Hwasun-gun, 40km south of Gwangju.

◉ Sights

Unju-sa   TEMPLE
(운주사; ☎061 374 0660; www.unjusa.org; 91-44 Cheontae-ro, Doam-myeon; adult/child/youth ₩3000/1000/2000; ⏰8am-7pm Mar-Oct, to 6pm Nov-Feb; 🚌218, 318-1) Legend has it that Unju-sa originally housed 1000 Buddhas and 1000 pagodas, built because, according to traditional geomancy, the southwest of the country lacked hills and needed the pagodas to 'balance' the peninsula. The remaining 23 pagodas and some 100 Buddhas still make up the greatest numbers of any Korean temple. Some are set on the hillsides, which you can scale.

According to another legend they were all built in one night by stonemasons sent down from heaven, but another theory is that Unju-sa was the site of a school for stonemasons. Whatever their origins, many works are unique and some are national treasures. Back-to-back twin Buddhas face their own pagodas, while another pair of Buddhas lying on their backs are said to have been the last works sculpted one evening; the masons returned back to heaven before the Buddhas could be stood upright.

ℹ Getting There & Away

Buses run from Gwangju bus terminal (₩3650, 1½ hours, every 30 minutes). Check with the driver as only some of the buses go all the way to Unju-sa. The last bus back to Gwangju leaves around 8pm.

Gurye   구례

Gurye is the gateway to the southwest entrance of Jirisan National Park. While the bulk of this park lies in the neighbouring province of Gyeongsangnam-do it is best approached from this direction if you plan to visit Hwaeom-sa, one of Korea's top temples.

◉ Sights

Hwaeom-sa   TEMPLE
(화엄사; ☎061 782 7600; www.hwaeomsa.org; 539 Hwaeomsa-ro, Masan-myeon; adult/child/youth ₩3500/1300/1800; ⏰7am-7.30pm) Founded by priest Yeongi in AD 544 after his return from India, this ancient temple dedicated to the Birojana Buddha is enveloped by the beautiful natural surroundings of Jirisan National Park. Last rebuilt in 1636, it has endured five major devastations in its history, including the Japanese invasion of 1592.

On the main plaza is Gakgwang-jeon, a huge two-storey hall. Inside are paintings that are national treasures, nearly 12m long and 7.75m wide, featuring Buddhas, disciples and assorted holies. Korea's oldest and largest stone lantern fronts Gakgwang-jeon, which was once surrounded by stone tablets of the Tripitaka Sutra (made during the Shilla era). These were ruined during the Japanese invasion.

Up many further flights of stairs is Hwaeom-sa's most famous structure, **Sasaja Samcheung** (사사자 삼층석탑), a unique three-storey pagoda supported by four stone lions. The female figure beneath the pagoda is said to be Yongi's mother; her dutiful son offers her tea from another lantern facing her. At the time of research, it was closed for restoration.

The temple is about 25 minutes' walk from the bus stop. Templestays (₩40,000) are possible at Hwaeom-sa. A large tourist village is at the park entrance with a number of restaurants and affordable accommodation, but prices rise on weekends.

It is possible to continue from the temple, along a trail through Hwaeom-sa Valley. After about 2½ to three hours the trail begins to ascend to a shelter, Nogodan Sanjang (a strenuous four-hour hike, p206). From the shelter, the trail continues to rise until you are finally on the long spine of the Jirisan ridge.

ℹ️ Getting There & Away

Buses (₩1300, 15 minutes, every 30 minutes) run between Hwaeom-sa and Gurye. From Gurye buses run to Suncheon (₩4200, 50 minutes, every 40 minutes) or Gwangju (₩7800, 1¼ hours, every 30 minutes). Reserved-seat express buses (₩8500, 1½ hours, five daily) also run to Hwaeom-sa from Gwangju.

Suncheon & Around   순천

The southern city of Suncheon (http://tour. suncheon.go.kr) is a convenient base for exploring several of the region's highlights, including the wetlands at Suncheon-man, the Nagan Folk Village and the temples inside Jogye-san Provincial Park.

⊙ Sights

Suncheon-man   NATURE RESERVE
(순천만; ☎061 749 3006; www.suncheonbay. go.kr; adult/child/youth ₩7000/3000/5000; ⊙8am-6pm; 🚌67) At this coastal estuary,

Suncheon   0 —— 200 m / 0 —— 0.1 miles

JEOLLANAM-DO SUNCHEON & AROUND

inscribed on the Ramsar list of protected wetlands, you can follow walkways through rustling reeds up to an observation hut on a neighbouring hill – a popular sunset viewing spot. Birdwatchers should be on the lookout for hooded cranes, black-faced spoonbills and swans, all of which stop by during their migrations.

If you'd like to get closer to the wildlife, take a birdwatching boat (adult/child ₩7000/2000, 35 minutes, six daily Sunday to Tuesday). There's also a museum with exhibitions on the local ecology. Buses (₩1200, 20 minutes) leave every 25 minutes from Suncheon bus terminal.

Naganeup-seong
Folk Village   HISTORIC SITE
(낙안읍성민속마을; ☎061 749 3893; 30 Chungmn-gil, Nagan-myeon; adult/child/youth ₩4000/1500/2500; ⊙9am-5pm Dec-Jan, 9am-6pm Feb-Apr & Nov, 8.30am-6.30pm May-Oct; 🚌63) Among Korea's many folk villages, Nagan is unique for its setting, surrounded by 1410m of Joseon-period fortress walls, built to protect the inhabitants from marauding Japanese pirates. It's Korea's best-preserved fortress town, crammed with narrow, dry-stone alleyways leading to vegetable allotments, and adobe and stone homes thatched with reeds. What's perhaps most interesting, however, is that people still live here.

Some homes double as *minbak* (private homes with rooms for rent, from ₩40,000), restaurants and souvenir shops. Buses (₩1200, 40 minutes) leave every 90 minutes from Suncheon bus terminal.

Jogyesan Provincial Park
PARK

(조계산도립공원; ☑061 749 8801) This park is home to two noteworthy temples, **Songgwang-sa** (송광사; ☑061 755 0107; www. songgwangsa.org; 12 Sinpyeong-ri, Songgwang-myeon; adult/child ₩3000/2000; ☺6am-7pm Mar-Oct, 7am-6pm Nov-Feb; 📷111) to the west and **Seonam-sa** (선암사; ☑061 754 9117; www. seonamsa.net; 802 Jukak-ri, Seungju-eup; adult/child/youth ₩2000/1000/1500; ☺6am-7.30pm Jun-Sep, 7am-7pm Oct-May; 📷1) to the east. A spectacular 8km hike (about four hours) connects the two temples. You can also take a detour over the peak of Janggun-bong (884m).

Songgwang-sa is considered one of the three jewels of Korean Buddhism (along with Tongdo-sa and Haein-sa, in Gyeongsangnam-do). Featured in the Little Monk movie, it is a regional head temple of the Jogye sect, by far the largest in Korean Buddhism. It is also one of the oldest Zen temples in Korea, founded in the 10th century, although most of the buildings date from the 17th century. Songgwang-sa is known for having produced many prominent Zen masters over the years, and today the temple is home to a community of monks. A templestay (₩50,000) is available here.

Seonam-sa is a quieter hermitage dating back to AD 875, where the monks study and try to preserve the old ways. Below Seonam-sa is **Seungseongyo**, one of Korea's most exquisite ancient granite bridges, with a dragon's head hanging from the top of the arch.

Buses leave approximately every 45 minutes to Seonam-sa (₩1200, one hour) and Songgwang-sa (₩1200, 1½ hours) from Suncheon bus terminal; there are also direct buses to Sonngwang-sa from Gwangju (₩1700, 1½ hours, five daily).

🛏 Sleeping & Eating

Suncheon Guesthouse Namdo
HOSTEL ₩

(순천게스트하우스 남도; ☑010 4356 3255; http://namdogeha.com; 30-17 Jangcheon 2-gil; dm ₩20,000; ❄❂@🛜) In a rambling old house a few minutes' walk north of the bus ter-

minal (turn right at Samoa Motel), Namdo makes for an excellent base. Amenities include cooking and laundry facilities. A colourful mural marks the entrance.

Yeongbunsik
KOREAN ₩

(영분식; ☑061 742 0933; 16 Isu-ro; meals ₩5000-6500; ☺11am-9pm) A favourite with local taxi drivers, Yeongbunsik does big portions of hearty staples such as *doenjang-jjigae* (된 장찌개; tofu soup), *dolsot bibimbap* (돌솥 비빔밥; bibimbap in a stone hotpot), and *donkkaseu* (돈까스; breaded pork cutlet). The restaurant is one block behind the bus terminal, on the left, with a red sign.

❶ Information

There is a tourist information centre inside the **bus terminal** (☑061 749 3839; ☺9am-6pm) and in front of the **train station** (☑061 749 3107; ☺9am-6pm). The city runs reasonably priced **tours**, with different schedules daily taking in some of the major sights, meaning you won't have to keep doubling back to the bus terminal. Inquire at the TIC.

❶ Getting There & Around

KTX trains run from Yongsan in Seoul to Suncheon (₩43,000, two hours, nine daily); there are also *saemaeul* (₩37,800, 4¼ hours, two daily) and *mugunghwa* (₩25,400, 4½ hours, 10 daily). Trains continue to Yeosu (KTX/saemaeul/mugunghwa ₩8400/4800/2600, 20 minutes). One *mugunghwa* train at 9.59am travels to Mokpo (₩12,000, 3¼ hours).

The intercity bus terminal is in the centre of town. Local buses depart from Palma-ro, in front of the bus terminal.

Yeosu
여수

☑061 / POP 291,000

The molar-shaped, port city of Yeosu (www. yeosu.go.kr) is halfway along Korea's steep, island-pocked and deeply indented southern coast. Its bustling city centre is nothing special, but its shoreline, peppered with cliffs, islands and peninsulas, is spectacular. The local hero is Admiral Yi Sun-shin (1545–98),

BUS DEPARTURES FROM SUNCHEON

DESTINATION	PRICE (₩)	DURATION	FREQUENCY
Gwangju	6900	1½hr	every 30min
Haenam	13,200	2¼hr	hourly
Mokpo	9000	1½hr	hourly
Yeosu	4400	30min	every 10min

Jogyesan Provincial Park

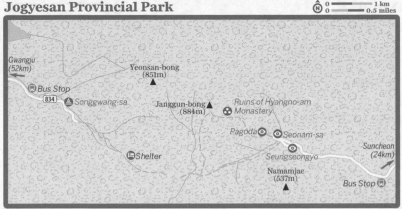

who repelled Japanese invaders with his 'turtle ships'. You'll see statues of him, and replicas of the ships, around town; he's also on the ₩100 coin. In 2012 Yeosu hosted the World's Fair International Exposition (called Expo 2012), which resulted in a redevelopment of the waterfront.

◉ Sights

Hyangir-am   TEMPLE
(향일암; ☎ 061 644 3650; 60 Hyangiram-ro, Dolsan-eup; adult/child/youth ₩2000/1000/1500; ⊗ dawn-dusk; ☐ 111, 113) A Buddhist hermitage with a 1350-year heritage, Hyangir-am has an enviable location perched halfway up a mountain at the tip of Dolsando, an island connected to Yeosu by a bridge. It's stunning anytime of day, but is most enchanting at sunrise, when you can watch daybreak over the ocean while listening to the monks chant. Buses (one hour; ₩1200) to Hyangir-am start around 4.30am to arrive in time for first light; pick up a schedule at the TIC.

It's a steep 10-minute walk from the bus stop through the tourist village up to the temple. Every restaurant along the way sells *gatkimchi* (갓김치; pickled mustard leaves), a local speciality.

Odongdo   ISLAND
(오동도; ☎ 061 690 7301; ☐ 2, 52, 61, 555) This small, craggy island, a favourite destination for locals, is covered in bamboo groves and camellia trees. Walking paths wend round the island in about half an hour. Take the lift up to the **lighthouse observatory** (9.30am to 5.30pm) for the best harbour views. The island is joined to the mainland by a 750m causeway that can be traversed by a **road train** (adult/child ₩800/500; every 20 minutes; ⊗ 9am to 5.30pm).

Buses stop at the causeway entrance; otherwise it's a pleasant 30-minute walk along the coast from Jungang-dong Rotary.

Jinnamgwan   HISTORIC BUILDING
(진남관; 11 Dongmun-ro; ⊗ 9am-6pm) **FREE** In the centre of town stands this national treasure, Korea's largest single-storey wooden structure (75m long and 14m high). The beautiful pavilion, first built in 1599 with 68 pillars supporting its massive roof, was originally used for receiving officials and for holding ceremonies. Jinnamgwan is set to undergo restorations sometime between 2015 and 2018, so may be closed when you visit.

On the right, a small but modern museum focuses on Admiral Yi Sun-sin (1545–98) and has maps explaining his naval tactics and victories over Japan in the 1590s.

Expo 2012 Yeosu Korea
Memorial Hall   MUSEUM
(1 Bangnamhoe-gil; adult/child ₩3000/2000; ⊗ 9am-7pm Tue-Sun; ☐ 2, 6, 7, 333) Originally the Korea Pavilion for Yeosu's 2012 World's Fair International Exposition, this museum showcases the latest in Korean maritime technology, such as tidal-wave power generators.

⌂ Sleeping

There's a cluster of budget and midrange hotels around the harbour. Newer midrange

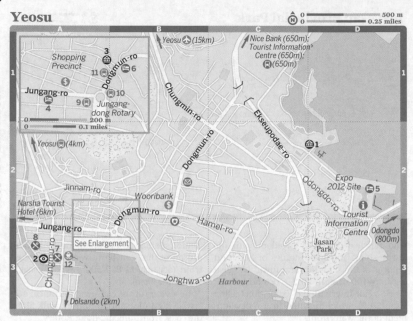

Yeosu

◉ Sights
1 Expo 2012 Yeosu Korea Memorial
Hall.. D2
2 Fish Market.. A3
3 Jinnamgwan A1

⊜ Sleeping
4 Motel Sky A1
5 MVL Hotel D2
6 Yeosu Guesthouse Flying Pig................B1

⊗ Eating
7 Gubaek Sikdang A3
8 Gyodong-sijang................................... A3

ℹ Transport
9 Airport Shuttle Stop............................. A1
10 Buses to Bus Terminal & Train
Station... B1
11 Buses to Hyangiram A1
12 Ferry Terminal A3

hotels can be found along the waterfront in Hak-dong.

Yeosu Guesthouse Flying Pig HOSTEL ₩
(여수게스트하우스; ☎061 666 1122; http://
yeosuhouse.com/xe; 16 Dongmun-ro; dm
₩20,000; ⊜❋@❂) The location here is
fantastic, right in the centre of town. There
are a few quirks, such as the steep stairs
and cramped shared bathrooms. On the
other hand, there's free breakfast and the
English-speaking owner is friendly and
helpful.

Narsha Tourist Hotel HOTEL ₩₩
(나르샤 관광호텔; ☎061 686 2000; www.
narshahotel.com; 200-24 Hak-dong; r ₩90,000-
120,000; ℙ❋@❂) Though not the cheapest

spot on the Hak-dong waterfront strip, this
solid midrange option is the most inviting,
with helpful English-speaking staff and
comfortable, well-appointed rooms, some
with sea views.

Motel Sky MOTEL ₩₩
(모텔스카이; ☎061 662 7780; 5-5 Gyodongnam
1-gil; r ₩50,000-60,000; ❋@❂) A friendly welcome awaits you at this dated but
well-maintained motel. The 6th floor has
the best views and more expensive rooms
have computers.

MVL Hotel HOTEL ₩₩₩
(☎061 660 5800; www.mvlhotel.com; 111
Odongdo-ro; r from ₩225,000; ℙ⊜❋@❂) The
glossy 'Most Valuable Life' hotel (really!) has

ultramodern rooms with plush beds and bay views.

✖ Eating & Drinking

The harbour front is loaded with restaurants serving fresh fish and seafood, although none are cheap. A row of new restaurants and bars surround Soho Yacht Marina in Hak-dong.

Gubaek Sikdang   KOREAN ₩₩
(구백식당; ☑061 662 0900; 18 Yeogaekseonte-omineol-gil; meals ₩12,000-25,000; ⊙7am-8pm) *Seodae-hoe* (서대회; thin slices of raw fish marinated in *makgeolli* (rice wine) vinegar and chilli paste) is a local speciality and this restaurant is famous for it. To eat it, mix the fish with the rice and stir. *Saengseongui* (생선구이; grilled fish) is another good bet. The *ajumma* (married or older women) staff are friendly and used to dealing with foreigners.

Gyodong-sijang   STREET FOOD ₩₩
(교동시장; meals ₩15,000-30,000) In the evening, this market fills with 'covered wagons' – makeshift eating and drinking joints. Several serve *haemul bokkeum* (해물볶음, ₩30,000), a huge two-person (or more) assorted seafood and vegetable sauté, set to bubble at your table.

❶ Information

Tourist Information Centre (☑061 690 2588; ⊙9am-9pm) The biggest of the tourist information centres is in front of the train station and usually has an English speaker.

❶ Getting There & Away

AIR
Yeosu airport, 17km north of the city, has flights to Seoul and Jeju-do. An airport shuttle (₩3000, 40 minutes) runs from Jungang-dong Rotary; buses are timed to meet departures.

BOAT
The ferry pier for island ferries is at the western end of the harbour. Ferries leave for Geomundo

(₩36,600, 2½ hours) at 7.40am and 1.40pm, and for Sado (₩11,500, 1½ hours) at 6am and 2.20pm.

BUS
The express bus terminal and intercity bus terminal are together, 4km north of the port area. Cross the pedestrian overpass to Pizza Hut and from the bus stop, almost any bus (₩1200, 15 minutes) goes to Jungang-dong Rotary.

TRAIN
Yeosu Expo station is the terminus for KTX trains running on the Jeolla line from Yongsan (₩46,000, 3½ hours, nine daily). There are also *saemaeul* (₩39,300, 4½ hours, one daily) and *mugunghwa* (₩26,400, five hours, nine daily) services.

❶ Getting Around

BUS
The most useful bus for getting around is no 2, which stops at Yeosu Expo station, Jinnamgwan and Odongdo.

TAXI
Fares start at ₩2800. It's roughly a 15-minute, ₩10,000 taxi ride from central Yeosu to Hak-dong.

Boseong   보성
☑061

Boseong (http://english.boseong.go.kr/index.boseong), famous as Korea's largest producer of green tea, is the gateway to the Daehan Dawon Tea Plantation. In May, Boseong hosts the **Green Tea Festival** (http://dahyang.boseong.go.kr/index.boseong).

⊙ Sights & Activities

Daehan Dawon Tea Plantation   GARDENS
(대한다원; ☑061 853 2595; 763-65 Nokcha-ro; adult/child ₩3000/2000; ⊙9am-6pm) One of Korea's most iconic sights, the Boseong Daehan Dawon Tea Plantation is spectacularly set on a hillside covered with curvy row after row of manicured green-tea bushes. It's

BUS DEPARTURES FROM YEOSU

DESTINATION	PRICE (₩)	DURATION	FREQUENCY
Busan	14,000	3hr	hourly
Gwangju	10,300	1½hr	every 30min
Mokpo	13,000	3hr	hourly
Seoul	30,800	4hr	hourly
Suncheon	4400	30min	every 30min

a popular setting for TV dramas and films. Spring, when the leaves are at their greenest, is the most congenial time to visit.

At the plantation's restaurant you can sample green-tea infused dishes (₩5000 to ₩8000) and drinks.

Korea Tea Museum   MUSEUM

(한국차박물관; ☑061 852 0918; www.koreateamuseum.kr; 775 Nokcha-ro; adult/child ₩1000/500; ⊙10am-5pm Tue-Sun) Here you can learn more than you ever thought you needed to know about tea, both in Korea and around the world, and also take part in a traditional tea service (₩2000). The museum is a 1km walk up the hill from the parking lot behind the bus station.

Yulpo Haesu Nokchatang   BATHHOUSE

(율포 해수 녹차탕; ☑061 853 4566; 678 Dongyul-ri, Hoecheon-myeon; adult/child ₩6000/4000; ⊙6am-8pm, last entry 7pm) Don't just settle for drinking tea – bathe in it at this local spa that includes a green-tea bath among its many tubs.

❶ Getting There & Around

Buses (₩6300, 50 minutes, every 30 minutes) and trains (₩3800, one hour, six daily) travel from Suncheon to Boseong; from Boseong, buses continue to Gangjin (₩4500, 45 minutes). One *mugunghwa* train at 6.31pm goes from Boseong to Gwangju (₩5200, two hours).

Buses run from Boseong bus terminal to Yulpo Haesu Nokchatang (₩1200, 30 minutes, once or twice an hour), stopping at Boseong train station and Daehan Dawon Tea Plantation (15 minutes).

Gangjin   강진

☑061

One of the most important ceramic centres in Korea, Gangjin has been associated with celadon (glazed green ceramic) for over 1000 years. Gangjin is specifically known for etched celadon, in which shallow patterns are cut out of the piece while it's still wet and filled in with special glazes through an inlay process.

⊙ Sights

Gangjin Celadon Museum   MUSEUM

(강진청자박물관; ☑061 430 3718; 33 Cheongjachon-gil, Daegu-myeon; adult/child/youth ₩2000/1000/1500; ⊙9am-6pm) The exquisite 800-year-old examples of Goryeo-dynasty celadon on display here

look startlingly contemporary. At the back are pottery workshops (Monday to Friday), where visitors can watch artisans at work on various processes. On the right is an excavated kiln site, discovered in 1968, that dates back to the 12th century. The museum and shops outside sell modern-made Goryeo celadon (the Seoul airport sells similar pieces for 10 times the price). The **Gangjin Ceramic Festival** is held here during midsummer.

❶ Getting There & Away

The museum is 18km south of Gangjin. Take a local bus from Gangjin bus terminal for Maryang and get off at the museum (₩1800, 25 minutes, every 40 minutes).

To get to Gangjin, hop on one of the buses running every 30 to 60 minutes along the southern coast from Suncheon (₩10,800, two hours) or Mokpo (₩5500, one hour). Buses also run from Gwangju (₩9800, 1½ hours, hourly). Then take a local bus for Maryang and get off at the museum (₩1800, 25 minutes, every 40 minutes).

Haenam   해남

☑061

Just southeast of the small, regional hub of Haenam (http://eng.haenam.go.kr) is Duryunsan Provincial Park, where a cluster of climbable peaks cradle the temple, Daeheung-sa.

⊙ Sights & Activities

Duryunsan Provincial Park   PARK

(두륜산도립공원; ☑061 530 5543; 400 Daeheungsa-gil; adult/child/youth ₩3000/1000/1500) Picturesque views of Korea's southern coastline reward hikers who scale the rocky path up to the peak, Duryun-bong (630m). The hike, which begins just behind the temple museum at Daeheung-sa, takes 1½ hours. It's a hard scramble near the top; it's an easier descent if you follow the stairs down and pick up the trail at the junction Jinburam.

There's also a **cable car** (☑061 534 8992; 88-54 Daeheungsa-gil; adult/child return ₩9000/6000; ⊙8am-5pm Dec-Mar, to 6pm Apr-Nov) that heads up to a different peak, Gogye-bong (638m), but does not operate on windy days.

Daeheung-sa   TEMPLE

(대흥사; ☑061 535 5775; www.daeheungsa.co.kr; 400 Daeheungsa-gil; ⊙sunrise-sunset) This major Zen temple is thought to date back a millenia, but it remained relatively unknown until it became associated with Seosan, a warrior monk who led a group against Japanese invaders between 1592 and 1598. The backdrop of mountains against the temple is said to be a silhouette of Buddha lying down on his back. Trails behind the temple lead to some mountain hermitages, such as **Bukmireuk-am**, with its Silla-era (850–932) Buddhist stone carvings.

The temple is inside Duryunsan Provincial Park, a 30-minute walk from the bus stop. Templestays are available (from ₩40,000).

🛏 Sleeping & Eating

Haenam Youth Hostel HOSTEL ₩
(해나유스호스텔; ☎ 061 533 0170; 88-88 Daeheungsa-gil; dm/r ₩10,000/30,000; P ⊜ ✳ @) A three-minute walk beyond the cable car inside Duryunsan Provincial Park is this excellent budget option, with clean modern rooms. Dorms have bunk beds while private rooms have *yo* (padded quilt mattresses on the floor); all rooms have bathrooms.

★**Yuseongwan** HANOK GUESTHOUSE ₩₩
(유선관; ☎ 061 534 2959; 376 Daeheungsa-gil; d ₩50,000; P ⊜) This idyllic traditional inn, built around a courtyard, is inside Duryun-san Provincial Park, about two-thirds of the way between the car park and Daeheung-sa. Rooms are small but cosy, decorated with ink-brush paintings; note that bathrooms are shared – and in a separate building. Don't miss the traditional breakfast (₩8000), brought to your room on a low table.

Next door is a rest stop with floor seating above the gurgling stream – it's a perfect place to stop for an ice cream or *makgeolli*.

★**Wonjo Jangsu Tongdak** KOREAN ₩₩
(원조장수통닭; ☎ 061 536 4410; 295 Gosan-ro; meal for four ₩50,000 ⏰ 11am-9pm) Hungry?

Come here to feast on *tongdak* (통닭), chicken served in two courses. First comes a tabletop stir-fry of chicken marinated in a tangy, spicy sauce, followed by the rest of the bird and mung-bean rice porridge. The whole thing, which costs ₩50,000, is meant to serve four. The restaurant is in a brick building with a red sign.

It's halfway between Haenam bus terminal and Daeheung-sa, along the bus route; get off at the Dolgogae bus stop.

ℹ Getting There & Around

Access to Duryunsan Provincial Park is by bus (₩1200, 15 minutes, every 40 minutes) from Haenam bus terminal.

Wando 완도
☎ 061 / POP 53,000

Most travellers view Wando (http://eng.wando.go.kr), an island connected to the mainland by a bridge, as a transit point for ferries to Jeju-do. However, it's also home to a fantastic beach and ever-changing views of scattered offshore islands.

◉ Sights

Myeongsasim-ni BEACH
(명사십리; ☎ 061 550 6929) The southern coast's best beach is a nearly 4km stretch of golden sand backed by a boardwalk and pine trees. There's a popular **campground** (20 June to 31 August; ₩10,000 per night) here, with raised platforms for tents and plenty of showers. Myeongsasim-ni is on the smaller, neighbouring island of Shinjido; buses (₩1900, 25 minutes, hourly) run here from the Wando bus terminal.

Gugyedeung PARK
(구계등; ☎ 061 554 1769; 131 Jeongdo-ri; ⏰ 9am-5pm) On Wando's south coast is a tiny park that offers views of distant cliffs and offshore islands, a pebbly beach and

BUS DEPARTURES FROM HAENAM

DESTINATION	PRICE (₩)	DURATION (HR)	FREQUENCY
Busan	25,700	6	7 daily
Gwangju	11,100	1¾	every 30min
Jindo	5900	1	hourly
Mokpo	6300	1	hourly
Seoul	34,400	5	6 daily
Wando	5400	1	hourly

Wando

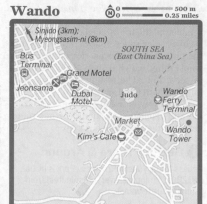

a 1km nature trail that runs through a thin slither of coastal woodland. Swimming is dangerous. The Seobu (western side) bus (₩1200, 10 minutes, hourly) runs from Wando bus terminal. Get off at Sajeong and walk 600m down to the park entrance.

Sleeping

Motels are clustered along the harbour, in between the bus terminal and the ferry terminal.

Grand Motel
MOTEL ₩₩

(그랜드 모텔; ☏061 535 0100; www.wandogrand.co.kr; 41 Gaepo-ro 56beon-gil; r ₩40,000-50,000; P❋@🖲) This is a comfortable, clean place with large rooms overlooking the harbour, fast PCs and free use of the in-house sauna.

Dubai Motel
MOTEL ₩₩

(두바이 모텔; ☏061 553 0688; 37 Haebyeo-ngongwon-ro; r ₩40,000-50,000; P❋@🖲) There's no desert in sight but this green waterfront hotel has smart rooms, both

Western-style and *ondol,* and harbour views. Pricier rooms have PCs.

Eating & Drinking

Wando is Korea's largest producer of *jeonbok* (전복; abalone), and you'll see tanks of them in most restaurants lining the harbour.

Jeonsama
KOREAN ₩₩₩

(전사마; ☏061 555 0838; 1273-13 Gunnae-ri; dishes ₩9,000-50,000; ☉10am-9pm) This popular restaurant serves abalone a bunch of different ways, but try what we dub a Korean version of surf-and-turf: *wanggalbi jeonbokjjim* (왕갈비전복찜; ₩50,000 for two people) – braised abalone and grilled spare ribs. Yum.

Kim's Cafe
CAFE

(40 Cheonghaejinnam-ro; coffee ₩3000-5000; ☉8.30am-10pm; 🖲) This cute-as-pie white cottage looks totally out of place on a street filled with grey, weathered shops. There are fresh juices, cakes and muffins on the menu along with the usual coffees and teas.

Getting There & Away

BOAT

Ferries depart from **Wando Ferry Terminal** (☏061 554 8000) for Jeju-do at 9.30am and 4pm on weekdays and at 9am, 3am and 4pm on weekends. The last ferry of the day takes three hours and costs ₩26,700; the others take 1½ hours and cost ₩37,000. Other ferries run to a dozen nearby islands including Cheongsando.

Getting Around

From Wando bus terminal, one local bus heads west (서부; *seobu*) while another heads east (동부; *dongbu*). Both go to the bridge to the mainland before heading back to Wando. The ferry terminal is a 25-minute walk from the bus terminal or a short taxi ride.

BUS DEPARTURES FROM WANDO

DESTINATION	PRICE (₩)	DURATION (HR)	FREQUENCY
Busan	31,900	6	5 daily
Gwangju	16,500	2¾	hourly
Haenam	5400	1	8 daily
Mokpo	11,800	2	3 daily
Seoul	37,200	6	4 daily
Suncheon	17,100	3¼ hours	5 daily
Yeongam	9800	1½	hourly

Mokpo 목포

✓ 061 / POP 250,000

The sprawling port city of Mokpo, set on a small peninsula jutting out into the West Sea, is the end of the line for trains and expressway traffic, and a starting point for sea voyages to Jeju-do and the western islands of Dadohae Haesang National Park. Korea's National Maritime Museum is appropriately located here, and the craggy peaks of Yudalsan Park rear up in the city centre, offering splendid sea, city and sunset views.

Mokpo is the hometown of late South Korean president and Nobel Peace Prize recipient Kim Dae-jung. It's also the base of the Formula 1 race, held at a racetrack 15km south of town – one of the many recent development projects awarded to long-neglected Jeollanam-do.

◉ Sights

Mokpo is a classic tale of two cities: the old city, crowded between the train station, craggy Yudalsan Park and the ferry terminals is a salty, port town with fish markets and narrow streets. To the east is the newer Hadang, with fashionable cafes, a big modern shopping centre and a popular waterfront promenade, Peace Park. In between, is the Gatbawi Culture District, full of museums.

Yudalsan Park PARK
(유달산; 180 Yudal-ro) Right on the coast, this park is filled with rocky cliffs and pavilions, with views across the island-scattered sea. Follow the main path for about 45 minutes to the peak Ildeung-bawi (일등바위; 228). To head down to **Yudal Beach**, double back to **Soyojeong** (소요정) pavilion for the path to **Arirang Gogae** (아리랑고개), then follow the sign to **Nakjo-dae** (낙조대) pavilion. From there it's a 10-minute walk down the steps to the beach.

The beach is just a tiny patch of sand, rocks and seaweed, so the main attractions are the island views (partially spoiled by a bridge) and a smattering of bars and restaurants. Bus 1 and most of the other buses that pass by can take you back to downtown.

Mokpo Modern History Museum MUSEUM
(목포근대역사관; ✓ 061 270 0878; 18 Beonwha-ro; ⊗ 9am-6pm Tue-Sun) **FREE** This museum is housed in the Mokpo branch of the Japanese Oriental Colonization Company, a building from the 1920s. It takes a hard look at the Japanese colonisation of Korea in the early 20th century, telling its story almost entirely through photographs, which also document Mokpo's rapid growth over the last century.

Gatbawi Culture District NEIGHBOURHOOD
(갓바위공원; 🚌 15) This area, 4km east of downtown, has a swathe of museums, the best of which is the National Maritime Museum. Just past the museums is the riverside **Gatbawi Rocks**, which have been heavily eroded into shapes that are supposed to look like two monks wearing reed hats. A pier extends into the river so you can get a good look at this city icon. Catch the bus (₩1200, 20 minutes, every 30 minutes) from outside the train station (across the street). A taxi costs ₩5000 from the train station.

➡ **National Maritime Museum**
(국립해양유물전시관; ✓ 061 270 2000; 136 Namnong-ro; ⊗ 9am-6pm Tue-Sun; ♿; 🚌 15) **FREE** This is the only museum in Korea dedicated to the country's maritime history. The highlights are two shipwrecks, one dating from the 11th century and the other from the early 14th century. Thousands of priceless items of Korean and Chinese celadon, coins and other trade items were salvaged from them. Fascinating film footage shows the treasures being salvaged, and part of the actual boats has been preserved. It has English signage.

➡ **Namnong Memorial Hall**
(남농기념관; 119 Namnong-ro; adult/child ₩1000/500; ⊗ 9am-6pm Tue-Sun; 🚌 15) This hall contains paintings by five generations of the Huh family, including work by Huh Gun, a master of Namjonghwa, a Korean art style associated with the Southern School of China.

🛏 Sleeping

There are countless love motels and *yeogwan* (small, family-run hotels) around the bus terminal and between the train station and ferry terminal. More modern hotels are in Hadang.

Mokpo 1935 HANOK ₩
(목포1935; ✓ 061 243 1935; http://cafe. daum.net/mokpo1935; 59 Yeongsan-ro; dm/d 25,000/100,000; ⊗ ❋ 🛜) This beautifully restored, 100-year-old *hanok* is in the heart of the old downtown, a short walk from the train station. There are dorm rooms in one building and family rooms in another, around a courtyard; bathrooms are shared. It's tricky to find: look up for the sign that

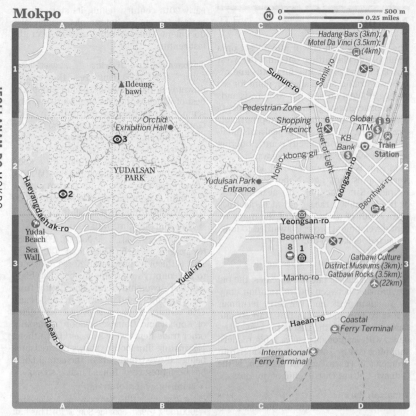

Mokpo

◎ Sights
1 Mokpo Modern History Museum	C3
2 Nakjo-dae	A2
3 Soyojeong	B2

🛏 Sleeping
4 F1 Motel	D2

🍴 Eating
5 Dokcheon	D1
6 Namupo	D2
7 Yeongran Hoet-jip	D3

🍷 Drinking & Nightlife
8 House Filled with Happiness	C3

ℹ Information
9 Tourist Information Centre	D2

says 'Cafe & Bar, Guesthouse' over the entrance to an alleyway.

Marina Bay Hotel　　　　　　　　HOTEL ₩₩
(마리나베이호텔; ☎061 247 9900; www.marina bayhotel.co.kr; 1 Haean-ro 249beon-gil; d from ₩70,000; 🅿❄🛜) Outside peak season, this new hotel – along the waterfront and just a few minutes' walk from the ferry terminals – is an excellent deal. (Prices rise by 20% on weekends and double during summer). Rooms are bright, airy and modern.

F1 Motel　　　　　　　　　　　MOTEL ₩₩
(에프원호텔; ☎061 244 7744; 29 Sugang-ro 12beon-gil; r ₩50,000-60,000; 🅿❄@🛜) The best of the cluster of motels between the train station and the ferry terminal is this dark high-rise. Modern, clean rooms have sofas, heated toilet seats and ultrafast PCs. Note that wi-fi is weak in some rooms.

Motel Da Vinci   LOVE MOTEL ₩₩
(모텔다빈치; ☏061 287 0456; 16 Beonyeong-ro; r ₩50,000-60,000; P❋@) This flashy motel in Hadang has rooms that are head and shoulders above the local competition (and are thankfully less flashy inside). Twin rooms, for example, come with two PCs and spa tubs.

✗ Eating

Mokpo is famous for its fresh seafood and you'll find many seafood restaurants in front of the ferry terminal along Haean-ro. Smart new restaurants and chains are in Hadang, and there are often street vendors along the Peace Park waterfront. The shopping precinct opposite the train station has bakeries, cafes and pizza joints alongside Korean restaurants.

★ Dokcheon   KOREAN ₩₩
(독천식당; ☏061 242 6528; 3-1 Honam-ro 64beon-gil; dishes ₩11,000-19,000; ⊙10am-9.30pm) Mokpo is known for its octopus, particularly for its *nakji tangtangi* (chopped live octopus). This is the best place in town to try it, and if you're not quite up for the challenge of eating it still wriggling, the *nakji bibimbap* (octopus, rice, egg and vegies with chilli sauce) and *nakji yeonpotang* (octopus soup) are excellent, too. It's an ordinary white-tiled building, with signs lit up at night. Seating is on the floor.

Namupo   KOREAN ₩₩
(나무포; ☏061 243 8592; 19-1 Sumun-ro; dishes ₩8000-35,000; ⊙9am-10pm) Not in a seafood mood? Try the *galbi* (갈비; beef ribs) grills at this local favourite located in the city centre. There's also a range of fan faves such as bibimbap and *naengmyeon* (cold buckwheat noodles).

Elephant House   INTERNATIONAL ₩₩
(☏061 284 6242; 48 Wonhyeong-ro; meals ₩18,000-22,000; ⊙10am-midnight; ✍) This Hadang joint is the place to go for your pasta fix. There are some clever fusion dishes on the menu such as 'currybonara' and spaghetti with Mokpo's local octopus.

Yeongran Hoet-jip   KOREAN ₩₩₩
(영란횟집; ☏061 243 7311; 47 Beonhwa-ro; dishes ₩45,000; ⊙10am-10pm) Though it may not look like much, this is one of Mokpo's finest *hoe* (raw fish) restaurants, where you can sample the local *mineo* (민어; croaker). Eat it as is or wrapped in *ssam* dipped in a sweet and spicy sauce. Dishes are meant for sharing. There's a blue sign out front.

🍺 Drinking

Mokpo's entertainment and nightlife district is in Hadang, behind the Peace Park waterfront promenade. Here you'll find an ever-changing assortment of bars, cafes, discos and karaoke clubs. From April to November, there's a **dancing water fountain** show nightly (except Mondays) at 8.40pm in front of Peace Park.

★ House Filled with Happiness   CAFE
(행복이가득한집; ☏061 247 5887; 48 Yudul-ro; drinks from ₩6600; ⊙11am-10pm) Mokpo's most attractive cafe, with dark polished wood, dim lights and a wrap-around veranda, is inside a restored Japanese colonial residence. Given the history, the name may seem ironic, but there's no denying that the building itself is beautiful, with a quiet calm.

Moe's Bar & Grille   BAR
(1102 Sang-dong; drinks from ₩5000; ⊙9pm-2am) You'll find this scruffy expat hangout on Rose St, a meandering pedestrian lane about 1km behind Peace Park. Don't read

---

WORTH A TRIP

JEONGNAMJIN SATURDAY MARKET

Elsewhere traditional markets may be losing out to newer shopping centres, but the **Jeongnamjin Saturday Market** (정남진토요시장; Yeyang-ri, Jangheung-eup; ⊙6am-6pm) in Jangheung (장흥) is definitely a happening place. In addition to the usual dried fish and hiking clothes, the market has live music and food stalls – including some run by members of the province's ethnic communities. Come around noon, when things are at their liveliest, then pick up some *mandu* (dumplings) and join the local families at the picnic tables.

Buses running every 30 to 60 minutes on the Suncheon to Mokpo route stop at Jangheung, which is closest to Boseong (₩2600, 30 minutes) and Gangjin (₩2000, 15 minutes). From Jangheung bus terminal it's a 10-minute walk to the market. Head right on the main road, then over the bridge; the market will be on your right.

too much into the name: it's more of a beer and darts sort of place than a restaurant. It's above 11am Cafe.

ℹ Information

Tourist Information Centre (☏ 061 270 8599; ⊗ 9am-6pm) Little English spoken but there is a helpful English map. At the train station.

ℹ Getting There & Away

AIR

Muan International Airport (☏ 1661 2626; http://muan.airport.co.kr; 970-260, Gonghang-ro, Mangun-myeon) is 25km north of the city and has flights to Jeju, Shanghai and Shenyang. There is no direct bus to the airport (a transfer is required at Muan). A taxi (around ₩30,000) is the best option.

BOAT

Mokpo's **Coastal Ferry Terminal** (연안여객선터미널) handles boats to smaller islands west and southwest of Mokpo. Sightseeing trips (adult/child ₩15,000/8000) depart from here and cruise around the nearby islands.

The **International Ferry Terminal** (국제 여객선 터미널) has two sailings a day to Jeju-do. Slower car ferries leave at 9am and take 4½ hours. Fares start at ₩30,000 and vary based on class; fares for under 12s are half-price. The faster, pricier *Pink Dolphin* (₩49,650) leaves at 2pm, taking three hours. Contrary to its name, there are no international routes from this terminal.

BUS

Mokpo's bus terminal is several kilometres from the centre of town. Turn left outside the bus terminal, then left at the end of the road and walk down to the main road where bus 1 (₩1200, every 20 minutes) stops on the left. It runs to the train station, the ferry terminals and then on to Yudal Beach.

TRAIN

KTX provides a fast service to Seoul's Yongsan station (₩52,800, 2½ hours, 16 daily), as well as *saemaeul* (₩39,600, 4½ hours, two daily) and *mugunghwa* (₩26,600, six hours, six daily) services. Trains to and from Seoul pass through Gwangju-Songjeong. There is one train daily to Boseong (₩8700, 2½ hours) at 9.20am.

ℹ Getting Around

It's a 15-minute walk from the train station to the ferry terminals or to the entrance to Yudalsan Park.

Local bus 1 (₩1200, every 20 minutes) serves the bus terminal, ferry terminals, train station and Yudal Beach. Bus 15 (₩1200, 20 minutes, every 30 minutes) runs to the Gatbawi Park museums and Hadang from the bus and train stations. Taxis are cheap and plentiful.

Around Mokpo

East of Mokpo, the small city of Yeongnam is the gateway to 42-sq-km Wolchulsan National Park

Wolchulsan National Park   NATIONAL PARK (월출산국립공원; ☏ 061 473 5210; http://english.knps.or.kr; adult/child/youth ₩2000/500/1000; ⊗ 5am-7pm Mar-Oct, 8am-6pm Nov-Feb) Korea's smallest national park has crags, spires and unusually shaped rocks around every corner, as well as an 8m Buddha rock carving, steel stairways and a 52m steel bridge spanning two ridges. The popular route is the 8km, six-hour hike from Dogap-sa in the west to Cheonhwang-sa in the east (or vice versa) over the park's highest peak, Cheonhwang-bong (809m). Tracks are well signposted, but steep and strenuous in places due to the rocky terrain. Bring lots of water.

BUS DEPARTURES FROM MOKPO

DESTINATION	PRICE (₩)	DURATION	FREQUENCY
Busan	22,500	4½hr	9 daily
Gwangju	5700	1¼hr	every 20min
Haenam	6300	1hr	hourly
Incheon Airport	39,100	4½hr	3 daily
Jindo	6500	2hr	every 30min
Seoul	30,400	4½hr	every 40min
Wando	11,800	2hr	3 daily
Yeongam	4400	30min	every 20min
Yeosu	13,000	3½hr	hourly

JINDO MYSTERIOUS SEA ROAD

Jindo (진도), Korea's third-largest island, boasts some of the world's largest tides. The island is famous for an unusual natural phenomenon: for a few days each year (usually in spring), the tide drops extremely low, exposing a 2.8km-long, 40m-wide causeway that connects Jindo to the tiny island of Modo-ri.

The experience is known as the **Ganjuyuk Gyedo** (Mysterious Sea Road) and has long been celebrated among Koreans in legend. As one story goes, a family of tigers was causing so many problems on Jindo that all the islanders moved to nearby Modo, but somehow Grandma Ppong was left behind. She was broken-hearted and prayed to the Sea God to be reunited with her family. In answer to her fervent prayers, the Sea God parted the sea, enabling her to cross over to Modo and meet her family again. Sadly, she died of exhaustion shortly afterward. Statues, shrines and paintings of her can be seen throughout Jindo.

With the spread of Christianity in Korea, the similarity to the Israelites' crossing of the Red Sea has only brought more enthusiasts. Some 300,000 people make the crossing each year – in long rubber boots (available for rent, naturally).

The **Jindo Miracle Sea Road Festival** (http://miracleseaeng.jindo.go.kr/index. html), which includes a torchlit procession, musical performances and a memorial cere-mony for Grandma Ppong, is held annually to coincide with the crossing.

Jindo is best accessed from Gwangju (₩12,200, 2¾ hours, every 40 minutes) or Mokpo (₩6500, one hour, every 30 minutes). From Jindo bus terminal, catch a local bus bound for Hoedong (₩1300, one hour, hourly) to the festival site; a taxi should cost about ₩13,000 and take 30 minutes.

If you're not up for a huge hike, head to the more popular Cheonhwang-sa end and hike an hour up a rocky path to the suspension bridge from where sprawling views of the surrounding country unfold.

From Yeongnam, buses run the 11km to Dogap-sa (₩1400, 20 minutes, 9.30am and 4.30pm) in the west and the 4km to Cheonhwang-sa (₩1200, 10 minutes, 7.10am, 9am, 10.10am and 4.50pm). Consider taking a taxi from Yeongam.

Dadohae Haesang National Park
다도해해상국립공원

Consisting of more than 1700 islands and islets and divided into eight sections, Dadohae Haesang (Marine Archipelago) National Park occupies much of the coast and coastal waters of Jeollanam-do. Some of the isles support small communities with fishing and tourism income; others are little more than tree-covered rocks.

Mokpo is the gateway to the western sector, including Hongdo and Heuksando, the most visited and scenic of the islands. In July and August the boats fill up, so book ahead.

⊙ Sights

Hongdo   ISLAND
(홍도; Red Island) This is the most popular and beautiful of the islands west of Mok-po. Some 6km long and 2.5km wide, it rises precipitously from the sea and is bounded by sheer cliffs, bizarre rock formations and wooded hillsides cut by ravines. The island is ringed by islets and sunsets can be spec-tacular, but the only way you can see most of it is by boat, because with the exception of the villages, Hongdo is a protected nature reserve; entry is prohibited.

It is possible to climb the hill **Gitdae-bong** for views. There's a small peb-bled beach on the south of the island.

Ferries to Hongdo arrive at a spanking new ferry-terminal building in **Ilgu** village, which is protected by a tiny cove. Boat tours (₩22,000, two hours, 7.30am and 12.30pm) around the island are the best way to appreciate the island and its rocky islets and arches, though the Korean com-mentary gets a little grating. Towards the end of the tour, a small boat pulls up and fishermen slice up live fish into plates of sashimi (₩35,000).

Ilgu has several minbak and motels, all charging about ₩50,000 per night. Try **1004 Hotel** (1004호텔; ☑061 246 3758; r ₩50,000; ❋), with its sea-facing rooms and

WORTH A TRIP

HAMPYEONG SEAWATER SAUNA

Too cold for a swim? Take a detour to the **Hampyeong Seawater Sauna** (함평해수찜; 1007-1 Gungsan-ri, Son-bul-myeon; r ₩30,000; ☉8am-5pm), where saltwater is mixed with medicinal herbs and heated with fire-baked stones. Private rooms are available for parties of up to four. You'll be given pyjamas to wear and towels to soak in the water and wrap around your body (don't get in the water – it's too hot).

Buses run roughly hourly from Mokpo to Hampyeong (₩4100, one hour), from where a taxi to the sauna will cost around ₩10,000. Last entry is 3pm.

balconies. Restaurants serve up seafood from ₩15,000 and a small supermarket beside 1004 Hotel serves the town.

Heuksando
ISLAND

(흑산도) Heuksando, on the way to Hongdo, is the larger, more populated and more accessible of the two islands. Views from its peaks show why Dadohae Haesang means 'marine archipelago'. Fishing villages are linked by trails, but walking around the island takes around nine hours. Fortunately, local buses (₩1200, hourly) circle most of the island – a recommended trip is up the **Bonghwa-dae** peak, on the north coast hill, Sangnasan.

Cycling is also a fun way to get around; look for shops offering mountain bikes for hire (₩20,000 per day) near the ferry terminal.

The largest village, **Yeri**, formerly a whaling centre, is where ferries dock and is home to several basic accommodation options of *minbak* and *yeogwan*. Seafood restaurants are plentiful but prices, ranging from ₩10,000 to ₩60,000, are higher than the mainland.

ℹ Getting There & Away

The same ferries serve Heuksando, 90km west of Mokpo, and Hongdo, another 20km further away. Leaving from Mokpo's Coastal Ferry Terminal, ferries run to Heuksando (adult/child one way ₩34,300/17,150, two hours) and continue on to Hongdo (adult/child one way ₩42,000/21,000, 2½ hours). Ferries depart Mokpo at 7.50am and 1pm. Return ferries depart from Hongdo at 10.20am and 3.30pm, stopping at Heuksando (₩11,200, 30 minutes) along the way.

Note that you will be asked to show your passport when buying a ferry ticket (and likely again when you board).

Jeju-do

♪ 064 / POP 621,500

Best Places to Eat

➜ Dasi Boesi (p244)

➜ Saesom Galbi (p251)

➜ Yetnal Patjuk (p247)

➜ Haejin Seafood
Restaurant (p238)

➜ Chocolate Castle
by the Sea (p250)

Best Places to Stay

➜ Hotel Little France (p251)

➜ Seaes Hotel
& Resort (p256)

➜ Ssari's Flower Hill (p244)

➜ Baume Couture
Boutique Hotel (p238)

➜ Hotel W (p238)

Why Go?

Jeju-do (제주도), Korea's largest island, has long been the country's favourite domestic holiday destination thanks to its beautiful beaches, lush countryside and seaside hotels designed for rest and relaxation.

There's plenty on Jeju-do to appeal to those who prefer to be active. Hike up South Korea's highest mountain, Hallasan, or climb the incredible tuff cone Seongsan Ilchul-bong, rising straight from the sea, to watch the sun rise from the ridge of a crater. For a less-demanding nature experience, meander along one of the Jeju Olle Trails and explore tangerine-trimmed country roads, jagged coasts and narrow lanes dotted with cottage-style homes made from black lava rock. The ocean is never far away, so plunge into blue seas to view coral as colourful as the sunsets and dig into Jeju-do's unique cuisine, including seafood caught by *haeneyo* (female free divers).

When to Go

Jeju-si

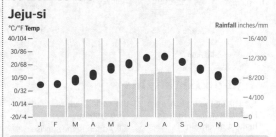

Feb/Mar Hike up to Hallasan's snow-covered peak.

Apr Join the cherry-blossom festivities across the island.

Oct Enjoy good weather and splendid autumn foliage along nature trails such as Saryeoni Park.

History

According to legend, Jeju-do was founded by three brothers who came out of holes in the ground and established the Tamna kingdom. Early in the 12th century the Goryeo dynasty took over, but in 1273 Mongol invaders conquered the island, contributing a tradition of horsemanship, a special horse (*jorangmal*) and quirks in the local dialect. During the Joseon period, Jeju-do was used as a place of political and religious exile.

The Japanese colonial period of the early 20th century can be traced through abandoned military bases and fortifications on the island. From 1947 to 1954, as many as 30,000 locals were massacred by right-wing government forces in events collectively labelled the 'April 3 Incident'.

Recent decades have seen Jeju-do's economy shift from mainly agriculture to tourism. In 2006 the island was made into a special autonomous province, giving it a level of self-government that is encouraging further economic development. The World Conservation Congress was held here in September 2012 and ambitious carbon-free electricity generation ventures are being tested. Jeju-do has come under fire from conservationists and other protesters for the Korean naval base under construction at Gangjeong on the island's south coast.

Since 2008 the Korean government has waived visa requirements for Chinese tourists coming to Jeju-do. In that year the island had about 400,000 visitors. In 2015 that number was expected to surpass five million. Coupled with a recent residency visa-investment program, some complain that financial pressures and high land costs are forever changing the once-sleepy nature of this resort island.

ℹ️ Getting Around

CAR

Driving on Jeju-do is quite unlike the *Mad Max* frenzy evident in some mainland cities. Traffic

Jeju-do Highlights

1 Hiking the trails of **Hallasan** (p257), Korea's highest mountain.

2 Exploring the **Jeju Olle** (p259), a magnificent network of walking trails.

3 Going underground at **Manjang-gul** (p242), part of the world's largest lava-tube cave system.

4 Admiring the sunrise from **Seongsan Ilchul-bong** (p245) volcanic tuff cone.

5 Grabbing a bite and strolling Seogwopo's youthful art district around Lee Jung-Seop Art Gallery & Park (p249).

6 Uncovering delights on **Udo** (p250), a tiny island off Jeju-do's east coast.

7 Finding Buddha in a cave in **Sanbanggul-sa** (p257) at Sagye-ri.

flows smoothly and the most common hazards are speed bumps and lost drivers making U-turns. Road signs are in English, most rental cars come with an English-language GPS system and the hire cost is reasonable (around ₩60,000 a day for a compact car, including insurance). You must be at least 21 years of age and have a current international driving permit.

BICYCLE

It's possible to pedal or scoot your way around the island (250km) in three to five days. The designated cycleway is relatively flat, with much of it parallel to the beautiful coast. Pack rain gear. Bicycles (₩10,000 a day) and scooters (₩15,000 to ₩25,000 a day) can be hired in Jeju-si and Seogwipo.

BUS

Services radiate from Jeju-si and Seogwipo and cover most of the island, running around the coast and across the centre roughly every 20 minutes. Pick up an English intercity bus map and timetable from the airport tourist office.

TAXI

Charge is ₩2800 for the first 2km; a 15km journey costs about ₩10,000. You can hire a taxi for around ₩150,000 a day.

JEJU-SI

POP 435,000

Chances are that you'll end up spending a day or two in the island's capital, Jeju-si (제주시), as this is the main entry point to Jeju-do, either by air or sea. The city centre, 4km east of Jeju International Airport, has a few historic structures, plenty of shopping and lively bars opposite the old City Hall – all fine, but nothing extraordinary. Tapdong-ro has an incredible number of seafood and pork restaurants. The coastal road starting at Yongduam Rock has nice seaside views and a panoply of restaurants, cafes, bars and pensions.

In the suburb of Shin Jeju, you'll find more accommodation, restaurants and bars. The most interesting sights, such as Jeju Stone Park and Jeju Loveland, are out of town, but easily accessed either by bus or taxi.

⊙ Sights & Activities

◎ City Centre

Tapdong Promenade & Waterbreak   WATERFRONT
(제주시내) Jeju-si itself doesn't have a beach, but along the Tapdong seafront

---

DOLHARUBANG

An ever-present symbol of Jeju-do is the volcanic stone statues known as *dolharubang* (grandfather rock). The original *dolharubang* were carved around 1750 and placed outside the island's fortresses – 47 of these *dolharubang* still exist.

It's generally believed the statues were set to ward off evil, but they may have also been fertility symbols. These phallic oddities are nearly life-sized with a helmet-style hat, bulging eyes, a squashed nose and hands on the stomach. Taking home your own *dolharubang* is easy as they're sold in all shapes and sizes as souvenirs.

---

runs this pleasant promenade. At the eastern end, walk along the mosaic-decorated sea wall. There's also a small **amusement park** and an outdoor **band shell** that hosts summer music and dance performances.

Yongduam Rock   VIEWPOINT
(용두암) 'Dragon Head Rock' (so called because the volcanic rocks are supposed to resemble a dragon) attracts coachloads of tourists. Besides rock watching, plane spotting is a popular activity – aeroplanes fly just a few hundred metres overhead on their final approach to the island.

Arario Museum   MUSEUM
(아라리오유지엄; ☑064 720 8201; www.arario museum.org; adult ₩6000-12,000, depending on gallery; ☉10am-7pm) One of the island's most interesting art projects, Arario has four galleries in renovated buildings in and around the Tapdong area hosting permanent and temporary exhibitions by Korean and international artists. The intriguing design of these galleries continues and expands a Jeju tradition of thoughtful and artful use of space.

Entry fee into the Tapdong Cinema gallery (₩12,000) also gets you into the next-door Tapdong Bike Shop gallery. Two galleries housed in old motels – **Arario Museum Dongmun Motel I** (동문모텔 I; ☑064-720 8202; adult/youth ₩10,000/6000) and **Dongmun Motel II** (동문모텔 II; ☑064 720 8203) – are a 20-minute walk from Tapdong, near Sanji-ro.

Folklore & Natural History Museum
MUSEUM

(민속자연사박물관; ☎064 710 7708; http://museum.jeju.go.kr/en; adult/youth ₩1100/500; ◷8.30am-6pm) Wide-ranging eco-museum with exhibits on Jeju-do's varied geological features, including volcanic bombs, lava tubes and trace fossils. Other highlights are excellent wildlife films, the bizarre oar fish and panoramas of the island's six ecological zones.

Global Sea Water Sauna
SPA

(탑동해수사우나; ☎064 758 4800; http://jejuzzim.com; bathhouse/jjimjil-bang & overnight sleeping ₩6000/8000; ◷24hr) Clean up and wind down at this public bath and *jjimjil-bang* (upmarket sauna) in Tapdong. It's a 24-hour facility, which also makes it the cheapest sleeping option in Jeju-si.

◉ Outside Jeju-si

Jeju Stone Park
PARK

(제주돌문화공원; ☎064 710 7731; http://jejustonepark.com/eng; adult/youth ₩5000/3500; ◷9am-6pm, closed 1st Mon of month) Creating a park dedicated to rocks on a rock-littered island might sound a snooze, but you'll quickly reassess that opinion after touring this beguiling sculpture park. Three walking

> ### ⓘ PLANNING FOR JEJU-DO
>
> July and August are peak season; hotels and car hire get booked up and rates are higher. Visit from September (excluding the Lunar New Year holiday period) and you'll avoid the crowds and pay less. The weather is still good and you'll have the beaches mostly to yourself.
>
> If time is short, make Seogwipo, the island's second-largest city on the south coast, your base. From here you can visit Hallasan National Park to the north, Seongsan Ilchul-bong to the east and Sanbanggul-sa and the Yongmeori coast to the west. Jeju-si, the island's capital to the north, is closer to the airport but is not as scenic.
>
> With a week or more it's possible to take in all of Jeju-do's top sights, as well as visit one of the smaller islands, such as Udo, or lounge on a deserted beach. Get off the beaten track by staying at a small village pension or guesthouse.

trails (between 560m and 970m in length) snake past outdoor exhibits, ranging from replicas of the original 47 *dolharubang* (grandfather rocks) to an enchanting forest with hundreds of *dongjasok* (pairs of stone tomb guardians). It's a stop on the Jeju City Tour Bus (p241) route.

Jeju Museum of Art
GALLERY

(제주도립미술관; ☎064 710 4300; http://jmoa.jeju.go.kr; adult/child/youth ₩1000/300/500; ◷9am-6pm Tue-Sun) View interesting permanent and temporary exhibits of contemporary visual art at this excellent gallery next to Jeju Loveland. The beautifully designed building appears to float on a pool of water. It's on the Jeju Golden Bus City Tour (p241) route.

Saryeoni Forest
FOREST

(사려니숲길; ☎064 900 8800; http://jejuforest.kfri.go.kr) **FREE** On the eastern border of Hallasan National Park, this is a popular weekend walking destination with 15km of forest paths shaded by maples, oaks and cedars, with the occasional roaming deer. Plan on four hours to walk the entire path between the two roadside entrances. The Jeju City Tour Bus (p241) stops at the two entrances on Rtes 1112 and 1118.

Iho Tewoo Beach
BEACH

(이호테우해변; 🚌702 to Hyeon-sa Village) The nearest beach to Jeju-si is blessed with an unusual mixture of yellow and grey sand, which means you can build two-tone sandcastles. There's shallow water that makes for safe swimming.

Buses from Jeju-si (₩1300, 15 minutes, every 20 minutes) run from the intercity bus terminal to Heon-sa Village.

🛏 Sleeping

There's a mix of high-end hotels and budget accommodation near the seafront in Tapdong, which is a ₩4000 taxi ride from the airport. Business and luxury hotels can be found in Shin Jeju, which is closer to the airport.

HK Jeju
HOSTEL ₩

(☎064 727 0027; www.hkjeju.com; Tapdong; dm/s/tw ₩15,000/39,000/55,000; ❋@🛜) The friendly staff speak English at this appealing backpackers joint that occupies an old-fashioned hotel. A bit of colourful paint brightens things up and there's a big kitchen and laundry.

JEJU-DO JEJU-SI

Jeju-si

⊚ Sights
1 Arario Museum	C1
2 Arario Museum Dongmun Motel I	C2
3 Arario Museum Dongmun Motel II	C1
4 City Hall	D4
5 Folklore & Natural History Museum	D3
6 Tapdong Promenade & Waterbreak	B1
7 Yongduam Rock	A1

⊕ Activities, Courses & Tours
8 Amusement Park	C1
9 Global Sea Water Sauna	B1
10 Jeju City Tour Bus	A4

🛌 Sleeping
11 Backpackers in Jeju	C4
12 HK Jeju	C1
13 Hotel W	C1

⊗ Eating
14 Bagdad Cafe	C4
15 Dombaedon	C1
16 D-Stone Pub	A1
17 E-Mart Food Court	B1
18 Factory Bakery	B1
19 Haejin Seafood Restaurant	C1

⊜ Drinking & Nightlife
20 Craft Han's	C4
21 Factory	D4
22 Nilmori Dong Dong	A1

⊕ Entertainment
23 Band Shell	C1

ⓘ Information
24 Korean Air	C3
25 Tourist Information Centre Tapdong	C1
26 Tourist Information Centre Yongduam	A1

ⓘ Transport
27 I Love Bike	C1
28 Jeju Intercity Bus Terminal	A4
29 Mr. Lee's Bike Shop	B4

1. Ulleungdo (p172)
All that remains of an extinct volcano, this island has some of the best scenery in Korea

2. Heyri (p98)
This charming village near the publishing centre of Paju Book City is devoted to books

3. Seoraksan National Park (p129)
Designed as a Biosphere Protection site, this stunning park has forests, temples and wildlife

4. Hahoe Folk Village (p179)
Centuries-old Joseon-era homes have been preserved in this beautiful region

JEJU'S SEX MUSEUMS

Although attitudes are changing, Koreans tend to be conservative in public about sex. Pornography, for example, is illegal. So how come Jeju-do has three graphic sex museums? Chatting to locals, a couple of answers come up. The island gives tax breaks to anyone who runs a museum (which explains why Jeju-do has so many 'museums') and many honeymooning and vacationing visitors are already in the mood for frisky fun – these museums provide inspiration and education.

Jeju Loveland (제주러브랜드; ☑ 064 712 6988; www.jejuloveland.com; admission ₩9000; ⊙ 9am-11pm) This erotic theme park created by art students and graduates of Seoul's Hongik University features hundreds of sexy and frequently comic sculptures, soft-core art galleries and adult-toy stores. The park is a short drive from Jeju-si on Rte 1139; it's also a stop on the **Jeju Golden Bus City Tour** (p241).

Museum of Sex & Health (건강과 성 박물관; ☑ 064 792 5700; www.sexmuseum.or.kr; 1736 Gamsan-ri, Andeok-myeon; admission ₩12,000; ⊙ 10am-8pm; 🚌 702) In Gamsan-ri in southern Jeju-do, this huge complex has extensive sections devoted to sex education and sex culture from around the world. Laudable for its inclusivity, covering usually taboo subjects in Korea such as homosexuality, it also has some very imaginative installations.

Buses running on Rte 1132 between Seogwipo (₩3300, one hour, every 20 minutes) and Hwasun-ri stop near the museum in Andeok-myeon.

World Eros Museum (제주 세계성문화박물관; ☑ 064 739 0059; admission ₩7000; ⊙ 9am-7pm, last entry 6pm) The smallest of Jeju-do's sex-themed museums and perhaps the most artful. There's a collection of world erotic art, though the lack of English signage makes it a bit inaccessible. The adult-only museum is on the 2nd floor of Seogwipo's **World Cup Stadium** (p250).

In Seogwipo, frequent local buses run from Jungang Rotary to the World Cup Stadium (₩1200).

Backpackers in Jeju
HOSTEL ₩

(제주여행자숙소; ☑ 064 773 2077; http://cafe.naver.com/chejukorea; dm ₩25,000, r from ₩44,000; ❄ @ 🛜) Handy if you want to be in the City Hall party district. This quirky, foreigner-friendly place has a large area map on a blackboard, an extensive LP vinyl collection in the basement cafe-bar and iPads instead of TVs in the private rooms. It's down a lane next to Baskin Robbins.

★ Hotel W
MOTEL ₩₩

(☑ 064 757 0314; http://jejuw.co.kr; r ₩70,000; ❄ @) The modern rooms are good value compared to the surrounding properties in Tapdong. Every room has a computer – the one in 506 works well and has Chrome, a rarity in Korean motels. Off-season rates are negotiable. Ask for a room facing away from the ocean – the amusement park across the street is noisy until 9.30pm.

★ Baume Couture Boutique Hotel
HOTEL ₩₩₩

(☑ 064 798 8000; www.baume.co.kr; 95, Singwang-ro, Shin Jeju; r from ₩210,000; ❄ @ 🛜 ⛱) Oh so chic, this boutique hotel is Jeju-si's most stylish place to sleep. Up at the rooftop pool (open July and August), there are great views of Halla-san, weather permitting. Look for the cool building near the intersection of Singwang-ro and Yeonbuk-ro.

✖ Eating

Factory Bakery
BAKERY ₩

(☑ 064 720 8223; Tapdong; items from ₩3000; ⊙ 8am-8pm) The air inside this open-kitchen bakery is filled with the aroma of freshly baked breads, cakes and sweets...and it's not the phoney smell found in some popular brand-name bakeries. Decent sandwiches and coffee are also available.

E-Mart Food Court
KOREAN ₩

(Tapdong; meals from ₩5000; ⊙ 10am-11pm) This 5th-floor food court has sea views and plenty of cheap eats. The basement supermarket is ideal for self-catering.

★ Haejin Seafood Restaurant
SEAFOOD ₩₩

(해진횟집; ☑ 064 757 4584; Raw Fish St; meals ₩10,000-60,000; ⊙ 10.30am-midnight) Of the many restaurants overlooking the harbour,

Haejin is the largest and one of the most popular places to try Jeju-do's seafood specialities such as cuttlefish, eel, squid, octopus, sea cucumber and abalone. The set meal (₩30,000) feeds two people.

Bagdad Cafe INDIAN ₩₩

(☑064 757 8182; 8 Seogwang-ro 32-gil; meals from ₩9000; ☺noon-11pm; 🛜) This top date spot in the City Hall district has English-speaking staff and fine halal food. Standard Indian fare is here such as tandoori chicken and peanut butter masala, which tastes great with a large serving of garlic nan. Look for the pink building two blocks west of Jungang-ro.

D-Stone Pub INTERNATIONAL ₩₩

(meals from ₩8000; ☺5pm-2am) There's an eclectic range of dishes on the menu, from sushi to burgers, plus a decent selection of imported beers on tap. But really, you'll come here to admire the stunning ocean views while sitting on a patio near Yongduam Rock.

Dombaedon BARBECUE ₩₩₩

(돔베돈; ☑064 753 0008; http://dombaedon .co.kr; Tapdong; 180g serving ₩16,000; ☺noon-midnight) One of the better options on *heukdwaeji geori,* a street dedicated to barbecue restaurants serving the island's tastiest speciality, black pig. It's the corner restaurant with floor-to-ceiling windows.

Drinking

The prime nightlife spots are around City Hall and Shin Jeju, around Singwang-no.

Factory BAR

(☑010 9184 3431; 6, Gwangyang 13-gil; ☺7pm-3am Tue-Sun) Named after Andy Warhol's studio, the Factory is a dark and moody bar that attracts artists, musicians and other hipsters. It's a favourite haunt for Jeju-si's expat community. There's occasional live music.

Nilmori Dong Dong BAR

(닐모리동동; ☑064 745 5008; www.nilmori. com; ☺11am-11pm; 🛜) On the coastal road behind the airport is this eclectic cafe-bar-restaurant that often stages craft exhibitions and other arty events. A ₩6000 taxi ride from Shin Jeju, it's a worthwhile stop if you're looking for a place to eat, drink and sample the local arts scene before or after strolling the oceanfront promenade.

Craft Han's BAR

(크래프트 한스; ☑064 721 3336; http://craft hans.fordining.kr; ☺5pm-2am) Craft beer is on tap along with a decent selection of imported bottled brew at this cosy bar in the City Hall area. Side orders include cheesy deep-dish Chicago-style pizza plus salmon and chips. Look for the small building with a woody exterior and dark-green trim.

☆ Entertainment

Aroma Night DANCE

(☑064 746 7000; Singwang-ro, Shin Jeju; admission ₩20,000, sets from ₩50,000; ☺8pm-3am) Partygoers looking for something different come here to dance into the early hours amid exotic dancers, live music, DJs and a spectacular laser-light show. Dress casual but smart and come with a group if you want to experience Korea's *booking* culture.

In this, a male customer tips a waiter to bring a female to his table – a process of meeting new people in a culture that doesn't normally see strangers walking up to one another and introducing themselves.

Let's Run Park HORSE RACING

(렛츠런파크 제주; ☑064 741 9114; www.kra. co.kr; admission ₩2000; ☺12.30-5pm Fri & Sat, schedule varies; 🚌780, Jeju Horse Racing Park stop) Watch *jorangmal,* descendants of horses brought to the island by invading Mongols centuries ago, race around this track, 15km southwest from Jeju-si. The facilities are first-class, and there is a separate lounge for foreigners.

Several cross-island buses from Jeju-si, including 780, stop here (₩1300, 20 minutes, every 20 minutes). A taxi from Jeju-si costs ₩18,000.

❶ Information

Central Post Office (제주우체국; ☑064 722 0084; ☺9am-6pm Mon-Fri) The post office on Gwandeok-ro.

Jeju Welcome Center (☑064 740 6000; www. ijto.or.kr; 23 Seondeok-ro, Yeon-dong, Shin Jeju; ☺9am-6pm; 🛜) Tourist information and internet access.

KTO Tourist Information Jeju Office (☑064 742 0032; 1st fl, Jeju International Airport terminal; ☺9am-8pm; 🛜) Free internet and lots of maps.

Tourist Information Centre Jeju Airport (☑064 742 8866; ☺6.30am-8pm) Helpful staff; be sure to get a bus map and schedule.

JEJU-DO JEJU-SI

Tourist Information Centre Tapdong (☑ 064 728 3919; ☺ 9am-6pm) This small office is near the band shell.

Tourist Information Centre Yongduam (☑ 064 711 1022; ☺ 9am-6pm) Near Yongduam Rock.

ⓘ Getting There & Away

AIR

Flights connect Jeju-si with several mainland cities, plus a handful of international destinations in China and Japan. From Gimpo in Seoul, flights depart every 10 to 30 minutes, dawn to dusk. Except for holidays and the summer season, it's rarely necessary to pre-book. Advance one-way fares can start as low as ₩34,000 from Seoul and Busan.

Air Busan (☑ 1666 3060; www.flyairbusan. com) Regional air carrier based in Busan.

Asiana (☑ 2 2669 8000; www.flyasiana.com) Korea's second-largest carrier, after Korean Air.

Eastar Jet (☑ 82 1544 0080; www.eastarjet. com) Based out of Gimpo International Airport in Seoul.

Jeju Air (☑ 82 1599 1500; www.jejuair.net) Low-cost airline based in Jeju-si.

Korean Air (☑ 82 1558 2001; www.koreanair. co.kr) Korea's largest air carrier.

T'way Air (☑ 82 1688 8686; www.twayair.com) Low-cost carrier.

BOAT

Comfortable ferries sail between Jeju-si and three ports on the peninsula. Most ships have three classes: 3rd-class passengers sit on the floor in big rooms; 2nd class gets you a seat; 1st class gets you a private cabin with bed and bathroom.

Ferries berth at either Jeju Ferry Terminal or the International Ferry Pier, 2km further east. City bus 90 (₩1200, every 20 minutes) runs to and from both ferry terminals, but a taxi is more convenient. Contrary to the latter terminal's name, there are no international routes.

ⓘ Getting Around

TO/FROM THE AIRPORT

Jeju International Airport (제주국제공항; ☑1661 2626; http://www.airport.co.kr/ jejueng/index.do) is 1km from Shin Jeju and 4km from central Jeju-si.

The limousine airport bus 600 (every 20 minutes) drops off and picks up passengers at major hotels and resorts all around the island, including Jungmun Resort (₩4500, one hour),

FERRIES FROM JEJU-SI

DESTINATION	SHIP	TELEPHONE; WEBSITE	PRICE FROM (₩)	DURATION	FREQUENCY
Busan	Seokyung Paradise	☑ 051 469 5994; http://skferry. haewoon.co.kr	51,500	12hr	Tue, Thu, Sat
Busan	Seokyung Island	☑ 064 751 1901; http://skferry. haewoon.co.kr	47,000	12hr	Tue, Thu, Sat
Goheung (Nokdong)	Namhae Express Carway 7	☑ 064 723 9700	27,000	1hr 10min	Sun-Fri
Mokpo, Chujado & Jindo	Pink Dolphin	☑ 064 758 4234; http://seaferry.co.kr	38,000	20min-3hr	daily, closed 4th Wed
Mokpo	Seastar Cruise	☑ 064 758 4234; http://seaferry.co.kr	30,000	4hr 30min	Tue-Sun
Wando	Blue Narae	☑ 064 751 5050; www.hanilexpress. co.kr	37,000	2hr	4 daily, 2nd & 4th Wed closed
Wando	Hanil Car Ferry I	☑ 064 751 5050; www.hanilexpress. co.kr	26,250	2hr 50min	daily, 3rd Wed closed
Wando & Chujado	Hanil Car Ferry 3	☑ 064 751 5050; www.hanilexpress. co.kr	26,250	2-5hr	daily

JEJU CITY & AREA TOUR BUSES

Jeju Golden Bus City Tour (☑ 064 742 8862; http://en.jejugoldenbus.com; adult/child ₩12,000/10,000; ⊘ 8am-8.40pm) Explore Jeju-si on a golden bus. Jump on and off the bus all day at the city's best sights, including **Yongduam Rock** (p233) and **Loveland** (p238). There's a stop at the airport.

Jeju City Tour Bus (☑ 064 748 3211; http://english.jeju.go.kr; adult/child ₩5000/3000; ⊘ 8 departures 8am-5pm) A day pass on the Jeju City Tour Bus is an economical way to explore 19 sights on a circuit in and around Jeju-si. Key stops include **Saryeoni Forest** (p234), **Jeju Stone Park** (p234) and **Jeju April 3 Peace Park** (p254). Buses start at the Jeju-si intercity bus terminal.

Yeha Bus Tours (☑ 064 713 5505; www.yehatour.com; adult/youth ₩79,000/69,000; ⊘ 8.30am-5.30pm) You get bus travel, sight entrance fees, lunch and a guide to explain everything on this one-day excursion. The company operates three routes that run to some of the most popular destinations on the island: east – includes **Seongsan Ilchul-bong** (p245) and **Manjang-gul** (p242); west – includes **Hallim Park** (p262) and **Sanbangsan trek**; and south – includes **Eoseungsaengak Trail** (p259) and **Yakcheon temple** (p255).

Seogwipo (₩5000, 1½ hours) and the World Cup Stadium (₩5500, 1¾ hours).

Bus 100 shuttles between the airport and the city's bus terminal (₩1200, 10 minutes, every 20 minutes); bus 500 goes to Shin Jeju (₩1200, 15 minutes, every 20 minutes).

BICYCLE & SCOOTER
I Love Bike (아이러브바이크; ☑ 064 723 7775; www.bikejeju.com/introduce/rentguide.php; Samdo2-dong 14-4 Beon-ji; bicycle per day ₩7000-30,000; ⊘ 7am-8pm) English speaking, with a large choice of bikes. Look for the shop close to a post-office building near the intersection of Bukseong-ro and Gwandeong-ro 7-gil.

Mr. Lee's Bike Shop (☑ 064 758 6640; www.jejubike.co.kr; 163 Seosa-ro; 125cc scooter for 24hr ₩40,000; ⊘ 9am-6.30pm Mon-Sat) Recommended for bikes, scooters and motorcycles with 125cc engines.

You must be an experienced rider with an international driving licence to rent a scooter or motorcycle.

BUS
Streams of city and round-island buses originate from the **intercity bus terminal** (☑ 064 753 1153) on Seogwang-ro; tourist information offices can provide a timetable. Fares start at ₩1200.

CAR
Cars come with English-language navigation systems.
Avis (☑ 064 726 3322; www.avis.co.kr; ⊘ 8am-10pm) In the arrivals terminal.

SK Hertz (☑ 064 751 8000; https://www.hertz.com) In the arrivals terminal beside other rental agencies.

EASTERN JEJU-DO

Eastern Jeju-do includes the coastal area along Rte 1132 from Gimnyeong to Pyoseon, some inland sites and the ferry to Udo.

Most of the coastal destinations can be accessed by bus 701 (₩1300 to ₩3300, every 20 minutes from 5.40am to 9pm) as it shuttles between Jeju-si and Seogwipo.

Gimnyeong Beach
김녕해수욕장

The white sand of small **Gimnyeong beach** (김녕해수욕장; ☐ 701, Gimnyeong beach stop) contrasts with the black-lava rocks and wind turbines spinning round nearby. It's popular in summer with families wading in the shallow waters.

Buses from Jeju-si (₩2300, 45 minutes, every 20 minutes) stop near the beach.

🛏 Sleeping

Emerald Pension Castle　　　PENSION ₩₩
(에메랄드펜션개슬; ☑ 064 782 1110; http://emeraldcastle.co.kr; r from ₩50,000; ☐ 701, Gimnyeong Beach stop) This modest pension close to Gimnyeong beach is run by a friendly old woman. Rooms on the 2nd floor have more scenic views.

Jeju-do

Chujado (40km);
Wando (85km);
Mokpo (160km)

Busan
(300km)

JEJU STRAIT

Samyang
Beach

Hamdeok
Beach

Jeju-do
Ferry Terminal

Chocheon

8

56

Jeju-Si

Shin Jeju

53
40
55

**Jeju April 3
Peace Park**

1

1118

97

10

Gwakji
Beach

Aewol

1132

33

13

Biyangdo
2

41

Hallim

Mysterious Rd

22

23

Geumneung &
Hyeopjae
Beaches 7

49

54

31

6

Hallasan
National
Park

1131

1118

1120

1136

1135

32

Halla-san
(1950m)

36

11

9

1139

38

30

115

1132

Gosan

25

12 50

19

45

1115

1136

44

51

3

Wolpyeong

Jeongbang
Pokpo

18 29

21

20 39 Hwasun
Beach

37 47 14 28

24

34

Moseulpo

Hamo Beach

Songaksan

27

Jungmun Beach

Jungmun

Jigwido

Gapado

Marado
17

Manjang-gul
만장굴

👁 Sights

Manjang-gul   CAVE
(만장굴; ☑ 064 710 7905; http://jejuwnh.jeju.go.kr;
adult/youth ₩2000/₩1600; ⏰ 9am-5pm; 🚌 701,
Manjang-gui stop) Manjang-gul is the main access point to the world's longest system of
lava-tube caves. In total the caves are 7.4km
long, with heights between 2m and 23m. In
this section you can walk around 1km underground to a 7m-high lava pillar, the cave's

outstanding feature. The immense black
tunnel with swirling walls looks like the lair
of a giant serpent and it's hard to imagine the
geological forces that created it aeons ago,
moulding rock as if it were Play-Doh.

Take a jacket, as the cave ceiling drips
and the temperature inside is a chilly 10°C.
The lighting is dim so a torch (flashlight) is
a good idea. The ticket office is about 2.5km
from the Manjang-gul bus stop on Rte 1132;
a transfer to local bus 990 (₩1000, every 45
minutes to two hours) is possible, but arrival times are inconvenient. A taxi from Gimnyeong costs ₩7000.

Woljeong Beach
월정해수욕장

Woljeong Beach BEACH

(월정리 해변; 🚌701, Woljeong-ri stop) This hideaway beach is fast becoming a hotspot for young couples looking for good times near the ocean. Year-round, it's a fun place to stroll the beach and spend time in the funky beachside cafes and restaurants. Commercial development, so far, has been small scale.

From Jeju-si (₩2300, 55 minutes, every 20 minutes) buses run on Rte 1132; the beach is 500m from the bus stop.

🛏 Sleeping & Drinking

Gaga Pension PENSION

(가가펜션; 🕿064 782 5009; r ₩60,000, higher weekends & summer; 🅿❄🛜; 🚌701, Woljeong-ri stop) Just steps from Woljeong beach, this decent property has clean rooms with kitchens and balconies.

Woljeong-ri Lowa CAFE

(월정리 LOWA; 🕿064 783 2240; ⊙9am-9pm; 🚌701, Woljeong-ri stop) Here's a cafe with a nice beach vibe. Funky interior design, decent drinks, Sam Miguel with a side of fries on the roof overlooking Woljeong beach, and friendly, English-speaking staff. Toasted rice cake sprinkled with bean powder is a house speciality. Heavy, gooey and sticky, one order is probably enough for two people.

Sehwa-ri & Hado-ri
신양리, 하도리

Tucked into the northeast corner of the island, this pocket of quiet, rural life is often overlooked by tourists in a hurry to get down the road to Seongsan Ilchul-bong. Travellers with a car, and extra time, might consider getting off the main highway here and driving the Sehwa seashore road for splendid ocean views.

⊙ Sights

Haenyeo Museum MUSEUM

(해녀 박물관; 🕿064 710 7771; www.haenyeo. go.kr; adult/youth ₩1100/800; ⊙9am-6pm; 🚌701, museum stop) The highlight of Hado-ri, a small east-coast fishing town, is this museum, which does an excellent job explaining the history and culture of the amazing **haenyeo** (p245).

Gimnyeong Maze Park PARK

(김녕미로공원; 🕿064 782 9266; http://jeju maze.com; adult/child/youth ₩3300/1100/2200; ⊙8.30am-6pm; 🚌701, Manjang-gul stop) This popular maze is fun for adults and children. Created by American expat Fred Dunstin from 2232 Leyland cypress trees, it's fiendishly clever.

Getting here by bus is inconvenient, as it's a 30-minute walk from the 701 bus stop. A ₩6500 taxi from Gimnyeong here, followed by a 15-minute walk to Manjang-gul, is a cost-effective way to combine both sights in one trip.

Jeju-do

Buses from Jeju-si (₩2800, 80 minutes, every 20 minutes) stop near the museum entrance.

🛏 Sleeping & Eating

★ Ssari's Flower Hill   PENSION ₩₩
(☑ 010 9134 7741, 064 782 5933; www.jejussari. com; r incl breakfast ₩60,000, higher weekends & May-Sep; ❄️🛜) Surrounded by farms and woods, this beautiful countryside guest-house is an ideal location to get away from it all. Go for lazy walks on Hado beach (a few kilometres down the road), or grab some quiet time with a book and glass of wine in the 1st-floor coffee shop. It's run by a Japa-nese woman and her shaggy dog.

★ Dasi Boesi   KOREAN ₩
(다시버시; ☑ 064 783 5575; meal for 2 people ₩12,000-20,000; ☺11am-8pm; 🚍701, museum stop) If you've spent time exploring the Haenyeo Museum, do yourself a favour and eat here. This shop serves delicious feasts of grilled mackerel and tofu stew. Near the beach road, it's a 10-minute walk from the museum. Note: it doesn't serve lone diners.

Seongsan-ri & Sinyang-ri
성산리, 시냥리

A must-see destination, Seongsan-ri (Fortress Mountain Village) and the neigh-

HAENYEO: JEJU'S FREE DIVERS

Jeju-do is famous in Korea for its women, in particular the hardy *haenyeo*. Statues celebrate these free divers all along the coast and it's not uncommon to spot the real deal preparing to dive on the seashore or bobbing in the ocean.

For centuries Jeju-do women have been engaged in this form of fishing to gather shellfish, sea cucumbers, spiky black sea urchins and anything else edible. Working as co-operatives and sharing their catch, they use low-tech gear – polystyrene floats, flippers, nets, knives and spears – but no oxygen tanks. Until recently they didn't wear wetsuits, despite diving for long hours in all weather. They are able to hold their breath underwater for up to two minutes and reach a depth of 20m. Great physical stamina is a prerequisite and yet many of the *haenyeo* are in their 60s, if not older.

With around 5000 *haenyeo* on Jeju-do (down from a peak of 30,000 in the 1950s), it's a dying profession – daughters these days are not keen to follow in their mothers' flippers. However, since 2008, at Hallim, a school has been helping to preserve the legacy by teaching anyone who wants to learn the *haenyeo*'s free-diving skills. Call ☑ 011 691 6675 to find out how to take part in a one-day experience.

Brenda Paik-Sunoo's book *Moon Tides: Jeju Island Grannies of the Sea* and the 2004 movie *My Mother the Mermaid* provide insights into the lives of *haenyeo*.

bouring village of Sinyang-ri are at the foot of a spectacular extinct volcano that rises straight out of the ocean. Black-sand beaches are nearby, as is the lovely island of Udo and the Seopji-koji peninsula, with breathtaking architecture by the Japanese master Ando Tadao.

⊙ Sights & Activities

★ **Seongsan Ilchul-bong** VOLCANO
(성산일출봉; http://jejuwnh.jeju.go.kr; adult/youth ₩2000/1000; ⊙1hr before sunrise-8pm; 🚊 701, Seongsan stop) This majestic 182m-high tuff volcano, shaped like a giant punchbowl, is one of Jeju-do's most impressive sights. The forested crater is ringed by jagged rocks, though there's no lake because the rock is porous. From the entrance, climbing the steep stairs to the crater rim only takes 20 minutes. Doing it in time to catch the sunrise is a life-affirming journey for many Koreans – expect plenty of company.

To do the sunrise expedition, you'll have to spend the night in Seongsan-ri, a sleepy village filled with motels and restaurants catering to the hiking crowd. The steps up the volcano are easy and clear, but if you're concerned, bring a torch. Not an early riser? It's also a popular daytime hike. The Seongsan Sunrise Festival, an all-night New Year's Eve party, is held here every 31 December.

Ilchul-bong Beach BEACH
(🚊 701, Seongsan stop) At the eastern base of Seongsan Ilchul-bong (p245), a long staircase leads down to this lovely crescent-shaped cove backed by weather-beaten lava cliff walls and boulders. On the left side of the beach, *haenyeo* divers run a small restaurant and put on a performance of their skills every day at 1.30pm and 3pm. Next to the restaurant, small **speedboats** (per trip ₩10,000) can whisk you out to sea for another perspective on Ilchul-bong.

Phoenix Island ARCHITECTURE
(☑ 064 731 7000; www.phoenixisland.co.kr; Seopji-koji; adult/child ₩2000/1000; ⊙9am-6pm) Coachloads of tourists disgorge here daily to view the scenic location that has been featured in several Korean TV dramas and movies. But the real stars of the Seopji-koji Peninsula are two pieces of architecture by Ando Tadao: **Glass House**, housing the restaurant Mint (p247), and the amazing **Genius Loci**, a gallery with site-specific works that aid meditation. Both buildings are angled to frame Seongsan Ilchul-bong (p245), providing yet more perspectives on the volcano.

A taxi here from Seongsan-ri is around ₩5000.

Sea Life Scuba DIVING
(씨라이프 다이브 리조트; ☑ 010 5283 8144, 064 783 0012; http://sealifekorea.com; Seongsan-po; ⊙7am-6pm) Mr Park speaks some English and can take you diving inside underwater caves and around coral reefs. A day trip with two dives costs ₩150,000, including guide and equipment.

Seongsan Ilchul-bong

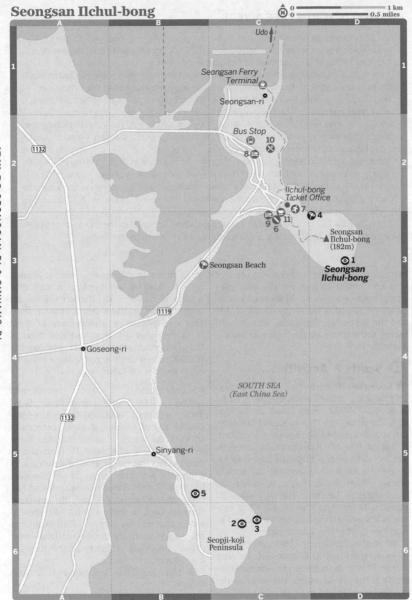

🛏 Sleeping

There's plenty of accommodation in Seongsan-ri. You'll also find grannies on the main road to Ilchul-bong offering *minbak* (private) rooms.

Seongsanpo Village HOTEL ₩₩
(성산포빌리지; ☎064 782 2373; r ₩40,000; ❀@) Sit out on a balcony with a wonderful view of the sea and anything going on along the harbour road. It also has a good restaurant on the ground floor.

Bomulseom   PENSION **WWW**
(보물섬; ☏064 784 0039; r from ₩50,000; ✳@☎✖) This hilltop pension has well-kept and equipped self-catering rooms with en-closed balconies. In July and August a swim-ming pool is available. It's on a hill, a block off the main road, surrounded by a few other motels.

Phoenix Island   APARTMENT **WWW**
(☏064 731 7000; www.phoenixisland.co.kr; apt from ₩300,000; ✳@☎✖) The enormous and comfortable self-catering apartments at this resort are great for families or groups of friends to share. You have ac-cess to plenty of on-site facilities, nearby beaches and beautiful views of Seongsan Ilchul-bong.

✖ Eating & Drinking

There's a good number of restaurants and cafes in and around the entrance of Seong-san Ilchul-bong.

Haeddeuneun   SEAFOOD **WW**
(해뜨는식당; ☏064 782 3380; mains from ₩10,000; ☺8am-9pm) At the top of a hill and close to a cliff with great ocean views, this place is a little apart from the cluster of restaurants at the foot of Seongsan Ilchul-bong. The menu covers many common local options, including abalone rice porridge, sea-urchin soup and seafood hotpot.

Mint   INTERNATIONAL **WWW**
(☏064 731 7000; www.phoenixisland.co.kr; set lunch/dinner from ₩40,000/56,000; ☺11.30am-10pm; ☎) Dining inside Ando Tadao's Glass House is a delightful experience, one best enjoyed during the day when you can take in the coastal views through the floor-to-ceiling windows. The menu offers high-grade local produce such as black pork.

Café It Suda   CAFE
(커피잇수다; ☏070 4416 2510; ☺9am-7pm; ☎) There are plenty of chain cafes around Seongsan Ilchul-bong, but this independent, artsy cafe has bags more charm. It also sells Olle Trail souvenirs and other attractive lo-cal items. It's on the village's main road, near the street leading to the Ilchul-bong ticket office.

ⓘ Getting There & Away

Buses (₩3300, 1½ hours, every 20 minutes) run to Seongsan-ri from Jeju-si and Seogwipo bus terminals. Make sure the bus goes right into Seongsan-ri as a few stay on the main road, dropping you 2.5km from the village centre.

From the Seongsan ferry terminal boats sail to Udo (return ₩5500, 15 minutes, at least hourly from 8am to 5pm) and Jangheung (one way adult/child ₩37,000/18,500, two hours 20 minutes, two to four daily) in Jeolla-do; see www. jhferry.com for details.

Seongeup Folk Village
성읍민속마을

Give yourself an hour to explore the narrow lanes zigzagging alongside lava rock walls, traditional homes with thatched roofs, more than a few *hareubang* (old grandfather) statues and the occasional baby black pig in this **folk village** (성읍민속마을; ☺24hr; ▣ 720, Seongeup Folk Village stop) **FREE**. If the gate poles are down, you're welcome to en-ter. Modern intrusions into the village in-clude souvenir shops, restaurants and car parks, but most of it still looks fantastically feudal. Look out for the Confucian school and the 1000-year-old zelkova tree.

The village is surrounded by a fortress wall punctuated by ornate entrance gates; Nammun (south gate) is the main gate.

✖ Eating

★**Yetnal Patjuk**   KOREAN **W**
(옛날 팥죽; ☏064 787 3357; mains from ₩5500; ☺10am-5pm Tue-Sun; ☎; ▣720, Seongeup Folk

Seogwipo

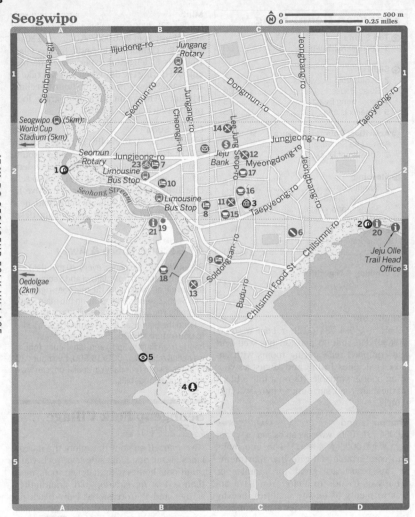

Village stop) Everything about this restaurant, housed in a traditional building, is inviting. Inside the door you're greeted by warm smiles and the sweet earthy aroma of red beans. Excellent soups and porridge are served here, including some made from lotus flowers, pumpkin and seaweed. Wooden tables, exposed beams and heavy earthenware add to the rustic charm.

Coming from the south gate, go to the first intersection and turn left. Go about 50m and turn left at the first street. The restaurant is down the road – Seongeup Minseok-ro – on the left. Look for the shop with a gravel parking lot.

Gwandangnae Sikdang KOREAN ₩₩
(관당네식당; ☑ 064 787 1055; mains from ₩12,000; ⊗ 8am-7pm; ☐ 720, Seongeup Folk Village stop) The ebullient owner of this restaurant is known for his succulent black-pig pork dishes – a massive banquet for two is ₩35,000. From the small retail plaza outside the south gate, walk about 50m into the hamlet of traditional buildings. Look for the shop with a weather-worn Korean flag.

Seogwipo

ⓘ Getting There & Away

From Jeju-si, take bus 720 (₩2300, one hour, every 20 minutes) and get off at the stop at the car park near Nammun. From Seogwipo, take bus 701 east to Pyoseon (₩2300, 50 minutes, every 20 minutes) and transfer to bus 720 to Seongeup (₩1200, 10 minutes, every 20 minutes). A taxi from Pyoseon is about ₩7000.

SOUTHERN JEJU-DO

If you only have a short time on Jeju-do, make Segwipo your base. It has the best climate and coastal scenery, plus easy access to Halla-san and Seongsan Ilchul-bong.

Seogwipo
서귀포

POP 155,000

Jeju-do's second-largest city is beautifully situated on a rocky volcanic coastline dotted with lush parks, a deep gorge and two waterfalls. The clear blue waters and mild ocean temperatures make Seogwipo Korea's best scuba-diving destination and it's also an ideal base for hiking.

The town centre (up a steep slope from the harbour) is full of motels and hotels. The main bus terminal and other attractions are clustered around the World Cup Stadium, 6km west of town in Shin Seogwipo. Jungmun Resort is also within easy day-trip distance.

⊙ Sights

Lee Jung-Seop Art Gallery & Park MUSEUM
(☑ 064 760 3567; http://jslee.seogwipo.go.kr; Lee Jung-Seob St; adult/youth ₩1000/500; ⊙ 9am-6pm Tue-Sun) On the street that is named after him, and decorated with images from his distinctive paintings and drawings, is this small museum devoted to Lee Jung-Seop (1916–56). Outside, on a lovely manicured lawn with fragrant trees, is the traditional Jeju house in which the artist lived for a short time in 1951. A four-day festival is held in September to celebrate Lee.

Saeyeon-gyo & Saeseom BRIDGE, ISLAND
(새연교 | 새섬; ⊙ dawn-11pm) FREE The attractive cable-stayed Saeyeon-gyo **bridge** at the mouth of Seogwipo Harbour provides access to densely wooded Saeseom (Sod Island), around which runs a shady 1.1km trail. It's a favourite spot to stroll at sunset and the bridge is also nicely illuminated at night.

Cheonjiyeon Pokpo WATERFALL
(천지연폭포; adult ₩2000, youth & child ₩1000; ⊙ 7am-10pm) This 22m-high waterfall is reached after a 10-minute walk through a beautifully forested, steep gorge. The waterfall can be impressive following heavy rain; at other times it's more noisy than wide. Well worth visiting in the evening, too, when the illuminated gorge takes on a romantic atmosphere. The falls are on Olle Trail 6.

WORTH A TRIP

JEJU-DO SEOGWIPO

UDO 우도

The largest of 62 islets surrounding Jeju-do, and supposedly shaped like a sprawled-out cow, Udo (Cow Island), 3.5km off the coast from Seongsan-ri, is a beautiful, occasionally barren, place that attracts throngs of tourists, particularly on weekends and holidays. Though light on interesting sights, Udo's main attractions for independent travellers are its rugged natural beauty and the allure of splendid isolation.

Entry to the island, which is a provincial maritime park, is included when you buy your ferry ticket. **Car ferries** (☑064 782 5671) cross to Udo's southern port in **Cheonjin** (천진항) or western port in **Haumokdong** (하우목동항) from Seongsan port (return ₩5500, 15 minutes, at least hourly from 8am to 5pm). The ticket office is at the far end of Seongsan port, a 15-minute walk from Seongsan-ri.

Plenty of operations at either Udo port rent bicycles (three hours ₩10,000), scooters (two hours ₩25,000) and quad bikes (two hours ₩30,000). An international driving licence is required to rent motorised vehicles. The easiest, though least convenient, option is to ride an island tour bus, which makes four slightly hurried stops: Udo-bong, Dongangyeonggul Cave, Hagosudong beach and Seobin White Sand Beach (₩5000, buy ticket at either ferry port). Departures follow ferry arrivals.

Hongjodangoe Haebin Beach (홍조단괴해빈 해수욕장) Gorgeous Hongjodangoe Haebin (sometimes called Red Algae beach) has brilliant white coral sand stretching out in a crescent-shaped beach. Located on the west coast, between the two ports, it's a popular family destination during the summer months.

Udo Lighthouse Park (우도 등대 공원; ☑064 783 0180; ⊗sunrise-sunset) A short drive from Cheonjin Port, expect grassy hills overlooking rugged rock formations, steep steps up to the lighthouse, spectacular views of rural Udo from **Udo-bong** (Udo Peak) and an endless parade of travellers taking selfies.

Jeju Olle Trail Route 1-1 A great way to explore Udo is following the 15.9km Jeju Olle Trail Rte 1-1. The moderately challenging trail runs past the island's two ports and main sites, including Hongjodangoe Haebin beach. There are plenty of *minbak* (private houses that rent rooms) and guesthouses here, as well as places to eat.

Chocolate Castle by the Sea (빨간머리 앤의 집; ☑064 784 2171; http://anne-of-udo. com; burgers from ₩10,000; ⊗9am-3pm Wed-Mon) This wonderfully eclectic shop serves oh-so-juicy hamburgers. There is no chocolate here, but you will find a delightful museum housing a nearly complete collection of **Anne of Green Gables memorabilia**, including a 1908 first edition of the Lucy Maud Montgomery book. It's opposite Hongjodangoe Haebin beach.

Jeongbang Pokpo WATERFALL
(정방폭포; adult/youth ₩2000/1000; ⊗9am-6pm) A favorite with photographers, this 23m-high waterfall is a 15-minute walk east of the town centre. At times less dramatic than the island's other waterfalls, its claim to fame is that it's the only waterfall in Asia that falls into the ocean.

World Cup Stadium STADIUM
(제주 월드컵 경기장; Shin Seogwipo; ⊗Dak Paper Doll Museum 9am-7pm; ℗) Six kilometres west of central Seogwipo, this graceful soccer stadium built for the 2002 World Cup is the centrepiece of an entertainment complex that includes a multiplex cinema, E-Mart discount store, a family water park, a paper doll museum and World Eros Museum (p238), one of Jeju's trio of museums devoted to sex.

🏃 Activities

Oedolgae WALKING
(외돌개; 🚌8, Oedolgae stop) At the junction of Rtes 6 and 7 on the Olle Trail, about 2km west of Seogwipo, is this impressive 20m-tall volcanic basalt pillar jutting out of the ocean. Oedolgae (meaning 'Lonely Rock') is a pleasant walk through pine forests to a beautiful cliffside lookout at Sammae-bong Park.

Catch the bus (₩1200, 20 minutes) at the Jungang Rotary and get off at the last stop.

Big Blue 33
DIVING

(☑019 9755 1733, 064 733 1733; www.big blue33.co.kr; Chilispri 4 ro; ⊙9am-7pm) Run by German expat Ralf Deutsch, a diving enthusiast who speaks English, German and Korean. A two-tank dive trip costs ₩120,000 with all equipment and guide. An eight-day Master Scuba Diver course costs ₩600,000.

🛏 Sleeping

Backpacker's Home
HOSTEL ₩

(☑064 763 4000; http://backpackershome.com; dm ₩24,000, private r from ₩66,000; ❄@☎) One of Seogwipo's better backpacker hostels, this one has spacious dorms, each with its own bathroom, sleeping four in sturdy pine bunks, English-speaking staff, a great outdoor terrace and a midnight curfew.

★Hotel Little France
HOTEL ₩₩

(☑064 732 4552; www.littlefrancehotel.co.kr; r ₩50,000-90,000; ❄@☎) This modern, stylish hotel is a cut above others in its class and provides guests with a choice of four room styles: modern, oriental, antique and royal classic. The manager speaks English.

Shinsung Hotel
MOTEL ₩₩

(신성호텔; ☑064 732 1415; r ₩50,000; ❄@) A classy motel with a hard-to-miss metal-and-chequerboard exterior. Rooms include a computer and spa. Some rooms have balconies and those with a sea view cost ₩10,000 extra, even if it's too misty to see the sea.

Sun Beach Hotel
HOTEL ₩₩

(☑064 732 5678; Taepyeong-ro 363, Seogwi-dong 820-1; r from ₩70,000; ❄☎) A reasonable option if you're into retro and hanker for those midrange tourist hotels that resemble a grand dame somewhat past her prime, but still retaining an air of faded gentility.

🍴 Eating

Seogwipo Olle Market
MARKET ₩

(서귀포 올레시장; Jungjeong-ro; ⊙6am-6pm) Browse stalls of wonderful fruit and live seafood. It's a good place to pick up snacks for a picnic.

Meokbo Bunsik
DUMPLING ₩

(먹보분식; ☑064 733 0059; meals from ₩2000; ⊙24hr) Handy for late-night snacking is this cheap diner with homemade *mandu* (dumplings) steaming in big pots outside and *gimbap* (Korean sesame-oil flavoured rice wrapped in seaweed) on the menu.

★Saesom Galbi
BARBECUE ₩₩

(새섬 갈비; ☑064 732 4001; mains ₩12,000-30,000; ⊙10am-11pm; ℗☎) Down an alley and perched on a cliff overlooking the harbour, this is the place for barbecued beef or pork. The atmosphere is informal and boisterous thanks to the weathered floors, open dining concept and giddy staff. Side dishes are modest, but the meat is top-notch.

Kkomjirak
INTERNATIONAL ₩₩

(꼼지락키친; ☑064 763 0204; Lee Jung Seob St; mains ₩7000-10,000; ⊙10am-11pm Mon-Sat; ☎) One of many convivial cafes on Seogwipo's art street, this one serves brunch with a bagel, scrambled eggs, bacon and salad as well as French toast with Canadian maple syrup.

🍷 Drinking

★Cafe Mayb
CAFE

(메이비; ☑070 4143 0639; Lee Jung Seob St; ⊙11am-1am; ☎) Creatively decorated inside, with tables spilling onto the street, Seogwipo's most laid-back cafe is the place to meet friends or enjoy downtime with a book.

Architecture Cafe Utopia
CAFE

(건축카페 유토피아; ☑064 762 2597; http://cafe.daum.net/jejuarchitecture; ⊙10am-10pm) One of the most inspired cafes you'll ever see. This multilevel complex is part cafe, beer bar, gallery and tree fort. If you visit at night, be sure to find the room with a model horse. It's on a corner, one block west of Lee Jung-Seob St.

Rose Marin
CAFE, BAR

(로즈마린 노천카페; ☑064 762 2808; ⊙noon-3am) Rose Marin is a tumbledown waterfront shack with giant trees growing through the floorboards. It's quirky, gritty and delightful. Be sure to try the dried squid, Korea's classic beer-bar side dish.

Ba Nong
CAFE, BAR

(바농; ☑064 763 7703; http://blog.naver.com/windsing1; Lee Jung Seob St; ⊙8am-midnight; ☎) A relaxed place with soothing music, serving a good selection of caffeinated drinks and beer. There's also a small selection of food, including pasta dishes and sandwiches. Look for the cafe with planters on the footpath.

ℹ Information

Bus Terminal Tourist Information Office (서귀포 시외버스터미널 관광안내소; ☑064 739

KEREN SU / GETTY IMAGES ©

MINGHU / GETTY IMAGES ©

1. Tap-sa (p269)
A pagoda temple inside Maisan Provincial Park; its stone towers all represent religious ideas

2. Triumphal Arch (p313)
The Pyongyang landmark celebrates Kim Il-sung's speech to Koreans at the end of Japanese occupation in 1945

3. Jirisan National Park (p206)
The mountains of Jirisan offer some of the best hiking in Korea

LOCAL KNOWLEDGE

JEJU'S GEMS

Douglas MacDonald, a 14-year resident of Jeju-do, is a photographer for the *Jeju Weekly* and Getty Images. His job regularly takes him off the tourist trail to some of the island's more intriguing sights. Here are his recommendations.

Kim Young Gap Gallery Dumoak (김영갑갤러리두모악; ☑ 064 784 9907; www.dumoak. com; adult/child/teen ₩3000/1000/2000; ☺ 9.30am-6pm Thu-Tue, daily Jul & Aug; ☒ 701, Samdal-ri 2 stop) The reason for pausing at Samdal-ri, a coastal village between Sinyang-ri and Pyoseon beach, is to view the stunning images at this countryside gallery. Kim (1957–2005) was a talented, self-taught photographer who documented the island's landscape. In the last years of his life he moved into an abandoned school, which he transformed into a studio (now gallery) and sculpture-filled garden.

From Samdal-ri 2 bus stop (from Jeju-si ₩3300, 1½ hours, every 20 minutes), the gallery is a 1.4km walk; it's also on Olle Trail Rte 3.

Jeju April 3 Peace Park (제주 4·3 평화공원; ☑ 064 710 8461; http://jeju43.jeju.go.kr/index.php; ☺ 9am-6pm, closed 1st & 3rd Mon of the month; ℗) Thoughtful and evocative, this museum chronicles the events that led up to and followed the 'April 3 Incident' – a series of island massacres between 1947 and 1954 that resulted in 30,000 deaths and the destruction of many homes. The reasons behind the deaths are complex and the museum takes a factual and artistic approach that heightens the emotional impact. It's on the **Jeju City Tour Bus** (p241) route.

Jeju Peace Museum (제주 전쟁역사평화박물관; ☑ 064 772 2500; www.peacemuseum. co.kr; adult ₩6000, youth & child ₩4000; ☺ 8.30am-6pm) Gama Oreum is a parasitic volcano that hides an underground fortress created by the Japanese army in the final stages of WWII. Explore some of the 2km of tunnels, and a good selection of Japanese military memorabilia, in this decent but modest museum that will appeal to hard-core history enthusiasts.

1391; ☺ 9am-6pm) Next to the bus terminal in the World Cup Stadium (p250).

Jeju Bank (Jungjeong-ro) Global ATM with a ₩1,000,000 withdrawal limit.

Jeongbang Pokpo Tourist Information (정방폭포 관광안내소; ☑ 064 733 1530) Kiosk located at Jeongbang Pokpo waterfall (p250).

Seogwipo Tourist Information Centre (서귀포 종합관광안내소; ☑ 1330; ☺ 9am-6pm) Next to the Cheonjiyeon Pokpo ticket office.

❶ Getting There & Around

The fastest way here from the airport in Jeju-si is bus 600 (₩6000, 1½ hours, every 20 minutes). Cross-island buses, such as the 780, are cheaper but slower (₩3300, two hours, every 20 minutes).

Seogwipo bus terminal is 6km west of the town centre, next to the World Cup Stadium. Frequent buses (₩1200, 10 minutes) run from here to the Jungang Rotary, the city-centre junction for local buses. Seogwipo itself is small enough to walk around, but taxis are plentiful and cheap.

From the World Cup Stadium terminal, buses (usually departing every 20 minutes) head east to Seongsan (701, ₩3300, two hours), west to Hallim (702, ₩3300, two hours), north to Seongpanak along Rte 1131, the eastern stop for

Hallasan (780, ₩2300, 40 minutes) and north to Yeongsil along Rte 1139 (also called Rd 1100), the western entrance to Hallasan (740, ₩2300, 40 minutes).

SCOOTER & BIKE

Scooter & Free Zone (스쿠터 앤 프리존; ☑ 064 762 5296; http://jejusfz.co.kr; Seomun-ro, 29 Beon-gil, 38-6 Seogwi-dong; 50/125cc scooter per 24hr ₩20,000/25,000, bicycle/electric bicycle ₩10,000/15,000; ☺ 9am-7pm) Explore Seogwipo and Jeju-do the easy way: with your own wheels. Travellers need an international driving licence to rent scooters and must be aged 21 or over. Higher prices in July and August.

Jungmun Resort & Around 중문 휴양지

Located a 25-minute bus ride west of Seogwipo, Jungmun Resort is South Korea's primary tourist-resort town. Because it's popular, sprawling development – luxury hotels, buffet restaurants and kitschy museums – surrounds the area's pockets of natural beauty.

The town's vibe is like Niagara Falls – filled with imaginative ways to extract money from honeymooning couples and busloads of travellers. Like Niagara, nature is the draw, and Jungmun does have a couple of nice spots, though they are less impressive than the marketing bumf might suggest. The coastline is breathtaking, the two waterfalls interesting and the beach rather small, packed during the summer, dead quiet at night and less scenic than many others on the island. If time is short and you're on a budget, take a pass on Jungmun and head to some of the island's truly interesting beach areas.

If you do come, be sure to visit the helpful and well-stocked **tourist information centre** (☑ 064 738 1393; ⊙ 9am-6pm), located near the town's busy intersection.

◉ Sights

Cheonjeyeon Pokpo WATERFALL
(천제연폭포; adult ₩2500, youth & child ₩1370; ⊙ sunrise-sunset) Jungmun's top natural attraction is this legendary waterfall, a three-tier cascade tucked inside a forested gorge. Above soars an arched footbridge decorated with sculptures of the nymphs who served the Emperor of Heaven and who, it is said, used to slide down moonbeams to bathe here. There's an entrance to the falls near the Yeomiji Botanical Garden.

Jusangjeollidae AREA
(주상절리대; ☑ 064 738 1532; adult/youth ₩2000/1000; ⊙ 8am-sunset) Just south of the Jeju International Convention Centre is a dramatic 2km stretch of coastline known for rectangular rock columns that look as if they were stamped out with a cookie cutter. The formations are the result of the rapid cooling and contraction of lava as it poured into the sea. This spectacular rock formation – called Daepo Jusangjeolli – is part of Olle Trail Rte 8.

Yakcheon-sa TEMPLE
(약천사; ☑ 064 738 5000; www.yakchunsa.org; ⊙ sunrise-sunset; ◻ 600, Yakcheon-sa stop) **FREE**
Although construction of this Buddhist temple was completed in 1997, it is one of Jeju-do's most impressive buildings. The ornate hall is filled with vibrant murals of scenes from Buddha's life and teachings. The main hall has galleries overlooking a 3m-tall statue of Buddha. The temple is about 2km east of Jungmun. It's not far from the start of Jeju Olle Rte 8.

Yakcheon-sa offers several English programs. There is a one-night Basic (₩30,000 per person) and Experience (₩50,000) Templestay program, the latter offering more things to do, as well as a two-night stay (₩60,000). Program schedules are not fixed but require a minimum of five guests. Travellers in a hurry might consider the Templelife program (₩20,000), a three-hour crash course that includes bead making, meditation walking and a back-breaking 108 deep bows.

Yeomiji Botanical Garden GARDENS
(여미지식물원; ☑ 064 735 1100; www.yeomiji. or.kr; adult/child/youth ₩9000/5000/6000; ⊙ 9am-6pm) This impressive botanical garden has a huge indoor section with areas that mimic rainforests, deserts and other landscapes. The surrounding plantings and designs include Italian, Japanese, palm and herb gardens. It's a 10-minute walk from the Teddy Bear Museum.

Jungmun Beach BEACH
(중문해수욕장; kayak/boogie board per 2hr ₩15,000/5000) The resort's palm-fringed beach becomes crowded in July and August. Walk up the steps to the Hyatt Regency Hotel, continue along the boardwalk and down the steps to reach an even more scenic and secluded beach – aquamarine water and golden sand backed by sheer black cliffs eroded into cylindrical shapes.

Teddy Bear Museum MUSEUM
(테디베어 유지엄; www.teddybearmuseum. com; adult/child/youth ₩8000/6000/7000; ⊙ 9am-8pm) A supremely kitsch gathering of stuffed teddies in poses ranging from Mona Lisa to Elvis.

🏃 Activities

Shangri-la Yacht Tour CRUISE
(요트투어 샹그릴라; ☑ 064 738 2111; www.y-tour.com; 30min/1hr cruise from ₩40,000/60,000) Local yacht tours provide a unique look at the incredible geological creations along the coast. Basic tours run for 30 minutes, though there are other options, including a 60-minute sunrise tour. Buy a ticket inside the Jungmun Tourist Complex.

Jungmun Beach Golf Club GOLF
(중문골프클럽; ☑ reservations 064 736 1202, 064 735 7241; green fees ₩90,000-130,000, cart & caddy extra) This PGA-calibre golf course, perched on a seaside cliff, might be the most scenic 18 holes in the country. At

6820m it's the country's longest course. Unlike some clubs, nonmembers can play here (reservations required). Right-hand clubs (no lefties) are available for hire (₩40,000).

🛏 Sleeping

Minbak, pensions and restaurants are strung along the main local road, Cheonjeyeon-ro, while the luxury hotels and the Jungmun Tourist Complex are beside or near the beach, all accessible from Jungmungwanggwan-ro.

Gold Beach Minbak
MOTEL **WW**

(골드비치민박; ☎ 064 738 7511; r ₩50,000; 🌣) Simple, clean, private rooms in a central location at a decent rate are surprisingly hard to find in Jungmun, but this modest property has all of those features. It's a 10-minute walk to the tourist information centre and 30 minutes to the beach. Look for a peach-and-green building with a ground-floor restaurant.

★ Seaes Hotel & Resort
HOTEL **WWW**

(씨에스호텔 앤 리조트; ☎ 064 735 3000; www.seaes.co.kr; r/ste from ₩300,000/410,000; P🌣@🛜) This gorgeous property delivers luxury with a rustic theme. Just 26 cottages, many with traditional stone walls and thatched roofs, coupled with landscaped gardens create a relaxed and secluded environment. Throw in a dramatic sunset and it's easy to understand why several Korean

---

JEJU-DO FOOD & DRINK

Jeju-do speciality meats include *heukdwaeji* (pork from the local black-skinned pig), *kkwong* (pheasant) and *basme* (horse), served in a variety of ways, including raw.

All kinds of fish and seafood are available from restaurants and direct from **haenyeo** (p245), the island's famous female divers. Try *galchi* (hairtail), *godeungeo* (mackerel) or *jeon-bok* (abalone), often served in *jeonbok-juk* (a rice porridge). *Okdomgui* is a tasty local fish that is semi-dried before being grilled.

Halla-bong tangerines are common. Also look out for prickly-pear jam, black *omija* tea and honey. Hallasan *soju* (vodka) is smoother than some.

TV dramas, including *Boys over Flowers*, have filmed here.

Lotte Hotel Jeju
HOTEL **WWW**

(롯데호텔 제주; ☎ 064 731 1000; www.lottehoteljeju.com; r from ₩340,000; 🌣@🛜) Las Vegas comes to Jeju-do with this over-the-top resort. The gardens have windmills, a boating lake and a swimming pool surrounded by fake rocks. A nightly outdoor show involves music, lights, fountains, volcanoes and dragons. There are plenty of kid-friendly activities and Hello Kitty fans will want to book one of the three themed rooms.

🍴 Eating

Ha Young
BARBECUE **WWW**

(하영; ☎ 064 738 6011; http://hayoung.ejeju.net; mains ₩25,000-50,000; ⏱10am-10pm) This popular barbecue restaurant specialises in Jeju-do's famous black pig. The meat is good, though the service is more hurried than friendly. It's on the main street, a couple of blocks from the tourist information centre. Look for the tall grey building with blue fairy lights.

Jeju Mawon
KOREAN **WWW**

(제주 마원; ☎ 064 738 1000; www.jejumawon.com; mains ₩15,000-45,000; ⏱11am-10pm; P🌣) Jeju-do's less famous speciality meat – horse – is served in this splendid traditional restaurant housed in a spacious *hanok* building. The food, which also includes beef and pork, is great and the presentation, wonderful. For best results, avoid overcooking horsemeat, otherwise it becomes rather tough.

ℹ Getting There & Away

Frequent buses, including 702 and 600, shuttle between Seogwipo and Jungmun's main street (₩1300, 25 minutes, every 20 minutes), 2.3km from the beach. From Jeju-si, the fastest bus is 600 (₩5000, one hour, every 20 minutes).

Sagye-ri

Hugging the southwest corner of the island, this sleepy village boasts a number of terrific sights, including the imposing Sanbang-san (395m), dramatic coastlines and incredible rock formations. There are several guesthouses on the narrow road running between Sanbang-san and Sagye's port, which is a good place to eat, if you like seafood.

Sights & Activities

Sanbanggul-sa
TEMPLE

(산방굴사; adult/child ₩2500/1000, parking ₩1000; ☉sunrise-sunset; Ⓟ) A steep, 20-minute walk up the south face of the craggy Sanbang-san is a stone Buddha in a 5m-high cave called Sanbanggul-sa. From Sagye-ri, the walk up looks more daunting than it really is, but after reaching the cave you'll be delighted because of the powerful 'wow' factor. Lower down, by the ticket office, are more-modern shrines and statues.

Hamel Memorial
MUSEUM

(하멜상선전시관; incl in Sanbanggul-sa ticket price) The Hamel Memorial is housed in a replica of a Dutch ship. Hendrick Hamel (1630–92), one of the survivors of a shipwreck near Jeju in 1653, was forced to stay in Korea for 13 years before escaping in a boat to Japan. Later he was the first Westerner to write a book on the 'hermit kingdom'.

★Yongmeori Coast
WALKING

(용머리해안; incl in Sanbanggul-sa ticket price; ☉8am-5.30pm) A short walk from Sanbanggul-sa towards the ocean brings you to the Yongmeori coast, a spectacular seaside trail with soaring cliffs pockmarked by erosion into catacombs, narrow clefts and natural archways. Some say the rock formation looks like a dragon's head, hence the name (dragon, 용, yong, and head, 머리, meori).

From the temple entrance, cross the street and walk towards the shipwreck. Note: the walk along the cliffs closes during very high seas.

Sleeping

One Fine Day Guesthouse
GUESTHOUSE ₩

(어느멋진날 게스트하우스; ☎010 8991 2983; http://mbbolam.blog.me; dm from ₩20,000, private r from ₩60,000) Kitsch meets comfort in these private and dorm rooms done up in pastel colours and teddy bears to give the place a warm, fuzzy feel. The friendly owner, Mr Park, a Seoul escapee who spent 15 years cooking at the Hilton Hotel, also operates a small on-site French restaurant.

It's on the village's main road, about halfway between Sanbang-san and the port. Look for the building with the words 'Restaurant and Private Guesthouse'.

Zen Hide Away
BOUTIQUE HOTEL ₩₩₩

(☎064 794 0188; http://zenhideawayjeju.com; r from ₩250,000, higher Fri & Sat) This property oozes a Zen-like appreciation for harmony with nature and balance in decor. Spas are standard in rooms, which also come with seaside views and earthy wood-stone finishings. Look for the brick building set back from the road running between Sanbang-san and the port.

Eating & Drinking

Yongrim Sikdang
SEAFOOD ₩₩

(용림식당; ☎064 794 3652; http://younglim.fordining.kr; meals from ₩10,000; ☉11am-10pm) A simple restaurant offering splendid seafood dishes such as maeuntang (매운탕, spicy seafood soup). A pair of travellers might choose the set meal (회정식, ₩30,000), which includes raw fish and loads of side dishes. If the weather is nice, ask for a seat on the outdoor patio overlooking the ocean.

It's near the port, on the narrow road running between the village and Sanbang-san.

Lazybox Café
CAFE

(☎064 792 1254; www.lazybox.co.kr; ☉10am-7pm; ☜) Located in the small retail strip at the foot of Sanbang-san, this cafe serves fair-trade coffee, freshly squeezed juices and homemade cakes. The owners, escapees from Seoul, also run a guesthouse (dm ₩20,000), 2km away.

Getting There & Away

Buses (₩2500, 50 minutes, every 40 minutes) depart Seogwipo bus terminal for Sanbang-san. You can also walk here along Olle Trail Rte 10 from Hwasun beach. From Jeju-si's intercity bus terminal, take bus 750-2 (₩2800, 45 minutes, every 40 minutes).

CENTRAL JEJU

Hallasan National Park
한라산국립공원

Halla-san
MOUNTAIN

(한라산; www.hallasan.go.kr) Hiking up or around 1950m Halla-san, South Korea's highest peak, is worth the effort. The densely wooded dormant volcano, the world's only habitat for Korean firs, is beautiful throughout the seasons, with

Hallasan National Park

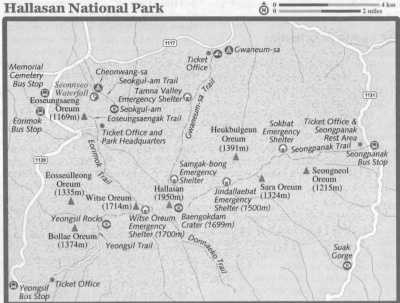

hillsides of flowering azaleas in April and May being a particularly notable sight. If you're lucky, you might spot deer. Be prepared for sudden weather changes and winter snow.

On Halla-san, refreshments are available at the Jindallaebat shelter (1500m) on the Seongpanak trail and at the Witse Oreum shelter (1700m), the meeting point of the Eorimok, Yeongsil and Donnaeko trails. Shelters are for emergency use only and cannot be used for overnight stays. There's a campground at the Gwaneum-sa entrance.

🏃 Activities

There are seven trails up and around Halla-san, but only Seongpanak and Gwaneum-sa go to the peak. Free maps are available from the information centres at the main trail entrances, but the paths are clearly marked so it's difficult to get lost. Besides, you'll seldom be climbing alone.

Noted climbing times are generous. However, set out early – if you don't reach the uppermost shelters by certain times (usually 1pm, or noon in the winter), rangers will stop you from climbing higher. Trails open at 6am (5am in summer), and hikers should be off the trails by sunset.

Seongpanak Trail HIKING

(성판악탐방로; ☎ 064 725 9950; 🚌 780, Seongpanak stop) This popular route (9.6km, 4½ hours) has the most gradual ascent and a side trail to Sara Oreum Observatory. With quick access to Rte 1131 and public transport – the bus stop is beside the car park – it's a busy place. Shops near the car park sell basic food and hiking supplies.

Buses from Jeju-si and Seogwipo (₩1800, 40 minutes, every 20 minutes) stop near the car park.

Gwaneum-sa Trail HIKING

(관음사탐방로; ☎ 064 756 9950) This challenging route (8.7km, five hours) is one of the most scenic trails on Halla-san. It's also the steepest, which can make it murder on your knees coming down. Some travellers recommend hiking up the Seongpanak trail and coming down via Gwaneum-sa.

There is no regular public transport to the Gwaneum-sa trailhead. A taxi from the Gwaneum-sa trailhead to the Seongpanak car park (a bus stop is here, too) costs about ₩17,000.

Eorimok Trail HIKING

(어리목탐방로; ☎ 064 713 9953; 🚌 740, Eorimok stop) After a 20-minute walk from the Eorimok bus stop, this trail (4.7km, three

JEJU OLLE TRAIL

Launched by former Korean journalist and Jeju native Suh Myeong-sook in 2007, the Jeju Olle Trail network is one of the great success stories of local tourism. The first route starts in Siheung near Seongsan-ri, and a further 25 routes of between 5km and 22.9km meander mainly along Jeju-do's coast (with some inland diversions) and three outer islands (Udo, Gapado and Chujado).

Olle is the local word for a pathway that connects a house to the main street, signifying one of the project's aims – to open up Jeju's unique culture and scenery to visitors. Although you could hike the entire 430km network of trails in around a month, the Olle's philosophy is one of slow, meandering travel. 'We recommend you don't rush,' says the Jeju Olle Foundation's Soojin Ivy Lee, 'It's not a race...we like people to feel spiritual healing and tranquility.'

If you hike any of the trails, it's worth investing in a passport (₩15,000) that comes with an excellent English-language guidebook providing detailed information on many sights and places to stay and eat along the routes. The passport also gets you discounts at many places. Passports are available at the foundation's head office in Seogwipo on Trail 6 and at stores or offices at the start/finish point of each trail. Visit www.jejuolle.org for details.

The three-day **Jeju Olle Walking Festival** (www.ollewalking.co.kr) generally occurs each October or November and includes many special events.

Olle Trail 1 (🚌 701, Siheung-ri stop) Where to begin your Olle Trail experience? Olle Trail 1 is a good place to start because of the up-close connection it provides with rural Jeju-do. The 15km trail (four to five hours) runs through farm plots worked by grandmothers, over grassy *oreum* (craters) where horses and cows graze freely and along a seaside path leading to one of Jeju-do's most impressive natural treasures, **Seongsan Ilchulbong** (p245).

Buses from Jeju-si (₩3300, 1½ hours, every 20 minutes) stop near the trailhead. It's near a wooden sign about 50m from the elementary school.

hours) begins in earnest with a steep climb through a deciduous forest. Halfway up, the dense trees give way to an open, subalpine moorland of bamboo, grass and dwarf firs. Some travellers recommend hiking up the Yeongsil trail and coming down via Eorimok, which has easy public-transport access from Jeju-si and Jungmun.

Buses from Jeju-si (₩1200, 40 minutes, every 30 minutes to 1½ hours) stop here.

Yeongsil Trail   HIKING
(영실탐방로; ☎ 064 747 9950; 🚌 740, Yeongsil stop) Yeongsil trail (5.1km, 2½ hours) is a short, easy course with grand scenery – panoramas of green oreum and pinnacle rocks atop sheer cliffs as you hike through a dwarf fir forest before reaching the mixed deciduous and evergreen forest lower down.

It begins with a 2.1km walk from a park office (first car park) to a resting area (second car park) and finishes with 3.7km of trails to the Witse Oreum shelter.

Buses from Jeju-si (₩2800, 50 minutes, every 30 minutes to 1½ hours) stop at the Yeongsil trail.

Donnaeko Trail   HIKING
(돈내코탐방로; ☎ 064 710 6920) This southern course (7km, 3½ hours) provides coastal views of Seogwipo and runs through a red pine forest. For the best views, some travellers recommend climbing up Yeongsil or Eorimok and then down Donnaeko. There is no easy public transport to the Donnaeko trailhead; a taxi from Seogwipo costs about ₩13,000.

Eoseungsaengak Trail   HIKING
(어승생악탐방로; ☎ 064 713 9953; 🚌 740, Eorimok stop) One of the shortest mountain trails (1.3km, 30 minutes), this easy hike begins at the Hallasan National Park Visitor Centre and finishes atop Eoseungsaeng Oreum, with sweeping views of the Jeju plains and the peak of Halla-san.

The trailhead is a 20-minute walk from the bus stop on Rte 1139. Bus service from

PODO HOTEL & PINX GOLF CLUB

Whether you come to golf, admire Japanese-Korean architect Itami Jun's designs, or simply enjoy the gently rounded *oreum*-scattered scenery of central Jeju-do, a visit to the Podo Hotel has much to offer.

Podo Hotel (포도호텔; ☑064 793 7000; www.thepinx.co.kr/podohotel; r from ₩440,000; P✳@☎) With its attractive use of stone and wood in a cottage concept that melds seamlessly with the surrounding environment, this architecturally extraordinary property draws guests from around the world.

Pinx Golf Club (☑064 792 8000; www.thepinx.co.kr; 18 holes weekday/weekend ₩85,000/97,000, caddy & cart extra) This exquisite 27-hole golf course was selected by US Golf Digest in 2005 as one of the world's top 100 clubs. Play a round while admiring views of Hallasan, the ocean blue and volcanic cones.

Jeju-si (₩1800, 40 minutes, every 30 minutes to 1½ hours) is irregular.

Seokgul-am Trail HIKING
(석굴암탐방로; ☐740, Memorial Cemetery stop) This short course (1.5km, 50 minutes) starts at Cheonwang-sa, runs through Ahheunahhop-gol (Ahheunahhop Valley) and terminates at Seokgul-am, a women's hermitage. Though novice hikers may wince at the occasional stretch of steep steps, the end is worth it.

From Jeju-si (₩1300, 25 minutes, every 20 minutes) get off at the Memorial Cemetery stop and walk towards Cheonwang-sa. The trail for Seokgul-am begins at the cemetery parking lot.

ⓘ Getting There & Away

Bus 780 between Jeju-si and Seogwipo stops at Seongpanak on Rte 1131. Bus 740 on Rte 1139 stops at Yeongsil, Eorimok, Eoseungsaengak and Seokgul-am trails; be sure to check the bus direction before boarding. There's no bus service to Gwaneum-sa or Donnaeko trails, and some hikers recommend catching a taxi from Seongpanak to the Gwaneum-sa campground, where the trail begins. A taxi from Seogwipo

is the best option for getting to the Donnaeko trailhead.

Sangumburi
산굼부리

Sangumburi VOLCANO
(산굼부리; ☑064 783 9900; www.sangumburi. net; adult ₩6000, youth & child ₩3000; ☺9am-5pm; ☐720-1, Sangumburi Crater stop) Sangumburi is an impressive volcanic crater. About 350m in diameter and 100m deep, it only takes a few minutes to walk up to the crater rim, so it's a short visit but you'll want to spend time admiring the expansive plains, distant craters and lush fields.

Buses from Jeju-si (₩1800, 50 minutes, every 25 minutes) stop near the ticket office.

WESTERN JEJU-DO

Bus 702 connects west-coast towns along Rte 1132 (every 20 minutes) between Seogwipo and Jeju-si, but if you want to see the inland sights, you're better off with your own transport.

Moseulpo
모슬포

Near the island's southwest tip, this sizeable fishing port is at the junction of Olle Trails 10 and 11 and a jumping-off point for Gapado and Marado. Ferry schedules from Molseupo to either island can change depending on the weather and seas. From Jeju-si, take bus 750-1, 750-2 or 750-3 (₩3300, one hour, every 30 to 45 minutes).

⊙ Sights

Gapado ISLAND
(가파도; ☑064 794 3500) Olle Trail 10-1 (5km, two hours) encircles Gapado (population 300), the nearer and larger of the two pizza-flat volcanic islands, just 5.5km off the coast of Moseulpo. The mostly flat trail meanders along windy coasts and through green fields of flowing barley. There are a few places to grab a bite and rent a bike.

Ferries (return adult/youth ₩12,400/6200 including park entrance fee, 20 minutes) depart four times daily (9am, 11am, 2pm and 4pm).

Marado   ISLAND

(마라도; ☑064 794 3500) This barren, wind-swept island with a rocky coastline has few sights, though you do get bragging rights for reaching Korea's most southerly point, 11km off the coast of Molseupo. Just 4.2km in circumference, it takes about two hours to walk the islet (population 100), which has a Buddhist temple and a Catholic church.

Ferries (return adult/youth ₩17,000/8500 including park entrance fee, 30 minutes) have hourly departures from 10am to 4pm.

🛏 Sleeping & Eating

Springflower Guesthouse   GUESTHOUSE ₩
(게스트하우스 봄꽃; ☑064 792 6008, 010 6816 8879; www.gojejeguesthouse.com; 1046 Hamo-ri, Daejeong-eup, Seogwipo; dm ₩18,000, r from ₩40,000; @🛜) Run by a friendly British-Korean couple, this convivial guesthouse is well set up for travellers. Rates include breakfast and it's a 10-minute walk to the Molseupo ferry terminal.

★ Hamo Restaurant   SEAFOOD ₩₩
(하모식당; ☑064 794 0139; mains from ₩8000; ☺8.30am-9pm) An excellent choice for travellers looking for breakfast before heading out on a ferry to the nearby islands, this seafood restaurant opens early and serves home-style fare such as *miyeokguk* (미역국, seaweed soup). It's a five-minute walk from the ferry terminal on Molseupo's main road.

Inland Region

These sights are best accessed by car. Local bus 967 from Hallim (₩1200, hourly departures) is possible, though infrequent service can mean long roadside waits. If driving, most of these sites are on local road Nokcha Bunjae Ro (녹차분재로, Green Tee-Bonsai Rd).

👁 Sights

O'Sulloc Tea Museum   MUSEUM
(오설록 녹차박물관; www.osulloc.com; ☺10am-5pm; ☐967, O'Sulloc stop) **FREE** Overlooking the verdant plantation of one of Korea's largest growers of *nokcha* (green tea), this museum displays a collection of ancient tea implements, some of which date back to the 3rd century. You can also stroll the fields and shop for its products, such as green-tea shampoo, green-tea cake and green-tea ice cream.

Jeju Glass Castle   AMUSEMENT PARK

(유리의성; ☑064 772 7777; www.jejuglasscastle .com; adult/child/youth ₩11,000/8000/9000; ☺9am-6pm; ☐967, Glass Castle stop) This fascinating park features more than 350 glass sculptures created by global artists, including the world's largest glass ball and glass diamond. Glass-blowing and glass-making classes are also run here.

Spirited Garden   GARDENS
(생각하는 정원; ☑064 772 3701; www.spiritedgarden.com; adult/child/youth ₩10,000/5000/6000; ☺8.30am-6pm Nov-Mar, to 7pm Apr-Oct; ☐967, Jeo-jiri stop) *Bunjae* (bonsai) trees may seem esoteric, but this bonsai park has excellent examples, some up to 500 years old. It's the life's work of Mr Sung Bum-young and has hosted dignitaries from all over the world.

**Jeju Museum of
Contemporary Art**   MUSEUM
(제주현대미술관; ☑064 710 7801; www.jejumuseum.co.kr; adult/youth ₩7000/5000; ☺9am-6pm Thu-Tue Mar-Oct, to 5pm Nov-Feb; ☐967, Shin Heung-dong stop) At the heart of the Artists Village in Jeoji is this excellent gallery. Permanent exhibitions by Kim Heng-sou and Park Kwang-jin are supplemented by regularly changing shows of other artists. The village is dotted with engaging pieces of modern and traditional architecture.

It's on Rte 1115, a short drive from Green Tee-Bonsai Rd.

🍴 Eating

Harubang Pizza   ITALIAN ₩₩
(피자굽는돌하르방; ☑064 773 7273; mains ₩13,000-59,000; ☺11am-6pm; ☐967,

> ### GATE POLE MESSAGES
>
> Jeju-do has traditionally described itself as having lots of rocks, wind and women, but no beggars, thieves or locked gates. Instead of locked fences in front of homes in the island's villages, you'll often see a *jeongnang* gate – two stone pillars that support three wooden poles between them. Three poles straight across means 'We're not home, please keep out'. Two down and one across means 'We're not home, but we are within shouting distance'. If all the poles are on the ground, it means 'We're home, please come in'.

Myeongri-dong stop) Tasty 1m-long pizzas topped with sweet potato, bulgogi (marinated beef) and kimchi are served in an old building in the middle of nowhere.

Coming from the southern part of the island, head north on Rte 1120 towards Jeju Glass Castle. Before the northern intersection of 1120 and Rte 1136, turn right on a local road called Cheongsu-ro (청수로) – look for the pizza sign. Drive straight to the yellow building on a corner lot. That's the pizza shop. It's about 600m from the Jeju Peace Museum (p254).

Mayflower CAFE **₩₩**
(카페 오월의 꽃; ☑ 064 772 5995; mains from ₩15,000; ◷ 11am-6pm) Enjoy coffee or tea in this self-service cafe that, on the outside, looks like a giant white cloud. Pizza, pasta and salad are also available.

It's on Green Tee-Bonsai Rd, between the Spirited Garden and Jeju Glass Castle.

Hallim 한림

On the northwest coast, this pretty town is close to lovely beaches, including **Geumneung** (금능해수욕장) and **Hyeopjae** (협재해수욕장), both with white sand and crystal-clear waters, perfect for snorkelling. Bus 702 from Jeju-si (₩2300, 50 minutes) and Seogwipo (₩3300, 80 minutes) stop here.

◉ Sights

Hallim Park PARK
(한림공원; ☑ 064 796 0001; www.hallimpark.co.kr; adult/child/youth ₩10,000/6000/8000; ◷ 8.30am-7pm Mar-Oct, to 6pm Nov-Feb; ℗) Hallim Park offers a botanical and bonsai

garden, a mini folk village and walks through a lava-tube cave. The caves are part of a 17km-long lava-tube system and are said to be the only lava caves in the world to contain stalagmites and stalactites.

Biyangdo ISLAND
(비양도; ☑ 064 796 7552) Just beyond Hyeopjae's sandy shores sits a tiny island that beckons. It's a curious place; just a hamlet, a couple of restaurants and *minbak* for overnight stays. A hike around the island takes about two hours, including time to reach the lighthouse.

Take a ferry (one way ₩3000, 15 minutes, departures 9am, noon and 3pm) from Hallim Port, which is a long walk or short taxi ride from Hyeopjae beach. The ticket office is next to a police station.

🍴 Sleeping & Eating

David House
Food & Guesthouse MOTEL **₩₩**
(데이빗하우스; ☑ 064 748 5162; r ₩60,000) The upper floors have positively large bedrooms, a separate dining area, a kitchen and two bathrooms. It's on the village's main street, so it's easy to find, plus it's a short walk to the beach and a long, leisurely stroll to Hallim Park.

Donatos ITALIAN **₩₩₩**
(도나토스; ☑ 064 796 1981; pizzas from ₩18,000; ◷ noon-9pm, closed end Feb-Mar) Delicious pizza from a wood-burning stove is served in a laid-back atmosphere with rock music in the background and cans of Italian tomatoes stacked here and there. It's opposite the beach, near the retail shops made from containers.

Jeollabuk-do

Best Places to Eat

➡ Hanguk-jip (p268)

➡ Yetchon Makgeolli (p268)

➡ Hyundai-ok (p267)

Best Places to Hike

➡ Naejangsan
National Park (p269)

➡ Daedunsan
Provincial Park (p270)

➡ Byeonsan-bando
National Park (p273)

Why Go?

The small southwestern province of Jeollabuk-do (전라북
도) punches above its weight. At the centre is the capital
Jeonju, famous for its *hanok maeul*, a village of hundreds
of tile-roofed traditional homes that house craft workshops,
boutiques and teahouses. Koreans also call the Unesco-
listed 'City of Gastronomy' Jeonju the country's number-one
foodie destination. Eat once in Jeonju, they say, and you're
spoiled for life. It makes sense: this fertile green province is
an agricultural heartland whose fresh produce stars in local
dishes such as bibimbap.

Much of rural Jeollabuk-do is also parkland, which
means, should you tire of Jeonju's charms, you can stretch
your legs on any number of fantastic hiking trails, from the
steep peaks of Naejangsan National Park to the gentle hills
of Seonunsan Provincial Park. There's also skiing on the
slopes of Muju to the east and sandy beaches on the West
Sea, from where you can catch ferries to sleepy islands.

When to Go
Jeonju

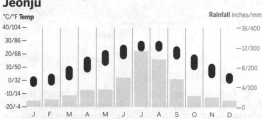

Apr–May The
camellias bloom
at Seonun-sa
and the Jeonju
International Film
Festival kicks off.

Jul–Aug Hit the
beaches and
islands; in August
catch the Jeonju
Sori Festival.

Dec–Jan Winter
means you'll be
able to hit the
slopes at Muju.

History

The Donghak rebellion, led by Chon Pong-jun, took place mainly in Jeollabuk-do in 1893 when a ragtag force of peasants and slaves seized Jeonju fortress and defeated King Gojong's army, before being destroyed by Japanese forces. Their demands included the freeing of slaves, better treatment of the *chonmin* (low-born), the redistribution of land, the abolition of taxes on fish and salt, and the punishment of corrupt government officials. Jeollabuk-do and Jeollanam-do were one joint province until 1896; Jeonju was the capital of this combined province.

Jeonju 전주

☎ 063 / POP 650,000

Jeonju (http://tour.jeonju.go.kr), the provincial capital, is famous for being the

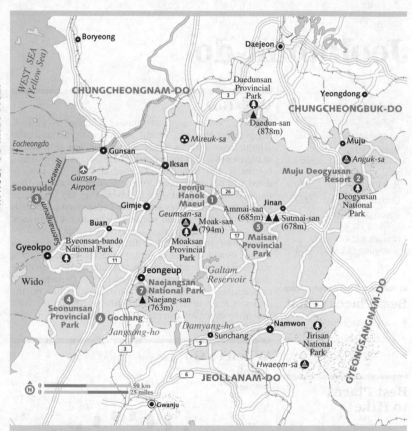

Jeollabuk-do Highlights

1 Getting lost exploring the alleys of **Jeonju Hanok Maeul** (p265) village.

2 Skiing or snowboarding the slopes at **Muju Deogyusan Resort** (p272).

3 Zipping round **Seonyudo** (p275) on a bicycle before relaxing on the beach.

4 Ambling through pretty **Seonunsan Provincial Park** (p273) to a giant Buddha carving on a cliff.

5 Being amazed by the unique rock-pinnacle temple in **Maisan Provincial Park** (p269).

6 Visiting the impressive Moyang Fortress and eerie dolmen sites in **Gochang** (p273).

7 Hiking the cradle of peaks that form **Naejangsan National Park** (p269).

birthplace of both the Joseon dynasty and Korea's most well-known culinary delight, bibimbap (rice, meat, egg and vegetables with a hot sauce). Centrally located, the city is the perfect base from which to explore Jeollabuk-do, as it's the regional hub for buses and trains. The central historical folk village has many outstanding *hanok* (traditional wooden homes), which house museums, cute teahouses and artisan workshops.

⊙ Sights & Activities

★ Jeonju Hanok Maeul   NEIGHBOURHOOD
(전주한옥마을) This *maeul* (village) – in the middle of modern Jeonju – has more than 800 *hanok*, one of the largest such concentrations in the country. Most of them now contain guesthouses, galleries, restaurants, teahouses and boutiques (rather than homes). Yes, it's touristy, but wandering the cobblestone lanes is still an enchanting experience, especially in the early morning or evening hours.

Some places in the village host workshops (making traditional paper or alcohol, for example). These usually require advance reservations and a minimum of two people; ask at a tourist information centre.

Gyeonggijeon   HISTORIC BUILDING
(경기전; ☑ 063 281 2891; 102 3-ga, Pungnam-dong; adult/child/student ₩1000/500/700; ⊙9am-6pm) Originally constructed in 1410 and reconstructed in 1614, this palace is home to shrines, storehouses and guard-rooms relating to the Confucian rituals once held here. There is also a replica portrait of Yi Seong-gye, the founder of the Joseon dynasty (1392–1910), whose family came from Jeonju. Portraits of six other Joseon monarchs, and palanquins, are also on display in the **Royal Portrait Museum**. English tours are held at 11am and 2pm daily.

Jeonju Hyanggyo   HISTORIC BUILDING
(전주향교; ☑ 063 288 4548; 145-20 Hyanggyo-gil, Wansan-gu; ⊙10am-6pm Mar-Sep, to 5pm Oct-Feb) FREE *Hyanggyo* were neighbourhood schools established by *yangban* (aristocrats) in the 1500s to prepare their sons for the *seowon* (Confucian academies), where the students took the all-important government service exams. This well-preserved and atmospheric example dates to 1603.

Traditional Wine Museum   MUSEUM
(전통술박물관; ☑ 063 287 6305; http://urisul. net; 74 Hanji-gil, Wansan-gu; ⊙9am-6pm Tue-Sun)

FREE Housed in a beautiful old *hanok,* this museum has a *gosori* (traditional still), displays (in Korean) explaining the process of making traditional liquors and a small gift shop.

Jeondong Catholic Church   CHURCH
(전동성당; ☑ 063 284 3222; 51 Taejo-ro, Wansan-gu) FREE The red-brick church was built by French missionary Xavier Baudounet on the spot where Korean Catholics were executed in 1781 and 1801. Built between 1908 and 1914, the architecture is a fusion of Asian, Byzantine and Romanesque styles. It's closed to the public except during mass, when you can respectfully peak inside at the stained-glass windows, which portray early martyrs.

Those executed were later interred on the hill southeast of Hanok Maeul known today as **Martyr's Mountain** (치명자산성지). There are 13 crosses on the hillside marking the burial spot and a small church, accessible by a trail. Locals know it as Jeonju's best sunset spot.

Pungnam-mun   GATE
(풍남문) This stone-and-wood gateway is all that remains of Jeonju's fortress wall. First built in 1398 but renovated many times since, it's now the ornate centrepiece of a busy roundabout.

Omok-dae   HISTORIC BUILDING
(오목대) On a hill overlooking the entire village is a pavilion where General Yi Seong-gye celebrated a victory over Japanese pirates in 1380, prior to his overthrow of the Goryeo dynasty. Cross the bridge to **Imok-dae** (이목대), a monument to one of Yi Seong-gye's ancestors.

Jaman Village   NEIGHBOURHOOD
(자만마을) Eclectic, colourful murals adorn the walls of this shantytown, on a hill overlooking Hanok Maeul. It's slowly gentrifying and several spots are now home to galleries and cafes, the best of which is **Kkojittap-pong** (꼬지따뽕; 31 Jamandong 2-gil, drinks from ₩5000; ⊙10.30am-6pm), a terrace cafe that looks like a child's dream house.

Jeonju Gaeksa   HISTORIC BUILDING
(전주 객사; 59 Chunggyeong-ro, Wansan-gu) FREE This rebuilt former government office is a central landmark that lends its name to the surrounding Gaeksa district.

Jeonju Hanji Museum   MUSEUM
(전주한지박물관; ☑ 063 210 8103; www. hanjimuseum.co.kr; 59 Palbok-ro, Deokjin-gu;

Jeonju

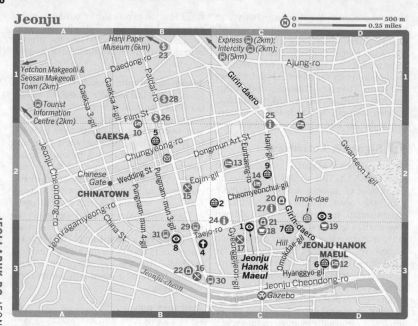

Jeonju

◎ Top Sights

◎ Sights

◎ Sleeping

◎ Eating

◎ Drinking & Nightlife

◎ Shopping

◎ Information

◎ Transport

⊙ 9am-5pm) FREE Adjacent to a modern-day paper factory, this museum covers the history and processes involved in making *hanji* (traditional Korean paper) and also shows some of the impressive things that can be made with it. At the end, you get to try making your own.

Take any of the buses in the 200 range leaving from the Jeondong Catholic Church bus stop to the Palbok Namyang Apt stop (about 20 minutes; ₩1200) and continue walking five minutes in the same direction.

✰ Festivals & Events

Jeonju International Film Festival   FILM
(www.jiff.or.kr) Nine-day event every April/May focusing mainly on indie, digital and experimental movies. Around 200 films from 40 countries shown in local cinema multiplexes.

Jeonju Sori Festival   MUSIC
(www.sorifestival.com) A week-long music festival, with an emphasis on traditional Korean music, held in autumn in the Jeonju Hanok Maeul (p265).

🛏 Sleeping

Budget and midrange hotels are located in the Gaeksa district; cheaper love motels surround the bus terminals and train station. For a truly unique experience, stay in a *hanok* in the Hanok Maeul. Look down alleys for English signs that say 'guesthouse'. Rooms start at ₩50,000 though typically rise 20% on weekends or during high season.

★ Carpe Diem   HOSTEL ₩
(☑063 902 9345; www.carpediemhostel.kr; 21 Gwanseon 1-gil, Wansan-gu; dm ₩20,000; ⊜❋@⊚) Run by the indefatigable, English-speaking Ashley, a veteran traveller and font of local knowledge, this tiny hostel sleeps just 10. It's in a renovated old home, brightly decorated, with a common cooking area. Excursions, barbecue parties and more can be arranged.

Jeonju Guesthouse   HOSTEL ₩
(전주 게스트하우스; ☑063 286 8886, 010 7668 3929; www.koreabackpackers.net; 46 Gyeonggijeon-gil, Wansan-gu; dm/s/d from ₩19,000/35,000/50,000; ⊜❋@⊚) Jeonju's original guesthouse is a sprawling, ramshackle place with friendly English-speaking owners. There are cooking and laundry facilities. It's located right on the edge of Hanok Maeul.

★ Cho Ga Jib   HANOK GUESTHOUSE ₩₩
(초가집; ☑063 288 2403, 010 5295 2403; http://blog.naver.com/cottage47; 25 Omokdae-gil, Wansan-gu; s/d/q ₩30,000/50,000/90,000) Only one thatched-roof commoner residence remains in Jeonju's old city (tile roofed *hanok* were for the upper class). It's now this charming guesthouse, whose cosy rooms have modern – though tiny – bath-

rooms. The woman who runs it (and grew up in the house) is delightful and speaks some English.

Seunggwangje   HANOK GUESTHOUSE ₩₩
(승광제; ☑063 284 2323; 12-6 Choemyeonghui-gil, Wansan-gu; r from ₩60,000; ⊜❋) This humble, 75-year-old *hanok* has the distinction of being owned by Lee Seok, a grandson of King Gojong, and photos of royalty adorn the courtyard. The tiny rooms have TV, fridge, *yo* (padded quilt or mattress on the floor) and small, modern bathrooms. The entrance is down an alleyway. Some English spoken.

Benikea Jeonju Hansung Tourist Motel   HOTEL ₩₩
(전주한성관광호텔; ☑063 288 0014; www.hotelhansung.kr; 143-3 Jeonju-gaeksa 5-gil, Wansan-gu; d incl breakfast from ₩70,000; P❋@⊚) This recently renovated hotel in the heart of the Gaeksa district offers Western and *ondol*-style rooms with TV and fridge. Staff speak some English. Note that rooms facing the main drag can be noisy on weekends.

🍴 Eating & Drinking

Hanok Maeul is big on street food, with countless vendors dishing up everything from dumplings to churros. More vendors set up inside **Nambu-sijang** (남부시장; 63 Pungnammun 2-gil, Wansan-gu) on Friday and Saturday evenings. Pack a picnic – and a bottle of *makgeolli* (milky rice wine) – and head to the public gazebo over the river. Modern restaurants, bars and Western fast-food chains are located in the Gaeksa shopping district.

Hyundai-ok   KOREAN ₩
(현대옥; Nambu Market 2-74, Wansan-gu; meals ₩5000; ⊙6am-2pm) Jeonju's most beloved restaurant is this 10-seater *kongnamul gukbap* (bean sprout and rice soup) shop inside labyrinthine Nambu Market. Ordering is easy: with squid (*ojingeo*; plus ₩3000 for two people) or without. You might also want to ask for it mild – the soup is pretty spicy otherwise.

To find it: enter the market through the south entrance and turn down the alley on your left, across from the shop selling baskets. But really, all you have to do is ask – everyone knows this place.

Veteran   KOREAN ₩
(베테랑; 135 Gyeonggijeon-gil, Wansan-gu; dishes ₩5000-7000; ⊙9am-9.30pm) This 'veteran'

JEONJU'S MAKGEOLLI BARS

Jeonju has a long history of brewing *makgeolli* and locals will tell you it is a *food* not a mere beverage. There are no less than seven 'makgeolli towns' – bar strips devoted to the milky rice wine – in the city. It's served by the kettle for the table, and with each kettle comes a complementary round of food. *Makgeolli* drinking is invariably social, and you'll need to pull together a group of at least four to do it proper justice. For an introductory experience, there is no better place in town than **Yetchon Makgeolli** (p268).

of the Jeonju dining scene has been dishing out delicious *mandu* (만두; dumplings) and noodle dishes such as *kalguksu* (칼국수) since 1977. The setting is decidedly no-frills but who cares with food this cheap and good.

⭐**Hanguk-jip**　　　　　　　　KOREAN ₩₩
(한국집; ☏063 284 2224; www.bibimbab.name; 119 Eojin-gil, Wansan-gu; meals from ₩11,000; ⊙9.30am-8.30pm) Jeonju locals say this is the best bibimbap restaurant in the city's historic district. The classic Jeonju dish comes served here with bright yellow mung-bean jelly, a hearty dollop of chilli paste and wild greens; get it in a hot stone pot (*dolsot*; 돌솥) or topped with raw beef (*yukhoe*; 육회). The building has a temple-like facade.

⭐**Yetchon Makgeolli**　　　　　KOREAN ₩₩
(옛촌막걸리; 8 Jungsanjungang-ro, Wansan-gu; ⊙4pm-2am) Simply put, Yetchon Makgeolli is Jeonju's best night out. Unlike other *makgeolli* bars, where the food is secondary, the dishes here are distractingly good. With the first kettle comes butter-soft pork belly and kimchi; with the second, grilled prawns (and more). It's exceedingly popular and you'll have to queue on weekends.

The first kettle is ₩20,000 and subsequent kettles are ₩15,000; dishes are included. It's a ₩5000 taxi-ride from Hanok Maeul; most taxi drivers know the place.

Gyodong Dawan　　　　　　　TEAHOUSE
(교동다완; ☏063 282 7133; 65-5 Eunhaeng-ro, Wansan-gu; tea ₩5000; ⊙11am-10pm) Hanok's best teahouse is this richly atmospheric spot, where the speciality is *hwangcha* (황차), a golden-hued tea once served exclu-

sively to kings (and grown here in the courtyard). It's served in a ritualistic manner (no photos during this, please).

🛍 Shopping

Youthful Gaeksa is Jeonju's shopping district.

Demiseam　　　　　　　　　CLOTHING
(데미샘; 100-7 Hanji-gil, Wansan-gu; ⊙10am-6pm) Silk scarves coloured with natural dyes and handmade traditional-meets-contemporary clothing from local artisan Han Seowoon.

Handicraft Exhibition Hall　　　CRAFTS
(공예품전시관; ☏063 285 0002; 15 Taejo-ro, Wansan-gu; ⊙10am-7pm) This large complex sells paper, lanterns, lacquerware and more.

ℹ Information

Hanok Village Tourist Information Centre
(☏063 282 1330; ⊙9am-6pm) There are several other TICs around Jeonju Hanok Maeul and also outposts at the bus terminal and train station.

ℹ Getting There & Away

BUS

The Express Bus Terminal and Intercity Bus Terminal are next to each other, 3km northwest of Hanok Maeul and a short (about ₩5000) taxi ride away.

TRAIN

KTX trains connect Jeonju with Seoul's Yongsan station (₩34,400; 1¾ hours, 11 daily). *Saemaul* (express; ₩26,200, three hours, two daily) and *mugunghwa* (semiexpress; ₩17,600, 3½ hours, nine daily) also run from Yongsan. Trains continue south to Jeollanam-do.

ℹ Getting Around

From the bus terminals, walk 500m away from the river to Geuman Sq bus stop, where any number of buses (₩1200) go to Pungnam-mun – useful for destinations around Hanok Maeul. From the train station catch bus 79. Other useful stops include Jeondong Catholic Church and Nambu Market. Taxis are plentiful and cheap (fares start at ₩2800).

Around Jeonju

Moaksan Provincial Park　　　PARK
(모악산도립공원; ☏063 290 2752; ⊙8am-7pm) This park, which contains Moak-san (794m), is a popular destination for hikers on weekends. The main attraction is the temple,

Geumsan-sa (금산사; ☑063 548 4441; www.
geumsansa.org; 9 Geumsan-ri, Geumsan-myeon,
Gimje-si; adult/child ₩3000/1000; ☺sunrise-
sunset), which dates to AD 599. While there
are no buildings here nearly that old, the
three-storey Mireukjeon dates to 1635 and
has an impressive air of antiquity. Inside
is a looming, golden statue of the Maitreya
Buddha – the Buddha of the future.

Geumsan-sa runs a foreigner-friendly
templestay program (shared/private room
₩70,000/90,000, including meals); see the
website for details. Near the entrance, sip
traditional teas, such as *daechucha* (대추
차; jujube tea) in the serene atmosphere of
Sanjang Dawon (산중다원; ☑063 548 4449;
teas ₩5000-8000).

Beyond the temple, a trail goes up
Janggun-dae (장군대) and along the ridge
to the peak in a relatively easy two hours.
Minor trails wend past temple hermitages.

Moaksan is easily reached by bus from
Jeonju. Get local bus 79 (₩1950, one hour,
every 40 minutes) from the stop at Nambu Market. Don't get on buses that go to
the other end of Moaksan park; ask for
Geumsan-sa, from where it's a 20-minute
walk to the temple.

Maisan Provincial Park   PARK
(마이신도립공원; ☑063 433 3313; ☺9am-
6pm) Maisan means 'Horse Ears Mountain',
which refers to two extraordinary rocky
peaks as they appear from the distance. The
east peak is **Sutmai-san** (Male Mai-san;
678m) while the west peak is **Ammai-san**
(Female Mai-san; 685m). Both ears are
made of conglomerate rock, which is rare
in Korea. The temple, **Tap-sa** (탑사; ☑063
433 0012; 367 Maisannam-ro, Maryeong-myeon,
Jinan-gun; adult/child/youth ₩2000/1000/1500),
at the base of the female ear, has a unique
sculptural garden of 80 stone towers or
pinnacles that were piled up by a Buddhist
mystic, Yi Kapmyong (1860–1957).

From Jeonju, buses run to Jinan (₩4600,
50 minutes, every 20 minutes), from where
you can catch a bus to the north entrance
of Maisan (₩1200, five minutes, hourly).
A path runs between the ears to Tap-sa in
about 40 minutes.

Naejangsan National Park
내장산국립공원
☑063

⊙ Sights

Naejangsan National Park   NATIONAL PARK
(내장산국립공원; ☑063 538 7875; http://
english.knps.or.kr; ☺sunrise-sunset) The mountainous ridge in this park is shaped like an
amphitheatre. A spider's web of trails leads

Naejangsan National Park

WORTH A TRIP

DAEDUNSAN PROVINCIAL PARK 대둔산도립공원

Daedunsan Provincial Park (대둔산 도립공원; ☑063 240 4560; ⏱8am-6pm) This small park has craggy peaks with spectacular views over the surrounding countryside. It also offers vertigo-inducing thrills: the climb to the summit of Daedun-san (878m) is a steep, stony track that includes a 50m-long cable bridge stretched precariously between two rock pinnacles and a long steel-cable stairway. A five-minute **cable-car ride** (one way/return ₩5000/9000) saves you an hour of uphill hiking.

Afterwards, you can unwind in the sauna (hotel guests/nonguests ₩4000/6000) attached to the **Daedunsan Tourist Hotel** (대둔산온천관광호텔; ☑063 263 1260; 611-70 Sanbuk-ri, Unju-myeon, Wanju-gun; r ₩75,000-90,000; ❋@). It has an *oncheon* (hot-spring bath).

Daedunsan can be reached by bus from Jeonju (₩6400, 1¼ hour, five daily) or from Seodaejeon bus terminal in Daejeon (₩3500, 40 minutes, three daily).

up to the ridge, but the fastest way up is by **cable car** (adult/child one way ₩5000/3000 return ₩7000/4000; ⏱9am-5pm). The hike around the rim is strenuous, but with splendid views on a fine day. The trail itself is a roller-coaster ride, going up and down six main peaks and numerous small ones before you reach Seorae-bong (622m), from where you head back down to the access road.

There are metal ladders, bridges and railings to help you scramble over the rocky parts. Give yourself six hours to hike around the amphitheatre, with an hour more for breaks and a picnic. If you find the hike too difficult, turn right at any time and follow one of the many trails back down to the temple **Naejang-sa** (내장사; adult/child/youth ₩3000/700/1200).

An easy and picturesque 1.2km walk from Naejang-sa goes through Geumseong valley. English trail maps are available at the **Tourist Information Centre** (☑063 537 1330; ⏱9am-5pm).

Naejang-san is particularly famous for its brilliant display of autumn leaves in October. Expect the park to be absolutely packed then.

🛏 Sleeping

A tourist village clusters around the park entrance, but it's not usually busy except in October. **Camping** (☑063 538 7875; high/low season from ₩7000/5000) is available before the tourist village.

Servill Hotel   MOTEL ₩₩
(세르빌 호텔; ☑063 538 9487; 937 Naejang-san-ro; d ₩40,000-60,000; ❒❋❉@❈) Clean, comfortable rooms and an owner who speaks a smattering of English make this an excellent place to rest your weary legs. The attached restaurant does a tasty *sanchae hanjeonsik* (a set meal of local wild vegetables) for ₩20,000 a person.

❶ Getting There & Away

Jeongeup is the nearest city. Buses (₩4300, one hour, every 15 minutes) run here from Jeonju. Jeongeup is also a stop on the KTX Honam line from Yongsan (₩39,500, 1¾ hours, 15 daily). Local bus 171 (₩1400, 30 minutes, every 20 minutes) runs from the train station and the bus terminal to Naejangsan National Park. It's a 2km, 20-minute walk between the ticket office and the cable-car terminal.

Muju & Deogyusan National Park
무주군, 덕유산국립공원

☑063

The small town of Muju is a jumping off point for Deogyusan National Park. The town itself holds little of interest, but it has a handy selection of simple hotels serving skiers and hikers.

Muju is also home to the **Muju Firefly Festival** (무주 반딧불축제; http://english. firefly.or.kr; Muju-eup, Muju-gun; adult/child ₩5000/3000; ⏱Jul-Aug), held in mid-June.

⊙ Sights & Activities

Deogyusan National Park   NATIONAL PARK
(덕유산국립공원; http://english.knps.or.kr; adult/student/child camping per person per day ₩2000/1500/1000; ⏱sunrise-sunset; ❒❉) This national park is a hiker's playground and home of Deogyusan Muju ski resort (p272). There's a tourist village with an **information centre** (구천동 탐방지원 센터; ☑063 322 3473; 418-24, Samgong-ri, Seolcheon-myeon, Muju-gun) at Gucheon-dong, which marks the start of the park's best **hike** (two hours, 6km). The trail follows the river and valley past 20 beauty spots to a small

Deogyusan National Park

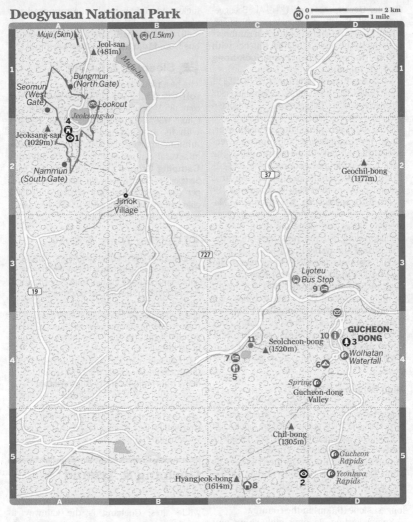

Deogyusan National Park

◉ Sights
1 Anguk-sa A2
2 Baengnyeon-sa C5
3 Deogyusan National Park D4
4 Jeoksangsan-seong A2

❂ Activities, Courses & Tours
5 Muju Deogyusan Resort C4

🛏 Sleeping
6 Deogyudae Camping Ground D4

7 Hotel Tirol C4
8 Hyangjeok-bong Shelter C5
9 Muju Deogyusan Leisure
   Biketel D3

❶ Information
10 Gucheon-dong Information
   Centre D4

❶ Transport
11 Seolcheon-bong Gondola C4

temple, **Baengnyeon-sa** (백련사; Baengne-onsa-gil 580, Seolcheon-myeon, Muju-gun) FREE, where fairies are said to slide down rainbows to bathe in the pools. The hike finishes with a steep, 1½-hour ascent of **Hyangjeok-bong** (향적봉; 1614m).

A basic **hikers' shelter** (향적봉대피소; ✆063 322 1614; http://english.knps.or.kr/Experience/Shelters/Default.aspx; Samgong-ri Seolcheon-myeon, Muju-gun; high/low season ₩8000/7000) accommodates trekkers overnight. Yew trees, azaleas and alpine flowers adorn the summit. In the northwest of the park is **Jeoksangsan-seong** (무주 적상산성), a fortress rebuilt in the 17th century. Encircled by an 8km wall is **Anguk-sa** (안국사; 1050, Sanseong-ro, Jeoksang-myeon, Muju-gun), a temple housing a Joseon-dynasty archive. Buses run along the main road to Gucheon-dong, so you must get off at the access road and walk (4km).

The **gondola** (adult/child single return journey ₩14,000/10,000; ◷8.30am-4.30pm) to the peak of **Seolcheon-bong** (설천봉; 1520m) is open year-round. Mountain bikes can be hired from **Muju Deogyusan Leisure Biketel** (무주 덕유산 레저바이크텔; ✆063 320 2575; http://4s.mj1614.com/index.9is; 968, Gucheondong-ro, Cheoncheon-myeon, Jangsu-gun; d ₩11,000, ondol from ₩105,000; P@), a cyclist hotel.

Muju Deogyusan Resort
SNOW SPORTS

(무주덕유산리조트; ✆063 322 9000; www.mdysresort.com; 185, Manseon-ro, Seolcheon-myeon, Muju-gun; lift tickets per day adult/child ₩85,000/65,000, equipment rental per day adult/child ₩33,000/28,000; ☒) Opened in 1990, Muju Deogyusan Resort (formerly known as Muju Ski Resort) is the only Korean ski resort located in a national park. It comprises 30 runs including the highest altitude and longest slope (6.1km) in the country.

Snowboarding, sledding, night skiing and lessons in English are on offer.

Taekwondo Park
MARTIAL ARTS

(무주태권도원; ✆Chinese 063 320 0120, English 063 320 0117; www.tkdwon.kr; 1482, Museol-ro, Seolcheon-myeon, Muju-gun; admission adult/child/student ₩6000/4500/5000; ◷10am-6pm Tue-Fri, to 7pm Sat-Sun Mar-Oct, to 5pm Tue-Fri, to 6pm Sat-Sun Nov-Feb; ☒) This park devoted to Korea's national sport houses the largest taekwondo stadium in the world. There is also a **museum** dedicated to the sport, as well as an **experience centre** where people can try

taekwondo for themselves. A **monorail** zips visitors around the park.

To reach the park, take a Seolcheon-bound bus from **Muju Intercity Bus Terminal**.

🛏 Sleeping & Eating

The best place to stay in the park is **Hotel Tirol** (티롤호텔; ✆063 320 7200; www.mdysresort.com; 185, Manseon-ro, Seolcheon-myeon, Muju-gun; r from ₩380,000, ste from ₩510,000; P❋@), with its Austrian-style chalets and condominium apartments. Camping is available at several campsites, including **Deogyudae Camping Ground** (덕유대야영장; San 60-5, Samgong-ri, Seolcheon-myeon; camping per person per day adult/child/student ₩2000/1000/1500; auto camping per car per day ₩11,000; P), which has showers and tent pitches.

ℹ️ Getting There & Away

Resort buses (₩20,000, three hours, 9am) go from Seoul's Jamsil station during ski season.

Intercity buses go to Muju from Seoul Nambu Bus Terminal (p91; ₩12,200, 3½ hours, five daily). Fast KTX trains (₩22,900, one hour, five daily) go from Seoul to Daejeon and require a transfer to Dongdaejeon Bus Terminal (p281) for an intercity bus (₩3900, 50 minutes, twice an hour) to Muju.

To reach the national park and ski resort, take the Gucheon-dong bus (₩3300, 40 minutes, 15 daily) from **Muju Intercity Bus Terminal** (무주시외버스공용정류장; ✆063 322 2245; Dangsan-ri 1229, Muju-eup), which drops you near the tourist village, or take the resort shuttle bus (free, 45 minutes, 10.30am, 2pm, 4.30pm and 7.20pm).

Gochang & Around   고창
✆063

In addition to having a handful of worthwhile sites, Gochang is the gateway to Seonunsan Provincial Park, with its temple Seonun-sa.

◎ Sights

Moyang Fortress
FORTRESS

(모양성; Gochangeupseong; ✆063 560 8067; 1 Moyangseong-ro; adult/child/youth ₩1000/600/800; ◷9am-7pm Mar-Oct, to 5pm Nov-Feb) Perched on a hill overlooking the town of Gochang, Moyang Fortress is an impressive structure built in 1453 during the Joseon dynasty. The ivy-covered, 1.6km-long fortress wall with three gates surrounds a complex of reconstructed buildings. A local legend says that if a woman walks three times around the wall with a stone on her head during a leap year, she will never become ill and will enter paradise.

Gochang Dolmen Site
ARCHAEOLOGICAL SITE

(고창 고인돌군; Gochang Goindolgun; ☑063 560 8662; http://gcdolmen.gochang.go.kr; 74 Goindolgongwon-gil; adult/child/youth ₩3000/1000/2000; ⏰9am-6pm Tue-Sun) The hills surrounding Gochang are eerily filled with thousands of dolmen, prehistoric tombs from the Bronze and Iron Ages now registered with Unesco. The site includes a small museum, behind which are trails leading in and around the huge boulders that dot the countryside.

Seonunsan Provincial Park
PARK

(선운산도립공원; ☑063 560 8682; 250 Seonunsa-ro, Asan-myeon) This pretty park has always been popular with monks and poets alike. A 20-minute walk along a rocky, tree-lined river brings you to **Seonun-sa** (선운사; ☑063 561 1422; www.seonunsa.org/eng; 250 Seonunsa-ro, Asan-myeon; adult/child/youth ₩3000/1000/2000; ⏰sunrise-sunset), a Zen temple founded in 577 and last rebuilt in 1720. Just behind the temple is a 500-year-old camellia forest that flowers around the end of April. Beyond, there are hiking trails leading to mountain hermitages.

It's a 30-minute hike to **Dosol-am Hermitage** (도솔암) and just beyond is a giant **Buddha rock carving** dating to the Goryeo dynasty; the amazing image is carved into the cliff face and is 15m high. On the right is a very narrow grotto, and next to it stairs lead up to a tiny shrine and a great view.

From Dosol-am, you can climb up to Nakjodae, and then loop back down to the temple, passing the hermitage **Chamdang-am** (참당암). It's a pleasant, easy hike that should take about three hours.

Seonun-sa has an English-language templestay (₩50,000), which includes a 'walking meditation' trip up to the hermitages. There are a handful of motels and restaurants at the entrance to the park, clustered around the bus stop.

🛏 Sleeping

Seonunsan Youth Hostel
HOSTEL ₩₩

(선운산유스호스텔; ☑063 561 3333; www.seonunsan.co.kr; 334 Samin-ri, Asan-myeon; ₩50,000-60,000; ⏰❄) The nicest place to

stay in the Seonunsan tourist village is, surprisingly enough, the youth hostel. With private rooms (both *ondol* and Western-style), it's more like a hotel. Note that it fills up fast on Fridays and Saturdays and sometimes closes on Sundays.

ℹ Getting There & Around

Buses serve Gochang from Jeonju (₩6000, 1½ hours, hourly) and Gwangju (₩5000, one hour, every 30 minutes). From Gochang bus terminal, there are four direct buses to the Dolmen Site (₩1300, 20 minutes); otherwise get a bus heading to Asan (20 daily) and tell the driver you want to go to *goindorugongwon*. Buses (₩2500, 30 minutes, hourly) run to Seonun-sa from Gochang.

Byeonsan-bando National Park
변산반도국립공원

☑063

Byeonsan-bando National Park (변산반도국립공원; ☑063 582 7808; http://english.knps.or.kr) is Korea's only national park with both mountains and sea. During the summer months, sandy **Byeonsan Beach**, backed by pines, and **Gyeokpo Beach**, with its dramatic cliffs and caves, are the top draws. From Gyeokpo, ferries depart for the island of **Wido**, which has a sandy beach. Year-round there is hiking in the peaks that frame the temple **Naeso-sa** (내소사; ☑063 583 7281; www.naesosa.org; 268 Seokpo-ri, Jinseo-myeon; adult/youth/child ₩3000/1500/500; ⏰8.30am-6pm).

Originally built in 633 and last renovated in the 19th century, Naeso-sa has a weathered elegance. Don't miss the lattice work on the doors of the main hall, and the painted ceiling with musical instruments, flowers and

Byeonsan-bando National Park

WEST SEA
(Yellow Sea)

Saemangeum Sea Wall — Gunsan (33km)
Buan (18km)
Byeonsan Beach
Buan-ho
Gosapo Beach
Byeonsanhaebyeon-ro (Byeonsan Coastal Road)
Ssangseon-bong (459m) — Silsang-sa Ruins
Unsan-ri
Tourist Information Centre
Nakjo-dae (448m) — Bus Stop
Seonin-bong
Gyeokpo Beach
Chaeseokgang Cliffs
Mangpo-dae (492m)
Wolmyeongam — Bongnae Valley — Jikso Pokpo — Seonyeotang
Gyeokpo Bus Terminal
Gyeokpo-hang (ferries for Wido)
Gwaneum-bong
Cheongnyeon-am
Sinseon-bong (486m)
Bus Stop
Naeso-sa
Sangnok Beach
Buan (18km)
Mohang Beach

dragons among the motifs. Naeso-sa has an English-language templestay (weekday/weekends ₩40,000/60,000) with hiking on the weekends.

From the temple you can hike up the unpaved road to the hermitage **Cheong-nyeon-am** (청련암; 20 minutes) for sea views; another 15 minutes brings you to the ridge where you turn left for Gwane-um-bong. From the peak follow the path, which goes up and down and over rocks for an hour until you reach **Jikso Pokpo** (직소폭포), a 30m-high waterfall with a large pool. For a more challenging hike head up **Nakjodae**, which is famous for its sunset views.

There's a tourist village at Gyeokpo Beach, with motels and splashier resorts. On Wido, every house in the little fishing village of **Jinli** is a *minbak* or restaurant.

ℹ Getting There & Around

Take a bus from Jeonju to Buan (₩5100, one hour, every 30 minutes) and then a local bus to Naeso-sa (₩2000, one hour, every 30 minutes). Buses (₩8900, two hours, 13 daily) also run from Jeonju to Gyeokpo Beach and the ferry terminal. Buses between Naeso-sa and Gyeokpo

Beach (₩2750, 40 minutes) run every two hours (9am to 7pm).

Ferries go from Gyeokpo to Wido (₩9100 one way, 40 minutes, three daily September to April, six daily May to August).

Gunsan & Seonyudo
군산, 선유도
☑ 063

The industrial port city of Gunsan was a former Japanese colonial town and has a smattering of architecturally interesting structures. But the main reason to visit is to catch a ferry to the island of Seonyudo.

◉ Sights

Gunsan Modern History Museum MUSEUM
(군산근대역사박물관; ☑ 063 454 7870; http://museum.gunsan.go.kr/index.jsp; 240 Haemang-ro; adult/child/youth ₩2000/500/1000; ⊙9am-6pm Tue-Sun) The highlight here is a reconstruction of a typical Gunsan block during the 1930s, under Japanese rule. Be sure to pick up a pamphlet, which includes a map of colonial-era buildings in the neighbourhood. The museum is a ₩5000 taxi ride from Gunsan bus terminal.

Seonyudo   ISLAND

(선유도) A 43km ferry trip from Gunsan brings you to the relaxing island of Seonyu-do, situated amid 60 mostly uninhabited small islands. Today there are more bicycle-hire stalls than fishing boats; you can hire bicycles (₩10,000 per day) to pedal around the laid-back fishing villages on Seonyudo and the three islands that are linked to it by bridges.

The main attraction is the 1.6km beach, a 10-minute walk from the ferry pier, on a spit of soft sand. All the island's peaks can be hiked for panoramic views of islands: just look for a trail or steps leading up to the top.

You'll find plenty of inexpensive restaurants and *minbak* (rooms from ₩40,000) in the main village just before the beach.

ℹ️ Getting There & Around

Buses (₩5600, one hour, every 15 minutes) leave from Jeonju for Gunsan. Ferries for Seo-nyudo (one-way adult ₩12,300 to ₩16,650, child ₩5000; 50 to 90 minutes) leave from the **Gunsan Coastal Ferry Terminal** (연안여객터미널; Yeonan Yeogaek; 📞 063 472 2711), a 15-minute, ₩10,000 taxi ride from Gunsan bus terminal. The ferry schedule is highly seasonal and dependent on tides; prices depend on whether you wind up with a fast or slow boat.

Chungcheongnam-do

Best Places to Eat

➜ Mushroom (p283)

➜ Gomanaru (p285)

➜ Gudurae Dolssambap (p288)

Best Places to Stay

➜ Pinocchio Pension (p292)

➜ Lotte Buyeo Resort (p287)

➜ Mudrin Hotel (p290)

Why Go?

Much of the buzz in the region has focused on the new administrative city of Sejong, but until it gets up and running, it's Daejeon that's the capital manqué with all the trappings of modern Korean life. More interesting, however, are the small towns left in its wake: Gongju and tiny Buyeo were once capitals of the ancient Baekje dynasty, and have retained a surprising number of old fortresses, tombs and relics.

Chungcheongnam-do (충청남도) also has the best beaches within striking distance of Seoul. Gorgeous Daecheon Beach is popular with the young, active crowd, while those preferring some solitude can hop on a ferry to one of the nearby islands. To the north is Taean-haean Marine National Park, dotted with more islands, beaches and the promise of wind-whipped fresh air. In 2012, a series of trails – more than 100km long and flitting in and out of the coast – opened in the park.

When to Go
Daejeon

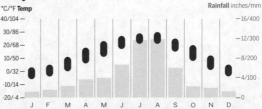

°C/°F Temp — Rainfall inches/mm

Apr See the spring blooms at the Cheollipo Arboretum and in Gyeryongsan National Park.

Jul Love it or loathe it, the Boryeong Mud Festival is one big (messy) throwdown.

Oct The region celebrates its rich links to the past via the Baekje Cultural Festival.

History

When the Baekje dynasty (57 BC – AD 668) was pushed south by an aggressive Goguryeo kingdom in AD 475, this is where the Baekje ended up, establishing their capital first in Ungjin (modern-day Gongju), then moving further south to Sabi (modern-day Buyeo). Its culture was fairly sophisticated, and coincided with the early flourishing of Buddhism in Korea, but after Sabi fell to the joint army of Shilla and China in AD 660, the region passed into obscurity.

Daejeon 대전

☎ 042 / POP 1.5 MILLION

The fifth-largest city in South Korea, Daejeon (www.daejeon.go.kr) is a major science and research centre, thanks no doubt to the presence of the Korea Advanced

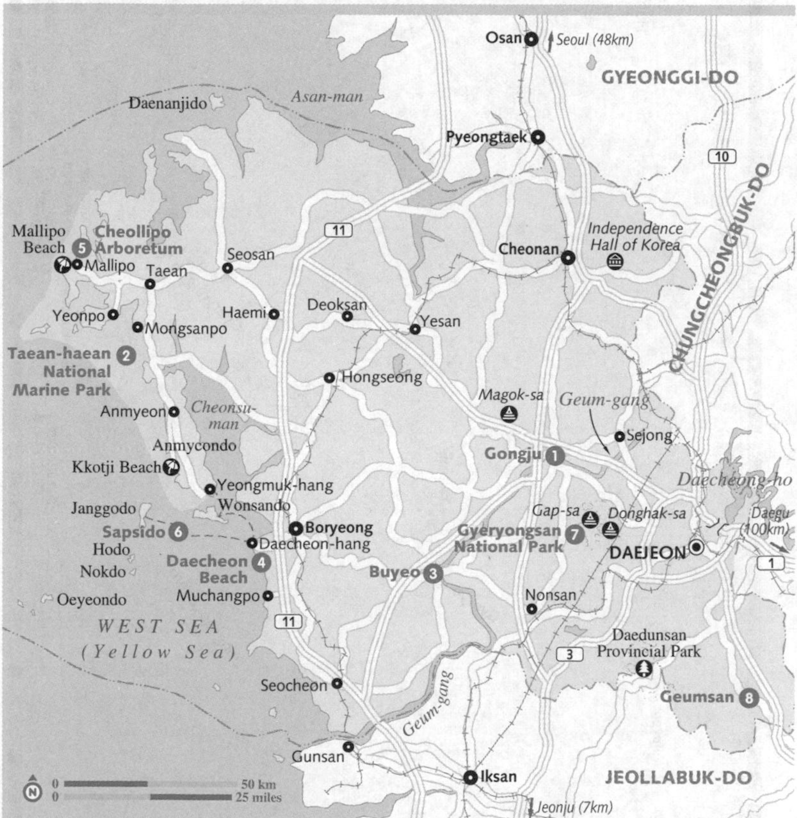

Chungcheongnam-do Highlights

1. Marvelling at the 1500-year-old treasures from King Muryeong's tomb in **Gongju** (p283).
2. Strolling from beach to beach along the new trails at **Taean-haean National Marine Park** (p291).
3. Climbing the fortress in **Buyeo** (p286), the site of the Baekje army's last stand.
4. Chilling out at **Daecheon Beach** (p289) and indulging in mud spa treatments.
5. Rejoicing at the variety of flora at the **Cheollipo Arboretum** (p292).
6. Unwinding at a beachfront hut in tiny **Sapsido** (p290).
7. Hiking from one end of **Gyeryongsan National Park** (p282) to the other.
8. Going gaga over ginseng in the trading town of **Geumsan** (p287).

Daejeon

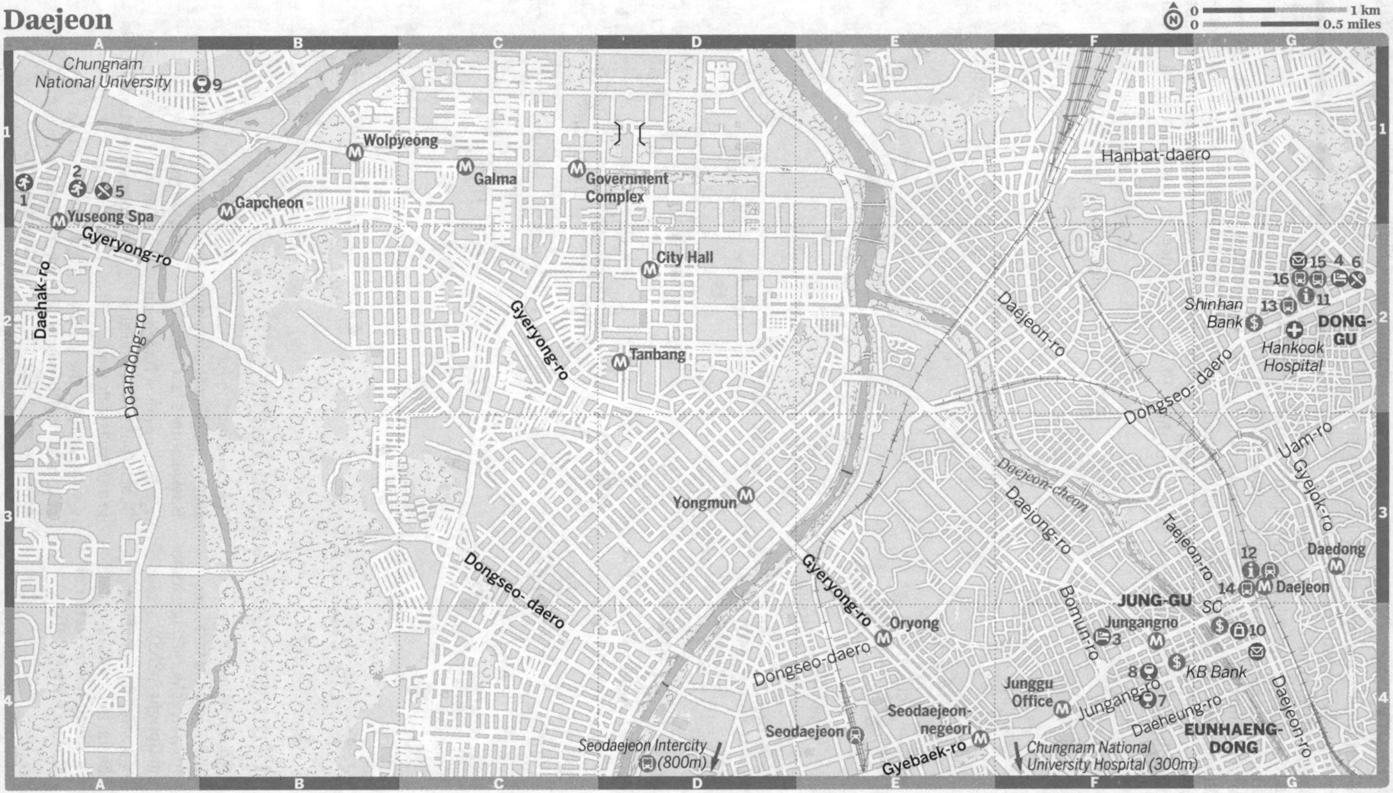

CHUNGCHEONGNAM-DO DAEJEON

DONG-GU

15 4 6
16 11
13
Hankook Hospital
Shinhan Bank

Gyejok-ro
Uam-ro
Daedong

12
14 Daejeon
Daejeon-ro
EUNHAENG-DONG

Taejeon-ro SC
10
KB Bank
JUNG-GU
Junggangno
8
3 17
Junga-ro
Daeheung-ro

Chungnam National University Hospital (300m)

Junggu Office

Bomun-ro
Daejeon-chem
Daejeong-ro
Dongseo-daero
Hanbat-daero
Daejeon-ro

Oryong
Gyeryong-ro
Seodaejeon-negeori
Seodaejeon
Gyebaek-ro

Dongseo-daero

Seodaejeon Intercity (800m)

Yongmun

City Hall
Tanbang
Government Complex

Gyeryong-ro
Galma
Dongseo-daero

Wolpyeong
Gapcheon

Chungnam National University
9

Yuseong Spa
2 5
1

Gyeryong-ro
Daehak-ro
Doandong-ro

1 km
0.5 miles

Daejeon

Institute of Science and Technology (KAIST, aka the 'MIT of South Korea').

Though just a small town up until the 1970s, Daejeon is now an overgrown suburb of Seoul, a cookie-cutter landscape of looming apartment buildings, squat research establishments and traffic-snarled streets.

In addition to being a major transit hub for the region, its principal attraction is Yuseong Hot Springs.

◉ Sights & Activities

Daejeon is a sprawling city. The 'old downtown' area of Eunhaeng-dong (은행동) is near Daejeon train station. The new centre is Dunsan-dong (둔산동), 5km to the east and home to City Hall. On the western edge are the hot springs in brassy, neon-lit Yuseong.

Yuseong Hot Springs　　　　　　SPRING
(유성 온천; www.yuseong.go.kr; Ⓢ Yuseong Spa) Yuseong Hot Springs draws its water from sources 350m underground. With more than 60 different minerals, the slightly alkaline water is said to be good for all sorts of ailments, from skin concerns to arthritis. There's a free public **foot bath** that is open 24 hours; from Exit 7 of the subway station, keep walking straight and turn right at the first traffic light.

Otherwise, several hotels have spas that are open to the public. **Yousung Spa** (☑ 042 820 0100; 9 Oncheon-ro, Yuseong-gu; admission ₩7000; ⊙ 5am-10pm; Ⓢ Yuseong Spa, Exit 6), at the eponymous hotel (유성호텔), has indoor and outdoor pools, with small waterfalls.

🛏 Sleeping

The biggest motel clusters are around Yuseong Hot Springs and the express bus terminal; both have some seedy corners, so it's best not to venture too deep.

Java Hotel　　　　　　　　　　MOTEL ₩
(자바 호텔; ☑ 042 256 6191; 36 Jungang-ro 109beon-gil, Jung-gu; d weekday/weekend ₩40,000/50,000; ✳@🛜; Ⓜ Jungangno, Exit 6) Pop accents liven up the spacious, clean rooms at this new motel. It's located in the old downtown, on the other (quieter) side of the street from the dining and drinking district; look for the neon sparks on top. The accommodating owners speak some English.

Limousine Motel　　　　　　LOVE MOTEL ₩
(리무진모텔; ☑ 042 621 1004; 34 Hanbat-dae-ro 1314beon-gil, Dong-gu; d weekday/weekend ₩40,000/50,000; ✳@) A love motel with all the trimmings: spacious rooms with huge flat-screen TV, bathtub, contemporary furnishings and windows that can be shuttered for complete privacy.

🍴 Eating

For cheap bites, visit the food outlets in the Daejeon bus-terminal complex. Dunsan-dong is packed with Korean faves such as barbecue and fried chicken. **Jungang Market** (중앙시장; 81-3 Jung-dong, Dong-gu; ⊙ 9am-7.30pm) has porridge and pancake vendors.

Cheongju Haejangguk　　　　KOREAN ₩
(청주해장국; ☑ 042 822 0050; 63 Oncheon-ro, Yuseong-gu; meals ₩5500-7000; ⊙ 24hr; Ⓜ Yuseong Spa, Exit 7) This 24-hour soup joint is an all-around pleaser: cheap and delicious, good for groups or solo diners. The

SEJONG: NOT THE NEW CAPITAL

In a controversial bid to decentralise the government in Seoul and to move some agencies further away from the northern border, the construction of Sejong (세종; www.sejongcitykorea.com) began in 2007. Sejong is not replacing Seoul as the capital; rather, it has been designated a 'special autonomous city'. As of 2015, 36 government agencies have been relocated here. The population is expected to grow from its current figure of 142,000 to 500,000 by 2030.

Built entirely from scratch (and still under construction), Sejong is 120km south of Seoul, and just north of Daejeon. There are ambitious plans to make the city a prototype for future developments: The new government complex is only six storeys, with green walkways running between buildings and along rooftops. At the centre is the large, human-made **Sejong Lake Park** (세종호수공원). Still, Sejong has been derided as a ghost town and many bureaucrats return to Seoul on the weekends to resume their social lives.

If you're curious to visit, take the Daejeon metro to Banseok, the end of the line. Then catch BRT bus 990 (₩1500, 20 minutes, every 15 minutes) to the Sejong Government Building (five stops).

---

speciality is *haejangguk* – known as 'hangover soup' – and there are several varieties on the menu. It's at the end of a strip of restaurants behind the public footbath in Yuseong.

Yeongsuni KOREAN ₩₩
(영순이; ☑ 042 633 4520; 1717 Dongseo-daero, Dong-gu; meals ₩6000-25,000; ⊙ 10.30am-10.30pm) Choose from a range of hearty set menus with *shabu kalguksu* (샤브칼국수), where you cook your own meat and noodles in a spicy mushroom and vegetable soup. More elaborate sets come with *sangchussam* (상추쌈; grilled meats wrapped in vegetable leaves). Look for a mushroom-headed caricature giving the thumbs up, and the picture menu out front.

 Drinking

There are two lively areas: Eunhaeng-dong and Dunsan-dong. The latter is brasher and where you'll find the city's nightclubs; in contrast, Eunhaeng-dong is a little quieter, with more artsy establishments.

Ranch Pub BAR
(☑ 042 825 4157; www.facebook.com/ranchpub-daejeon; 88 Gungdong-ro 18beon-gil, Yuseong-gu; ⊙ 5pm-2am; ☑ 105) With 10 beers on tap and a relaxed atmosphere, this is a favourite haunt of expats and beer lovers. It's run by the former head brewer at Hand & Malt, a Seoul craft brewery, and his wife. The food is better than the usual pub grub: try the air-fried chicken.

The bar is near Chungnam University, four bus stops past Yuseong Spa. From the

bus stop, turn left down the side street and the bar will be on your left, with a cinder-block wall.

Mustang Pub BAR
(33 Daeheung-ro 127beon-gil, Jung-gu; drinks from ₩5500; ⊙ 5pm-2am Mon-Sat; Ⓜ Jungangno, Exit 3) This small bar, with a neighbourhood-bistro vibe, serves yummy pints of Kabrew, one of Korea's better microbrews. Sister bar **Mustang's Brickhouse** (☑ 10 5457 5016; www.facebook.com/brickhouse.daejeon; 53 Junggyo-ro, Jung-gu; drinks from ₩5000; ⊙ 9pm-late Wed-Sun; Ⓢ Jungangno, Exit 3), across the street, is a bigger, louder affair (sometimes with live music), though the beer isn't as good. For both bars, head straight from Exit 3 of the metro and turn right at the church.

🛍 **Shopping**

Young people clog the pedestrianised streets of Eunhaeng-dong. The more upscale shopping area is in Dunsan-dong around **Time-World Galleria**.

ℹ **Information**

Chungnam National University Hospital
(충남대학교병원; ☑ 042 280 7100; www.cnuh.co.kr; 282 Munhwa-ro, Jung-gu; Ⓢ Seodaejeon Sageori, Exit 1) Medical services in English.

Tourist Information Centre Inside Daejeon train station and at the arrivals platform at the bus terminal complex (☑ 042 632 1335); there's usually someone who speaks good English.

ℹ Getting There & Away

AIR

The nearest airport is at Cheongju, 40km north. Trains (₩3900, one hour) run 11 times a day from Daejeon station to Cheongju Airport station. Buses run from Dongdaejeon intercity bus terminal to the airport (₩3700, 45 minutes, five daily). There are also buses to Incheon International Airport (₩15,900, three hours, every 20 minutes).

BUS

Daejeon has four bus terminals: Yuseong intercity bus terminal, Seodaejeon (west) intercity bus terminal, Dongdaejeon (east) intercity bus terminal and the express bus terminal; the last two are located in the new Daejeon bus terminal complex.

TRAIN

KTX trains run every 30 minutes (and more frequently in the morning and evening) from Seoul (₩23,700, one hour) and from Busan (₩35,200, 1¾ hours).

From Seoul, there are also hourly *saemaul* (₩16,000, 1¾ hours) and *mugunghwa*

(₩10,800, two hours) services to Daejeon. From Busan, *mugunghwa* trains (₩17,800, 2¼ hours) run hourly; *saemaul* trains (₩26,500, three hours) run seven times a day.

KTX trains also run from Yongsan to Seodaejeon train station (₩23,400, one hour, every 30 minutes) in the west of the city; some trains continue on to Mokpo and Yeosu in Jeollanam-do.

ℹ Getting Around

BUS

City buses are very regular and bus stops have GPS-enabled signs with arrival information. From outside the express bus terminal, useful buses (₩1200, every 10 to 15 minutes) include the following:

Bus 2, 201, 501 or 701 (15 minutes) To Daejeon train station and Eunhaeng-dong. The bus stop for the latter is along Jungang-ro after Daejeon train station.

Bus 102 or 106 (25 minutes) To Yuseong.

Bus 106 (20 minutes) To City Hall and Dunsan-dong. The bus stop for the latter is just after TimeWorld Galleria.

BUS DEPARTURES FROM DAEJEON

Express Bus Terminal Departures

DESTINATION	PRICE (₩)	DURATION (HR)	FREQUENCY
Busan	23,300	3¼	6 daily
Daegu	13,600	2	hourly
Gwangju	16,300	3	hourly
Jeonju	6900	1½	every 30min
Seoul	14,000	2	every 20min

Dongdaejeon Intercity Bus Terminal Departures

DESTINATION	PRICE (₩)	DURATION	FREQUENCY
Cheongju	3800	50min	every 15min
Gongju	4400	1hr	every 40min

Seodaejeon Intercity Bus Terminal Departures

DESTINATION	PRICE (₩)	DURATION	FREQUENCY
Buyeo	7100	1¼hr	every 30min
Daedunsan	3500	40min	3 daily

Yuseong Intercity Bus Terminal Departures

DESTINATION	PRICE (₩)	DURATION	FREQUENCY
Boryeong	10,800	1¾hr	every 40min
Gongju	3100	45min	every 20min

CHUNGCHEONGNAM-DO DAEJEON

Bus 701 (35 minutes) To Seodaejeon intercity bus terminal.

METRO

Daejeon's metro line (per trip ₩1200 to ₩1300) has 22 stations. Useful stops for travellers are Daejeon station, Jungangno (near Eunhaeng-dong), City Hall (near Dunsan-dong) and Yuseong Spa.

TAXI

Taxis are plentiful; fares start at ₩2800.

Gyeryongsan National Park
계룡산국립공원

♪ 041

Gyeryongsan is the region's most popular park, perhaps because of the sense of accomplishment it offers: you can easily hike from one end to the other in a day. There are two park entrances: the eastern one closer to Daejeon and the western one closer to Gongju.

◎ Sights & Activities

Gyeryongsan National Park   NATIONAL PARK
(계룡산국립공원; ☎ 0428253003; http://gyeryong.knps.or.kr; adult/child/youth ₩2000/400/700; ◎6am-7pm) Gyeryongsan, one of Korea's smallest parks, means 'Rooster Dragon Mountain', because locals thought the mountain resembled a dragon with a rooster's head. At the eastern entrance is the temple **Donghak-sa** (동학사; 462 Donghaksa 1-ro; adult/child/youth ₩2000/400/700; ◎8am-6pm); at the western entrance, **Gap-sa** (갑사; 567-3 Gapsa-ro; adult/child/youth ₩2000/400/700;

◎8am-6pm). A trail between the two temples runs along streams and small waterfalls (and a few peaks if you wish). The total hike takes between four and six hours, depending on the route. There is excellent English signage throughout.

With easy access from Daejeon, most people start at the eastern entrance, from where it's a 15-minute walk to Donghak-sa, noteworthy for being one of Korea's few nunneries. Just before the temple, look for the trail that leads you on an easy one-hour trek up to the **Brother & Sister Pagodas** (Nammaetap; 남매탑) – twin Shilla-era pagodas that are said to represent the brother and sister who founded the original hermitage here.

Continue up to **Sambul-bong Gogae** (Sambul-bong Ridge), where the trail splits: From here you can decide to continue on to the peaks **Sambul-bong** (775m), **Gwaneum-bong** (816m) and **Yeoncheong-bong** (738m), before wending down to Gap-sa (5.5km, four hours), or to head directly to Gap-sa (2.8km, 1½ hours). The latter route passes the small waterfall **Yongmun Pokpo** and the hermitage **Sinheung-am**.

Gap-sa's main hall contains three gleaming Buddha statues, while a smaller shrine houses three shamanist deities – Chilseong, Sansin and Dokseong. From Gap-sa, it's another 15 minutes to the bus stop. The hike is slightly more difficult going in the other direction.

🛏 Sleeping & Eating

The Donghak-sa entrance has the larger tourist village, with a motel strip. Both

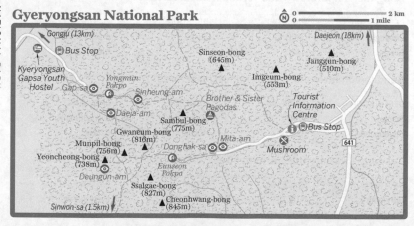

Gyeryongsan National Park

N | 0 ———— 2 km
0 ———— 1 mile

Gongju (13km)

Bus Stop

Kyeryongsan Gapsa Youth Hostel

Gap-sa

Yongmun Pokpo

Sinheung-am

Daeja-am

Sinseon-bong (645m)

Daejeon (18km)

Janggun-bong (510m)

Imgeum-bong (553m)

Brother & Sister Pagodas

Tourist Information Centre

Bus Stop

Sambul-bong (775m)

Gwaneum-bong (816m)

Munpil-bong (756m)

Yeoncheong-bong (738m)

Donghak-sa

Mita-am

Mushroom

641

Deungun-am

Eunseon Pokpo

Ssalgae-bong (827m)

Sinwon-sa (1.5km)

Cheonhwang-bong (845m)

sides have restaurants serving up the usual *sanchae bibimbap* (rice, egg, meat and mountain vegies with chilli sauce).

Kyeryongsan Gapsa Youth Hostel
HOSTEL ₩

(계룡산갑사 유스호스텔; ☑ 041 856 4666; www.kapsayouthhostel.com; 136-1 Jungjang-ri; dm/f ₩13,000/55,000; ☀) Guests sleep on *yo* (padded quilts) at this well-managed youth hostel at the Gap-sa entrance to Gyeryongsan National Park. It's a red brick building across from the bus stop. Call ahead, as it's sometimes booked out with school groups. Prices rise (extra ₩1000 to ₩2000 for dorms; ₩5000 to ₩10,000 for rooms) on weekends and during high season.

★ Mushroom
KOREAN ₩₩

(머쉬룸; ☑ 042 825 1375; 145 Donghaksa 2-ro, Banpo-myeon; dishes ₩8000-60,000; ☺10am-9pm) The best restaurant at the Donghak-sa entrance to Gyeryongsan National Park is styled after its namesake – you can't miss it. Naturally, it specialises in local mushroom dishes. For groups, there's *beseot jeongol* (버섯전골; mushroom hotpot; ₩60,000); solo diners can try the delicious *beoseot deopbap* (버섯덮밥; sauteed mushrooms over rice; ₩10,000). Seating is on plush sofas around a blazing hearth.

❶ Information

The information centre at the Donghak-sa entrance has trail maps (in English) and bus schedules (in Korean).

❶ Getting There & Away

TO/FROM DONGHAK-SA

From Daejeon take bus 107 (₩1200, 25 minutes, every 20 minutes) from the Yuseong Spa Exit 5 bus stop. From the local bus terminal in central Gonju, bus 350 (₩1400, one hour) runs three times a day; the first one leaves at 9.15am and the last one returns at 5.10pm. Bus 48 runs from Gyeryong station on the KTX Honam line (₩1200, one hour, every 45 minutes).

TO/FROM GAP-SA

From the local bus terminal in central Gonju, take bus 320 (₩1400, 40 minutes, hourly). From Gonju station on the KTX Honam line, take bus 205 (₩1400, 25 minutes, seven daily).

There are seven buses daily (numbered 340, 341 or 342) between Gap-sa and Yuseong Spa (₩3000, one hour); the first one leaves at 8am, from the Exit 6 bus stop, and the last one returns at 5.20pm.

Gongju
공주

☑ 041 / POP 116,800

From AD 475 to 538, Gonju (www.gonju.go.kr) was the capital of the Baekje Kingdom and there are a handful of sights here that draw on that legacy; the most notable is the Tomb of King Muryeong. All are within walking distance in the old city south of the river.

◉ Sights

Tomb of King Muryeong ARCHAEOLOGICAL SITE
(백제 무령왕릉; ☑041 856 0331; 37 Wangreung-ro; adult/child/youth ₩1500/700/1000; ☺9am-6pm Mar-Oct, to 5pm Nov-Feb) In 1971 the tomb of King Muryeong, the 25th Baekje king, was discovered – miraculously intact and completely by accident. The tomb and the six others in the vicinity aren't open to the public, though you can walk over the lumpy earth that covers them. Instead, the on-site **museum** has models of two of them that you can enter, as well as English information about the tombs and the history of the Baekje kingdom.

At the entrance to the site, the **Ungjin Baekje Historical Museum** (웅진백제역사관; ☑041 856 0331; 37 Wangreung-ro; ☺9am-6pm) FREE has more historical info and a **tourist information centre**. To see the actual artefacts recovered from the tombs, visit the Gongju National Museum.

Gongsan-seong FORTRESS
(공산성; 280 Ungjin-ro; adult/child/youth ₩1200/600/800; ☺9am-6pm Mar-Oct, to 5pm Nov-Feb) This commanding hilltop fortress is a reminder of a time when Gongju (then called Ungjin) was Baekje's capital. It was during the Joseon dynasty that the original mud structure was rebuilt into today's stone fortress. You can walk along the perimeter, on the wall. Along the way you'll pass numerous pavilions, rebuilt according to archeological evidence of their original structures. The best views are in the northwest overlooking the river. In the evening the fortress is lit by floodlights.

A changing of the guards ceremony takes place hourly between 11am and 4pm on weekends during April, May, June, September and October at the main entrance gate.

Gongju National Museum MUSEUM
(국립공주박물관; ☑041 850 6300; http://gongju.museum.go.kr; 34 Gwangwangdanji-gil; ☺9am-6pm Tue-Fri, to 7pm Sat & Sun) FREE This

Gongju

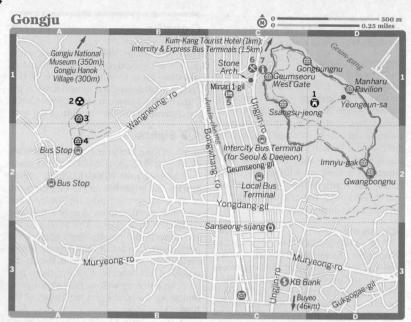

Gongju

◎ Sights
1 Gongsan-seong....................................D1
2 Tomb of King Muryeong.....................A1
3 Tomb of King Muryeong Museum......A1
4 Ungjin Baekje Historical Museum......A2

🛏 Sleeping
5 I-Motel..C1

✖ Eating
6 Gomanaru..C1

ⓘ Information
Tourist Information.....................(see 4)
7 Tourist Information Centre................C1

excellent museum exhibits the treasures discovered in the tomb of King Muryeong, including the intricate and distinctive gold diadem ornaments that you'll see images of all over Gongju. While only a few hundred of the 2906 tomb artefacts are on display here, together with some videos (with English subtitles) they paint a vivid picture of Baekje culture.

The museum is a 15-minute, signposted walk north from the royal tombs.

✦ Festivals & Events

Baekje Cultural Festival CULTURAL
(www.baekje.org) Gongju and Buyeo together host this extravagant festival in October, with a huge parade, games, traditional music and dancing, and a memorial ceremony for its erstwhile kings.

🛏 Sleeping

Kum-Kang Tourist Hotel HOTEL ₩
(금강관광호텔; ☎041 852 1071; www.hotel-kumkang.com; 16-11 Jeonmak 2-gil; r incl breakfast ₩40,000-50,000; ❈@ⓢ) Located on the northern side of the river near the express bus terminal, this hotel has neat rooms with large bathrooms and is a class above the usual love motels.

I-Motel MOTEL ₩
(아이 모텔; ☎041 853 1130; 6-5 Minari 3-gil; d ₩35,000; ❈@) One of a dozen motels clustered opposite the fortress, this one is run by a friendly older couple, and has a homey feel with clean rooms, huge TVs and computers. Look for the 'I' sign surrounded by swans.

Gongju Hanok Village HANOK GUESTHOUSE ₩₩
(공주한옥마을; ☎041 840 8900; http://hanok.gongju.go.kr; 12 Gwangwangdanji-gil; r from ₩100,000; Ⓟ❈) This recently built *hanok*

village is geared for local families to learn about their cultural heritage. As everything is shiny new, it's not exactly atmospheric of old Korea, but you do get the smell of wood smoke from the traditional *ondol*.

✘ Eating & Drinking

If you're itching for a drink, head to the back gate of Gongju National University (공주대 후문; Gongjudae humun), a few hundred metres behind the express bus terminal, which has scads of bars, cheap eateries and cafes.

★ Gomanaru   KOREAN ₩₩
(고마나루; ☑ 041 857 9999; www.gomanaru.co.kr; 5-9 Baekmigoeul-gil; meals ₩8000-25,000; ⊙ 9am-10pm) This restaurant serves the prettiest *ssambap* (assorted ingredients with rice and lettuce wraps) around: not only do you get a fragrant array of leaves, but you also get handfuls of colourful edible flowers. Solo diners can get a bibimbap that looks like a bouquet. Grab a seat by the window for views of Gongsan-seong lit up at night.

ℹ Information

Tourist Information Centre (☑ 041 856 7700) Staff here usually speak English. Ask about weekend city tours held March through November.

ℹ Getting There & Away

The new intercity and express bus terminals are together north of the river. The old intercity bus terminal south of Gongsan-seong also has buses to Seoul and Daejeon, though with less frequent departures than the new terminal. Bus 200 (₩1400, 30 minutes, 12 daily) runs between the new Gongju station on the KTX Honam line and the new bus terminal.

Bus 101 (₩1400, 15 minutes, every 20 minutes) connects the express bus terminal to the Gongsan-seong area, though the route is circuitous; it's quicker to walk (about 15 minutes). Buses 101 and 125 (₩1400, five minutes, every 15 minutes) run between Gongsan-seong and the Tomb of King Muryeong; otherwise it's a 15-minute walk.

Magok-sa   마곡사
☑ 041

Magok-sa, 25km from Gongju, makes for a pleasant half-day trip. The utterly serene temple enjoys a pastoral setting beside a river, and sees surprisingly few visitors.

⊙ Sights

Magok-sa   TEMPLE
(마곡사; ☑ 041 841 6220; www.magoksa.or.kr; 966 Magoksa-ro, Sagok-myeon; adult/child/youth ₩2000/1000/1500; ⊙ sunrise-sunset) Magok-sa was founded in the 7th century AD and, like most Korean temples, has had its buildings restored and reconstructed through the years. Unlike most temples, however, its extant buildings are being allowed to age gracefully, and there are quite a few atmospheric halls, stumpy pagodas and pavilions. The elaborate entry gates feature colourful statues of various deities and bodhisattvas. Cross the 'mind-washing bridge' to reach the main hall, behind which stands a rare, wooden, two-storey prayer hall, **Daeungbojeon**.

From Magok-sa, three hiking trails head up the nearby hills (there's a signboard with a map, in Korean only), passing small hermitages. The longest trail (10km, 4½ hours) hits the two peaks, **Nabal-bong** (나발봉; 417m) and **Hwarin-bong** (활인봉; 423m).

A templestay can be arranged for ₩50,000.

🛏 Sleeping & Eating

Magok-sa has a small tourist village, with restaurants serving typical country fare (₩8000 to ₩25,000): *sanchae bibimbap, pyogo jjigae jeongsik* (표고찌개정식; shiitake mushroom stew with side dishes) and *tokkitang* (토끼탕; spicy rabbit soup).

Magok Motel   MOTEL ₩
(마곡모텔; ☑ 041 841 0042; www.magokmotel. com; 855 Magoksa-ro, Sagok-myeon; weekday/weekend ₩40,000/50,000; P ❋) If the idyllic, hassle-free setting of Magok-sa appeals, you

CHUNGCHEONGNAM-DO MAGOK-SA

BUS DEPARTURES FROM GONGJU

DESTINATION	PRICE (₩)	DURATION	FREQUENCY
Boryeong	7700	1¾hr	every 40min
Buyeo	4300	45min	every 40min
Cheonan	5400	1hr	every 30min
Daejeon	4400	1hr	every 10min
Seoul	9000	1¾hr	every 40min

can stay the night at this surprisingly modern motel. There a porch with picnic tables and BBQ facilities, and usually someone around who can speak a little English.

ℹ Getting There & Away

Bus 707 (₩1400, 45 minutes, hourly) runs from Gongju's local bus terminal to Magok-sa's tourist village. The temple is a 20-minute walk from the bus stop along a road flanked by a stream.

Buyeo   부여

☑ 041 / POP 84,000

Buyeo (www.buyeo.go.kr) is home to several Baekje-era sites and relics. King Seong, a statue of whom presides over the roundabout in the town centre, moved the capital here in AD 538, when it was known as Sabi. It lasted till AD 660, when the combined Shilla-Tang army destroyed it. Though Buyeo was considered a better site for the capital, today it is more of a backwater than Gongju; it's a compact, walkable town, with no buildings taller than five storeys.

◉ Sights

Busosan-seong   FORTRESS
(부소산성; adult/child/youth ₩2000/1000/1100; ⊙8am-6pm Mar-Oct, 9am-5pm Nov-Feb) This mountain fortress covers the forested hill of Buso-san (106m) and shielded the Baekje capital of Sabi within its walls. Structures such as the **Banwollu Pavilion** (반월루) offer lovely views of the surrounding countryside. Sandy paths weave through pine trees past temples and pavilions.

One temple, **Samchung-sa** (삼충사), is dedicated to three loyal Baekje court officials, including General Gyebaek. Despite being outnumbered 10 to one, he led his army of 5000 in a last stand against the final Shilla and Chinese onslaught in AD 660. The Baekje army dauntlessly repulsed four enemy attacks but were defeated in the fifth – the *coup de grâce* for the kingdom.

In response, it is said, on the northern side of the fortress, 3000 court ladies threw themselves off a cliff into the river Baengma-gang, rather than submit to the conquering armies. The rock where they jumped is now called **Nakhwa-am** (낙화암), 'falling flowers rock', in their honour.

From Nakhwa-am there's a rocky and somewhat steep path down to the tiny temple at the bottom of the cliff, **Goran-sa** (고란사). Behind it is a spring that provided the favourite drinking water of Baekje kings. Slaves collecting the water had to present it along with a leaf from a nearby plant that only grows near here, to show that the water came from this spring.

At Goran-sa, pleasure boats (₩28,000 for up to seven people) make a 10-minute trip down the river to the **Gudurae Sculpture Park** (구드래조각공원).

Buyeo National Museum   MUSEUM
(국립부여박물관; ☑ 041 833 8562; http://buyeo.museum.go.kr; 5 Geumseong-ro; ⊙9am-6pm Tue-Sun) ▐FREE▌ This museum houses one of the best collections of Baekje artefacts. It has extensive English captions, making it a good place to get a primer on pre-Baekje and Baekje culture. The highlight of the collection is a glittering Baekje-era incense burner. Weighing 12kg, the burner and its pedestal are covered with incredibly intricate and well-preserved metalwork, crested with the legendary *bonghwang* bird.

Baekje Royal Tombs   ARCHAEOLOGICAL SITE
(백제왕릉; 16-1 Neungsan-ri; adult/child/youth ₩1000/400/600; ⊙8am-6pm Mar-Oct, to 5pm Nov-Feb; 🚌701) Buyeo has seven royal tombs, dating from AD 538 to 660. They're sealed for protection, but there's a re-creation of the most impressive one, which is painted with the four celestial creatures that guard the compass points (dragon, tiger, tortoise and phoenix). There's also a small museum with a model of the oldest tomb, believed

BUS DEPARTURES FROM BUYEO

DESTINATION	PRICE (₩)	DURATION	FREQUENCY
Boryeong	5200	1hr	8 daily
Cheongju	9800	2½hr	every 45min
Daejeon	7100	1hr	every 30min
Gongju	4300	45min	every 30min
Seoul	15,300	2¾hr	every 30min

GAGA OVER GINSENG

It's stumpish and a woody colour, with wispy roots trailing from its ends. Use your imagination and you might see the shape of a body, complete with limbs, perhaps even a head-shaped tip with thinning 'hair'. No wonder the Chinese call it ginseng (literally, 'man root'). To the Koreans it's *insam* (인삼), and they have been cultivating it for more than 1500 years. It's credited with myriad health benefits, from relieving pain and fatigue to curing cancer and improving sexual stamina.

The centre of the Korean ginseng business is **Geumsan** (금산; www.geumsan.go.kr), which despite its size (population 22,000) handles 80% of the ginseng trade. There are hundreds of stores, from mum-and-dad operations to wholesalers, and you'll find ginseng sold raw *(susam)*, as a potent extract and in soap, tea and candy. The street vendors make fresh *insam twigim* (인삼튀김; fried ginseng in batter; ₩1500), which you can wash down with *insam makgeolli* (인삼막걸리; rice wine made with ginseng; ₩2000).

If you're buying ginseng, the most prized variety is *hongsam* or red ginseng (홍삼), which is four to six years old and has been steamed and dried to concentrate its medicinal properties.

The best days to visit Geumsan are on market days: every second, seventh, 12th, 17th, 22nd and 27th day of the month. In September the town hosts a 10-day **Insam Festival**, with tours and activities to show how ginseng is grown, harvested, processed and served.

To get to Geumsan, take an intercity bus from Daejeon's Dongdaejeon intercity bus terminal (₩4100, one hour, every 15 minutes) or Seoul's Express Bus Terminal (₩11,700, 2¾ hours, every two hours). After you exit the Geumsan bus terminal, turn left and follow the canal for about 10 minutes. When you see SAE-Kumsan Hospital, turn right onto the road Bihoro. The market lies ahead, after you cross the wide road Insam-ro.

to be that of King Seong. Outside is the now-empty temple site, where the famous Baekje incense burner was unearthed in 1993.

The tombs are on a hillside 3km east of Buyeo, a five-minute bus ride (₩1400, every 15 minutes) from Busosan-seong.

Baekje Cultural Land   CULTURAL CENTRE
(백제역사문화관; ☑041 830 3400; www. bhm.or.kr; 374 Baekjemun-ro; adult/child/youth ₩4000/2000/3000; ☺9am-6pm Mar-Oct, to 5pm Nov-Feb, closed Mon; 🚌403-406) This recently built 'historical theme park' imagines what the Baekje palace and attendant village might have looked like, with structures you can enter (and plenty of room for kids to run around). There's a history museum too, with English signage; note that the displays here are all replicas. A taxi ride from the town centre costs around ₩8000.

Jeongnimsaji   HISTORIC BUILDING
(정림사지; 83 Jeongnim-ro; adult/child/youth ₩1500/700/900; ☺9am-6pm Mar-Oct, to 5pm Nov-Feb) This is the site of the Baekje-era temple, Jeongnim-sa. All that remains is a 8.3m five-storey stone pagoda – though this alone is certainly impressive. There's also

a museum on Baekje culture but it's all in Korean.

🛏 Sleeping

There are plenty of motels clustered around the bus terminal in the centre of town.

Samjeong Buyeo Youth Hostel   HOSTEL ₩
(삼정부여유스호스텔; ☑041 835 3101; www.buyeoyh.co.kr; 50 Naruteo-ro; dm/f ₩16,000/48,000; 🅿❄❀@🏊) You're as likely to stumble upon a bunch of kids on a field trip as you are a wedding party at this airy hostel that feels more like a hotel. Dorm rooms have two double bunks and good bathrooms. Family rooms have twin beds.

Arirang Motel   MOTEL ₩
(아리랑 모텔; ☑041 832 5656; www.arirang hotel.com; 55-1 Cheongrim-ro; d from ₩40,000; ❀@🛜) This motel looks as generic as its neighbours, but the rooms are modern and low on love-motel vibes. It's run by a cheerful *ajumma* (middle-aged woman); staff will clean the room daily if you stay for more than one night.

Lotte Buyeo Resort   HOTEL ₩₩₩
(롯데부여리조트; ☑041 939 1000; www.lotte buyeoresort.com; 400 Baekjemun-ro; r from

Buyeo

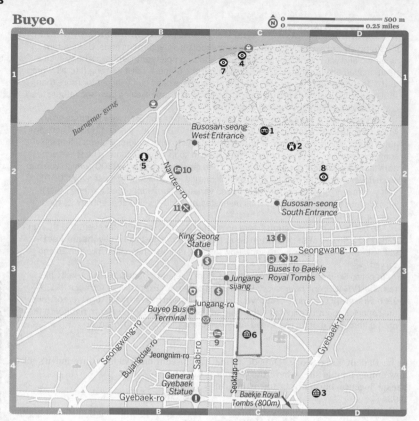

Buyeo

₩270,000; ⊖❄@✉🐾) Located opposite Baekje Cultural Land, this high-end condo-style hotel by conglomerate Lotte is a hunk of gleaming glass and concrete complete with ultraplush and modern rooms on par with the best in Seoul.

✗ Eating & Drinking

Gudurae Dolssambap   KOREAN ₩₩
(구드래돌쌈밥; ☑041 836 9259; 31 Naruteo-ro; meals ₩7000-22,000; ⊙10am-10pm) This popular restaurant serves delicious *ssambap* (rice and side dishes with lettuce wraps), with fragrant leaves and a whole host of sides. The *dolssambap* (hotpot rice and lettuce wraps), served with succulent braised pork, is particularly recommended. Look for the *jangseung* (totem poles with faces) out front.

House of Baekje   KOREAN ₩₩
(백제의집; ☑041 834 1212; 248 Seongwang-ro; meals ₩7000-18,000; ⊙10am-10pm) The house

speciality here is duck, such as *ori hunje* (오리훈제; smoked duck), served with sides and *ssam* (lettuce wraps). For solo diners, there's *yeonibap* (연잎밥; rice steamed in lotus leaf), served as a set meal that's plenty filling.

ℹ Information

Tourist Information Centre (☏ 041 830 2527) The main tourist information centre is below the entrance to Busosan-seong and usually has English-speaking staff.

Boryeong & Around 보령
☏ 041 / POP 107,350

Boryeong (www.boryeong.chungnam.kr) is the gateway to sandy Daecheon Beach (10km away) and the harbour Daecheon-hang (a further 2km), from where ferries sail to a dozen rural islands. Though it's well supplied with motels, restaurants, bars, cafes and *norae-bang* (karaoke rooms), Daecheon Beach is less a proper town than a resort outpost, surrounded by rice paddies and the sea. Developed only in the 1990s, it has all the aesthetic finesse of a tawdry Las Vegas – think neon nightscapes and plastic palm trees, with more hotels and amenities in the works.

◉ Sights & Activities

Daecheon Beach   BEACH
(대천해수욕장) This popular strip of almost golden-hued sand runs 3.5km long and is about 100m wide during low tide. The main hub of activity is at its southern end, near the **Citizen's Tower Plaza** (시민탑 광장), but in summer the entire stretch gets overrun with beachgoers, especially during the increasingly bacchanalian Boryeong Mud Festival. There's also waterskiing, canoeing, windsurfing, horse-and-carriage rides, and speedboat, banana-boat and jet-ski rides.

Boryeong Mud Skincare Center   SPA
(보령 머드체험관; ☏ 041 931 4021; http://mud.brcn.go.kr; 897-15 Daehae-ro; adult/child ₩5000/3000; ⊗8am-6pm) This modern sauna has baths with Boryeong's famous mud, said to be full of health-giving minerals. You can also tack on massages and mud packs (₩20,000 to ₩30,000). At the time of research it was closed for an upgrade. It's on the beachfront near the Citizen's Tower Plaza, to the left if you're approaching from Boryeong.

🛏 Sleeping & Eating

The older establishments are near Citizen's Tower Plaza, while Fountain Plaza (분수광장) to the north has newer outfits. Prices are an additional ₩10,000 to ₩20,000 on weekends and easily triple in summer.

Restaurants lining the beachfront have aquariums of fish, eels, crabs and shellfish outside, and you can get a platter of *modeumhoe* (모듬회; assorted raw fish) or *jogae modeumgui* (조개 모듬구이; mixed shellfish), to be barbecued at your table, for ₩30,000 to ₩40,000. Try the local speciality *kkotgejjim* (꽃게찜; steamed blue crab), or round off your meal with some spicy *haemultang* (해물탕; assorted seafood soup). If it gets too touristy, head to the harbour Daecheon-hang (대천항), which has more rustic seafood restaurants.

MUD, GLORIOUS MUD

Boryeong Mud Festival (www.boryeongmudfestival.com) Every July, Daecheon Beach is the principal venue for the nine-day Boryeong Mud Festival. It began in 1997 as a way of promoting the health benefits of the mud, which is rich in germanium and other minerals. Now it attracts 1.5 million attendees, and has developed a reputation for the unabashed, alcohol-fuelled frolics of expats, Korean students and international travellers.

After being baptised in a vat of the oozing grey stuff, participants can enter the 'mud prison' and get doused with buckets of warmed mud. There's a mud super-slide, a mud rain tunnel and a number of muddy pools where groups run, splash and generally get covered in mud. The festival grounds are just above the beach, where every evening there's a concert or rave and it's easy to zip out to the ocean for a quick swim or de-mudding. The festival is bookended by parades and fireworks.

Many English-speaking volunteers are on hand and there are free lockers, a campsite and basic clean-up facilities, making this one of the most foreigner-friendly events in Korea. Accommodation is booked up months in advance, even in Boryeong, so many come for the day or on tours run by outfits such as **Adventure Korea** (www.adventurekorea.com).

Sapsido

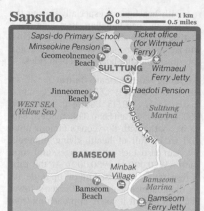

Sapsi-do Primary School
Minseokine Pension
Geomeolnemeo Beach
SULTTUNG
Ticket office (for Witmaeul Ferry)
Witmaeul Ferry Jetty
Haedoti Pension
Jinneomeo Beach
WEST SEA (Yellow Sea)
Sapsido 1-gil
Sulttung Marina
BAMSEOM
Minbak Village
Bamseom Marina
Bamseom Beach
Bamseom Ferry Jetty

0   1 km
0   0.5 miles

Mudrin Hotel

HOTEL ₩₩

(호텔머드린; ☎041 934 1111; www.mudrin. com; 28 Haesuyokjang 8-gil; d from ₩150,000; ☺❄@🛜) Daecheon newest hotel represents its move into the big leagues: Mudrin has big picture windows overlooking the beach, soft white linens and a 24-hour front desk with staff who speak some English. Still, the walls are a bit thin and you can hear noise from the hallways. The hotel is at the far end of the strip, towards Daecheon Harbour.

Motel Coconuts

MOTEL ₩₩

(모텔코코넛스; ☎041 934 6595; 7 Haesuyokjang 2-gil; r ₩50,000; ❄🛜) Decorated in bright colours, this family-run motel has a contemporary zing lacking in most of its competitors. Rooms on the upper level might have a snatch of sea view. It's around the corner from the Lotteria at Citizen's Tower Plaza.

🛈 Information

The **tourist information centre** (☎041 932 2023) is inside Daecheon train station. Interpretation services for English (☎010 5438 4865), Chinese (☎010 2031 2270) and Japanese (☎010 6717 5759) are available. There's another small kiosk at Citizen's Tower Plaza at Daecheon Beach.

🛈 Getting There & Around

BUS

Buses 100 and 101 (₩1400, every 10 minutes) run from Boryeong bus terminal and Daecheon train station to Daecheon Beach and on to Daecheon-hang (harbour). For Citizen's Tower Plaza, get off at the intersection where the access road meets the main strip. A taxi will cost about ₩10,000.

TRAIN

Though it's called Daecheon station, the train station is in Boryeong, located across a plaza from the bus terminal. Regular *saemaul* (₩17,400, 2½ hours, seven daily) and *mugunghwa* (₩11,700, 2¾ hours, nine daily) trains run between Daecheon station and Yongsan station in Seoul.

Sapsido

삽시도

☑ 041

If you like undeveloped beaches and the salty smell of fish, skip out to Sapsido, 13km from Daecheon. There isn't much to do here except hit the beach or wander between the two villages, Sulttung and Bamseom. You'll see locals mending fishing nets, collecting shellfish at low tide or working in the rice paddies. The pace speeds up in summer, with three beaches and more than 50 *minbak* (private homes with rooms for rent) drawing visitors from the mainland.

🔾 Sights

Geomeolneomeo Beach

BEACH

(거멀너머 해수욕장) Curving between two rocky headlands, this flat, wide beach is backed by sand dunes and fir trees. Except at high tide, you can clamber over the rocks on the left to the smaller **Jinneomeo Beach** (진너머 해수욕장). From Sulttung Marina, turn right before you hit the police station; you're on the right track if you pass a primary school.

Bamseom Beach

BEACH

(밤섬 해수욕장) The largest of Sapsido's three beaches is Banseom Beach, a broad stretch of golden sand on the island's southern coast. To find it, follow the road to the

BUS DEPARTURES FROM BORYEONG

DESTINATION	PRICE (₩)	DURATION (HR)	FREQUENCY
Buyeo	5200	1	7 daily
Daejeon	12,000	2	hourly
Seoul	10,900	2½	hourly

left of the *minbak* village at Witmaeul marina.

🛏 Sleeping & Eating

Expect prices to rise during the summer. Note that there are no shops on the island; either arrange meals at your *minbak* or bring provisions with you.

Minseokine Pension   MINBAK ₩₩
(민석이네펜션; ☎010 3920 7140; r from ₩40,000; 🅿) This is the only place right on Geomeolneomeo beach. The basic *ondol* cottages are a little shabby but have cooking facilities. The young couple that runs it are friendly and will pick you up from the marina.

Haedoti Pension   MINBAK ₩₩
(해돋이펜션; ☎041 935 1617; 168-28 Sapsido 1-gil; r from ₩50,000; 🅿) Centrally located on the island's one and only road, this red-brick *minbak* has rooms that are of motel standard, equipped with a fridge and kitchenette. Out front is a homey dining area, where the menu depends on the catch of the day (meals ₩6000 to ₩25,000).

ℹ Getting There & Around

Ferries (☎041 934 8896; www.shinhanhewoon. com/index.html in Korean; one way adult/child ₩9900/4700) run from Daecheon Ferry Terminal (대천 연안 여객선 터미널) to Sapsido at 7.30am, 1pm and 4pm (slightly earlier October to March). The trip takes 40 minutes, longer if the ferry is rerouted to other islands on the way. Ferries go to one of two marinas: Witmaeul marina (윗마을 선착장) in Sulttung village or Bamseom marina (밤섬 선착장), depending on the tides; check before you board (and check your return). The island has no public transport, though locals will often offer you a lift. It's a 40-minute walk from one end of the island to the other.

Daecheon Ferry Terminal is at the harbour Daecheon-hang, a 20-minute bus ride from Boryeong. Other ferries from Daecheon (adult ₩4950 to ₩16,500, child ₩2500 to ₩7850) run to even more remote islands – Hojado, Wonsando, Hodo, Nokdo and Oeyeondo – where few foreigners have ventured. Ferries may be delayed or cancelled on misty or rainy days.

Taean-haean National Marine Park
태안해안국립공원

📱 041

This beautiful **marine park** (태안해안국립 공원; ☎041 672 7267; http://english.knps.or.kr/ knp/taeanhaean; ☉ sunrise-sunset) covers 327 sq km of land and sea, with 130 islands and islets, and more than 30 beaches. It was badly hit by South Korea's worst-ever oil spill in December 2007, but the coast has been cleaned up and fishing and tourism have resumed with aplomb.

At the southern end is Anmyeondo (www. anmyondo.com), the park's largest island (and Korea's sixth largest). Further north, on the mainland, is the peninsula Taean (www. taean.go.kr).

Anmyeondo

◉ Sights

Kkotji Beach   BEACH
(꽃지해수욕장) Of the many beaches on Anmyeondo, one of the best is Kkotji Beach (꽃지해수욕장), a gentle 3.2km-long stretch that's a glorious 300m wide at low tide and popular with photographers at sunset. On weekends and during summer, snack vendors sell fried prawns and crabs.

You can get to Kkotji by bus (₩1300, 15 minutes, hourly) from the bus terminal in Anmyeondo's main town, Anmyeon (안면). There's a pension village a short walk back from the beach; the same bus services it.

ℹ Getting There & Around

You can get to Anmyeon by bus from Seoul (₩11,000, 2¾ hours, hourly), Daejeon (₩12,900, three hours, two daily) and Taean (₩3700, one hour, every 30 minutes). But the most picturesque journey is to take a ferry from Daecheon Ferry Terminal (₩8000, three daily) bound for Yeongmok-hang (영목항). The

---

TAEAN'S COASTAL TRAIL

Opened in 2012, the Haebyeongil (해변길) is a series of trails stretching nearly 100km through **Taean-haean National Marine Park**. The trail is divided into seven parts. It's not entirely contingent and some parts run along existing roads; however, there are daylong hikes running from beach to beach, over hills and along cliffs, past fishing and farming villages. It starts way down at the tip of Anmyeondo, in the port of Yeongmok – from where you can hike to Kkotji (29km, about seven hours) – and finishes north of Mallipo. The whole route is well-signposted.

journey takes 45 minutes to two hours depending on the ferry route. Once you disembark at Yeongmok-hang, turn right and then fork left for the two-minute uphill walk to the bus stop. The bus for Anmyeon (₩2100, 30 minutes, hourly) takes a rugged, circuitous route along back-country roads between rice paddies and rustic farmhouses.

Taean

⊙ Sights

Cheollipo Arboretum   GARDENS
(천리포수목원; ☑ 041 672 9982; www.chollipo. org; 187 Cheollipo 1-gil; Nov-Mar ₩6000, Apr-Oct ₩9000; ⊙ 9am-6pm Apr-Oct, to 5pm Nov-Mar) The Cheollipo Arboretum is among Asia's top botanical institutions, with a collection of more than 13,000 species from over 60 countries, laid out with diligent care across 64 hectares of lush coastal property. Only a fraction of it is open to the public, but even that is spectacular – particularly in spring when the magnolias bloom.

Oddly enough, the arboretum was founded and built by a man without formal training in that field: American Carl Ferris Miller was a banker in Seoul when he bought his first plot of farmland in Cheollipo in the 1970s, intending it as a weekend retreat. He continued to add it until he died in 2002 at the age of 81. He also relocated several Korean *hanok* (traditional wooden homes) to the arboretum in order to preserve them. You

can stay in one; rooms start at ₩100,000 per night.

Cheollipo Arboretum is a 20-minute walk from the Mallipo bus terminal.

Mallipo Beach   BEACH
(만리포) Though Mallipo is seeing more and more development every year, it's still a fine stretch of sand, a gentle crescent bookended by piney headlands. It's a 15-minute walk from here to the quieter Cheollipo Beach.

🛏 Sleeping & Eating

Pinocchio Pension   COTTAGE ₩₩
(피노키오 펜션; ☑ 041 672 3824; www.pinocchi-opension.com; 184 Mallipo 2-gil; r from ₩80,000; ⊛ ❀) Keep walking past the worn motels to the northern end of Mallipo Beach, stopping only when you see the wooden terrace of Pinocchio Pension. Here, comfortable cottages, with fridges, face the sea. Call directly for best rates; the owners speak some English. Complimentary breakfast is served at the attached beachfront cafe. Note that rates double from 20 July to 15 August.

❶ Getting There & Around

Taean is well served by buses from Seoul (₩9000, 2¼ hours, every 30 minutes) and Daejeon (₩9200, 2¾ hours, hourly). You can get to Mallipo Beach by local bus (₩2000, 25 minutes, hourly) from Taean's bus terminal, or directly from Seoul (₩11,000, three hours; six daily, hourly in summer).

Chungcheongbuk-do

Best Places to Eat

➜ Sangdangjip (p296)

➜ Satgatchon (p301)

➜ Doljip Sikdang (p304)

Best Places to Stay

➜ Birosanjang (p299)

➜ Hotel Lin (p295)

➜ Rio 127 (p303)

Why Go?

The only landlocked province in the South, Chungbuk (충청 북도) as it's known informally, is largely mountainous and agricultural. The province is a sleepy sort of place and its major cities are not particularly compelling, though bibliophiles may be inclined to make a pilgrimage to Cheongju, where in 1377 Buddhist monks printed the world's oldest extant book with movable metal type.

The province's charms can be better appreciated in its smaller towns and three national parks, which are home to an assortment of intriguing Buddhist sites. There's plenty to see and do here: climb the azalea-covered peaks of Sobaek-san, descend into the otherworldly caverns of Gosu Donggul, or simply savour the views along the river and at nearby Chungju-ho. Then there's Guin-sa, a Buddhist temple ensconced in a tight valley, as imposing as the mountain slopes on either side of it. If you have a few days to while away, this is the place to do it.

When to Go
Cheongju

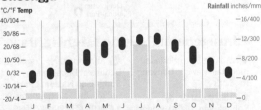

Apr The flowers in the national parks come alive, plus the weather is mercifully cool for hiking.

Jun Low season; you'll get in just before the heat wave, summer rains and price hikes.

Dec Sure it's cold but the sights are often coated in picturesque sheets of snow.

Cheongju 청주

☎043 / POP 668,000

Like most provincial capitals, Cheongju (http://english.cjcity.net) – not to be confused with nearby Chungju – is not terribly captivating. Its primary claim to fame is as the place where the world's oldest book was printed using movable metal type.

As a modern city it's somewhat redeemed by a youthful vibe, thanks to its universities, but if not for its proximity to Songnisan National Park and presidential villa Cheongnamdae, there'd be little reason to stop here.

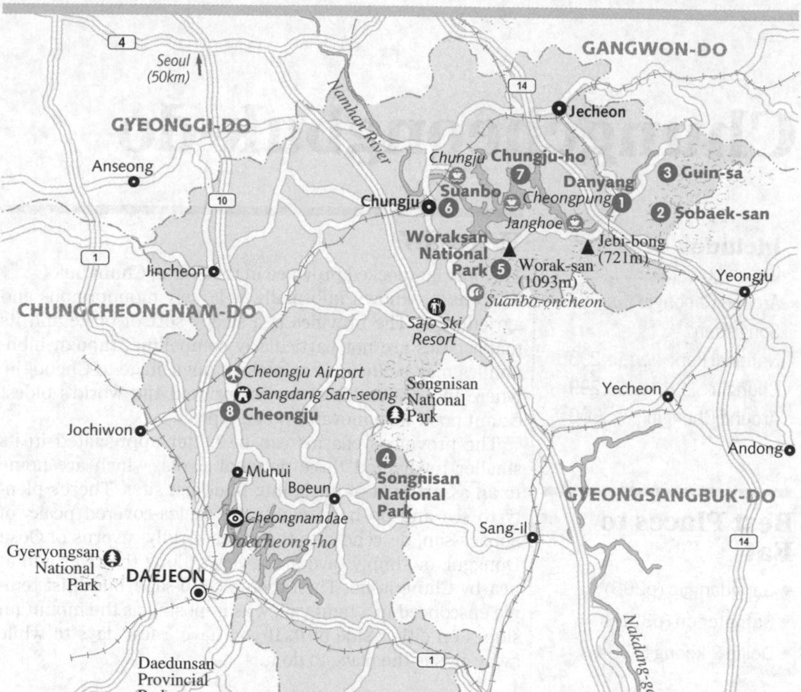

Chungcheongbuk-do Highlights

1. Waking up to glorious mountain views in **Danyang** (p302).
2. Hiking up nearby **Sobaek-san** (p304), where azaleas bloom in May.
3. Signing up for a templestay at bustling **Guin-sa** (p304), a modern but awe-inspiring hillside temple complex.
4. Admiring the gold-plated Buddha at Beopju-sa in **Songnisan National Park** (p298), then overnighting at a charming *yeogwan* beside a burbling river.
5. Contemplating ancient Buddhist carvings and the evocative ruins of Mireuksaji at **Woraksan National Park** (p302).
6. Soothing your stresses at an *oncheon* (hot-spring spa) in **Suanbo** (p300).
7. Admiring the scenery as you cruise down **Chungju-ho** (p300).
8. Learning all about the *Jikji*, the first book printed by movable type, in the province's capital of **Cheongju** (p294).

◉ Sights

Early Printing Museum
MUSEUM

(고인쇄박물관; ☏043 269 0556; ⏰9am-6pm Tue-Sun) FREE This small museum tells you everything about the *Jikji*, the oldest book in the world printed with movable metal type. Unfortunately the book is not here – it's in the National Library of France. Still, the museum exhibits many early books of Korea, including handwritten sutras and books printed using woodblocks, and there is extensive information in English. Book nerds will be enthralled by the slightly creepy Korean-speaking wax models that replicate the various steps in the creation of the *Jikji*.

Look out for Korea's oldest printed document, the *Dharani Sutra,* dating back to at least AD 751. It's accompanied by the woodblocks used in its creation.

The museum stands beside the site of **Heungdeok-sa**, where the *Jikji* was printed and where you can find a replica temple. To get there, catch bus 831 or 831-1 (₩1300, 15 minutes) from the bus stop opposite the tourist information centre. Get off at the bus stop beside the pedestrian bridge with green and yellow arches. The museum is about 50m ahead on the left.

Sangdang San-seong
FORTRESS

(상당산성) FREE This large fortress is 4km northeast of Cheongju, on the slopes of the mountain Uam-san. Originally built in the 1590s and renovated in the 18th century, it has walls that stretch 4.2km around wooded hillsides, offering great views of farms, mountains and the city. Its size makes it easy to imagine that it once housed three temples and several thousand soldiers and monks. Today, Korean families decamp to the fields outside the south gate for family picnics.

A hike around the top of the wall takes about 1½ hours. The route is completely exposed and can be steep-going. The easier direction is counter-clockwise. From where the bus drops you, walk back along the road and look on the left for a paved path that ascends to the top of the wall. Along the walk, there are hardly any signs or resting places, and no food stalls, vending machines or toilets – so bring your own water and a hat. If you're up for a challenge, follow the path beside the pond and up the steep hill on the right to do a clockwise circuit. There are restaurants and shops near the bus stop.

Bus 862 (₩1150, 30 minutes, hourly) goes from Cheongju Stadium bus stop and up to the fortress. To get to the stadium, hop on any bus heading downtown to Sajing-no (사직로) from outside the intercity bus terminal. The stadium bus stop is just after a five-storey **golden pavilion** FREE. A taxi from the bus terminal should cost ₩15,000. The last bus back to town leaves at 9.50pm.

✹ Festivals & Events

Jikji Festival
CULTURAL

(www.jikjifestival.com) Cheongju hosts the Jikji Festival every September with a demonstration of ancient printing techniques, exhibitions of old printed books, and traditional music and drama performances.

🛏 Sleeping

There are *a lot* of love motels around the bus terminals if you care to shop for price and varying degrees of 'look at me!' decor.

★ Hotel Lin
MOTEL ₩₩

(호텔린; ☏043 231 0207; r ₩40,000-50,000; ❄@) It may have faux-castle exteriors but the interiors are Santorini-inspired and a huge class above its neighbours. White walls accompany large beds and ultramodern bathrooms come complete with cute touches such as floral-patterned sinks and colourful tiling. Some rooms even have plexiglass-encased models of Santorini houses.

Hotel YaJa
LOVE MOTEL ₩₩

(☏043 238 3216; 8 Gyeongsan-ro 5beon-gil; d ₩45,000, tw/tr ₩55,000; P❄@🛜) This slick, quiet love motel is convenient for the bus station but offers plenty of little pluses to keep you lingering in the comfy beds or deep spa. A late 3pm checkout, PCs, wall-mounted mini clothes-washer and complimentary snacks – popcorn, ramen, coffee and hot ginseng. Prices rise ₩5,000 to ₩10,000 on Friday and Saturday.

✗ Eating & Drinking

There are bars and cheap eats galore (everything from fried chicken to bulgogi) in both the downtown shopping area around Young Plaza (known as Seongan-gil) and the area around Chungbuk National University (충대 중문; Chungdae jungmun), which buzzes with students.

There are also budget restaurants and snacks in and around the food and homewares market just east of the bus terminals.

Cheongju

From outside the intercity bus terminal, bus 105 takes you to Seongan-gil; to get to the university area, take bus 821 or 50-1 headed downtown and get off at the stop for Sachang Intersection, which is after the Cheongju High School stop.

Cheongju House
KOREAN ₩₩

(청주본가; ☑043 231 0588; meals ₩10,000-35,000) Meat-lovers can check out the range of *galbi* (beef ribs) and *samgyeopsal* (streaky pork belly) here. For something easier on the arteries, there's *naengmyeon* (buckwheat noodles in cold broth), *galbi-tang* (beef-rib soup) and *ttukbaegi bulgogi* (뚝배기불고기; beef simmered in an earthenware dish). Look for a red sign with an image of a house.

Sangdangjip
KOREAN ₩₩₩

(상당집; meals ₩6000-25,000; ☑) Opposite the bus stop at Sangdang San-seong, this popular restaurant makes its own tofu in a giant cauldron inside the entrance. A light starter is *dubujijim* (두부지짐; steamed tofu); for a fuller meal, try the *jeongol* (전골; hotpot) or *duruchigi* (두루치기; spicy stew). Dishes may include meat. For a quick taster, sample free tofu soup near the cauldron.

The Bugle
PUB

(beer from ₩3000, shots from ₩4000; ☑6pm-late) A stalwart on the local bar scene, this Irish pub attracts plenty of expats and has occasional live music on weekends. There's Guinness on tap, lots of imported beer, wine and bar bites such as burgers and Tex-Mex (₩9000 to ₩12,000), as well as weekend brunch. The friendly owner Andy speaks excellent English. Diagonally opposite a GS25 convenience store.

ⓘ Information

The **tourist information centre** (☑043 233 8431; ☑9am-6pm) is outside the intercity bus terminal in a two-storey blue-green building. There's free wi-fi and internet access, and staff who speak excellent English.

ⓘ Getting There & Away

AIR

Cheongju Airport (☑043 210 6110) has flights to Jeju-do and China. It's 18km from the city. Take bus 747 from outside the intercity bus terminal (₩1300, one hour, every 25 minutes). A taxi costs ₩15,000 to ₩20,000.

TRAIN

Cheongju station (청주역; ☑043 232 7788) connects primarily with Daejeon (₩3100, 40

Cheongju

◉ Sights
  1 Early Printing Museum.........................D1
  2 Golden Pavilion D2

⬛ Sleeping
  3 Hotel Lin...A3
  4 Hotel YaJa...A3

✖ Eating
  5 Cheongju House................................A3

● Drinking & Nightlife
  6 The Bugle...C2

Daejeon (₩8200, 16 minutes, every 20 to 50 minutes). Buses 500, 511 and 519 run between the intercity bus terminal and Osong station (one hour).

Around Cheongju

◉ Sights

Cheongnamdae　　　　　HISTORIC BUILDING
(청남대; ☎043 220 5677; http://chnam. cb21.net; adult/child incl return shuttle bus ₩8000/7000; ⊙9am-6.30pm Tue-Sun) Once the holiday home of South Korean presidents, this villa is no Camp David, but it's a beautiful lakeside park, with 185 hectares of well-manicured grounds and 2.3km of paths along the lakefront and across the gently rolling hills. You can linger in the Chogajeong Pavilion where President Kim Dae-jung liked to sit, or look over the golf

minutes, eight daily). Or you can travel to **Jochiwon station** (조치원역) for a connection to Seoul (₩8400, 1½ hours, every 30 minutes). To/from the intercity bus terminal, take bus 717 for Cheongju station (20 minutes), or 502 for Jochiwon (one hour). You can get a fast KTX train to/from Cheongju from **Osong station** (오송역), about 10km southwest of Cheongju centre. From Osong station there are trains to Seoul (₩18,500, 45 minutes, every 20 minutes) and

BUS DEPARTURES FROM CHEONGJU

Express Bus Terminal Destinations

DESTINATION	PRICE (₩)	DURATION (HR)	FREQUENCY
Busan	21,500	3½	every 30min
Daegu	12,800	2½	hourly
Dong-Seoul	9000	1¾	every 30min
Seoul	7400	1¾	every 5-10min

Intercity Bus Terminal Destinations

DESTINATION	PRICE (₩)	DURATION (HR)	FREQUENCY
Chuncheon	14,400	3	every 20-40min
Chungju	8200	2	every 20min
Daejeon	7400	1-2	every 15min
Danyang	16,100	4	6 daily

Songnisan National Park

Map labels:
- Myo-bong (874m)
- Gwaneum-bong (985m)
- Munjang-dae (1033m)
- Oseong Pokpo
- Munsu-bong (1031m)
- Sinseon-dae
- Spring
- Ipseok-dae
- Birosanjang
- Biro-bong (1032m)
- Beopju-sa
- Cheonhwang-bong (1058m)
- Tourist Information Centre
- Eorae Motel
- Ticket Office
- Lake Hills Hotel Songnisan
- SONGNI-DONG
- Bus Terminal

0   1 km
0   0.5 miles

course that President Roh Tae-woo favoured but President Kim Young-sam disapproved of (too many associations with corruption).

Cheongnamdae was built in 1983 by President Chun Doo-hwan (whose takeover of power sparked the Gwangju Uprising in 1980). Twenty years later, the much-loved President Roh Moo-Hyun opened it to the public.

The parkland is more attractive than the surprisingly modest two-storey villa, with trails around the compound and a musical fountain (ABBA features on the soundtrack). Where the bus stops, there's a building with a hagiographic exhibition (mostly Korean) on all the presidents as well as displays of items used by the presidents in residence (polo mallets, Colgate shaving cream, cutlery etc).

Take local bus 311 (₩1300, 50 minutes, 15km, hourly) from outside Cheongju's intercity bus terminal to the final stop at Munui. Walk out of Munui's small bus depot and turn left. In a few minutes you'll reach the car park and ticket office for the shuttle bus (15 minutes, every 30 minutes) to Cheongnamdae, which runs 9am to 4.30pm February to November, to 3.30pm December and January.

Songnisan National Park
속리산국립공원

📷 043

With forested mountains and rocky granite outcrops, this park covers one of central Korea's finest scenic areas and includes a secluded temple complex. There is a **tourist information centre** (📷 043 542 5267) diagonally across the road from the bus terminal.

⊙ Sights

Songnisan National Park   NATIONAL PARK
(속리산국립공원, Sokrisan National Park; 📷 043 542 5267; http://english.knps.or.kr; adult/child/youth ₩4000/1000/2000; ⊙6am-7pm) This park has easy hikes and year-round beauty among the craggy cliffs. It's atmospheric and misty in winter and alive with pink azaleas in spring. Though it often goes by the touristy catchword Chungbuk Alps, its name has a more solemn meaning – 'Remote from the Ordinary World Mountain', referring to the park being smack bang in the middle of the country.

After passing through the Beopju-sa, you'll find hiking trails leading to a series of 1000m-high peaks. A popular hike is the relatively easy 6km climb up **Munjangdae**

(1033m). In 1464 King Sejo was carried up in a palanquin; using your own feet, it's three hours up and two hours down. You can also return via Sinseondae, further south via Biro-bong or, for the gung-ho, push on to the highest peak **Cheonhwang-bong** (1058m).

Beopju-sa
BUDDHIST TEMPLE

This temple dates to AD 553 and lies about 1km from the entrance to Songnisan National Park (p298). It features a 33m-high gold-plated Maitreya Buddha statue, a unique five-storey wooden pagoda, a weather-worn Shilla-era bodhisattva statue, a lotus-shaped fountain and an enormous iron cauldron, once used for cooking for up to 3000 monks. Templestays are offered (₩70,000 per person, cash only).

🛏 Sleeping & Eating

Two camping grounds (₩1000) are available. Templestays are offered at Beopju-sa. There are plenty of motels in the lanes to the left of the main road (looking towards the park entrance). Lining the main road are many restaurants, offering the usual tourist-village fare: *sanchae jeongsik* (산채 정식; banquet of mountain vegetables), *beoseot jeongsik* (버섯 정식; mushroom set menu) and *sanchae bibimbap* (bibimbap with mountain vegetables). Prices range from ₩6000 to ₩35,000.

Eorae Motel
MOTEL ₩

(어래모텔; ☑ 043 543 3882; r ₩30,000; ❄) The closest budget option to the park entrance. Rooms are clean and adequate, with wood laminate floors and *ondol* rooms available.

★ Birosanjang
GUESTHOUSE ₩₩

(비로산장; ☑ 043 543 4782; r with shared bathroom ₩40,000, Sat & Sun ₩50,000, summer ₩60,000) If only every national park had this – a homely, delightful *yeogwan* (small family-run hotel) beside a gurgling river in the middle of the park. There's nothing fancy, just nine *ondol* (heated-floor) rooms and meals such as bibimbap (rice, egg, meat and vegies with chilli sauce; ₩8000) and *sanchae jeongsik* (banquet dishes; ₩15,000) whipped up by the friendly owner, who speaks a little English.

Try the refreshing *makgeolli* (fermented rice wine). It's on the trail between Beopju-sa (p299) and Sinseon-dae so don't lug a heavy backpack in. The local police station will help keep your luggage. Reservations recommended.

Lake Hills Hotel Songnisan
HOTEL ₩₩₩

(레이크힐스호텔속리산; ☑ 043 542 5281; www.lakehills.co.kr; r ₩150,000; ❄) The area's 'nicest' digs, right by the park entrance, are a little dated, with balconies and faded carpets. The back rooms face the woods. Rates are discounted during low season.

❶ Getting There & Away

Buses leave Cheongju's intercity bus terminal (₩8000, two hours, every 30 minutes) for Songnisan National Park. There are also direct buses to the park from Dong-Seoul (₩16,000, 3½ hours) and Daejeon (₩7200, 1¾ hours), or via Cheongju from Seoul Gangnam (₩15,400, four hours). When planning your trip, note that Songnisan is sometimes spelled Sokrisan.

Chungju
충주

☑ 043 / POP 202,000

Chungju (www.cj100.net/english) might be the town where UN Secretary-General Ban Ki-moon grew up, but there are really only three reasons to come to here: to get the bus to the Chungju Lake ferries or Woraksan National Park, to attend the World Martial Arts Festival or because you really, *really* like apples (there's an Apple Festival every October).

A **tourist information centre** (☑ 043 850 7329) is inside the bus terminal with English pamphlets but zero spoken English.

🛏 Sleeping & Eating

Unlike most towns, there are no motels around the bus terminal. There's a clump of love motels opposite the train station, in an area otherwise populated by car workshops.

From the bus terminal (turn right as you exit) it's a 15-minute walk or five-minute taxi ride (₩2200) across a treeless urban landscape.

Good eats aren't easy to scare up in Chungju and the better options are actually the Korean and Japanese restaurants in the bus terminal. There are also some good options along the perpendicular road to the left as you exit from the bus terminal. For self-caterers, there's a Lotte Mart beside the train station and one under the bus terminal.

Titanic Motel
LOVE MOTEL ₩
(타이타닉모텔; ☎043 842 5858; 168-2 Bongbang-dong; r without/with computer ₩30,000/35,000; ✴@) The Titanic has decent, if dated, rooms with all the usual love-motel trimmings. Look for the *Titanic* movie poster outside on the white, castle-inspired building.

3800
KOREAN ₩
(dishes ₩5000-12,000; ⊙24hrs) Choices are few but flavours fresh at this casual 24-hour place. Local workers flock for the simple and satisfying *kalguksu* (wheat noodles in a clam and vegetable broth). Exiting the bus terminal, turn left, then right at the intersection and look for a green awning.

❶ Getting There & Away

TRAIN
Chungju receives only one direct (evening) train from Seoul (₩13,400, 2½ hours). Alternatively, take a train from Seoul to Jochiwon station (조치원역, ₩8400, 1½ hours, every 30 minutes) and change for Chungju (₩5200, 1¼ hours, 10 daily).

Around Chungju
☑043

Chungju-ho
충주호

◉ Sights & Activities

Cheongpung Cultural Heritage Complex
HISTORIC SITE
(☎043 641 4301; adult/child ₩3000/1000; ⊙9am-6pm) When the area around here was

flooded to create the Chungju dam and lake, a number of villages were submerged (the residents were resettled, of course).

In order to preserve some of the rich heritage, 43 cultural properties, several private residences and more than a thousand artefacts were relocated here from Cheongpung, a historic port during the Joseon dynasty. You can take the ferry to Cheongpung, get off and walk up the hill to the complex.

Chungju-ho Cruise
CRUISE
(☑043 851 5771; www.chungjuho.com) The artificial Chungju-ho was formerly a valley that was deliberately flooded in 1985. This cruise across the lake is a scenic way to make your way towards Danyang. The cruises get very busy on weekends and there's prerecorded sightseeing commentary (Korean only), so it's not the most relaxing experience – though the placid scenery is beautiful.

There are numerous routes but the most popular cruise (adult/child one-way ₩17,000/8500, return ₩25,000/17,000; fast boat 1½ hours, ferry 2¼ hours) is from Chungju Dam to Janghoe via Cheongpung (and in reverse); the rocky cliffs are most dramatic between the later stops.

❶ Getting There & Away

Buses run from Janghoe to Danyang.

Ferries depart hourly in summer and every other hour in winter, though it is subject to weather conditions, water levels and passenger volume, so ask at the tourist information centre in **Chungju** (☑043 850 7329) or **Danyang** (☑043 422 1146) before you head to the terminal.

To get to the Chungju Dam ferry terminal (충주댐 선착장) take any bus from opposite the Chungju bus terminal to City Hall (시청; seven minutes) and swap to bus 301 (₩1300, 25 minutes, six daily). A taxi will cost ₩15,000.

Suanbo
수안보
☑043

This tiny town, known for its hot springs, has *jjimjilbang,* restaurants and motels clustered snugly across several streets. The

BUS DEPARTURES FROM CHUNGJU

DESTINATION	PRICE (₩)	DURATION (HR)	FREQUENCY
Cheongju	8200	2	every 20min
Daejeon	9500	2½	hourly
Danyang	7900	1¾	2 daily
Seoul	7400	2	every 20min

THE PRINTED WORD, MADE BY MONKS

While the Gutenberg Bible needs no introduction, the *Jikji* languished for many years in obscurity, even though it is the oldest book in the world printed with movable metal type. It was printed in 1377 (78 years before the Gutenberg) at the temple of Heungdeok-sa in modern-day Cheongju. In the mid-19th century it was acquired by a French official in Korea, who took it to France. After it was put on display at the 1900 World's Fair in Paris, it disappeared without fanfare from the public eye, and it was only in 1972 that Korean historian Park Byeng-Sen rediscovered it at the National Library of France.

The *Jikji* itself is a small book: 38 sheets of thin mulberry paper, each one measuring just 24.6cm x 17cm. Its full title is *Baegun hwasang chorok buljo jikji simche yojeol* – that is, an anthology of the monk Baegun Gyeonghan's teachings on Seon Buddhism (more commonly known in the West as Zen Buddhism). It's the second and only extant volume of a two-volume collection of these teachings, delivered at Heungdeok-sa in the 1370s. The last page of the book indicates that it was printed by two of Baegun's disciples, Seokchan and Daldam, with funding from a nun named Myodeok.

The *Jikji* has been exhibited at international book fairs since 1972 and South Korea lobbied till it was admitted to Unesco's Memory of the World Register in 2001. However, the book still resides within the National Library of France, along with other cultural relics from Korea's early dynasties. Understandably South Korea would like to see the book returned, but there's no indication that's likely to happen.

town looks as if it's seen better days, but makes a handy base for exploring Woraksan National Park (p302).

The modest **Eagle Valley Ski Resort** (이글밸리스키리조트 스키장; ☎043 846 0750; www.eaglevalley.co.kr; 197, Jujeongsan-ro, Suanbo-myeon; lift tickets per day adult/child ₩42,000/32,000, equipment rental per day adult/child ₩25,000/15,000), about 2km from town, has seven slopes and offers night skiing.

There's a **tourist information centre** (☎043 845 7829) near the town entrance.

🛏 Sleeping & Eating

Near the ski slopes are **Hanwha Resort** (☎043 846 8211; www.hanwharesort.co.kr; 321-36 Suanbo-ro; r ₩360,000; P ❄ @ 🛜 🛌) and a youth hostel (both closed in low season), but you can stay in Suanbo and use the free shuttle buses during ski season.

Restaurants specialise in rabbit (*tokki;* 토끼), duck (*ori;* 오리) and pheasant (*kkwong;* 꿩). Try *tokki doritang* (토끼도리탕; rabbit stew) or *sanchae deodeok jeongsik* (산채더덕정식), a set meal with mountain vegetables and a ginseng-like herbal meal.

Suanbo Sangnok Hotel
HOTEL ₩₩
(수안보상록호텔; ☎043 845 3500; www.sangnokhotel.co.kr; 22, Jujeongsan-ro; r/ste ₩130,000/240,000; ❄@🛌) This upmarket hotel has an restaurant, a tennis court and a nightclub. The carpeted rooms are smart and modern. The main attraction is the *oncheon* (guests/nonguests ₩5000/8000).

Suanbo Royal Hotel
HOTEL ₩₩
(수안보 로얄호텔; ☎043 846 0190; www.suanbo53c.com; 3734-82, Chungjeol-ro, Gyuam-myeon; d/ste ₩90,000/130,000; ❄@) This concrete-and-glass hotel looks sterner but is newer than the others on Suanbo's main road. Rooms are cosy and warm, and there's an *oncheon* (guests/nonguests ₩4000/6000).

Satgatchon
KOREAN
(삿갓촌식당; ☎846 2529; meals ₩6000-50,000) This restaurant serves up Suanbo specialties, such as *kkwong shabu shabu* (꿩샤브샤브) with pheasant served in seven different ways: kebabs, dumplings, meatballs, barbecued, *shabu shabu*-style, raw and in soup. To find it, walk down the side road by Suanbo Sangnok Hotel (p301) to the bridge and turn left. Walk ahead 50m and look for the restaurant with a wooden-man sculpture at the door.

ℹ Getting There & Away

From the front of Chungju's bus terminal (outside), catch bus 240 or 246 (₩1300, 40 minutes, every 40 minutes) to Suanbo's bus station, located on the north side of town. You can also return via a more comfortable intercity bus (₩2400, 30 minutes). Tickets are sold at the grocery store beside the station; look for a yellow and blue sign beside some orange seats. Other buses go to Daegu (₩15,000, 2½ hours, 11am and 7.20pm), Dong-Seoul (₩13,000, 2½ hours, hourly) and Woraksan National Park (₩1400, 30 minutes, every two hours).

Woraksan National Park
월악산국립공원

Spread across two serene valleys, this **park** (☏043 653 3250; http://worak.knps.or.kr; ☉sunrise-sunset) **FREE** offers fine hiking through picturesque forests, with pretty waterfalls, ancient Buddhist structures and, if you climb high enough, views all the way to Chungju-ho. Worak-san (Moon Crags Mountain) is also home to the endangered long-tailed goral.

A road runs through the park; the bus that plies it stops at the villages of Mireuk-ri in the south, Deokju in the middle and Songgye-ri in the north. Around 1km from Mireuk-ri lie the remains of **Mireuksaji**, a small Buddhist temple which was built in the late Shilla or early Goryeo period. Although a new temple has been constructed beside it, the stark, weather-beaten ruins – an enigmatic Buddha statue, stone lantern and five-storey pagoda – can be quite atmospheric.

The most popular of the hiking routes starts from Deokju. A gentle path leads past **Deokjusan-seong**, a late Shilla-era fortress that has been partly restored, up to **Deokju-sa** temple. The trail continues for 1.5km to **Ma-aebul**, a rock face with a Buddha image carved out of it, then it's pretty tough going for 3.4km more to the summit of **Yeong-bong** (1097m). Allow about 3½ hours to get from Deokju-sa to Yeong-bong. You can also approach Yeong-bong from Songgye-ri (three hours, 4.3km).

There are shops, restaurants, and pensions and *minbak* (private homes with rooms for rent) at all three villages, Songgye-ri being the most developed. There's camping (₩2000 per night) at Deokju and Datdonjae, but no mountain shelters.

❶ Getting There & Away

Bus 246 (₩4600, one hour, six daily) leaves from outside Chungju's bus terminal for Mireuk-ri. It can also be picked up in Suanbo's main street (₩1300, 30 minutes). Bus 222 (₩4600, 45 minutes, five daily) from Chungju's bus terminal goes directly to Songgye-ri. Bus stops and place names in the park are not well signposted, so ask the bus driver to alert you for your stop.

Danyang   단양
☏ 043 / POP 37,000

A little gem of a resort town, Danyang (http://english.dy21.net) is cosied right up to the mountains of Sobaeksan National Park, at a bend in the river Namhan-gang. This is small-town Korea at its most charming: you can stay at a riverfront motel and explore limestone caves, hiking trails and a one-of-a-kind Buddhist temple, basking in mountain views wherever you go. It's a great place to dawdle for a couple of days.

The annual highlight is the 10-day **Royal Azalea Festival** in May. Hikers come to see the flowers bloom on Sobaek-san, while the riverside comes alive with concerts, fireworks, food stalls and a funfair.

A **tourist information centre** (☏043 422 1146; ☉9am-6pm) with English-speaking staff is in the Danyang Danuri building next to the bus terminal. Another **tourist office** (☏043 422 1146; ☉9am-6pm) is just across the bridge and staff speak German but not English.

Woraksan National Park

◉ Sights & Activities

Gosu Donggul   CAVE

(고수동굴; ☑043 422 3072; adult/child/youth ₩5000/2000/3000; ⊘9am-6pm, last entry 5pm) This stunning limestone cave is a rabbit's warren of metal catwalks and spiral staircases running through 1.7km of dense, narrow grottoes. It's quite an intimate experience where you get up close with the rock formations. Unlike garishly lit caves, Gosu Donggul feels old and drippy – perhaps not as old as its 150,000 years, but it's certainly authentic.

There are few explanatory signs, except for a few earnest exhortations to, 'for a moment, look back please!'. Walkways are narrow – definitely not for the claustrophobic.

The cave is about a 15-minute walk from Danyang. Cross the bridge to the tourist information centre and follow the road to the right to a busy tourist village. The cave entrance is tucked away up a stone staircase behind the village. At the village you can refresh yourself with a cup (or jar) of local flavours such as *omija* (five-flavour berry), honey (꿀; *kkul*) or yam (마; *ma*) drinks.

Dansim Mugung   PARAGLIDING

(단심무궁 패러글라이딩; ☑010 9072 4553; http://cafe.daum.net/dypara) Offers paragliding (₩100,000) from Yangbaek-san, the peak overlooking the town. At the top of this peak is an astronomical observatory.

Aquaworld   AMUSEMENT PARK

(아쿠아월드; ☑043 420 8370; adult/child Mon-Fri ₩29,000/22,000, Sat & Sun ₩33,000/29,000, sauna ₩10,000/8000; ⊘10am-6pm Mon-Thu, 9am-9pm Fri & Sat, to 7pm Sun) Swimming at this indoor water park at Daemyung Resort is a tamer option than the caving or paragliding that usually draw visitors to Danyang. Alternatively, drop by its **sauna**, which has mineral baths, or jade, charcoal and amethyst saunas.

🛏 Sleeping

Most of the riverside motels are dated and faded but can't be beat for location.

Rio 127   GUESTHOUSE ₩₩

(리오127; ☑043 422 2619; dm ₩20,000, d/tw ₩50,000/80,000; ℗❄@⊚) The rooms may be plain but the mountain and river views give personality aplenty, while the cafe has one of the warmest vibes in town. Staff speak some English and will help with travel information. Each dorm room has a

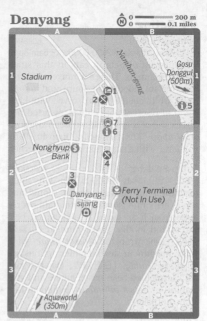

Danyang

⊜ **Sleeping**
1 Hotel Luxury B1
  Rio 127 ....(see 1)

⊗ **Eating**
2 Doljip Sikdang A1
3 Gimbap Heaven.......................................A2
4 Kujib Ssogari B2

ℹ **Information**
5 Tourist Information Centre B1
6 Tourist Information Centre B2

ℹ **Transport**
7 Bus Terminal B1

two-person bunk. Rates rise by 20% on Friday and Saturday.

You'll find it along the river, after the convenience store and opposite the bus terminal.

Hotel Luxury   LOVE MOTEL ₩₩

(럭셔리 호텔; ☑043 421 9911; www.hotel-luxury.co.kr; r/ste/VIP ₩50,000/70,000/80,000; ❄@) A slick choice for love-motel chic in Danyang with stylish rooms decorated with darkened mirrors and bold colours. The VIP suite sleeps three and has a whirlpool bath. Rooms cost an extra ₩20,000 on weekends.

CHUNGCHEONGBUK-DO AROUND CHUNGJU

Eating

Gimbap Heaven
KOREAN ₩

(김밥천국; meals ₩2500-6000; ⊙6am-8pm) Scrounge up dirt-cheap eats in this small chain restaurant. There's a range of *ramyeon* (instant noodles in soup) and *udong* (thick white noodle broth), served with kimchi. It also serves pork cutlets, assorted rice dishes and of course, half-a-dozen variations of *gimbap* (Korean sushi). Opposite Paris Baguette, with a supermarket on the corner.

Doljip Sikdang
KOREAN ₩₩

(돌집식당; meals ₩7000-15,000) This busy restaurant has private dining rooms and serves elaborate *jeongsik,* with main-course options such as *suyuk* (수육; boiled beef slices) and locally grown *maneul* (마늘쌈 정식; garlic wrap) or *beoseot jjigae* (버섯 찌개; mushroom stew). Lighter options are *doenjang sotbap* (된장솥밥; clay-pot rice with fermented-bean paste, jujube and vegetables) or *dolsot bibimbap* (bibimbap in a stone hotpot).

Kujib Ssogari
KOREAN ₩₩₩

(그집쏘가리; ☑043 423 2111; meals ₩9000-85,000) This riverfront restaurant serves the mandarin fish *ssogari* raw (쏘가리회; *ssogari hoe*) or as a spicy soup (쏘가리매운탕; *ssogari maeuntang*). A milder option is the catfish bulgogi (메기불고기; *megi* bulgogi).

Getting There & Away

BOAT
The closest ferry terminal for the Chungju-ho ferry is at Janghoe. After you exit the terminal, turn right at the main road and walk down for about 100m. Beside the trail entrance to Woraksan National Park is the waiting point for the bus to Danyang (₩2300, 30 minutes, 21km, every 2½ hours). It's marked with a circular red sign that reads '단양버스정류소'.

BUS
The **bus terminal** (☑043 421 8800) complex is in front of the bridge. Local buses don't have numbers but signs (Korean only) indicating the destination at the front of the bus.

TRAIN
The train station is in old Danyang, about 3km from the main town. Eight trains run daily from Seoul's Cheongnyangni station (₩10,700, two hours, every two hours). A taxi into town costs ₩6000, the local bus ₩1300.

Sobaeksan National Park
소백산국립공원

 043

This park is the third largest in South Korea and the daintily named Sobaek-san (Little White Mountain) is one of the highest mountains in the country.

Sights

Sobaeksan National Park
NATIONAL PARK

(☑043 423 0708; http://english.knps.or.kr; ⊙2hr before sunrise to 2hr after sunset) FREE While the climbs are not particularly steep, Sobaek-san can be demanding, wending through dense forests, picturesque valleys and even a waterfall. The main trail (7km, 2½ hours) heads from the park entrance at Darian to the highest peak of **Biro-bong** (1439m), famous for royal azaleas which bloom in late May. Views are incredible from the grassy mountaintop. It can also be approached from the campground at Samga (5.7km, 2½ hours).

From Biro-bong, you can push on to the three peaks of **Yeonhwa-bong** (2.5km to 6.8km); the National Astronomical Observatory is here but not open to visitors.

Guin-sa
BUDDHIST TEMPLE

(구인사; ☑043 420 7315; http://temple.cheontae. org/001_eng.html) FREE This stately complex's 30-odd buildings are wedged into a valley, with steep, forested slopes on either side. The gold-roofed buildings are as elaborate as you'd expect, very close together and connected with elevated walkways. You may stumble upon monks chanting and drumming as you climb towards the opulent three-storey hall (대조사전) at the top dedicated to the temple's founder. It's worth the

BUS DEPARTURES FROM DANYANG

DESTINATION	PRICE (₩)	DURATION	FREQUENCY
Chungju	7900	2hr	2 daily
Daejeon	17,400	4hr	4 daily
Guin-sa	3300	30min	hourly
Seoul	12,700	3½hr	every 30min

Sobaeksan National Park

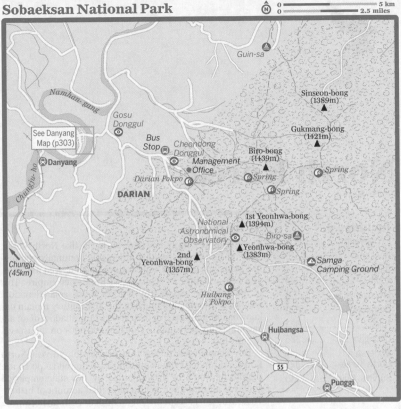

short hike just for the views of the temples and mountains vanishing into the horizon.

The temple is the headquarters of the Cheontae sect of Korean Buddhism, which was reestablished by Sangwol Wongak in 1945. From the main hall, it's a further steep climb of 30 minutes to his tomb atop the hill.

The communal kitchen serves free vegetarian meals (6am to 7.30am, 11.30am to 1.30pm and 6.30pm to 9.30pm) and templestays are held twice a month. The midway point has a tourist information office with English-speaking staff, maps and free lockers.

🛏 Sleeping & Eating

There is a delightful *minbak* village at Darian and many have restaurants. They are spread out so it doesn't feel too crowded or noisy. Rooms cost from ₩40,000 and you can wake up right next to the mountains. There are campsites here (₩12,000). Camping (₩2000) is also available at Samga. Take the bus (₩1300, every 30 minutes) heading to Yeongju (영주).

❶ Getting There & Away

Buses (₩1300, 10 minutes, hourly) leave from the stop outside Danyang's bus terminal for Darian (다리안). Direct buses (₩3300, 30 minutes, hourly) head from Danyang's bus terminal and terminate at the Guin-sa entrance archway. It's hardly worth getting out at the tourist village (penultimate stop) for the hourly free shuttle bus as it only shuttles you a short distance to the centre of Guin-sa.

From Guin-sa, there are hourly buses to Dong-Seoul (₩16,700, three hours).

North Korea

POP 24.9 MILLION

Best Places to Eat

➡ Pyongyang Number One
Duck Barbeque (p316)

➡ Pizza Restaurant (p316)

➡ Lamb Barbeque
Restaurant (p316)

➡ Chongryu Hotpot
Restaurant (p316)

Best Places to Stay

➡ Minsok Folk Hotel (p320)

➡ Koryo Hotel (p316)

➡ Yanggakdo Hotel (p315)

➡ Masik-Ryong Hotel (p323)

Why Go?

There is quite simply nowhere on Earth like North Korea. Now on its third hereditary ruler, this nominally communist state has defied all expectations and survived a quarter of a century since the collapse of the Soviet empire. This is your chance to visit the world's most isolated nation, where the internet and much of the 21st century remain unknown, and millions live their lives in the shadow of an all-encompassing personality cult that intrudes on all aspects of daily life.

Few people even realise that it's possible to visit North Korea, and indeed the compromises required to do so are significant. You'll be accompanied by two state-employed guides at all times and hear a one-sided account of history. Those who can't accept this might be better off staying away – but those who can will be able to undertake a fascinating journey into another, unsettling world.

When to Go
Pyongyang

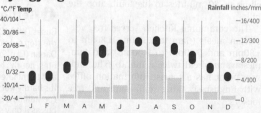

Feb The country is empty and annual celebrations to mark the birth of Kim Jong-il are impressive.

Apr Clear skies and the 15 April national holiday make this a great time to visit.

Sep & Oct With the summer humidity gone, these months offer some of the best travel conditions.

Tours

North Korean tours are all ultimately arranged by the national travel agency, Korean International Travel Company (KITC), though they are best booked through agencies specialising in travel to the Democratic People's Republic of Korea (DPRK). Specialists include the following.

➡ **Koryo Tours** (www.koryotours.com)

➡ **Regent Holidays** (www.regent-holidays.co.uk)

➡ **Young Pioneer Tours** (www.youngpioneertours.com)

➡ **Juche Travel Services** (www.juchetravelservices.com)

➡ **Lupine Travel** (www.lupinetravel.co.uk)

➡ **New Korea Tours** (www.newkoreatours.com)

➡ **KTG Tours** (www.north-korea-travel.com)

SET YOUR BUDGET

The cost of a trip to North Korea is considerable. Visitors have to pay for their guides, food and hotels in advance as part of an all-inclusive tour. The only real way to cut costs is to join a large group and share the expenses between many travellers.

It's difficult to travel to North Korea for much less than €1000 for five days, though competition between the various travel agencies is fierce.

Itineraries

➡ **Five Days** The standard tour of North Korea gives you a couple of days visiting the extraordinary monuments of Pyongyang, a day trip to Kaesong and the Demilitarized Zone (DMZ) and sometimes a visit to the mountains at Myohyangsan.

➡ **10 Days** Trips of more than a week can be exhausting, but very rewarding. As well as doing everything in the five-day itinerary, groups will have the opportunity to visit truly remote and little-visited cities such as Nampo, Wonsan or Hamhung, giving a great chance to see real life in North Korea.

AT A GLANCE

➡ Locals use North Korean won as currency, but travellers must use euros or Chinese RMB.

➡ The local language is Korean.

➡ Visas are needed by everyone and are normally issued the day before you travel by the North Korean embassy in Beijing.

NORTH KOREA

Fast Facts

➡ **Area** 120,540 sq km

➡ **Capital** Pyongyang

➡ **Telephone** North Korea's country code is ☎ 850. Your phone won't work in North Korea unless you purchase a local SIM card.

➡ **Internet** Unavailable anywhere in the country unless you buy a 3G SIM card.

Exchange Rates

Australia	A$1	KPW 102
China	RMB1	KPW 22
Euro Zone	€1	KPW 147
Japan	Y100	KPW 107
UK	UK£1	KPW 204
USA	US$1	KPW 133

Resources

➡ **North Korea News:** www.nknews.org

➡ **Koryo Tours:** www.koryogroup.com

➡ **North Korean Economy Watch:** www.nkeconwatch.com

0   100 km
0   50 miles

CHINA

RUSSIA

Onsong
Saebyol
Vladivostok
Sonbong
Rajin
Musan
Chongjin

Fushun

Shenyang (20km);
Beijing (500km)

Paekdusan **3**
Samjiyon
Chunggang
Chasong
Hwapyong
Hyesan
Manpo
Kapsan
Kilju
Orang
4 Mt Chilbosan
Kanggye
Chosan
Changjin
Pukchong
Tanchon
Kimchaek
Sakchu
Seoho
Dandong
Myohyangsan
(1909m)
Shinpo
Sinuiju
Hyangsan
5 Hamhung
Sonchon
Kaechon
Chongju
Kowon
EAST SEA
(Sea of Japan)
Mundok
Pyongsong
Yangdok
Pyongyang 1
Kangdong
5 Wonsan
Masik-
Ryong
Tongchon
Onjong-ri
Nampo
Ichon
Kumgang
Kumgangsan (1639m)
Kuwolsan
Sariwon
Sohung
Sinchon
Hwajinpo
Ganseong
Suyangsan
Kumchon
DMZ
Ryongyon **Haeju**
Kaesong
Sincheorwon
Yangyang
Yonan
Janggok
SOUTH
KOREA
2 Panmunjom
Kumchon

North Korea Highlights

1 Marvel at the architecture, monuments and general totalitarian weirdness of **Pyongyang** (p308).

2 Feel the full force of Cold War tensions during a visit to **Panmunjom** (p320) in the Demilitarized Zone (DMZ),

where an uneasy armistice holds.

3 Explore the remote far north and Korea's highest peak and holy mountain, **Paekdusan** (p324).

4 Enjoy pristine mountain walks and some lovely

beaches along the coast in and around **Chilbosan** (p325).

5 Come as close as you can to everyday life in the provincial cities of **Wonsan** (p322) and **Hamhung** (p322).

PYONGYANG

02 / POP 3.25 MILLION

An ideological statement forged in concrete, bronze and marble, Pyongyang (평양; 'flat land') is the ultimate totalitarian metropolis, built almost entirely from scratch following its destruction in the Korean War. It's a fascinating yet simultaneously inaccessible place, where a busy populace go about their

daily lives tantalisingly out of reach of the visitor.

Every visit to North Korea focuses heavily on the capital. Your guides will be falling over themselves to show you monuments, towers, statues and buildings that glorify Kim Il-sung, Kim Jong-il and the Juche idea. These include the Triumphal Arch, the Tower of the Juche Idea and the Mansudae Grand Monument, a rendering of the Great

Leader and the Dear Leader in bronze, to which every visitor is expected to pay floral tribute.

While these are all impressive, if surreal, the real delights of Pyongyang are to be had in the quieter moments when you can get glimpses of everyday life. A gentle stroll on Pyongyang's relaxed Moran Hill, for example, is a great chance to see the locals having picnics, playing music and idling away sunny afternoons. As you wander the streets between sights, you'll still be able to find a semblance of normality surviving in the capital. You just have to look hard for it.

History

It seems incredible to think it, given its stark, thoroughly 20th-century appearance, but Pyongyang is ancient, stretching back to when the Goguryeo dynasty built its capital here in AD 427. By the 7th century the kingdom of Goguryeo had started to collapse under the strain of successive, massive attacks from Sui and Tang China. Cutting a deal with the Tang Chinese, the Shilla kingdom in the south was able to conquer Koryo in 668, creating the first unified Korea.

The city was completely destroyed by the Japanese in 1592 and then again by the Manchus at the beginning of the 17th century. Pyongyang remained a relative backwater until the arrival of foreign missionaries in the 19th century, who constructed more than 100 churches in the city. Pyongyang was once again destroyed during the Sino-Japanese War (1894–95) and remained neglected until the occupying Japanese developed industry in the region.

The US practically wiped out Pyongyang between 1950 and 1953, and it rose from the ashes in the late 1950s as the ideological theme park it is today. Few historic buildings remain, but there are some in evidence, including a couple of temples and pavilions, the Taedong Gate and a few sections of the ancient city's inner and northern walls.

⊙ Sights

Pyongyang is divided into East and West Pyongyang by the Taedong River. Most sights, museums and hotels are in West Pyongyang, which is focused on Kim Il-sung Sq. A large area of this part of Pyongyang, known to foreign residents as the 'forbidden city', is back behind Kim Il-sung Sq west of Changgwang St and is a closed-off area for senior party members and their families.

Pyongyang's sights divide neatly into two categories: the impressive yet fairly pointless proliferation of statues, monuments and museums glorifying the Kims; and the far more interesting slices of daily North Korean life to be found in excursions to funfairs, cinemas, parks and on public transport. You don't have to be a genius to work out which your guides will prefer to show you, or to guess which most tour groups will enjoy more.

Mansudae Grand Monument   MONUMENT
Every itinerary features this larger-than-life bronze statue of the Great Leader, to which a statue of Kim Jong-il in his trademark parka was added in 2012 following the Dear Leader's death. The first statue was unveiled in 1972 to celebrate Kim Il-sung's 60th birthday. It was originally covered in gold leaf, but apparently at the objection of the Chinese, who were effectively funding the North Korean economy, this was later removed in favour of the scrubbed bronze on display today.

This is the epicentre of the Kim cult, so visitors need to be aware of the seriousness (officially, at least) with which North Koreans regard this monument and the respect they believe foreigners should accord it. Your tour leader will usually buy flowers and elect one member of the group to place them at the statue's feet. As this is done, the whole group will be expected to bow. Photographers will be instructed never to photograph one part of the monument – all pictures should be of the entire statue to avoid causing offence.

Chollima Statue   MONUMENT
This impressive statue portrays Chollima, the Korean Pegasus. It's an interesting example of how the North Korean state has incorporated traditional Korean myths into its cult. According to legend, Chollima could cover hundreds of kilometres a day and was untameable. Kim Il-sung appropriated the myth

---

WARNING

Travellers to North Korea should be aware that customs officials, particularly in Pyongyang airport, have been known to confiscate Lonely Planet guides to Korea. The best way to avoid this is to travel with an e-book or PDF preloaded on your tablet or smartphone. PDFs are available for purchase at http://shop.lonelyplanet.com.

Pyongyang

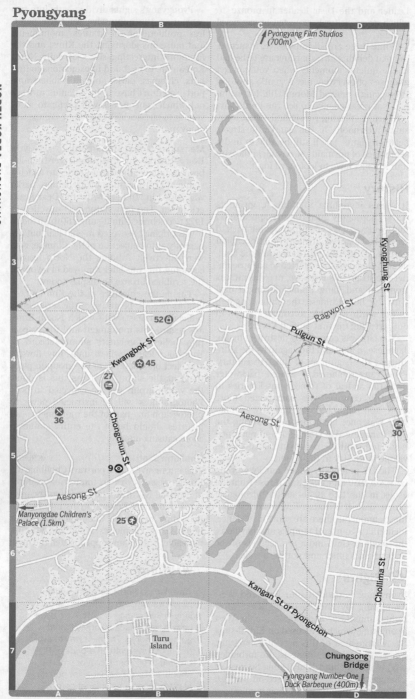

Pyongyang Film Studios
(700m)

Kyonghung St

Ragwon St

Pulgun St

52

Kwangbok St

45

27

Aesong St

36

30

Chongchun St

9

53

Aesong St

Manyongdae Children's
Palace (1.5km)

25

Kangan St of Pyongchon

Chollima St

Turu
Island

Chungsong
Bridge

Pyongyang Number One
Duck Barbeque (400m)

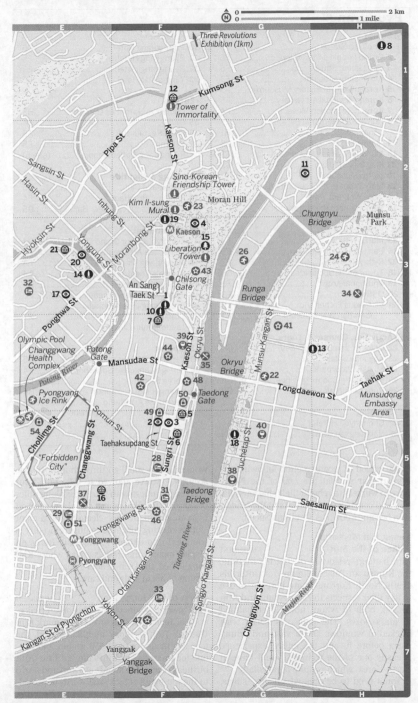

Pyongyang

in the period of reconstruction following the Korean War so that the zeal of the North Korean workers to rebuild their shattered nation and construct monuments to the leadership became known as 'Chollima Speed'.

Kumsusan Memorial Palace of the Sun   MONUMENT

Kim Il-sung's residence during his lifetime, the Kumsusan Palace remained so after his death. North Koreans come here en masse to pay their respects to Kim Il-sung and Kim Jong-il, both of whom now lie embalmed in glass boxes. The palace is eerie, with bricked-in windows and a vast and empty plaza before it, and the entire experience is easily one of the weirdest you'll have in North Korea, which is quite an accolade.

You'll need to be dressed smartly (shirts, ties and trousers for men, modest dress for women), then you'll go through airport-style security – you're allowed to take only your wallet and camera with you – pass along miles of slow red travelators and then be dusted off by both automatic shoe cleaners and a giant clothes-dusting machine to ensure no dirt is trampled into either viewing hall. Items on display include the train carriage where Kim Jong-il died, the Dear Leader's boat and a collection of his medals and cars.

Tower of the Juche Idea   MONUMENT

This tower honours the North Korean philosophy of Juche and was unveiled to mark Kim Il-sung's 70th birthday in 1982. Indeed, the tower is made up of 25,550 granite blocks – one for every day of Kim's life until his 70th birthday. The tower stands at 170m and a trip to the top by lift (€5) is well worth it, providing a great view over the capital on a clear day.

Triumphal Arch   MONUMENT
Your guides will tell you with barely concealed glee that the Triumphal Arch is 6m higher than its cousin in Paris, making it the largest of its kind in the world. The arch marks the site where Kim Il-sung first addressed the liberated Koreans after the end of Japanese occupation in 1945. The gloss you hear will omit the fact that the Soviets liberated Pyongyang, not the partisans, who themselves gave full credit to the Soviets at the time.

An impressive mural a short walk away details the event according to the legend, and pictures a young Kim addressing a wildly enthusiastic local population. Set back from the arch is the Kim Il-sung Stadium, where you'll often see pioneers and school children practising for parades.

Kim Il-sung Square   SQUARE
Pyongyang's central square is where North Korea's massive military parades normally take place. The plaza is ringed by austere-looking buildings: most impressive of these is the **Grand People's Study House**, the country's largest library and national centre of Juche studies, where any North Korean over 17 can come for free lectures.

With over 30 million books, finding what you want is inevitably quite a challenge – and you will be proudly shown the impressive system of conveyor belts that can deliver books in seconds. You'll also normally visit a reading room, a classroom, the intranet room and a room full of late-'80s cassette recorders.

Other buildings on the square include the **Korean National Art Gallery**, which is worth a visit to see the postwar socialist realist art collection. There are 14 rooms of prewar Korean art that are of very high quality, too. There's also the ho-hum **Korean Central History Museum** on the opposite side of the square. There's a great view from the riverside bank across the Taedong to the Tower of the Juche Idea, where groups usually go to take photos. There's also the Austrian joint venture Ryongwang Coffee Shop (p317) here, where you can get a decent cappuccino.

Victorious Fatherland Liberation War Museum   MUSEUM
Perhaps the best museum in Pyongyang, this mouthful of an institution opened its new home in 2013 to mark the 60th anniversary of the end of the Korean War. Outside you'll see war-damaged tanks, weapons and aircraft used by both sides in the conflict, while inside there are interactive exhibits and a 360-degree diorama of the Battle of Daejeon. In the foyer look out for the statue of a young Kim Il-sung, where he looks exactly like his grandson.

Nearby, opposite the little Potong tributary of the Taedong, there's the impressive **Monument to the Victorious Fatherland Liberation War**, unveiled in 1993 to mark the 40th anniversary of the war's end. The sculptures reflect the different battles of the war; the Victory Sculpture is the centrepiece.

Monument to the Foundation of the Workers' Party MONUMENT
This startlingly bombastic monument has starred on the cover of more books about North Korea than almost any other. The three hands portrayed represent the worker (holding a hammer), the peasant (holding the scythe) and the intellectual (holding the writing brush). It's an enjoyable visit, not least because you're in the middle of the city and curious locals often pass by.

Ryugyong Hotel   LANDMARK
This extraordinary hotel, begun in 1987, has still not been completed three decades later. Planned as a prestige project, but abandoned following the collapse of the USSR, its haunting skeleton sat for years as an unavoidable symbol of North Korea's economic failure. In 2008 work began on the hotel again. It was clad in glass, and looks far better than before. However, it remains totally empty inside and cannot be visited.

Mangyongdae Children's Palace   ARTS CENTRE
This centre for extracurricular activity – from martial arts to the playing of traditional instruments – makes for a great visit. The

---

FAUX PAS

➡ Don't take photos of one part of a statue of the Kims; get the whole thing in.

➡ Don't ever fold, tear or throw away a newspaper with one of the Kims on the cover.

➡ Don't wander away from your group; this can result in serious consequences for your guides.

➡ Take it seriously when your guides ask you not to take photographs.

palace visit includes displays of incredibly talented martial artists, gymnasts and musicians, all beaming at you with permanent smiles as they perform. The tour usually culminates in the main auditorium with a stellar display by fantastically regimented youth.

Moran Hill   PARK

This is Pyongyang's top recreation ground: couples wander, families picnic and there are people playing guitars and sometimes even dancing in an incongruously relaxed area of the capital. It's particularly busy on a Sunday and a lovely place to stroll and absorb something of daily life away from politics and propaganda.

USS Pueblo   HISTORIC SITE

The USS *Pueblo* is a US surveillance vessel that was seized by the North Koreans off the east coast of Korea in January 1968 during a heightening of tensions between the North and South. It's been preserved since then and is currently moored in the Pottong River. You can step aboard and watch a film on the violations of the ceasefire agreement by the US.

Korean Revolution Museum   MUSEUM

Despite the museum's rather misleading name, its main function is to document the death of Kim Il-sung (including a film of the extraordinary public reaction to it) and the succession of Kim Jong-il during the turbulent 1990s. One of the more bizarre items on display is a tin of Nivea hand cream that the Dear Leader thoughtfully gifted to fac-tory workers with sore hands. There is also a display of the various Kim regime loyalty badges worn by locals.

Party Founding Museum   MUSEUM

Located on the southern slope of Haebang Hill is this museum that originally housed the Central Committee of the Korean Workers' Party, as well as Kim Il-sung's office from where he 'led the building of a new democratic Korea'. Next door is the Great Leader's conspicuously modest residence, used after coming to power (and before he had numerous palaces built for him).

Three Revolutions Exhibition   MUSEUM

A surreal, enormous exhibition complex, North Korea's answer to Florida's Epcot theme park details the 'three revolutions' Kim Il-sung brought about in postwar Korea: ideological, technical and cultural. The six halls detail advances across the board in electronics, heavy industry, light industry, agriculture and technology (advances appear to be fairly slim, though, with all the technical exhibits looking more like a display of antiques).

The world's weirdest planetarium can be found within the electronics industry hall, which looks like a silver rendering of Saturn. There's also an interesting outdoor display of vehicles produced in North Korea.

Pyongyang Film Studios   FILM LOCATION

Several films a year are still churned out by the country's main film studios in the suburbs of Pyongyang. Like most things North Korean, the two main focuses are the anti-Japanese struggle and the anti-American war. The main complex is a huge, propaganda-filled suite of office buildings where apparently post-production goes on, even though it feels eerily empty. A short uphill drive takes you to the large sets, however, which are far more fun.

Here you'll find a generic ancient Korean town for historic films (you can even dress up as a king or queen and be photographed sitting on a 'throne' carpeted in leopard skin), a 1930s Chinese street, a Japanese street, a South Korean street (look for the massage signs that illustrate their compatriots' moral laxity) and a fairly bizarre range of structures from a collection of 'European' buildings.

Mangyongdae   NEIGHBOURHOOD

Located 8km from the centre of Pyongyang, Mangyongdae has long been a destination

---

PYONGYANG HIGHLIGHTS

➡ Take the lift to the top of the **Tower of the Juche Idea** (p312) for a magnificent view of the sprawling cityscape on a clear day.

➡ Ride the impressively deep and spectacularly adorned **Pyongyang metro** with the locals.

➡ See where Kim Il-sung lies in state at the **Kumsusan Memorial Palace of the Sun** (p312), which makes Lenin's mausoleum look like a shoebox.

➡ Escape the relentless grandeur of the city centre and have a walk on relaxed **Moran Hill**.

➡ Experience the iconic **Monument to the Foundation of the Workers' Party** (p313), one of Pyongyang's most famous symbols.

THE MYSTERY UNDERGROUND

Visiting the Pyongyang metro has traditionally involved a one-stop trip between Puhung (Rehabilitation) and Yonggwang (Glory) stations, the two most elaborately decorated and thus photogenic of the network's 17 stations. But in recent years a longer trip has become possible, allowing you to pass through several stations and quashing the long-standing rumours that power cuts and lack of repair meant that the rest of the system was no longer working on a day-to-day basis and that the 'passengers' tourists see on the network are extras bussed in to make the system look functional. Some specialist tours now even offer the chance to travel the entire length of the Pyongyang metro along its two lines, something very few foreigners have ever seen.

The entire system's construction was, inevitably, overseen by the Great Leader, who offered his famous 'on-the-spot guidance'. Indeed, the **Metro Museum**, next to the Tower of Immortality, covers almost exclusively the role of the two leaders in the construction of the metro and gives almost no technical information, although there is a very cool diorama. Rumours of a parallel metro system connecting government offices and military installations have persisted for years, although as with most rumours about North Korea, no evidence of its existence has ever been given.

for day trippers from the capital, due to its idyllic setting amid the gentle hills where the Sunhwa River flows into the Taedong. The suburb houses the place of Kim Il-sung's birth, a typical Korean peasant house with a thatched roof and a block of living rooms, as well as a small barn, most of which looks as if it were built in the past few decades.

The **Mangyongdae Revolutionary Museum**, located nearby, continues the theme of the Great Leader's childhood and underscores the point that all his family members were Korean patriot revolutionaries of the humblest possible order.

The nearby **Mangyongdae Funfair** is a pleasant oasis built around the base of Song Hill, where you can relax with day trippers from the capital. You can throw a ball at American imperialists at the coconut shy, take a ride on a North Korean roller coaster and nauseate yourself on the Mad Mouse (a harmless-looking mini roller coaster that is quite terrifying).

🏃 Activities

Funfairs are big in Pyongyang and there are currently four that can be visited. The best are the newly renovated **Kaeson Funfair** (Kaeson St) and **Rungna Funfair** (Rungna Island), both of which are kitted out with brand new Italian rides and are open evenings between April and October. Rides for foreigners cost €2 to €5.

⭐ **Munsu Waterpark**　　　　AMUSEMENT PARK
(admission €10) This vast indoor and outdoor water park opened at the end of 2013

and has proven exceptionally popular with Pyongyang's emerging middle class. Open to foreigners on weekends and holidays, the park can easily take up a whole day. Indoor and outdoor pools include water slides, wave machines, fountains and saunas. Swimming costume rental is included with your entry fee. It's the best place in the whole country to mingle with relaxing locals.

**Pyongyang
Shooting Range**　　　　　　SHOOTING RANGE
A trip to the Pyongyang shooting range off Chongchun St, where all Pyongyang's sporting facilities are concentrated, makes for an unusual evening. It costs €1 for three bullets using a 2.2mm rifle or pistol, and you may be shown how to shoot by former Olympic marksmen.

Golden Lane Bowling Alley　　　BOWLING
(Munsu-Kangan St) The huge Golden Lane Bowling Alley is a good chance to mix with locals and watch some stellar displays of local bowling talent, as well as beer drinking.

🛏 Sleeping

Pyongyang has a range of hotels, though in reality nearly all tour groups stay at the Yanggakdo Hotel, situated in the centre of the city on its own island.

Yanggakdo Hotel　　　　　　HOTEL ₩₩
(📞02-381 2134; fax 02-381 2931; Yanggak Island; ❄🌐) The tallest building in the country, a mid-'90s tower on its own island right in the middle of Pyongyang, is where nearly all tour groups stay. The rooms are already

showing their age, but they are spacious and comfortable, with great views over the city from most and hot water in the mornings and evenings.

As well as a pool and sauna, there are numerous restaurants, a microbrewery, a bowling alley, a billiards hall, a karaoke lounge, several shops and a casino. One advantage of the Yanggakdo is that you can wander around outside without your guides as the grounds are so large, something you aren't able to do in other Pyongyang hotels.

Haebangsan Hotel
HOTEL WW

(Sungri St) Centrally located, this hotel has decent-enough rooms, a good shop, pool tables and an office for booking international train tickets.

Pyongyang Hotel
HOTEL WW

(Sungri St) Popular with foreign residents in the capital mainly for its excellent Arirang restaurant (supposedly one of the city's best, though tourists aren't usually taken here), the Pyongyang Hotel is basic, though some floors have been redone to a good standard. It's mainly used by overseas Koreans visiting the motherland.

Chongnyon Hotel
HOTEL WW

(Chongchun St; ☎) The 'Youth' Hotel is in the bizarrely empty sports district around Chongchun St, and while it boasts an outdoor pool, its rooms are damp and depressing. There's a hamburger restaurant just outside, which is an interesting quirk in a neighbourhood otherwise given over to Olympian physical perfection.

Ryanggang Hotel
HOTEL WW

(Chongchun St) Also in the sports district of Chongchun St, this place is one of the cheapest hotels in the city and it shows: there's a revolving restaurant that doesn't revolve, beds are hard and rooms are rather dusty.

Koryo Hotel
HOTEL WWW

(☎ 02-381 4397; fax 02-381 4422; Changgwang St; ✳ ☎) This striking 1985 twin-towered structure is commonly used for business travellers and NGO staff, although some tour groups stay here too. Each of its twin towers has a revolving restaurant on top, though only one of them is open as, in a spectacular failure of forethought, the other overlooks the 'forbidden city', home to the country's highly secretive political elite.

The rooms are quirky, with small bathrooms and curious alcoves for sitting in, but it's comfortable and clean and has several bars, restaurants and shops to occupy guests. Avoid the overpriced ground-floor coffee shop.

Potonggang Hotel
HOTEL WWW

(☎ 02-381 2229; fax 02-381 4428; Saemaul St; ✳ ☎) Famously the only hotel in North Korea to get CNN, the pink-painted Potonggang was owned by the late Unification Church leader Reverend Moon and has the best rooms in the city. However, it's rare for groups to stay here as it's about 4km from the city centre. It nevertheless offers some good restaurants, a bar, pool, karaoke and indoor golf.

✗ Eating

Pyongyang has by far the best restaurants in North Korea, though that's not saying a huge amount. Any restaurant used by tour groups will be run by the KITC and therefore the exclusive preserve of foreigners and the local elite.

On tours all eating out will be included in your price, although there are extra charges for additional beers or specialities such as the local favourite: cold noodles.

★ Pyongyang Number One Duck Barbeque
KOREAN

One of the best places in town, this will often be where groups go on their last evening. Here you'll be served delicious strips of duck meat you cook at your table.

★ Lamb Barbecue Restaurant
KOREAN

This restaurant has some of the friendliest and most boisterous staff in the country, and once the delicious lamb barbecue has been served at your table, the waitresses will burst into song and encourage diners to dance with them.

Chongryu Hotpot Restaurant
KOREAN

The Chongryu Hotpot Restaurant is nearly always on the itinerary. It's a pleasant place where you make your own hotpot dish on little individual gas stoves. There's a second branch of this restaurant in a boat-shaped building overlooking the Potong River by the ice rink.

Pizza Restaurant
PIZZA

(Kwangbok St) Pyongyang's imaginatively named first pizza joint caused a sensation when it opened in 2009 after Kim Jong-il reportedly sent a team of chefs to Italy to learn how to make the perfect pizza. The

SHOULD YOU VISIT?

North Korea is a police state with a human-rights record that is considered among the worst on Earth. Concentration camps, executions, state-orchestrated terror and mass control by a vast propaganda machine are a daily reality for millions here. The revenue from your trip will largely go to the state, and given the cost of just one traveller's tour, this totals a sizeable amount. So should you visit, and is it morally acceptable to do so?

The case against visiting, as outlined above, is strong. On the other hand, those who argue that you *should* visit point out that tourism is one of the few ways of encouraging openness in the DPRK, of letting people see that the West is interested and, more importantly, friendly – not an insignificant fact for a population brought up on a relentless diet of anti-US propaganda.

Part of the fascination of travelling in North Korea is trying to divine the real from the fake and attempting to see past the ideology. While you may be horrified, amazed or awestruck by what you see in North Korea, you won't be able to help yourself seeing the world from a different perspective once you've been here.

If you do decide to come, listen to the version of history given to you by the guides, accept that this is their version and leave serious criticism until you are back at your hotel, or better, out of the country.

results are pretty decent, although if you don't fancy pizza, there's a full range of pasta dishes, as well as the ubiquitous after-dinner karaoke.

Okryu
KOREAN

One of the city's best-known restaurants is a recently renovated faux-traditional structure on the riverside that's famed for its cold noodles and is very popular with locals. For this reason it's not usually on the schedule for groups, but you may get lucky.

Pyulmori
CAFE

Pyulmori is a refreshingly well-run joint-venture restaurant, coffee shop and bar. You can get decent food, coffee and excellent cake here, and in the evenings it's a popular bar and something of an expat hang-out (this being a relative term in North Korea, of course).

Ryongwang Coffee Shop
CAFE

Right in the centre of the city, just off Kim Il-sung Sq, is this joint-venture project set up by Austrian investors in partnership with North Koreans. It's the best place in town for coffee and cake between sights.

 Drinking

Nightlife in Pyongyang is almost nonexistent, although hotel bars can be rowdy, especially in high season when there are plenty of tour groups in town. The sizeable diplomatic and NGO presence in town means that there are some private clubs where

foreigners can relax away from the strictures of everyday Pyongyang life, though these are usually inaccessible to foreign tourists. Ask your guides nicely if you'd like a night out on the town, as they'll have to accompany you on top of their already gruelling schedules.

Diplomatic Club
BAR

The Diplomatic Club is a complex full of bars, karaoke rooms and restaurants and it boasts an excellent pool aimed at foreign residents, although tourists are regularly taken here. More often than not, it's utterly deserted. It's one of the few places open until late at night in Pyongyang, though.

Taedonggang No 3 Beer Bar
BAR

This bar near the Juche Tower has seven different types of beer on tap, plus cocktails and meals. It's a good chance to see how the local middle classes spend their time, and is a world away from typical North Korean bars that tend to be full of smoking men drinking beer while standing around tables.

Paulaner Brauhaus
BEER HALL

Inside the Haemaji Shopping Centre you'll find this German-run venture where beer is served up to a mixture of locals and foreigners. Beer is pricey here and not necessarily any better than in a local bar, but it's perhaps a vision of the future sitting in a genuine foreign bar in North Korea, and popular with groups.

DON'T LEAVE HOME WITHOUT...

Anything medical or electrical that you will need during your stay – this includes simple everyday products such as painkillers, tampons, condoms, memory cards and batteries. Such basic items are sometimes available, but their price and quality can be quite different from elsewhere. Bringing a bag of fruit or energy snacks from China is a great idea for snacking between sights and sharing with other members of your tour group. Small change in euros and yuan (€1 and 10 yuan notes) is a huge help, as there's rarely hard-currency change in shops. Small token gifts for your guides will be appreciated, though they are not essential (and a cash tip won't be expected, whatever else you give them). Popular gifts include cigarettes (for male guides only), chocolates and quality beauty products. Most of all, bring a sense of humour and an open mind – you'll need both to make North Korea enjoyable and rewarding.

 Entertainment

The ultimate Pyongyang night out is the unforgettable **Mass Games**, a unique show that in the past took place nightly between August and October at the **May Day Stadium** and involved more than 100,000 participants in a dazzling display of coordinated political sloganising, gymnastics, dance, music and drama. The long-running *Arirang Mass Games,* the story of Korea's history, was finally retired in 2012 and a new show is purportedly in the works, although this was not confirmed at the time of writing. If the games do come back, jump at the chance to attend. Tickets are steeply priced, starting at €80 for a 'third-class' ticket and rising to €300 for VIP tickets, but the experience is worth every cent.

Cinema, theatre and opera trips are also possible (although rare), and while performances aren't likely to be particularly gripping, again it's the experience that's interesting. The two cinemas on offer are the **Taedongmun Cinema** (Sungri St) and the **Pyongyang International Cinema**, a six-screen complex on Yanggak Island. The biennial **Pyongyang Film Festival** (www.pyongyanginternationalfilmfestival.com) is held here in September of even-numbered years. The main theatres are the **Pyongyang Grand Theatre**, the **East Pyongyang Grand Theatre** (Munsu-Kangan St), the **Moranbong Theatre** and the **Mansudae Art Theatre**, although spectacles vary little from one to the other. The **People's Theatre**, part of the new buildings along Mansudae St, stages some of the most prestigious spectacles in the city.

Instead of drama you'll usually see orchestras performing classical and traditional Korean music, or one of the five North Korean revolutionary operas such as the

Flower Girl and *A Daughter of the Party*. Jump at the chance to see these, as they are sumptuous productions with very high production values.

Soccer, a very popular local spectator sport, is a good way to spend an evening with ordinary Koreans. These days any local match can be attended in Pyongyang, the schedule is often not known far in advance but is posted on a board outside **Kim Il-sung Stadium**, so keep an eye out for this if you want to go to a game. Expect low attendance and a low quality of football, unless you attend a women's game, where the quality of play tends to be far higher.

Pyongyang Circus　　　　　LIVE PERFORMANCE
The Pyongyang Circus is a popular afternoon or evening out, though it's housed in a palatial building a million miles away from your standard big top and sawdust floor. Here you'll see a stellar display of acrobatics, some very funny clowns and some deeply sad-looking bears who skip rope while dressed in outlandish costumes.

 Shopping

Every Pyongyang sight has a small stand selling books, postcards and other souvenirs. There are good bookshops at both the Yanggakdo and Koryo Hotels and the **Foreign Language Bookshop** is the best in the city.

Department stores are often visited, and they can be a fascinating insight into what's available. The one most regularly visited is the **Ragwon (Paradise) Department Store**, which tends to have few local shoppers or products and is consequently not that interesting. Sadly, **Department Store Number One**, the city's busiest, is off-limits to foreigners.

Kwangbok Supermarket   DEPARTMENT STORE
(Kwangbok St; ☺ Tue-Sun) Notable as the venue for Kim Jong-Il's final public appearance, this multi-storey department store stocks a good range of mostly imported goods, but also a good amount of local produce. You can roam freely inside, change money at the market rate and see what the middle class are spending their money on.

Some great street snacks are sold in the food court on the top floor.

Korea Stamp   SOUVENIRS
Next door to the Koryo Hotel is Korea Stamp, a good place to buy North Korean stamps (spectacular propaganda pieces). T-shirts and postcards are also on sale.

Mansudae Art Studio   ARTS
(Saemaul St) Art is another popular purchase in Pyongyang. The Mansudae Art Studio is a centralised art studio employing thousands of painters, embroiderers and sculptors. There's a large selection of socialist realist art available for sale, as well as more traditional landscape paintings.

❶ Information

There is no tourist office in Pyongyang, but there are numerous English-language publications designed for visitors detailing various aspects of North Korean life. The English-language *Pyongyang Times* is an amusing weekly paper full of propaganda, although a copy will enliven even the dullest coffee table back home.

Hotels, as the only place the authorities are happy to have visitors spend any time, provide all necessary services. Most tourists will not need to do laundry, as trips are rarely longer than a week, although the facilities exist in all

Pyongyang hotels. Most hotels also have a 24-hour doctor on call.

❶ Getting Around

All tourists will be driven around Pyongyang either by car, minibus or coach. Using public transport is not possible, save for the novelty metro ride most visitors do in Pyongyang. Foreign residents in the city, however, have more freedom to use the extensive bus, tram, trolleybus and metro network.

Taxis are available outside all hotels for you to travel in with your guide, should the need arise. Reception can also book taxis for you if there are none outside the hotel.

AROUND NORTH KOREA

Nearly all tours begin and end in Pyongyang, but all but the very shortest also include a trip to at least some other parts of the country. Nearly all travellers visit the DMZ at Panmunjom and the nearby city of Kaesong, typically overnight. Visits to mountain resorts elsewhere on the peninsula, and even the far-flung mountains in the country's northeast, are also sometimes included, as are a slew of industrial cities with few traditional attractions, but that hold plenty of interest to anyone fascinated with North Korean daily life.

Kaesong   개성
POP 330,000

Though just a few miles from the DMZ and the world's most concentrated build-up of military forces, Kaesong is a fairly relaxed place just off the Reunification Hwy from

---

IS NORTH KOREA SAFE?

North Korea isn't a dangerous destination, but you'd be foolhardy to openly criticise the regime in general, or any of the Kims in particular. Spare a thought for your guides – despite being official representatives of the regime, they're the ones who are vulnerable should you decide to speak your mind, make any form of protest or insult the leadership. Likewise, escaping the group, disobeying photography instructions or otherwise stirring up trouble will be far more dangerous for them than for you.

When meeting North Koreans in the street, take your lead from the guides. Ask before you take photographs, keep conversations nonpolitical and accept that at present you're unable to freely mix with locals – exchanging a few brief pleasantries is normally the furthest you can get with anyone before the guides get nervous.

The obligation to be with your guides at all times outside the hotel is a serious one. It means that individual exploration is totally impossible and often leads to frustration for seasoned travellers unused to the confines of group travel. However, until the rules change, it's important for travellers to accept and conform to them.

Pyongyang. The city is dominated by a massive statue of Kim Il-sung atop a large hill, while the city's main street runs from the hill to the highway.

Once the capital of the Koryo dynasty, Kaesong has an interesting old quarter as well as the country's most atmospheric hotel, but tours rarely spend much time here. You are usually billeted at the hotel for the night before returning to Pyongyang having seen the DMZ, although a fascinating walk through the town to the top of the hill with your guides is usually possible.

◉ Sights

Kaesong is a modern city with wide streets and an old town consisting of traditional tile-roofed houses sandwiched between the river and the main street. Within the town is a number of lesser tourist sights: the **Sonjuk Bridge**, a tiny clapper bridge built in 1216 and, opposite, the **Songin Monument**, which honours neo-Confucian hero Chong Mong-ju; the **Nammun** (South Gate), which dates from the 14th century and houses an old Buddhist bell; the **Sungyang Seowon** (Confucian academy); and **Chanamsan**, the hill from which Kim Il-sung's statue stares down at the city (and from where there are good views over the old town).

Songgyungwan
Neo-Confucian College   MUSEUM
This well-preserved college, originally built in AD 992 and rebuilt after being destroyed in the 1592 Japanese invasion, today hosts the **Koryo Museum**, which contains celadon pottery and other Buddhist relics. The buildings surround a wide courtyard dotted with ancient trees, and there are also two good souvenir shops, one selling ginseng and the other selling commemorative stamps and souvenirs. It's a short drive northeast of town.

Tomb of King Kongmin   TOMB
The 31st Koryo king, Kongmin reigned between 1352 and 1374 and his tomb is the best preserved and most elaborate in the country. It is richly decorated with traditional granite facing and statuary, including sheep statues (in honour of his Mongolian wife, also buried here) and plenty of vaguely Aztec-looking altars. It's a very secluded site, about 13km west of Kaesong.

🛏 Sleeping

★ Minsok Folk Hotel   HOTEL ₩₩
If you stay over in Kaesong, you'll normally be based at this wonderful hotel consisting of 20 traditional Korean *yeogwan* (small, well-equipped en-suite rooms), all off small courtyards, and featuring a charming stream running through it. There's no electricity during the day, but there's usually light in the evening and hot water.

It's basic (the rice-husk pillows are distinctly hard!) but fascinating and far more atmospheric than anywhere else you'll stay in the country.

Panmunjom & the DMZ
판문점&비무장지대

The sad sight of a pointlessly divided nation remains one of the most memorable parts of any trip to North Korea. While military-history buffs will really be in their element, you don't have to be an expert to appreciate the weirdness of the site where the bloody Korean War ended in an unhappy truce more than 60 years ago. Seeing the situation from the North, facing off against US troops to the south, is a unique chance to witness things from a new perspective.

The eerily quiet drive from Pyongyang down the six-lane Reunification Hwy – the road is deserted save for military checkpoints – gives you a sense of what to expect. Just before you exit to the DMZ, the sign saying 'Seoul 70km' is a reminder of just how close and yet how far is normality.

There are several aspects to the DMZ visit. Your first stop will be at a **KPA post** just outside the DMZ. Here a soldier will show you a model of the entire site, pointing out South Korean as well as North Korean HQ and watchtowers. Then you'll be marched (single file!) through an anti-tank barrier to rejoin your bus and you'll drive down a long concrete corridor. Look out for the tank traps either side – huge slabs of concrete ready to be dropped into the road at any minute in the event of a land invasion.

The next stop is the **Armistice Talks Hall**, about 1km into the DMZ. Here negotiations were held between the two sides from 1951 until the final armistice, which was signed here on 27 July 1953. You'll see two copies of the agreement on display in glass cases, along with the original North Korean and UN flags. Next door there's an exhibition of photos from the war. Outside, a plaque in red script best sums up the North Korean version of the ceasefire. It reads: 'It was here on July 27, 1953 that the American imperialists got down on their knees before the heroic Chosun people to sign the ceasefire for the war they had provoked June 25, 1950.'

From here you'll reboard the bus and drive to the **Demarcation Line** itself, and you'll be reminded in more than usually severe language about sticking together 'for your own safety'. The site consists of two sinister-looking headquarters staring at each other across the line (the North Korean is built to be the bigger of the two) and several huts built over the line for meetings. Amazingly, you can cross a few metres into South Korea within the huts, but the doors out to the south are closed and guarded by two soldiers.

Being at the centre of the biggest military face-off on Earth is rather like being in the eye of a storm – tension is in the air, but it is so peaceful that it makes the very idea of imminent combat seem ridiculous. South Korean and American soldiers eyeball their northern counterparts as they have done every day since 1953. Do not be fooled by the prevailing air of calm, though; any attempt to even approach the border proper will result in you being shot on the spot, possibly from both sides. In the 1980s, however, a Soviet tourist found a unique way to flee the communist bloc, defecting amid gunfire from both sides. Unless you are really short of time, this is not an advisable way to get to Seoul.

The other interesting sight at the DMZ is the **Concrete Wall**, a US-constructed anti-tank barrier that runs the length of the 248km border. It has been hijacked as an emotive propaganda weapon by the North, which since 1989 has been comparing it with the Berlin Wall. Indeed, the issue has proved an emotive one in the South as well, where students have demanded it be dismantled. You will inspect the wall with binoculars and be shown a particularly funny North Korean propaganda video.

Myohyangsan 묘향산

A trip to this pretty resort area, just 150km north of Pyongyang, provides an easy chance to experience the pristine North Korean countryside, along with an inevitable slice of personality cult. Mt Myohyang and the surrounding area of hills, mountain trails and waterfalls make for a charming trip.

Myohyangsan means 'mountain of mysterious fragrance' and it's certainly no misnomer. The scenery is quite wonderful, and in summer the area is awash with flowers. The focus of all trips, however, are the two vast shrines that make up the International Friendship Exhibition (IFE).

Having completed a tour of both exhibits, the perfect way to unwind from the seriousness is with some walking on the beautiful mountain trails. The nearby Sangwon Valley is the most common place for a hike.

⊙ Sights

International Friendship Exhibition   MUSEUM

If you begin to miss the relentless pomp and propaganda of Pyongyang, this massive display of the gifts given to Kim Il-sung and Kim Jong-il, housed in a mountainside vault that is vaguely reminiscent of a Bond villain's hideout, will remind you that you are still very much in North Korea.

Before entering, you will be asked to put on shoe covers in keeping with the reverential attitude shown by one and all. A member of your group may be honoured with the task of opening the vast doors that lead into the exhibit – after putting on ceremonial gloves to protect the polished doorknob.

Kim Il-sung's gifts are very impressive. Particularly noteworthy is the beautiful armoured train carriage presented to him by Mao Zedong and a limousine sent by that great man of the people, Josef Stalin. The exhibits are arranged geographically, although you will thankfully only be shown the highlights of the 100,000-plus gifts spread over 120 rooms. Gifts from heads of state are displayed on red cloth, those from other officials on blue and gifts from individuals on brown. The undeniable highlight is a stuffed crocodile holding a tray of wooden glasses, presented to the Great Leader by the Sandinistas.

The tone of the visit is very strict and sombre, so avoid the very real temptation to ice skate across the over-polished floor in your foot covers. The most reverential and surreal part of the exhibit is the final room, in which there is a grinning life-sized waxwork of the Great Leader, to which you will be expected to bow your head before leaving respectfully.

Next is Kim Jong-il's similarly spectacular warehouse, where gifts given to him have been housed in a vault built into the cave wall. Kim Jong-il's gifts include those from Hyundai and CNN, as well as a good-luck note from Jimmy Carter and a basketball from Madeleine Albright. Indeed, some parts of the exhibit look like any upmarket electronics showroom – row after row of widescreen TVs and stereo equipment donated by industrialists. There's also a rendering of the Dear Leader in wax here.

Pyohon Temple   TEMPLE
The most historically important Buddhist temple in western North Korea, the Pyohon Temple complex dates back to 1044, with numerous renovations over the centuries. It features several small pagodas and a large hall housing images of Buddha, as well as a museum that sports a collection of woodblocks from the Buddhist scriptures, the *Tripitaka Koreana*.

It's just a short walk from the IFE, at the entrance to Sangwon Valley.

Ryongmun Big Cave   CAVE
It's common for tours to visit this 6km-long limestone cave either prior to or after a visit to Myohyangsan. It has some enormous caverns and a large number of stalactites. Enjoy sights including the Pool of the Anti-Imperialist People's Struggle, the Juche Cavern and the Mountain Peak of the Great Leader.

🛏 Sleeping

Chongchon Hotel   HOTEL ₩₩
(Hyangsan) Tourists usually stay overnight in the Chongchon Hotel in Hyangsan town, a simple three-storey 1970s place that has a couple of bars, but limited hot water and electricity.

Hamhung   함흥
North Korea's massively industrial second city is now open to tour groups and it's a great place to visit, boasting such North Korean delights as a fertiliser factory and a collective farm. Tours inevitably begin with a Kim Il-sung & Kim Jong-il Statue on the central street, and include a visit to the monumental Hamhung Grand Theatre, the largest theatre in the country (and sadly only viewable from the outside at present), and the far more interesting Home of Ryi

Song Gye, an impressive complex of historic buildings set in attractive gardens and to which a particularly bawdy tale is attached. The suburbs of Hamhung are made up of factory after factory, the air is horribly polluted and chimneys belch noxious yellow fumes into the air. The Hungnam Fertiliser Factory can sometimes be visited, where you will be shown how ammonia is made deep inside the enormous industrial complex, an experience like no other, even by North Korean standards. Some way outside the city is the Tongbong Co-operative Farm, which can also be visited by groups. While you're unlikely to see any actual farming (except from a distance), you will be able to visit a kindergarten, a quite beautifully presented gift shop and see the inside of a collective-farm worker's home.

🛏 Sleeping

Sin Hung San Hotel   HOTEL ₩₩
On the city's main drag is Hamhung's main hotel. The rooms are basic, but there's running water and some unique interiors to enjoy.

Majon Beach Guesthouse   GUESTHOUSE ₩₩
Rather isolated some way out of town, but this place enjoys beach access and similarly spectacular interiors in its main building.

Wonsan   원산
POP 300,000
This port city on the East Sea is not a big tourist draw but makes for an interesting stop en route to Kumgangsan from Pyongyang. The city is an important port, a centre of learning with 10 universities and a popular holiday resort for Koreans, with lovely sandy beaches at nearby Lake Sijung and Lake Tongjong, as well as a newly built ski resort.

The city is surrounded by mountains and is full of high-rise buildings in its centre.

◉ Sights & Activities

Songdowon   BEACH
A clean sandy beach where the Jokchon Stream runs into the East Sea and some antique metallic diving boards. Foreigners swim at the 'foreigners only' section of the beach, but interaction with North Koreans is possible on the small pier and the diving platform, which you reach by swimming out into the bay.

Songdowon Schoolchildren's Camp
LANDMARK

At this camp you can meet holidaying schoolkids and see a very curious collection of disintegrating taxidermy, a state-of-the-art aquarium and a rather colourful water slide.

Masik-Ryong Ski Resort
SKIING

Just outside Wonsan is the Masik-Ryong Ski Resort, a pet project of Kim Jong-un that was completed in record time by the army. With several runs, one over 5km long, bunny slopes, skidoos, skating and the very impressive and luxurious **Masik-Ryong Hotel** (@☒) (with in-room internet access for US$10 per hour), this is truly unlike anything else in North Korea.

In the non-winter months it's possible to visit the area to stay in the hotel, but the real highlight is hitting the powder with locals. Access to the slopes costs US$40 per day and all kit, including snowboards, can be rented.

🛏 Sleeping

Tongmyong Hotel
HOTEL ₩₩

This large '70s hotel in a lurid shade of green is right on the harbour and has decent, spacious rooms, many with sea views. There's sometimes hot water and a decent restaurant. Don't miss the hilarious lift instructions.

Songdowon Tourist Hotel
HOTEL ₩₩

A second-class hotel right on the waterfront in the centre of the city, the Songdowon nonetheless boasts absolutely first-class '70s socialist interiors and a better-than-average souvenir shop.

Kumgangsan 금강산

South of the port city of Wonsan on the east of the Korean Peninsula, the most dramatic scenery in the entire country begins to rise. Kumgang is divided into the Inner, Outer and Sea Kumgang regions. The main tourist activities are hiking, mountaineering, boating and sightseeing. The area is peppered with former Buddhist temples and hermitages, waterfalls, mineral springs, a pretty lagoon and a small museum. Maps of the area are provided by park officials to help you decide where you want to go among the dozens of excellent sites.

If your time here is limited, the best places to visit in the Outer Kumgang Region are the **Samil Lagoon** (try hiring a boat, then rest at Tanpung Restaurant); the **Manmulsang Area**, where there are fantastically shaped crags; and the **Kuryong and Pibong Falls**, a 4.5km hike from the Mongnan Restaurant.

In the Inner Kumgang Region, it's worth visiting the impressively reconstructed **Pyohon Temple**, founded in AD 670 and one of old Korea's most important Zen monasteries. Hiking in the valleys around Pyohon Temple or, really, anywhere in the park is rewarding and memorable. **Pirobong** (1639m) is the highest peak out of at least 100.

The usual route to Kumgangsan is by car from Pyongyang to Onjong-ri via Wonsan along the highway (around 315km, a four-hour drive). Along the way to Wonsan, your car or bus will usually stop off at a teahouse by Sinpyeong Lake. From Wonsan, the road more or less follows the coastline south and you'll get glimpses of the double-wired electric fence that runs the entire length of the east coast. There may also be a stop for tea at Shijung Lake.

Your final destination is the village of Onjong-ri and the **Kumgangsan Hotel**. The hotel is quite a rambling affair, consisting of a main building and several outer buildings that include chalets, a shop, a dance hall and bathhouse fed by a hot spring.

Nampo 남포

POP 730,000

On the Taedong delta, 55km southwest of Pyongyang, is Nampo, North Korea's most important port and centre of industry. Nampo made its name for being the 'birthplace of the Chollima movement', after the workers at the local steel plant supposedly 'took the lead in bringing about an upswing in socialist construction', according to local tourist pamphlets. Sadly there's nothing much to see in the town itself, though it makes for an interesting glimpse at provincial life.

On the other side of the West Sea Barrage, there are nice beaches about 20km from Nampo. Here, if you are lucky enough to go, you will see the locals enjoying volleyball and swimming.

◉ Sights

West Sea Barrage
LANDMARK

The reason tourists come here (usually on an overnight stop en route to Kaesong) is to see this barrage, built across an 8km estuary of the Taedong to solve the area's irrigation and drinking-water problems. The impressive structure, built during the early 1980s, is nevertheless a rather dull visit – in every way a classic piece of socialist tourism.

You'll drive across it, then up to a hill at the far end from where you'll get good views and enjoy a quick video at the visitor centre. You'll then drive down to the sluice gates and watch them open, ostensibly the highlight of the trip.

🛏 Sleeping

Ryonggang
Hot Spring House
GUESTHOUSE ₩₩

It's now common to include Nampo in an overnight trip from Pyongyang and your group will sleep some way outside the city at this former state guesthouse now open to tourists. It's a unique place – 20 well-appointed villas with several bedrooms each are spread out in the sprawling grounds.

Each room contains its own spa bath, where you can take the waters for a maximum of 15 minutes a time – it's not clear what will happen if you stay in for longer than 15 minutes, but the guides make it clear it would be bad.

Sinchon 신천

This small, nondescript place is often visited on trips between Nampo and Kaesong. You're here to visit the **Sinchon Museum**, which details the atrocities allegedly carried out here against civilians during the Korean War. That US atrocities were committed here and in other places is not in question (both sides frequently violated the Geneva Convention), but the typically hyperbolic portrayal of these sad events does little to restore the dignity of those who suffered.

On arrival you'll be given a long lecture about how Americans 'never change' and how the bloodthirsty US soldiers enjoyed carrying out the murders of some 35,000 people here. The museum presents 'historic' paintings of American brutality (which was apparently endlessly complex and ingeniously esoteric: people having their heads sawed open, a man being pulled in two by two cows attached to either arm, people being burned at the stake) that only serve to undermine the real suffering that occurred during this brutal conflict.

Following the museum, the standard tour includes laying a wreath at a memorial next door and then travelling to the site of two barns where mothers and children were allegedly burned alive by the US army.

There is no hotel in Sinchon, but from here it's a three-hour drive to Kaesong, or it's possible (for non-American travellers) to stay at the **8th March Hotel** in the nearby small town of Sariwon.

Paekdusan 백두산

One of the most stunning sights on the Korean Peninsula, Paekdusan (Mt Paekdu) straddles the Chinese–Korean border in the far northeastern tip of the DPRK. Apart from it being the highest mountain in the country at 2744m, and an amazing geological phenomenon (it's an extinct volcano now containing a crater lake at its centre), it is also of huge mythical importance to the Korean people.

Paekdusan is not included on most tours, as it involves chartering an internal flight to Samjiyon and then driving 1½ hours into the mountains from there. However, if you have the time and money to include a visit on your trip, you will not be disappointed. It's also possible to approach Paekdusan from the Chinese side of the border on a ferry and bus tour from Sokcho in South Korea.

The natural beauty of the extinct volcano, now containing one of the world's deepest lakes, is made all the more magical by the mythology that surrounds the lake, both ancient and modern. The legend runs that Hwanung, the Lord of Heaven, descended onto the mountain in 2333 BC, and from here formed the nation of Choson – 'The Land of Morning Calm', or ancient Korea. It therefore only seems right and proper that, four millennia later, Kim Jong-il was born nearby 'and flying white horses were seen in the sky', according to official sources. In all likelihood, Kim Jong-il was born in Khabarovsk, Russia, where his father was in exile at the time, but the all-important Kim myth supersedes such niggling facts.

Trips here are strictly organised as this is a sensitive border region and a military zone. Having arrived at the military station at the bottom of the mountain, you'll be checked in and will take the funicular railway up the side of the mountain. From here it's a 10-minute hike up to the mountain's highest point, past some superb views down into the crater lake. You can either walk down to the shore of Lake Chon (an easy hike down, but somewhat tougher coming back up!) or take the cable car (€7 per person return) for the easy option. Bring warm clothing; it can be freezing at any time of year, with snow on the ground year-round.

Much like Myohyangsan, an area of great natural beauty is further enhanced by revolutionary 'sights' such as Jong-il peak and the **Secret Camp**, the official birthplace of Kim Jong-il and the spot from where Kim Il-sung supposedly directed some of the key battles during the anti-Japanese campaigns of WWII – no historians outside the DPRK have ever claimed the area was the site of battles.

North Korea's current history books also claim that Kim Il-sung established his guerrilla headquarters at Paekdusan in the 1920s, from where he defeated the Japanese. To prove this, you'll be shown declarations that the Great Leader and his comrades carved on the trees – some so well preserved you might think that they were carved yesterday.

The Dear Leader's birthplace is a nondescript log cabin that you aren't allowed to enter (though you can peer in through the windows) and it's a bit of a let-down after a long drive. But with the revolutionary sites out of the way, you can enjoy the real reason to come here: the glories of nature – the vast tracts of virgin forest, abundant wildlife, lonely granite crags, fresh springs, gushing streams and dramatic waterfalls.

◉ Sights

Samjiyon, the slightly sinister nearby resort town where most travellers stay overnight on the visit to Paekdusan, also boasts a couple of attractions.

Samjiyon Grand Monument   MONUMENT
Set in a huge clearing in the woods with views to Paekdusan and overlooking a large lake, this must be the most impressive paean to the leadership in the country outside Pyongyang. The monument commemorates the battle of Pochombo, where the anti-Japanese forces first moved from guerrilla tactics to conventional warfare and took the town of the same name.

The centrepiece is a 15m-high statue of a 27-year-old Kim Il-sung, as well as a smaller version of Pyongyang's Juche Tower and several large sculptures of various revolutionary scenes.

Paekdu Museum   MUSEUM
This museum in Samjiyon houses a ho-hum re-creation of all the sights of the region.

Children's Palace   THEATRE
Tour groups will sometimes be shown a performance here by local schoolchildren.

🛏 Sleeping

Pegaebong Hotel   HOTEL ₩₩
Just outside the resort town of Samjiyon, this hotel is a decent option with modern rooms and hot running water in its newest wing.

Hyesan Hotel   HOTEL ₩₩
In the town of Hyesan, further away from Paekdusan than Samjiyon, you can stay at the second-class Hyesan Hotel.

ℹ Getting There & Away

Paekdusan is only accessible from around late June to mid-September; at all other times it is forbiddingly cold and stormy. Access to the mountain is by air only, followed by car or bus. These charter flights can hold up to 40 people, for around €4600 per plane per round-trip flight. In a decent-sized group it isn't unreasonable, but it's rather pricey otherwise.

Chilbosan   칠보산

The area around Chilbosan (sometimes called Mt Chilbo) is one of the most beautiful places in North Korea. It's also incredibly remote – the only way to get here in reasonable time is to charter a flight from Pyongyang to Orang airport (approximately €4600 return per plane and usually combined with a trip to Paekdusan), from where Chilbosan is a three-hour drive down a rather Mediterranean-looking coastline of high jagged cliffs, small fishing villages and sandy beaches. The World Tourism Organization has pioneered the **Mt Chilbo Homestay Program** here, though it's some way from what you might imagine from the term 'homestay' – a purpose-built village of large traditional-style houses (as well as some 'European'-style ones) where one family lives in part of the house, and guests in the other. While it does feel rather contrived, it's still one of the best opportunities in the country to meet and talk with North Koreans, though the main problem is communicating, unless you speak some Korean or Chinese. There's a restaurant and a shop in the homestay and another restaurant on the nearby beach where squid barbecues are often laid on. Elsewhere in Chilbosan there's the **Waechilbo Hotel**, where Americans must stay, as they're currently not allowed to visit the homestay.

There's little to do here save enjoy the spectacular scenery, and you'll usually be driven around the attractive valleys, peaks and viewpoints of Chilbosan, including a stop at various beaches and the **Kaesim Buddhist Temple**, which dates from the 9th century.

Chongjin   청진

Jump at the chance to visit Chongjin (tours rarely go there), North Korea's third-largest city and a great spot to see how North Koreans really live. This huge industrial centre and port is a world away from gleaming Pyongyang, and despite a few attempts to ape the capital's socialist grandeur around the city centre, it's a poor, ugly, polluted and depressing place.

Coming here is fascinating, though – most locals have never seen foreigners and this is about as 'real' an experience of the country as you'll ever get. The rules about photography are very strict here, your guides will become far more stern and you'll see little of the city save what you glimpse out of the bus as it races through the city's deserted yet apparently endless avenues at high speed.

Chongjin is an hour's drive north of Orang airport, and while trains run here from Pyongyang, foreigners aren't able to travel on them unless they're chartered for private group use, a unique way to see the country. Koryo Tours (p307) can arrange this from Pyongyang. It is also possible to get to Chongjin without going to Pyongyang at all by entering the country from the northeast (via Rason or Hoeryong) and travelling down the coast by road to Chongjin.

It's usually possible to visit Chongjin on an overnight stop after visiting Chilbosan.

◉ Sights

Kim Il-sung &
Kim Jong-il Statue   MONUMENT
On Chongjin's main square, these twin statues are always on the itinerary. You'll be expected to bow after presenting flowers as a group.

Revolutionary Museum   MUSEUM
Adjacent to the Kim Il-sung and Kim Jong-il statues, this museum tells the truly grotesque story of how locals were burned alive protecting trees with revolutionary slogans on them during a forest fire.

North Hamgyong
Province E-Library   LIBRARY
This 'E-Library' is full of occasionally working computers that are theoretically linked to the national intranet. In the building next door, a highly aspirational model of the future development of Chongjin can be seen.

Chongjin Kindergarten   SCHOOL
Most tours end with a visit to the Chongjin Kindergarten, where scarily intense children with glued-on smiles perform for tourists. In an odd gesture afterwards, visitors are encouraged to pick the children up and pose with them for photographs.

⊨ Sleeping

Chongjin Hotel   HOTEL ₩₩
Accommodation is at this imaginatively named hotel, which has a very friendly manager and a team of frustrated singers working in the restaurant as waitresses, who love to perform songs and dance for the guests after dinner. There's usually no hot water in the rooms, but there's a communal sauna for a wash.

Rajin-Sonbong   라진-선봉

This eccentric corner of North Korea, right on the border with China and Russia, has been designated a 'free trade zone' since 1991. The two towns of Rajin and Sonbong (sometimes referred to collectively as Rason) are both unremarkable industrial ports surrounded by attractive hills, wetlands and forest.

Tours here take in the fascinating **Rajin Market**, the only market in the country tourists are allowed to visit, the **Rajin City Port** and the **Taehung Trading Corporation**, a large seafood-processing plant and mushroom wine factory.

Rajin-Sonbong's rocky cliffs, lakes and sandy coastline are uniquely beautiful, but it feels like the end of the world and tourists only visit on special tours.

The Chinese-owned five-star **Emperor Hotel**, the best in the country, is here, though there are also several far more reasonably priced hotels and guesthouses.

UNDERSTAND NORTH KOREA

North Korea Today

Since coming to power in 2012, Kim Jong-un, the third member of the Kim clan to rule this country, has made an enormous impact internationally despite having met with no other world leaders. Indeed, his apparently conscious cultivation of an air of mystery (nobody knows his actual age or place of birth, for example) seems only to have made him more feared as a volatile, unknown quantity. Initially dismissed by many as immature, unready and lacking the strategic vision and political nous for leading a country such as North Korea, Jong-un has effectively silenced his critics with a reported wave of brutality and brinkmanship.

That the 2014 Hollywood movie *The Interview* made Kim Jong-un the best known dictator of modern times is an irony that won't be lost to many. The extraordinary events around the film's release, when producer Sony was hacked on a huge scale and a multitude of compromising material was published online, still remain somewhat opaque, with no final word about whether North Korea was indeed to blame for the hacking. But the film, in which two American journalists travel to North Korea to interview Kim Jong-un and are recruited by the CIA to kill him, culminating in Jong-un's head exploding, has certainly set the tone for the increasingly histrionic relationship between North Korea and the outside world.

Domestically however, Kim Jong-un's rule has never faced any serious challenge. His avuncular manner, smiling face and the speeches he's given have massively boosted his popularity among a people that hadn't heard its last leader's voice more than once throughout his reign. With an appearance and manner reminiscent of his grandfather and North Korea's founder, Kim Il-sung, Kim Jong-un has arguably earned the respect of a nation that has grown up with enormous reverence for the late Great Leader.

That's not to say that factionalism, real or imagined, has not played a role in North Korea's tiny and secluded elite. Shortly after assuming power, Kim Jong-un very publicly purged his uncle, whom many Korea watchers had assumed was the power behind the throne. Jang Sung-taek was arrested, paraded on national television and described by state media as 'worse than a dog' before being publicly executed. His wife, Kim Jong-un's aunt, also subsequently disappeared from view and is believed to have either committed suicide or been killed.

While Pyongyang's politics may have changed forever with the ascent of the young Kim, for the vast majority of North Koreans life has changed little in decades. While the terrifying famine and unspeakable sufferings of the 1990s may now be a distant memory, the effect it had in breaking the social contract between the loyal people and their authoritarian leaders endures. While lip service is played to the Kims, it's safe to say that few today believe in the system, which has morphed from communist to feudalist and black market capitalist since then. Almost anything can be had for the right price in North Korea today, and Transparency International has repeatedly ranked North Korea as the most corrupt nation on earth.

For most people, day-to-day life remains incredibly hard. Fear of arrest or denouncement is never far away, food is never plentiful, consumer goods remain unimaginable luxuries for most citizens, propaganda is ubiquitous and relentless, electricity is scant, work is demanding and often weeks on end will be spent doing back-breaking manual work in the rice fields during transplantation and harvesting seasons.

Against all odds though, the country has survived for a quarter of a century since the end of the Cold War, and the Kim regime still has an iron grip on the country – once more going against the predictions of many Korea watchers. After 60 years of total repression of all opposition, it appears there are simply no surviving networks of dissent. How long the status quo can go on remains a mystery, but the fact that North Korea is now on its third hereditary leader and has survived devastating famine, complete international isolation and recurring energy crises suggests that the quick dissolution of the 'hermit kingdom' is not necessarily inevitable.

History

Division of the Peninsula

The Japanese occupation of the Korean Peninsula between 1910 and 1945 was one of the darkest periods in Korean history. The occupation forces press-ganged many Korean citizens – particularly in the north – into slave-labour teams to construct factories, mines and heavy industry. Moreover, the use of Korean girls as 'comfort women' for Japanese soldiers – a euphemism for enforced prostitution – remains a huge cause of resentment and controversy in both Koreas.

Most of the guerrilla warfare conducted against the Japanese police and army took place in the northern provinces of Korea and neighbouring Manchuria – northerners are still proud of having carried a disproportionate burden in the anti-Japan struggle. In fact, some modern history books would have you believe that Kim Il-sung defeated the Japanese nearly single-handedly (with a bit of help from loyal comrades and his infant son).

While his feats have certainly been exaggerated, Kim Il-sung was a strong resistance leader, although not strong enough to rid Korea of the Japanese. This task was left to the Red Army, which, in the closing days of WWII, entered Manchuria and northern Korea as the Japanese forces retreated. The USA, realising the strategic importance of the peninsula was too great for it to be left in Soviet hands, similarly began to move its troops to the country's south. Despite an agreement at Yalta to give joint custodianship of Korea to the USSR, the USA and China, no concrete plans had been made to this end, and the US State Department assigned the division of the country to two young officers, who, working from a *National Geographic* map, divided Korea across the 38th parallel.

American forces quickly took possession of the southern half of the country, while the Soviets established themselves in the north, with both sides stopping at the largely arbitrary dividing line. The intention to have democratic elections across the whole peninsula soon became hostage to Cold War tensions, and after the North refused to allow UN inspectors to cross the 38th parallel, the Republic of Korea was proclaimed in the South on 15 August 1948. The North proclaimed the Democratic People's Republic just three weeks later on 9 September 1948.

The Korean War

Stalin, it is rumoured, personally chose the 33-year-old Kim Il-sung to lead the new republic. The ambitious and fiercely nationalistic Kim was an unknown quantity, although Stalin is said to have favoured him due to his youth. He would have had no idea that Kim would outlive not only him and Mao Zedong, but communism itself, to become the one of the world's longest-serving heads of state. As soon as Kim had assumed the leadership of North Korea, he applied to Stalin to sanction an invasion of the South. The 'man of steel' refused Kim twice in 1949, but perhaps bolstered by Mao's victory over the nationalists in China the same year, and the USSR's own A-bomb project, he gave Kim the green light a year later.

The brutal and pointless Korean War of 1950–53 saw a powerful North Korean advance into the South, where it almost drove US forces into the sea, followed by a similarly strong counterattack by the US and the UN, which managed to occupy most of North Korea. As the situation began to look bleak for the North, Kim advocated retreating to the hills and waging guerrilla warfare against the South, unaware that China's Mao Zedong had decided to covertly help the North by sending in the People's Liberation Army in the guise of 'volunteers'. Once the PLA moved in, the North pushed the front down to the original 38th parallel and, with two million dead, the original stalemate was more or less retained. The armistice agreement obliged both sides to withdraw 2km from the cease-

THE HERMIT KINGDOM & THE GENERAL SHERMAN

During the 'hermit kingdom' phase of the Joseon dynasty, one of Korea's first encounters with Westerners was the ill-fated attempt of the American ship, the *General Sherman*, to sail up the Taedong River to Pyongyang in 1866. It arrogantly ignored warnings to turn around and leave, and insisted on trade. When it ran aground on a sandbar just below Pyongyang, locals burnt it and killed all those on board, including a Welsh missionary and the Chinese and Malay crew. An American military expedition later pressed the Seoul government for reparations for the loss, but otherwise the incident was virtually forgotten in South Korea. However, northerners have always regarded it with great pride as being their first of many battles with, and victories over, the hated Yankee imperialist enemy. Also of great pride to the North Koreans is the 'fact' that none other than the Great Leader's great-grandfather had participated in burning the ship.

fire line, thus creating the Demilitarized Zone (DMZ), still in existence today.

Rebuilding the Country

Despite the Chinese having alienated Kim by taking control of the war – Chinese commander Peng Dehuai apparently treated Kim as a subordinate, much to the future Great Leader's anger – the Chinese remained in North Korea and helped with the massive task of rebuilding a nation all but razed to the ground by bombing.

Simultaneously, following his ill-fated attempt to reunite the nation, Kim Il-sung began a process of political consolidation and brutal repression. He executed his foreign minister and those he believed threatened him in an attempt to take overall control of the Korean Workers' Party. Following Khrushchev's 1956 denunciation of Stalin's personality cult, Central Committee member Yun Kong-hum stood up at one of its meetings and denounced Kim for similar crimes. Yun was never heard from again, and it was the death knell for North Korean democracy.

Unlike many communist leaders, Kim's personality cult was generated almost immediately – the sobriquet *suryong* or 'Great Leader' was employed in everyday conversation in the North by the 1960s – and the initial lip service paid to democracy and multiparty elections was soon forgotten.

The first decade under Kim Il-sung saw vast material improvements in the lives of workers and peasants. Literacy and full health care were soon followed by access to higher education and the full militarisation of the state. However, by the 1970s North Korea slipped into recession, from which it has never recovered. During this time, in which Kim Il-sung had been raised to a divine figure in North Korean society, an *éminence grise*, referred to only as the 'party centre' in official-speak, began to emerge from the nebulous mass of Kim's entourage. At the 1980 party congress this enigmatic figure, to whom all kinds of wondrous deeds had been attributed, was revealed to be none other than the Great Leader's son, Kim Jong-il. He was awarded several important public posts, including a seat in the politburo, and even given the honorific title 'Dear Leader'. Kim Jong-il was designated hereditary successor to the Great Leader and in 1991 made supreme commander of the Korean army, despite never having served a day in it. From 1989 until 1994, father and son were almost always pictured together, praised in tandem and generally shown to be working in close proximity, preparing the North Korean people for a hereditary dynasty far more in keeping with Confucianism than communism.

Beyond Perestroika

It was during the late 1980s, as communism shattered throughout Eastern Europe, that North Korea's development began to differ strongly from that of other socialist nations. Its greatest sponsor, the Soviet Union, disintegrated in 1991, leaving the North at a loss for the subsidies it ironically needed to maintain its facade of self-sufficiency.

North Korea, having always played China and the USSR off against one another, turned to the Chinese, who have acted as the DPRK's greatest ally and benefactor ever since, despite the fact that Chinese 'communism' has produced the fastest-expanding economy in the world and any ideological ties with Maoism remain purely superficial. China's increasingly close relationship to the South and Japan also makes its reluctant support for the Kim regime all the more incongruous. Yet China has remained the North's one trusted ally, although several times since the early '90s Beijing has laid down the law to Pyongyang, even withholding oil deliveries to underscore its unhappiness at the North's continuous brinkmanship.

The regime's strategy did pay off in 1994, however, when North Korea negotiated an agreement with the Clinton administration in which it agreed to cancel its controversial nuclear program in return for US energy supplies in the short term. This was to be followed by an international consortium constructing two light-water reactors for North Korean energy needs in the long term.

Midway through negotiations, Kim Il-sung suffered a massive heart attack and died. He had spent the day personally inspecting the accommodation being prepared for the planned visit of South Korean president Kim Young-sam. This summit between the two leaders would have been the first-ever meeting between the heads of state of the two nations, and Kim Il-sung's stance towards the South had noticeably changed in the last year of his life.

Kim's death rendered the North weaker and even less predictable than before. Optimistic Korea watchers, including many within South Korea's government, expected the collapse of the regime to be imminent without its charismatic leader. In a move that was to further derail the reunification process, Kim Young-sam's government in Seoul did not therefore send condolences for Kim's death to the North – something even then US President Bill Clinton felt obliged to do. This slight to a man considered to be a living god was a miscalculation that set back any progress another five years.

While the expected collapse did not occur, neither did any visible sign of succession by the Dear Leader. North Korea was more mysterious than ever, and in the three years following Kim Il-sung's death, speculation was rampant that a military faction had taken control in Pyongyang and that continuing power struggles between them and Kim Jong-il meant there was no overall leader.

Kim Jong-il finally assumed the mantle of power in October 1997 after a three-year mourning period. Surprisingly, the presidency rested with the late Kim Il-sung, who was declared North Korea's 'eternal' president, making him the world's only dead head of state. However, the backdrop to Kim Jong-il's succession was horrific. While the North Korean economy had been contracting since the collapse of vital Soviet supplies and subsidies to the DPRK's ailing industrial infrastructure in the early 1990s, the terrible floods of 1995 led quickly to disaster. Breaking with a strict tradition of self-reliance (one that had never reflected reality – aid had long been received secretly from both communist allies and even the South two months previously), the North appealed to the UN and the world community for urgent food aid.

So desperate was the state that it even acceded to UN demands for access to the whole country for its own field workers, something that would have previously been unthinkable in North Korea's staunchly secretive military climate. Aid workers were horrified by what they saw – malnutrition everywhere and the beginnings of starvation, which led over the next few years to deaths estimated anywhere from hundreds of thousands to 3.5 million people.

An 'Axis of Evil'

Kim Jong-il's pragmatism and relative openness to change came to the fore in the years following the devastation of the famine, and a series of initiatives to promote reconciliation with both the South and the US were implemented. These reached their height with a swiftly convened Pyongyang summit between the South's Kim Dae-jung and the Dear Leader in June 2000. It was the first-ever meeting on such a level between the two countries. The two leaders, their countries ready at any second to launch Armageddon against one another, held hands in the limousine from the airport to the guesthouse in an unprecedented gesture of solidarity. The summit paved the way for US Secretary of State Madeleine Albright's visit to Pyongyang later the same year. Kim Jong-il's aim was to have his country legitimised through a visit from the US president himself. However, as Clinton's second term ended and George W Bush assumed power in 2001, the international climate swiftly changed.

In his 2002 State of the Union address, President Bush labelled the North (along with Iran and Iraq) part of an 'Axis of Evil', a phrase that came to haunt Kim Jong-il in his final years. This speech launched a new era of acrimonious relations between the two countries, exemplified the following year by North Korea resuming its nuclear program, claiming it had no choice due to American oil supplies being stopped and the two promised light-water reactors remaining incomplete. Frustrated at being ignored by the US throughout the Bush presidency, North Korea test launched several missiles in July 2006, followed by the detonation of a nuclear device on its own soil three months later.

An Uncertain Future

Kim Jong-il appeared to suffer a serious stroke in 2008, following which he lost a great deal of weight and became visibly frail. Shortly afterwards he began promoting his third son, Kim Jong-un, to whom great feats were accorded and who was soon accompanying the Dear Leader on public appearances. Kim Jong-il died from a massive heart attack on his private train on 17 December 2011, with the announcement of his passing causing similar scenes to that of Kim Il-sung in 1994. An enormous state funeral was presided over by Kim Jong-un, who, as predicted, went on to succeed his father.

Almost nothing was known about Kim Jong-un either domestically or internationally, but since taking over the running of the country he has given long speeches in public, something his reclusive father never did. In a relatively short period of time, he established himself as North Korea's third dynastic ruler by a combination of shrewd populism and unflinching brutality. He has also publicly taken a wife, Ri Sol-ju, a former singer for local pop group the Pochonbo Electronic Ensemble, and had a daughter, Kim Ju-ae. While maintaining the enormously complex system of vested interests making up the North Korean political system that he inherited (and some believe, he does not fully control), Kim Jong-un has nonetheless brought his own style to ruling – it's hard to imagine either his father or grandfather entertaining Dennis Rodman and his entourage in Pyongyang, as Kim Jong-un has now done on more than one occasion.

The Culture

The National Psyche

To say the North Korean national psyche is different from that of its southern cousin is an extraordinary understatement. While North Korean individuals are generally exceptionally polite people, if rather shy at first, their psyche as a nation is one defined by a state-promulgated obsession with the country's victimisation by the forces of American and Japanese imperialism and one most notable for its refusal to move on in any way from the Korean War. Of course, the Korean War was horrific and its legacy of a divided nation is the source of great sorrow for people on both sides of the DMZ, but the North's constant propaganda about how the war was everyone's fault but North Korea's is quite extraordinary, especially given the true history of the conflict. One of the key ingredients to a pleasant trip here is understanding that this persecution complex is inculcated from birth and that it's borne of ignorance rather than wilful rewriting of history on the part of individuals.

The North Koreans are also a fiercely nationalistic and proud people, again largely due to endless nationalist propaganda fed to the population since birth. Even more significant is the cult of Kim Il-sung (the Great Leader) and Kim Jong-il (the Dear Leader), which pervades everyday life to a degree that most people will find hard to believe. There are no Kim Il-sung jokes, there is no questioning of the cult and almost no resistance to it. Indeed, all adult members of the population must wear a loyalty badge to Kim Il-sung or Kim Jong-il.

While North Koreans will always be polite to foreigners, there remains a large amount of antipathy towards the USA and Japan. Both due to propaganda and the very real international isolation they feel, North Koreans have a sense of being hemmed in on all sides – threatened particularly by the South and the USA, but also by Japan. The changes over the past two decades in China and Russia have also been cause for concern. These two big brothers who guaranteed survival and independence have both sought rapprochement with the South.

On a personal level, Koreans are typically good humoured and hospitable, yet remain extremely socially conservative after centuries of Confucianism and decades of communism. By all means smile and say 'hello' to people you see on the street, as North Koreans have been instructed to give foreigners a warm welcome, but don't take photos of people without their permission – it may be far more relaxing for both of you to simply leave the camera in its bag. Similarly, giving gifts to ordinary people could result in unpleasant consequences for them, so ask your guide what is appropriate and they will advise.

Far easier is interaction with children, who are remarkably forthcoming and will wave back and smile ecstatically when they see a foreign tour group. Some older children are even able to manage a few phrases in English. Personal relationships with North Koreans who are not your tour guides or business colleagues will be impossible. Men should bear in mind that any physical contact with a Korean woman will be seen as unusual, so while shaking hands is perfectly acceptable, do not greet a Korean woman with a kiss in the European manner. Korea is still a patriarchal society and despite the equality of women on an ideological level, this is not the case in day-to-day life.

Lifestyle

Trying to give a sense of day-to-day North Korean life is a challenge indeed. It's difficult to overstate the ramifications of half a century of Stalinism – and it is no overstatement to say that North Korea is the most closed and secretive nation on Earth. Facts meld with rumour about the real situation in the country, but certain things are doubtless true: power cuts are regular and food shortages remain facts of everyday life. Outside Pyongyang (and even in the capital after 10pm) you'll notice how few

TOP FIVE DPRK DOCUMENTARIES

The following documentaries are all highly recommended for a glimpse into the DPRK, and are a great way for prospective visitors to get an idea of what to expect.

➡ **A State of Mind** (www.astateofmind.co.uk) Unprecedented access to the lives of normal North Koreans is the hallmark of this beautiful documentary about two young Korean girls preparing for the Mass Games in Pyongyang.

➡ **Friends of Kim** (www.friendsofkim.com) A wry look at the pro-regime Korea Friendship Association's annual pilgrimage to North Korea and a wonderful portrait of the eccentrics who truly believe the country is paradise on Earth.

➡ **Seoul Train** (www.seoultrain.com) This superb documentary looks at the huge problems facing North Korean refugees, how they escape the North, survive in China and – if they're lucky – make it to South Korea.

➡ **Crossing the Line** Telling the incredible story of an American soldier who defected to the DPRK in the 1960s and continues to live there today, this bittersweet film provides haunting insight into life in the North.

➡ **The Red Chapel** (www.theredchapel.com) Mags Brügger's satirical documentary follows two Danish-Korean comedians, one of whom is mentally handicapped, on a very uncomfortable journey to Pyongyang, where North Korean reality grinds against the European mentality.

lights there are, with most windows lit only by candlelight, if at all. While at the time of writing famine was no longer an imminent threat in North Korea, most North Koreans will eat meat only a few times a year, living the rest of the time off a diet of rice and soup that is often limited to just two meals a day.

The system of political apartheid that exists in North Korea has effectively created a three-strata society. All people are divided up by *taedo* – a uniquely North Korean caste system whereby people are divided into loyal, neutral or hostile categories in relation to the regime. The hostile are deprived of everything and often end up in forced labour camps in entire family groups, maybe for nothing more than having South Korean relatives, or for one family member having been caught crossing into China. The neutral have little or nothing but are not persecuted, while the loyal enjoy everything from Pyongyang residency and desk jobs (at the lower levels) to Party membership and the privileges of the elite. At the top of the tree, the Kim dynasty and its courtiers, security guards and other staff are rumoured to enjoy great wealth and luxury, although evidence of this is hard to produce – the North Korean elite is also obsessed with secrecy.

North Korea is predictably austere. The six-day week (which even for office workers includes regular stints of back-breaking labour in the rice fields) makes for an exhausted populace, but it makes Sundays a real event and Koreans visibly beam as they relax, go on picnics, sing songs and drink in small groups all over the country. A glance at the showcase shops and department stores in Pyongyang confirms that there is only a small number of imported goods, highly priced and of variable quality, available to the general population.

While in the 20 years following the Korean War it could genuinely be claimed that Kim Il-sung's government increased the standard of living in the North, bringing literacy and health care to every part of the country, the regression since the collapse of communism throughout the world has been spectacular. Most people are now just as materially poor as their grandparents were in the early 1950s. Outside Pyongyang the standard of living is far worse, and this is visible on the streets, although your carefully planned bus journeys will never fully expose the poverty of the nation to the casual tourist. Still, glimpses of life in rural villages from the bus can be chilling.

Population

A 2008 UN-sponsored census was the first in 15 years and pronounced North Korea's population to be just over 24 million people, which surprised many DPRK watchers, who expected the population to have declined following a series of famines in the late 1990s during which millions of people starved to death.

North Korea is conspicuous for its ethnic homogeneity, a result of the country's long history of isolation and even xenophobia, dating back to the 'hermit kingdom' days. The number of foreigners living in North Korea is very small and all of them are either diplomats or temporary residents working in the aid or construction industries. All of the three million inhabitants of Pyongyang are from backgrounds deemed to be loyal to the Kim regime. With a complete lack of free movement in the country (all citizens need special permission to leave their town of residence), no visitor is likely to see those termed 'hostile' – anyway, most people in this unfortunate category are in hard-labour camps miles from anywhere. All North Korean adults have been obliged to wear a 'loyalty' badge since 1970 featuring Kim Il-sung's portrait (and more recently, that of Kim Jong-il). You can be pretty certain that anyone without one is a foreigner.

Sport

Soccer is the national sport, and seeing an international match in Pyongyang is sometimes a possibility. Volleyball is the game you're most likely to see locals playing though, as both sexes can play together, making it popular among work groups.

The North's greatest sporting moment came at the 1966 World Cup in England, when it thrashed favourites Italy, stunning the world. It subsequently went out to Portugal in the quarter finals. The story of the team is told in a strangely touching documentary – one of the few ever to be made by Western crews in the DPRK – called *The Game of Their Lives*.

Weightlifting and martial arts are the other sporting fields in which North Korea has had an international impact, although its bronze- and silver-medal-winning shooter Kim Jong-su was disqualified from the Beijing Olympics in 2008 after failing a drug test.

Religion

In North Korea traditional religion was for a long time regarded, in accordance with Marxist theory, as an expression of a 'feudal mentality' and was effectively banned since the 1950s. However, as the Kim family became more and more deified in the 1990s, official propaganda against organised religion accordingly stopped, although one guide on a recent visit told us that Juche was a religion and that one could not follow both it and Buddhism. Despite the effective ban on traditional religion, a number of Buddhist temples are on show to tourists, although they're always showpieces – you won't see locals or any real Buddhist community. In recent years three churches have been built in Pyongyang, catering to the capital's diplomatic community.

TRADITIONAL RELIGIONS

The northern version of Korean shamanism was individualistic and ecstatic, while the southern style was hereditary and based on regularly scheduled community rituals. As far as is known, no shamanist activity is now practised in North Korea. Many northern shamans were transplanted to the South, chased out along with their Christian enemies, and the popularity of the services they offer (fortune telling, for instance) has endured there. Together with the near destruction of southern shamanism by South Korea's relentless modernisation, there's the curious situation where the actual practice of North Korean shamanism can only be witnessed in South Korea.

Northern Korea held many important centres of Korean Buddhism from the 3rd century through the Japanese occupation period. The Kumgangsan and Myohyangsan mountain areas, in particular, hosted large Zen-oriented (Jogye) temple complexes left over from the Koryo dynasty. Under the communists, Buddhism in the North (along with Confucianism and shamanism) suffered a fate identical to that of Christianity.

Some historically important Buddhist temples and shrines still exist, mostly in rural or mountainous areas. The most prominent among them are Pyohon Temple at Kumgangsan, Pyohon Temple at Myohyangsan and the Confucian Shrine in the Songgyungwan Neo-Confucian College just outside Kaesong.

Arts

North Korean film enjoys something of a cult following with movie buffs, mainly as cinema was a lifelong passion for Kim Jong-il and the industry was relatively well financed for decades. Perhaps the most famous North Korean film is Shin Sang-ok's *Pulgasari*, a curious socialist version of *Godzilla* made by the kidnapped South Korean director, who escaped back to the

South in 1986. Since his escape and subsequent 'non-person' status in the DPRK, his involvement in the film is no longer credited by the North Koreans.

Separating truth from myth is particularly hard with the film industry in North Korea – despite claims that scores of films are produced annually, the reality is probably far less impressive. Cinema visits are sometimes included on tours, when local films are shown with English subtitles, and are a fascinating experience. You can also request a visit to the Pyongyang Film Studios when booking your tour – and you may even be lucky enough to see a political-propaganda piece in production.

North Korean literature has not profited from the Kim dynasty, which has done nothing to encourage original writing. Despite an initial artistic debate in the 1950s, all non-party-controlled forms of expression were quickly repressed. Bookshops stock an unimaginably restrictive selection of works, focusing heavily on the writing of Kim Il-sung and Kim Jong-il.

Tourists with an interest in traditional arts can request visits to performances of traditional Korean music, singing and dance, though these are rarely available. More feasible is a visit to a (revolutionary) opera or a classical-music concert in Pyongyang.

Environment

North Korea is spookily litter-free, with streets cleaned daily and no graffiti save that scratched onto the windowpanes of the Pyongyang Metro, explained by the fact that carriages were bought from Berlin after German reunification. However, the country's cities are polluted and there is little or no environmental consciousness.

The varying climatic regions on the northern half of the Korean Peninsula have created environments that are home to subarctic, alpine and subtropical plant and tree species. Most of the country's fauna is contained within the limited nature reserves around the mountainous regions, as most of the lower plains have been converted to arable agricultural land. An energetic reforestation program was carried out after the Korean War to replace many of the forests that were destroyed by the incessant bombing campaigns, a notable exception being the area to the north of the DMZ, where defoliants are used to remove vegetation for security purposes. The comparatively low population has resulted in the preservation of most mountainous regions.

Areas of particular biodiversity are the DMZ, the wetlands of the Tumen River and the Paekdusan and Chilbosan mountains in the far north. For those interested in tours with a greater emphasis on nature, it is possible to organise an itinerary with your travel company, though any hopes of a truly nature-focused tour are likely to be dashed by the ubiquitous revolutionary sights that always take priority over hikes.

Two particular flora species have attracted enormous attention from the North Koreans, and neither of them are native. In 1965 Indonesia's then-president Sukarno named a newly developed orchid after Kim Il-sung – *kimilsungia* – with popular acclaim overcoming Kim's modest reluctance to accept such an honour. Kim Jong-il was presented with his namesake, *kimjongilia,* a begonia developed by a Japanese horticulturist, on his 46th birthday. The blooming of either flower is announced annually as a tribute to the two leaders and visitors will notice their omnipresence at official tourist sites.

Environmental Issues

The main challenges to the environment in North Korea are from problems that are harder to see. The devastating floods and economic slowdown during the 1990s wreaked havoc not only on property and agricultural land, but also on the environment. Fields were stripped of their topsoil, which, combined with fertiliser shortages, forced authorities to expand the arable land under cultivation. Unsustainable and unstable hillside areas, riverbanks and road edges were brought under cultivation, further exacerbating erosion, deforestation, fertiliser contamination of the land and rivers and the vulnerability of crops. The countryside is slowly recovering from the devastation of the 1990s, though the threat of floods and famine remains.

Food & Drink

Staples & Specialities

While tour groups eat sumptuously by North Korean standards, the standard fare is usually fairly mediocre. There is no danger of tourists going hungry though, and you'll find you get by very well on a diet of kimchi, rice, soups, noodles and fried meat. Vegetarians will be catered for without a problem, but their meals will usually be bland and heavy on rice, egg and cucumber. One culinary highlight is the barbecued duck and squid often given to tourists.

Drinks

Taedonggang, a pleasant locally produced lager, is the most commonly found beverage, although imported beers such as Heineken are also common.

Other drinks on offer include a range of North Korean fruit juices and sodas, and Coke and Fanta are also available in some Pyongyang hotels and restaurants.

Soju (the local firewater) is also popular; it's rather strong stuff. Visitors might prefer Korean blueberry wine – the best is apparently made from Paekdusan blueberries. Blueberry wine comes in two forms: the gently alcoholic, which tastes like a soft drink; and the reinforced version, which could stun an elephant.

SURVIVAL GUIDE

❶ North Korea Directory A–Z

ACCOMMODATION

All accommodation in North Korea is in state-run hotels, which are nearly all of a passable standard – particularly those in Pyongyang. You won't usually have much control over where you stay unless you organise your own private group tour, but you can always make requests. All hotels have the basics of life: a restaurant, a shop (although bring everything you need if you're outside Pyongyang) and usually some form of entertainment, from the ubiquitous karaoke to pool tables and a bar.

A homestay scheme (p325) in Chilbosan opened in 2006, although it's about as far from a homestay as you can imagine, being set in something of a showcase village. Elsewhere, homestays are not possible.

While many hotels may indeed be bugged, there's only a very small chance that anyone's listening, so there's really no need to worry about what you say in your room.

CHILDREN

While North Koreans love children, a DPRK tour is not suitable for kids. The long, exhausting days and endless sightseeing may tire out even the most diehard Kimophiles and they are likely to bore a child to tears. Equally, the lack of creature comforts and facilities for foreign children may make prospective foreign residents think twice before bringing their families.

CUSTOMS REGULATIONS

North Korean customs procedures vary in severity from general polite inquiries to thorough goings-over. We have had reports that the Lonely Planet *Korea* guide and other guidebooks to the country have been confiscated in some cases, although it's not always common for bags to be searched. Cameras of almost any size and nonprofessional video recorders are fine, though huge zoom lenses and enormous tripods are not allowed. Mobile phones and laptops, once not allowed, are now fine to bring with you, though there is no roaming in the country at all, so phones will only work if you purchase a local SIM card. Religious materials for personal use are also fine.

EMBASSIES & CONSULATES

North Korea now enjoys diplomatic relations with many countries, although very few maintain embassies in Pyongyang. North Korean embassies abroad can all process visa applications, but most travellers will have theirs processed at the Beijing embassy by their tour agency the day before they travel.

Embassies & Consulates in North Korea

The UK Embassy represents the interests of Australians, New Zealanders and citizens of the Republic of Ireland, while the Swedish legation looks after US and Canadian citizens as well as EU citizens whose own country does not have representation in Pyongyang. All embassies are in the Munsudong diplomatic compound.

Chinese Embassy (📞 02-381 3116, 02-381 3133; fax 02-381 3425)
German Embassy (📞 02-381 7385; fax 02-381 7397)
Indian Embassy (📞 02-381 7274, 02-381 7215; fax 02-381 7619)
Russian Embassy (📞 02-381 3102, 02-381 3101; fax 02-381 3427)
Swedish Embassy (📞 02-381 7485; fax 02-381 7663)
UK Embassy (📞 02-381 7980, 02-382 7980; fax 02-381 7985)

INTERNET ACCESS

There is now finally some degree of internet access in North Korea, though it's still more hassle than it's worth for most people on a short trip. It is possible to buy a 3G SIM card at Pyongyang airport for unrestricted internet access. However this costs US$200 to set up, and costs at present US$22 per month, plus 20c per MB of data. It is designed for foreign residents rather than tourists, but it is available to short-term visitors, should you be dying to Instagram from the DPRK. 3G coverage outside Pyongyang is restricted to larger cities.

With the exception of the Masik-Ryong Hotel near Wonsan, there is no wi-fi in hotels, nor any other way of getting online in North Korea.

LEGAL MATTERS

It is extremely unlikely that a tourist will experience legal problems with the North Korean authorities, but if this does occur, stay calm and ask to speak to your country's diplomatic representative in North Korea. Usually, tourists who break the law in North Korea are deported immediately, though in recent years North Korea has used cases where foreigners break the law as a form of international leverage. Only the truly reckless and foolhardy would travel to DPRK with the intention of proselytising or protesting against the regime.

MONEY

The unit of currency is the North Korean won (KPW), though most travellers will never even see them. Banknotes come in denominations of five, 10, 50, 100, 200, 500, 1000, 2000 and 5000KPW and coins come in denominations of one, five, 10 and 50 chon, as well as one won. Visitors can pay for everything with euros or Chinese yuan (but bring small change of both; big notes can be impossible to change). US dollars and Japanese yen can also be exchanged, but generally at poor rates. While you're unlikely to use the won, it may be possible to get some from your guides as a souvenir (it's officially illegal to take it out of the country, so hide it deep in your luggage).

Credit cards are completely useless everywhere in the country, so bring as much cash as you'll need with some leeway for any unexpected expenses. Bring your cash in euros or yuan. Travellers cheques are not usable in North Korea and there are no ATMs anywhere in the country.

PHOTOGRAPHY & VIDEO
Equipment

Memory cards are not easily available in North Korea, so bring as many as you'll need. Visitors nearly always take huge numbers of shots, so come prepared! Having a laptop on which to download your pictures gives you double protection if your camera is checked and any photos deleted when you leave the country.

Restrictions

Always ask before taking photos and obey the reply. North Koreans, acutely aware of the political power of an image in the Western press, are especially sensitive about foreigners taking photos of them without their permission. Your guides are familiar with the issue of tourists taking photos that end up in a newspaper article that contains anti-DPRK content, and it's quite normal for customs officers to give your pictures a quick look through at the border – they will ask you to delete any offending content. Taking photographs from the bus is officially banned, though in practice it's not a big deal as long as you are discreet and are not photographing sensitive objects. Avoid taking photos of soldiers or any military facilities, although you're actually encouraged to do just that at the DMZ.

Video

Restrictions are similar to those with a still camera. But as a number of journalists have made video documentaries about the country in the guise of simply filming tourist sights, the guides and customs officers have become far stricter about their use.

POST

Like all other means of communication, the post is monitored. It is, however, generally reliable and the colourful North Korean stamps, featuring everything from tributes to the Great Leader to Princess Diana commemoratives, make great souvenirs. Some people have suggested that postcards arrive more quickly than letters, as they do not need to be opened by censors. In either medium, keep any negative thoughts about the country to yourself to ensure your letter gets through.

PUBLIC HOLIDAYS

Note that North Korea does not celebrate Christmas or the Lunar New Year, or many of South Korea's major traditional holidays. National holidays are a good time to visit North Korea – try to be in Pyongyang during May Day or Liberation Day as both are celebrated with huge extravaganzas featuring military parades that rank among North Korea's most memorable sights.

New Year's Day 1 January
Kim Jong-il's birthday 16 February
Kim Il-sung's birthday 15 April
Armed Forces Day 25 April
May Day 1 May
The Death of Kim Il-sung 8 July
Victory in the Fatherland Liberation War 27 July
National Liberation (from Japan) Day 15 August
National Foundation Day 9 September
Korean Workers' Party Foundation Day 10 October
Constitution Day 27 December

TELEPHONE

North Korean telephone numbers are divided into ☑ 381 numbers (international) and ☑ 382 (local). It is not possible to call a ☑ 381 number from a ☑ 382 number or vice versa. International calls start at €3 per minute to China and €8 to Europe. To dial North Korea, the country code is ☑ 850. Nearly all numbers you dial from abroad will be Pyongyang numbers, so dial ☎ +850-2-381 and then the local number.

Mobile phones are not used by the vast majority of locals, although a network does exist in Pyongyang and most other large towns, but it's not accessible internationally. You are now allowed to bring mobile phones into the country, though they will only work if you purchase a local SIM card, as there is no roaming at all.

TIME
In 2015, North Korea created its own time zone 30 minutes behind Seoul to commemorate the 70-year anniversary of the end of Japanese colonial rule (the Japanese put Korea on Tokyo time in the 1940s). The time in North Korea is GMT plus eight and a half hours. When it is noon in Pyongyang, it is 12.30pm in Seoul, 1.30pm in Sydney, 3.30am in London, 10.30pm the previous day in New York and 7.30pm the previous day in Los Angeles.

You will also see years such as Juche 8 (1919) or Juche 99 (2011). Three years after the death of Kim Il-sung, the state adopted a new system of recording years, starting from Juche 1 (1912) when Kim No 1 was born. Despite the wide use of these dates internally, they are always clarified with 'normal' years.

TOILETS
In Pyongyang and around frequently visited tourist sites, toilet facilities are basic and smelly, usually with squat toilets. There are regular cuts in the water supply outside Pyongyang, and often a bucket of water will be left in your hotel room or a public toilet for this eventuality. Toilet paper is supplied in hotels but it's always a good idea to carry tissues for emergencies, especially as diarrhoea is a common problem for visitors. Hand sanitiser is also handy to bring with you, as soap is as scarce as running water in public toilets.

TRAVELLERS WITH DISABILITIES
North Korean culture places great emphasis on caring for the disabled, especially as the Korean War left such a brutal legacy among young recruits. Despite this, seeing disabled people on the streets is actually relatively rare. Facilities are basic, but manageable, and even in situations where disabled access is a problem, the guides are likely to find some locals to help out. Most hotels have lifts due to their large size and many floors.

VISAS
People of all nationalities need a visa to visit North Korea. Despite what many people think, US and Israeli citizens are able to visit the DPRK, though at the time of writing it was not possible for citizens of South Korea.

Restrictions have relaxed somewhat for visa applicants, and you currently just have to supply the name of your employer and your job. If you work in the media, human rights or any other potentially controversial professions, be sure not to put this on the application form. Each visa needs approval from Pyongyang, so apply at least one month before you travel. Your travel agency will normally handle the application for you, and in most cases the visa is a formality if you travel with an established agency.

Tour groups usually have visas issued in Beijing the day before travel, so don't worry about leaving home without one in your passport. It does mean that you need to spend 24 hours in Beijing before going on to Pyongyang though, but you won't have to go to the embassy yourself in most cases. Individual visas can usually be issued at any North Korean embassy around the world.

The embassy visa charges (€50 in Beijing) are included in some, but not all, packages. North Korean visas are not put into passports, but are separate documents taken from you when you exit the country. If you want a souvenir, make a photocopy. No stamp of any kind will be made in your passport.

WOMEN TRAVELLERS
While communist ideology dictates equality of the sexes, this is still far from everyday reality in a traditionally patriarchal society. However, women travellers will have no problems at all in the country, as no North Koreans would be foolhardy enough to get themselves in trouble for harassing a foreigner. There is an increasing number of female guides and it is possible to request two of them for individual travel. Normally all tour groups get one male and one female guide.

ℹ Getting There & Away

Beijing is the only real transport hub for entering North Korea, offering regular trains and flights to Pyongyang. The only other cities with regular air connections to Pyongyang are Vladivostok in Russia and Shenyang in northern China. As tourists are often obliged to pick up their visas in Beijing anyway, other routes would generally be impossible even if there were more transport options.

ENTERING THE COUNTRY
Once you've got your visa you can breeze into North Korea, even if the welcome at immigration is rather frosty. Your guides will take your passport for the duration of your stay in the country. This is totally routine, so do not worry about it being lost.

Air
Pyongyan's Susan International Airport is the only airport in the country open to flights from abroad. A brand new airport was opened to much fanfare in 2015, and while it now looks much like any small airport anywhere in the world, the similarities end there.

Only Air Koryo and Air China connect Pyongyang to the outside world. The national airline, Air Koryo runs a fleet of old Soviet Tupolevs

SPECIALIST TOURS

While the day-to-day realities and restrictions of travel in North Korea remain similar no matter who you travel with, one option for seeing and doing something rather different is to take a specialist tour of the country. These are offered by many tour operators and range from sporting trips, where teams travel together to DPRK and play matches with their North Korean counterparts, to the more obscure (and often very expensive) tours such as bird-watching and surfing. **Koryo Tours** (p307) offers a train tour, which charters a North Korean train and makes the journey from Pyongyang to the northern city of Chongjin, the only chance at present to see much of this part of the country. Also on offer are architecture tours, marathon tours (allowing participants to take part in the mid-April Pyongyang Marathon), cycling tours, aviation tours and golf tours.

In 2014 **Juche Travel Services** (p307) began organising stints for foreign volunteers to teach English in North Korea. Despite being unpaid positions, there's still a considerable price tag attached. While this is very far from being an organised tour, volunteers still live in hotels and have their movements as restricted as tourists do, so unless you get a job as a diplomat or NGO worker in North Korea, your chances to experience the country as a local remain thin.

and Ilyushins, as well as a few more modern Russian-made planes on international routes. Air Koryo flies regularly to Beijing, Shenyang and Vladivostok. By far the most commonly used route is the flight from Beijing, operated every day except Sunday on either Air Koryo or Air China. Air Koryo flies between Shanghai and Pyongyang every Tuesday and Friday. On Wednesday and Saturday there's a flight between Pyongyang and Shenyang in both directions as well, and on Thursday there's a return flight between Pyongyang and Vladivostok on Air Koryo. Pyongyang's airport code is FNJ.

The **Air Koryo** (☑ 010 6501 1557, 010 6501 1559; fax 010 6501 2591; Swissôtel Bldg, Hong Kong-Macau Center, Dongsi Shitau Lijiao) building adjoins the Swissôtel in Beijing, but the entrance is around the back. You must have a visa before you can pick up your ticket, though if you're travelling in a group your travel agency will arrange the ticket.

Train

There are four weekly overnight trains in either direction between Beijing and Pyongyang. The journey takes about a day, though delays are not uncommon. Trains run on Monday, Wednesday, Thursday and Saturday. On each day, train No 27 leaves Beijing at 5.30pm and arrives at Pyongyang the next day at 6pm. Going the other way, train No 26 departs from Pyongyang at 10.10am arriving in Beijing at 8.34am the next morning. In contrast to the plane, it's possible to pick up your train tickets to Pyongyang without a DPRK visa.

The North Korean train is actually two carriages attached to the main Beijing–Dandong train, which are detached at Dandong (Chinese side) and then taken across the Yalu River Bridge to Sinuiju (Korean side), where more carriages are added for local people. You'll remain in the same carriage for the entire journey, however, and can mingle with locals in the dining car on both legs of the trip. Accommodation is in four-berth compartments, though sometimes two-berth compartments are available.

Trains usually spend about four hours at the border – two hours at Dandong and two hours at Sinuiju – for customs and immigration.

If Sinuiju station is your introduction to North Korea, the contrasts with China will be quite marked. Everything is squeaky-clean and there are no vendors plying goods. A portrait of the Great Leader looks down from the top of the station, as it does at all train stations in North Korea.

Food is available from the restaurant car on both legs of the journey. Make sure you have some small-denomination euro or yuan notes to pay for meals (€6) from the North Korean buffet car, as this is not usually included in tours. There are no money-changing facilities on-board or at Sinuiju.

Your guide will meet you on arrival at Pyongyang train station and accompany you to your hotel. Be very careful taking pictures from the train in North Korea. While you'll get some great opportunities to snap everyday DPRK scenes, do not take pictures in stations as these are considered to be military objects.

As well as the service to Beijing, there's a weekly train each way between Moscow and Pyongyang, which travels via Dandong and through northern China along the route of the Trans-Manchurian Railway. The trip takes seven days.

ℹ Getting Around

All accommodation, guides and transport must be booked through the state-run KITC, or via a travel agency that will deal with Ryohaengsa itself.

The main office of **KITC** (Ryohaengsa; ☑ 010 8576 9465; kitcbri@gmail.com) is in Beijing, but is not open to the public; you can only call or email. There are branches in Dandong, Liaoning Province and in Yanji in Jilin.

Understand Korea

Korea Today

With consumer spending and industrial output both down, the *Sewol* ferry tragedy and the deadly outbreak of the MERS (Middle East Respiratory Syndrome) in 2015, it's been rocky times of late for South Korea. The popularity ratings of the country's first female president, Park Geun-hye, have plummeted to 30%. Her saving grace is a fractured opposition, though it could be in a winning position should popular Seoul mayor Park Won-soon throw his hat into the ring for the 2018 presidential election.

Best on Film

The Host (2006) Seoul-based classic monster movie that juggles humour, poignancy and heart-stopping action.

Poetry (2010) Lee Chang-dong directs this drama about a woman in her 60s struggling with Alzheimer's disease who enrols in a poetry-writing course.

In Another Country (2012) Hong Sang-soo, director of award-winning *Hahaha*, casts Isabelle Huppert as three different women whose stories intersect in the seaside resort of Mohang.

Best in Print

I'll Be Right There (Shin Kyung-sook; 2014) A city wracked by pro-democracy protests in the 1980s is elegantly evoked by this award-winning Korean author.

Three Generations (Yom Sang-seop; 2005) Originally published in newspaper serialisations in the 1930s, this epic novel focuses on the travails of a family under colonisation.

A Geek in Korea (Daniel Tudor; 2014) Fully illustrated and covering topics from religion and traditional martial arts to K-Pop, Samsung and the *hallyu* (pop-culture wave).

Sinking of the Sewol

On 16 April 2014, while sailing from Incheon to Jeju-do, the ferry MV *Sewol* capsized while attempting to make a sharp turn in a channel with strong underwater currents. Of the 476 passengers and crew aboard, 304 people drowned, most of them teenagers from a high school in Ansan, Gyeonggi-do. Many of the survivors were rescued by fishing boats and other commercial vessels that arrived at the scene well before either the coast guard or the Korean navy.

Grief over the tragedy was swiftly followed by national outrage when it was discovered that not only was the ferry carrying more than twice the legal limit of cargo (which was also improperly secured), but that Captain Lee Jun-seok – who had not been on the bridge at the time disaster struck – had abandoned ship, along with many of the crew, while passengers had been instructed to stay in their cabins. The captain was later found guilty of negligence and sentenced to 36 years' imprisonment.

Fighting for Justice

The owner of the shipping line that operated the *Sewol* was found dead under suspicious circumstances a few months after the sinking. The government was also in the figurative dock for its botched role in the rescue operation and poor regulation of the shipping industry in general. Approval ratings for President Park Geun-hye sank amid rumours that she was out of reach on the day of the disaster. The president's office strongly denied this and charged a Japanese reporter with defamation when those rumours were printed in Japan's *Sankei Shimbun*.

The shadow of the *Sewol* continued to loom large in 2015. Tensions ran particularly high in central Seoul around the first anniversary of the tragic sinking. Thousands of police and national-service conscripts blocked streets around Gwanghwamun Sq, where a sea of yellow ribbons, flickering memorial candles and placards demanding truth and justice, marked the encampment of the families and friends of the bereaved. Their stand-off with the government over further investigation of the sinking and punishment of those involved resulted in violent clashes and shows little sign of abating, despite President Park's accession to one of their key demands: the raising of the 6825-tonne vessel, which could take up to 18 months and cost over US$140 million.

Anyone who doubts how tenacious Koreans can be in these matters need only look at the protest that has been going on every Wednesday at noon since 1992 in front of Seoul's Japanese Embassy over full acknowledgement of the Japanese military's use of sexual slavery during WWII.

Territorial Disputes

The supposed lack of a sincere apology for Japan's past actions in Korea is not the only issue the Republic of Korea (ROK) has with its neighbour across the East Sea. Japan calls this same body of water the Sea of Japan and lays claim to a group of islets it calls Takeshima and which Koreans know as Dokdo (p152; to confuse matters further, they are also called Liancourt Rocks internationally). The islets are closer to Korean territory than Japanese and only have two permanent inhabitants (Koreans). They have been squabbled over for decades as a point of pride as much as for their rich fishing grounds and possible reserves of natural gas. For more about Dokdo/Takeshima see www.dokdo-takeshima.com.

Even though territorial disputes are also a small part of the diplomatic dance between South Korea and China, relations between the two are generally rosier than they are between Korea and Japan. In June 2015 the ROK signed a free-trade deal with China, which was already its largest trading partner. However, it hasn't gone unnoticed in the South that China lends both economic and political support to an often-belligerent North Korea and that the ROK's economic dependence on China is at odds with its military dependence on the US, which still maintains 28,500 troops in the country, 60 years after the end of the Korean War.

Foes in the North?

Less than 50km from the border, Seoul is literally on the front line with North Korea. Provocations such as North Korea's bombing of the South Korean island of Yeonpyeongdo in November 2010, its third underground nuclear bomb test in 2013 and the test firing of a submarine-launched ballistic missile in May 2015, are inevitably taken very seriously by the South. Not for nothing was Seoul the venue for the 2012 Nuclear Security Summit. US President Barack Obama chose that occasion to make a visit to the DMZ and speak

South Korea facts

POPULATION: **51.3 MILLION**

AREA: **100,210 SQ KM**

GDP: **₩1,428,294.60 (2013)**

GDP GROWTH: **3% (2013)**

INFLATION: **0.4%**

UNEMPLOYMENT: **2.7%**

if South Korea were 100 people

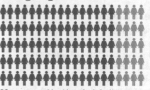

80 women would not have had plastic surgery
20 women would have had plastic surgery

belief systems
(% of population)

No formal religion · Protestantism

Buddhism · Roman Catholicism · Other

population per sq km

KOREA · UK · USA

≈ 35 people

Best North Korea Books

Nothing to Envy: Ordinary Lives in North Korea (Barbara Demick; 2009) Award-winning account of life in Chongjin, a bleak North Korean town near the border with China, that reads like a thriller.

Aquariums of Pyongyang: 10 years in the North Korean Gulag (Kang Chol-hwan; 2006) Harrowing tale of a defector who survived a decade in the notorious Yodok camp.

Without You, There Is No Us (Suki Kim; 2015) An account of Kim's 2011 stint teaching at an elite Pyongyang all-male university.

Best Blogs

The Marmot's Hole (www.rjkoehler. com) Eye-opening, entertaining, addictive round-up of Korea-related posts and news.

Ask A Korean (http://askakorean. blogspot.co.uk) Go on, ask him. You may be surprised by the answer.

Hermit Hideaways (http://hermit hideaways.com) Beautiful inspirational photos of South Korea by Gregory Curley.

of his country's continued military support for South Korea against aggression from the North.

Even so, South Korean President Park has made more conciliatory noises towards Pyongyang than her predecessor Lee Myung-bak, who took a hard line against the North. The North has openly referred to Park as a 'crafty prostitute' controlled by her 'pimp', Barack Obama. Despite this, Park has said she's amenable to holding a summit meeting with the North Korean leader, Kim Jong-un.

Bribery Allegations

In April 2015 President Park suffered another blow when the prime minister, Lee Wan-koo, tendered his resignation after just two months in the job following bribery accusations by a business tycoon who had recently committed suicide, leaving a letter detailing alleged corruption. Lee was the fifth of Park's prime ministers since 2013 and charges against him followed hard on his declaration of an 'all-out war' on corruption by the government.

Others close to Park in the ruling Saenuri Party were named by the dead tycoon, and while at the time of writing nothing had been proved, the accusations alone caused an extra level of trouble for the increasingly lame-duck president. In Park and Saenuri's favour is the ongoing factional fighting plaguing the opposition party, New Politics Alliance for Democracy (NPAD), which fared poorly in 2015 by-elections. The next test of power is in the 2016 National Assembly elections. Going forward, all eyes are on whether left-of-centre Seoul mayor Park Won-soon will declare his candidacy for the presidential election in 2018.

History

Koreans can trace a continuous history and presence on the same territory going back thousands of years. The present politically divided peninsula is mirrored by distant eras such as the Three Kingdoms period (57 BC–AD 668) when the kingdoms of Goguryeo, Shilla and Baekje jockeyed for control of territory that stretched deep into Manchuria. Korea's relationship with its powerful neighbours of China and Japan has also defined the country's fortunes right up to current times.

The First Korean

The imagined beginning of the Korean nation was the 3rd millennium BC, when a legendary king named Dangun founded old Joseon. Joseon (also spelled Choson) remains the name of the country in North Korea, but South Koreans use the term Hanguk, a name dating from the 1890s.

Real or not, Dangun has been a continuous presence from his time up to the present, a kingly vessel filled by different people at different times who drew their legitimacy from this eternal lineage. Under its first president, for example, South Korea used a calendar in which Dangun's birth constituted year one – setting the date at 2333 BC. If the two Koreas can't agree on many things, including what to call their country, they can agree on Dangun.

Unfortunately there is no written history of Korea until a couple of centuries BC, and that history was chronicled by Chinese scribes. But there is archaeological evidence that humans have inhabited this peninsula for thousands of years, and that an advanced people were here seven or eight thousand years ago in the Neolithic period. These Neolithic people practised agriculture in a settled communal life and are widely supposed to have had family clans as their basic social grouping. Nationalist historians also trace many Korean social and cultural traits back to these people.

Bronze Age (c 10,000 BC) people on the Korean Peninsula built dolmen or stone burial chambers such as those found on the island of Ganghwado.

The Three Kingdoms

Around the time of Christ three kingdoms emerged on the Korean Peninsula: Baekje (also spelled Paekche), Goguryeo (Koguryŏ) and Shilla (Silla).

TIMELINE	2333 BC	57 BC	AD 372
	Dongguk Tonggam, a chronicle of early Korean history compiled in the 15th century, gives this date for the founding of Gojoseon by the mythical leader Dangun.	Start of the Three Kingdoms period in which the ancient kingdoms of Goguryeo, Baekje and Shilla rule over the Korean Peninsula and parts of Manchuria.	Chinese monk Sundo brings Buddhism to Goguryeo, where it blends with local shamanism. It takes two centuries for the religion to spread throughout the peninsula.

In 1971 the tomb of King Muryeong, the longest-ruling Baekje king, was discovered in Gongju. It contained a wealth of funerary objects that had not seen the light of day in 1500 years, including remains of the king and queen's wooden coffins, golden diadem ornaments, jewellery, clothing accessories and the king's sword.

The Korean Peninsula is divided by a major mountain range about three quarters of the way down at the 37th parallel. This southwest extension of mountains framed Baekje's historic territory, just as it did the Shilla kingdom to the east. Goguryeo, however, ranged over a wild region consisting of northeastern Korea and eastern Manchuria, giving rise to contemporary dreams of a 'greater Korea' in territories that now happen to be part of China and Russia. While South Korea identifies itself with the glories of the Shilla kingdom, which it says unified the peninsula in AD 668, the North identifies with Goguryeo and says the country wasn't truly unified until the founding of the Goguryeo dynasty.

Central Kingdom

Baekje was a centralised, aristocratic state melding Chinese and indigenous influence. By the 3rd century AD, Baekje was strong enough to demolish its rivals and occupy what today is the core area of Korea, around Seoul. The kingdom controlled much of western Korea up to Pyongyang and, if you believe certain controversial records, coastal regions of northeastern China, too.

By the time it moved its capital to Chungnam, however, its influence was under siege. Its centre of power, Hanseong (in the modern-day Seoul region), had fallen to Goguryeo from the north, and in 475 Baekje had to relocate its capital to Gongju (then known as Ungjin), where the mountains offered some protection.

The dynasty thrived anew, nurturing relations with Japan and China, and in 538 King Seong moved the capital further south to Buyeo (then known as Sabi). Unfortunately his Shilla allies betrayed him, killing him in battle. Baekje fell into decline and was finally vanquished in 660 by a combined army from Shilla and China's Tang dynasty, though pockets of resistance lingered for some years.

The common Korean custom of father-to-son royal succession is said to have begun with Baekje king Geun Chugo. His grandson inaugurated another long tradition by adopting Buddhism as the state religion in AD 384.

Northern Kingdom

Goguryeo conquered a large territory by 312 and expanded in all directions, especially towards the Taedong River, which runs through Pyongyang, in the south. By the 5th century Goguryeo was in the ascendancy on the peninsula, and under warrior kings such as Gwanggaeto the Great (391–412) and his son Jangsu (413–419), it was also in control of huge chunks of Manchuria.

Southern Kingdom

Shilla emerged victorious on the peninsula in 668. However, in this process the country had come under the long-term sway of the great Tang dynasty in China. Chinese statecraft, Buddhist and Confucian philoso-

427	668	721	918
King Jangsu, the 20th monarch of the Goguryeo dynasty, moves his capital south from the present-day Chinese–Korean border to Pyongyang on the banks of the Taedong River.	Having allied his kingdom with China's Tang dynasty, Munmu of Shilla defeats Goguryeo to become the first ruler of a unified southern Korean Peninsula.	King Seongdeok orders the construction of a wall along Shilla's northern border to protect against the forces of Balhae, the successor state to Goguryeo.	The Goryeo dynasty is established by King Taejo. It rules Korea until 1392, during which time the territory under its rule expands to the whole Korean Peninsula.

phy, Confucian practices of educating the young, and the Chinese written language were all entrenched.

Shilla sent many students to Tang schools and had a level of civilisation high enough to merit the Chinese designation of 'flourishing land in the East'. Its capital at Gyeongju was renowned as the 'city of gold', where the aristocracy pursued a high culture and extravagant pleasures.

Chinese historians wrote that elite officials possessed thousands of slaves, with like numbers of horses, cattle and pigs. Their wives wore solid-gold tiaras and earrings of delicate and intricate filigree. Scholars studied the Confucian and Buddhist classics and developed advanced methods for astronomy and calendrical science. 'Pure Land' Buddhism, a simple doctrine, united the mass of common people who, like today's Hare Krishnas, could become adherents through the repetition of simple chants.

Artists from Goguryeo and Baekje also perfected a mural art found on the walls of tombs and took it to Japan, where it deeply influenced that country's temple and burial art. But it was the blossoming of Shilla that still astounds contemporary visitors to Korea and makes its ancient capital at Gyeongju one of the most fascinating tourist destinations in East Asia.

Shilla vs Balhae

In spite of Shilla's military strength, broad territories of the old Goguryeo kingdom were not conquered and a section of the Goguryeo elite established a successor state known as Balhae (Parhae), above and below the Amnok and Tuman boundaries that now form the border between China, Russia and Korea. Balhae's continuing strength forced Shilla to build a northern wall in 721 and kept Shilla forces permanently below a line running from present-day Pyongyang in the east to the west coast. As one prominent South Korean historian wrote, 'Shilla and Balhae confronted each other hostilely much like southern and northern halves of a partitioned nation'.

Like Shilla, Balhae continued to be influenced deeply by the Chinese civilisation of the Tang, sending students to the capital at Ch'angan, on which it modelled its own capital city.

Unification under Goryeo

A formidable military leader named Wang Geon had defeated Shilla as well as some Baekje remnants by 930 and established a flourishing dynasty, Goryeo, from which came the name Korea. Korea was now fully unified with more or less the boundaries that it retains today. Wang was a magnanimous unifier. Regarding himself as the proper lineal king of Goguryeo, he embraced that kingdom's survivors, took a Shilla princess as his wife and treated Shilla aristocracy with unprecedented generosity.

Based on primary sources, the superbly illustrated *Joseon Royal Court Culture* by Shin Myung-ho (2004) details the unique Confucian royal-court lifestyle.

Bulguk-sa (Pulguk-sa) temple and the nearby Seokguram Grotto in Gyeongju were built around AD 750 and are home to some of the world's finest Buddhist sculptures. Buddhists came on pilgrimages to Gyeongju from as far away as India, and Arab sojourners sometimes came to the temple to stay.

1231	1251	c 1270	1274
As part of a general campaign to conquer China, Mongols invade the Korean Peninsula, forcing the Goryeo royal court to regroup on the island of Ganghwado.	Monks at Jeondeung-sa, Ganghwado, complete the second *Tripitaka Koreana*, 80,000 woodblocks of Buddhist scriptures; the first had been destroyed by the Mongols in 1232.	Although some military leaders in the south refuse to surrender, Goryeo's rulers agree a peace treaty with the Mongols, becoming a vassal state.	With help from Korea, a Mongol army attempts to conquer Japan but is thwarted by a heavy sea storm (*kamikaze*). Similar storms in 1281 scupper a second invasion.

His dynasty ruled for nearly 500 years and in its heyday was among the most advanced civilisations in the world.

Goryeo Culture

With its capital at Kaesong, the Goryeo dynasty's composite elite also forged a tradition of aristocratic continuity that lasted down to the modern era. By the 13th century there were two government groupings: civil officials and military officials. At that time the military people were stronger, but thereafter both were known as *yangban* (the two orders), which became the Korean term for aristocracy. Below the hereditary aristocracy were common people such as peasants and merchants. Below them were outcaste groups of butchers, tanners and entertainers, who were called *cheonmin* and who lived a caste-like existence, often in separated and ostracised villages, and whose status fell upon their children as well. Likewise, slavery was hereditary (matrilineally), with slaves making up as much as 30% of Goryeo society.

The Goryeo aristocracy admired and interacted with the splendid Chinese civilisation that emerged during the contemporaneous Song dynasty (960–1279). Official delegations and ordinary merchants took Korean gold, silver and ginseng to China in exchange for silk, porcelain and woodblock books. Finely crafted Song porcelain stimulated Korean artisans to produce an even finer type of inlaid celadon pottery – unmatched in the world before or since for the pristine clarity of its blue-green glaze and the delicate art of its inlaid portraits.

Buddhism was the state religion, but it coexisted with Confucianism throughout the Goryeo period. Buddhist priests systematised religious practice by rendering the Korean version of the Buddhist canon into mammoth woodblock print editions, known as the *Tripitaka*. The first was completed in 1087 after a lifetime of work, but was lost. Another, completed in 1251, can still be viewed today at Haein-sa.

The Rise of the Mongols

This high point of Goryeo culture coincided with internal disorder and the rise of the Mongols, whose power swept most of the known world during the 13th century. Korea was no exception, as Kublai Khan's forces invaded and demolished Goryeo's army in 1231, forcing the government to retreat to the island of Ganghwado, a ploy that exploited the Mongol horsemen's fear of water.

After a more devastating invasion in 1254, in which countless people died and around 200,000 people were taken captive, Goryeo succumbed to Mongol domination and Goryeo kings came to intermarry with Mongol princesses. The Mongols then enlisted thousands of Koreans in ill-fated invasions of Japan in 1274 and 1281, using craft made by Korea's

The Balhae bequeathed a lasting invention to the Korean people: sleeping on *ondol* floors. This system, which uses flues from a central hearth to heat the floors of each room, is still in wide use in contemporary Korea, with the stone flues covered by waxed and polished rice paper.

By 1234, if not earlier, Koreans had invented movable metal type, two centuries before its inception in Europe.

1377	1392	1394	1399
Monks at Cheong-ju's Heundeok-sa temple beat Johannes Gutenberg by 78 years by creating the *Jikji*, the world's first book printed using moveable metal type.	Having had King Gong-yang and his family murdered, General Yi Seong-gye names himself King Taejo and establishes the Joseon dynasty that will rule Korea for the next 500 years.	King Taejo employs geomancy, or feng shui (*pungsu* in Korean), to select Hanyang (Seoul) as Joseon's capital. He also adopts Neo-Confucianism as the country's religion.	As his sons battle to become his successor, Taejo abdicates. His second son, Yi Bang-gwa, becomes the Joseon monarch Jeongjong, but his reign lasts only a year.

great shipwrights. The Kamakura Shogunate turned back both invasions with help, as legend has it, from opportune typhoons known as the 'divine wind' or *kamikaze*.

Joseon: The Last Dynasty

The overthrow of the Mongols by the Ming dynasty in China (1316–1644) gave an opportunity to rising groups of Korean military men to contest for power. One of them, Yi Seong-gye, grabbed the bull by the horns and overthrew Goryeo leaders, thus becoming the founder of Korea's longest and last dynasty (1392–1910). The new state was named Joseon, harking back to the old Joseon kingdom 15 centuries earlier, and its capital was built at Seoul.

General Yi announced the new dynasty by mobilising some 200,000 labourers to surround the new capital with a great wall that was completed in 1396. Around 70% of it still stands today, including Sungnyemun (Namdaemun; the Great South Gate) and the Heunginjimun (Dongdaemun; the Great East Gate).

The deep Buddhist influence on the previous dynasty led the literati to urge the king to uproot Buddhist economic and political influence, which led to exile in the mountains for monks and their disciples – this is one of the reasons why many of Korea's Buddhist temples are located in mountain areas.

Influential literati in the Joseon dynasty were ideologues who wanted to restore Korean society to its proper path as they saw it, by using the virtues to discipline the passions and the interests. Over many decades the literati thus accomplished a deep Confucianisation of Joseon society. The reforming came in the name of Neo-Confucianism and Chu Hsi, the

Chihwaseon (2002), which won a prize for director Im Kwon-taek at Cannes, is a visually stunning film based on the true story of a talented, nonconformist painter who lived at the end of the Joseon dynasty.

KING SEJONG'S GIFT

Hangeul is a phonetic script: concise, elegant and considered one of the most scientific in the world in rendering sounds. It was developed in 1443, during the reign of Korea's greatest king, Sejong, as a way of increasing literacy – it is much simpler and easier to learn than Chinese characters. But the Confucian elite opposed its wide use, hoping to keep the government exams as difficult as possible so only aristocratic children had the time and money to pass.

Hangeul didn't come into general use until after 1945, and then only in North Korea. South Korea used a Sino-Korean script requiring the mastery of thousands of Chinese characters until the 1990s. Today, though, Chinese characters have mostly disappeared from Korea's public space, to the consternation of Chinese and Japanese travellers who used to be able to read all the street and commercial signs. King Sejong's face, meanwhile, is etched on the ₩10,000 note.

1400	**1418**	**1446**	**1450s**
Yi Bang-won is crowned King Taejong and he sets about creating a stronger central government and absolute monarchy. Private armies are banned and many relatives and rivals are killed.	Following King Taejong's abdication, his third son becomes King Sejong, later to be known as Sejong the Great. His father continues to wield power until his death in 1422.	Sejong the Great oversees the invention of *hangeul*, Korea's unique script, which is announced to the public in the document known as the *Hunmin-jeongeum*.	Following Sejong the Great's death, several of his sons take the throne in quick succession. In 1455 Sejo, Sejong's second son, becomes king and reigns until 1468.

Chinese progenitor of this doctrine. The result was that much of what we now see as 'Korean culture' or 'tradition' arose from major social reorganisation by self-conscious 15th-century ideologues. Foreign observers declared that Korea was 'more Confucian than China'.

Korea & China: A Special Relationship

General Yi Seong-gye founded his dynasty when he refused to send his troops into battle against a Chinese army, instead using them to overthrow his own government and make himself king. Not surprisingly, he received the blessing and support of the Chinese emperor, and Korea became a 'tributary' country to China – but more than that, it became the ideal tributary state, modelling itself on Chinese culture and statecraft.

From 1637 until the end of the practice in 1881, Korea sent a total of 435 special embassies and missions to China. The emperor sent gifts in return, but the lavish hospitality provided to the Chinese emissaries when they came to Seoul could take up 15% of the government's revenue.

Most of the time China left Korea alone to run its own affairs, and Korea was content to look up to China as the centre of the only world civilisation that mattered. This policy was known as *sadae* (serving the great). Because of this special relationship, when Japan attacked in the 1590s, Chinese troops were sent to help repel them. In just one battle, as many as 30,000 Chinese soldiers died.

Sadae was in the background during the Korean War as well, when a huge Chinese army intervened in late 1950 and helped rescue the North from certain defeat. Meanwhile, many South Koreans felt that the behaviour of the Chinese troops during the Korean War was superior to that of any other force, including the American troops. Today China is South Korea's largest trading partner, with thousands of Korean students studying there, while China maintains its long-term alliance with North Korea.

It isn't clear what the common people thought about China until the modern period, nor were they asked. The vast majority were illiterate in a country that marked its elite according to their literacy – in Chinese. The aristocrats were enthusiastic Confucianists, adopting Chinese painting, poetry, music, statecraft and philosophy. The complicated Chinese script was used for virtually all government and cultural activities throughout the Joseon period, even though the native alphabet, *hangeul*, was an outstanding cultural achievement.

Royal Pomp & Ceremony

Many of the premier cultural attractions in Korea today, such as Seoul's palaces, are imperial relics of the long-lived Joseon dynasty. They are windows into a time in Korea's history when absolute monarchs ruled. Pomp and ritual became an essential aspect of royal power, with atten-

Historic Fortresses

Mongchon-to-seong, Seoul

Old City Wall, Seoul

Hwaseong, Suwon

Namhan Sanseong

Banwolseong, Gyeongju

Men wearing a topknot was widespread during Korea's pleasant relations with the Ming dynasty, but later it became a symbol of 'Ming loyalists' in Korea after that dynasty fell. In 1895 King Gojong had his topknot cut off, but conservatives didn't follow his example or share his enthusiasm for reforms.

1592	1666	1767	1776
Seoul falls to Japan during the Imjin War. Korean forces use metal-covered 'turtle boats' to win several decisive naval battles in the successful quest to expel the invaders.	Dutchman Hendrick Hamel, held prisoner in the country for 13 years after being shipwrecked off Jeju-do, writes the first Western account of the Joseon dynasty.	Confucianism reaches its height under King Yeongjo. He imprisons his possibly mentally disturbed son Sado in a large rice chest, starving him to death in eight days.	Jeongjo, Sado's son, comes to the throne. He establishes a royal library and shakes up the social order by opening government positions to the middle classes.

tion to ritual and protocol developed into an art form. Koreans appeared to break sharply with this royal system in the 20th century, but when you look at the ruling system in North Korea, or the families that run most of South Korea's major corporations, you can see the family and hereditary principles of the old system continuing in modern form.

In these more democratic times it is difficult to imagine the wealth, power and status of Joseon kings. The main palace, Gyeongbokgung, contained 800 buildings and more than 200 gates – in 1900, for example, palace costs accounted for 10% of all government expenditures. In the royal household were 400 eunuchs, 500 ladies-in-waiting, 800 other court ladies and 70 *gisaeng* (female entertainers who were expert singers and dancers). Only women and eunuchs were allowed to live in the palace – male servants, guards, officials and visitors had to leave at sunset.

Most of the women lived like nuns and never left the palace. A *yangban* woman had to be married for years before daring to move in the outer world of society, and then only in a cocoon of clothing inside a cloistered sedan chair, carried by her slaves. In the late 19th century foreigners witnessed these cloistered upper-class women, clothed and swaddled from head to toe, wearing a green mantle like the Middle Eastern chador over their heads and bringing the folds across the face, leaving only the eyes exposed. They would come out after the nightly curfew, after the bells rang and the city gates were closed against tigers, and find a bit of freedom in the darkness.

Lives of the Eunuchs

The only 'male' staff allowed to live inside the palaces, eunuchs were privy to all the secrets of the state and had considerable influence because they waited upon the king and were around the royal family 24 hours a day. All access to the king was through them, as they were the royal bodyguards and responsible for the safety of their master. This was an easy way to earn money and they usually exploited it to the full. These bodyguard eunuchs, toughened by a harsh training regime of martial arts, were also personal servants to the king and even nursemaids to the royal children. They played so many roles that life must have been very stressful for them, particularly as any mistake could lead to horrific physical punishments.

Although often illiterate and uneducated, a few became important advisers to the king, attaining high government positions and amassing great wealth. Most were from poor families and their greed for money was a national scandal. Eunuchs were supposed to serve the king with total devotion, like monks serving the Buddha, never thinking about mundane matters like money or status.

Hendrick Hamel's fascinating account of his 13 years in Korea, after he and 36 other sailors were shipwrecked on Jeju-do in 1653, is available in Gari Ledyard's *The Dutch Come to Korea*, with full scholarly annotation.

The Dongnimmun (Independence Gate), built in Seoul in 1898 by the Independence Club, stands where envoys from Chinese emperors used to be officially welcomed to the city.

1796	1800	1834	1849
King Jeongjo moves the royal court to Suwon to be closer to Sado's grave, and builds the Hwaseong fortress (now a World Heritage Site) to protect the new palace.	Sunjo succeeds his father as the 23rd king of the Joseon dynasty and reigns for 34 years, during which time Korean Catholics are increasingly persecuted.	The eight-year-old Heonjong, Sunjo's grandson, is named the 24th Joseon king. During his 15-year reign, power resides with his mother's family, the Andong Kim clan.	Following Heonjong's death, the Andong Kims track down the great-grandson of King Yeongjo, living in poverty on Ganghwado. The illiterate and easily manipulated 18-year-old is crowned King Cheoljong.

Surprisingly, eunuchs were usually married and adopted young eunuch boys who they brought up to follow in their footsteps. The eunuch in charge of the king's health would pass on his medical knowledge to his 'son'. Under the Confucian system, eunuchs had to get married. The system continued until 1910 when the country's new Japanese rulers summoned all the eunuchs to Deoksugung and dismissed them from government service.

Korea & Japan

In 1592, 150,000 well-armed Japanese troops, divided into nine armies, rampaged throughout Korea, looting, raping and killing. Palaces and temples were burned to the ground and priceless cultural treasures were destroyed or stolen. Entire villages of ceramic potters were shipped back to Japan, along with thousands of ears clipped from dead Koreans, which were piled into a mound in Japan, covered over and retained into modern times as a memorial to this war.

A series of brilliant naval victories by Admiral Yi Sun-sin helped to turn the tide against the Japanese. Based in Yeosu, Yi perfected the *geobukseon* (turtle ship), a warship protected with iron sheets and spikes against the Japanese 'grapple and board' naval tactics. The standard Korean warship was the flat-bottomed, double-decked *panokseon,* powered by two sails and hard-working oarsmen. It was stronger and more manoeuvrable than the Japanese warships and had more cannons. With these advantages, clever tactics and an intimate knowledge of the complex patterns of tides and currents around the numerous islands and narrow channels off the southern coast, Admiral Yi was able to sink hundreds of Japanese ships and thwart Japan's ambition to seize Korea and use it as a base for the conquest of China.

Ming troops also arrived from China and by 1597 the Japanese were forced to withdraw. Stout resistance on land and sea thwarted Japanese ambitions to dominate Asia, but only at the cost of massive destruction and economic dislocation in Korea.

Japanese Takeover

Japan's ambitions to seize Korea resurfaced at the end of the 19th century, when the country began to rapidly transform into Asia's first modern industrialised power. Seizing on the Donghak peasant rebellion in Korea, Japan instigated war with China, defeating it in 1895. After another decade of imperial rivalry over control of the peninsula, Japan smashed Russia in lightning naval and land attacks, stunning the Western world, which had previously viewed Asians as people to be subjugated rather than feared as economic and military rivals.

Isabella Bird Bishop visited Gyeongbokgung in 1895 and noted: 'What with 800 troops, 1500 attendants and officials of all descriptions, courtiers and ministers and their attendants, secretaries, messengers and hangers-on, the vast enclosure of the palace seemed as crowded and populated as the city itself.'

War Diary of Admiral Yi Sun-sin, edited by Sohn Pow-key (1977), is a straightforward and fascinating account by Korea's greatest admiral of the battles, floggings and court intrigues that were his daily preoccupations.

1864	1866	1871	1876
The 11-year-old Gojong, son of the shrewd courtier Yi Ha-eung (later called the Daewongun or 'Prince of the Great Court'), is crowned Joseon's 26th ruler.	French forces invade Ganghwado, ostensibly in retaliation for the execution of French Catholic priests who had been illicitly proselytising in Korea. They are forced to retreat after six weeks.	Ganghwado witnesses another international tussle as a US diplomatic mission is rebuffed, leading to an armed conflict on the island that leaves 243 Koreans and three Americans dead.	The Japanese prevail in getting Korea to sign the Treaty of Ganghwa, formally opening up three of the nation's ports – Busan, Incheon and Wonsan – to international trade.

Japan was now in a secure position to realise its territorial ambitions with regard to Korea, which became a Japanese protectorate in 1905. Following King Gojong's abdication in 1907, Korea became a full colony of Japan in 1910, with the acquiescence of all the great powers, even though progressive calls were beginning to emerge to dismantle the entire colonial system. Furthermore, Korea had most of the prerequisites for nationhood long before most other countries in colonised areas of the world: common ethnicity, language and culture, and well-recognised national boundaries since the 10th century.

Samurai Invasion by Stephen Turnbull (2002) is a detailed account of the Japanese invasions of Korea in the 1590s.

Colonisation

Once fully in control Japan tried to destroy the Korean sense of national identity. A Japanese ruling elite replaced the Korean *yangban* scholar-officials; Japanese modern education replaced the Confucian classics; Japanese capital and expertise were built up in place of the Korean versions – Japanese talent for Korean talent; and eventually even the Korean language was replaced with Japanese.

DONGHAK DEMANDS

The Donghak Rebellion, which had been building for decades, erupted in 1894 in Jeolla province, attracting large numbers of peasants and low-born groups of people. The rebels were only armed with primitive, homemade weapons, but they defeated the government army. The rebellion then spread to neighbouring provinces, and when King Gojong called in Chinese troops, Japanese troops took advantage of the uproar to march into Seoul. The rebels were defeated and their leaders (including Jeon Bong-jun, who was known as the 'Green Pea General' because of his small size) were executed by Japanese firing squads. The demands of the rebels revealed their many grievances against the Joseon social system:

➡ Slaves should be freed.

➡ The low-born should be treated fairly.

➡ Land should be redistributed.

➡ Taxes on fish and salt should be scrapped.

➡ No unauthorised taxes should be levied and any corrupt *yangban* (aristocrat) should be severely punished.

➡ All debts should be cancelled.

➡ Regional favouritism and factions should be abolished.

➡ Widows should be allowed to remarry.

➡ Traitors who supported foreign interference should be punished.

1882	1884	1894	1895
A military insurrection, supported by the Daewongun, seeks to overthrow King Gojong and reform-minded Queen Min. They escape Seoul in disguise, returning when support arrives from China.	Progressive forces, backed by Japan, attempt a coup at the royal palace. Again Queen Min calls on the Chinese for help and the revolt is suppressed after three days.	Peasants rise up in the Donghak Rebellion. The rebels are defeated but the Joseon court responds with the Gabo Reform, abolishing slavery, among other sweeping changes.	Queen Min is assassinated at Gyeongbokgung palace. Posthumously named Empress Myeongseong, Min is considered a national heroine for her reforms and attempts to maintain Korea's independence.

Few Koreans thanked the Japanese for these substitutions, or credited Japan with any social improvements. Instead they saw Japan as snatching away the ancient regime, Korea's sovereignty and independence, its indigenous if incipient modernisation and, above all, its national dignity. Most Koreans never saw Japanese rule as anything but illegitimate and humiliating. The very closeness of the two nations – in geography, in common Chinese civilisational influences and in levels of development until the 19th century – made Japanese dominance all the more galling to Koreans and gave a peculiar hate/respect dynamic to their relationship.

During colonisation there were instances when Koreans fought back. The South Korean national holiday on 1 March honours the day in 1919 when the death of ex-king Gojong and the unveiling of a Korean declaration of independence sparked massive pro-independence demonstrations throughout the country. The protests were ruthlessly suppressed, but still lasted for months. When it was over, the Japanese claimed that 500 were killed, 1400 injured and 12,000 arrested, but Korean estimates put the casualties at 10 times those figures.

Collaborating with Japan

A certain amount of Korean collaboration with the Japanese was unavoidable given the ruthless nature of the regime under the Japanese colonialists. Also in the last decade of colonial rule, when Japan's expansion across Asia caused a shortage of experts and professionals throughout the empire, educated and ambitious Koreans were further co-opted.

The burst of consumerism that came to the world in the 1920s meant that Koreans shopped in Japanese department stores, banked at Japanese banks, drank Japanese beer, travelled on the Japanese-run railway and often dreamed of attending a Tokyo university.

Ambitious Koreans found new careers opening up to them just at the most oppressive point in the colony's history, as Koreans were commanded to change their names and not speak Korean, and millions were used as mobile human fodder by the Japanese. Koreans constituted almost half of the hated National Police, and young Korean officers (including Park Chung-hee, who seized power in 1961, and Kim Jae-gyu, who, as intelligence chief, assassinated Park in 1979) joined the aggressive Japanese army in Manchuria. Pro-Japanese *yangban* were rewarded with special titles, and some of Korea's greatest early nationalists, such as Yi Gwang-su, were forced into public support of Japan's empire.

Such Korean collaboration during the Japanese occupation was never punished or fully and frankly debated in South Korea, leaving the problem to fester until 2004, when the government finally launched an official investigation into collaboration – along with estimates that upwards of

Korea by Angus Hamilton (1904) is a rare and lively description of life in Korea under the last dynasty.

The Dawn of Modern Korea (Andrei Lankov, 2007) is a fascinating, accessible look at Korea in the early 20th century and the cultural and social impacts of Westernisation as King Gojong tried to modernise his tradition-bound hermit kingdom.

1897	1900	1905	1907
As an independence movement grows in Korea, King Gojong declares the founding of the Korean Empire, formalising the end of the country's ties to China.	Korea's modernisation continues with the opening of a railroad between the port of Incheon and Seoul. In the capital an electricity company provides public lighting and a streetcar system.	The treaty of Portsmouth ends the Russo–Japanese war over Manchuria and Korea. Russia recognises Korea as part of Japan's sphere of influence, further imperilling Korea's attempts to become independent.	Having angered Japan by trying to drum up international support for his sovereignty over Korea, Gojong is forced to abdicate in favour of his son, Sunjong.

90% of the pre-1990 South Korea elite had ties to collaborationist families or individuals.

The colonial government implemented policies that developed industries and modernised the administration, but always in the interests of Japan. Modern textile, steel and chemical industries emerged, along with new railroads, highways and ports. Koreans never thanked Japan for any of this, but it did leave Korea much more developed in 1945 than other countries under colonial rule, such as Vietnam under the French.

WWII & After

By 1940 the Japanese owned 40% of the land and there were 700,000 Japanese living and working in Korea – an enormous number compared to most other countries. But among large landowners, many were as likely to be Korean as Japanese – most peasants were tenant farmers working their land. Upwards of three million Korean men and women were uprooted from their homes and sent to work as miners, farm labourers, factory workers and soldiers abroad, mainly in Japan and Manchukuo, the Japanese colony in northeast China.

More than 130,000 Korean miners in Japan – men and women – worked 12-hour days, were paid wages well under what Japanese miners earned, were poorly fed and were subjected to brutal, club-wielding overseers. The worst aspect of this massive mobilisation, however, came in the form of 'comfort women' – the hundreds of thousands of young Korean women who were forced to work as sex slaves for the Japanese armed forces.

It was Korea's darkest hour, but Korean guerrilla groups continued to fight Japan in Manchukuo – they were allied with Chinese guerrillas, but Koreans still constituted by far the largest ethnic group. This is where we find Kim Il-sung, who began fighting the Japanese around the time they proclaimed the puppet state of Manchukuo in 1932 and continued into the early 1940s. After murderous counter-insurgency campaigns (participated in by many Koreans), the guerrillas numbered only about 200. In 1945 they returned to northern Korea and constituted the ruling elite from that point up to the present.

Mutual Animosity

Japan's surrender to the Allies in 1945 opened a new chapter in the stormy relationship between the two countries. Thanks to munificent American support, Japan began growing rapidly in the early 1950s and South Korea got going in the mid-1960s. Today companies in both countries battle each other to produce the best ships, cars, steel products, computer chips, mobile phones, flat-screen TVs and other electronic

At the Court of Korea by William Franklin Sands gives a first-hand account of King Gojong and his government between 1890 and 1910.

Although only a handful were deployed, replicas of *geobukseon* battleships can be found on Odongdo and in museums throughout the country, including Seoul's War Memorial of Korea.

1909	1910	1919	1926
Independence activist An Jung-geun assassinates Hirobumi Ito, Korea's ex-resident-general, at the train station in Harbin, Manchuria. Japan uses the incident to move towards annexation of the Korean Peninsula.	Emperor Sunjong refuses to sign the Japan–Korea Annexation Treaty, but Japan effectively annexes Korea in August. Terauchi Masatake is the first Japanese governor general of Korea.	The March 1st Movement sees millions of Koreans in nonviolent nationwide protests against Japanese rule. A declaration of independence is read out in Seoul's Tapgol Park.	Emperor Sunjong dies. His half-brother, Crown Prince Euimin, who had married into a branch of the Japanese royal family, is proclaimed King Ri of Korea by the Japanese.

THE HOUSE OF SHARING

An hour's journey south of Seoul, in bucolic countryside, is the **House of Sharing** (http://nanum.org; 65 Wongdang-ri, Twoichon-myon, Gwangju-si, Gyeonggi-do; adult/student ₩5000/3000; ⊙10am-5pm Tue-Sun), a very special retirement home and museum. Here live a handful of women, now in their late 70s and 80s, who were forced to work in Japanese military brothels across Asia before and during WWII. 'Comfort women' is the euphemism coined by the Japanese military for these women, 70% of whom were Korean. A study by the UN has put the number of women involved at around 210,000 (the Japanese government claims the figure was 50,000).

At the House of Sharing they prefer the respectful term *halmoni,* which means grandmother. In the museum here you can learn more about the atrocious conditions and experiences these women were forced to endure. Most of them were aged between 13 and 16, and had to service between 30 and 40 soldiers a day.

'We must record these things that were forced upon us.' These words by Kim Hak Soon, one of the first Korean *halmoni* to testify about her experiences, introduces the museum exhibition which includes a display of the artworks created by the *halmoni* that reflect their feelings and experiences. Video documentaries about the *halmoni* are screened and discussions are held about their plight and the ongoing sexual trafficking of women around the world. The overall picture painted by the guides of these frail, sometimes crotchety women, is of pillars of strength who after a lifetime of shame and sorrow have chosen to spend their twilight years as campaigners for social justice.

It's a heavy-going experience but one not without a sense of hope – both at the resilience of the human spirit and the prospect for reconciliation. The greatest number of visitors to the House come from Japan and every year a Peace Road Program brings Korean and Japanese students together to help further understanding of their countries' painfully entwined history and how they might be better neighbours in the future.

equipment. The new rivalry is a never-ending competition for world markets.

Several generations have passed since the end of WWII and Japan and South Korea are both democracies and natural trading partners and allies. However, a high degree of mistrust and mutual animosity remains between the countries. Sticking points include perceptions of what happened during the colonisation period and territorial issues over the islands of Dokdo/Takehima. A survey by a Tokyo think tank in 2015 found that 52.4% of Japanese have a negative impression of Korea, while 72.5% of Koreans feel the same about Japan. In South Korea, one survey found that Japan's current right-wing prime minister, Abe Shizo, is less popular than the North Korean leader, Kim Jong-un.

A New History of Korea by Lee Ki-baik (1984) takes a cultural and sociological perspective of the country's history.

1929	1945	1947	1948
A nationwide student uprising in November leads to the strengthening of Japanese military rule in 1931, after which freedom of the press and expression are curbed.	With the Allied victory in WWII, Korea is liberated from Japan and divided into two protectorates – the Soviets handling the North and the US the South.	Between 1947 and 1953 as many as 30,000 islanders on Jeju-do are massacred by right-wing government forces in events collectively labelled the 'April 3 Incident'.	The Republic of Korea is founded in the southern part of the peninsula, with Seoul designated the capital city. The Democratic People's Republic of Korea (DPRK, or North Korea) is also founded.

The Korean War

The 38th Parallel

In the immediate aftermath of the obliteration of Nagasaki, three Americans in the War Department (including Dean Rusk, later Secretary of State) drew a fateful line at the 38th parallel in Korea. The line was supposed to demarcate the areas in which American and Soviet forces would receive the Japanese surrender, but Rusk later acknowledged that he did not trust the Russians and wanted to get the nerve centre of the country, Seoul, into the American zone. He consulted no Koreans, no allies and not even the president in making this decision. But it followed on from three years of State Department planning in which an American occupation of part or all of Korea was seen as crucial to the postwar security of Japan and the Pacific. The US then set up a three-year military government in southern Korea that deeply shaped postwar Korean history.

The Soviets came in with fewer concrete plans for Korea and moved more slowly than the Americans in setting up an administration. They thought Kim Il-sung would be good as a defence minister in a new government, but sought to get him and other communists to work together with Christian nationalist figures such as Jo Man-sik. Soon, however, the Cold War rivalry overshadowed everything in Korea, as the Americans turned to Rhee Syngman (an elderly patriot who had lived in the US for 35 years) and the Russians to Kim Il-sung.

By 1948 Rhee and Kim had established separate republics and by the end of the year, Soviet troops had withdrawn, never to return again. American combat troops departed in June 1949, leaving behind a 500-man military advisory group. For the first time in its short history since 1945, South Korea had operational control of its own military forces. Within a year war had broken out and the US took back that control and has never relinquished it.

The War Begins

In 1949 both sides sought external support to mount a war against the other side, and the North succeeded where the South failed. Its greatest strength came from tens of thousands of Koreans who had been sent to fight in China's civil war, and who returned to North Korea in 1949 and 1950. Kim Il-sung also played Stalin off against Mao Zedong to get military aid and a critical independent space for himself, so that when he invaded he could count on one or both powers to bail him out if things went badly. After years of guerrilla war in the South (fought almost entirely by southerners) and much border fighting in 1949, Kim launched a surprise invasion on 25 June 1950, when he peeled several divisions off in the midst of summer war games; many high officers were unaware of

The Korean Sohn Kee-chung won the marathon gold medal at the 1936 Berlin Olympics, but he was forced to compete as Kitei Son under the flag of Japan, Korea's occupying power.

South Korea punished very few citizens who collaborated with the Japanese, partly because the US occupation (1945–48) re-employed so many of them and partly because they were needed in the fight against communism.

25 June 1950	September 1950	1953	1960
North Korea stages a surprise invasion of the South over the 38th parallel border, triggering the Korean War. By the end of the month, it occupies Seoul.	UN troops led by US General MacArthur mount a daring counter-attack in the Battle of Incheon. By 25 September Seoul is recaptured by South Korean forces.	The armistice ending the Korean War is signed by the US and North Korea, but not South Korea. The DMZ is established around the 38th parallel.	Popular protest ousts President Rhee Syngman. Attempts at democratic rule fail – a military coup topples the unstable elected government and installs General Park Chung-hee into power in 1961.

the war plan. Seoul fell in three days, and soon North Korea was at war with the US.

The Americans responded by getting the United Nations to condemn the attack and gaining commitments from 16 other countries, although Americans almost always bore the brunt of the fighting, and only British and Turkish combat forces had a substantial role. The war went badly for the UN at first and its troops were soon pushed far back into a small pocket around Busan (Pusan). But following a daring landing at Incheon (Inchon) under the command of General Douglas MacArthur, North Korean forces were pushed back above the 38th parallel.

Creating the DMZ

The question then became whether the war was over. South Korea's sovereignty had been restored and UN leaders wanted to call it a victory. But for the previous year, high officials in the Truman administration had been debating a more 'positive' strategy than containment, namely 'rollback' or liberation, and so Truman decided to march north to overthrow Kim's regime. Kim's long-time relations with Chinese communists bailed his chestnuts out of the fire when Mao committed a huge number of soldiers, but now the US was at war with China.

By the start of 1951, US forces were pushed back below the 38th parallel, and the communists were about to launch an offensive that would retake Seoul. This shook America and its allies to the core, Truman declared a national emergency and WWIII seemed to be at the doorstep. But Mao did not want general war with the US and did not try to push the UN forces off the peninsula. By spring 1951 the fighting had stabilised roughly along the lines where the war ended. Truce talks began, dragging on for two years amid massive trench warfare along the lines. These battles created the Demilitarized Zone (DMZ).

At the end of the war, Korea lay in ruins. Seoul had changed hands no less than four times and was badly damaged, but many prewar buildings remained sufficiently intact to rebuild them much as they were. The US Air Force pounded the North for three years until all of its cities were destroyed and some were completely demolished, leaving the urban population to live, work and go to school underground, like cavemen. Millions of Koreans died (probably three million, two-thirds of them in the North), millions more were left homeless, industries were destroyed and the entire country was massively demoralised because the bloodletting had only restored the status quo. Of the UN troops, 37,000 were killed (about 35,000 of them Americans) and 120,000 were wounded.

US Academic Bruce Cumings' *The Korean War: A Modern History* (2010) and UK journalist Max Hastings' *The Korean War* (1988) are two takes on this pivotal conflict, analysing its causes, progress and repercussions.

Sourcebook of Korean Civilisation (1993), edited by Peter Lee, has a wide selection of original historical documents and materials, in translation and with commentary.

1963	1967	1968	1971
Following pressure from the US, civilian rule is restored. However, the Democratic Republican Party, a political vehicle for Park, wins the general election.	Even with rigged elections, and the economic revitalisation of the country well underway, Park only just manages to be re-elected president.	In January North Korean agents are halted just 800m from the presidential Blue House, foiling a daring assassination attempt on Park Chung-hee.	The constitution is amended so Park can run for a third term of office. He wins against Kim Dae-jung. The following year Park dissolves parliament and suspends the constitution.

Postwar Recovery

The 1950s was a time of depressing stagnation for the South, but rapid industrial growth for the North. Then, over the next 30 years, both Koreas underwent rapid industrial growth. The North's growth was as fast as any in the world from the mid-1950s into the mid-1970s, and even in the early 1980s its per-capita GNP was about the same as the South's. But then the South began to build an enormous lead that soon became insurmountable and by the 1990s huge economic disparities had emerged. The North experienced depressing stagnation that led finally to famine and massive death, while the South emerged as a major global economic power.

Rise of the Jaebeol

Much of the credit for what came to be known as the 'Miracle on the Han' (after the Han River running through Seoul) belongs to Korea's industrial conglomerates or *jaebeol* (also spelled *chaebol*). Although their origins as family-owned business organisations stretch back to the days of Japanese colonisation, it was in the 1960s that the *jaebeol* came into their own. In 1963 the key companies came together to form the Federation of Korean Industries to promote their interests and support President Park Chung-hee's drive for economic development.

Operating under a motto of 'if it doesn't work, make it work', Hyundai in particular made huge strides for Korea – for example, building the 400km-long Gyeongbu Expressway connecting Seoul to Busan in less than 2½ years, and building a successful shipyard from scratch as a new business. In contrast to this gung-ho approach, Samsung had a reputation for reviewing all the options before making a choice – something that served it equally well as it became the country's largest *jaebeol,* its revenue accounting for close to 20% of South Korea's GDP.

This great triumph came at enormous cost, as South Koreans worked the longest hours in the industrial world for decades and suffered under one military dictatorship after another. Corrupt, autocratic rulers censored the media, imprisoned and tortured political opponents, manipulated elections and continually changed the country's constitution to suit themselves. Washington backed them up (except for a brief moment in the 1960s) and never did more than issue tepid protests at their authoritarian rule. Student protests and less frequent trade-union street protests were often violent, as were the police or military forces sent to suppress them. But slowly a democratisation movement built strength across the society.

The fascinating *Times Past in Korea: An Illustrated Collection of Encounters, Customs and Daily Life Recorded by Foreign Visitors* (2003) was compiled by Martin Uden, former British ambassador to South Korea.

Korea's Place in the Sun: A Modern History by Bruce Cumings (2005) offers an overview of Korean history from year 1 to the 1860s, followed by a close examination of the modern period.

1972	1979	1980	1987
The new constitution, which includes no limits on re-election, turns Park's presidency into a virtual dictatorship. He's re-elected with no opposition in both 1972 and 1978.	After surviving a couple of assassination attempts (one of which killed his wife), Park is shot dead by the trusted head of his own Central Intelligence Agency.	The military brutally suppresses a pro-democracy uprising in the southern city of Gwangju, killing at least 154 civilians and wounding or arresting more than 4000 others.	Following sweeping national protests, with the strongest concentration in Seoul, Korea's last military dictatorship under Chun Doo-hwan steps down to allow democratic elections.

Dictatorship & Massacre

When the Korean War ended in 1953, Rhee Syngman continued his dictatorial rule until 1961, when he and his wife fled to Hawaii following widespread demonstrations against him that included university professors demonstrating in the streets of Seoul. Ordinary people were finally free to take revenge against hated policemen who had served the Japanese. Following a military coup later in 1961, Park Chung-hee ruled with an iron fist until the Kennedy administration demanded that he hold elections. He narrowly won three of them in 1963, 1967 and 1971, partly by spreading enormous amounts of money around (peasants would get envelopes full of cash for voting).

In spite of this, the democracy activist Kim Dae-jung nearly beat him in 1971, garnering 46% of the vote. That led Park to declare martial law and make himself president for life. Amid massive demonstrations in 1979 his own intelligence chief, Kim Jae-gyu, shot him dead over dinner one night, in an episode never fully explained. This was followed by five months of democratic discussion until Chun Doo-hwan, a protégé of Park, moved to take full power.

In response the citizens of Gwangju took to the streets on 18 May 1980, in an incident now known as the May 18 Democratic Uprising. The army was ordered to move in, on the pretext of quelling a communist uprising. The soldiers had no bullets, but used bayonets to murder dozens of unarmed protesters and passers-by. Outraged residents broke into armouries and police stations and used seized weapons and ammunition to drive the troops out of their city.

For over a week pro-democracy citizen groups were in control, but the brutal military response came nine days later, on 27 May, when soldiers armed with loaded rifles, supported by helicopters and tanks, retook the city. Most of the protest leaders were labelled communists and summarily shot. At least 154 civilians were killed, with another 74 missing, presumed dead. An additional 4141 were wounded and more than 3000 were arrested, many of whom were tortured.

The Return of Democracy

Finally, in 1992, a civilian, Kim Young-sam, won election and began to build a real democracy. Although a charter member of the old ruling groups, Kim had resigned his National Assembly seat in the 1960s when Rhee tried to amend the constitution and had since been a thorn in the side of the military governments along with Kim Dae-jung. Among his first acts as president were to launch an anti-corruption crusade, free thousands of political prisoners and put Chun Doo-hwan on trial.

The former president's conviction of treason and monumental corruption was a great victory for the democratic movement. One of the

Since 1948 South Korea has had a presidential system of government. The president, who is head of state, head of government and commander-in-chief of the armed forces, is elected every five years and can only sit for one term of office.

For eyewitness accounts of the still-controversial Gwangju massacre of 1980, read *Memories of May 1980* by Chung Sang-yong (2003), or the website of the May 18 Memorial Foundation (www.518.org).

1988	1991	1992	1994
Seoul hosts the Summer Olympic Games, bulldozing and/or concealing slums to build a huge Olympic park south of the Han River and a major expressway.	Following two years of talks, an Agreement of Reconciliation is signed between Seoul and Pyongyang. One of the aims is to make the Korean Peninsula nuclear free.	The first civilian to hold the office since 1960, Kim Young-sam is elected president. During his five-year term he presides over a massive anti-corruption campaign.	During nuclear-program negotiations with the US, and prior to what would have been a historic summit with Kim Young-sam, North Korea's Kim Il-sung dies of a heart attack.

strongest labour movements in the world soon emerged and when former dissident Kim Dae-jung was elected at the end of 1997, all the protests and suffering and killing seemed finally to have effected change.

Kim was ideally poised to solve the deep economic downturn that hit Korea in 1997, as part of the Asian financial crisis. The IMF demanded reforms of the *jaebeol* as the price for its $57 million bailout, and Kim had long called for a restructure of the conglomerates and their cronyism with the banks and the government. By 1999 the economy was growing again.

Sunshine Policy

In 1998 Kim also began to roll out a 'Sunshine Policy' aimed at reconciliation with North Korea, if not reunification. Within a year Pyongyang had responded, various economic and cultural exchanges began and, in June 2000, the two presidents met at a summit for the first time since 1945. Seen by critics as appeasement of the North, this engagement policy was predicated on the realist principles that the North was not going to collapse and so had to be dealt with as it was, and that the North would not object to the continued presence of US troops in the South during the long process of reconciliation if the US normalised relations with the North – something Kim Jong-il acknowledged in his historic summit meeting with Kim Dae-jung in June 2000.

Between 2000 and 2008, when Lee Myung-bak's administration suspended the policy, tens of thousands of South Koreans were able to visit the North, some for heartbreakingly brief meetings with relations they hadn't seen for half a century. Big southern firms established joint ventures using northern labour in a purpose-built industrial complex at Kaesong. In 2000 Kim Dea-jung was awarded the Nobel Peace Prize for implementing the Sunshine Policy.

After Kim

When President Kim retired after his five-year term his party selected a virtual unknown, Roh Moo-hyun, a self-taught lawyer who had defended many dissidents in the darkest periods of the 1980s. To the surprise of many, including officials in Washington, he narrowly won the 2002 election and represented the rise to power of a generation that had nothing to do with the political system that emerged in 1945 (even Kim Dae-jung had been active in the 1940s). That generation was mostly middle-aged, having gone to school in the 1980s with indelible images of conflict on their campuses and American backing for Chun Doo-hwan. The result was a growing estrangement between Seoul and Washington, for the first time in the relationship.

Roh continued Kim's policy of engagement with the North, but his mismanagement of the economy and the decision to send South

The Gwangju Prize for Human Rights has been awarded since 2000 in memory of the 1980 pro-democracy martyrs. Recipients have included Aung San Suu Kyi, the pro-democracy politician of Myanmar (Burma).

Elections for the 300-seat National Assembly, South Korea's parliament, are held every four years and result in 246 directly elected members, with the other 54 appointed through proportional representation.

HISTORY POSTWAR RECOVERY

1996	1997	1998	2000
Two ex-presidents, Chun Doo-hwan and Roh Tae-woo, are put on trial and jailed for corruption charges. A year later they are both pardoned by President-elect Kim Dae-jung.	Long-time democracy champion Kim Dae-jung is elected president in the midst of a region-wide economic crisis. The International Monetary Fund offers the country a $57 million bailout.	Kim Jong-il takes full power on the 50th anniversary of the founding of North Korea, at the same time as his deceased father is proclaimed the country's 'eternal leader'.	In June Kim Dae-jung and Kim Jong-il meet in Pyongyang at the first-ever summit of the two countries. Kim Dae-jung is awarded the Nobel Peace Prize.

Korean troops to Iraq saw his public support plummet. The opposition tried to impeach Roh when, ahead of national parliamentary elections in 2004, he voiced support for the new Uri Party – a technical violation of a constitutional provision for the president to remain impartial. The impeachment failed, but Roh's popularity continued to slip and the Uri Party, suffering several defeats by association with the president, chose to distance itself from him by reforming as the Democratic Party.

The end result was a swing to the right that saw Lee Myung-bak of the Grand National Party elected president in 2007, and Roh retire to the village of Bongha, his birthplace in Gyeongsangnam-do. Eighteen months later, as a corruption investigation zeroed in on his family and former aides, Roh committed suicide by jumping off a cliff behind the village. The national shock at this turn of events rebounded on President Lee, who was already suffering public rebuke for opening Korea to imports of US beef.

Changes of Guard

Succession issues have dominated the Korean Peninsula in recent years. North of the border, Kim Jong-un was hailed the 'great successor' following the death of his father, Kim Jong-il, in December 2011. At the time little was known about Kim Jnr, the third in the family dynasty that has ruled the repressive single-party state since 1948 – even his birthday (1982–1984?) was unclear. North Korea analysts have since scrambled to interpret scraps of news from the secretive country, such as the public appearances of Ri Sol-ju, officially acknowledged as Kim's wife, and the public execution of Kim's uncle, Jang Sung-taek, who had previously been believed to be pulling the strings of power behind the scenes.

In the South, President Lee Myung-bak served out his five-year term of office and was replaced in the December 2012 national election by Park Geun-hye, the daughter of former dictator Park Chung-hee. Born in 1952, Park had served as the country's first lady in the 1970s, following the assassination of her mother in 1974 and before the killing of her father in 1979. She has publically apologised for the suffering of pro-democracy activists under her father's dictatorial regime and was first elected as an MP in 1998. Quite apart from her political stance, Park is not married, which in South Korea's conservative society elevates the significance of her presidential election win even more.

In October 2011 Park Won-soon, a former human-rights lawyer and independent candidate, was elected Seoul's mayor, ending a decade of right-wing political domination of the capital. In February 2012 Park affiliated himself with the DUP (Democratic Union Pary) and in 2014 won a second term of office in the most powerful post in South Korea after

---

Top Jaebeol

Samsung Represents 20% of Korean exports.

LG Plastics and electrical goods producer.

Hyundai-Kia Construction and Korea's largest automaker.

SK Textiles, petrochemicals, telecommunications and leisure.

Korea: The Impossible Country by Daniel Tudor (2012) is a good primer on modern life and times in Korea, including aspects of the country's history and politics.

2002	2003	2005	2006
Human-rights lawyer Roh Moo-hyun becomes South Korea's 16th president and continues the 'Sunshine Policy' of engagement with the North. South Korea and Japan co-host soccer's World Cup.	North Korea withdraws from the Nuclear Non-Proliferation Treaty. The first round of the so-called 'six-party talks' between North and South Korea, China, Japan, Russia and the US begin.	The death of King Gojong's 74-year-old grandson, Lee Gu, in Tokyo ends the Joseon dynasty's bloodline and any possibility of the return of a monarchy in Korea.	In October North Korea claims to have successfully conducted an underground nuclear test explosion. By the end of the month North Korea rejoins the six-party disarmament talks.

the president. That same year the DUP merged with the New Political Vision Party to form the New Politics Alliance for Democracy (NPAD), but performed poorly in by-elections in 2015.

The Nuclear Question

After a tumultuous 20th century, South Korea is by any measure one of the world's star performers of the 21st century. Its top companies, such as Samsung, LG and Hyundai, make products the world wants. Korea is now possibly the most wired nation on earth. The talented younger generation has produced such a dynamic pop culture that *hallyu* (the Korean Wave) is a huge phenomenon across Asia and is gaining popularity in the West.

The single anachronism in South Korea's progress, however, remains its fractious relations with North Korea. For decades the North's nuclear ambitions have loomed large on the peninsula. In 2003 China sponsored six-party talks (China, Japan, Russia, the US and both Koreas) to get Washington and Pyongyang talking and negotiating. These intermittent discussions have yet to yield a significant result. On the contrary, the North has successfully tested nuclear bombs, first in October 2006, again in May 2009 and for a third time in 2013.

> Korean Foundation (www.kf.or.kr) has video lectures on history and a link to *Koreana*, an excellent quarterly magazine with some history articles.

TAMING KOREA'S UNRULY PARLIAMENT

In 2009 *Foreign Policy* magazine cited South Korea's National Assembly as one of the most unruly parliaments in the world, where debates often get out of hand and even resort to violence. Such were the scenes in 2004 when then-President Roh Moo-hyun was being impeached. In 2008 angry opposition lawmakers reached for sledgehammers and electric saws to break into a locked committee room where the governing Grand National Party (now renamed Saenuri, or New Frontier Party) was attempting to rush though a free-trade bill. This was followed by a 12 day sit-in before the matter was resolved. Fist fights again broke out during the heated debate over media privatisation in July 2009. And in 2011, during a vote to ratify the nation's free-trade agreement with the US, an opposition lawmaker exploded a tear-gas canister in the chamber.

In early December 2014, no such scenes accompanied the passing of the 2015 budget – the first time since 2002 that the budget had been passed within the constitutional deadline of 30 days before its implementation at the start of January. However, it wasn't exactly that politicians had mended their brawling ways. The deadline for budget approval was met because of new legislation mandating that the budget bill is automatically forwarded to a plenary session by 30 November. Speaking to the *Korea Herald*, Myongji University professor of politics Chung Jin-min said that the law attempted to create a 'culture of handshaking' among lawmakers.

2007	2008	2009	2010
Former South Korean foreign minister Ban Ki-moon becomes the eighth UN Secretary General. Lee Myung-bak, ex-CEO of Hyundai Engineering and Construction and Seoul mayor, becomes South Korea's 17th president.	President Lee faces his first major domestic challenge as 20,000 people take to Seoul's streets to protest a government plan to resume US beef imports.	The nation mourns as former president Roh Moo-hyun, under investigation for corruption, commits suicide in May. Another former premier, Kim Dae-jung, succumbs to natural causes in August.	Seoul hosts the G20 Economic Summit and becomes World Design Capital, but its centrepiece – Dongdaemun Design Plaza & Park, by architect Zaha Hadid – remains uncompleted.

WOMEN IN KOREA

Park Geun-hye made women's rights one of the cornerstones of her campaign to become South Korea's first female president in 2012. She promised a 'women's revolution' for the country, which ranks 15th on the United Nations Development Programme's Gender Inequality Index. Women here can expect to make an average of 32% less than a man in the same job.

The roots of such inequality stretch way back to the 15th century, when the Joseon dynasty established new reforms and laws that led to a radical change in women's social position and an expropriation of women's property. Where many women were prominent in Goryeo society, they were now relegated to domestic chores of child-rearing and housekeeping, as so-called 'inside people'.

From then on, the latticework of Korean society was constituted by patrilineal descent. The nails in the latticework, the proof of its importance and existence over time, were the written genealogies that positioned families in the hierarchy of property and prestige. In succeeding centuries a person's genealogy would be the best predictor of his or her life chances – it became one of Korea's most lasting characteristics. Since only male offspring could prolong the family and clan lines, and were the only names registered in the genealogical tables, the birth of a son was greeted with great fanfare.

Such historical influences remain strong in both Koreas today, where first sons and their families often live with the male's parents, and all stops are pulled out to father a boy.

Go to the Korea Society's website (www.korea society.org) to listen to podcasts about Korean current affairs and the country's recent history.

Even though Park Geun-hye had promised greater engagement with North Korea than under her predecessor, President Lee, that third nuclear test and a subsquent test launch of submarine-based ballistic missiles in 2015 have done nothing to engender the evolution in relations. In fact, in 2014 Park asked China for help in reigning in its rogue neighbour – China is North Korea's largest source of trade and foreign aid, so is thought to exert some influence over Pyongyang.

However, while China is no more desirous than South Korea of having a nuclear-armed North Korea on its doorstep, it also has no appetite to destabilise Kim Jong-un's regime and face the consquences of a collapsed state – be it chaos or the reunification of the Korean Peninsula with US troops in the mix.

2011	2012	2013	2014
Independent candidate and former human-rights lawyer Park Won-soon is elected Seoul's mayor. He puts the brakes on major construction projects, focusing instead on welfare spending.	Park Geu-hye, daughter of South Korea's former dictator Park Chung-hee, wins the presidential election for the right-of-centre Saenuri Party and becomes the country's first female leader.	Tensions between North and South Korea ratchet up as Pyongyang carries out an underground nuclear bomb test and, in response to subsequent UN sanctions, says it's scrapping the 1953 truce.	Protestors are arrested as a candlelight vigil in Seoul turns into angry demands for the Park Geun-hye government to resign over the *Sewol* ferry disaster.

The Korean People

Once divided strictly along nearly inescapable social-class lines, South Koreans today are comparatively better off in terms of economic opportunities and are more individualistic in their world view. Nuclear rather than extended families have become the norm, and birth rates are among the lowest in the developed world. Still, there linger strong traces of Korea's particular identity; remnants of its Confucian past coexist alongside 'imported' spiritual beliefs and a striking devotion to displays of material success.

The Main Belief Systems

Confucianism

The state religion of the Joseon dynasty, Confucianism lives on as a kind of ethical bedrock in the minds of most Koreans.

The Chinese philosopher Confucius (552–479 BC) devised a system of ethics that emphasised devotion to parents and family, loyalty to friends and dedication to education. He also urged that respect and deference be given to those in positions of authority. These ideas led to the system of civil-service examinations (gwageo), where one could gain position through ability and merit rather than from noble birth or connections. Confucius preached against corruption and excessive taxation, and was the first teacher to open a school to all students solely on the basis of their willingness to learn.

As Confucianism trickled into Korea it evolved into Neo-Confucianism, which combined the sage's original ethical and political ideas with the quasireligious practice of ancestor worship and the idea of the eldest male as spiritual head of the family.

Korean Buddhism operates a templestay (http://eng.templestay.com) program at facilities across the country. Many Koreans as well as international visitors take part in these programs, regardless of whether they are Buddhist or not, as a chance to escape societal pressures and clear their minds.

Buddhism

When first introduced during the Koguryo dynasty in AD 370, Buddhism coexisted with shamanism. Many Buddhist temples have a samseiong-gak (three-spirit hall) on their grounds, which houses shamanist deities such as the Mountain God.

Buddhism was persecuted during the Joseon period, when temples were tolerated only in remote mountains. The religion suffered another sharp decline after WWII as Koreans pursued worldly goals. But South Korea's success in achieving developed-nation status, coupled with a growing interest in spiritual values, is encouraging a Buddhist revival. Temple visits have increased and large sums of money are flowing into temple reconstruction. According to 2003 data from Statistics Korea, about 25% of the population claims to be Buddhist.

About 90% of Korean Buddhist temples belong to the Jogye sect (www.korean buddhism.net). The Buddha's birthday is a national holiday, and celebrations include an extravagant lantern parade in Seoul.

Christianity

Korea's first exposure to Christianity was in the late 18th century. It came via the Jesuits from the Chinese Imperial court when a Korean aristocrat was baptised in Beijing in 1784. The Catholic faith took hold and spread so quickly that it was perceived as a threat by the Korean government and was vigorously suppressed, creating the country's first Christian martyrs.

THE CONFUCIAN MINDSET

Not everyone follows the rules, but Confucianism does continue to shape the Korean paradigm. Some of the key principles and practices:

➡ Public, symbolic displays of obedience and respect towards seniors – parents, teachers, the boss, older brothers and sisters – are crucial. Expect a heavy penalty if you step out of line.

➡ Seniors get obedience, but it's not a free ride. Older sisters help out younger siblings with tuition fees, and the boss always pays for lunch.

➡ Education is the mark of a civilised person. A high-school graduate, despite having built a successful business, still feels shame at the lack of scholastic credentials.

➡ Obvious displays of one's social status, from winter-coat brand names worn by middle-school children to overzealous criticisms by an airline executive about the way a steward presents a bag of nuts, are paramount. Every action reflects on the family, company and country.

➡ Everything on earth is in a hierarchy. Never, ever, forget who is senior and who is junior to you.

➡ Families are more important than individuals. Everyone's purpose in life is to improve the family's reputation and wealth. No one should choose a career or marry someone against their parents' wishes – a bad choice could bring about family ruin.

➡ Loyalty is important. A loyal liar is virtuous.

Christianity got a second chance in the 1880s with the arrival of American Protestant missionaries who founded schools and hospitals and gained many followers. Today, about 27% of the population claims some sort of affiliation with a Christian church.

Shamanism

Historically, shamanism influenced Korean spirituality. It's not a religion but it does involve communication with spirits through intermediaries known as *mudang* (female shamans). Although not widely practised today, shamanist ceremonies are held to cure illness, ward off financial problems or guide a deceased family member safely into the spirit world.

Ceremonies involve contacting spirits who are attracted by lavish offerings of food and drink. Drums beat and the *mudang* dances herself into a frenzied state that allows her to communicate with the spirits and be possessed by them. Resentments felt by the dead can plague the living and cause all sorts of misfortune, so their spirits need placating. For shamanists, death does not end relationships. It simply takes another form.

On Inwangsan, in northwestern Seoul, ceremonies take place in or near the historic Inwangsan Guksadang shrine.

Koreans give their family name first followed by their birth name, which is typically two syllables, eg Lee Myong-bak. There are fewer than 300 Korean family names, with Kim, Lee, Park and Jeong accounting for 46% of the total.

Competitive Lives

Koreans don't think much of happiness. It's not a state of mind that people generally aspire to. When discussing the human condition, *stress* is a much more descriptive word. People here, it seems, are in a continual state of stress or are seeking ways to escape it through faddish elixirs. Much of that stress comes from the way life is manifest: it's a zero-sum game. From corporate manoeuvres to elementary-school maths class, everything is competitive.

Take, for example, the country's hypercompetitive education system. To get into a top Korean university, high-school students go through a gruelling examination process, spending 14 hours a day or more memorising reams of data for the annual college entrance test. But that's only part of the story. A good number of students give up the game, feign studying or simply sleep in class because the race to the top is no longer a reflection of one's abilities or willpower. Vast amounts of money for private education are required to be competitive at school. As a result, higher education is no longer a social leveller, it exacerbates social divisions.

To stay competitive, Korean fanaticism extends to health. The millions of hikers who stream into the mountains at weekends are not only enjoying nature but also keeping fit. Thousands of health foods and drinks are sold in markets and pharmacies, which stock traditional as well as Western medicines. Nearly every food claims to be a 'well-being' product or an aphrodisiac – 'good for stamina' is the local phrase.

KOREA'S SPORTING CULTURE

Baseball rules as the most popular spectator sport (2014 league average was 11,300 spectators per game). Among the young, soccer is a popular game to play or watch on TV if the match involves the Korean national team in a World Cup match. Interest in soccer peaked with Park Ji-sung, the most decorated player in Asian history. Since his retirement in 2014, Park has served as a Global Ambassador for Manchester United.

Baseball

There are 10 professional teams in the Korean Baseball Organization (KBO; www.korea baseball.com), all sponsored by *jaebeol* (business conglomerates). Five teams are based in or around Seoul. The LG Twins and Doosan Bears share Jamsil Stadium in Seoul. The other five teams play in Korea's largest cities and regions. The season runs from April to October and each team plays 144 games. Since 2014, teams have been allowed to sign up to three foreign players (in the past, two players), a strategy designed to increase the calibre of play. Salary caps and mandatory one-year contracts for foreign players were abolished by the league in the same year.

Soccer

There are two divisions in Korean professional soccer: 12 teams play in the top tier K-League Classic and 11 teams in the second division K-League Challenge. Matches are played between March and November. The Korean national team's greatest accomplishment was finishing fourth in the 2002 World Cup.

Basketball

Ten teams play in the Korean Basketball League (KBL; www.kbl.or.kr). Each team plays 54 games during the regular season, October to March. Two foreign players (usually Americans) are allowed on each team. KBL games tend to be a lot of fun for fans, playing in comparatively small centres. League average attendance is about 4300 per game.

Taekwondo

By some accounts taekwondo is the world's most popular martial art (measured by number of participants). This is despite only having been cobbled together at the end of WWII by fighters who wanted a sport that, on the surface at least, was unrelated to anything Japanese. Bits were taken from (ahem) karate and blended with lesser-known Korean fighting skills such as *taekyon,* which relies primarily on leg thrusts. By the mid-1950s the name 'taekwondo' was born.

Today, taekwondo thrives as a sport that most boys practise as elementary-school students. It is also part of the physical training program that young men complete as part of their compulsory military service. Taekwondo in Korea is not a popular spectator sport. Matches are not broadcast on TV and few tournaments draw popular attention outside Olympic contests. In 2014, the World Taekwondo Federation opened a training facility and museum in Deogyusan National Park in Muju-gun.

FORTUNE-TELLING

These days most people visit street-tent fortune tellers for a bit of fun, but no doubt some take it seriously. For a *saju* (reading of your future), inform the fortune teller of the hour, day, date and year of your birth; another option is *gunhap* (a love-life reading), when a couple give their birth details and the fortune teller pronounces how compatible they are. Expect to pay ₩10,000 for *saju* and double that for *gunhap*. If you don't speak the language, you'll need someone to translate.

Contemporary & Traditional Culture

Culture Books

The Koreans: Who They Are, What They Want, Where Their Future Lies, *Michael Breen (1998)*

Still Life With Rice, *Helie Lee (1997)*

The Birth of Korean Cool: How One Nation is Conquering the World Through Pop Culture, *Euny Hong (2014)*

Korea: The Impossible Country, *Daniel Tudor (2012)*

Driven by the latest technology and fast-evolving trends, Korea can sometimes seem like one of the most cutting-edge countries on the planet. People tune into their favourite TV shows via their smart phones. In PC *bang* (computer-game rooms) millions of diehard fans battle at online computer games.

General fashions too tend to be international and up to the moment. However, it's not uncommon to see some people wearing *hanbok,* the striking traditional clothing that follows the Confucian principle of unadorned modesty. Women wear a loose-fitting short blouse with long sleeves and a voluminous long skirt, while men wear a jacket and baggy trousers.

Today *hanbok* is worn mostly at weddings or special events, and even then it may be a more comfortable 'updated' version. Everyday *hanbok* is reasonably priced but formal styles, made of colourful silk and intricately embroidered, are objects of wonder and cost a fortune.

Multiculturalism

Korea is a monocultural society. As of 2014, *foreigners* (the local name given to foreign nationals) numbered 1.5 million or 3% of the population. Foreign residents tend to congregate in pockets, such as international tradespeople working in the shipbuilding industry on Geojedo, though none qualify as a distinct cultural community.

In the Korean Kitchen

Most people think Korean food means kimchi and barbecue, which exhibit quintessentially Korean flavours – the ripe tartness of fermented leaves, the delicate marinade of grilled meat. But that's just the starting point. A Korean meal is packed with flavours, unrepentant and full. While the basic building blocks of the cuisine are recognisably Asian (garlic, ginger, green onion, black pepper, vinegar and sesame oil), Korean food strikes out on its own in combining them with three essential sauces: *ganjang* (soy sauce), *doenjang* (fermented soybean paste) and *gochujang* (hot red-pepper paste).

The other distinctive feature is that the main course is always served not only with *bap* (boiled rice), soup and kimchi, but also a procession of *banchan* (side dishes). Diners eat a bit from one dish, a bite from another, a little rice, a sip of soup, mixing spicy and mild any way they want. Above all, mealtimes are a group affair with family, friends or colleagues – always convivial and rarely, if ever, alone.

Dining options range from casual bites at a market stall to an elaborate multicourse *jeongsik* (set menu or table d'hôte) at a lavish restaurant. Many places serve a small menu of less than 10 specialities; those at national parks and tourist villages tend to have a wider range. Restaurants outside major cities are unlikely to have English menus.

Eating out is a social activity, so lone travellers may encounter a quizzical '*honja?*' ('alone?'). Occasionally a restaurant may turn away solo diners because they only serve meals in portions for two (especially for *jeongsik* and barbecue).

Seoul is the best place to take cookery courses in English. A great online resource is Maangchi's recipe archive (www.maangchi.com/recipes), which includes demonstration videos.

Restaurant Types & Typical Dishes

Barbecue

Perhaps the most recognisable of Korean restaurants, these are often boisterous establishments where every table has its own small grill and the main selling point is the quality of the meat and the marinade. The menu typically consists of a mind-boggling array of meat cuts. Beef, usually local, is highly prized and more expensive; pork is more affordable. Bulgogi is thin slices of meat, marinated in sweetened soy sauce, while *galbi* are short ribs, similarly flavoured. These terms usually refer to beef but can also be used for pork (*dwaeji*). Another popular cut is *samgyeopsal* (streaky pork belly).

Diners cook their own meat on the grill, though servers will assist foreign customers. Grilled meats are often eaten wrapped in *ssam* (vegetable leaves) with slices of fresh garlic, green pepper, kimchi and a daub of spicy *ssamjang* (soybean and red-pepper sauce). The vegetables used for *ssam* are lettuce, perilla (similar to shiso leaf, and what Koreans call wild sesame), crown daisy and seaweed. Rounding off the meal – or just something to munch on while the meat is cooking – are dishes such as *bossam* (steamed pork and kimchi), *pajeon* (green-onion pancake) or *jjigae* (stew). Expect to pay ₩15,000 to ₩50,000 per person.

All-seafood barbecues (sometimes called grilled seafood) on the coast focus on oily fish such as mackerel, but also include flounder and squid,

In 2012, Jeonju in Jeollabuk-do was recognised as a Unesco City of Gastronomy for safeguarding its culinary heritage. One visit to its hugely popular street-food stalls and you can see and taste why.

SAY KIMCHI

It appears at every meal (including breakfast) and often as an ingredient in the main course too. What began as a pickling method to preserve vegetables through Korea's harsh winters has become a cornerstone of its cuisine. With its lurid reddish hues and limp texture, kimchi doesn't look that appealing, but just one bite packs a wallop of flavours: sour, spicy, with a sharp tang that often lingers through the meal.

The most common type is *baechu* kimchi, made from Chinese cabbage, but there are more than 180 varieties, made with radish, cucumber, eggplant, leek, mustard leaf and pumpkin flower, among others. Some are meant to be eaten in tiny morsels while others, such as *bossam* kimchi, are flavour-packed packages containing vegetables, pork or seafood.

To make kimchi, vegetables are salted to lock in the original flavour, then seasoned with garlic, red-pepper powder, green onions, ginger, fish sauce and other spices, and left in earthenware jars to ferment for hours, days or even years. Kimchi can be made all year round using seasonal vegetables, but traditionally it is made in November. Many regions, restaurants and families have their own recipes, jealously guarded and handed down through the generations. High in fibre and low in calories, kimchi is said to lower cholesterol, fight cancer and prevent SARS and H1N1 swine flu.

served with an array of *banchan*. Expect to pay ₩10,000 to ₩20,000 per person.

Soups, Stews, Jeongol & Jjim

Many Korean dishes are served as boiling or sizzling hot off the stove. Besides the soup that accompanies every meal, there are many hearty, piquant main-course soups called *tang* or *guk*. Soup restaurants usually specialise in just a few dishes.

Samgyetang is a ginseng chicken soup, infused with jujube, ginger and other herbs. It's not spicy and is very easy on the palate – the idea is to savour the hint of ginseng and the quality of the chicken. Though it originated as court cuisine, it is now enjoyed as a summer tonic.

A stouter alternative is *gamjatang*, a spicy peasant soup with meaty bones and potatoes. Other meat broths are delicate, even bland, such as *galbitang* or *seolleongtang*. *Haejangguk* or 'hangover soup' (to dispel the night's excesses) is made from a *doenjang* base, with bean sprouts, vegetables and sometimes cow's blood.

Jjigae are stews for everyday eating, often orangey, spicy and served in a stone hotpot. The main ingredient is usually *dubu* (tofu), *doenjang* or kimchi, with vegetables and meat or fish. *Budae jjigae* ('army stew') was concocted during the Korean War using leftover hot dogs, Spam and macaroni scrounged from American bases.

Jeongol is a more elaborate stew, often translated as a casserole or hotpot. Raw ingredients are arranged in a shallow pan at the table, then topped with a spicy broth and brought to a boil. *Jjim* are dishes where the main ingredient is marinated in sauce, then simmered in a broth or steamed until the liquid is reduced. It's a popular (and extremely spicy) serving style for prawns, crab and fish.

Soup and stew meals cost ₩6000 to ₩20,000 per person. *Jeongol* and *jjim* are rarely served in individual portions, unlike *jjigae*.

Fish & Seafood

Hoe (raw fish) is extremely popular in coastal towns, despite the high prices. *Modeumhoe* or *saengseonhoe* is raw fish served with *ssam* or *ganjang* with wasabi, usually with a pot of spicy *maeuntang* (fish soup) to complete the meal. *Chobap* is raw fish served over vinegar rice. Restau-

A helpful guide to the dizzying range of meat choices at a barbecue restaurant is Kimchimari's *Know Your Beef Cut!* (http://kimchimari.com/2012/01/28/know-your-beef-cut).

rants near the coast also serve squid, barbecued shellfish, octopus and crab. More gung-ho eaters can try *sannakji* (raw octopus, not live but wriggling from post-mortem spasms) or *hongeo* (ray, served raw and fermented, or steamed in *jjim* – neither of which masks its pungent ammonia smell). A seafood meal costs from ₩15,000 per person.

Jeongsik

Often translated as a set menu or table d'hôte, this is a spread of banquet dishes all served at once: fish, meat, soup, *dubu jjigae* (tofu stew), rice, noodles, shellfish and a flock of *banchan*. It's a delightful way to sample a wide range of Korean food in one sitting. *Hanjeongsik* (Korean *jeongsik*) may denote a traditional royal banquet spread of 12 dishes, served on *bangjja* (bronze) tableware. Expect to pay from ₩20,000 for a basic *jeongsik* to more than ₩100,000 for a high-end version.

Everyday Eats

Not every meal in Korea is a *banchan* or meat extravaganza. For casual dining, look for one-dish rice or noodle dishes. Bibimbap is a perennial favourite: a tasty mixture of vegetables, sometimes meat and a fried egg on top of rice. The ingredients are laid out in a deep bowl according to the five primary colours of Korean food – white, yellow, green, red and black – which represent the five elements. Just stir everything up (go easy on the red *gochujang* if you don't want it too spicy) and eat. A variant is *dolsot* bibimbap, served in a stone hotpot; the highlight of this is *nurungji*, the crusty rice at the bottom. Vegetarians can order bibimbap without meat or egg.

As in much of East Asia, noodle joints are plentiful. A common dish is *naengmyeon*, buckwheat noodles served in an icy beef broth, garnished with vegetables, Korean pear, cucumber and half a boiled egg. You can add *gochujang, sikcho* (vinegar) or *gyeoja* (mustard) to taste. *Naengmyeon* is especially popular in summer. Sometimes it's served with a small bowl of meat broth, piping hot, that you can drink with your meal (but it's not for pouring onto the noodles).

Japchae are clear 'glass' noodles stir-fried in sesame oil with strips of egg, meat and vegetables. A Koreanised Chinese dish is *jajangmyeon*, wheat noodles in a black-bean sauce with meat and vegetables. *Gimbap* joints often serve *ramyeon* (instant noodles) in spicy soup.

Gimbap are colourful rolls of *bap* (rice) flavoured with sesame oil and rolled in *gim* (dried seaweed). Circular *gimbap* contain strips of vegetables, egg and meat. *Samgak* (triangular) *gimbap* are topped with a savoury fish, meat or vegetable mixture. Just don't call it sushi – the rice does not have vinegar added and it is not topped with raw fish.

Mandu are dumplings filled with meat, vegetables and herbs. Fried, steamed or served in soup, they make a tasty snack or light meal. Savoury pancakes, often served as a side dish, can also be ordered as a meal. *Bindaetteok* are made with mung-bean flour and are heavier on the batter,

South Koreans eat 1.5 million tonnes of kimchi every year. When the country's first astronaut went into space in 2008, she took a specially engineered 'space kimchi' with her.

IN THE KOREAN KITCHEN RESTAURANT TYPES & TYPICAL DISHES

SAUCY SIDE DISHES

It's not a Korean meal unless there's kimchi and *banchan* (side dishes). *Banchan* creates balance with saltiness, spiciness, temperature and colour. The number of *banchan* varies greatly, from three in an ordinary meal to 12 in traditional royal cuisine, to an incredible 20 or more in *jeongsik* (set menu or table d'hôte).

Besides the archetypal cabbage kimchi, it's common to see radish or cucumber kimchi, and dishes with spinach, seaweed, bean sprouts, tofu, *jeon, bindaetteok,* small clams, anchovies – just about anything the chefs can concoct. You don't have to eat it all, though if you like a particular dish you can ask for refills (within reason).

LOCAL SPECIALITIES

➡ *jjimdak* (simmered chicken) – Andong

➡ *ureok* (rockfish) – Busan

➡ *dakgalbi* (spicy chicken grilled with vegetables and rice cakes) – Chuncheon

➡ *maneul* (garlic) – Danyang

➡ *sundubu* (soft or uncurdled tofu) – Gangneung

➡ *oritang* (duck soup); *tteokgalbi* (grilled patties of ground beef) – Gwangju

➡ *okdomgui* (grilled, semidried fish); *jeonbok-juk* (abalone rice porridge); *heukdwaeji* (black-pig pork) – Jeju-do

➡ bibimbap – Jeonju

➡ *ojing-eo* (squid) served *sundae* (sausage) style – Sokcho

➡ *galbi* – Suwon

➡ *chungmu gimbap* (rice, dried seaweed and kimchi) – Tongyeong

➡ *gatkimchi* (leafy mustard kimchi) – Yeosu

while *jeon* are made with wheat flour. Common fillings are kimchi, spring onion *(pajeon)* and seafood *(haemul pajeon)*.

Some eateries specialise in *juk* (rice porridge). Savoury versions are cooked with ginseng chicken, mushroom or seafood, sweet ones with pumpkin and red bean. The thick, black rice porridge is sesame. *Juk* is considered a healthy meal, good for older people, babies or anyone who's ill.

Rice and noodle dishes cost ₩6000 to ₩10,000 each, a meal-sized *jeon* is ₩7000 to ₩10,000, and *gimbap* or *mandu* meals cost ₩3000 to ₩7000.

Cooking at Home

Growing Up in a Korean Kitchen *by Hisoo Shin Hepinstall*

Eating Korean *by Cecilia Hae-Jin Lee*

A Korean Mother's Cooking Notes *by Sun-Young Chang*

Desserts

While desserts are not traditional in Korean dining, sometimes at the end of a meal you'll be served fruit or *sujeonggwa,* a cold drink made from cinnamon and ginger.

The classic summer dessert is *patbingsu,* a bowl heaped with shaved ice, *tteok* (rice cakes) and sweet red-bean topping with a splash of condensed milk. Modern toppings include strawberries, green-tea powder and fresh or canned fruit. It costs ₩2500 to ₩7000 at cafes.

Bakeries and street vendors sell bite-sized *hangwa* (Korean sweets) such as *dasik* (traditional cookies), and *tteok* flavoured with nuts, seeds and dried fruit.

Drinks

Tea is a staple and the term is also used to describe drinks brewed without tea leaves. The most common leaf tea is *nokcha* (green tea), grown on plantations in Jeju-do and Jeollanam-do. Black tea is harder to find. Nonleaf teas include the ubiquitous *boricha* (barley tea), *daechucha* (red-date tea), *omijacha* (five-flavour berry tea), *yujacha* (citron tea) and *insamcha* (ginseng tea).

Koreans have taken to coffee, or *keopi,* in a big way in recent decades. Aside from the ever-present vending machines which churn out an overly sweet three-in-one (coffee, cream and sugar) instant coffee mix (₩300), the number of gourmet coffee shops has multiplied by about 10 since 2006 – from Korean chains such as Angel-in-us Coffee and Hollys, to homegrown speciality roasters and slow-brewers, to foreign imports like Starbucks. In Seoul, expect to pay from ₩4000 for coffee at a chain outlet to ₩10,000 for a speciality brew.

STREET FOOD

Korean street food runs the gamut from snacks to full meals. Expect to pay ₩500 to ₩2000 per serve, although some meals at *pojangmacha* (street tent bars) cost up to ₩15,000 per dish.

➡ *bungeoppang* (red-bean waffles) – Fish-shaped sweet cakes with a golden brown, waffle-like exterior and a hot, sweet, red-bean-paste interior.

➡ *dakkochi* (grilled chicken skewers) – Skewers of chicken and spring onion with a smoky charred flavour under a sticky, tangy barbecue sauce.

➡ *gyeranppang* (egg muffins) – Literally egg bread, *gyeranppang* is a golden oblong muffin with a still-moist whole egg baked on top with a dusting of parsley.

➡ *haemul pajeon* (seafood pancakes) – These savoury seafood pancakes are a full meal on the go. Lots of squid and sometimes prawns or mussels are fried in a batter with lashings of leeks.

➡ *hotteok* (Korean doughnuts) – Spiced, plump pancakes filled with a mixture of sunflower seeds, cinnamon and brown sugar. Other fillings include black sesame seeds, peanuts, red beans and honey.

➡ *jjinppang* (steamed buns) – Soft fluffy buns with various fillings, but usually coarse red-bean paste, pork or kimchi.

➡ *mandu* (dumplings) – Fried or steamed Korean dumplings, often including a tofu or vermicelli-noodle filling. *Kogi mandu* are stuffed with a gingery minced pork and spring onions. Kimchi *mandu* adds spicy kimchi.

➡ *odeng* (fishcake skewers) – Flat fishcakes on a skewer, either long or folded over. They jut from vats of broth, which is a seafood and spring-onion soup that Koreans say cures hangovers.

➡ *sundae* (blood sausage) – Slices of black sausage eaten with toothpicks or chopsticks.

➡ *ttcokbokki* (spicy rice cakes) – Chewy rice cakes that resemble penne pasta in pans of spicy, saucy *gochujang* (hot red-pepper paste). Variations add slices of fish cakes, boiled eggs or *ramyeon* (ramen or wheat noodles).

➡ *twigim* (Korean-style tempura) – Various batter-fried (like Japanese tempura but more substantial) ingredients such as squid, a hash of vegetables, sweet potatoes and even boiled eggs.

Every restaurant serves *mul* (water) or tea. Most serve alcohol, but not usually soft drinks. Some unusual Korean canned soft drinks, readily available from convenience stores, are grape juice with whole grapes inside and *sikhye*, rice punch containing rice grains.

Alcoholic Drinks

Drinking, and drinking heavily, is the mainstay of Korean socialising, and an evening out can quickly turn into a blur of bar-hopping. The most common poison of choice is *soju*, the mere mention of which tends to elicit looks of dismay from foreigners who have overindulged before. The stuff is, to put it bluntly, ethanol mixed with water and flavouring. If you think that it goes down easy, remember it can also leave you with a killer hangover.

The cheaper varieties (sold in convenience stores for as little as ₩1500) have all the subtlety of really awful moonshine, while those distilled from grain (₩7000 and up) offer a far more delicate flavour. The cheap stuff has an alcohol content of 20% to 35%, while the good stuff goes up to 45%. The latter includes Andong *soju* and white *soju*, available in Gyeongsangbuk-do and Gyeongsangnam-do respectively.

Makgeolli is a traditional farmer's brew made from unrefined, fermented rice wine. Much lower in alcohol content than *soju*, it has a cloudy

Koreans drink so much *soju* that the brand Jinro Soju has been the top-selling brand of spirits worldwide for the last 11 years.

INSIDE THE COVERED WAGON

Spend time walking at night on a busy street in a large Korean city and you're likely to come across a *pojangmacha* (also *pojenmacha*), an orange piece of Korean street culture. Literally meaning 'covered wagon', these food-and-drink carts draped in a tarpaulin are more than a convenient late-night street pub; they're an institution that delivers a unique social and sensory experience.

According to Mrs Lee, the woman who runs Emo (이모), a *pojangmacha* in Seomyeon, Busan, 'People who love drinking come to the covered wagon because they feel comfortable.' Comfort, in this case, does not mean physical amenities, as most *pojangmacha* are equipped with bench seating, dim lighting and off-site washrooms that require a short stumble to a nearby car park. Comfort instead means a respite from the outside world.

Inside the *pojangmacha*, traditional barriers that prevent Koreans from socialising easily give way to conviviality. As customer talk rambles on between shots of *soju* and whiffs of cigarette smoke, Mrs Lee sits behind the counter watching over a charcoal grill. Plumes of smoke rise to the top of the tent. The aroma of grilled chicken anus (닭똥집), sea eel (꼼장어구이) and mackerel (고등어), commingled with the plasticky smell of a decades-old tarpaulin, induces childhood memories of an overnight camping trip. It all seems like another world.

appearance and a sweetish yoghurt flavour. It has gained popularity and credibility in recent years with artisanal *makgeolli* bars in Seoul serving quality drops minus the dreaded aspartame found in many commercial varieties. In Seoul, Makgeolli Mamas & Papas (http://mmpkorea.wordpress.com) and Makgeolli Makers (www.facebook.com/makgeollimakers) are a community of *makgeolli* lovers and educators who run *makgeolli*-making courses.

Dongdongju is similar to *makgeolli*, with rice grains floating in it. Both are popular tipples in national parks, where it's practically ritual to swig down a bowl or two after (or during) an arduous hike. They cost ₩1000 to ₩2500 in supermarkets, double that in restaurants and bars. Sweeter on the palate are a host of traditional spirits, brewed or distilled from grains, fruits and roots. *Bokbunjaju* is made from wild raspberries, *meoruju* from wild fruit, *maesilju* from green plums and *insamju* from ginseng. Beer, or *maekju*, is the least exciting. Local brands, all lagers, are the rather bland Cass, Hite and OB. Interesting microbreweries have taken off, mainly in Itaewon in Seoul, and imported beers are increasingly available. Local beers cost ₩2000 to ₩5000 in a restaurant or bar.

During an evening of drinking, Koreans usually order *anju* (bar snacks), which traditionally meant kimchi, *dotorimuk* (acorn jelly) or *dubu* kimchi. Nowadays you're more likely to get heaped plates of oil-soaked food – fried chicken, French fries or vegetable *twigim* (fritters). Chain bars that serve just beer and French fries have taken off in university areas. A *hof*, a term inspired by German beer halls, is any watering hole that serves primarily Korean beer, with the requisite plate of fried chicken and other *anju*.

Vegetarians & Vegans

Although Korean cuisine uses lots of vegetables, much of it is pickled or cooked with meat or seafood. *Dubu jjigae* may be made from beef or seafood stock, and *beoseot deopbap* (mushrooms on rice) may contain a little pork. Even kimchi is often made with fish sauce. The only assuredly meat-free meals are those served at Buddhist temples or restaurants. Seoul Veggie Club (www.facebook.com/groups/seoulveggieclub) and www.happycow.net are good resources.

The safest approach is to ask about ingredients or order something such as bibimbap without the ingredients you don't eat. Be as specific

Food Sites

An American foodie's Seoul food blog (www.seouleats.com)

Guide to Korean food and cooking (http://english.visitkorea.or.kr)

Korean food and pop-up restaurant journal (www.zenkimchi.com)

about your requirements as you can be – for instance, saying 'no meat' may not suffice to omit seafood.

Dining & Drinking Etiquette

From casual eateries to high-end restaurants, you're as likely to encounter traditional floor seating as Western-style chair seating. If it's the former, remove your shoes at the door and sit on floor cushions (stack a few for more comfort). The menu is often posted on the wall. Main courses come with rice, soup, kimchi and *banchan* (usually included in the price). Don't worry about not finishing the *banchan* as no one is expected to eat everything.

Meals are eaten communally. If the table is not set, there will be an oblong box containing metal chopsticks and long-handled spoons, as well as metal cups and a bottle of water or tea. The spoon is for rice, soup and any dish with liquids; chopsticks are for everything else. Don't touch food with your fingers, except when handling *ssam*. Remember not to let the chopsticks or spoon stick up from your rice bowl – this is taboo, only done with food that is offered to deceased ancestors.

Koreans eat out – a lot – and love to sit and sup on a main course for several hours (and over several bottles of *soju*). Seniors or elders begin eating first. Dining companions usually pour drinks for each other – traditionally, never for themselves. It's polite to use both hands when pouring or receiving a drink.

To call a server, say '*Yogiyo*', which if translated seems rude (it means 'here') but is a bona fide way of hailing attention. Tipping is not expected, though high-end restaurants often add a 10% service charge.

Bosintang (dog-meat soup) is said to make men more virile and it's eaten on the hottest days of the year. It's less popular with the younger generation and there are growing concerns about animal protection.

IN THE KOREAN KITCHEN DINING & DRINKING ETIQUETTE

Food Glossary

Fish & Seafood Dishes

chobap	초밥	raw fish on rice
garibi	가리비	scallops
gwang-eohoe	광어회	raw halibut
jangeogui	장어구이	grilled eel
kijogae	키조개	razor clam
kkotgejjim	꽃게찜	steamed blue crab
modeumhoe	모듬회	mixed raw-fish platter
nakji	낙지	octopus
odeng	오뎅	processed seafood cakes
ojingeo	오징어	squid
saengseongui	생선구이	grilled fish
saeugui	새우구이	grilled prawns

Kimchi 김치

baechu kimchi	배추김치	cabbage kimchi; the classic spicy version
kkakdugi	깍두기	cubed radish kimchi
mul kimchi	물김치	cold kimchi soup

Meat Dishes

bossam	보쌈	steamed pork with kimchi, cabbage and lettuce wrap
bulgogi	불고기	barbecued beef slices and lettuce wrap

dakgalbi	닭갈비	spicy chicken pieces grilled with vegetables and rice cakes
dwaeji galbi	돼지갈비	pork ribs
galbi	갈비	beef ribs
heukdwaeji	흑돼지	black pig
jjimdak	찜닭	spicy chicken pieces with noodles
metdwaejigogi	멧돼지고기	wild pig
neobiani/tteokgalbi	너비아니/떡갈비	large minced-meat patty
samgyeopsal	삼겹살	barbecued (bacon-like) streaky pork belly
tangsuyuk	탕수육	Chinese-style sweet-and-sour pork
tongdakgui	통닭구이	roasted chicken
yukhoe	육회	seasoned raw beef

Noodles

bibim naengmyeon	비빔냉면	cold buckwheat noodles with vegetables, meat and sauce
bibimguksu	비빔국수	noodles with vegetables, meat and sauce
jajangmyeon	자장면	noodles in Chinese-style black-bean sauce
japchae	잡채	stir-fried 'glass' noodles and vegetables
kalguksu	칼국수	wheat noodles in clam-and-vegetable broth
kongguksu	콩국수	wheat noodles in cold soybean soup
makguksu	막국수	buckwheat noodles with vegetables
mulnaengmyeon	물냉면	buckwheat noodles in cold broth
ramyeon	라면	instant noodles in soup

Rice Dishes

bap	밥	boiled rice
bibimbap	비빔밥	rice topped with egg, meat, vegetables and sauce
bokkeumbap	볶음밥	Chinese-style fried rice
boribap	보리밥	boiled rice with steamed barley
chamchi gimbap	참치김밥	tuna *gimbap*
chijeu gimbap	치즈김밥	cheese *gimbap*
daetongbap	대통밥	rice cooked in bamboo stem
dolsot bibimbap	돌솥비빔밥	bibimbap in stone hotpot
dolsotbap	돌솥밥	hotpot rice
dolssambap	돌쌈밥	hotpot rice and lettuce wraps
gimbap	김밥	rice flavoured with sesame oil and rolled in dried seaweed
gulbap	굴밥	oyster rice
hoedeopbap	회덮밥	bibimbap with raw fish
honghapbap	홍합밥	mussel rice
jeonbokjuk	전복죽	rice porridge with abalone
juk	죽	rice porridge
modeum gimbap	모듬김밥	assorted *gimbap*
pyogo deopbap	표고덮밥	mushroom rice
sanchae bibimbap	산채비빔밥	bibimbap with mountain vegetables
sinseollo	신선로	meat, fish and vegetables cooked in broth

| ssambap | 쌈밥 | assorted ingredients with rice and wraps |

Snacks

beondegi	번데기	boiled silkworm larvae
bungeoppang	붕어빵	fish-shaped waffle with red-bean paste
dakkochi	닭꼬치	spicy grilled chicken on skewers
gukhwappang	국화빵	flower-shaped waffle with red-bean paste
hotteok	호떡	wheat pancake with sweet filling
jjinppang	찐빵	giant steamed bun with sweet-bean paste
norang goguma	노랑고구마	sweet potato strips
nurungji	누룽지	crunchy burnt-rice cracker, often at the bottom of *dolsot* bibimbap
patbingsu	팥빙수	shaved-iced dessert with *tteok* and red-bean topping
tteok	떡	rice cake
tteokbokki	떡볶이	pressed rice cakes and vegetables in a spicy sauce

Soups

bosintang	보신탕	dog-meat soup
dakbaeksuk	닭백숙	chicken in medicinal herb soup
dakdoritang	닭도리탕	spicy chicken and potato soup
galbitang	갈비탕	beef-rib soup
gamjatang	감자탕	meaty bones and potato soup
haejangguk	해장국	bean-sprout soup ('hangover soup')
haemultang	해물탕	spicy assorted seafood soup
kkorigomtang	꼬리곰탕	oxtail soup
maeuntang	매운탕	spicy fish soup
manduguk	만두국	soup with meat-filled dumplings
oritang	오리탕	duck soup
samgyetang	삼계탕	ginseng chicken soup
seolleongtang	설렁탕	beef and rice soup

Stews

budae jjigae	부대찌개	'army stew' with hot dogs, Spam and vegetables
dakjjim	닭찜	braised chicken
doenjang jjigae	된장찌개	soybean-paste stew
dubu jjigae	두부찌개	tofu stew
galbijjim	갈비찜	braised beef ribs
gopchang jeongol	곱창전골	tripe hotpot
kimchi jjigae	김치찌개	kimchi stew

Other

bindaetteok	빈대떡	mung-bean pancake
donkkaseu	돈까스	pork cutlet with rice and salad
dotorimuk	도토리묵	acorn jelly
gujeolpan	구절판	eight snacks and wraps
hanjeongsik	한정식	Korean-style banquet
jeongsik	정식	set menu or table d'hôte, with lots of side dishes
mandu	만두	filled dumplings

omeuraiseu	오므라이스	omelette filled with rice
pajeon	파전	green-onion pancake
sujebi	수제비	dough flakes in shellfish broth
sundae	순대	blood sausage
sundubu	순두부	uncurdled tofu
twigim	튀김	seafood or vegetables fried in batter

Nonalcoholic Drinks

boricha	보리차	barley tea
cha	차	tea
daechucha	대추차	red-date tea
hongcha	홍차	black tea
juseu	주스	juice
keopi	커피	coffee
mukapein keopi	디카페인커피	decaffeinated coffee
mul	물	water
nokcha	녹차	green tea
omijacha	오미자차	five-flavour berry tea
saengsu	생수	mineral spring water
seoltang neo-eoseo/ ppaego	설탕널어서/빼고	with/without sugar
sikhye	식혜	rice punch
sujeonggwa	수정과	cinnamon and ginger punch
uyu	우유	milk
uyu neo-eoseo/ppaego	우유널어서/빼고	with/without milk
yujacha	유자차	citron tea

Alcoholic Drinks

bokbunjaju	복분자주	wild-berry liquor
dongdongju/makgeolli	동동주/막걸리	fermented rice wine
maekju	맥주	beer
maesilju	매실주	green-plum liquor
soju	소주	local vodka

Arts & Architecture

Historically, Korea was a land of scholar artists, meditative monks and whirling shamans, all of whom have left a mark on the country's artistic traditions. See it in the elegant brush strokes of a calligraphic scroll, the serene expression on a Buddhist statue or in an impassioned folk dance. Contemporary Korea, meanwhile, punches above its weight in cinema and pop culture, and is rediscovering its artistic heritage, too. Its built space includes monumental palaces, charming early-20th-century *hanok* (traditional wooden homes) and dramatic structures of glass and steel.

The Arts

Traditional Visual Arts

Traditional visual arts in Korea were heavily influenced first by China and Buddhism and then, in the Joseon period, by neo-Confucian ideals. Typical styles include landscape and ink-brush painting, religious statuary, calligraphy, ceramics and ornate metal craft (such as incense burners). In painting, particular attention is paid to the brush stroke, which varies in thickness and tone. The painting is meant to surround the viewer and there is no fixed viewpoint. The National Museum of Korea in Seoul has the best collection of traditional art. Cast-iron Buddhist statues and murals depicting scenes from Buddha's life can be found in temples and museums around the country.

Of all the traditional arts, Korea is especially known for its ceramics. Originally using techniques brought over from China, Korean pottery came into its own in the 12th century with the production of Goryeo celadon. The beautiful, jade-coloured works were highly prized in trade on the Silk Road, and today earn thousands of dollars at auction. Another noteworthy style is *buncheong* (less-refined pottery than celadon), which came into vogue in the early years of the Joseon dynasty. In bold shapes, dipped in white glaze and decorated with sgraffito and incising, *buncheong* ware has a vibrant, earthy quality and still looks modern today.

The Leeum Samsung Museum of Art in Seoul has an outstanding and informative display of traditional ceramics. You can also go right to the source, to the ancient celadon kilns in Gangjin, now home to the Gangjin Celadon Museum.

Modern & Contemporary Visual Art

The most important movement of the modern era was the *dansaekhwa* (monochrome paintings) of the 1970s. Though similar in many ways to abstract expressionism, *dansaekhwa* is noted for its tactile nature and use of traditional Korean materials, such as *hanji* (mulberry paper). There's been a recent resurgence of interest in the movement, with exhibitions featuring key artists such as Chung Sang-hwa, Yun Hyong-keun, Ha Chong-hyun and Lee Ufan popping up in New York, Los Angeles and cities across Asia.

However, the most famous Korean artist is, hands down, Nam June Paik (1932–2006; www.paikstudios.com). Paik, who eventually settled in

Traditional folk art includes *jangseung* (wooden shamanist guardian posts) and the *dolharubang* (grandfather stones) of Jeju-do.

Korea is the first known country to develop metal type printing. The oldest existing artefact is the *Jikji* (1377), but records indicate that printing began at least a century earlier. Learn all about it at the Early Printing Museum in Cheongju.

K-DRAMA, K-POP & THE NEW KOREAN WAVE

Psy – the rapper whose *Gangnam Style* music video was a YouTube sensation in 2012 – may have been the first emissary of Korean pop culture to become a universal household name; however, Korean stars have been making waves around Asia since the early 2000s.

It started with the soap opera *Winter Sonata* (2002), whose star Bae Yong-joon made Japanese housewives swoon when the show later aired in Japan. More recently, the drama *My Love from a Star* (2013–14), about the budding romance of an alien stranded on Earth and an ice-queen actress, became a sensation in China, notably bumping up sales of fried chicken (the main character's favourite snack); an American remake is in the works.

Currently, the most popular show is *Running Man* (official YouTube channel: www.youtube.com/user/newsundaysbs), a variety show that sends cast members on various missions around Korea and – due to the show's growing international following – around Asia.

K-Pop, too, with its catchy blend of pop R&B, hip hop and EDM – complete with synchronized dance moves – shows no sign of fading away. As soon as critics declare it over, new groups emerge to capture hearts (and endorsements) around Asia. Top groups of the moment include the eight-member Girls' Generation and boy-band Big Bang.

But it's not just about covetable hairstyles and infectious tunes: In 2013, the Korean culture export industry was worth US$5 billion; it plans to double that by 2017. The government has invested heavily in the content industry, and it is paying dividends in terms of gross national cool. Film sites have been known to become overnight hotspots – a huge boon for the tourist industry. Meanwhile, popular tabloid websites such as Soompi (www.soompi.com) cover the behind-the-scenes gossip in English, French and Spanish – showing just how far the appeal goes.

---

the US, is considered the founder of video art, though he was essentially a multimedia artist. He used sound, circuits and performance to make insightful and playful cultural critiques. One of his larger creations, *The More the Better*, is an 18m tower with 1000 monitors on display at the National Museum of Contemporary Art inside Seoul Grand Park.

While Seoul is still far and away the centre of the arts scene, Gwangju, home to the Gwangju Biennale and the new Asian Culture Centre (2015), is a burgeoning hub. Meanwhile, the 2014 opening of the Arario Museum earned Jeju-si a star on the country's art map.

Performing Arts

Pansori is an impassioned, operatic form of storytelling that's been around for centuries (and was named a Masterpiece of Intangible Heritage by Unesco in 2013). It's usually performed solo by a woman, who flicks her fan at dramatic moments, singing to the beat of a male drummer. *Changgeuk* is an opera performed by a larger cast.

Samulnori is a lively folk style combining music and dance, originally played by travelling entertainers. It died out during Japanese colonial rule but was reinvented in the 1970s to mean musicians playing four traditional percussion instruments. *Samulnori* troops sometimes play overseas and the style has influenced contemporary productions such as the incredibly popular show *Nanta*. Other forms of folk performance include *talchum* (mask dance) and solo, improvisational *salpuri* (shamanist dance).

Music

Gugak (traditional music) is played on stringed instruments, such as the *gayageum* (12-stringed zither) and *haegeum* (two-stringed fiddle), and

---

K-Indie is the artist-driven alternative to K-Pop. Hunt for new underground bands at Korean Indie (www.koreanindie.com) and their shows at Korea Gig Guide (www.koreagigguide.com). Don't miss the July music festivals Pentaport Rock Festival MUSIC (www.pentaportrock.com) – Korea's answer to Glastonbury – and Ansan Valley Rock Festival (www.valleyrockfestival.com).

on chimes, gongs, cymbals, drums, horns and flutes. Notable forms of traditional music include: *jeongak*, a slow court music often combined with elegant dances; *bulgyo eumak* (Buddhist music) played and chanted in Buddhist temples; and *arirang*, folk songs.

Recently, the younger generation of Koreans raised on pop music are rediscovering *gugak*. Bands such as Jambinai, a post-rock group made up of musicians classically trained on traditional instruments, are a hit on the festival circuit. Another noteworthy indie band that draws on traditional music – this time folk music – is Danpyunsun and the Sailors.

Cinema

Korean cinema's first big moment came in the late 1950s and early '60s, after the war and before government censorship made free expression near impossible. The most renowned director of this period is Kim Ki-young (1919–98), the auteur behind *The Housemaid* (1961), a chilling tale of a seductive maid who terrorises a bourgeois family.

However, no director did more to put Korean cinema on the map than Im Kwon-taek (1936–). The prolific filmmaker (102 titles and counting) won best director at Cannes in 2002 for *Chihwaseon* – about influential 19th-century painter Jang Seung-up – and was awarded an honorary Golden Bear at the Berlin Film Festival in 2005. He is also considered to have helped pave the way for the art-house movement that took off in the mid-1990s and has been going on ever since.

Today, Korean cinema is embraced by both local audiences (thanks partly to government quotas that mandate a certain amount of screen time for domestic films) and the international festival circuit. Some films worth watching include: the jaw-dropping action-revenge flick *Oldboy* (Park Chan-Wook; 2003); the critically acclaimed monster epic *The Host* (Bong Joon-ho; 2006); the controversial, and hypersexual, *Pieta* (Kim Ki-duk; 2012), a Golden Lion winner at Venice; and anything by low-budget, shoe-gazer Hong Sang-soo – his latest, *Our Sunhi* (2013) has won a handful of awards.

Literature

The watershed moment for Korean literature occurred with the introduction of the *hangeul* writing system in the 15th century, which exponentially increased who could create and consume literature. Previously, all texts were penned in classical Chinese (which continued to be used by the predominantly male elite until the Japanese occupation). Newly

Korean films are occasionally shown with English subtitles in cinemas, but the best way to see them is on DVD at one of Korea's numerous DVD-*bang*. For must-sees past and present check out www.koreanfilm.org.

DAWON: CONTEMPORARY PERFORMING ARTS

Seunghyo Lee, curator of the annual Festival Bo:m (www.festivalbom.org) in Seoul spoke to us about *dawon* – literally 'miscellaneous arts'. This latest movement in the Korean performing-arts scene includes genre-bending, often participatory works that take place in unconventional venues.

What is dawon? It's art that's not characterised. It has no specific form or context. Say someone wants to do something crazy: it's not theatre, it's not dance, so there's a problem of funding. *Dawon* was created by the Arts Council in 2005 as a framework for art that didn't fit into an existing context. But *dawon* is different from subculture. It's something that very established artists are participating in.

Where can you find it? Good question! In the 1990s, Hongdae was one of the main spots for creators and artists. But it started getting more and more commercial so people started leaving, and now the scene is very fragmented. B:om is a platform for bringing people together. Indie Art Hall Gong is also a good place to visit. Even if no event is happening, people can visit and have a chat.

ARTS & ARCHITECTURE ARCHITECTURE

in translation, the 18th century *Memoirs of Lady Hyegyong*, penned by the lady herself, provides a fascinating inside look at the downfall of her famous husband, Prince Sado.

The modern period brought an increased proliferation of voices, including the experimental (read: Yi Sang's *Wings*; 1936). It also brought a crisis of language: the Japanese occupation mandated that Japanese be taught in schools. Consequently the generation of writers born after WWII are known as the *hangeul* generation, meaning they were raised neither on classical Chinese nor Japanese but rather in their own native tongue. Important authors include Cho Se-hui, whose novel *The Dwarf* (1978) recounts the daunting social costs of rapid industrialisation on the working poor during the 1970s, and Choe In-ho, whose award-winning *Deep Blue Night* (1982) tells the story of two wayward Koreans tearing through California. Kim Young-ha, author of the existentialist, urbane *I Have the Right to Destroy Myself* (1996) is considered one of the leading voices among contemporary writers. His works are just now coming out in translation.

More and more women are breaking into the literary world long dominated by men and, with translation, onto the international stage. Works to read include: Park Wan-suh's plain-talking, semiautobiographical portrait of a family torn by the Korean War, *Who Ate up All the Shinga* (1992) and Shin Kyung-sook's melancholy meditation on modern families, *Please Look After Mom* (2011).

Architecture
Temples & Palaces

Traditional Korean buildings are made from stone and wood, with construction techniques originally imported from China, and emphasise a harmony with the natural environment. Sturdy wooden beams – set on a stone foundation and often joined with notches instead of nails – support heavy, sloping roofs. Location is determined by principles of Chinese geomancy (feng shui). Korea's best known architectural innovation is the *ondol*, the radiant floor-heating system that makes use of flues under the floor. Archaeological records show that this ingenious invention is likely a thousand years old, and originated in the harsh climes of what is now North Korea.

During the Joseon period, palace design became increasingly influenced by neo-Confucian principles of geometry and restraint. Meanwhile, Buddhist temples, whose reconstruction was often sponsored by merchants, reflected the tastes of this increasingly wealthy demographic. Lavish decoration, such as colourful painted ceilings and intricate latticework, became popular.

Centuries of war and invasion mean that Korea has few truly old structures, though reconstructed temples and palaces are often faithful replicas (Joseon dynasty civil servants were meticulous record keepers).

MURAL VILLAGES

Daldongne (moon village) is the euphemistic term for the shanty towns that appeared on urban hillsides during the postwar reconstruction years – built by those who had been left out of reconstruction. Considered eyesores by some, memories of humbler times by others, many *daldongne* were slated for demolition. However, a decade ago, local municipalities, residents and artists hit upon an idea: decorating the villages with murals. Today there are around a dozen 'mural villages' scattered around Korea and they've become big tourist draws. Look for them in Seoul (Ihwa-dong), Suwon, Tongyeong and Jeonju. Many artists have since settled in the neighbourhoods, bringing with them galleries and cafes.

HANOK: SAVING KOREA'S TRADITIONAL HOMES

Hanok are traditional one-storey, wooden homes insulated with mud and straw and topped with clay-tiled roofs. Unlike the ostentatious manor homes of Europe, even an aristocrat's lavish *hanok* was designed to blend with nature; they are typically left unpainted, their brown and tan earth tones giving off a warm, intimate feel. All rooms look onto a courtyard (*madang*). Life was lived on the floor and people sat and slept on mats rather than chairs and beds.

Today few people live in *hanok*: '35 years ago there were around 800,000 *hanok* in South Korea, now there are less than 10,000,' says Peter Bartholomew, an American who has lived in Korea since 1968 and is one of the most outspoken proponents of greater preservation measures for *hanok*.

The Japanese colonisation destroyed Korea's monumental architecture – its palaces and fortresses – explains Bartholomew, but it was modern development that doomed the *hanok*, which were seen as 'old, dirty, rundown buildings'.

Scheming contractors and perhaps well-intended but ultimately ineffective government measures didn't help. In the Bukchon neighbourhood of Seoul, for example, which has been a preservation zone since 1977 (and is the only such zone in the country), only one-third of the *hanok* are original; the rest have been scrapped and rebuilt. (For more about preservation issues in Bukchon, see www.kahoidong.com.)

However it seems that the tides are starting to turn: the last five years have seen a proliferation of guesthouses, restaurants and coffee shops setting up inside former homes. Ahn Young-hwan, owner of Rak-Ko-Jae, a *hanok* guesthouse in Bukchon, was one of the first people to suggest that *hanok* be used in this way. 'People thought I was crazy,' he says, 'but now many more people are doing it'.

For Ahn, *hanok* are the 'vessels that contain Korean culture' and a way of experiencing the joys of an analogue life in an increasingly digital society. Bartholomew believes that the re-evaluation of *hanok* is part of a larger generational shift: 'Young people have no memory of *hanok* and are baffled at the automatic knee-jerk prejudice against them.'

ARTS & ARCHITECTURE ARCHITECTURE

Meanwhile, the oldest structures you'll likely come across are granite pagoda in temple courtyards, some of which date to the Shilla period.

Postwar & Contemporary Architecture

The Korean War reduced the peninsula to the worst kind of blank slate, and hurried reconstruction resulted largely in a landscape of drab concrete towers. There are some notable exceptions: the most prominent architect of the reconstruction era was Kim Swoo-geun (1931–86), who along with his contemporary, Kim Joong-eop (1922–88), laid the foundation for a modern Korean aesthetic. Among Kim Swoo-geun's most notable structures is the Seoul Olympic Stadium, with curves said to be inspired by traditional pottery.

As Korea becomes richer, design is becoming more and more prominent, especially in cities such as Seoul and Busan. Spurred on by its winning bid to be the World Design Capital in 2010, Seoul went on a construction spree, hiring world-renowned architects such as Zaha Hadid for the Dongdaemun Design Park (2013). Of Korea's contemporary homegrown architects, Seung H-Sang is the biggest name; a protege of Kim Swoo-geun, Seung was named Seoul's official architect in 2014. He also worked on Paju Book City in Gyeonggi-do.

Since its launch in 1996, the Busan International Film Festival (BIFF; www.biff.kr) has grown to become the most respected festival in Asia.

The Natural Environment

At 96,920 sq km, South Korea is a similar size to Portugal. Bordered only by North Korea, the country has 2413km of coastline along three seas – the West Sea (also known as the Yellow Sea), the East Sea (Sea of Japan) and the South Sea (East China Sea). Its overall length from north to south (including Jeju-do) is 500km, while the narrowest point is 220km wide.

Birds Korea (www.birdskorea. org) is a conservation NGO with an online bird-ID guide.

The largest of some 3400 islands is 1847-sq-metre Jeju-do, a volcanic landmass with spectacular craters and lava tubes. Off the east coast is Ulleungdo, another scenic volcanic island. Korea is not in an earthquake zone, but there are dozens of mineral-laden *oncheon* (hot springs) that bubble up through the ground, some of which have been developed into health spas.

Forested mountains cover 70% of the land, although they are not very high – Halla-san (1950m) on Jeju-do is the highest peak. Many mountains are granite with dramatic cliffs and pinnacles, but there are also impressive limestone caves to visit. The 521km Nakdong-gang and 514km Han River are the country's longest. They, like most other larger rivers, have been dammed, creating scenic artificial lakes.

The plains and shallow valleys are still dominated by irrigated rice fields that are interspersed with small orchards, greenhouses growing vegetables, and barns housing cows, pigs and chickens. In the south are green-tea plantations and on Jeju-do citrus fruit is grown.

The hundreds of sparsely populated islands scattered off the western and southern coasts of the peninsula have relaxed atmospheres; a few have attractive sandy beaches. Here you can go way off the beaten track to islands where the inhabitants have never seen a foreigner.

Animals

Korea's largest environmental NGO is Korea Federation for Environmental Movements (KFEM; www. kfem.or.kr), which has around 80,000 members and 31 branch offices across the country.

Korea's forested mountains used to be crowded with Siberian tigers, Amur leopards, bears, deer, goral antelopes, grey wolves and red foxes. Unfortunately these wild animals are now extinct or extremely rare in Korea.

Small efforts are being made to build up the number of wild animals in the country – goral antelopes have been released into Woraksan National Park and there's an ongoing project to protect the tiny population of Asiatic black bears (known in Korea as moon bears) in Jirisan National Park. In Seoul, small populations of roe deer and elk live on Bukak-san and in Seoul Forest Park.

Jindo is home to a special breed of Korean hunting dog, Jindogae. Brave, intelligent, loyal and cute as any canine on the planet, the breed can be a challenge to train and control, but they possess an uncanny sense of direction – one dog was taken to Daejeon but somehow made its way back to the island, a journey of hundreds of kilometres. Being hunting dogs, they are an active, outdoor breed that is not suited to an urban environment. Any other breed of dog found on Jindo is immediately deported to the mainland in order to maintain the breed's purity.

Magpies, pigeons and sparrows account for most of the birds in towns and cities, but egrets, herons and swallows are common in the countryside, and raptors, woodpeckers and pheasants can also be seen. Although many are visiting migrants, more than 500 bird species have been sighted, and Korea has a growing reputation among birdwatchers keen to see Steller's sea eagles, red-crowned cranes, black-faced spoonbills and other rarities.

Plants

Northern parts of South Korea are the coldest and the flora is alpine: beech, birch, fir, larch and pine. Further south, deciduous trees are more common. The south coast and Jeju-do are the warmest and wettest areas, so the vegetation is lush. Cherry trees blossom in early spring followed by azaleas and camellias.

Korea's mountainsides are a pharmacy and salad bar of health-giving edible leaves, ferns, roots, nuts and fungi. Many of these wild mountain vegetables end up in restaurant side dishes and *sanchae* bibimbap (a meal of rice, egg, meat and mountain vegetables). Wild ginseng is the most expensive and sought-after plant.

Jeju-do World Heritage Sites

Hallasan National Park

Seongsan Ilchul-bong

Geomunoreum Lava Tube System

National & Provincial Parks

With an abundance of river valleys, waterfalls and rocky outcrops, plus brightly painted wooden Buddhist temples and hermitages gracing many mountains, it's not surprising that many visitors rate Korea's national and provincial parks as its top attractions.

Since the first national park, Jirisan, was established in 1967 it has been joined by 19 others covering 3.7% of the country. For more details see Korea National Parks (http://english.knps.or.kr). There are also 22 smaller provincial parks (covering 747 sq km) and 29 county parks (covering 307 sq km). All the parks have well-marked hiking trails; some

JEJU'S ENVIRONMENTAL INITIATIVES

It's no accident that Jeju was chosen to host the World Conservation Congress in September 2012, a 10-day symposium where experts exchanged ideas for tackling pressing environmental issues including climate change, biodiversity and green growth. South Korea's largest island, recognised by Unesco for its extraordinary ecosystem and natural features, is pushing ahead with various schemes in its aim to be crowned, in the words of Korea's environment minister Yoo Young-sook, as the 'environment capital of the world'.

A trust has been set up to protect gotjawal (forests on rocky terrain), which cover around 12% of the island. Considered the 'lungs of Jeju' they are not only an essential part of the island's groundwater supply system but also a species-rich biosphere. Three of Jeju's wetland regions are also listed under the Ramsar Convention as being of 'international importance'. In 2015, Jeju's Governor Won Hee-ryong declared that he would push skyrocketing Chinese investment in property development on the island towards renewable energy. You will already find 44% of South Korea's electric cars on Jeju.

Along the northeast coast of Jeju, giant wind farms form part of the island's **Smart Grid Testbed** (www.smartgrid.or.kr) – an attempt to use information technology to transmit power and cut down on CO_2 emissions. The long-term plan is to make Jeju carbon-free and self-sustainable by 2030 through renewable energy resources. Already the island of Gapado off Jeju's southwest coast is carbon-free: its power comes from wind farms and solar panels, its cars have been replaced with electric vehicles and its water comes from a desalination plant.

MOON BEARS: A GLIMMER OF HOPE

According to legend, the Korean nation was born from a bear – one of the reasons why Asiatic black bears (also called moon bears because of the crescent moon of white fur on their chests) are accorded the status of a national treasure and a protected species. However, by the late 20th century the hunting of bears for their meat and use in traditional medicine had contributed to them being thought extinct in the wild in South Korea.

Then in 2001, video footage proved that up to six wild bears were living in a remote part of Jirisan National Park. Soon after, the park established a project with the aim of building up a self-sustaining group of 50 wild bears in Jirisan (as of 2010 it was believed there were 19 bears). However, according to Moonbears.org (http://moonbears.org), one of several Korean groups campaigning for protection of the animal, even these few are threatened by poaching. This is despite the fact that more than 1000 bears are bred on farms across the country for the lucrative bear-meat and gall-bladder trade. The conditions that the bears are kept in are often horrific.

Moonbears.org, Bear Necessity Korea (http://bearnecessitykorea.wordpress.com), Green Korea and other pressure groups have long campaigned for the government to ban such farms. In 2012, the National Assembly voted through a proposal to 'prepare measures to end the practice of bear farming through investigation of the current status of bear farming and its management plan'. A budget of ₩200 million has been set aside for the proposal.

have been so popular that they've had to be closed to protect them from serious erosion.

The parks can be enjoyed in every season. In spring, cherry blossoms, azaleas and other flowers are a delight; in summer, the hillsides and river valleys provide a cool escape from the heat and humidity of the cities; during the summer monsoon, the waterfalls are particularly impressive; in autumn, red leaves and clear blue skies provide a fantastic sight; and in winter, snow and ice turn the parks into a white wonderland, although crampons and proper clothing are needed for any serious hikes. Korean winters can be arctic, especially if you're high up in the mountains.

All the parks have tourist villages near the main entrances with restaurants, market stalls, souvenir and food shops, and budget accommodation where big groups can squeeze into a small room. Camping grounds (₩2000 to ₩3000 per person per day) and mountain shelters (₩5000 to ₩8000 for a bunk) are cheap, and while some have modern facilities, most are very basic.

With an average of five million visitors a year, Bukhansan National Park, located on Seoul's doorstep, has qualified for a Guinness World Record as the national park with the highest number of visitors per sq ft in the world.

Environmental Issues

South Korea's economic growth since 1960 has transformed the country from an agricultural to an industrial society. Sprawling apartment-block cities and huge industrial complexes have been constructed, rivers have been dammed and freeways have been bulldozed through the countryside. Authoritarian governments stamped on any opposition to development projects, and the environmental effects of the projects were ignored.

Fortunately the 70% of Korea that is mountainous and forested is still largely undeveloped, and the hundreds of offshore islands are also unspoilt. For a developed country Korea is surprisingly green, as 90% of the population is packed into high-rise city apartments.

Nowadays politics is more democratic, politicians win votes by promising green policies and environmental groups are no longer ignored by the media. Unpopular construction projects can face fierce opposition. Among the country's most contentious environmental flashpoints are land reclamation and what to do with nuclear waste.

A DMZ NATIONAL PARK?

The dearth of human intervention in the Demilitarized Zone (DMZ) for more than 50 years has made it something of an environmental haven. The zone is home to 2716 wild plants and animals, including 67 endangered species such as the Siberian musk deer, the Amur goral (a mountain goat that resembles an antelope), a third of the world's remaining red-crowned cranes and half the remaining white-naped cranes. Environmentalists hope that the day the two Koreas cease hostilities, the DMZ will be preserved as a nature reserve, a plan that has the support of the South Korean government. As a first step towards this goal, trekking and cycling paths are being created within the Civilian Control Zone, a buffer zone that runs along the southern border of the DMZ.

Nuclear Power & Waste Disposal

South Korea faces a green-energy dilemma. Even if each of the country's marine and national parks were converted to wind farms, all the wetlands were used for hydropower, and every one of its buildings was plastered in solar panels, the electricity pumped out from these 'green' sources would still only supply about 30% of the electricity that was consumed in 2010.

For now South Korea relies on 23 nuclear-power plants concentrated in four locations (Gori, Ulchin, Wolseong, Yonggwang) to generate around 40% of its electricity – this compares to a 15.7% average worldwide. As part of its 'low-carbon, green-growth' strategy there are plans to add up to 13 more nuclear facilities by 2029 to boost the level of electricity generation.

Field Guide to the Birds of Korea by Lee, Koo & Park (2000) is the standard bird guide, but doesn't include all feathered visitors.

However, Korea's nuclear-power industry has long struggled to find a permanent storage site for the radioactive waste that it produces. In November 2005 Gyeongju was chosen as the site of the country's first permanent dump for low- and middle-grade nuclear waste. Despite protests and claims of the site's geological instability, the site became fully functional from January 2013, sweetened by the annual ₩300 billion (US$323 million) in economic subsidies that the central government had promised the region. With Gyeongju, South Korea bought itself some time, as without the new facility, by 2025 the storage sites at each of the plants would have reached full capacity.

Frighteningly, the operator of the country's plants, Korea Hydro & Nuclear Power, claimed in March 2015 that North Korea had hacked their computer system in an attempt to gain remote control. They were unsuccessful, with only partial blueprints of power plants leaked to the public, but it did open up a dark possibility.

Land Reclamation

Reclaiming the mud flats off Korea's west coast for farming and construction has become a highly emotive and divisive issue. According to Korean Federation for Environmental Movements (KFEM), since 1990 more than 140,000 hectares of coastal wetlands have been reclaimed or are in the process of being reclaimed.

Beautiful Wildflowers in Korea (2002), published by the Korea Plant Conservation Society, has photos of 200 native flowers and will encourage you to stop and ID flowers on your travels.

The environmental impact that such projects can have is seen at Saemangeum in Jeollabuk-do where in 2006 a 33km sea wall was built to reclaim 40,000 hectares of mud flats. Opponents, who battled hard against the project during its construction, stressed the importance of the mud flats as a fish and shellfish breeding area and as a vital feeding ground for more than 100,000 migrant birds, including black-faced spoonbills and 12 other threatened species.

In response to the Saemangeum protests, the government declared 60 sq km of wetlands at the Han River estuary in Gyeonggi-do a protected area. Ten smaller wetland areas (covering a total of 45 sq km) had already been protected. The Ministry of Environment has since increased the number of protected wetlands, and with the addition of Sumeunmulbaengdui on Jeju-do and the Hanbando Wetland in Gangwon-do in May 2015, Korea's list of Ramsar Wetlands stands at 21. In one of these wetlands, Suncheon-man – the winter nesting ground of five endangered species of crane – the cancellation of a land-reclamation project in favour of the area's promotion as an ecotourism destination is a positive sign for the future.

Caves by Kyung Sik Woo (2005) is a lavishly illustrated book on Korean caves by a geological expert and cave enthusiast.

Green Korea?

In June 2015 South Korea announced it would aim to cut greenhouse gas emissions by 37% by 2030. This was another step in the strategy mapped out in 2008 to create jobs using green technology and clean energy. The government reached a milestone in 2012 by completing the 'Four Rivers Project', which saw the cleanup of four major rivers (the Han, Nakdong, Geum and Yeongsan) and their surroundings to reduce flooding by building water-treatment facilities, banks and 20 new dams. It also included a 1757km bicycle route running alongside the four rivers. The project was such a success that both Turkey and Paraguay looked to it as a model for cleaning their own waterways.

Among the other 'ecofriendly' success stories on the government's green agenda was the construction of a 20-mile solar-panel-covered bicycle lane between Daejeon and Sejong, south of Seoul; and converting all of Seoul's 8750-plus buses to low-polluting natural-gas, full-hybrid or fuel-cell electric vehicles by 2014.

Ongoing work includes more high-speed railway lines; the provision of energy-saving 'green homes' and energy-recycling projects including the production of gas from garbage.

Many of these policies were given the thumbs up from the UN Environment Program, but local environmental groups felt the Four Rivers Project opened the door to reviving a plan for a grand canal between Seoul and Busan.

Green Korea (www.greenkorea. org) is a pressure group with practical ideas such as Buy Nothing Day, Car Free Day (22 September in Seoul) and Save Paper Day.

Despite commitments to preserve wetland and coastal areas, Seoul is also pushing ahead to build two more tidal-power plants along the west coast, in addition to the two already in operation there – Uldolmok in Jeollanam-do and Sihwa Lake in Gyeonggi-do, which is the largest in the world.

Cutting greenhouse gases may come at the expense of other aspects of Korea's natural environment.

What Can You Do?

Travellers can do their bit for Korea's environment by keeping in mind the following:

➡ Use the country's excellent public transport system or rent a bicycle.

➡ Place your rubbish in the appropriate recycling bins for paper, cans and plastic.

➡ Refuse unnecessary packaging in shops – carry your own shopping bag.

➡ Patronise organic and vegetarian restaurants and businesses that have a seal of approval from **LOHAS** (Lifestyles of Health & Sustainability; http://korealohas .or.kr).

Survival Guide

Directory A–Z

Accommodation

In general you don't need to worry about where to stay in Korea – motels are so numerous that there is usually no need to book ahead. Outside the big cities and towns – where you'll find regular hotels and hostels – the most common type of accommodation will be *minbak* – private homes with rooms for rent.

Accommodation is normally charged per room, so solo travellers receive little or no discount. Still, it's always worth asking. If you're staying a few days or if it's low season (outside July and August on the coast or outside July, August, October and November in national parks), you can always try for discounts. Some hostels and *hanok* (traditional wooden home) guesthouses include a simple breakfast in their rates; most hotels don't.

Budget and midrange places usually include VAT of 10% in their rates. All top-end hotels will slap a service charge of 10% on the bill as well as VAT (so a total of 21%

over the quoted rate); rates usually include all taxes.

Watch for internet-access charges. This can be as much as ₩35,000 a day. Check whether there's free wi-fi access in the hotel lobby first.

Only staff in Seoul guesthouses and upper-midrange and top-end hotels are likely to speak any English. An extra bed or *yo* (mattress or futon on the floor) is usually available. Check-out time is generally noon. Prices can rise on Friday and Saturday and at peak times (July and August near beaches or national parks, and October and November near national parks).

Although some places offer use of a washing machine (and sometimes a dryer), laundry can be a problem – outside Seoul you may find yourself having to wash your clothes in the bathroom and hanging them up in your room to dry, or laying them on the *ondol*-heated floor.

Backpacker Guesthouses & Hostels

The backpacker scene is well established in Seoul, and is starting to become popular

elsewhere in Korea. When you find them, these internationally minded hostels are ideal for budget-oriented tourists, and have staff who are friendly and speak English. Hostels offer dormitories (from ₩15,000 per night) and double rooms (from ₩40,000), some of which have private bathrooms. Communal facilities include toilets, showers, satellite TV, a kitchen and washing machine. Free internet and breakfast is typically provided.

Camping & Mountain & Forest Huts

Camping at beaches and in or near some national and provincial parks is possible. The cost is ₩2000 to ₩3000 per person per night but facilities are very basic and they are usually only open in July and August.

Only a few major hikes in Seoraksan and Jirisan National Parks require an overnight stay in a mountain hut or shelter. Huts and camping grounds can be fully booked at weekends and during high season. For more information see http://english.knps.or.kr.

Hanok Guesthouses

Traditional *hanok* are increasingly being turned into guesthouses. Staying in one of these is a unique and memorable experience. Rooms are small and you'll sleep on *yo* (padded quilts and mattresses) on the floor, but underfloor heating

FINDING AN ADDRESS

Under an old system of addresses, big cities such as Seoul were divided into districts (*gu*, eg Jongno-gu) with these districts further divided into subdistricts (*dong*, eg Insa-dong). Buildings were then numbered according to their chronology within the subdistrict. It was pretty confusing, so Korea has decided to move over to a new address system of logically numbered buildings on named streets (*gil*).

However, until the end of 2013 the old address system existed alongside the new one and you will still find that giving a description to a local works better than a new address.

If you have the correct full address (either system), or the telephone number, these can be used by satellite navigation in taxi or on phones to find your location. For more information on the address changeover including an address converter, see www.juso.go.kr/openengpage.do. There is also a free app (search for Juso or 주소 찾아, Korean only).

systems (*ondol*) keep them snug in winter. At the cheaper *hanok* you'll be sharing the bathroom, but many guesthouses do offer en-suite rooms. Rates often include breakfast, and traditional cultural experiences may be offered too.

For more about *hanok* guesthouses across Korea see the KTO site **Hanokstay** (www.hanokstay.or.kr). **Jongno-gu** (http://homestay.jongno.go.kr) in Seoul also runs a *hanok* homestay program.

Homestays

These are the best way to experience Korean food, customs and family life at close quarters. Most Korean families sign up to such schemes to meet and make friends with foreigners and to practise their English. Some families offer pick-ups and dinner, and rates are greatly reduced if you stay longterm. The charge for bed and breakfast per night can be as low as ₩30,000 per person.

BnB Hero (www.bnbhero.com)

Go Homestay (www.go-homestay.com)

Homestay Korea (www.homestaykorea.com)

Koreastay (www.koreastay.or.kr)

Lex (www.lex.or.kr)

Hotels

Luxury hotels are relatively scarce outside major cities and Jeju-do. The lobbies,

fitness centres, restaurants and other services are often their strong points – when it comes to room design and facilities, motels tend to offer a better deal. We list rack rates (including service and taxes), but discounts or packages are nearly always available.

Minbak & Pension

Most *minbak* provide simple accommodation (and usually meals) on islands, near ski resorts, in rural areas and near beaches and national parks. Expect to pay ₩40,000 for a room but double that in peak seasons. You sleep on a *yo* on an *ondol*-heated floor, usually with a TV and a heater or fan in the room. Facilities may not include private bathrooms. Lots of people can squeeze into one room – an extra person usually costs ₩10,000. More upmarket *minbak* cost ₩50,000 or more and provide smart, stylish rooms with beds and kitchenettes.

Pension are more luxurious than most *minbak* and cost from ₩50,000 upwards with spacious rooms,

often with stylish furniture, balconies and kitchens.

Motels & Love Motels

Motels and love motels are by far the most common form of accommodation across Korea. The rooms are always on the small size but they are packed with facilities – private bathroom, TV, DVD, phone, fridge, drinking water, air-con and heating, toiletries and even computers. However, staff rarely speak English and motels lack communal areas beyond the lobby, which is not designed for lingering.

Love motels cater for couples seeking some by-the-hour privacy, but they also accept conventional overnight guests. They're usually easy to spot by the plastic curtains shielding the parked cars from prying eyes. If you can cope with the clandestine trappings (and possibly intrusive noise from neighbouring rooms), they can be an excellent option; some of the extravagantly decorated rooms are a bargain compared with what

ACCOMMODATION PRICE RANGES

The following price ranges refer to a double room with private bathroom.

PRICE INDICATOR	SEOUL	KOREA
$	up to ₩60,000	up to ₩40,000
$$	₩60,000-250,000	₩40,000-150,000
$$$	over ₩250,000	over ₩150,000

ACCOMMODATION BOOKING SITES

Apart from booking directly with hotel websites, you can also book rooms via the following:

Benikea (www.benikea.com)

Korean Hotel Reservation Center (www.khrc.com)

Lonely Planet (hotels.lonelyplanet.com)

you'd pay for similar facilities at a top-end hotel. Some love motels, however, require a late check-in, around 9pm; earlier check-ins cost more.

Rental Accommodation

Renting an apartment can be tricky because of the traditional payment system, which involves paying a huge deposit to the landlord and/or having to pay all your rent up front. Browse Seoul websites www.nicerent.com or www.nearsubway.com for what's on offer. Real estate is measured in *pyeong* (one *pyeong* is 3.3 sq metres). Backpacker guesthouses and motels sometimes offer reduced rates for long-term tenants. Go to www.korea4expats.com for useful information on this topic under the 'Moving To Korea' section.

Sauna Dormitories

Saunas and *jjimjilbang* (luxury saunas) usually have a dormitory or napping room. They are not really meant for overnight sleepovers, but they can be used for that purpose. Pay the entry fee (usually under ₩10,000), use the facilities and then head for the dormitory. Don't expect much in the way of bedding, and the pillow may be a block of wood. Be sure that your belongings and locker key are secure while you sleep, as thefts can occur.

Serviced Apartments

Seoul has several serviced-apartment complexes, which can be a good alternative to hotels and the hassle of finding and renting an apartment. They're known locally as residences or suites; prices start at ₩90,000 a day for a studio apartment, with big discounts for month-long stays.

Templestays

Around 100 temples across the country provide overnight accommodation in the form of a **Templestay program** (☏054 429 1716; http://eng.templestay.com; per night ₩50,000-70,000), most charging ₩50,000 to ₩70,000 per night including all meals. No attempt will be made to try to convert you to Buddhism and they provide a chance not only to experience the life of a monk but also to stay in some incredibly beautiful places. This is an increasingly popular choice of accommodation, with more temples geared towards accepting foreigners, while others will also happily let you stay if you bring along a Korean to help translate.

Yeogwan

'Adequate but shabby' sums up most *yeogwan* (small, family-run hotels), which provide old-fashioned budget rooms, but are only ₩5000 to ₩10,000 cheaper than much better modern motels. Quilts are usually aired rather than washed so you may want to bring sheets with you.

Youth Hostels

Hostelling International Korea (www.kyha.or.kr) runs 70 large modern youth hostels around the country. The dormitories offer a good deal for solo travellers on a budget, at around ₩20,000 a night. Private and family rooms cost as much as motel rooms and are unlikely to be as good. They also can be rather institutional and inconveniently located, and are sometimes full of noisy children on a school trip. Sort out a YHA card in your home country as you need to have been a resident in South Korea for more than a year before you can apply for a local card (annual membership ₩33,000).

Children

Koreans adore children and make them the centre of attention, so travelling with your offspring here is highly recommended. Expect the locals to be particularly helpful and intrigued. Check out www.travelwithyourkids.com for general advice and a first-hand report on Seoul for kids, which gives the city a thumbs up.

Only luxury hotels are likely to be able to organise a cot, but you could always ask for a *yo*. Few restaurants have high chairs. Nappy-changing facilities are more common in Seoul toilets than in the provinces. Baby-sitting services are almost nonexistent.

Zoos, funfairs and parks can be found in most cities along with cinemas, DVD rooms, internet rooms, video-game arcades, ten-pin bowling alleys, *norae-bang* (karaoke rooms), pool tables and board-game cafes. Children will rarely be more than 100m away from an ice cream, cake or fast-food outlet. In winter hit the ski slopes, and in summer head for the water parks or beaches. For general advice pick up a copy of Lonely Planet's *Travel with Children*.

Customs Regulations

Visitors must declare all plants, fresh fruit, vegetables and dairy products that they bring into South Korea. Meat is not allowed in without a certificate. Go to www.customs.go.kr for further information. Antiques

of national importance are not allowed to be exported.

Electricity

South Korea is on the 220V standard at 60Hz and uses the same shape (but not necessarily voltage) as many European, South American and Asian countries.

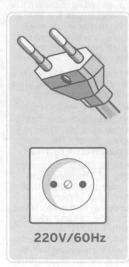

220V/60Hz

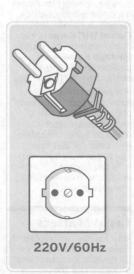

220V/60Hz

Embassies

Most embassies are located in Seoul.

Australian Embassy (Map p58; ☑02 2003 0100; www. southkorea.embassy.gov.au; 19th fl, Kyobo Bldg, 1 Jong-ro, Jongno-gu; ⓢLine 5 to Gwanghwamun, Exit 4)

Canadian Embassy (Map p46; ☑02 3783 6000; www. canadainternational.gc.ca/korea-coree; 21 Jeong-dong-gil, Jung-gu; ⓢLine 5 to Seodaemun, Exit 5)

Chinese Embassy (Map p46; ☑02 738 1038; www.chinaemb.or.kr; 27 Myeong-dong 2-gil, Jung-gu; ⓢLine 4 to Myeongdong, Exit 5)

French Embassy (Map p46; ☑02 3149 4300; www.ambafrance-kr.org; 43-12 Seosomun-ro, Seodaemun-gu; ⓢLine 2 or 5 to Chungjeongno, Exit 3)

German Embassy (Map p46; ☑02 748 4114; www. seoul.diplo.de; Seoul Sq, 8th fl, 416 Hangang daero, Jung-gu; ⓢLine 1 or 4 to Seoul Station, Exit 8)

Irish Embassy (Map p58; ☑02 721 7200; www.embassyofireland.or.kr; 13th fl, Leema Bldg, 2 Jong-ro 1-gil, Jongno-gu; ⓢLine 5 to Gwanghwamun, Exit 2)

Japanese Embassy (Map p58; ☑02 765 3011; www. kr.emb-japan.go.jp; 64 Yulgok-ro, Jongno-gu; ⓢLine 3 to Anguk, Exit 6)

New Zealand Embassy (Map p58; ☑02 3701 7700; www.nzembassy.com/korea; 15th fl, Kyobo Bldg, Jongno 1-ga, Jongno-gu; ⓢLine 5 to Gwanghwamun, Exit 4)

UK Embassy (Map p46; ☑02 3210 5500; www.gov.uk/government/world/organisations/british-embassy-seoul; 24 Sejong-daero 19-gil, Jung-gu; ⓢLine 1 or 2 to City Hall, Exit 3)

US Embassy (Map p58; ☑02 397 4114; seoul.usembassy.gov; 188 Sejong-daero, Jongno-gu; ⓢLine 5 to Gwanghwamun, Exit 2)

Emergency

If no English-speaking staff are available, ring the 24-hour tourist information and help line on ☑1330.

Ambulance (☑119)

Fire Brigade (☑119)

Police (Map p58; ☑112)

Food

In this guide, restaurant listings are by author preference and are accompanied by the symbols ₩ (budget), ₩₩ (midrange) or ₩₩₩ (top end).

For more about eating and drinking, see p367.

Gay & Lesbian Travellers

Korea has never passed any laws that mention homosexuality, but this shouldn't be taken as a sign of tolerance or acceptance. Attempts to include sexual orientation in antidiscrimination laws by the Democratic Party in 2013 were shot down by conservative religious groups. Some older Koreans insist that there are no queer people in Korea – even though there are at least several very high profile ones such as the TV personality and Seoul restaurateur Hong Seok-chun and transgender celebrity Ha Ri-su.

Attitudes are changing, especially among young people, but virtually all local gays and lesbians choose to stay firmly in the closet. Gay and lesbian travellers who publicise their sexual orientation tend to receive less-than-positive reactions. However, there are openly gay areas of Seoul where few will blink an eye at displays of affection, and other cities have gay bars too. Gays and lesbian locals use the English loan words *gei*

MEDICAL TOURISM

In image-conscious South Korea, medical tourism is a booming industry with annual visitor numbers expected to reach nearly one million by 2020. The focus might be on cosmetic surgery but can include anything from cutting-edge cancer treatments to simple check-ups. Health tourism is heavily promoted by the **Korea Tourism Organization** (www.visitmedicalkorea.com), with specialised information booths (and even festivals) in Seoul, Incheon, Daegu and Busan. Staff keep lists (but not prices) of medical practitioners who speak English, Chinese and other languages and have surgeries that resemble high-end hotel lobbies. Speak with your own doctor and health-insurance company before considering getting anything done; despite the gloss, botched work still happens.

and *lejeubieon* as the other term in Korean, *ivan*, can mean 'second-class citizen'.

Chungusai (Between Friends; ☏02 745 7942; www.chingusai. net) Korean GLBT human-rights group.

iShap (www.ishap.org) Gay HIV/AIDS awareness project; produces a free Korean guidebook to gay bars and clubs – ask for it at bars such as Barcode in Nagwon-dong.

Utopia (www.utopia-asia.com) Check the Korea section for maps and reviews to gay bars, clubs and services.

Health

The quality of medical care in Seoul is high. You need a doctor's prescription to buy most medications and it may be difficult to find the exact medication you use at home, so take extra. A letter from your physician outlining your medical condition and a list of your medications (using generic names) could be useful.

There are no special vaccination requirements for visiting Korea, but you should consider vaccination against hepatitis A and B. Most people don't drink the tap water, but those who do seem to come to no harm and Korea's water ranks higher in purity than that of the USA. Filtered or bottled water is free in most restaurants and machines with free purified hot and cold water are available in most motels and guesthouses.

Insurance

A policy covering theft, loss, medical expenses and compensation for cancellation or delays in your travel arrangements is highly recommended. If items are lost or stolen, make sure you obtain a police report straight away – otherwise your insurer might not pay up. There is a wide variety of policies available, but always check the small print.

Worldwide travel insurance is available at www.lonelyplanet.com/travel_services. You can buy, extend and claim online any time – even if you're already on the road.

Internet Access

With the world's fastest connections and one of the highest rates of internet usage, you'll find abundant free internet access, either via a computer or wi-fi in cafes, public streets, guesthouses, hotels and tourist information centres.

➡ Some motels and nearly all hotels provide computers with broadband access.

➡ Internet rooms (or PC 방) are ubiquitous across the country, mainly serving young gamers. They charge around ₩2000 per hour.

➡ Major phone companies offer USB dongle devices (known as 'pocket wi-fi' or a 'wi-fi egg') to rent, in the same way as mobile phones, to connect all your devices to the internet from your own portable wi-fi hotspot. If you are travelling outside Seoul or major cities, make sure your device plan covers the whole country. Reliable services are available from **Pocket WiFi Korea** (www.pocketwifikorea.com) and **Package Korea** (www.packagekorea.com) and charge from ₩7150 per day.

➡ If you just need internet access on your (unlocked) phone, a Korean SIM geared towards foreigners might be a cheaper option, with plans for 1GB data starting at ₩30,000, widely available from stores aimed at tourists in Itaewon and Hongdae in Seoul.

Legal Matters

Most tourists' legal problems involve visa violations or illegal drugs. In the case of visa transgressions, the penalty is normally a fine and possible expulsion from the country. If

EATING PRICE RANGES

PRICE INDICATOR	SEOUL	KOREA
$	up to ₩10,000	up to ₩7000
$$	₩10,000-25,000	₩7000-18,000
$$$	over ₩25,000	over ₩18,000

caught using or selling narcotics, you'll either be deported or spend a few years researching the living conditions in a South Korean prison.

Money

The South Korean unit of currency is the won (₩), with ₩10, ₩50, ₩100 and ₩500 coins. Notes come in denominations of ₩1000, ₩5000, ₩10,000 and ₩50,000.

See www.xe.com for up-to-date exchange rates.

ATMs

ATMs that accept foreign cards are common. ATMs often operate from 7am to 11pm but some are 24-hour. Restrictions on the amount you can withdraw vary. It can be as low as ₩100,000 per day. Lotte ATMs in 7-Eleven stores allow you to select from international banks for the transaction, including Citibank.

Moneychangers

Many banks offer a foreign-exchange service. In big cities there are also licensed moneychangers, that keep longer hours than the banks and provide a faster service, but may only exchange $US cash.

Credit Cards

Increasingly accepted across the board, but plenty of places, including budget accommodation, stalls and small restaurants, still require cash. Always have handy a stash of ₩10,000 notes in case.

Opening Hours

The following are general business hours:

Banks 9am to 4pm Monday to Friday

Post offices 9am to 6pm Monday to Friday

Shops 10am to 8pm

Cafes 7am to 10pm

Restaurants 11am to 10pm

Bars 6pm to 1am, longer hours Friday and Saturday

Photography & Video

➡ All the major camera and video brands are available including the local ones, such as Samsung. Yongsan Electronics Market and Namdaemun Market in Seoul are the best places to buy the latest camera and video equipment.

➡ Some Koreans are shy, reluctant or even hostile about being photographed, so always ask first.

➡ Never take photographs inside Buddhist shrines or of shamanist ceremonies without asking permission first, and don't expect Seoul's riot police to be too happy to be snapped either. In and around the Demilitarized Zone (DMZ) there are very strict rules about what can and can't be photographed.

For professional hints on how to improve your pictures, purchase *Lonely Planet's Guide to Travel Photography*.

Post

For postal rates see **Korea Post** (www.koreapost.go.kr); post offices are fairly common and have a red/orange sign.

Public Holidays

Eight Korean public holidays are set according to the solar calendar and three according to the lunar calendar, meaning they fall on different days each year. Restaurants, shops and tourist sights stay open during most holidays, but may close over the three-day Lunar New Year and Chuseok (Thanksgiving) holidays. School holidays mean that beaches and resort areas are busy in August.

New Year's Day 1 January

Lunar New Year 8 February 2016, 28 January 2017, 16 February 2018

Independence Movement Day 1 March

Children's Day 5 May

Memorial Day 6 June

Constitution Day 17 July

Liberation Day 15 August

Chuseok 14 September 2016, 3 October 2017, 23 September 2018

National Foundation Day 3 October

Christmas Day 25 December

Telephone

Mobile Phones

➡ Korea uses the WCDMA 2100 mHz network system, which few other countries use (wi-fi will work from your

PRACTICALITIES

→ **Daily newspapers** Korea Herald (www.koreaherald.co.kr), Korea JoongAng Daily (http://joongangdaily.joins.com) and Korea Times (www.koreatimes.co.kr).

→ **Monthly magazines** 10 Magazine (10mag.com), Groove Korea (groovekorea.com) and Seoul (www.seoulselection.com).

→ **TV & Radio** KBS World (http://world.kbs.co.kr) news, features; Arirang (www.arirang.co.kr) English language TV and radio; Radio Gugak (www.gugakfm.co.kr) traditional Korean music; TBS (http://tbsefm.seoul.kr) music and news.

→ **DVD** Region 3; some with English-language option.

→ **Weights & Measures** Uses the metric system, but real estate is often measured in pyeong (3.3 sq metres or almost 6ft x 6ft), and some traditional markets still use wooden measuring boxes.

own phone, regardless of the network or if it is locked). Phone models (unlocked, with a SIM slot) that work include the iPhone 5 and newer, Samsung Galaxy, Google Nexus, Moto G/X. Otherwise you will probably have to rent a mobile (cell) phone while you're in Seoul. The best place to do this is at Incheon International Airport as soon as you arrive, although some top-end hotels will have phones available for guests, and discount electronic stores in Itaewon sell new and used phones.

→ Mobile-phone and sim-card hire is available from four companies, which all have counters on Incheon's arrivals floor:

→ Each company offers similar (but not identical) schemes; you'll pay more for smart-phone rentals.

→ Online discounts can cut daily rental fees.

→ Incoming calls are free and outgoing domestic calls cost around ₩600 a minute, while calls to the US, for example, cost ₩700 a minute and to the UK ₩1050 a minute. Check that prices quoted include the 10% VAT.

→ Korean mobile-phone numbers have three-digit area codes, always beginning with ☑01, eg ☑011 1234 5678.

→ When you call from your mobile phone you always input the area code, even if you're in the city you're trying to call. For example, in Seoul when calling a local Seoul number you would dial ☑02 123 4567.

KT (http://roaming.kt.com)

LG Telecom (www.uplus.co.kr)

SK Telecom (www.sktroaming.com/tworld/gate.html)

S'Roaming (www.sroaming.com)

Phone Codes

→ Korea's nine provinces and seven largest cities have their own area codes.

→ The major cities have their own codes – thus Gwangju City's code (☑062) is one digit different to the surrounding province of Jeollanam-do (☑061).

→ South Korea's country code is ☑82.

→ Do not dial the first zero of the area codes if you are calling from outside Korea.

→ Phone numbers that begin with a four-figure number starting with ☑15 do not have an area code.

→ The international access code is ☑001.

Public Phones & Phonecards

With practically everyone having a mobile phone it's increasingly rare to find public pay phones; the best place to look is subway stations. Ones accepting coins (₩50 or ₩100) are even rarer. Telephone cards usually give you a 10% bonus in value and can be bought at convenience stores. There are two types of cards so if your card does not fit in one type of pay phone, try a different-looking one. The squat pay phones accept the thin cards. A few public phones accept credit cards. Local calls cost ₩70 for three minutes; calls to mobile phones cost ₩70 for 38 seconds.

Time

South Korea is nine hours ahead of GMT/UCT (London) and does not have daylight saving. When it is noon in Seoul it is 7pm the previous day in San Francisco, 10pm the previous day in New York and 1pm the same day in Sydney.

Toilets

Korea has plenty of clean, modern and well-signed *hwajangsil* (public toilets). Virtually all toilets are free, some are decorated with flowers and artwork, and a few even have music. Toilet paper is usually outside the cubicles. As always, it's wise to carry a stash of toilet tissue around with you just in case. Asian-style squat toilets are losing their battle with European-style ones, but there are still a few around. Face the hooded end when you squat.

Tourist Information

In Seoul the excellent **KTO tourist information centre** (Map p46; ☎02 1330; www.visitkorea.or.kr; Cheonggye-cheon-ro, Jung-gu; ⏰9am-8pm; 👪; [S]Line 1 to Jonggak, Exit 5) has stacks of brochures on every region plus helpful and well-informed staff. They can book hotels for you and advise you about almost anything. Chat to them also about the nationwide system of **Goodwill Guides** (http://english.visitkorea.or.kr/enu/index.kto), who are volunteer tour guides.

Many tourist areas have their own tourist information centres, so it's not a problem to locate one.

Travellers with Disabilities

Facilities for travellers with disabilities in Seoul and some other cities are far from perfect but are improving. Most Seoul subway stations have stair lifts, elevators and toilets with wheelchair access and handrails, while buses have ramps to aid wheelchair access. Tourist attractions, especially government-run ones, offer generous discounts or even free entry for people with disabilities and a helper. There are also some hotels with accessible rooms. For more information go to http://english.visitkorea.or.kr/enu/gk/gk_en_2_5_2.jsp.

Before setting off get in touch with your national support organisation (preferably with the travel officer, if there is one). For general travel advice in Australia contact **Nican** (www.nican.com.au; ☎02 6241 1220); in the UK contact **Tourism For All** (www.tourismforall.org.uk; ☎0845 124 9971); in the USA try **Accessible Journeys** (www.disabilitytravel.com; ☎800 846 4537), an agency specialising in travel for the disabled, or **Mobility International USA** (www.miusa.org; ☎541 343 1284).

Visas

Tourist Visas

➡ With a confirmed onward ticket, visitors from the USA, nearly all Western European countries, New Zealand, Australia and around 30 other countries receive 90-day permits on arrival. Visitors from a handful of countries receive 30-day permits, while 60-day permits are given to citizens of Italy and Portugal. Canadians receive a six-month permit.

➡ About 30 countries – including the Russian Federation, India and Nigeria – do not qualify for visa exemptions. Citizens from these countries must apply for a tourist visa, which allows a stay of 90 days.

➡ Visitors cannot extend their stay beyond 90 days except in situations such as a medical emergency. More info is at www.mofat.go.kr and www.moj.go.kr.

➡ Holders of a passport from China must apply for a tourist visa but are allowed an exemption of 120 hours (five days) if they join a tour group to visit Jeju-do and arrive through certain airports. This list is always increasing but includes the airports Gimpo (Seoul), Incheon (near Seoul), Gimhae (Busan), Daegu (Gangwon-do), Yangyang (Gangwon-do) and Cheongju (Chungcheongbuk-do). Other incentives aimed at wooing Chinese tourists include being able to apply online for electronic visas and increased visa application centres in China.

➡ As rules are always changing, see www.hikorea.go.kr for more visa information.

Work Visas

Applications for a work visa can be made inside Korea but you must leave the country to pick up the visa. You can also apply for a one-year work visa before entering Korea but it can take a few weeks to process. Note that the visa authorities will want to see originals (not photocopies) of your educational qualifications. This a safeguard against fake degree certificates.

You don't need to leave Korea to renew a work visa as long as you carry on working for the same employer. But if you change employers you must normally apply for a new visa and pick it up outside Korea.

If you are working or studying in Korea on a long-term visa, it is necessary to apply for an alien registration card (ARC) within 90 days of arrival, which costs ₩10,000. This is done at your local immigration office.

The main **Seoul Immigration Office** (☎02-2650 6212; www.immigration.go.kr/hp/imm80/index.do; 319-2 Sinjeong 6 dong, Yangcheon-gu; ⏰9am-6pm Mon-Fri; [S]Line 5 to

GOVERNMENT TRAVEL ADVICE

The following government websites offer travel advisories and information on current hotspots:

Australian Department of Foreign Affairs & Trade (www.smarttraveller.gov.au)

British Foreign Office (www.fco.gov.uk)

Canadian Department of Foreign Affairs (www.dfait-maeci.gc.ca)

US State Department (http://travel.state.gov)

TRANSLATION & INFORMATION SERVICES

If you need interpretation help or information on practically any topic, day or night you can call the following:

BBB (☎1588 5644; www.bbbkorea.org)

Tourist Phone Number In Seoul ☎1330 or ☎02 1330 from a mobile phone; outside Seoul dial the provincial or metropolitan code first – so for information on Gangwon-do, dial ☎033 1330.

Omokgyo, Exit 7) is always busy, so take something to read. To reach it, take line 5 to Omokgyo, Exit 7. Carry straight on from the subway exit and walk along the road until it ends, where you'll see a white-tiled building on your left with a big blue sign in English. An immigration office at **Seoul Global Centre** (Map p58; ☎02-2075 4180; global.seoul.go.kr; 38 Jong-ro, Jongno-gu; 🕒9am-6pm Mon-Fri; [S]Line 1 to Jonggak, Exit 6) can help with issues related to D8 and any C-type visa.

Volunteering

Many travellers find that volunteering to teach English or work in orphanages can be a fulfilling way to experience the local culture. Koreans are very reluctant to adopt children, partly because of the huge educational costs and partly because of the traditional emphasis on blood lines. Charities working in this area include US-based **Korean Kids & Orphanage Outreach Mission** (http://kkoom.org) and **HOPE** (Helping Others Prosper through English; www.alwayshope.or.kr), a Korean-based nonprofit run by foreign English teachers that helps out at orphanages, assists low-income and disadvantaged children with free English lessons and serves food to the homeless.

The **Seoul Global Center** (http://global.seoul.go.kr) is a good place to start looking for other volunteer possibilities. More charities and organisations with volunteer opportunities include:

Amnesty International (http://amnesty.or.kr/english) Raises awareness in Korea about international human-rights issues.

Cross-Cultural Awareness Program (CCAP; www.koreaunesco.or.kr/eng/activ/active5.htm) Unesco-run program; activities include presenting a class about your culture to young people in a Korean public school, or on a weekend trip to a remote area.

Korea Women's Hot Line (KWHL; http://eng.hotline.or.kr; ☎02 3156 5400) Nationwide organisation that also runs a shelter for abused women.

Korean Federation for Environmental Movement (KFEM; http://kfem.or.kr; ☎02 735 7000) Volunteer on environmental projects and campaigns.

Korean Unwed Mothers' Families Association (KUMFA; www.facebook.com/groups/kumfa) Supports single mothers.

Seoul International Women's Association (www.siwapage.com) Organises fundraising events to help charities across Korea.

Seoul Volunteer Center (http://volunteer.seoul.go.kr; ☎070 8797 1861) Teach language and culture, take part in environmental clean-ups and help at social welfare centres.

World Wide Opportunities on Organic Farms (WWOOF; http://wwoofkorea.org; ☎02 723 4458) Sends volunteers to farms across Korea who provide labour in exchange for board and lodging.

Work

The biggest demand in Korea is for English teachers.

Native English teachers on a one-year contract can expect to earn around ₩2.5 million or more a month, with a furnished apartment, return flights, 50% of medical insurance, 10-days paid holiday and a one-month completion bonus included in the package. Income tax is very low (around 4%), although a 4.5% pension contribution (reclaimable by some nationalities) is compulsory.

Most English teachers work in a *hagwon* (private language school) but some are employed by universities or government schools. Company classes, English camps and teaching over the phone are also possible, as is private tutoring, although this is technically illegal. Teaching hours in a *hagwon* are around 30 hours a week and are likely to involve split shifts, and evening and Saturday classes.

Any degree is sufficient as long as English is your native language. However, it's a good idea to obtain an English-teaching qualification before you arrive, as this should help you to find (and do) a better job.

Some *hagwon* owners are not ideal employers and don't pay all they promise; research before committing yourself. Ask prospective employers for the email addresses of foreign English teachers working at the *hagwon*, and contact them for their opinion and advice. If you change employers, you will usually need a new work visa, which requires you to leave the country to pick up your new visa. Your new employer may pick up all or part of the tab for this.

The best starting point for finding out more about the English-teaching scene is the **Association for Teachers of English in Korea** (ATEK; www.atek.or.kr).

Transport

GETTING THERE & AWAY

Entering the Country

Many visitors don't need a visa, but if your country is not on the visa-free list, you will need one. See p395 for more information.

Air

Airports & Airlines

Most international flights leave from Incheon International Airport, connected to Seoul by road (80 minutes) and train (60 minutes). There are also some international flights (mainly to China and Japan) from Gimpo International Airport, Gimhae International Airport for Busan and Jeju International Airport. Go to www.airport.co.kr for information on all the airports.

Tickets

Good deals can be found online and with discount agencies. Korean airport departure taxes are included in the ticket price.

Prices of flights from Korea can increase 50% in July and August, and special offers are less common during holiday periods. The peak period for outbound flights is early August, when it can be difficult to find a seat.

Sea

International ferries are worth considering if you're travelling around North Asia.

China

Ferries link a dozen Chinese ports with Incheon.

Japan

Regular ferries shuttle between Busan and four Japanese cities: Fukuoka, Shimonoseki, Osaka and Tsushima. Faster services

are available on **hydrofoils** (www.jrbeetle.co.jp/internet/english) from Busan to Fukuoka.

A **Korea-Japan Joint Railroad Ticket** via Korail (www.letskorail.com) lasts a week. It offers discounts of up to 30% on train fares in Korea and Japan, and on ferry tickets between the two countries from Busan.

Russia

DBS Cruise Ferry Co (www.dbsferry.com) runs the ferry 'Eastern Dream' that makes the trip from Donghae in Gangwon-do to Vladivostok on a regular basis; check the company website for fares and the schedule, which varies by season.

GETTING AROUND

South Korea is a public-transport dream come true. Planes, trains and express buses link major cities,

---

CLIMATE CHANGE & TRAVEL

Every form of transport that relies on carbon-based fuel generates CO_2, the main cause of human-induced climate change. Modern travel is dependent on aeroplanes, which might use less fuel per kilometre per person than most cars but travel much greater distances. The altitude at which aircraft emit gases (including CO_2) and particles also contributes to their climate change impact. Many websites offer 'carbon calculators' that allow people to estimate the carbon emissions generated by their journey and, for those who wish to do so, to offset the impact of the greenhouse gases emitted with contributions to portfolios of climate-friendly initiatives throughout the world. Lonely Planet offsets the carbon footprint of all staff and author travel.

SUSTAINABLE TRAVEL

Unless you're already based in Asia, a journey to Korea is likely to be by aeroplane. When the train link between North and South Korea resumes it will open the way to the development of a Seoul–London train journey. For now, such a trip remains a distant dream.

The most direct rail route for getting to this side of the world from Europe or Asia is to ride the Trans-Siberian Railway: Lonely Planet's *Trans-Siberian Railway* guide provides the low-down on how to get to Vladivostok, from where it's possible to hop on a ferry to Sokcho. There are also regular ferries to Korea from several ports in China or from Japan.

Once in Korea you can do your bit for the environment by using the country's excellent public transport system. Seoul's extensive subway and train system is particularly impressive and the city moved all its 8750-plus buses over to low-polluting natural-gas as well as full-hybrid and fuel-cell electric buses in 2014.

intercity buses link cities and towns large and small, while local buses provide a surprisingly good service to national and provincial parks and villages in outlying rural areas. Car ferries ply numerous routes to offshore islands. Local urban buses, subways and taxis make getting around cities and towns easy. All transport works on the Korean *ppalli ppalli* (hurry hurry) system, so buses and trains leave on time, and buses and taxis tend to be driven fast with little regard to road rules.

Air

Korean Air and Asiana, the two major domestic airlines, provide flights to and from a dozen local airports, and usually charge identical but reasonable fares – competition is being supplied by a handful of budget airlines. Gimpo International Airport handles nearly all Seoul's domestic flights, but Incheon International Airport also has a handful of domestic flights to Busan, Daegu and Jeju-do. Budget T'way Airlines now run more domestic fights to Jeju-do, from Gimpo, Daegu

or Gwangju. The longest flight time is just over an hour between Seoul Gimpo and Jeju-do.

Fares are 15% cheaper from Monday to Thursday, when seats are easiest to obtain. Flights on public holidays have a surcharge and are often booked out. Students and children receive discounts, and foreigners should always carry their passports on domestic flights for ID purposes.

Airlines in Korea

South Korea has a number of domestic carriers.

Air Busan (☎02 1666 3060; www.airbusan.com; Gimpo International Airport)

Asiana Airlines (☎02 2669 8000; www.flyasiana.com)

Eastar Jet (☎82 1544 0080; www.eastarjet.com) Based out of Gimpo International Airport in Seoul.

Jeju Air (☎82 1599 1500; www.jejuair.net) Low-cost airline based in Jeju-si.

Korean Air (☎82 1588 2001; www.koreanair.com; 9th Fl Korean Air Bldg, 117 Seosomun-Ro, Seosomun-dong, Chung-gu; ⊙8.30am-5.30pm Mon-Fri)

T'way Air (☎82 1688 8686; www.twayair.com) Low-cost carrier.

Bicycle

The Korean government has been promoting cycling as a green and healthy means of transport. Seoul's metropolitan government has also expanded cycling infrastructure in the city. However, something will have to be done about poor local driving habits, because currently these make cycling in Korea a less than pleasurable experience, especially in urban areas.

That said, hiring a bike for short trips in areas with bike paths or little traffic is a good idea. Bicycle hire starts at ₩3000 per hour, with discounts available for one-day's hire. You'll have to leave your passport or negotiate some other ID or deposit. Helmets are typically not available and you may need your own bikelock.

Jan Boonstra's website **Bicycling in Korea** (http://user.chollian.net/~boonstra/korea/cycle.htm) has some useful information.

Boat

Korea has an extensive network of ferries that connects hundreds of offshore islands to each other and to the mainland. Services from Incheon's Yeonan Pier connect to a dozen nearby and more distant islands, while other west-coast islands further south can be reached from Daecheon harbour and Gunsan.

ISLAND	MAINLAND PORT(S)
Jeju-do (Jeju-si)	Incheon, Mokpo, Wan-do, Sam-chunpo
Jeju-do (Seongsan-ri)	Jangheung
Ulleungdo	Pohang

Bus

Long-distance buses whiz to every nook and cranny of the country, every 15 minutes between major cities and towns, and at least hourly to small towns, villages, temples, and national and provincial parks. Listed bus frequencies are approximate, as buses don't usually run on a regular timetable and times vary throughout the day. Bus terminals have staff on hand to ensure that everyone boards the right bus, so help is always available. Most buses don't have toilets on board, but on long journeys drivers take a 10-minute rest at a refreshment stop every few hours. When buses aren't busy, locals ignore designated seating and sit where they like.

Express buses link major cities, while intercity buses stop more often and serve smaller cities and towns. The buses are similar, but they use separate (often neighbouring) terminals. Expressways have a special bus lane that operates at weekends and reduces delays due to heavy traffic. Buses always leave on time (or even early) and go to far more places than trains, but are not as comfortable (sometimes overheated) or smooth, so for travelling long distances, trains can be the better option.

Udeung (superior-class express buses) have three seats per row instead of four, but cost 50% more than *ilban* (standard buses). Buses that travel after 10pm have a 10% surcharge and are generally superior class.

Expect to pay around ₩4000 for an hour-long journey on a standard bus.

Buses are so frequent that it's unnecessary to buy a ticket in advance except on weekends and during holiday periods. Buy tickets at the bus terminals. You can check schedules on www.kobus.co.kr and www.hticket.co.kr.

Car & Motorcycle

Bring Your Own Vehicle

Contact **Korea Customs** (http://english.customs.go.kr) for information on regulations concerning importing your own car. The vast majority of cars running in the country are Korean-made, although a few luxury cars are imported. Repairs and spare parts are not generally available for most imported cars.

Driving Licence

Drivers must have a current (issued the year of travel) International Driving Permit, which should be obtained in your home country before arrival in Korea; they are not available in Korea and many car-rental companies will not rent you a vehicle unless you have one.

Car Hire

Not recommended for first-time visitors, but travellers who wish to hire a car must be 21 years or over and must by law have an International Driving Permit (a driving licence from your own country is not acceptable). Rates start at around ₩65,000 per day for a compact car but can be discounted by up to 50%. Insurance costs around ₩10,000 a day, but depends on the level of the excess you choose. It is better to rent a Korean car because in the event of an accident, it is much cheaper to fix, resulting in a lower deductible. Chauffeur service is also an option.

Incheon International Airport has a couple of car-rental agencies. Try **KT Kumho** (☎02-797 8000; www.ktkumhorent.com) or **Avis** (☎032 743 3300; www.avis.com; Incheon International Airport). GPS is likely to be in Korean only.

Insurance

Insurance is compulsory for all drivers in Korea. Since the chance of having an accident is higher than in nearly all other developed countries obtain as much cover as you can, with a low excess.

Road Conditions

Korea has an appalling road-accident record, and foreign drivers in large cities are likely to spend most of their time lost, stuck in

---

K-SHUTTLE BUS TOURS

The foreigner-only **K-shuttle** (www.k-shuttle.com) tour-bus service departs Seoul with a couple of three days/two nights packages (₩448,000), which include accommodation, breakfast, a guide who speaks English, Japanese or Chinese, and admission fees to various tourist sites along the way:

➡ **Southwest Course** Stops in Buyeo, Jeonju, Yeosu and Busan before returning to Seoul.

➡ **Southeast Course** Stops in Gangneurig, Pyeonchang, Wonju, Andong, Gyeongju and Busan before returning to Seoul.

It's also possible to use the service to cover one or more sectors of a tour without the package component; for example, the fare from Seoul to Jeonju is ₩42,000 or to Andong ₩70,000.

Reserve your place on the 35-seater coaches at least five days in advance. There is no designated seating.

traffic jams, looking for a parking space or taking evasive action. Impatient and careless drivers are a major hazard and traffic rules are frequently ignored.

Driving in rural areas or on islands such as Jeju-do or Ganghwado can be much smoother but public transport is so good that there's little incentive to sit behind a steering wheel.

Road Rules

➡ Vehicles drive on the right side of the road.

➡ The driver and front-seat passenger must wear seatbelts.

➡ Drunk drivers receive heavy fines, and victims of road accidents are often paid a big sum by drivers wanting to avoid a court case.

Hitching

Accepting a lift anywhere has an element of risk so we don't recommend it.

Hitching is not a local custom and there is no particular signal for it. However, Korea is relatively crime-free, so if you get stuck in a rural area, stick out your thumb and the chances are that some kind person will give you a lift. Drivers often go out of their way to help foreigners.

Normally bus services are frequent and cheap enough,

even in the countryside, to make hitching unnecessary.

Local Transport
Bus

Local city buses provide a frequent and inexpensive service (from ₩1150 a trip, irrespective of how far you travel), and although rural buses provide a less frequent service, many run on an hourly or half-hourly basis. Put the fare in the glass box next to the driver – make sure you have plenty of ₩1000 notes because the machines only give coins in change.

The main problem with local buses is finding and getting on the right bus – bus timetables, bus-stop names and destination signs on buses are rarely in English, and bus drivers don't speak English. Writing your destination in big *hangeul* (Korean phonetic alphabet) letters on a piece of paper will be helpful. Local tourist information centres usually have English-speaking staff; these are the best places to find out which local bus goes where, and where to pick it up.

Subway

Six cities have a subway system: Seoul, Busan, Daejeon, Daegu, Gwangju and Incheon. The subway (also referred to as the metro) is a cheap and convenient

way of getting around these major cities, and since signs and station names are in English as well as Korean, it is foreigner-friendly and easy to use.

Taxi

Taxis are numerous almost everywhere and fares are inexpensive. Every taxi has a meter that works on a distance basis but switches to a time basis when the vehicle is stuck in a traffic jam. Tipping is not a local custom and is not expected or necessary.

Ilban (regular taxis) cost around ₩2400 for the first 2km with a 20% surcharge from midnight to 4am, while the pricier *mobeom* (deluxe taxis; black with a yellow top) that exist in some cities cost around ₩4500 for the first 3km but with no late-night surcharge.

Any expressway tolls are added to the fare. In the countryside check the fare first as there are local quirks, such as surcharges or a fixed rate to out-of-the-way places with little prospect of a return fare.

Since few taxi drivers speak English, plan how to communicate with the driver; if you have a mobile phone you can also use the ☑1330 tourist advice line to help with interpretation. Ask to be dropped off at a nearby landmark if the driver doesn't understand what you're saying or doesn't know where it is. It can be useful to write down your destination or a nearby landmark in *hangeul* on a piece of paper.

Train

South Korea has an excellent but not comprehensive train network operated by **KoRail** (www.letskorail.com, ☑1544 7788). Trains are clean, comfortable and punctual, and just about every station has a sign in Korean and English. Trains are the best option for long-distance travel.

T-MONEY CARDS

Bus, subway, taxi and train fares can all be paid using the rechargeable, touch-and-go **T-Money Card** (http://eng.t-money.co.kr); the card provides a ₩100 discount per trip. The basic card can be bought for a nonrefundable ₩3000 at any subway-station booth, bus kiosks and convenience stores displaying the T-Money logo across the country. Reload it with credit at any of the aforementioned places and get money refunded that hasn't been used (up to ₩20,000 minus a processing fee of ₩500) at subway machines and participating convenience stores before you leave.

If you plan to travel by train a lot over a short period consider buying a 'KR pass' – see the website for details.

Classes

The fastest train is the Korea Train Express (KTX). A grade down are *saemaeul* services, which also only stop in major towns. *Mugunghwa* trains are comfortable and fast but stop more often.

Many trains have a train cafe where you not only buy drinks and snack foods but also surf the internet, play computer games, even sing karaoke. If a train is standing-room only, hanging out in the train cafe for the journey is the best way to go.

Costs

The full range of discounts is complicated and confusing. For fares and schedules see the Korail website (www. letskorail.com). KTX trains are 40% more expensive than *saemaul* trains (and KTX 1st class is another 40%). *Saemaul* 1st class is 22% more than the standard *saemaul* fare. *Saemaul* standard fares are 50% more than *mugunghwa* class. KTX tickets are discounted 7% to 20% if you buy them seven to 30 days before departure. Tickets are discounted 15% from Monday to Friday, and *ipseokpyo* (standing tickets) are discounted 15% to 30% depending on the length of the journey; with a standing ticket, you are allowed to sit on any unoccupied seat. Children travel for half price any time; over 65-year-olds receive a 30% discount Monday to Friday.

Reservations

The railway ticketing system is computerised and you can buy tickets up to a month in advance online, on the Korail app (Korean only; from the Apple App Store or Google Play), at train stations and many travel agencies. Seat reservations are sensible and necessary on weekends, holidays and other busy times.

Train Passes

Foreigners can buy a **KoRail Pass** (www.letskorail.com) at overseas travel agencies or online; it offers unlimited rail travel (including KTX services) for one (₩66,900), three (₩93,100), five (₩139,700) or seven (₩168,400) consecutive days. Children (four to 12 years) receive a 50% discount, and youths (13 to 25 years old) receive a 20% discount.

However, distances in Korea are not great, and trains don't go everywhere, so the pass is unlikely to save you much, if any, money unless you plan to shuttle more frequently than a Lonely Planet researcher back and forth across the country.

Language

Korean belongs to the Ural-Altaic language family and is spoken by around 80 million people. The standard language of South Korea is based on the dialect of Seoul.

Korean script, *hangeul*, is simple and accessible, as each character represents a sound of its own. There are a number of competing Romanisation systems in use today for *hangeul*. Since 2000, the government has been changing road signs to reflect the most recent Romanisation system, so you may encounter signs, maps and tourist literature with at least two different Romanisation systems.

Korean pronunciation is pretty straightforward for English speakers, as most sounds are also found in English or have a close approximation. If you follow our coloured pronunciation guides, you should be understood just fine. Korean distinguishes between aspirated consonants (formed by making a puff of air as they're pronounced) and unaspirated ones (pronounced without a puff of air). In our pronunciation guides, aspirated consonants (except for s and h) are followed by an apostrophe ('). Syllables are pronounced with fairly even emphasis in Korean.

BASICS

Hello.	안녕하세요.	an·nyŏng ha·se·yo
Goodbye. (if leaving/ staying)	안녕히 계세요/ 가세요.	an·nyŏng·hi kye·se·yo/ ka·se·yo
Yes.	네.	né
No.	아니요.	a·ni·yo
Excuse me.	실례합니다.	shil·lé ham·ni·da
Sorry.	죄송합니다.	choé·song ham·ni·da
Thank you.	고맙습니다./ 감사합니다.	ko·map·sŭm·ni·da/ kam·sa·ham·ni·da
You're welcome.	천만에요.	ch'ŏn·ma·ne·yo

How are you?
안녕하세요? · an·nyŏng ha·se·yo

Fine, thanks. And you?
네. 안녕하세요? · ne an·nyŏng ha·se·yo

What is your name?
성함을 여쭤봐도 될까요? · sŏng·ha·mŭl yŏ·tchŏ·bwa·do doélk·ka·yo

My name is ...
제 이름은 ...입니다. · che i·rŭ·mŭn ...im·ni·da

Do you speak English?
영어 하실 줄 아시나요? · yŏng·ŏ ha·shil·jul a·shi·na·yo

I don't understand.
못 알아 들었어요. · mot a·ra·dŭ·rŏss·ŏ·yo

ACCOMMODATION

Do you have a ... room?	... 룸 있나요?	... rum in·na·yo
single	싱글	shing·gŭl
double	더블	tŏ·bŭl
twin	트윈	t'ŭ·win

How much per ...?	...에 얼마예요?	...é ŏl·ma·ye·yo
night	하룻밤	ha·rup·pam
person	한 명	han·myŏng
week	일주일	il·chu·il
air-con	냉방	naeng·bang
bathroom	욕실	yok·shil
internet	인터넷	in·t'ŏ·net
toilet	화장실	hwa·jang·shil
window	창문	ch'ang·mun

Is breakfast included?
아침 포함인가요? · a·ch'im p'o·ha·min·ga·yo

DIRECTIONS

Where's a/the ...?
... 어디 있나요?　... ŏ·di in·na·yo

What's the address?
주소가 뭐예요?　chu·so·ga mwŏ·ye·yo

Could you please write it down?
적어 주시겠어요?　chŏ·gŏ ju·shi·gess·ŏ·yo

Please show me (on the map).
(지도에서) 어디인지　(chi·do·e·sŏ) ŏ·di·in·ji
가르쳐 주세요.　ka·rŭ·ch'ŏ ju·se·yo

Turn left/right.
좌회전/　chwa·hoé·jŏn/
우회전 하세요.　u·hoé·jŏn ha·se·yo

Turn at the ... ...에서 도세요. ...·e·sŏ to·se·yo

corner	모퉁이	mo·t'ung·i
pedestrian crossing	횡단 보도	hoéng·dan· bo·do

It's ... ... 있어요. ... iss·ŏ·yo

behind ...	... 뒤에	... dwi·é
in front of ...	... 앞에	... a·p'é
near ...	... 가까이에	... kak·ka·i·é
next to ...	... 옆에	... yŏ·p'é
on the corner	모퉁이에	mo·t'ung·i·é
opposite ...	... 반대 편에	... pan·dae· p'yŏ·né
straight ahead	정면에	chŏng·myŏ·né

EATING & DRINKING

Can we see the menu?
메뉴 볼 수 있나요?　me·nyu bol·su in·na·yo

What would you recommend?
추천　ch'u·ch'ŏn
해 주시겠어요?　hae·ju·shi·gess·ŏ·yo

Do you have any vegetarian dishes?
채식주의 음식　ch'ae·shik·chu·i ŭm·shik
있나요?　in·na·yo

I'd like ..., please.
... 주세요.　... ju·se·yo

Cheers!
건배!　kŏn·bae

That was delicious!
맛있었어요!　ma·shiss·ŏss·ŏ·yo

Please bring the bill.
계산서 가져다　kye·san·sŏ ka·jŏ·da
주세요.　ju·se·yo

I'd like to reserve a table for ... ... 테이블 예약해 주세요. ... t'e·i·bŭl ye·ya·k'ae ju·se·yo

KEY PATTERNS

To get by in Korean, mix and match these simple patterns with words of your choice:

When's (the next bus)?
(다음 버스) 언제　(ta·ŭm bŏ·sŭ) ŏn·jé
있나요?　in·na·yo

Where's (the train/subway station)?
(역) 어디예요?　(yŏk) ŏ·di·ye·yo

I'm looking for (a hotel).
(호텔) 찾고　(ho·t'el) ch'ak·ko
있어요.　iss·ŏ·yo

Do you have (a map)?
(지도) 가지고　(chi·do) ka·ji·go
계신가요?　kye·shin·ga·yo

Is there (a toilet)?
(화장실) 있나요?　(hwa·jang·shil) in·na·yo

I'd like (the menu).
(메뉴) 주세요.　(me·nyu) ju·se·yo

I'd like to (hire a car).
(차 빌리고)　(ch'a pil·li·go)
싶어요.　shi·p'ŏ·yo

Could you please (help me)?
(저를 도와)　(chŏ·rŭl to·wa)
주시겠어요?　ju·shi·gess·ŏ·yo

How much is (a room)?
(방) 얼마예요?　(pang) ŏl·ma·ye·yo

Do I need (a visa)?
(비자) 필요한가요?　(pi·ja) p'i·ryo·han·ga·yo

(eight) o'clock	(여덟) 시	(yŏ·dŏl)·shi
(two) people	(두) 명	(tu)·myŏng

Key Words

bar	술집	sul·chip
bottle	병	pyŏng
bowl	사발	sa·bal
breakfast	아침	a·ch'im
chopsticks	젓가락	chŏk·ka·rak
cold	차가운	ch'a·ga·un
dinner	저녁	chŏ·nyŏk
fork	포크	p'o·k'ŭ
glass	잔	chan
hot (warm)	뜨거운	ddŭ·gŏ·un
knife	칼	k'al
lunch	점심	chŏm·shim
market	시장	shi·jang
plate	접시	chŏp·shi
restaurant	식당	shik·tang

Signs

영업 중	Open
휴무	Closed
입구	Entrance
출구	Exit
... 금지	... Prohibited
금연 구역	No Smoking Area
화장실	Toilets
신사용	Men
숙녀용	Women

snack	간식	kan·shik
spicy (hot)	매운	mae·un
spoon	숟가락	suk·ka·rak

Meat & Fish

beef	쇠고기	soé·go·gi
chicken	닭고기	tak·ko·gi
duck	오리	o·ri
fish	생선	saeng·sŏn
herring	청어	ch'ŏng·ŏ
lamb	양고기	yang·go·gi
meat	고기	ko·gi
mussel	홍합	hong·hap
oyster	굴	kul
pork	돼지고기	twae·ji·go·gi
prawn	대하	tae·ha
salmon	연어	yŏ·nŏ
seafood	해물	hae·mul
tuna	참치	ch'am·ch'i
turkey	칠면조	ch'il·myŏn·jo
veal	송아지 고기	song·a·ji go·gi

Fruit & Vegetables

apple	사과	sa·gwa
apricot	살구	sal·gu
bean	콩	k'ong
capsicum	고추	ko·ch'u
carrot	당근	tang·gŭn
corn	옥수수	ok·su·su
cucumber	오이	o·i
eggplant	가지	ka·ji
fruit	과일	kwa·il
legume	콩류	k'ong·nyu
lentil	렌즈콩	ren·jŭ·k'ong
lettuce	양상추	yang·sang·ch'u

mushroom	버섯	pŏ·sŏt
nut	견과류	kyŏn·gwa·ryu
onion	양파	yang·p'a
orange	오렌지	o·ren·ji
pea	완두콩	wan·du·k'ong
peach	복숭아	pok·sung·a
pear	배	pae
plum	자두	cha·du
potato	감자	kam·ja
pumpkin	늙은 호박	nŭl·gŭn ho·bak
spinach	시금치	shi·gŭm·ch'i
strawberry	딸기	ddal·gi
tomato	토마토	t'o·ma·t'o
vegetable	야채	ya·ch'ae
watermelon	수박	su·bak

Other

bread	빵	bbang
cheese	치즈	ch'i·jŭ
egg	계란	kye·ran
honey	꿀	ggul
noodles	국수	kuk·su
rice (cooked)	밥	pap
salt	소금	so·gŭm
soup	수프	su·p'ŭ
sugar	설탕	sŏl·t'ang

Drinks

beer	맥주	maek·chu
coffee	커피	k'ŏ·p'i
juice	주스	jus·sŭ
milk	우유	u·yu
mineral water	생수	saeng·su
red wine	레드 와인	re·dŭ wa·in

Question Words

how	어떻게	ŏt·tŏ·k'é
what (object)	무엇을	mu·ŏ·sŭl
what (subject)	뭐가	mwŏ·ga
when	언제	ŏn·jé
where	어디	ŏ·di
which	어느	ŏ·nŭ
who (object)	누구를	nu·gu·rŭl
who (subject)	누가	nu·ga
why	왜	wae

soft drink	탄산 음료	t'an·san ŭm·nyo
tea	차	ch'a
water	물	mul
white wine	화이트 와인	hwa·i·t'ŭ wa·in

ATM	현금인출기	hyŏn·gŭ·min· ch'ul·gi
internet cafe	PC방	p'i·shi·bang
post office	우체국	u·ch'e·guk
tourist office	관광안내소	kwan·gwang an·nae·so

EMERGENCIES

Help!	도와주세요!	to·wa·ju·se·yo
Go away!	저리 가세요!	chŏ·ri ka·se·yo
Call ...!	... 불러주세요!	... pul·lŏ·ju·se·yo
a doctor	의사	ŭi·sa
the police	경찰	kyŏng·ch'al

I'm lost.
길을 잃었어요.   ki·rŭl i·rŏss·ŏ·yo

Where's the toilet?
화장실이   hwa·jang·shi·ri
어디예요?   ŏ·di·ye·yo

I'm sick.
전 아파요.   chŏn a·p'a·yo

It hurts here.
여기가 아파요.   yŏ·gi·ga a·p'a·yo

I'm allergic to ...
전 ...에   chŏn ...é
알레르기가 있어요.   al·le·rŭ·gi·ga iss·ŏ·yo

SHOPPING & SERVICES

I'm just looking.
그냥   kŭ·nyang
구경할게요.   ku·gyŏng halk·ke·yo

Do you have (tissues)?
(휴지) 있나요?   (hyu·ji) in·na·yo

How much is it?
얼마예요?   ŏl·ma·ye·yo

Can you write down the price?
가격을 써   ka·gyŏ·gŭl ssŏ
주시겠어요?   ju·shi·gess·ŏ·yo

Can I look at it?
보여 주시겠어요?   po·yŏ ju·shi·gess·ŏ·yo

Do you have any others?
다른 건 없나요?   ta·rŭn·gŏn ŏm·na·yo

That's too expensive.
너무 비싸요.   nŏ·mu piss·a·yo

Please give me a discount.
깎아 주세요.   ggak·ka·ju·se·yo

There's a mistake in the bill.
계산서가   kye·san·sŏ
이상해요.   i·sang·hae·yo

TIME & DATES

What time is it?
몇 시예요?   myŏs·shi·ye·yo

It's (two) o'clock.
(두) 시요.   (tu)·shi·yo

Half past (two).
(두) 시 삼십 분이요.   (tu)·shi sam·ship·pu·ni·yo

At what time ...?
몇 시에 ...?   myŏs·shi·é ...

At (five) o'clock.
(다섯) 시에.   (ta·sŏs)·shi·é

Numbers

Use pure Korean numbers for hours when telling the time, for counting objects and people, and for expressing your age.

1	하나	ha·na
2	둘	tul
3	셋	set
4	넷	net
5	다섯	ta·sŏt
6	여섯	yŏ·sŏt
7	일곱	il·gop
8	여덟	yŏ·dŏl
9	아홉	a·hop
10	열	yŏl

Use Sino-Korean numbers for minutes when telling the time, for dates and months, and for addresses, phone numbers, money and floors of a building.

1	일	il
2	이	i
3	삼	sam
4	사	sa
5	오	o
6	육	yuk
7	칠	ch'il
8	팔	p'al
9	구	ku
10	십	ship

morning	아침	a·ch'im
afternoon	오후	o·hu
evening	저녁	chŏ·nyŏk
yesterday	어제	ŏ·jé
today	오늘	o·nŭl
tomorrow	내일	nae·il
Monday	월요일	wŏ·ryo·il
Tuesday	화요일	hwa·yo·il
Wednesday	수요일	su·yo·il
Thursday	목요일	mo·gyo·il
Friday	금요일	kŭ·myo·il
Saturday	토요일	t'o·yo·il
Sunday	일요일	i·ryo·il
January	일월	i·rwŏl
February	이월	i·wŏl
March	삼월	sa·mwŏl
April	사월	sa·wŏl
May	오월	o·wŏl
June	유월	yu·wŏl
July	칠월	ch'i·rwŏl
August	팔월	p'a·rwŏl
September	구월	ku·wŏl
October	시월	shi·wŏl
November	십일월	shi·bi·rwŏl
December	십이월	shi·bi·wŏl

TRANSPORT

Public Transport

A ... ticket (to Daegu), please.	(대구 가는) ... 표 주세요.	(tae·gu ka·nŭn) ... p'yo chu·se·yo.
1st-class	일등석	il·dŭng·sŏk
one-way	편도	p'yŏn·do
return	왕복	wang·bok
standard class	일반석	il·ban·sŏk
standing room	입석	ip·sŏk
When's the ... (bus)?	... (버스) 언제 있나요?	... (bŏ·sŭ) ŏn·jé in·na·yo?
first	첫	ch'ŏt
last	마지막	ma·ji·mak
Which ...	어느 ...이/가	ŏ·nŭ ...i/·ga

goes to (Myeongdong)?	(명동)에 가나요?	(myŏng·dong)·é ka·na·yo?
boat	배	pae
bus	버스	bŏ·sŭ
metro line	지하철 노선	chi·ha·ch'ŏl no·sŏn
train	기차	ki·ch'a
platform	타는 곳	t'a·nŭn·got
ticket machine	표 자판기	p'yo cha·pan·gi
timetable display	시간표	shi·gan·p'yo
transportation card	교통카드	kyo·t'ong k'a·dŭ

At what time does it get to (Busan)?
(부산)에 언제 도착하나요? (pu·san)·é ŏn·jé to·ch'a·k'a·na·yo

Does it stop at (Gyeongju)?
(경주) 가나요? (kyŏng·ju) ka·na·yo

Please tell me when we get to (Daejeon).
(대전)에 도착하면 좀 알려주세요. (tae·jŏn)·é to·ch'a·k'a·myŏn chom al·lyŏ·ju·se·yo

Please take me to (Insa-dong).
(인사동)으로 가 주세요. (in·sa·dong)·ŭ·ro ka·ju·se·yo

Driving & Cycling

I'd like to hire a ...	... 빌리고 싶어요.	... pil·li·go shi·p'ŏ·yo
4WD	사륜구동	sa·ryun·gu·dong
car	차	ch'a

I'd like to hire a bicycle.
자전거 빌리려고요. cha·jŏn·gŏ pil·li·ryŏ·go·yo

Do I need a helmet?
헬멧 써야 하나요? hel·met ssŏ·ya ha·na·yo

Is this the road to (Donghae)?
이게 (동해) 가는 길인가요? i·gé (tong·hae) ka·nŭn ki·rin·ga·yo

(How long) Can I park here?
(얼마 동안) 여기 주차해도 되나요? (ŏl·ma·dong·an) yŏ·gi chu·ch'a·hae·do doé·na·yo

Where's a petrol station?
주유소가 어디있나요? chu·yu·so·ga ŏ·di in·na·yo

I need a mechanic.
자동차정비사가 필요해요. cha·dong·ch'a chŏng·bi·sa·ga p'i·ryo·hae·yo

I'd like my bicycle repaired.
자전거 고치려고요. cha·jŏn·gŏ ko·ch'i·ryŏ·go·yo

GLOSSARY

For more food and drink terms, see the Food Glossary (p373).

ajumma – a married or older woman

~am – hermitage

anju – snacks eaten when drinking alcohol

bang – room

bawi – large rock

~bong – peak

buk~ – north

buncheong – Joseon-era pottery with simple designs

celadon – green-tinged pottery from early 12th century

cha – tea

~cheon – small stream

Chuseok – Thanksgiving Day

dae~ – great, large

dancheong – ornate, multi-coloured eaves that adorn Buddhist temples and other buildings

Dangun – mythical founder of Korea

DEP – Democratic Party

DMZ – the Demilitarized Zone that runs along the 38th parallel of the Korean peninsula, separating North and South

-do – province, also island

-dong – neighbourhood or village

dong~ – east

donggul – cave

DPRK – Democratic People's Republic of Korea (North Korea)

DVD-bang – room for watching DVDs

-eup – town

-ga – section of a long street

~gang – river

geobukseon – 'turtle ships'; iron-clad warships of the late 16th century

gil – small street

-gu – urban district

gugak – traditional Korean music

~gul – cave

-gun – county

~gung – palace

gwageo – Joseon government service exam

hae – sea

haenyeo – traditional female divers of Jeju-do

hagwon – private school where students study after school or work

hallyu – (Korean Wave) increasing global interest in Korean pop culture

hanbok – traditional Korean clothing

hang – harbour

hangul – Korean phonetic alphabet

hanja – Chinese characters

hanji – traditional Korean hand-made paper

hanok – traditional Korean one-storey wooden house with a tiled or thatched roof

harubang – lava-rock statues found only on Jeju-do

~ho – lake

hof – local pub

insam – ginseng

jaebeol – huge family-run corporate conglomerate

~jeon – hall of a temple

~jeong – pavilion

jjimjil-bang – upmarket spa and sauna

Juche – North Korean ideology of economic self-reliance

KTO – Korea Tourism Organization

KTX – Korea Train Express; fast 300km/h train service

minbak – private homes with rooms for rent

mudang – female shaman

Mugunghwa – semi-express train

~mun – gate

~myeon – township

~myo – shrine

nam~ – south

~neung – tomb

~no – street

norae-bang – karaoke room

~nyeong – mountain pass

oncheon – hot-spring bath

ondol – underfloor heating system

pansori – traditional Korean solo opera

PC-bang – internet cafe

pension – upmarket accommodation in the countryside or near beaches

pocketball – pool

pokpo – waterfall

pyeong – real-estate measurement equal to 3.3 sq m

~reung – tomb

-ri – village

~ro – street

ROK – Republic of Korea (South Korea)

~ryeong – mountain pass

-sa – temple

Saemaul – luxury express train

samulnori – drum-and-gong dance

~san – mountain

sanjang – mountain hut

sanseong – mountain fortress

seo~ – west

Seon – Korean version of Zen Buddhism

~seong – fortress

seowon – Confucian academy

shamanism – set of traditional beliefs; communication with spirits is done through a *mudang*

~si – city

sijang – market

sijo – short poems about nature and life; popular in the Joseon period

soju – the local firewater; often likened to vodka

ssireum – Korean-style wrestling

taekwondo – Korean martial art

tap – pagoda

tonggeun – commuter-class train

yangban – aristocrat

yeogwan – motel with small en suite

yeoinsuk – small, family-run budget accommodation with shared bathroom

yo – padded quilt that serves as a mattress or futon for sleeping on the floor

Behind the Scenes

SEND US YOUR FEEDBACK

We love to hear from travellers – your comments keep us on our toes and help make our books better. Our well-travelled team reads every word on what you loved or loathed about this book. Although we cannot reply individually to postal submissions, we always guarantee that your feedback goes straight to the appropriate authors, in time for the next edition. Each person who sends us information is thanked in the next edition – the most useful submissions are rewarded with a selection of digital PDF chapters.

Visit **lonelyplanet.com/contact** to submit your updates and suggestions or to ask for help. Our award-winning website also features inspirational travel stories, news and discussions.

Note: We may edit, reproduce and incorporate your comments in Lonely Planet products such as guidebooks, websites and digital products, so let us know if you don't want your comments reproduced or your name acknowledged. For a copy of our privacy policy visit lonelyplanet.com/privacy.

OUR READERS

Many thanks to the travellers who used the last edition and wrote to us with helpful hints, useful advice and interesting anecdotes:

Kim Aeran, Rod Bennett, Martina Bieri, Larry Cannon, DongKwon Choi, Abilio Gomez, Molly Harder, Kim Ha-ye-ram, Kenneth Holmes, Maria Kamsäter, David Kerkhoff, Dan Krechmer, Maureen Liston, Melanie Luangsay, Marcos Mendonca, Serhat Narsap, Triin Saag, Nico Scherer, Susanne Stigsson, Hal Swindall, Charlotte Toolan, Jennifer Ward, Wim Westervoorde, Julie Woods

AUTHOR THANKS

Simon Richmond

Many thanks to my fellow authors, as well as Maureen O'Crowley and Kim Daegeun at Seoul Tourism, Seunghyo Lee, Daniel Durrance, Charles Usher, Alistair Gale, Joshua Hall, Joshua Davies, Joshua Park, David and Jade Kilburn, Robert Koehler, Monica Cha, Becca Baldwin, Daniel Lenaghan and Julia Mellor.

Megan Eaves

Many thanks are due to the outstanding authors on this project who let me into their chapters and were flexible in working with me to make the winter activities great. Thanks to

David Carroll and Nóirín Hegarty for letting me go skiing for a living. And massive gratitude to my husband, Bill, who unfailingly supports me when the need for a solo adventure strikes.

Trent Holden

Thanks first up to Megan Eaves for giving me the opportunity to work on *Korea* – a wonderful gig – as well as to my co-authors, especially Simon for all the help and tips along the way. A shout out to all the good folk I met on the road and shared a beer with. But as always my biggest thanks goes to my beautiful girlfriend Kate, and my family and friends who I miss back home in Melbourne.

Rebecca Milner

A huge thank you to my husband Chikara, as always, for your company and support. To Ashley and Pedro for your invaluable help and friendship. To Hyo Yun Kim, the best TIC lady in the country. And thank you to Seunghyo, Peter, David, Robert, Luis, Su Bae Yang, Cho Seung-ki, Kim Keun Su, Choi, Mori, Rachel, Calen, Jae Hyeon, Ted, Morgan, Jonathan, Moon Yumi, Will, another Ashley, my inspiring co-authors and my ever-patient editor Megan.

Phillip Tang

Thanks to the travellers and locals who shared their experiences, the very helpful ladies at Cheongju tourist information centre, and Megan Eaves for having me on board. Thanks to Jack Kennerley for Tour Le Jours taste testing, the abandoned theme park and Bone Henge. Big thanks to Daniel Belfield for four seasons on one train, oh they have popcorn, and *jjimdak* sharing. Cheers to Pukyong National University and Do Be for lending a hand. *Muchas gracias* to Ernesto A. Alanis Cataño, Vek Lewis, Da Sel Lee and Lisa N'Paisan.

Rob Whyte

Many thanks to many good folk. In Seogwipo, Mrs Lee at the tourism office and Mr Kim at the ferry terminal went way out of their way to help me understand schedules and routes. Mrs Kim inside the Tongyeong passenger ferry terminal for her patience. Ian for his

insights. And, my understanding friends in Busan, Tae-ho, Kim, Levi and Richard. Thanks.

ACKNOWLEDGMENTS

Cover photograph: Young woman in traditional attire, Seoul; Jim Zuckerman/Alamy

Climate map data adapted from Peel MC, Finlayson BL & McMahon TA (2007) 'Updated World Map of the Köppen-Geiger Climate Classification', Hydrology and Earth System Sciences, 11, 1633–44.

THIS BOOK

This 10th edition of Lonely Planet's *Korea* guidebook was researched and written by Simon Richmond, Megan Eaves, Trent Holden, Rebecca Milner, Phillip Tang and Rob Whyte. The previous two editions were also written by Simon, with Shawn Low, Timothy N Hornyak, Yu-Mei Balasingamchow and César G Soriano. This guidebook was produced by the following:

Destination Editor
Megan Eaves
Product Editor
Sarah Billington
Assisting Editors
Andrew Bain, Bridget Blair, Helen Koehne, Kellie Langdon, Susan Paterson, Erin Richards, Adela Shin, Jeanette Wall
Senior Cartographer
Corey Hutchison
Cartographer
Alison Lyall

Book Designer
Michael Buick
Cover Researcher
Campbell McKenzie

Thanks to David Carroll, Simon Cockerell, Jo Cooke, Nóirín Hegarty, Andi Jones, Katherine Marsh, Claire Murphy, Catherine Naghten, Karyn Noble, Monique Perrin, Martine Power, Samantha Russell-Tulip, Dianne Schallmeiner, Jaeyoon Shin, Ellie Simpson, Vicky Smith, Angela Tinson, Lauren Wellicome

Index

NOTES

Map Legend

Sights
- Beach
- Bird Sanctuary
- Buddhist
- Castle/Palace
- Christian
- Confucian
- Hindu
- Islamic
- Jain
- Jewish
- Monument
- Museum/Gallery/Historic Building
- Ruin
- Shinto
- Sikh
- Taoist
- Winery/Vineyard
- Zoo/Wildlife Sanctuary
- Other Sight

Activities, Courses & Tours
- Bodysurfing
- Diving
- Canoeing/Kayaking
- Course/Tour
- Sento Hot Baths/Onsen
- Skiing
- Snorkelling
- Surfing
- Swimming/Pool
- Walking
- Windsurfing
- Other Activity

Sleeping
- Sleeping
- Camping

Eating
- Eating

Drinking & Nightlife
- Drinking & Nightlife
- Cafe

Entertainment
- Entertainment

Shopping
- Shopping

Information
- Bank
- Embassy/Consulate
- Hospital/Medical
- Internet
- Police
- Post Office
- Telephone
- Toilet
- Tourist Information
- Other Information

Geographic
- Beach
- Gate
- Hut/Shelter
- Lighthouse
- Lookout
- Mountain/Volcano
- Oasis
- Park
- Pass
- Picnic Area
- Waterfall

Population
- Capital (National)
- Capital (State/Province)
- City/Large Town
- Town/Village

Transport
- Airport
- Border crossing
- Bus
- Cable car/Funicular
- Cycling
- Ferry
- Metro/MRT/MTR station
- Monorail
- Parking
- Petrol station
- Skytrain/Subway station
- Taxi
- Train station/Railway
- Tram
- Underground station
- Other Transport

Routes
- Tollway
- Freeway
- Primary
- Secondary
- Tertiary
- Lane
- Unsealed road
- Road under construction
- Plaza/Mall
- Steps
- Tunnel
- Pedestrian overpass
- Walking Tour
- Walking Tour detour
- Path/Walking Trail

Boundaries
- International
- State/Province
- Disputed
- Regional/Suburb
- Marine Park
- Cliff
- Wall

Hydrography
- River, Creek
- Intermittent River
- Canal
- Water
- Dry/Salt/Intermittent Lake
- Reef

Areas
- Airport/Runway
- Beach/Desert
- Cemetery (Christian)
- Cemetery (Other)
- Glacier
- Mudflat
- Park/Forest
- Sight (Building)
- Sportsground
- Swamp/Mangrove

Note: Not all symbols displayed above appear on the maps in this book

OUR STORY

A beat-up old car, a few dollars in the pocket and a sense of adventure. In 1972 that's all Tony and Maureen Wheeler needed for the trip of a lifetime – across Europe and Asia overland to Australia. It took several months, and at the end – broke but inspired – they sat at their kitchen table writing and stapling together their first travel guide, *Across Asia on the Cheap*. Within a week they'd sold 1500 copies. Lonely Planet was born.

Today, Lonely Planet has offices in Franklin, London, Melbourne, Oakland, Beijing and Delhi, with more than 600 staff and writers. We share Tony's belief that 'a great guidebook should do three things: inform, educate and amuse'.

OUR WRITERS

Simon Richmond

Coordinating author, Seoul UK-born writer and photographer Simon first co-ordinated Lonely Planet's *Korea* guide in 2009 when he explored Seoul and its surroundings over several weeks. He liked the place so much that his next visit, to update the 9th edition of *Korea* and 7th edition of *Seoul*, saw him spend over two months living in Seoul and travelling down to Jeju-do. For *Korea 10*, Simon co-ordinated the general coverage of the country and covered central, northern and western areas of Seoul; he also hiked around the old city walls on a beautiful spring day and had an enjoyable but messy time learning to make *makgeolli*. Follow him on Twitter, Instagram and at www.simonrichmond.com. Simon also wrote the Plan Your Trip section, as well as the Korea Today and History chapters.

Megan Eaves

Lonely Planet's North Asia Destination Editor, Megan has worked on Lonely Planet's *China* guide and is a recent convert to the delights of the Korean peninsula. Originally from New Mexico, she is a mountain girl at heart and an avid skier. For this edition, she researched Korea's winter activities, downing as much kimchi, fried chicken and *soju* as she could in between stints on the country's many snowy slopes. You can follow her on Twitter @megoizzy. Megan contributed to the chapters Gangwon-do, Around Seoul, Chungcheongbuk-do and Jeollabuk-do.

Read more about Megan at:
http://auth.lonelyplanet.com/profiles/meganeaves

Trent Holden

Around Seoul Having covered the length of the peninsula on other writing assignments, this is Trent's first gig working on the *Korea* book for Lonely Planet. He researched the regions surrounding Seoul, where he was blown away by the area's diversity and beauty. Trent has worked on over 20 books for Lonely Planet, covering mainly Asia and Africa. You can catch him on twitter @hombreholden.

OVER MORE
PAGE WRITERS

Published by Lonely Planet Publications Pty Ltd
ABN 36 005 607 983
10th edition – February 2016
ISBN 978 1 74321 500 5
© Lonely Planet 2016   Photographs © as indicated 2016
10 9 8 7 6 5 4 3 2 1
Printed in China

32953012478246

Rebecca Milner

Jeollanam-do, Jeollabuk-do, Chungcheongnam-do Lucky for Rebecca, Korea is just a short flight from her home in Tokyo. Previous trips had already sold her on the charms of *makgeolli* and *jjimjilbang*, so she jumped at the chance to explore the country's southern reaches for this edition. Highlights included eating live octopus in Mokpo, steaming in the saltwater baths in Hampyeong and having morning tea on the veranda of a 100-year-old home in Jeonju. Rebecca has also written Lonely Planet's guides to Tokyo and Japan. Follow her on Twitter @tokyorebecca. Rebecca also wrote the Arts & Architecture chapter.

Phillip Tang

Gangwon-do, Gyeongsangbuk-do, Chungcheongbuk-do Phillip Tang spent this trip inviting himself to Korean homes, tagging along to local street eats and being out-hiked by Koreans twice his age bolting up mountains. He writes about travel on his two loves, Asia and Latin America, and has contributed to Lonely Planet's guides to China, Japan, Mexico and Peru, and for other publishers. Find his photos, tweets and articles from this Korea visit through philliptang.co.uk. Phillip also wrote the In the Korean Kitchen, The Natural Environment and Survival Guide chapters.

Rob Whyte

Busan & Gyeongsangnam-do, Jeju-do A Busan resident for more than 15 years, Rob spends several weeks each year backpacking across the country in search of secluded getaways. One memorable discovery on this journey was a hamburger restaurant on Udo, which has an amazing collection of *Anne of Green Gables* memorabilia including a first edition of the book. That discovery was a reminder that we have everything we need for a magnificent journey. Rob also wrote the Korean People chapter.

Contributing Author

North Korea The author of our North Korea chapter has chosen to remain anonymous.